Why Do You Need This New Edition?

If you're wondering why you need this new edition of *The Little, Brown Reader*, here are five good reasons!

1. **Two new chapters—on Social Networking (Ch. 11) and Our Environment: Present and Future (Ch. 14)**— offer compelling insights into two significant contemporary topics.

2. **Thirty new readings** enhance this already rich collection of classic and contemporary selections and provide engaging models for your own writing.

3. New **Casebooks**, on the emergence of **Twitter (Ch. 11)** and the reprehensible behavior of **bullying (Ch. 12)**, demonstrate how persuasive writing occurs in nontraditional settings and offer support for developing skills in critical analysis.

4. A new quiz on **plagiarism and citing sources (Ch. 3)** allows you to test yourself on this difficult and sometimes confusing skill.

5. **New essays, checklists, and images** in the first five chapters offer more guidance on the writing process than any other composition reader.

Marcia Stubbs • Sylvan Barnet

The Little, Brown Reader

Custom Edition for Burlington County College

Taken from:
The Little, Brown Reader, Twelfth Edition
by Marcia Stubbs and Sylvan Barnet

Pearson Learning Solutions, 501 Boylston Street, Suite 900, Boston,
MA 02116
A Pearson Education Company
www.pearsoned.com

Printed in the United States of America

4 5 6 7 8 9 10 V202 16 15 14 13 12 11

000200010270781780

SE/JG

ISBN-10: 1-256-32830-8
ISBN-13: 978-1-256-32830-8

Detailed Contents

3   Academic Writing   47

4   Writing an Argument   83

A Casebook on Testing and Grading   312

A Casebook: College Advice from People Who Have Been There Awhile   320

9   Work and Play   327

A Casebook on Virtual Worlds   423

A Casebook on Twitter: Three Essays and Two Cartoons   431

12   Law and Disorder   443

ILLUSTRATIONS

Readings   571

Preface

Overview

Books have been put to all sorts of unexpected uses. Tolstoy used Tatishef's dictionaries as a test of physical endurance, holding them in his outstretched hand for five minutes, enduring "terrible pain." Books (especially pocket-sized Bibles) have served as armor by deflecting bullets. And they have served as weapons: Two hundred years ago the poet and essayist Samuel Johnson knocked a man down with a large book.

In a course in writing, what is the proper use of the book in hand? This anthology contains some 140 essays, together with a few poems and numerous "Short Views"—that is, paragraphs and aphorisms. But these readings are not the subject matter of the course; the subject matter of a writing course is writing, particularly the writing the students themselves produce. The responsibilities we felt as editors, then, were to include selections that encourage and enable students to write well and to exclude selections that do not.

Our selections and writing exercises also reflect our own experience, over many years, as teachers of writing courses. We think it's important for the selections to lead not only to good written work by students but also to lively discussion and debate. The more that students are engaged by the readings and led to explore and examine their own responses in relation to those of their classmates, the more they feel there's something at stake in the writing they are doing. We have found—like all our colleagues—that students improve the most when their work on papers is connected with lively classroom discussions about the readings, and we have tried to keep this point in mind in choosing selections and in preparing our topics for Joining the Conversation: Critical Thinking and Writing.

What's New in the Twelfth Edition?

William Hazlitt said that he always read on old book when a new one was published. This new edition allows instructors to read both at once. We have retained those essays and the special features (for example, Checklists for Writers, headnotes, and topics for Critical Thinking and Writing at the end of each essay) that in our experience and the experience of many colleagues have consistently been of value to instructors and to students. But guided by suggestions from users of the eleventh edition, we have made many changes and additions. Among the most evident changes in the five introductory chapters devoted to reading and writing are:

- In Chapter 1, two new essays and a new checklist, "Analyzing Letters of Response"
- In Chapter 2, new material about incorporating reading into one's thinking
- In Chapter 3, a new quiz on plagiarism and citing sources
- In Chapter 4, a new argument about phoning while driving
- In Chapter 5, new images (an advertisement and a cartoon)

Thirty readings are new to the book. These include:

- Two new chapters: "Social Networking" and "Our Environment"
- A casebook on college advice
- A casebook on Twitter
- A casebook on bullying

We have retained the popular casebooks on testing and grading and on race.

Purpose

Students, like all other writers, write best when they write on fairly specific topics that can come within their experience and within their command in the time that they have available to write. A glance at our table of contents reveals the general areas within which, we believe, students can find topics they have already given some thought to and are likely to also be encountering in other courses: family relationships; love and courtship; schools, work and play; the environment.

Although other sections ("Messages" and "Consumer Culture") are also on familiar subjects—language, popular culture, the Web—the sections themselves offer ways of thinking about these subjects that may be less familiar. For example, advertisements can be thought of as networks that articulate and transmit values implicit in a culture.

Some essays are about areas of experience that, while hardly remote from students' interest, are perhaps more difficult for all of us to grasp concretely: the tension between civil rights and liberties and the need for law and order; matters of gender and ethnic identity; our desires and our treatment of other species and of wilderness. In these essays, therefore, we have taken particular care to exclude writing that is, for our purposes, too abstract, or too technical, or too elaborate.

As editors, we have tried to think carefully about whether selections we were inclined to use—because they were beautifully written or on a stimulating topic—would encourage students to write. Such encouragement does not come, we feel, solely from the subject of an essay or from its excellence; it comes when the essay engenders in the reader a confidence in the writing process itself. No one quality in essays automatically teaches such confidence: not length or brevity, not difficulty or simplicity, not necessarily clarity, and almost certainly not brilliance. But essays that teach writing demonstrate, in some way, that the writers had some stake in what they were saying, took some pains to say what they meant and took pleasure in having said it.

The selections we include vary in length, complexity, subtlety, tone, and purpose. Most were written by our contemporaries—but not all. The authors include historians, sociologists, scientists, saints, philosophers, U.S. presidents, and undergraduates as well as journalists and other professional writers. And we have included some pictures in each section. The pictures—beautiful things in themselves—provide immediate or nearly immediate experiences for students to write about.

We offer substantial help to students who want to write about pictures: In Chapter 5, "Reading and Writing About Pictures," we set forth our own ideas about the topic; we reprint a helpful introductory essay, Lou Jacobs's "What Qualities Does a Good Photograph Have?"; and we print a sample essay by a first-year student.

We hope that everything in the book will allow students to establish connections between the activities that produced the words (and pictures) in these pages and their own work in putting critical responses to them on paper.

Flexible Arrangement

Any arrangement of the selections—thematic, rhetorical, alphabetical, chronological, or random—would have suited our purposes, but we prefer the thematic arrangement. For one thing, by narrowing our choices, it helped us to make decisions. But more importantly, we know that in the real world, what people write about is subjects, and we don't want to miss any opportunity to suggest that what goes on in writing courses is something like what goes on outside. The thematic categories are not intended to be rigid, however, and they do not pretend to be comprehensive; some of the questions following the selections suggest that leaping across boundaries is permitted—even encouraged. Finally, we append a glossary of terms for students of writing.

Although the organization of the essays in *The Little, Brown Reader* is thematic, most of the essays can be classified as

- **Argument** or **Persuasion**.

Within this mode however, instructors will find a notable diversity of rhetorical structures such as—and these are cited merely as examples—

- **Narration** (Langston Hughes, Jonathan Foer, Maya Angelou);
- **Cause and Effect** (Natalie Angier, James Twitchell, Stephen Jay Gould, Thomas Jefferson);
- **Comparison and Contrast** (Edward T. Hall, C. S. Lewis, Mary Eberstadt);
- **Definition** (Lewis Coser, Nancy Mairs, Plato), along with many others.

Additional Resources

An updated instructor's manual is available to instructors who adopt the twelfth edition.

Pearson's MyCompLab is a unique collection of resources and assignments that integrates a composing space and assessment tools with market-leading instruction, multimedia tutorials, and exercises for writing, grammar and research. Students can use MyCompLab on their own, benefiting from self-paced diagnostics and a personal study plan, or may be directed to assignable and gradable activities and exercises. Learn more at www.mycomplab.com.

Acknowledgments

As usual, we are indebted to readers-in-residence. Morton Berman, William Burto, and Judith Stubbs have often read our material and then told us what we wanted to hear. We are deeply indebted to Marlon Kuzmick of Harvard University for preparing most of the unit on social networking and to William Cain of Wellesley College for calling our attention to several essays and for preparing the relevant apparatus. We also wish to thank Pat Bellanca of Harvard University, Virginia L. Blanford and Rebecca Gilpin of Longman, and the staff of PreMediaGlobal—all of whom have given us valuable assistance.

We are grateful also to colleagues at other institutions who offered suggestions for the twelfth edition: Michael Hricik, Westmoreland County Community College; Terrence McNulty, Middlesex Community College; Carol Myers, Athens Technical College; Roseanne Giannini Quinn, Santa Clara University; Kevin Scott, Albany State University.

Marcia Stubbs
Sylvan Barnet

CHAPTER 1

A Writer Reads

*One reads well only when one reads with some personal goal in mind. It may
be to acquire some power. It may be out of hatred for the author.*

–Paul Valery

Good writers are also good readers—of the works of other writers and of
their own notes and drafts. The habits they develop as readers of others—
for instance, evaluating assumptions, scrutinizing arguments, and perceiving irony—empower them when they write, read, and revise their own
notes and drafts. Because they themselves are readers, when they write,
they have a built-in awareness of how their readers might respond. They
can imagine an audience, and they write almost as if in dialogue with it.

Active reading (which is what we are describing) involves writing at the
outset: annotating a text by highlighting or underlining key terms, putting
question marks or brief responses in the margin, writing notes in a journal.
Such reading, as you already may have experienced, helps you first of all to
understand a text—to get clear what the writer seems to intend. Later, skimming your own notes will help you to recall what you have read.

But active reading also gives you confidence as a writer. It helps you
treat your own drafts with the same respect and disrespect with which
you read the work of others. To annotate a text or a draft is to respect it
enough to give it serious attention, but it's also to question it—to assume
that the text or draft is not the last word on the topic.

But let's start at the beginning.

Previewing

By *previewing* we mean getting a tentative fix on a text before reading it
closely.

If you know something about the **author**, you probably already know
something about a work even before you read the first paragraph. An
essay by Martin Luther King Jr. will almost surely be a deeply serious discussion centering on civil rights, and because King was a Baptist clergyman, it is likely to draw on traditional religious values. An essay by
Woody Allen will almost surely differ from King's in topic and tone.
Allen usually writes about the arts, especially film. Both writers are serious (although Allen also writes comic pieces), but they are serious about
different things and serious in different ways. We can read both with interest, but when we begin with either of them, we know we will get something very different from the other.

King and Allen are exceptionally well-known, but you can learn something about all the authors represented in *The Little, Brown Reader* because
they are introduced by means of biographical notes. Make it a practice to
read these notes. They will give you some sense of what to expect. For example, you may have never heard of Gary Steiner, but when you learn

from the note that he is a professor of philosophy at Bucknell University, you can tentatively assume that the essay will have a philosophic dimension. Of course, you may have to revise this assumption—the essay may be about how to bake an apple pie—but in all probability, the biographical note will have given you some preparation for reading the essay.

The original place of publication may also give you some sense of what the piece will be about. The essays in *The Little, Brown Reader* were originally published in books, magazines, or newspapers, and these sources (specified when relevant in the biographical notes) may in themselves provide a reader with clues. For example, because *The American Scholar* is published by Phi Beta Kappa and is read chiefly by college and university teachers or by persons with comparable education, articles in *The American Scholar* usually offer somewhat academic treatments of serious matters. They assume that the readers are serious and capable of sustained intellectual effort. Whereas a newspaper editorial runs about 1,000 words, articles in *The American Scholar* may be 8,000 or 10,000 words, running 15 or so pages long.

Some journals have an obvious political slant, and the articles they publish are to some degree predictable in content and attitude. For example, the late William F. Buckley's *The National Review* is politically conservative. Its readers want to hear certain things, and *The National Review* tells them what they want to hear. Its readers also know that the essays will be lively and can be read fairly rapidly. Similarly, readers of *O, The Oprah Magazine*, expect highly readable essays with a strong feminist slant.

The **form,** or **genre** (a literary term for type or kind of literature), may provide another clue as to what will follow. Newspaper editorials are fairly short (and the paragraphs are also usually short), and of course the letters of response are even shorter. (Martin Luther King Jr.'s "Letter from Birmingham Jail," a response to a letter from eight clergymen, is a famous exception.)

The **title** may provide a clue. Again, King provides an example; even before studying "I Have a Dream," a reader can assume that the essay will be about King's vision of the future. Another example of a title that announces its topic is "We Have No 'Right to Happiness.'" This title is straightforward and informative, but suppose you pick up an essay called "Do-It-Yourself Brain Surgery." What do you already know about the essay?

Skimming

"Some books are to be tasted, others to be swallowed, and some few to be chewed and digested." You may have already encountered this wise remark by Francis Bacon, a very good reader (and a good writer too, although he did not write Shakespeare's plays). The art of reading includes the art of skimming—that is, the art of gliding rapidly over a piece of writing and getting its gist.

Skimming has three important uses: to get through junk mail and other lightweight stuff; to locate what is relevant to your purpose in a mass of material—for example, when you are working on a research paper; and (our topic now) to get an overview of an essay, especially to get the gist of its argument. Having discovered what you can from the name of the author, the title of the work, and the place of publication, you may want to skim the essay before reading it closely.

The **opening paragraph or paragraphs** will often give you a good idea of the topic or general area of the essay (for example, the ethics of eating meat). And if the essay is essentially an argument, it may announce the writer's **thesis**—the point that the writer will argue (for example, eating meat is acceptable—or, on the contrary, is barbaric).

Taking into account the author's profession (teacher of philosophy), the title of the essay ("Animal, Vegetable, Miserable"), and the first few paragraphs, a reader assumes that Steiner's essay will argue that despite the claim that some animals are raised humanely, their lives are miserable and that therefore it is immoral to raise animals for the purpose of satisfying our appetites.

If the title and first paragraph do not seem especially informative (the first paragraph may be a sort of warmup, akin to the speechmaker's "A funny thing happened to me on my way here"), look closely at the next two or three paragraphs. Then, as you scan subsequent paragraphs, look especially for topic sentences (often the first sentence in a paragraph), which summarize the paragraph, and look for passages that follow key phrases, such as "the important point to remember," "these two arguments can be briefly put thus," in short, "it is essential to recall," and so on.

In skimming an essay, pay special attention to the final paragraph, which usually reformulates the writer's thesis. The final paragraph in Steiner's essay picks up the idea that if we think that laws protect animals from cruelty, we should remember that these laws were formulated by persons who believe that "animals are fundamentally inferior to human beings."

> Think about that when you're picking out your free-range turkey, which has absolutely nothing to be thankful for on Thanksgiving. All it ever had was a short and miserable life, thanks to us intelligent, compassionate humans.

The fury in his final line, with its ironic characterization of humans as "compassionate," is evident. Later, when you carefully reread his essay, you will be in a position to judge whether or not he has made a sufficiently convincing case so a reader finds his tone acceptable.

As you scan an essay, you will find it useful to highlight phrases or sentences or to draw vertical lines in the margin next to passages that seem to be especially concise bearers of meaning. In short, even while you are skimming, you are using your pen.

If the essay is divided into sections, **headings** may give you an idea of the range of coverage. You probably won't need to highlight them—they already stand out—but there's no harm in doing so.

When you skim, you are seeking to get the gist of the author's **thesis**, or **point**. But you are also getting an idea of the author's methods and the author's purpose. For example, skimming may reveal that the author is using statistics (or an appeal to common sense, or the testimony of authorities, or whatever) to set forth an unusual view. Because Steiner's essay originally appeared in a newspaper, we know that it is aimed at the general public, not (for example) only at philosophers, and we see that his purpose is to inform us and indeed to persuade us that we have not fully understood the indecency of eating meat.

During this preliminary trip through a piece of writing, you may get a pretty good idea of the writer's personality. More precisely, since you are not encountering the writer in the flesh but only the image that the writer presents in the essay, you may form an impression of the voice, or **persona,** that speaks in the essay. That speaker may be genial or cool or hearty or whatever. In general, writers of arguments do well to convey that they are decent folks who are chiefly concerned with the good of the reader. Why? Because most readers don't wish to associate themselves with—to share the ideas of—unpleasant people, such as egotists or smart alecks. We will return to this important matter of persona on pages 00–00.

Let's now look at Steiner's essay. We suggest that in your first reading that you skim it—perhaps highlighting, underlining, or drawing vertical lines next to passages that strike you as containing the chief ideas. To this extent, you are reading for information. But because you have ideas of your own and because you do not accept something as true simply because it appears in print, you may also want to put question marks or expressions of doubt ("Really?" "Check this") in the margin next to any passages that strike you as puzzling. Furthermore, you may want to circle any words that you are not familiar with, but at this stage, don't bother to look them up. In short, run through the essay, seeking to get the gist and briefly indicating your responses, but don't worry about getting every detail of the argument.

Gary Steiner

Gary Steiner (Ph.D., Yale University), a professor of philosophy at Bucknell University, is the author of Animals and the Moral Community: Mental Life, Moral Status and Kinship *(2008). The following essay was published in* The New York Times *on November 22, 2009–the Sunday before Thanksgiving Day.*

Animal, Vegetable, Miserable

Lately more people have begun to express an interest in where the meat they eat comes from and how it was raised. Were the animals humanely treated? Did they have a good quality of life before the death that turned them into someone's dinner?

Some of these questions, which reach a fever pitch in the days leading up to Thanksgiving, pertain to the ways in which animals are treated. (Did your turkey get to live outdoors?) Others focus on the question of how eating the animals in question will affect the consumer's health and well-being. (Was it given hormones and antibiotics?)

None of these questions, however, make any consideration of whether it is wrong to kill animals for human consumption. And even when people ask this question, they almost always find a variety of resourceful answers that purport to justify the killing and consumption of animals in the name of human welfare. Strict ethical vegans, of which I am one, are customarily excoriated for equating our society's treatment of animals with mass murder. Can anyone seriously consider animal suffering even remotely comparable to human suffering? Those who answer with a resounding no typically argue in one of two ways.

Some suggest that human beings but not animals are made in God's image and hence stand in much closer proximity to the divine than any non-human animal; according to this line of thought, animals were made expressly for the sake of humans and may be used without scruple to satisfy their needs and desires. There is ample support in the Bible and in the writings of Christian thinkers like Augustine and Thomas Aquinas for this pointedly anthropocentric way of devaluing animals.

Others argue that the human capacity for abstract thought makes us capable of suffering that both qualitatively and quantitatively exceeds the suffering of any non-human animal. Philosophers like Jeremy Bentham, who is famous for having based moral status not on linguistic or rational capacities but rather on the capacity to suffer, argue that because animals are incapable of abstract thought, they are imprisoned in an eternal present, have no sense of the extended future and hence cannot be said to have an interest in continued existence.

The most penetrating and iconoclastic response to this sort of reasoning came from the writer Isaac Bashevis Singer in his story "The Letter Writer," in which he called the slaughter of animals the "eternal Treblinka."[1] The story depicts an encounter between a man and a mouse. The man, Herman Gombiner, contemplates his place in the cosmic scheme of things and concludes that there is an essential connection between his own existence as "a child of God" and the "holy creature" scuffling about on the floor in front of him. Surely, he reflects, the mouse has some capacity for thought; Gombiner even thinks that the mouse has the capacity to share love and gratitude with him. Not merely a means for the satisfaction of human desires, nor a mere nuisance to be exterminated, this tiny creature possesses the same dignity that any conscious being possesses. In the face of that inherent dignity,

---

[1]**Treblinka** Nazi death camp in Poland, where 850,000 persons (mostly Jews) were killed [all notes are the editors'].

Gombiner concludes, the human practice of delivering animals to the table in the form of food is abhorrent and inexcusable.

Many of the people who denounce the ways in which we treat animals in the course of raising them for human consumption never stop to think about this profound contradiction. Instead, they make impassioned calls for more "humanely" raised meat. Many people soothe their consciences by purchasing only free-range fowl and eggs, blissfully ignorant that "free range" has very little if any practical significance. Chickens may be labeled free-range even if they've never been outside or seen a speck of daylight in their entire lives. And that Thanksgiving turkey? Even if it is raised "free range," it still lives a life of pain and confinement that ends with the butcher's knife.

How can intelligent people who purport to be deeply concerned with animal welfare and respectful of life turn a blind eye to such practices? And how can people continue to eat meat when they become aware that nearly 53 billion land animals are slaughtered every year for human consumption? The simple answer is that most people just don't care about the lives or fortunes of animals. If they did care, they would learn as much as possible about the ways in which our society systematically abuses animals, and they would make what is at once a very simple and a very difficult choice: to forswear the consumption of animal products of all kinds.

The easy part of this consists in seeing clearly what ethics requires and then just plain doing it. The difficult part: You just haven't lived until you've tried to function as a strict vegan in a meat-crazed society. What were once the most straightforward activities become a constant ordeal. You might think that it's as simple as just removing meat, eggs and dairy products from your diet, but it goes a lot deeper than that. To be a really strict vegan is to strive to avoid all animal products, and this includes materials like leather, silk and wool, as well as a panoply of cosmetics and medications. The more you dig, the more you learn about products you would never stop to think might contain or involve animal products in their production—like wine and beer (isinglass, a kind of gelatin derived from fish bladders, is often used to "fine," or purify, these beverages), refined sugar (bone char is sometimes used to bleach it) or Band-Aids (animal products in the adhesive). Just last week I was told that those little comfort strips on most razor blades contain animal fat. To go down this road is to stare headlong into an abyss that, to paraphrase Nietzsche,[2] will ultimately stare back at you.

The challenges faced by a vegan don't end with the nuts and bolts of material existence. You face quite a few social difficulties as well, perhaps the

[2]**Nietzsche** Friedrich Nietzsche (1844–1900), German philosopher.

chief one being how one should feel about spending time with people who are not vegans. Is it O.K. to eat dinner with people who are eating meat? What do you say when a dining companion says, "I'm really a vegetarian—I don't eat red meat at home." (I've heard it lots of times, always without any prompting from me.) What do you do when someone starts to grill you (so to speak) about your vegan ethics during dinner? (Wise vegans always defer until food isn't around.) Or when someone starts to lodge accusations to the effect that you consider yourself morally superior to others, or that it is ridiculous to worry so much about animals when there is so much human suffering in the world? (Smile politely and ask them to pass the seitan.[3])

Let me be candid: By and large, meat-eaters are a self-righteous bunch. The number of vegans I know personally is . . . five. And I have been a vegan for almost 15 years, having been a vegetarian for almost 15 before that.

Five. I have lost more friends than this over arguments about animal ethics. One lapidary conclusion to be drawn here is that people take deadly seriously the prerogative to use animals as sources of satisfaction. Not only for food, but as beasts of burden, as raw materials and as sources of captive entertainment—which is the way animals are used in zoos, circuses and the like. These uses of animals are so institutionalized, so normalized, in our society that it is difficult to find the critical distance needed to see them as the horrors that they are: so many forms of subjection, servitude and—in the case of killing animals for human consumption and other purposes—outright murder.

People who are ethical vegans believe that differences in intelligence between human and non-human animals have no moral significance whatsoever. The fact that my cat can't appreciate Schubert's late symphonies and can't perform syllogistic logic does not mean that I am entitled to use him as an organic toy, as if I were somehow not only morally superior to him but virtually entitled to treat him as a commodity with minuscule market value.

We have been trained by a history of thinking of which we are scarcely aware to view non-human animals as resources we are entitled to employ in whatever ways we see fit in order to satisfy our needs and desires. Yes, there are animal welfare laws. But these laws have been formulated by, and are enforced by, people who proceed from the proposition that animals are fundamentally inferior to human beings. At best, these laws make living conditions for animals marginally better than they would be otherwise—right up to the point when we send them to the slaughterhouse.

Think about that when you're picking out your free-range turkey, which has absolutely nothing to be thankful for on Thanksgiving. All it ever had was a short and miserable life, thanks to us intelligent, compassionate humans.

---

[3]**seitan** Japanese word for *gluten*, a high-protein substitute for meat made from whole grain wheat.

Highlighting, Underlining, Annotating

Now that you have read Steiner's essay, go back and reread it; this time, highlight or underline key passages as though you were marking the text so that you might later easily review it for an examination. Your chief purpose now is to make sure that you know what Steiner is getting at, but you may find it impossible not to add an occasional marginal comment such as "Yes!" or "Not so fast" or "Does this really follow?" You may strongly disagree with him on details or even on large matters, and you would certainly make clear your differences with him if you were to write about his essay; but for the moment, your purpose is to make sure that you know what his position is. See if in each paragraph you can find a sentence that contains the topic idea of the paragraph. If you find such sentences, mark them.

Caution: Do not allow yourself to highlight or underline whole paragraphs. Before you start to mark a paragraph, read it to the end and then go back and mark what you now see as the key word, phrase, or passage. If you simply start marking a paragraph from the beginning, you may end up marking the whole and you will thus defeat your purpose, which is to make highly visible the basic points of the essay.

You may also want to jot down in the margins questions or objections, and you may want to circle any words that puzzle you.

Here are the first three paragraphs of Steiner's essay, with the annotations that one of our students made. (Of course, no two readers of the essay will make exactly the same annotations.)

Isn't this a good question to ask?

Lately more people have begun to express an interest in where the meat they eat comes from and how it was raised. Were the animals humanely treated? *Sounds a bit flip?* Did they have a good quality of life before the death *really?* that turned into someone's dinner?

Some of these questions, which reach a fever pitch in the days leading up to Thanksgiving, pertain to the ways in which animals are treated. (Did your turkey get to live outdoors?) Others focus on the question of how eating the animals in question will affect the consumer's health and well-being. (Was it given hormones and antibiotics?)

None of these questions, however, make any consideration of whether it is wrong to kill animals for human consumption. And even when people ask this question, they almost always find a variety of *probably true* resourceful answers that purport to justify the killing and consumption of animals in the name of human welfare. *Same as vegetarian or not same?* Strict ethical vegans of which I am one, are customarily *meaning?* excoriated for equating our society's treatment of animals with mass murder. Can anyone seriously consider animal suffering even remotely comparable to human suffering? Those who answer with a resounding no typically argue in one of two ways.

Of course, different readers will find different passages of special interest and importance. Our personal histories, our beliefs, our preconceptions, and our current preoccupations to some extent determine how we read. For example, when they come to the third paragraph, a meat-eater may mark the passage in which Steiner says that he's a "strict ethical vegan" with something like:

> What's a vegan, and how does it differ from a vegetarian?

However, a vegan might mark it with:

> I'd begin by saying I'm a strict vegan, and I'd define the term.

As these examples indicate, even when you simply set out to make a few notes that will help you follow and remember the essayist's argument, you may find yourself making notes that record your responses (where you agree, what you question)—notes that may start you thinking about the validity of the argument.

As we have already said, *what* you annotate will partly depend on what interests you, what your values are, and what your purpose is. True, you read the essay because it was assigned, but Steiner's original readers read it for other reasons. It first appeared in a newspaper, so the original readers were people who freely picked it up because they found the title interesting and wanted to hear more.

Let us now examine the evidence that Steiner uses to support his argument.

Critical Thinking: Analyzing the Text

When you annotate a text—even if you're not doing much more than underlining or putting a check mark next to an occasional sentence that seems especially important or putting an occasional question mark next to an assertion that seems doubtful to you—you are engaging in critical thinking. "Critical" here does not mean finding fault ("Don't be so critical"); rather, it means judging, especially judging the ways in which the parts are related to the whole. In this sense, to read critically is to read analytically.

We have already said that you will probably find yourself putting question marks in the margins next to words that you don't know and that don't become clear in the context and next to statements that you find puzzling or dubious. These marks will remind you to take action— perhaps to check a dictionary, to reread a paragraph, or to jot down your objection in the margin or at greater length in a journal.

But analytic readers also engage in another sort of questioning, although they may do so almost unconsciously. They are almost always asking themselves—or rather asking the text—several questions. You'll notice that these questions concern not only the writer's point but also the writer's craft. By asking such questions, you will learn about subject matter and also about some of the tricks of the writer's trade (for example, effective ways of beginning). If you read actively, asking the following questions, you will find that reading is not a solitary activity; you are conversing with a writer.

- What's the writer's thesis?
- How does the writer support the thesis?
- What's the writer's purpose (to persuade, to rebut, to entertain, to share an experience, or whatever)?
- How do the writer's audience and purpose help shape the writing? (The place of publication is often a clue to the audience.) For example, does the writer use humor or does the writer speak earnestly? Are terms carefully defined or does the writer assume that the audience is knowledgeable and doesn't need such information?
- What's the writer's tone?

These questions will help you to understand what you are reading and how writers go about their business. But you are also entitled to evaluate what you are reading, hence some other questions of a rather different sort:

- How successful is the piece?
- What are its strengths and weaknesses?
- What do I especially like or dislike about it? Why?

We recommend that when you read an essay that you ask each of these questions—not, of course, during an initial skimming but during a second and third reading after you have some sense of the essay.

These questions can almost be boiled down to one question:

What is the writer up to?

That is, a reader who is not content merely to take what the writer is handing out asks such questions as, "Why this way of opening?" "Why this way of defining the term?" The assumption that the writer has a purpose may be false. (We are reminded of a comment that Metternich, the keenly analytic Austrian statesman and diplomat, uttered when he learned that the czar had died: "I wonder why he did that.") Yes, the writer may just be blundering along, but its reasonable to begin with the assumption that the writer is competent. If under questioning the writer fails, you have at least learned that not everything in print is worthy.

Tone and Persona

Perhaps you know the line from Owen Wister's novel The *Virginian:* "When you call me that, smile." Words spoken with a smile mean something different from the same words spoken through clenched teeth. But while speakers can communicate by facial gestures, body language, and changes in tone of voice, writers have only words in ink on paper. Somehow, the writer has to help us to know whether, for example, he or she is solemn or joking in earnest.

Consider the first paragraph of Gary Steiner's "Animal, Vegetable, Miserable."

> Lately more people have begun to express an interest in where the meat they eat comes from and how it was raised. Were the animals humanely treated? Did they have a good quality of life before the death that turned them into someone's dinner?

Steiner's first sentence could have run thus:

> I have observed over the last decade, or (to be more precise) perhaps decade and a half, that there has been a substantial increase in the number of people in America and probably elsewhere who have expressed their serious concern. . . .

This version contains nothing that is certifiably wrong, and the grammar and spelling are satisfactory, but we think you will agree that the speaker of this version is windy, relatively pompous, and is probably not someone you want to hear at length.

As writers build their essays sentence by sentence, they are establishing a persona, and this persona may somewhat change. For example, the writer may begin by coming across as a nice guy and, having gained the reader's trust, end by coming across as a hard-hitting speaker of the truth. Or if the writer is less skilled, he or she may come across as a windbag or a nag. Good writers take pains to make certain that their readers respect them.

Of course, we do not know a great deal about any essayist. For example, we don't know if Steiner is a fair grader of students or what kinds of movies he likes. But even from this brief essay, we do get a sense of personality. What sort of person does Steiner appear to be? Point to sentences in the essay that cause you to see him as you do.

How do readers form an impression of a persona? By listening, so to speak, with a third ear—listening for the writer's *attitude toward*

- himself or herself,
- the subject, and
- the audience.

Of course, different readers will respond differently. To take a simple example, readers who do not wish to hear arguments concerning the alleged wrongs of meat-eating may dismiss Steiner as radical or as lacking in common sense. But we think most readers will agree with us in saying that Steiner conveys the persona of someone who is (1) educated, (2) sincere, and (3) concerned with a significant issue. It's also our guess that Steiner hoped to be seen as this sort of person. However, if most readers of his first paragraph conclude that he is conceited, stuffy, full of hot air, a threat to society, and so on—in short, if he turns his readers away—he has failed as a writer.

(Please note: We do *not* think his opening fails.)

What is the lesson? When you reread your own drafts and essays, try to get out of yourself and into the mind of an imagined reader, such as a classmate. Try to hear how your words will sound *in this other person's ear*; that is, try to imagine what impression this reader will form of your attitude toward yourself, your subject, and your reader.

Letters Responding to Gary Steiner

When Steiner wrote his piece for *The New York Times*, he hoped he would get people thinking—and thinking in *his* direction. Inevitably, however, some readers were stimulated to respond with severe criticisms of his position. Here are several letters that were published in *The New York Times* in response.

The Ethical Choices in What We Eat

To the Editor:

Soon after I read Gary Steiner's article, my wife asked me to kill a spider, which I did. This made me feel guilty. Spiders are living creatures, too; perhaps I should have gently caught it and carried it outdoors?

It is hard to imagine where a line can be drawn. We kill so many living creatures when we build a house, construct a road, drive down that road or just walk on a path. How far do we go in protecting them?

When we plant and harvest crops that vegans would find acceptable to eat, many animals are killed and their habitats are destroyed.

If we all decide to consider animals as precious as humans, the only logical place for us is back in the jungle. But even then if we were to survive we would have to kill some animals in self-defense.

Alexander Mauskop
New York, Nov. 22, 2009

To the Editor:

Gary Steiner's case for veganism founders on the facts. First, the human digestive system has evolved to accommodate an omnivorous diet, not a purely vegetable one.

Indeed, many paleoanthropologists maintain that the evolution of the large, energy-hungry human brains depended on a transition of our ancestors' diets to include meat.

And vegans must tread a very narrow line to avoid all sorts of deficiency diseases, while omnivores have very broad latitude in diet, as a survey of world cuisines makes evident.

Letters to the Editor by Sandy Asirvatham, Alice Desaulniers, Lisa Dinhofer, Lawrence S. Lerner, Alexander Mauskop, M.D and L. David Peters published in *The New York Times*, November 24, 2009. Reprinted by permission of the authors.

Second, our food animals have co-evolved with us. Cows, domestic sheep, chickens and many others would not survive if they were not raised for human consumption, protected from malnutrition, disease and predators.

Professor Steiner is entitled to his beliefs and his tofurkey; most of the rest of us will enjoy our turkey without guilt (but with vegetables stuffing).

Lawrence S. Lerner
Woodside, Calif., Nov. 22, 2009
The writer is professor emeritus
at the College of Natural Sciences and Mathematics
at California State University, Long Beach.

To the Editor:

Gary Steiner recognizes that many of us justify eating animals because we believe we are superior to them. Mr. Steiner rightly rejects this view as morally flawed.

Humans can acceptably consume animals precisely because we are not superior to them at all. Wolves eat sheep. Tuna eat mackerel. We are animals ourselves—and are no more (or less) than the animals we consume, or than the predators that would otherwise consume them.

If we are not justified in eating mackerel ourselves, are we not also morally obligated to stop the slaughter brought on by the tuna?

Such an obligation would make us the protectors of all species, and the destroyers of every ecosystem on earth.

L. David Peters
New York, Nov. 22, 2009

To the Editor:

As a vegetarian for 18 years, I have been confronted with the same questions that Gary Steiner faces from those challenging his dietary habits. I learned an effective response long ago that has benefited both my blood pressure and friendships.

I say with a big smile: "My vegetarianism is a personal choice that I usually don't discuss in detail. I'm happy to eat with nonvegetarians." And then I'm quiet.

That has pleasantly ended many potentially uncomfortable exchanges. Being vegetarian, as with being a member of a political party or a religious denomination, does not bestow license to convert others to one's own way of thinking.

On my deathbed, I'll be happy to have lived life as a vegetarian and also (I hope) comforted by many who were not alienated through heated discussions about my dietary choices.

Lisa Dinhofer
Frederick, Md., Nov. 22, 2009

To the Editor:

I will rise to the challenge Gary Steiner presents. He's right: I don't care deeply about the suffering of animals I eat, wear or otherwise benefit from. Suffering and injustice are inherent in life, and time is short.

Moreover, I find no way to shine a moral spotlight on one corner without letting shadows fall on another. I radically limit my conscious sphere of concern (just as Mr. Steiner must).

My moral boundaries may be rational or reflexive, expansive or selfish—who can judge?

I also recognize that alleviating suffering in one area may cause pain elsewhere. My mind and spirit are continually tested by outrages, from the countless dead innocents in current wars to the limited life prospects of my son's first-grade classmates with drug dealers for parents.

Were I also to internalize the pain experienced by animals, I'd simply shut down. Whose lot could that possibly help?

Sandy Asirvatham
Baltimore, Md., Nov. 22, 2009

To the Editor:

I was shocked to read that Gary Steiner thinks his cat can't appreciate Schubert's late symphonies. It's not the feline lack of musical discernment that I found disturbing (I don't "get" Schubert's symphonies either), but rather that Mr. Steiner owns a pet.

If he wishes to make no distinction between animal and human life and rights, how does he justify keeping an animal in what amounts to captivity?

And where does he draw the line between keeping a cow for milk and keeping a cat or dog for comfort or gratification?

Alice Desaulniers.
Irvington, N.Y., Nov., 23, 2009

✓ A Checklist: Analyzing Letters of Response

After reading the letters responding to an editorial or to a previous letter, go back and ask yourself if you have thought about each of the following topics:

- ☐ What's the writer's claim? Thesis? Point?
- ☐ What assumption(s) does the letter-writer make? Do I share the assumption(s)?
- ☐ What evidence, if any, does the writer offer to support the claim?
- ☐ What qualities in the letter especially affected my response to the letter? The evidence? The writer's tone? Or what?

✓ A Checklist: Reading, Analyzing, and Evaluating an Essay

☐ What's the **topic** of the essay? Try to state the topic as specifically as possible.

☐ What's the essay's **thesis?** Its point? Its argument?

☐ What does the **title** do?

☐ What's the function of the **opening paragraph** (or paragraphs)? What claim on your attention or beliefs does it make?

☐ What **speaker** or **persona** does the writer create, and how does the writer create it? What's the **tone?** Does the tone shift as the essay progresses? If so, why?

☐ What **audience** is the writer addressing? The general, literate public or a more specialized group?

☐ **How is the argument set forth?** By logic? By drawing on personal experience? What other kinds of evidence support the essay's claim? What are the author's underlying assumptions? Are they stated or implied, and are they acceptable to you or can you challenge them?

☐ **Is the essay persuasive** (whether because of its logic or because of the power of the speaker's personality)?

☐ Does the essay give **pleasure?**

Now let's look at another essay.

Brent Staples

Brent Staples, born in 1951, received a bachelor's degree from Widener University in Chester, Pennsylvania, and a Ph.D. from the University of Chicago. After working as a journalist in Chicago, he joined The New York Times *in 1985, and he is now on the newspaper's editorial board, where he writes on politics and culture. His essay was first published in* Ms. *magazine in 1986 and reprinted in a slightly revised form—the form we give here—in* Harper's *in 1987.*

Black Men and Public Space

My first victim was a woman—white, well dressed, probably in her late twenties. I came upon her late one evening on a deserted street in Hyde Park, a relatively affluent neighborhood in an otherwise mean, impoverished section of Chicago. As I swung onto the avenue behind her, there seemed to be a discreet, uninflammatory distance between us. Not so. She cast back a worried glance. To her, the youngish black man—a broad six feet two inches with a beard and billowing hair, both hands shoved into the pockets of a bulky military jacket—seemed menacingly close. After a few more quick glimpses, she picked up her pace and was soon running in earnest. Within seconds, she disappeared into a cross street.

That was more than a decade ago. I was twenty-two years old, a graduate student newly arrived at the University of Chicago. It was in the echo of that terrified woman's footfalls that I first began to know the unwieldy inheritance I'd come into—the ability to alter public space in ugly ways. It was clear that she thought herself the quarry of a mugger, a rapist, or worse. Suffering a bout of insomnia, however, I was stalking sleep, not defenseless wayfarers. As a softy who is scarcely able to take a knife to a raw chicken—let alone hold one to a person's throat—I was surprised, embarrassed, and dismayed all at once. Her flight made me feel like an accomplice in tyranny. It also made it clear that I was indistinguishable from the muggers who occasionally seeped into the area from the surrounding ghetto. That first encounter, and those that followed, signified that a vast, unnerving gulf lay between nighttime pedestrians—particularly women—and me. And I soon gathered that being perceived as dangerous is a hazard in itself. I only needed to turn a corner into a dicey situation, or crowd some frightened, armed person in a foyer somewhere, or make an errant move after being pulled over by a policeman. Where fear and weapons meet—and they often do in urban America—there is always the possibility of death.

In that first year, my first away from my hometown, I was to become thoroughly familiar with the language of fear. At dark, shadowy intersections, I could cross in front of a car stopped at a traffic light and elicit the *thunk,* thunk, thunk, thunk of the driver—black, white, male, or female—hammering down the door locks. On less traveled streets after dark, I grew accustomed to but never comfortable with people crossing to the other side of the street rather than pass me. Then there were the standard unpleasantries with policemen, doormen, bouncers, cabdrivers, and others whose business it is to screen out troublesome individuals *before* there is any nastiness.

I moved to New York nearly two years ago and I have remained an avid night walker. In central Manhattan, the near-constant crowd cover minimizes tense one-on-one street encounters. Elsewhere—in SoHo, for example, where sidewalks are narrow and tightly spaced buildings shut out the sky—things can get very taut indeed.

After dark, on the warrenlike streets of Brooklyn where I live, I often see women who fear the worst from me. They seem to have set their faces on neutral, and with their purse straps strung across their chests bandolier-style, they forge ahead as though bracing themselves against being tackled. I understand, of course, that the danger they perceive is not a hallucination. Women are particularly vulnerable to street violence, and young black males are drastically overrepresented among the perpetrators of that violence. Yet these truths are no solace against the kind of alienation that comes of being ever the suspect, a fearsome entity with whom pedestrians avoid making eye contact.

It is not altogether clear to me how I reached the ripe old age of twenty-two without being conscious of the lethality nighttime pedestrians attributed to me. Perhaps it was because in Chester, Pennsylvania, the small, angry industrial town where I came of age in the 1960s, I was scarcely noticeable against a backdrop of gang warfare, street knifings, and murders. I grew up one of the good boys, had perhaps a half-dozen fistfights. In retrospect, my shyness of combat has clear sources.

As a boy, I saw countless tough guys locked away; I have since buried several, too. They were babies, really—a teenage cousin, a brother of twenty-two, a childhood friend in his mid-twenties—all gone down in episodes of bravado played out in the streets. I came to doubt the virtues of intimidation early on. I chose, perhaps unconsciously, to remain a shadow—timid, but a survivor.

The fearsomeness mistakenly attributed to me in public places often has a perilous flavor. The most frightening of these confusions occurred in the late 1970s and early 1980s, when I worked as a journalist in Chicago. One day, rushing into the office of a magazine I was writing for with a deadline story in hand, I was mistaken for a burglar. The office manager called security and, with an ad hoc posse, pursued me through the labyrinthine halls, nearly to my editor's door. I had no way of proving who I was. I could only move briskly toward the company of someone who knew me.

Another time I was on assignment for a local paper and killing time before an interview. I entered a jewelry store on the city's affluent Near North Side. The proprietor excused herself and returned with an enormous red Doberman pinscher straining at the end of a leash. She stood, the dog extended toward me, silent to my questions, her eyes bulging nearly out of her head. I took a cursory look around, nodded, and bade her good night.

Relatively speaking, however, I never fared as badly as another black male journalist. He went to nearby Waukegan, Illinois, a couple of summers ago to work on a story about a murderer who was born there. Mistaking the reporter for the killer, police officers hauled him from his car at gunpoint and but for his press credentials would probably have tried to book him. Such episodes are not uncommon. Black men trade tales like this all the time.

Over the years, I learned to smother the rage I felt at so often being taken for a criminal. Not to do so would surely have led to madness. I now take precautions to make myself less threatening. I move about with care, particularly late in the evening. I give a wide berth to nervous people on subway platforms during the wee hours, particularly when I have exchanged business clothes for jeans. If I happen to be entering a building behind some people who appear skittish, I may walk by, letting them clear the lobby before I return, so as not to seem to be following them. I have been calm and extremely congenial on those rare occasions when I've been pulled over by the police.

And on late-evening constitutionals I employ what has proved to be an excellent tension-reducing measure: I whistle melodies from Beethoven and Vivaldi and the more popular classical composers. Even steely New Yorkers hunching toward nighttime destinations seem to relax, and occasionally they even join in the tune. Virtually everybody seems to sense that a mugger wouldn't be warbling bright, sunny selections from Vivaldi's *Four Seasons*. It is my equivalent of the cowbell that hikers wear when they know they are in bear country.

[1986]

 ## Joining the Conversation: Critical Thinking and Writing

1. In "Black Men and Public Space," what do you take to be Staples's *purpose*? Do you think he was writing chiefly to clarify some ideas for himself—for instance, to explore how he came to discover the "alienation that comes of being ever the suspect"? Or writing to assist blacks? Or to assist whites? Or what? (You may of course conclude that none of these suggestions, or all, are relevant.)

2. If you think the essay is effective, try to account for its effectiveness. Do certain examples strike you as particularly forceful? If so, why? Do certain sentences seem especially memorable? Again, why? For example, if the opening and concluding paragraphs strike you as effective, explain why. On the other hand, if you're unimpressed by part or all of the essay, explain why.

3. The success of a narrative as a piece of writing often depends on the reader's willingness to identify with the narrator. From an examination of "Black Men and Public Space," what explanations can you give for your willingness (or unwillingness) to identify yourself with Staples? (You'll probably want to say something about his persona as you sense it from the essay.) In the course of a 500-word essay explaining your position, very briefly summarize Staples's essay and state his thesis.

4. Have *you* ever unintentionally altered public space? For example, you might recall an experience in which, as a child, your mere presence caused adults to alter their behavior—for example, to stop quarreling. Write an essay in which you recall that experience and its effect on you. For your opening paragraph, you might want to imitate the strategy Staples adopted for his first paragraph. (Suggested length: 750 words.)

5. If you have ever been in the position of one of Staples's "victims"—that is, if you have ever shown fear or suspicion of someone who, it turned out, meant you no harm (or if you can imagine being in that position)—write an essay from the "victim's" point of view. Explain what happened and what you did and thought. Did you think at the time about the feelings of the person you avoided or fled from? Has reading Staples's essay prompted further reflections on your experience? (Suggested length:750 words.)

CHAPTER 2

A Reader Writes

All there is to writing is having ideas. To learn to write is to learn to have ideas.

–Robert Frost

In the previous chapter, we proposed that students, as *critical readers* (we might say *active readers*), should be able to

- Locate the thesis (the point, the claim) of an argument;
- Locate the assumptions, stated and unstated; and
- Analyze and evaluate the strength of the evidence and the soundness of the reasoning offered in support of the thesis.

Those were our concerns in the chapter called "A Writer Reads." Our concerns in the present chapter, "A Reader Writes," are closely related. Students and instructors will probably agree that, *as thoughtful writers*, students should be able to

- Imagine an audience and write effectively for it (for example, by using the appropriate tone and providing the appropriate amount of detail);
- Present information in an orderly and coherent way;
- Be aware of their own assumptions;
- Locate sources and incorporate them into their own writing, not simply by quoting extensively or by paraphrasing but also by having digested material so they can present it in their own words;
- Properly document all borrowings—not merely quotations and paraphrases but also borrowed ideas; and
- Do all of these things in the course of developing a thoughtful argument of their own.

All these activities help you to think about what you are reading.
"It is thinking," the philosopher John Locke wrote, "that makes what we read ours," and in writing college essays, part of your job will be to incorporate what you have read *into your own thinking*. Sometimes you will briefly summarize what you have read—perhaps from more than one source—but almost always, your essay will also present your own view, or argument, in which you reveal to what extent you agree with your sources and where you question, disagree, or build on them.

A Note on Writing a Summary

We have just said that although an academic essay customarily requires you to set forth your own thoughts, you may sometimes want to summarize a position—for example, the gist of an essay that you will go on to analyze or to argue against. That is, you may want to offer a condensation or abridgment, briefly giving the reader the gist of a longer work. Here are a few principles that govern summaries:

1. A summary is much briefer than the original. It is not a paraphrase—a word-by-word translation of someone's words into your own—for a paraphrase is usually at least as long as the original, whereas a summary is rarely longer than one-fourth the original and may even be much briefer—perhaps condensing an entire essay into a sentence or two.

2. A summary usually achieves its brevity by omitting almost all the concrete details of the original and presenting only the sum that the details add up to.

3. A summary is accurate; it has no value if it misrepresents the point of the original.

4. The writer of a summary need not make the points in the same order as that of the original. In fact, a reader is occasionally driven to write a summary because the original author does not present the argument in an orderly sequence; the summary is an attempt to disengage the author's argument from the confusing presentation.

5. A summary is normally written in the present tense because the writer assumes that although the author wrote the piece last year or 100 years ago, the piece speaks to us today. (In other words, the summary is explicitly or implicitly prefaced by "The author says," and all that follows is in the present tense.)

6. Because a summary is openly based on someone else's views, not your own, some instructors believe you need not use quotation marks around any words that you take from the original, but other instructors strongly disagree. Check with your instructor.

Here is a summary of this discussion on summary:

> A summary is a condensation or abridgment. These are some characteristics: (1) It's rarely more than one-fourth as long as the original; (2) its brevity is usually achieved by leaving out most of the concrete details of the original; (3) it is accurate; (4) it may rearrange the organization of the original, especially if a rearrangement will make things clearer; (5) it normally is in the present tense; (6) some instructors say quoted words need not be enclosed in quotation marks; check with your instructor.

In your composition courses, in other courses across the disciplines, and, we expect, during your whole life, you will be reading or listening, and you will often want to respond in writing. Often, you will also find that you cannot assume that your readers are familiar with the work to which you are responding, and in these instances, you probably will offer a brief summary, such as this passage about Steiner's essay (page 5) on veganism:

> Gary Steiner's "Animal, Vegetable, Miserable" argues that the human use of animals—not only for food but also for clothing and even (as in circuses) for

entertainment—is immoral. The important point, he says, is not whether we slaughter animals humanely but whether it is or is not wrong to make use of them. For example, he insists that is a mistake to think that eating "free range" animals is acceptable, and he also insists that animal welfare laws are inadequate because they are written by persons who regard animals as inferior creatures. He recognizes that being a vegan (a person who avoids using all animal products) is difficult, but he argues that the behavior of nonvegans is immoral.

The student's essay on the issue might then continue:

> Let's look both at Steiner's assumptions and at his evidence.

Incorporating Your Reading into Your Thinking: The Art and Science of Synthesis

A much-quoted passage—at least, it is much-quoted by teachers of composition—is by Kenneth Burke (1897–1993), a college drop-out who became one of America's most important twentieth-century students of rhetoric. Burke wrote:

> Imagine that you enter a parlor. You come late. When you arrive, others have long preceded you, and they are engaged in a heated discussion, a discussion too heated for them to pause and tell you exactly what it is about. In fact, the discussion had already begun long before any of them got there, so that no one present is qualified to retrace for you all the steps that had gone before. You listen for a while, until you decide that you have caught the tenor of the argument; then you put in your oar. Someone answers; you answer him; another comes to your defense; another aligns himself against you, to either the embarrassment or gratification of your opponent, depending upon the quality of your ally's assistance. However, the discussion is interminable. The hour grows late, you must depart. And you do depart, with the discussion still vigorously in progress.

> *The Philosophy of Literary Form* (Baton Rouge: Louisiana State University Press, 1941), 110–111.

Why do we quote this passage? Because it is your turn to join the unending conversation.

Notice that Burke says in this metaphoric discussion of the life of a thoughtful person, "You listen for a while, until you decide that you have caught the tenor of the argument; then you put in your oar." There may be times in your daily life when it is acceptable to make use of Twitter and to shoot off 140 characters, but for serious matters, you will want to think about what you are saying before you give it to the world, and you will want to convey more than 140 characters. (We admit that quite a lot can be said in 140 characters—for example, the forceful words in *Brown v. Board of Education of Topeka* that "Separate educational facilities are inherently unequal" or the anonymous insight that "There is no such thing as a free lunch"—but most of us lack the genius that will enable us to produce such compressed wisdom.)

During the process of reading and especially afterward, you will want to listen, think, say to yourself something such as:

- "No, no, I see things very differently; it seems to me that . . . "or
- "Yes, of course, but on one large issue, I think I differ . . . "or
- "Yes, sure, I agree, but I would go further and add . . . "or
- "Yes, I agree with your conclusion, but I hold this conclusion for reasons very different from the ones that you offer."

During at least your composition courses—and, we think, during your entire life—you will be reading or listening and will sometimes want to put in your oar or will sometimes want to respond in writing—for example, in the form of a Letter to the Editor or in a memo at your place of employment. In the course of your response, you almost surely will have to summarize very briefly the idea or ideas you are responding to so your readers will understand the context of your remarks. These ideas may not come from a single source; you may be responding to several sources—for example, to a report and also to some comments that the report evoked. In any case, you will state these ideas briefly and fairly, and will then set forth your thoughtful responses, thereby giving the reader a statement that you hope represents an advance in the argument, even if only a tiny one. That is, you will **synthesize** sources—combining existing material into something new, drawing nourishment from what has already been said (giving credit, of course), and converting it into something new: a view that you think is worth considering.

A Controversial Essay

C. S. Lewis

*Clive Staples Lewis (1898–1963) taught English literature at Oxford and at Cambridge, but he is most widely known not for his books on literature but for his books on Christianity (*The Screwtape Letters *is one of the most famous), his children's novels (collected in a seven-volume set called* The Chronicles of Narnia*), and his science fiction (for example,* Perelandra*). Lewis also wrote autobiographical volumes and many essays on literature and on morality. The essay printed here—the last thing that he wrote—was published in* The Saturday Evening Post *in December 1963, shortly after his death.*

We Have No "Right to Happiness"

After all, said Clare, "they had a right to happiness."

We were discussing something that once happened in our own neighborhood. Mr. A. had deserted Mrs. A. and got his divorce in order to marry Mrs. B., who had likewise got her divorce in order to marry Mr. A. And there was certainly no doubt that Mr. A. and Mrs. B. were very much in love with one another. If they continued to be in love, and if nothing went wrong with their health or their income, they might reasonably expect to be very happy.

It was equally clear that they were not happy with their old partners. Mrs. B. had adored her husband at the outset. But then he got smashed up in the war. It was thought he had lost his virility, and it was known that he had lost his job. Life with him was no longer what Mrs. B. had bargained for. Poor Mrs. A., too. She had lost her looks—and all her liveliness. It might be true, as some said, that she consumed herself by bearing his children and nursing him through the long illness that overshadowed their earlier married life.

You mustn't, by the way, imagine that A. was the sort of man who nonchalantly threw a wife away like the peel of an orange he'd sucked dry. Her suicide was a terrible shock to him. We all knew this, for he told us so himself. "But what could I do?" he said. "A man has a right to happiness. I had to take my one chance when it came."

I went away thinking about the concept of a "right to happiness."   5

At first this sounds to me as odd as a right to good luck. For I believe—whatever one school of moralists may say—that we depend for a very great deal of our happiness or misery on circumstances outside all human control. A right to happiness doesn't, for me, make much more sense than a right to be six feet tall, or to have a millionaire for your father, or to get good weather whenever you want to have a picnic.

I can understand a right as a freedom guaranteed me by the laws of the society I live in. Thus, I have a right to travel along the public roads because society gives me that freedom; that's what we mean by calling the roads "public." I can also understand a right as a claim guaranteed me by the laws, and correlative to an obligation on someone else's part. If I have a right to receive £100 from you, this is another way of saying that you have a duty to pay me £100. If the laws allow Mr. A. to desert his wife and seduce his neighbor's wife, then, by definition, Mr. A. has a legal right to do so, and we need bring in no talk about "happiness."

But of course that was not what Clare meant. She meant that he had not only a legal but a moral right to act as he did. In other words, Clare is—or would be if she thought it out—a classical moralist after the style of Thomas Aquinas, Grotius, Hooker and Locke. She believes that behind the laws of the state there is a Natural Law.[1]

I agree with her. I hold this conception to be basic to all civilization. Without it, the actual laws of the state become an absolute, as in Hegel. They cannot be criticized because there is no norm against which they should be judged.

The ancestry of Clare's maxim, "They have a right to happiness," is august. In words that are cherished by all civilized men, but especially by Americans, it has been laid down that one of the rights of man is a right to "the pursuit of happiness." And now we get to the real point.

What did the writers of that august declaration mean?

It is quite certain what they did not mean. They did not mean that man was entitled to pursue happiness by any and every means—including, say, murder, rape, robbery, treason and fraud. No society could be built on such a basis.

They meant "to pursue happiness by all lawful means"; that is, by all means which the Law of Nature eternally sanctions and which the laws of the nation shall sanction.

Admittedly this seems at first to reduce their maxim to the tautology that men (in pursuit of happiness) have a right to do whatever they have a right to do. But tautologies, seen against their proper historical context, are not always barren tautologies. The declaration is primarily a denial of the political principles which long governed Europe: a challenge flung down to the Austrian and Russian empires, to England before the Reform Bills, to Bourbon France.[2] It demands that whatever means of pursuing happiness are lawful for any should be lawful for all; that "man," not men of some particular caste, class, status or religion, should be free to use them. In a century when this is being unsaid by nation after nation and party after party, let us not call it a barren tautology.

But the question as to what means are "lawful"—what methods of pursuing happiness are either morally permissible by the Law of Nature or should be declared legally permissible by the legislature of a particular nation—remains exactly where it did. And on that question I disagree with Clare. I don't think it is obvious that people have the unlimited "right to happiness" which she suggests.

[1]**Thomas Aquinas . . . Natural Law** Lewis names some philosophers and theologians from the thirteenth century through the eighteenth who believed that certain basic moral principles are evident to rational people in all periods and in all cultures. (Editors' note)
[2]**England . . . France** England before the bills that liberalized representation in Parliament in the nineteenth century, and France before the French Revolution of 1789–99. (Editors' note)

For one thing, I believe that Clare, when she says "happiness," means simply and solely "sexual happiness." Partly because women like Clare never use the word "happiness" in any other sense. But also because I never heard Clare talk about the "right" to any other kind. She was rather leftist in her politics, and would have been scandalized if anyone had defended the actions of a ruthless man-eating tycoon on the ground that his happiness consisted in making money and he was pursuing his happiness. She was also a rabid teetotaler; I never heard her excuse an alcoholic because he was happy when he was drunk.

A good many of Clare's friends, and especially her female friends, often felt—I've heard them say so—that their own happiness would be perceptibly increased by boxing her ears. I very much doubt if this would have brought her theory of a right to happiness into play.

Clare, in fact, is doing what the whole western world seems to me to have been doing for the last forty-odd years. When I was a youngster, all the progressive people were saying, "Why all this prudery? Let us treat sex just as we treat all our other impulses." I was simple-minded enough to believe they meant what they said. I have since discovered that they meant exactly the opposite. They meant that sex was to be treated as no other impulse in our nature has ever been treated by civilized people. All the others, we admit, have to be bridled. Absolute obedience to your instinct for self-preservation is what we call cowardice; to your acquisitive impulse, avarice. Even sleep must be resisted if you're a sentry. But every unkindness and breach of faith seems to be condoned provided that the object aimed at is "four bare legs in a bed."

It is like having a morality in which stealing fruit is considered wrong—unless you steal nectarines.

And if you protest against this view you are usually met with chatter about the legitimacy and beauty and sanctity of "sex" and accused of harboring some Puritan prejudice against it as something disreputable or shameful. I deny the charge. Foam-born Venus . . . golden Aphrodite . . . Our Lady of Cyprus[3] . . . I never breathed a word against you. If I object to boys who steal my nectarines, must I be supposed to disapprove of nectarines in general? Or even of boys in general? It might, you know, be stealing that I disapproved of.

The real situation is skillfully concealed by saying that the question of Mr. A.'s "right" to desert his wife is one of "sexual morality." Robbing an orchard is not an offense against some special morality called "fruit morality." It is an offense against honesty. Mr. A.'s action is an offense against good faith (to solemn promises), against gratitude (toward one to whom he was deeply indebted) and against common humanity.

Our sexual impulses are thus being put in a position of preposterous privilege. The sexual motive is taken to condone all sorts of behavior

20

---

[3]**Foam-born Venus . . . Aphrodite . . . Cyprus** The Roman goddess Venus was identified with the Greek goddess of love, Aphrodite. Aphrodite sprang from the foam (*aphros*), and was especially worshipped in Cyprus. (Editors' note)

which, if it had any other end in view, would be condemned as merciless, treacherous and unjust.

Now though I see no good reason for giving sex this privilege, I think I see a strong cause. It is this.

It is part of the nature of a strong erotic passion—as distinct from a transient fit of appetite—that it makes more towering promises than any other emotion. No doubt all our desires make promises, but not so impressively. To be in love involves the almost irresistible conviction that one will go on being in love until one dies, and that possession of the beloved will confer, not merely frequent ecstasies, but settled, fruitful, deep-rooted, lifelong happiness. Hence *all* seems to be at stake. If we miss this chance we shall have lived in vain. At the very thought of such a doom we sink into fathomless depths of self-pity.

Unfortunately these promises are found often to be quite untrue. Every experienced adult knows this to be so as regards all erotic passions (except the one he himself is feeling at the moment). We discount the world-without-end pretensions of our friends' amours easily enough. We know that such things sometimes last—and sometimes don't. And when they do last, this is not because they promised at the outset to do so. When two people achieve lasting happiness, this is not solely because they are great lovers but because they are also—I must put it crudely— good people; controlled, loyal, fairminded, mutually adaptable people.

If we establish a "right to (sexual) happiness" which supersedes all the ordinary rules of behavior, we do so not because of what our passion shows itself to be in experience but because of what it professes to be while we are in the grip of it. Hence, while the bad behavior is real and works miseries and degradations, the happiness which was the object of the behavior turns out again and again to be illusory. Everyone (except Mr. A. and Mrs. B.) knows that Mr. A. in a year or so may have the same reason for deserting his new wife as for deserting his old. He will feel again that all is at stake. He will see himself again as the great lover, and his pity for himself will exclude all pity for the woman.

Two further points remain.

One is this. A society in which conjugal infidelity is tolerated must always be in the long run a society adverse to women. Women, whatever a few male songs and satires may say to the contrary, are more naturally monogamous than men; it is a biological necessity. Where promiscuity prevails, they will therefore always be more often the victims than the culprits. Also, domestic happiness is more necessary to them than to us. And the quality by which they most easily hold a man, their beauty, decreases every year after they have come to maturity, but this does not happen to those qualities of personality—women don't really care twopence about our *looks*—by which we hold women. Thus in the ruthless war of promiscuity women are at a double disadvantage. They play for higher stakes and are also more likely to lose. I have no sympathy with moralists who frown at the increasing crudity of female provocativeness. These signs of desperate competition fill me with pity.

Secondly, though the "right to happiness" is chiefly claimed for the sexual impulse, it seems to me impossible that the matter should stay there. The fatal principle, once allowed in that department, must sooner or later seep through our whole lives. We thus advance toward a state of society in which not only each man but every impulse in each man claims *carte blanche*.[4] And then, though our technological skill may help us survive a little longer, our civilization will have died at heart, and will—one dare not even add "unfortunately"—be swept away.

Responding to an Essay

After you have read Lewis's essay at least twice, you may want to jot down your responses to the basic questions that we introduced on page 11 after Steiner's essay. Here they are yet again, slightly abbreviated:

- What's the writer's thesis?
- How does the writer support the thesis?
- What's the writer's purpose?
- How does the writer shape the purpose to the audience?
- What's the writer's tone?
- How successful is the piece? What are its strengths and weaknesses?

And here, to help you to think further about Lewis's essay, are some specific questions to answer and points to consider:

- Having read the entire essay, look back at Lewis's first five paragraphs and point out the ways in which he is not merely recounting an episode but is already conveying his attitude and seeking to persuade.
- Lewis argues that we do not have a "right to (sexual) happiness." What *duty* or *duties* do we have, according to Lewis?
- In paragraph 25, Lewis writes:

  When two people achieve lasting happiness, this is not solely because they are great lovers but because they are also—I must put it crudely—good people; controlled, loyal, fairminded, mutually adaptable people.

  If you know of a couple who in your opinion have achieved "lasting happiness," do you agree with Lewis's view that their achievement is largely because they are "good people"?

- Evaluate Lewis's comment in paragraph 28 on the differences between men and women.

If you find yourself roughing out responses to any of these questions, you may be on the way toward writing a first draft of an essay.

[4]***Carte blanche*** Full permission to act (French for "blank card"). (Editors' note)

The Writing Process

An essay is a response to experience. In Chapter 1, Gary Steiner is responding to people who "express an interest in where the meat they eat comes from" (page 5). C. S. Lewis heard (or says that he heard) someone utter a comment about a right to happiness, and he was set to thinking and then to writing about it (page 26). Their essays came out of their experience. By *experience*, we don't mean only what they actually saw: Their experience included things they had read about and had reflected on. After all, Steiner's and Lewis's reports of behavior were at most only triggers, so to speak. A good deal of previous experience and a good deal of later experience—chiefly in the form of reading and of *thinking* about what they had read—went into the production of their essays.

In short, writers think about their responses to experience. You have been actively reading their responses—engaging in a dialogue with these authors—and so you have been undergoing your own experiences. You have things to say, though on any given topic you probably are not yet certain of *all* that you have to say or of how you can best say it. You need to get further ideas, to do further thinking. How do you get ideas? The short answer is that you will get ideas if you engage in an imagined dialogue with the authors whom you are reading. When you read an essay, you will find yourself asking such questions as, What evidence supports this assertion? Is the writer starting from assumptions with which I don't agree? Why do I especially like (or dislike) this essay?

Many writers—professionals as well as students—have found it useful to get their responses down on paper, either as annotations in the margins or as entries in a journal or both. Here, as a sample, are the annotations that one student jotted next to Lewis's third and fourth paragraphs.

It was equally clear that they were not happy with their old partners. Mrs. B. had adored her husband at the outset. But then he got smashed up in the war. It was thought he had lost his virility, and it was known that he had lost his job. Life with him was no longer what Mrs. B. had <u>bargained</u> for. Poor Mrs. A., too. She had lost her looks—and all her liveliness. It might be true, as some said, that she consumed herself by bearing his children and nursing him through the long illness that overshadowed their earlier married life.

These examples are caricatures. They really defeat L's purpose.

Loaded word. Makes her too calculating.

You mustn't, by the way, imagine that A. was the sort of man who nonchalantly threw a wife away like the peel of an orange he'd sucked dry. Her suicide was a terrible shock to him. We all knew this, for <u>he told us so himself</u>. "But what could I do?" he said. "A man has a right to happiness. I had to take my one chance when it came."

Is CSL making him too awful?

Annotations of this sort are often the starting point for entries in a journal.

Keeping a Journal

A journal is not a diary, a record of what the writer did during the day ("Today, I read Lewis's 'We Have No "Right to Happiness"'"). Rather, a journal is a place to store some of the thoughts that you may have scribbled on a bit of paper or in the margin of the text—for example, your initial response to the title of an essay or to something you particularly liked or disliked. It is also a place to jot down further reflections. You can record your impressions as they come to you in any order—almost as though you are talking to yourself. Because no one else is going to read your notes, you can be entirely free and at ease. The student whose annotations we reproduced a moment ago wrote the following entry in his journal:

> I find Lewis's writing is very clear and in its way persuasive,
> but I also think that his people—A. and B. and Clare—are not real
> people. They are almost caricatures. Anyway, he certainly has
> chosen people (or invented them?) who help him make his case.
> What if Mrs. B.'s husband had been a wife-beater, or maybe
> someone who molested their daughter? Would Lewis still think
> Mrs. B. was wrong to leave Mr. B.?

A second student wrote a rather different entry in her journal:

> Lewis at first seems to be arguing against a "right to happiness,"
> but really he is arguing against adultery and divorce, against what
> we can call the Playboy morality—the idea that if a middle-aged
> man divorces his middle-aged wife because he now finds his
> young secretary attractive, he is acting maturely.

Here is a third entry:

> Terrific. That story about A. and B. really got to me. But is it true?
> Does it matter if it isn't true? Probably not; there are people like
> the A.'s and the B.'s. Lewis really is awfully good at holding my
> interest. And I was really grabbed by that business about a right
> to happiness being as strange as a right to be six feet tall. But my
> question is this: I agree that we don't have a right to be six feet
> tall, but why, then, do we have any rights? Lewis talks about
> Natural Law, but what is that?

> Is the idea of one husband and one wife "Natural Law"? If so, how
> come so many societies don't obey it? When Bertrand Russell
> talks about natural instincts and emotions "which we inherit from
> our animal ancestors," is this like Natural Law?

> Still, I think Lewis is terrific. And I think he is probably right about
> the difference between men and women. It seems obvious to me

that men care more about a woman's looks than women care about a man's looks. How can this be checked?

You might even make a journal entry in the form of a letter to the author or in the form of a dialogue. Or you might have Mr. A. and Mrs. B. give *their* versions of the story that Clare reports.

Questioning the Text Again

We have already suggested that one way to increase your understanding of an essay and to get ideas that you may use in an essay of your own is to ask questions of the selection that you have read. Let's begin by thinking about the questions we asked following C. S. Lewis's "We Have No 'Right to Happiness'" (pages 26–30). All of these could provide topics for your own essays. Some were questions that might be asked of any essay—about the author's thesis, the way in which the author supports the thesis, the author's purpose, the author's persona or tone, and your evaluation of the essay. And there were questions specifically about Lewis's essay, concerning Lewis's comments on rights and his comments about the differences between men and women.

Probably the most obvious topic for an essay such as Lewis's is:

What's the author's thesis, and how sound is it?

One student formulated the thesis as follows:

We not only do not have a "right" to sexual happiness, but we probably cannot achieve lasting happiness if we allow sex to govern behavior that otherwise "would be condemned as merciless, treacherous and unjust."

An essay concerning Lewis's thesis might be narrowed to:

Does Lewis give a one-sided view of divorce?

or

Does Lewis underestimate (or overestimate) the importance of sexual satisfaction?

But other topics easily come to mind:

- Lewis's methods as a writer
- The logic of Lewis's argument

Take the matter of Lewis's methods, a topic of special interest if you are trying to become a better writer. One student who planned to write about this topic made the following notes.

Summaries, Jottings, Outlines, and Lists

(Parenthetic numbers refer to Lewis's paragraphs.)

1. Purpose is obviously to persuade. How does he do it?
2. Very informal manner:
    a. Begins by telling of a conversation he had (1).
    b. Often uses "I"; for instance, "I went away thinking" (5); "this sounds to me" (6); "I can understand" (7); "I was simple-minded enough to believe" (18). So the tone is personal, as if he and the reader were having a conversation.
3. Though informal, seems very educated:
    a. Cites authorities, apparently philosophers, in par.8 (check these names); refers to Austrian, Russian, English, and French history (14).
    b. Educated vocabulary ("tautologies" in par. 14).
4. But also uses easy examples: Mr. and Mrs. A. and Mr. and Mrs. B. in first paragraph; stealing fruit (19–21).
5. Makes the abstract clear by being concrete. In par. 18, when he says that our impulses have to be controlled, he says, "Absolute obedience to your instinct for self-preservation is what we call cowardice. . . ."
6. Sentences are all clear. Some are very short ("I agree with her" 9), but even the long sentences—several lines of type—are clear. Give one (or maybe two) examples?
7. In next-to-last par., frankly speaks as a male: "domestic happiness is more necessary to them [that is, women] than to us." And "the quality by which they [that is, women] most easily hold a man," and "women don't really care twopence about our <u>looks</u>" (all in 28). Sense of a man talking heart-to-heart to men. But how might it strike a woman? Sexist? Ask Jane and Tina.

You may prefer to record your thoughts in the form of lists:

Methods:
    Examples
    Anecdote about A. and B. (par.1)
    Stealing fruit (19–21)
Informal style:
    Uses "I" (many places)
    Also uses "we"
Clear sentences (give examples)
Vocabulary:
    Usually simple words
    A few hard words ("tautologies" in par. 14)
Beginning: an individual listening
End: rather authoritative; generalizes about men vs. women

Further thinking and further readings of Lewis's essay produced more evidence, and the material then had to be reorganized into a clear and effective sequence, but these notes and lists were highly promising. The student who wrote them was well on the way to writing a strong first draft.

After converting his notes into a draft and then revising the draft, an interesting—yet rather common—thing happened. The student found himself dissatisfied with his point. He now felt that he wanted to say something different. It turned out that the annotations and the drafts were a way of helping him to get to a deeper response to Lewis's essay, so he rewrote his essay with a different focus. But we are getting ahead of our story.

✓ A Checklist: Getting Started

- ☐ Have I adequately previewed the work?
- ☐ Can I state the thesis?
- ☐ If I have jotted down a summary,
  - ☐ Is the summary accurate?
  - ☐ Does the summary mention all the chief points?
  - ☐ If there are inconsistencies, are they in the summary or the original selection?
  - ☐ Will the summary be clear and helpful?

Getting Ready to Write a Draft

After jotting down notes (and further notes stimulated by rereading and further thinking), you can probably formulate a tentative thesis: a point such as "Lewis argues with great skill," or "Lewis does not make clear the concept of Natural Law," or "Lewis generalizes too freely," or "Lewis has a narrow idea of why people divorce." At this point, most writers find it useful to clear the air by glancing over their preliminary notes and by jotting down the thesis and a few especially promising notes— brief statements of what they think their key points may be. These notes may include some key quotations that the writer thinks will help support the thesis.

Draft of an Essay

On "We Have No 'Right to Happiness'"

When I first read the title of C. S. Lewis's essay, I was interested and also somewhat resistant. Without having given much thought to it, I believe that I do have a right to happiness. I don't want to give up this right or this belief. Still I was intrigued to know what Lewis had to say. After reading the essay, it seemed entirely reasonable to say that if there is a right to happiness there are also limits to it. So I decided to look at how Lewis managed to make me change my mind—at least part way.

C. S. Lewis is persuasive, especially because of three things. First, although Lewis (a professor) is obviously very learned, he uses an informal manner that sounds very natural and honest. Second, he gives clear examples. Three, his sentences are always clear. This is true even when they are not especially short. All of these things combine together to make his essay clear and interesting. Lewis is an Englishman, not an American.

Lewis's informal manner, especially seen in his use of the first-person pronoun, appears right away. In the second sentence, when he says "We were discussing something. . . ." He uses "I" in the fifth paragraph and in many later paragraphs.

Another sign of Lewis's informality is his use of such expressions as "It might be true, as some said," and "You mustn't, by the way, imagine," and "for one thing." It sounds like an ordinary person talking, even though Lewis also mentions the names of philosophers in paragraph 8, and in paragraph 14 mentions several historical matters.

Next I will deal with Lewis's examples. The examples help him to be clear to the reader. The essay begins with a story about four people. Two said they had a "right to happiness." In this story Lewis lets us see two people (Mr. A. and Mrs. B.) who behave very badly. They justify their behavior simply by saying they have a right to happiness. They behave so badly—Mr. A. deserts the wife who nursed him through a long illness, and Mrs. B. deserts her husband, who is a wounded veteran—that just to hear them talk about a "right to happiness" is almost enough to make you say they should not be happy and they certainly do not have a right to happiness. The example of Mr. and Mrs. A. and Mr. and Mrs. B. is the longest example that Lewis gives, but Lewis several times gives short examples. These short examples make his point clear. For instance, when he wants to show how silly it is to treat sex differently from all other impulses, he says that it is "like having a morality in which stealing fruit is considered wrong—unless you steal nectarines."

Another thing Lewis does to persuade the reader is to write very clear sentences. Some of his sentences are long—about three lines of print—but the reader has no trouble with them. Here is an example of this sort of sentence.

> A right to happiness doesn't, for me, make much more sense than a right to be six feet tall, or to have a millionaire for your father, or to get good weather whenever you want to have a picnic.

The only thing that causes any trouble is a few unfamiliar words such as "tautologies" (paragraph 14) and "tycoon" (paragraph 16), but you can understand the essay even without looking up such words.

Revising and Editing a Draft

To write a good essay, you must be a good reader—not only of the essay you are writing about but also of the essay you yourself are writing. We're not talking about proofreading or correcting spelling errors, although you must also engage in those activities.

Revising. In revising their work, writers ask themselves such questions as,

- Do I mean what I say?
- Do I say what I mean? (Answering this question will cause you to ask yourself such questions as "Do I need to define my terms?" "Add examples to clarify?" "Reorganize the material so a reader can grasp it?")

During this part of the writing process, you do your best to read the draft in a skeptical frame of mind. In taking account of your doubts, you will probably unify, organize, clarify, and polish the draft.

- **Unity** is achieved partly by eliminating irrelevancies. For example, in the second paragraph of the draft, the writer says that "Lewis is an Englishman, not an American," but the fact that Lewis is English is not clearly relevant to the student's argument that Lewis writes persuasively. The statement should be deleted—or its relevance should be demonstrated.

- **Organization** is largely a matter of arranging material into a sequence that will assist the reader to grasp the point. If you reread your draft and jot down a paragraph outline of the sort shown on pages 13–14, you can then see if the draft has a reasonable organization—a structure that will let the reader move easily from the beginning to the end.
- **Clarity** is largely achieved by providing concrete details, examples, and quotations to support generalizations and by providing helpful transitions ("for example," "furthermore," "on the other hand," "however").
- **Polish** involves small-scale revision. For example, you may delete unnecessary repetitions. In the first sentence of the second paragraph, "C. S. Lewis" can effectively be changed to "Lewis"—there really is no need to repeat his initials—and in the second sentence of the second paragraph "Lewis" can be changed to "he." Similarly, in polishing, a writer combines choppy sentences into longer sentences and breaks overly long sentences into shorter sentences.

Editing. After producing a draft that seems good enough to show to someone, writers engage in yet another activity. They edit; that is, they check the accuracy of quotations by comparing them with the original, check a dictionary for the spelling of doubtful words, check a handbook for doubtful punctuation—for example, whether a comma or a semicolon is needed in a particular sentence.

A Revised Draft

Persuasive Strategies in C. S. Lewis's

~~On~~ "We Have No 'Right to Happiness'"

~~When I first read the title of C. S. Lewis's essay I was interested and also somewhat resistant. Without having given much thought to it, I believe that I do have a right to happiness. I don't want to give up this right or this belief. Still I was intrigued to know what Lewis has to say. After reading the essay it seemed entirely reasonable to say that if there is a right to happiness there are also limits to it. So I decided to look at how Lewis managed to make me change my mind, at least part way.~~

C. S. Lewis's "We Have No 'Right to Happiness'" is surprisingly persuasive—"surprisingly" because I believe in the right to happiness which is mentioned in the Declaration of Independence. Lewis, an Englishman writing in an American magazine, probably knew he was facing an audience who did not hold his view, and he apparently decided to begin by stating his position as directly as possible in his title, "We Have No 'Right to Happiness.'" How does he win his reader over?

C. S. Lewis is persuasive because in addition to thinking carefully, he writes effectively. Three features of his writing especially contribute to his effectiveness.

~~C. S. Lewis is persuasive especially because of three things.~~ First,
although Lewis (a professor) is obviously very learned, he uses an informal
manner that ~~sounds very natural and honest~~. *helps to establish a bond between him and his reader* Second, he gives clear
examples. ~~Three~~, *Third* his sentences are always clear. This is true even when
they are not especially short. All of these things combine together to make
his essay clear and interesting. ~~Lewis is an Englishman, not an American.~~

Lewis's informal manner, especially seen in his use of the first-
person pronoun, appears right away. ~~In~~ *in* the second sentence, when he
says "We were discussing something. . . ." He uses "I" in the fifth
paragraph and in many later paragraphs.

Another sign of Lewis's informality is his use of such expressions
as "It might be true, as some said," and "You mustn't, by the way,
imagine," and "for one thing." It sounds like an ordinary person talking,
even though Lewis also mentions the names of philosophers in paragraph
8, and in paragraph 14 mentions several historical matters.

As for ~~Next I will deal with Lewis's~~ examples. ~~The examples~~ *which* help him to
be clear ~~to the reader. The essay begins with a story about four people.~~ *, the story of Mr. & Mrs. A. and Mr. & Mrs. B. is a good illustration.*
~~Two said they~~ *Mr. A. & Mrs. B. both of whom believed they* had a "right to happiness.~~" In this story Lewis lets us see~~
~~two people (Mr. A. and Mrs. B.) who behave very badly. They justify their~~
~~behavior simply by saying they have a right to happiness.~~ They behave
so badly—Mr. A. deserts the wife who nursed him through a long illness,
and Mrs. B. deserts her husband, who is a wounded veteran—that just to
hear them talk about a "right to happiness" is almost enough to make you
~~say they should not be happy and they certainly do not have a right to~~ *doubt that there can be such a right*
~~happiness~~. The example of Mr. and Mrs. A. and Mr. and Mrs. B. is the
longest example that Lewis gives, but ~~Lewis~~ *he* several times gives short
examples. ~~These short examples~~ *that* make his point clear. For instance, when
he wants to show how silly it is to treat sex differently from all other

impulses, he says that it is "like having a morality in which stealing fruit is considered wrong—unless you steal nectarines."

Lewis's third persuasive technique

~~Another thing Lewis does to persuade the reader~~ is to write very clear sentences. Some of his sentences are long—about three lines of print—but the reader has no trouble with them. Here is an example of this sort of sentence.

> A right to happiness doesn't, for me, make much more
>
> sense than a right to be six feet tall, or to have a
>
> millionaire for your father, or to get good weather
>
> whenever you want to have a picnic.

The sentence is fairly long, partly because the second half gives three examples, but because these examples are given in a parallel construction ("to be," "or to have," "or to get") the reader easily follows the thought.

True,

~~The only thing that causes any trouble is~~ a few unfamiliar words such as

may cause a bit of trouble

tautologies (paragraph 14) and tycoon (paragraph 16), but ~~you~~ can

a reader

understand the essay even without looking up such words.

Of course Lewis has not absolutely proved that there is no "right to happiness," but he has made a good, clear case. The clarity, in fact, is part of the case. Everything that Lewis says here seems so obvious that a reader is almost persuaded by Lewis's voice alone.

Rethinking the Thesis: Preliminary Notes

You'll probably agree that the student improved his draft—for example, by deleting the original first paragraph and replacing it with a more focused paragraph. But as we mentioned earlier, when the student thought further about his revision, he was still dissatisfied with it because he no longer fully believed his thesis.

He found that although he continued to admire Lewis's persuasive techniques, he remained unpersuaded by Lewis's argument. He therefore felt obliged to change the thesis of his essay from (approximately) "Lewis's chief persuasive techniques are..." to "Although Lewis is highly skilled as a persuasive writer, even his rhetorical skill cannot overcome certain weaknesses in his thesis."

Here are some of the annotations that the student produced after he recognized his dissatisfaction with his revised draft.

Mr. and Mrs. A. and B. may or may not be real people, but they certainly seem UNREAL: too neatly suited (all good or bad) to L's purpose.

> The villains: Mr. A. (he tosses out his wife after she loses her looks, despite the fact that she wore herself out with his children and nursed him through long illness; even after wife commits suicide he doesn't see that he continues to talk selfishly); Mrs. B. (she leaves her husband when he gets wounded and he loses his "virility" and loses his job). Aren't these people a bit too awful? Are they really typical of people who divorce?
>
> The heroes—or saints? Mrs. A. (nursed husband through long illness, wore self out with the children); Mr. B. (injured in war; loses job).

Clare: She also seems too suited to CSL's thesis; she's pretty terrible, and stupid too.

Lewis on Divorce: He seems to think it is always motivated by a desire for sex, and that it is always wrong. But what if a husband abuses his wife—maybe physically, or maybe verbally and emotionally? Maybe chronic alcoholic, refuses treatment, etc.? Or what if wife abuses husband—probably not physically, but verbally, and maybe she assaults kids? Or take another angle: what if woman married at too young an age, inexperienced, married to escape from an awful family, and now finds she made a mistake? Should she stay married to the man for life? In short, does Lewis see divorce from enough angles?

First five paragraphs are extremely interesting, but are unfair for three reasons:

1. Lewis loads the dice, showing us goodies and baddies, and then says (par.5) that they set him to thinking about the "right to happiness";
2. He overemphasizes the importance of sex, neglects other possible reasons why people divorce;
3. His discussion of "Natural Law," is not convincing to me. I simply am not convinced that there is a "Law of Nature" that "eternally sanctions" certain things.

Sexist??? Although CSL seems to be defending women (esp. par. 28, in which he says that promiscuity puts women at a double disadvantage), there is something sort of sexist in the essay, and I imagine that this will turn off women, and maybe even men. I know that I'm a little bothered by it.

The Final Version

We won't take you through the drafts that the student wrote, but in reading the final version, you will notice that although some of the points from the draft are retained, the thesis has shifted. For example, notice that the first paragraph of the revised draft is used in the final version but with two significant changes: In the first sentence, the student now adds that he finds Lewis's essay "finally unconvincing," and in the last sentence of the paragraph, he implies that he will discuss why the essay is "not finally convincing."

Jim Weinstein

Professor Valdez

English Composition 12

Style and Argument:

An Examination of C. S. Lewis's

"We Have No 'Right to Happiness'"

C. S. Lewis's "We Have No 'Right to Happiness'" is, though finally unconvincing, surprisingly persuasive—"surprisingly" because I believe in the right to happiness, which is mentioned in the Declaration of Independence. Lewis, an Englishman writing in an American magazine, probably knew he was facing an audience who did not hold his view, and he apparently decided to begin by stating his position as directly as possible in his title: "We Have No 'Right to Happiness.'" How does he nearly win his reader over? And why is he not finally convincing?

Lewis is highly (though not entirely) persuasive because he writes effectively. Three features of his writing especially contribute to his effectiveness. First, although Lewis (a professor) is obviously very learned, he uses an informal manner that helps to establish a bond between him and his reader. Second, he gives clear examples. Third, his sentences are always clear, even when they are not especially short. All of these things combine to make his essay clear and interesting—and almost convincing.

His informal manner, especially his use of the first-person pronouns, appears right away in the second sentence, when he says "We were discussing something. . . ." He uses "I" in the fifth paragraph and in many later paragraphs. Another sign of his informality is his use of such expressions as "It might be true, as some said," and "You mustn't, by the way, imagine." It sounds like an ordinary person talking.

Most of his examples, too, seem ordinary. They make his points seem almost obvious. For instance, when he wants to show how silly it is to treat sex differently from all other impulses, he says that it is "like having a morality in which stealing fruit is considered wrong—unless you steal nectarines" (p. 25). The touch of humor drives the point home.

Still, although Lewis seems thoughtful and he makes his argument very clear, the essay somehow does not finally persuade. The trouble may largely be Mr. and Mrs. A. and B., but there are other difficulties, too.

Mr. and Mrs. A. and B. are just too simple a case, too neat an illustration. Lewis of course wanted to make a clear-cut case, but a reader does not really believe in these people. They are caricatures: Mr. A. tosses out his wife after she loses her looks (and she lost them not only through the natural process of aging but through taking care of the family), and Mrs. B. leaves her husband, a wounded veteran. Of course it is conceivable that there really were a Mr. A. and a Mrs. B., but surely the pros and cons of divorce ought not to be based on cases like this, where it is so clear that Mr. A. and Mrs. B. are irresponsible. They are, one might say, as morally stupid as Clare is. But the fact that these people are selfish and stupid and that they each get a divorce does not prove that only selfish and stupid people seek divorce.

Nor do the experiences of the A.'s and the B.'s show that people who seek a divorce always are seeking sexual pleasure. We can imagine, for instance, a woman married to a wife-beater. Does she not have a right to be free of her abusive husband, a "right to happiness"? Nor need we limit our case to physical abuse. A husband (or a wife) can abuse a spouse verbally and emotionally and can be impossibly neglectful of the children. Or we can imagine a couple who married when very young—perhaps partly for the sake of defying their parents, or maybe in order to escape from a bad family situation. In any case, we can imagine that one member of the couple now sees that a bad mistake was made. Need they stay tied to each other?

Lewis's essay is powerful, partly because it clearly advances a thesis that must seem strange to many Americans; and it is interesting, partly because Lewis makes his points clearly and he seems to be such a thoughtful and decent person. But in the end, the essay is not convincing. It is just a little too simple in its examples and in its suggestion that people who claim a right to happiness are really just saying that they want to get divorced so they can live legally with another sexual partner.

Work Cited

Lewis, C. S. "We Have No 'Right to Happiness.'" *The Little, Brown Reader.* Ed. Marcia Stubbs and Sylvan Barnet. 12th ed. New York: Longman, 2012. 26-30. Print.

A Brief Overview of the Final Version

- First, a mechanical matter: A bibliographic note on a separate page headed "Work Cited" tells the reader where the essay can be found.
- The title, although not especially engaging, is informative—more so than, say, "On an Essay by C. S. Lewis." Readers know that the writer will discuss Lewis's style and argument in a particular essay.
- The student's final essay is *not* simply a balanced debate—a statement of the pros and cons that remains inconclusive. Rather, the student argues a thesis: Although Lewis's essay is in some ways admirable, it remains unconvincing.
- The student's thesis is stated in the first paragraph. It's almost always a good idea to let your reader know early where you're going.
- Quotations are used as evidence, not as padding. For example, see paragraphs 3 and 4.
- The writer has kept his reader in mind. He has not summarized Lewis's essay in needless detail, but on the other hand, he has not assumed that the reader knows the essay inside out. For example, he does not simply assert that Mr. A. behaves very badly; rather, he reminds us that Mr. A. rejects his wife after she loses her looks. When he uses a quotation, he guides the reader to where in Lewis's essay the quotation can be found.
- He also keeps the reader in mind by using helpful transitions. In paragraph 2, notice "First," "Second," and "Third"; in paragraph 5, "Still" indicates a reversal of direction. Also, notice that key words and phrases are repeated. Repetition of this sort, like transitions, makes it easy for the reader to follow the writer's train of thought.

For example, in the second paragraph, he cites Lewis's "informal manner" as the first of three points of style. His next paragraph begins, "His informal manner. . . ." Similarly, the last sentence of paragraph 3 contains the words "ordinary person." The next paragraph begins, "Most of his examples, too, seem ordinary."

- So far, we have talked about what is in the essay. But what is *not* in it is also worth comment. In the final essay, the student does *not* include all the points he jotted down in his preliminary notes. He does not take up either Natural Law or the issue of sexism, probably because he felt unsure about both. Notes are points of departure; if when you get going you find you are going down a blind alley, don't hesitate to go back and drop the point.

 ## Joining the Conversation: Thinking Further about an Essay

1. A scholar who generally admires Lewis's work has recently conceded, "One must admit that in some ways this essay, first published in 1963, has dated." Do you agree? Which features, if any, of the essay strike you as "dated" and which do not? Please point to evidence from the text to support your responses.

2. Another scholar, also an admirer of Lewis's work, has made a different claim about it: "The message of 'We Have No Right to Happiness' is as timely today as it was when Lewis wrote it." Do you agree or disagree? Make sure that you cite evidence from the text to support your argument.

✓ A Checklist: Analyzing Your Analysis

- ☐ Have I fairly summarized the writer's thesis?
- ☐ Have I considered and evaluated the kinds of evidence—for example, personal experience, statistics, authoritative testimony—the writer offers?
- ☐ Have I considered the writer's strategies from the beginning (the title) to the end, including the writer's tone?
- ☐ Is my essay organized so the reader can move through it easily without wondering where I am going?

CHAPTER 3

Academic Writing

Kinds of Prose

Traditionally, prose is said to be of four kinds: **exposition** (its chief purpose is to explain), **description** (it sets forth a detailed account of appearances or sensations), **narration** (it recounts a sequence of events, telling a story), and **persuasion** or **argument** (it attempts to get readers to accept or act on the writer's views). Thus, an essay or a book on how to improve one's game of tennis chiefly will be an

- *exposition*—a putting forth of information.
- In fact, however, the essay or book on how to improve one's game probably will also include a good deal of *description* (it will describe as accurately as possible the motion of the arm),
- and it may include some *narration* ("Tennis seems to have originated in the courts of fourteenth-century France, originally was played with balls stuffed with horse hair, and from France the game traveled to Germany and England . . ." or "You may already be familiar with the story of how Venus Williams became the great player that she now is, but the story is worth repeating here").
- However, the discussion of how to improve our tennis probably will not contain much *persuasive* writing because the author assumes that the readers are already sold on the game. On the other hand, we can reasonably say that simply by writing about how to improve your game, the author is in effect persuading you to stay with the game, implicitly telling you that, gee, even *you* can become a pretty good player.

When you think about it, almost *all* writing is persuasive because it says, in effect, "I find this interesting and I want you to find it interesting too." Even a note on a refrigerator door—"Egg salad sandwich and apple on lower shelf"—is partly an attempt to persuade the reader to leave the cold roast beef and the ice cream alone. Consider for a moment Thomas Jefferson's Declaration of Independence (page 447). On the surface, it's chiefly *expository*. Jefferson explains why the time has come for certain people to declare their independence from England; that's the expository part—the setting forth of information—although it also includes a good deal of narration because Jefferson tells us that the King of England did this ("He has dissolved Representative Houses repeatedly") and the king did that ("He has kept among us, in times of peace, Standing Armies"). Jefferson offers this information because he wishes to *persuade* the international community—especially the French—to support the revolution.

Or consider a very different piece of writing by another political figure: Lincoln's Gettysburg Address (page 361). Surely, Lincoln was not chiefly concerned with exposition or narration or description. True, he tells his hearers that "four score and seven years ago our fathers brought forth on this continent, a new nation" (narration), but they already knew *that* story; and he explains to them that they cannot dedicate the cemetery because the dead men have already hallowed it (exposition). But the speech is essentially meant to celebrate the heroism of the dead, and by reminding the audience of the heroism of the fallen soldiers, the speech seeks to inspire—to persuade—the living to continue the battle. Of these two essays, the Declaration of Independence is closer to academic writing than is the Gettysburg Address.

More about Critical Thinking: Analysis and Evaluation

In Chapter 1, we talked briefly about critical thinking and about analysis. We now want to amplify our discussion, but first, we should devote a few more words to the term "academic writing."

Exactly what is "academic writing"? *Academic* comes from the Greek *Academus,* a garden near Athens where the philosopher Plato taught. Because of its connection with a great teacher, the name of the garden came to refer to any place where the arts or sciences or both are taught or fostered. Academic writing is the sort of writing done in the academy—in colleges and universities. However, because each academic discipline requires its own sort of writing, several kinds of writing are done in an academic setting. In literature courses, students chiefly analyze and evaluate works of literature—but they may also be required to write a story, poem, or play. In sociology courses, students may be asked to analyze and evaluate the views of a particular sociologist—but they may also be asked to interview authorities or perhaps ordinary folk and to then present their findings in writing.

Still, at the heart of most academic writing—most of the writing that you will do in college—is an activity that can be called *critical thinking,* which consists chiefly of *analyzing* and *evaluating.* Exactly what is analysis? Literally, it is "separating into parts," and a good way to get going on an analysis is to ask what the parts are. Let's talk briefly about "hate speech." Is the display of a Nazi flag "hate speech"? Of course, it's not literally speech, but most people would probably agree that the act of displaying the flag might be closely comparable to verbally expressing some ideas. But exactly what is hate speech? Suppose *X* uses an ethnic term that *Y* finds offensive but *X* says he used it playfully. Or suppose *X* admits that the word was used aggressively, and suppose we all agree that such aggressive language is bad; we still have to think about *how bad* it is. Bad enough so that it ought to be regulated by the college? Punishable by a reprimand? Suspension? Expulsion?

If in an effort to think analytically we ask ourselves such questions (and perhaps even take notes to help us advance our thoughts), we might find we are thinking along these lines:

- What is hate speech? How is it distinguished from mere unthinking expression or high spirits? Must the speech concern race, religion, ethnicity, or sexual preference? If *X* calls *Y* a fat pig, does this show an offensive hatred of obesity? (In asking the question, "What is . . . ?" we are getting into matters of *definition.*)

- The First Amendment to the Constitution guarantees freedom of speech, but it does *not* protect *all* speech (for instance, libel, false advertising, incitements to violence). Does hate speech belong to protected speech or does it belong to *un*protected speech? (Here we are concerned with *classification*—with trying to see to what larger class of things something belongs.)
- After all, how bad is hate speech? Bad, yes, but probably no one would suggest that it is as bad as murder or rape or that it should be punished by long-term jail sentences. By one day in jail? By a reprimand? (Here, we are concerned with quality—with evaluation.)

As you ask yourself questions such as these, and as you seek to answer them, you will probably find that your views are changing—perhaps slightly (maybe you are refining them); perhaps radically. The writer E. M. Forster tells of a little girl who when instructed to think before she spoke, shrewdly replied, "How do I know what I think until I hear what I say?" Only by the process of hearing what we say and then testing and pressing further in a mental conversation with ourselves can we hope to have ideas that our fellow students and our instructors will value. When you write an academic paper, your instructor will expect you to have done this sort of work, and if you have done it, you will recognize that you have indeed been thinking—been educating yourself.

The essays in *The Little, Brown Reader* contain a good deal of information, but you'll chiefly read them not for the information they contain—the world is changing, and today's facts will not be tomorrow's facts-but instead for the ideas they advance and for the habits of thought that they display. And you will respond to them largely by setting forth arguments of your own. Writing based on serious *thinking* is what's expected of you. One of the reasons you are attending college is to acquire practice in thinking. As William Cory said, one goes to school not only for knowledge—facts, we might say—but for

> the art of assuming at a moment's notice a new intellectual posture, for the art of entering quickly into another person's thought, for the habit of submitting to censure and refutation, for the art of indicating assent or dissent in graduated terms. . . .

For a moment, let's put aside the writings in this book and instead look at a photograph of Sitting Bull and Buffalo Bill taken in 1886 by William Notman. William Cody got his nickname from his work as a supplier of meat for workers on the Kansas Pacific Railway, but he got his fame from his exploits as an army scout and a fighter against the Sioux Indians. Sitting Bull, a chief of the Sioux Indians, had defeated Custer at the Battle of Little Big Horn some 10 years before this picture was taken, but he soon fled to Canada. In 1879, he was granted amnesty, and he returned to the United States, where for a while he appeared in Buffalo

Sitting Bull and Buffalo Bill, 1886

Bill's Wild West Show. In 1890, whites—fearful of an Indian uprising—attempted to arrest Sitting Bull, and he was killed during the encounter.

What you have just read cannot pass for an example of critical thinking. We hope the writing is clear, but about the only thinking that we were forced to do was to decide how much information to give. Should we have added that Sitting Bull encouraged the Sioux not to sell their lands, which thus enraged the whites? Should we have added that Buffalo Bill rode for the Pony Express? Or that he invented some of his greatest exploits? Probably none of these points needs to be made here in a brief introduction to the photograph. In short, we made some choices—we decided to give minimal information—and that was that. But now let's think—think critically—about the picture. We can begin (and this may sound like a contradiction) with our emotional response—our gut feelings. We are interested in this picture—but why?

We begin to ask ourselves questions—a method that, we have seen, almost always helps to develop one's thoughts. What is going on here? There are two figures, but they are very different. Buffalo Bill, head brightly illuminated, is looking off into the distance—rather like a modern-day political candidate, whose upward and outward glance implies that he or she is looking into the future. His right hand is on his heart in a patriotic or noble gesture; his left leg is thrust forward. He wears a mammoth buckle, a fancy jacket, and shiny hip boots. His hand is above Sitting Bull's on the gun, and he is both behind Sitting Bull and (by virtue of his left leg) in front of Sitting Bull. Buffalo Bill, in short, is all showbiz. If we look closely at the setting, we see that the meeting is not taking place in the great outdoors; rather, the setting is a sort of stage set, presumably in a photographer's studio.

What about Sitting Bull? Whereas Buffalo Bill was clearly striking a pose for the camera, Sitting Bull seems indifferent to the camera. Later in this chapter we will discuss comparing at length, but here, we want only to mention that comparing is an excellent way to perceive what is unique about each of the things being compared. By comparing these two figures, we can more clearly see Buffalo Bill's flamboyance—and Sitting Bull's reserve. Sitting Bull seems withdrawn; his face, tilted downward, is mostly in shadow; his body seems inert; his right arm hangs lifelessly; his headdress is splendid, but his trousers are baggy, and his belt dangles beneath his shirt. His hand on the rifle is subordinated to Buffalo Bill's.

May we say that now we are really *thinking* about the picture? An *un*thinking description would say, "The picture shows the two figures, dividing the space approximately equally, each in costume." This statement is true, and it might indeed find a place in the early stage of an analytic essay on the photograph, but your teachers—you are writing in an academy—expect more than an accurate, neatly typed description.

Here is the final paragraph from one of the best student essays we have received on this photograph. (The earlier paragraphs specified the differences in pose, costume, and so on, along the lines that we have just set forth.)

> Buffalo Bill is obviously the dominant figure in this photograph, but he is not the outstanding one. His efforts to appear great only serve to make him appear small. His attempt to outshine Sitting Bull strikes us as faintly ridiculous. We do not need or want to know any more about Buffalo Bill's personality; it is spread before us in this picture. Sitting Bull's humility and dignity make him more interesting than Buffalo Bill, and make us wish to prove our intuition and to ascertain that this proud Sioux was a great chief.

Of course, the photograph might lead a student to another, related topic. For instance, a student might want to know more about the photographer, William Notman. What did Notman think the photograph said to viewers? Was Notman setting forth a compassionate statement about the American Indian? Or was he just doing a job for Buffalo Bill? One might do some research on Notman—perhaps first by turning to a handsome book of his photographs: *Portrait of a Period,* edited by J. Russell Harper and Stanley Triggs. Research on Notman might lead you to conclude that his pictures often subtly undermine the pretensions of his heroic sitters or you might find that Notman celebrates heroism of all kinds, white and Indian. Or you might find that, for some strange reason, his pictures of Indians are far more interesting than his pictures of whites.

If a student writing about Notman's photographs does no more than tell us that the book has 75 pictures, that they are black and white, that all are portraits, that . . . , the student is not presenting the sort of writing expected in an academic community. Such information if presented briefly is acceptable as a start acceptable as establishing a framework—but it is only a start; it is *not* critical thinking and it is *not* academic writing.

One last example of a related essay that would exemplify critical thinking. You might want to read the entries on Sitting Bull and Buffalo Bill in two versions of the *Encyclopaedia Britannica:* the 9th edition (1911) and the most recent edition. If you do, take note of the differences between the two versions and then think about what these differences tell us about the early 20th century and the early 21st century.

✔ A Checklist: Critical Thinking

Attitudes

- ☐ Does my thinking show imaginative open-mindedness and intellectual curiosity?
  - ☐ Am I willing to examine my assumptions?
  - ☐ Am I willing to entertain new ideas—both those that I encounter while reading and those that come to mind while writing?
  - ☐ Am I willing to exert myself—for instance, to do research—to acquire information and to evaluate evidence?

Skills

- ☐ Can I summarize an argument accurately?
- ☐ Can I evaluate assumptions, evidence, and inferences?
- ☐ Can I present my ideas effectively—for instance, by organizing and by writing in a manner appropriate to my imagined audience?

Joining the Conversation: Writing About Differing Views

Your instructor will probably ask you to read more than one essay in some section of this book. The chief reason for such an assignment is to stimulate you to think about some complex issue. After all, no one essay on any topic of significance can claim to say all that needs to be said about the topic. Essays that advocate similar positions on, say, capital punishment may—because of slightly different emphases—usefully supplement one another; even two radically opposed essays may both contain material that you find is essential to a thoughtful discussion of the topic.

Let's say that you read an essay supporting the death penalty. Perhaps as an aid to grasping the author's argument, you prepared a summary of the essay, and you notice that the writer's chief points are these:

1. The death penalty serves as a deterrent.
2. Justice requires that murderers pay an appropriate price for their crimes.

These basic points are probably supported by some evidence, but you have been reading critically, and you have wondered whether this or that piece of evidence is compelling. You have also wondered if more can't be said on the other side—not only by specific refutation of certain arguments but perhaps also by arguments that the first essayist has not raised. You turn to a second essayist—someone who opposes the death penalty and who (you find when you summarize the essay) in effect offers these arguments:

1. The death penalty does not serve as a deterrent.
2. If the death penalty is inflicted mistakenly, the error cannot be corrected.
3. The death penalty is imposed unequally; statistics indicate that when blacks and whites are guilty of comparable offenses, blacks are more likely to be sentenced to death.

It is now evident that the two writers are and are not talking about the same thing. They are talking about the death penalty, but for the most part, they are not confronting the same issues. On only one issue—deterrence—do they face each other. On this issue you will want to think hard about the evidence that each offers. Possibly you will decide that one author makes a compelling case at least on this issue, but it is also possible that you will decide that the issue cannot be resolved. Or you may find that you can make a better case than did either writer.

Think about the other arguments offered—on the one hand that justice requires the death penalty and on the other hand that it can be mistakenly inflicted and is awarded unequally. You will not only want to think hard about each of these points, but you will also wonder why only one of the two essayists took them up. Is one or the other argument so clearly mistaken that it is not worth discussing? Or is a particular argument one that can't be proved either true or false? Or are the writers working from different **assumptions** (unexamined beliefs)? For instance, the writer who argues that the death penalty is capriciously enforced may assume that race prejudice cannot be overcome, whereas a writer who rejects the argument may assume that the courts can and will see to it that the death penalty is imposed impartially. As a critical reader, you will want to be alert to the assumptions that writers make. You'll have to ask yourself often, *What assumption lies beneath this assertion?* That is, what belief is so firmly held and is assumed to be so self-evident that the writer does not bother to assert it? Do I share this assumption? Why?

If you are asked to compare two essays that offer sharply differing views, you'll probably want to point out where the two face each other and where they don't. You'll probably also want to offer an evaluation of the two. Or depending on the assignment, you may use the two merely as a point of departure for your own essay on the topic. That is, you may want to draw on one or both—giving credit of course—and then offer your own serious thoughts.

Interviewing

In preparing to write about some of the essays in *The Little, Brown Reader,* you may want to interview faculty members or students or persons not on the campus. For instance, if you are writing about the essays by Steiner or Lewis, you may want to talk to instructors who teach ethics—or you may simply want to collect the views of people who have no special knowledge but who may offer thoughtful responses. Obviously, topics such as divorce, vegetarianism and almost all the other topics addressed in this book are matters that you might profitably discuss with someone whose experience is notably different from your own.

A college campus is an ideal place to practice interviewing. Faculties are composed of experts in a variety of fields, and distinguished visitors are a regular part of extracurricular life. In the next few pages, we'll offer some advice on conducting interviews and writing essays based on them. If you take our advice, you'll acquire a skill you may well put to further, more specialized use in social science courses; at the same time, you'll be developing skills in asking questions and shaping materials relevant to all research and writing.

Guidelines for Conducting the Interview and Writing the Essay

You can conduct interviews over the telephone or online by using electronic mail, but in the following pages, we assume that you are conducting the interview face-to-face.

1. *Finding a subject for an interview.* If you are looking for an expert, in the college catalog, scan the relevant department and begin to ask questions of students who have some familiarity with the department. Then, with a name or two in mind, you may want to see if these faculty members have written anything on the topic. Department secretaries are good sources of information not only about the special interests of the faculty but also about guest speakers scheduled by the department in the near future. Investigate the athletic department if you're interested in sports or the departments of music, art, and drama for the names of resident or visiting performing artists. Other sources of newsworthy personalities or events: the publicity office, the president's office, the college newspaper, bulletin boards. All are potential sources for information about recent awards, or achievements, or upcoming events that may lead you to a subject for an interview and a good story.

2. *Doing preliminary homework.* Find out as much as you can about your potential interviewee's work from the sources we mentioned above. If the subject of your interview is a faculty member, ask the department secretary if you may see a copy of that person's vita (Latin for "life" and pronounced vee-ta). Many departments have these brief biographical sketches on file for publicity purposes. Among other things, the vita will list publications and current research interests.

3. *Requesting the interview.* In making your request, don't hesitate to mention that you are fulfilling an assignment, but also make evident your own interest in the person's work or area of expertise. (Showing that you already know something about the work—that you've done some preliminary homework—is persuasive evidence of your interest.) Request the interview, preferably in writing, at least a week in advance, and ask for ample time (probably an hour to an hour and a half) for a thorough interview.

4. *Preparing thoroughly.* If your subject is a writer, read and take notes on the publications that most interest you. Read book reviews if available; read reviews of performances if your subject is a performing artist. As you read, write out the questions that occur to you. As you work on them, try to phrase your questions so they require more than a yes or no answer. A "why" or "how" question is likely to be productive, but don't be afraid of a general question such as "Tell me something about. . . ."

Revise your questions and then put them in a reasonable order. Work on an opening question that you think your subject will find both easy and interesting to answer. "How did you get interested in . . . " is often a good start. Type your questions or write them boldly so you will find them easy to refer to.

Think about how you will record the interview. Although a tape recorder may seem like a good idea, there are good reasons not to rely on one. First of all, your subject may be made uneasy by its presence and freeze up. Second, the recorder (or the operator) may malfunction, leaving you with a partial record or nothing at all. Third, even if all goes well, when you prepare to write, you will face a mass of material—some of it inaudible and all of it daunting to transcribe.

If despite these warnings you decide (with your subject's permission) to tape, expect to take notes anyway. It's the only way you can be sure you will have a record of what was important to you out of all that was said. Think beforehand, then, of how you will take notes, and if you can manage to, practice by interviewing a friend. You'll probably find that you'll want to devise some system of shorthand—perhaps no more than using initials for names that frequently recur, dropping the vowels in words that you transcribe, or whatever assists you to write quickly but legibly. But don't think you must transcribe every word. Be prepared to do a lot more listening than writing.

5. Presenting yourself for the interview. Dress appropriately, bring your prepared questions and a notebook or pad for your notes, and appear on time.

6. Conducting the interview. At the start of the interview, try to engage briefly in conversation—without taking notes—to put your subject at ease. Even important people can be shy. Remembering that will help keep you at ease too. If you want to use a tape recorder, ask your subject's permission, and if it is granted, ask where the microphone may be conveniently placed.

As the interview proceeds, *keep your purpose in mind.* Are you trying to gain information about an issue or a topic or are you trying to get a portrait of a personality? Listen attentively to your subject's answers and be prepared to follow up with your own responses and spontaneous questions. Here is where your thorough preparation will pay off.

A good interview develops like a conversation. Keep in mind that your prepared questions—however essential—are not sacred. At the same time, don't hesitate to steer your subject, courteously, from apparent irrelevancies (what one reporter calls "sawdust") to something that interests you more. "I'd like to hear a little more about . . . " you can say. Or "Would you mind telling me about how you. . . ." It's also perfectly acceptable to ask your subject to repeat a remark so you can record it accurately, and if you don't understand something, don't be afraid to admit it. Experts are accustomed to knowing more than others do and are particularly happy to explain even the most elementary parts of their lore to an interested listener.

7. Concluding the interview. Near the end of the time you have agreed upon, ask your subject if he or she wishes to add any material or to clarify something said earlier. Express your thanks, and at the appointed time, leave promptly.

8. Preparing to write. As soon as possible after the interview, review your notes, amplify them with details you wish to remember but might have failed to record, and type them up. You might have discovered during the interview or you might see now that there is something more that you want to read by or about your subject. Track it down and take further notes.

9. Writing the essay. In writing your first draft, think about your audience. Unless a better idea occurs to you, consider your college newspaper or magazine or a local newspaper as the place you hope to publish your story. Write with the readers of that publication in mind. Thinking about your readers will help you to be clear—for instance, to identify names that have come up in the interview but which may be unfamiliar to your readers.

As with other writing, begin your draft with any idea that strikes you, and write at a fast clip until you have exhausted your material (or yourself).

When you revise, remember to keep your audience in mind; as it unfolds, your material should tell a coherent and interesting story. Interviews, like conversations, tend to be delightfully circular or disorderly. But an essay, like a story, should reveal its contents in a sequence that captures and holds attention.

If you've done a thorough job of interviewing, you may find that you have more notes than you can reasonably incorporate without disrupting the flow of your story. Don't be tempted to plug them in anyway. If they're really interesting, save them—perhaps by copying them into your journal; if not, chuck them out.

In introducing direct quotations from your source, choose those that are particularly characteristic, or vivid, or memorable. Paraphrase or summarize the rest of what is usable. Although the focus of your essay is almost surely the person you interviewed, it is your story, and most of it should be in your own words. Even though you must keep yourself in the background, your writing will gain in interest if your reader hears your voice as well as your subject's.

You might want to use a particularly good quotation for your conclusion. Now make sure that you have an attractive opening paragraph. Identifying the subject of your interview and describing the setting is one way to begin. Give your essay an attractive title. Before you prepare your final draft, read your essay aloud. You're almost certain to catch phrases you can improve and places where a transition will help your reader to follow you without effort. Check your quotations for accuracy; check with your subject any quotations or other details you're in doubt about. Type your final draft and then edit and proofread carefully.

10. Going public. Make two copies of your finished essay: one for the person you interviewed and one for yourself. The original is for your instructor; hand it in on time.

Topics for Writing

Write an essay based on an interview. You needn't be limited in your choice of subject by the examples we've given. A very old person, a recent immigrant, the owner or manager of an interesting store or business, a veteran of the war in Afghanistan or Iraq, a gardener are only a few of the possibilities. If you can manage to do so, include a few photographs of your subject, with appropriate captions.

Using Quotations

Here, we remind you of procedures for using quotations. These procedures are not noteworthy when handled properly, but they become noticeable and even ruinous to your essay when bungled. Read over the following reminders, and consult them again the first few times you write about an essay.

- *Quote.* Quotations from the work under discussion provide evidence and indispensable support for your analysis. Quotations that strike you as especially engaging will also provide your readers with a welcome change of voice.
- *Don't overquote.* Most of your essay should consist of your own words.
- *Quote briefly.* Use quotations as evidence, not as padding.
- *Comment on what you quote*—immediately before or immediately after the quotation. Make sure your reader understands why you find the quotation relevant. Don't count on the quotation to make your point for you.
- *Take care with embedded quotations* (quotations within a sentence of your own). A quotation must make good sense and must fit grammatically into the sentence of which it is a part.

Incorrect:

Steiner says that he "have been a vegan for almost fifteen years. . . ."

Steiner does indeed use the words that are quoted (he says, "I have been a vegan for almost fifteen years"), but the student's "he have" is ungrammatical.

Improved:

Steiner says that he has "been a vegan for almost fifteen years. . . ."

Or:

Steiner says, "I have been a vegan for almost fifteen years. . . ."

- Don't try to fit a long quotation into the middle of one of your own sentences. It is almost impossible for the reader to come out of the quotation and pick up the thread of your sentence. It is better to lead into a long quotation with "Steiner says" followed by a colon, and then, after quoting, to begin a new sentence of your own.
- *Quote exactly.* Any material that you add or edit (to make the quotation coherent with your sentence) must be in square brackets. Thus:

Steiner says that "Strict ethical vegans, of which [he is one], are customarily excoriated for equating our society's treatment of animals with mass murder."

An ellipsis (any material that you omit from a quotation) must be indicated by three spaced periods:

> Steiner says there is "support in the Bible and in the writings of Christian thinkers . . . for this . . . way of devaluing animals."

If you end the quotation before the end of the author's sentence, add a period and then three spaced periods to indicate the omission:

> Steiner says this view is supported "in the Bible and in the writings of Christian thinkers. . . ."

- *Quote fairly.* For example, it would not be fair to say that C.S. Lewis says, "After all, . . . they had a right to happiness." The words do in fact appear in Lewis's essay, but he is quoting them in order—ultimately—to refute them.
- *Identify the quotation* clearly for your reader. Use such expressions as "Lewis says," "Steiner argues."
- *Identify the source of quotations* in a list called "Works Cited."
- *Check your punctuation.* Remember: Periods and commas go *inside* the closing quotation marks; semicolons and colons go outside. Question marks and exclamation points go inside if they are part of the quotation; outside if they are your own.

Avoiding Plagiarism

Acknowledging Sources

Your purpose as an academic writer is to develop your own ideas about the topic you are writing about. Secondary sources will help you shape and develop your thoughts about your topic, but your purpose is to develop an argument and an analysis that is your own. It is crucial, then, to be clear about the distinction between your words and ideas and those of your sources. Not to do so is to risk charges of **plagiarism**. To plagiarize is to use someone else's words or ideas without attributing them to a source; it is to pass off someone else's work as your own. In short, it's theft. The institutional consequences of plagiarism vary from school to school and from case to case. In the university where one of us teaches, students who are found guilty of plagiarism are, among other things, banned from the campus for a year. At other schools, students can be expelled permanently; at still others, they simply receive a failing grade for the course and are put on academic probation.

Respect for your readers and for your sources requires that you acknowledge your indebtedness for material when

- you quote directly from a work, or
- you paraphrase or summarize someone's words (the words of your paraphrase or summary are your own, but the ideas are not), or
- you use an idea that is not common knowledge.

Most commonly, the words, ideas, and information you'll cite in a research essay will come from printed and electronic sources. But you must also acknowledge the advice of peer editors and ideas that come from lectures and class discussions, unless your instructor tells you not to do so. (Consult a handbook for instructions on formatting citations of sources.)

Let's suppose you want to make use of William Bascom's comment on the earliest European responses to African art:

> The first examples of African art to gain public attention were the bronzes and ivories which were brought back to Europe after the sack of Benin by a British military expedition in 1987. The superb technology of the Benin bronzes won the praise of experts like Felix von Luschan who wrote in 1899, "Cellini himself could not have made better casts, nor anyone else before or since the present day." Moreover, their relatively realistic treatment of human features conformed to the prevailing European aesthetic standards. Because of their naturalism and technical excellence, it was at first maintained that they have been produced by Europeans—a view that was still current when the even more realistic bronze heads were discovered at Ife in 1912. The subsequent discovery of new evidence has caused the complete abandonment of this theory of European origins of the bronzes of Benin and Ife, both of which are in Nigeria.

> —William Bascom, *African Art in Cultural Perspective*
> (New York: Norton, 1973), p. 4

Acknowledge a direct quotation. A student wanting to use some or all of Bascom's words might write something like this:

> According to William Bascom, when Europeans first encountered Benin and Ife works of art in the late nineteenth century, they thought that Europeans had produced them, but the discovery of new evidence "caused the complete abandonment of this theory of European origins of the bronzes of Benin and Ife, both of which are in Nigeria" (4).

In this example, the writer introduces Bascom with a signal phrase ("According to William Bascom"); then, she summarizes several sentences from Bascom; then, she uses quotation marks to indicate the passage that comes directly from Bascom's book. Note that the summary does not borrow Bascom's language; the words are all the writer's own. Note also that what appears inside the quotation marks is an exact transcription of Bascom's words: The writer has not changed any word endings or omitted any words or any punctuation of her own. (The "4" inside parentheses at the end of the passage is the page reference.)

Acknowledging a paraphrase or summary. Summaries (abridgments) are usually superior to paraphrases (rewordings—usually phrase by phrase—of approximately the same length as the original) because summaries are briefer. When you are using sources, you will for the most part be writing summaries, *not* paraphrases—unless the language of the source is especially complex. If Bascom's sentences had been obscure—for instance, if they used highly technical language—there would have been a reason to paraphrase them—to translate them (so to speak) into clearer English. In that case, the writer of the essay would explicitly have said she was paraphrasing Bascom, and she would have explained why.

Occasionally, you may find that you cannot summarize a passage in your source and yet you don't want to quote it word for word—perhaps because it is too technical or because it is poorly written. In that case, you need to paraphrase the passage; that is, you need to put it into your own words. Even though you have put the idea into your own words, you must give credit to the source because the idea is not yours. *Both summaries and paraphrases must be acknowledged*. In both cases, the author must be identified by name, and the location of the source—a page reference if you are using a print source—must be given.

Here's an example of an **acceptable summary**:

> William Bascom, in *African Art in Cultural Perspective*, points out that the first examples of African art brought to Europe—Benin bronzes and ivories—were thought by Europeans to be of European origin because they were realistic and well-made, but evidence was later discovered that caused this theory to be abandoned (4).

The summary is adequate, and the page reference indicates where the source is to be found. But if the writer had omitted the signal phrase "William Bascom, in *African Art in Cultural Perspective*, points out that," the result would have been plagiarism. Not to give Bascom credit would be to plagiarize, even if the words are the writer's own. The offense is just as serious as not acknowledging a direct quotation.

The following paragraph is an example of an **unacceptable summary**. Why is it unacceptable, since the writer cites Bascom as her source? It is unacceptable because she uses too much of Bascom's language, and she follows his organization of the material; she has not turned the material into her own writing.

> William Bascom points out that the earliest examples of African art to become widely known in Europe were bronzes and ivories that were brought to Europe in 1897. These works were thought to be of European origin, and one expert said that Cellini could not have done better work. Their technical excellence as well as their realism fulfilled the European standards of the day. The later discovery of new evidence at Benin and Ife, both in Nigeria, refuted this belief.

Again, all the ideas are Bascom's and so is the way in which the ideas are presented. The writer simply substitutes one phrase for another, maintaining much of the structure and organization of Bascom's sentences. The writing is Bascom's in a thin disguise. She substitutes

"The earliest examples of African art"

for Bascom's

"The first examples of African art";

she substitutes

"to become widely known"

for

"to gain public attention";

she substitutes

"Their technical excellence as well as their realism"

for

"their naturalism and technical excellence."

The writer here is plagiarizing—perhaps without even knowing it. But it should be clear that neither the words nor the ideas in this passage are the writer's own. This form of plagiarism—where a writer simply substitutes his or her own phrases here and there but retains the form and content of the original passage—is one of the most common forms of plagiarism that writing instructors see. We believe that much of it occurs because students don't know it's wrong—and because they don't see their job as developing their own ideas in relation to their sources.

As we have noted, it is unlikely that a writer would paraphrase a passage that is as straightforward and as free of technical language as Bascom's. The main reason for paraphrasing is to clarify a text that might be confusing to a reader—for example, a literary text or a particularly complex or technical piece of writing.

Acknowledging an idea. Let's say you have read an essay in which Irving Kristol argues that journalists who pride themselves on being tireless critics of national policy are in fact irresponsible critics because they have no policy they prefer. If this strikes you as a new idea and you adopt it in an essay—even though you set it forth entirely in your own words and with examples not offered by Kristol—you must acknowledge your debt to Kristol. Not to acknowledge such borrowing is plagiarism. Your readers will not think the less of you for naming your source; rather, they will be grateful to you for telling them about an interesting writer.

Fair Use of Common Knowledge

If in doubt as to whether to give credit (either with formal documentation or merely in a phrase such as "Carol Gilligan says . . ."), give credit. But as you begin to read widely in your field or subject, you will develop a sense of what is considered common knowledge.

Unsurprising definitions in a dictionary can be considered common knowledge, so there is no need to say "According to Webster, a *novel* is a long narrative in prose." (That's weak in three ways: It's unnecessary, it's uninteresting, and it's inexact because "Webster" appears in the titles of several dictionaries—some good and some bad.)

Similarly, the date of Freud's death can be considered common knowledge. Few can give it when asked, but it can be found out from innumerable sources, and no one need get the credit for providing you with the date. Again, if you simply know from your reading of Freud that Freud was interested in literature, you need not cite a specific source for an assertion to that effect, but if you know only because some commentator on Freud said so and you have no idea whether the fact is well-known, you should give credit to the source that gave you the information. Not to give credit—for ideas as well as for quoted words—is to plagiarize.

"But How Else Can I Put It?"

If you've just learned—say, from one of the readings in this book or from an encyclopedia—something that you sense is common knowledge, you may wonder how to change into your own words the simple, clear words that this source uses in setting forth this simple fact. For example, if before writing an analysis of a photograph of Buffalo Bill and Sitting Bull (p. 51), you look up these names in the *Encyclopaedia Britannica*, you will find this statement about Buffalo Bill (William F. Cody): "In 1883 Cody organized his first Wild West exhibition." You could not use this statement as your own, word for word, without feeling uneasy. But to put in quotation marks such a routine statement of what can be considered common knowledge and to cite a source for it seems pretentious. After all, the *Encyclopedia Americana* says much the same thing in the same routine way: "In 1883 . . . Cody organized Buffalo Bill's Wild West." It may be that the word "organized" is simply the most obvious and the best word and perhaps you will end up using it. Certainly, to change "Cody organized" into "Cody presided over the organization of" or "Cody assembled" or some such thing in an effort to avoid plagiarizing would be to make a change for the worse and still to be guilty of plagiarism. What, then, can you do? You won't get yourself into this mess of wondering whether to change clear, simple wording into awkward wording if, in the first place, when you take notes, you summarize your sources: "1883: organized Wild West" or "first Wild West: 1883." Later (even if only 30 minutes later), when drafting your paper, if you turn this nugget—probably combined with others—into the best sentence you can, you will not be in danger of plagiarizing, even if the word "organized" turns up in your sentence. The sentence will be your own sentence, not your source's sentence.

Of course, even when dealing with material that can be considered common knowledge—and even when you have put it into your own words—you'll probably cite your source if you are drawing more than just an occasional fact from a source. For instance, if your paragraph on Buffalo Bill uses half a dozen facts from a source, cite the source. You do this both to avoid charges of plagiarism and to protect yourself in case your source contains errors of fact.

Joining the Conversation: Critical Thinking and Writing

1. Write a paragraph that acknowledges the author of an essay in this book but nevertheless illustrates plagiarism. (Your instructor will probably choose the paragraph.)

2. Write a paragraph in which you make honest use of a source, quoting some words and summarizing a passage or an idea. (Your instructor will probably choose the paragraph.)

✓ A Checklist: Avoiding Plagiarism

☐ In using my sources, did I *summarize* (rather than paraphrase) material and did I give credit to the source for the facts and ideas? (A paraphrase in the student's essay, even if a source is cited, is considered plagiarism because the sequence of ideas is the source's not the student's. The writing is essentially the source's translated into the student's language.)

☐ Is *all* quoted material—in notes and in the submitted essay— enclosed within quotation marks and is the source cited?

☐ Are all borrowed *ideas* credited to the appropriate sources?

☐ Common knowledge—the term includes indisputable material that can be found in countless sources, such as the date of the Battle of the Bulge and the fact that Lincoln was assassinated—is *not* cited, but if you are in doubt about whether something is "common knowledge," choose the safer course and cite your source.

How Much Do You Know About Citing Sources?
A Quiz with Answers

> *Taking the quiz below will let you test yourself and will assist you in any discussion you have with your classmates about how to cite sources accurately and honestly.*

Quiz Yourself: How Much Do You Know About Citing Sources?

Section 1: Plagiarism and Academic Dishonesty

Which of the following examples describe violations of academic integrity? Check all the examples that are punishable under university rules.

_____ 1. You buy a term paper from a Web site and turn it in as your own work.

_____ 2. You ask a friend to write a paper for you.

_____ 3. You can't find the information you need, so you invent statistics, quotes, and sources that do not exist and cite these in your paper as if they were real.

_____ 4. Your professor requires you to use five sources, but you find one book written by one person that has all the information you need, so you cite that book as if it were information coming from other books and authors in order to make it look like you used five different sources.

_____ 5. Your history professor and your political science professor both assign a term paper. To save time, you write one paper that meets both requirements and hand it in to both professors.

_____ 6. You don't want to have too many quotes in your paper, so you do not put quotation marks around some sentences you copied from a source. You cite the source correctly at the end of the paragraph and in your bibliography.

_____ 7. You have copied a long passage from a book into your paper, and you changed some of the wording. You cite the source at the end of the passage and again in the bibliography.

_____ 8. While writing a long research paper, you come across an interesting hypothesis mentioned in a book, and you incorporate this hypothesis into your main argument. After you finish writing the paper, you can't remember where you initially found the hypothesis, so you don't bother to cite the source of your idea.

Section 2: Common Knowledge

Common knowledge is information that is widely known within a society or an intellectual community; therefore, if you include common knowledge in your paper, you do not need to cite where you found that information.

Answer *Yes* or *No* to the following questions:

_____ 1. In a high school class on American government, you learned about the checks-and-balances system of government that separates power into the judicial, executive, and legislative branches. Now you are writing a paper for an introductory political science class, and you mention the concept of checks-and-balances you learned in high school. Should you cite your old high school textbook?

_____ 2. In writing a paper about pop culture in the 1980s, you want to include the year that Reagan was shot, but you cannot remember if it was 1980 or 1981, so you look up the correct date in an encyclopedia. Do you have to include that encyclopedia as a source for the date on which Reagan was shot?

_____ 3. You do most of your research online and find lots of interesting Web sites from which you quote several passages. After you write the first draft, you ask your older and more experienced roommate if he knows how to cite Web sites. He says that Web sites are in the public domain and constitute common knowledge, and they therefore do not need to be cited. Is this true?

_____ 4. In writing a research paper on astrophysics, you come across something called the Eridanus Effect several times. You have never heard of this effect nor discussed it in your class, but after reading about it in six different astrophysics journal articles, you have a pretty clear idea of what it is and its most common characteristics. Is the Eridanus Effect common knowledge within astrophysics?

_____ 5. Your older sister works for a nonprofit organization that runs adult literacy programs in factories and unemployment centers in several major cities. During winter break, she tells you about the success of one of the programs in St. Louis and the innovative curricula it has designed. Several weeks into spring semester, you remember your conversation as you are writing an economics term paper on empowerment zones and unemployment in the inner city. If you include a description of the program, do you need to cite a source, even if it's just your sister?

_____ 6. You are writing a paper on Shakespeare's *Hamlet*. Your textbook's introduction to the play mentions that Shakespeare was born in 1564 in Stratford-upon-Avon. You mention these facts in your paper's introduction. Do you need to cite the introduction to your textbook?

_____ 7. You are writing a paper on Shakespeare's *Hamlet*. A footnote in your textbook mentions that some literary historians now believe that Shakespeare himself played the ghost when the play was first performed. If you mention Shakespeare playing the ghost, do you need to cite this footnote in your textbook?

_____ 8. You are writing a paper on the assassination of Robert F. Kennedy. The three major biographies on him mention when he was killed and by whom. Do you have to cite all these biographies when you mention the date and murderer of RFK?

_____ 9. You are writing a paper on the assassination of Robert F. Kennedy. The most influential biography on him mentions a controversial conspiracy theory first put forward in the early 1970s by a journalist for the *Washington Post*. When you mention this conspiracy theory, should you cite the biography?

Section 3: Quoting, Paraphrasing, and Summarizing Texts

Read the following passage excerpted from an online edition of a foreign policy magazine. Determine whether any of the sample sentences that follow are improperly cited within the sentence or plagiarized.

> The illegal trade in drugs, arms, intellectual property, people, and money is booming. Like the war on terrorism, the fight to control these illicit markets pits governments against agile, stateless, and resourceful networks empowered by globalization. Governments will continue to lose these wars until they adopt new strategies to deal with a larger, unprecedented struggle that now shapes the world as much as confrontations between nation-states once did.
>
> —from Moisés Naím, "The Five Wars of Globalization."
> *Foreign Policy* Jan.–Feb. 2003: Web. 13 January 2003.

Read the following passages and then mark *OK* if the passage is fine. If the passage is plagiarized, improperly paraphrased, or otherwise cited inadequately, mark it with *X*.

_____ 1. In his essay on "The Five Wars of Globalization," Moisés Naím argues that governments need to find new ways to handle the kinds of borderless illegal activity increasing under globalization.

_____ 2. In describing the "illegal trade in drugs, arms, intellectual property, people, and money" as "booming," Moisés Naím asserts that governments need to adopt new strategies to deal with this unprecedented struggle that now shapes the world (http://www.foreignpolicy.com).

_____ 3. Like the war on terror, the struggle to control illegal trade in drugs, arms, money, etc., pits governments against cunning, stateless, and enterprising networks empowered by globalization (Moises 2003).

_____ 4. Many experts believe that globalization is changing the face of foreign policy.

Read the following passage from a book on romance novels and soap operas and then read the citations of it that follow to determine whether any are plagiarized or improperly cited within the sentence.

> The complexity of women's responses to romances has not been sufficiently acknowledged. Instead of exploring the possibility that romances, while serving to keep women in their place, may at the same time be concerned with real female problems, analysts of women's romances have generally seen the fantasy embodied in romantic fiction either as evidence of female "masochism" or as a simple reflection of the dominant masculine ideology. For instance, Germaine Greer, referring to the idealized males of women's popular novels, says, "This is the hero that women have chosen for themselves. The traits invented for him have been invented by women cherishing the chains of their bondage."[9] But this places too much blame on women, and assumes a freedom of choice which is not often in evidence—not in their lives and therefore certainly not in their popular arts.

> —from Tania Modleski, *Loving with a Vengeance: Mass-Produced Fantasies for Women* (New York and London: Methuen, 1982), 37–38. Print.

Read the following passages and then mark *OK* if the passage is fine. If the passage is plagiarized in part or whole or is otherwise cited improperly, mark it with *X*.

_____ 1. Tania Modleski claims that Germaine Greer oversimplifies why women read romance novels (38).

_____ 2. Modleski states that although romance novels may keep women in their place, they also address real female problems (37).

_____ 3. Feminist critics see the fantasy embodied in romance novels either as evidence of female "masochism" or as a simple reflection of male chauvinism (Modleski 37–38).

_____ 4. One feminist writer, Germaine Greer, says that the idealized male featured in women's popular romance novels "is the hero that women have chosen for themselves. The traits invented for him have been invented by women cherishing the chains of their bondage."(38).

_____ 5. Tania Modleski rejects the idea that the fantasies expressed in romance novels are merely a reflection of some innate masochism in women who, in the words of Germaine Greer, "cherish[. . .] the chains of their bondage" (37; Greer qtd. in Modleski, 38).

Section 4: Miscellaneous

_____ 1. You read *Time* magazine every week and notice that the writers in the magazine never use footnotes or parenthetical citations. Why don't news-writers cite their sources?
   a. Citing sources is only required of students, not professional writers.
   b. Professional publications are free to decide if they will require footnotes or citation of any kind.
   c. By law, journalists are exempt from revealing their sources of information.
   d. Newspapers and magazines have limited space on the page, so they cut off the citations or footnotes to make room for more copy.

_____ 2. What is *not* the proper way to document a Web site in a bibliography?
   a. Naím, Moisés. (2003, Jan.–Feb.) The Five Wars of Globalization [Electronic version]. *Foreign Policy.* Retrieved Jan. 15, 2003, from www.foreignpolicy.com/wwwboard/fivewars.html
   b. Naím, Moisés. "The Five Wars of Globalization," *Foreign Policy* Jan.–Feb. 2003: Online Edition. <http://www.foreignpolicy.com>. Jan. 15, 2003.
   c. [12]Naím, Moisés. (2003, Jan.–Feb.) The Five Wars of Globalization [Electronic version]. *Foreign Policy.* Retrieved Jan. 15, 2003, from www.foreignpolicy.com/wwwboard/fivewars.html
   d. http://www.foreignpolicy.com/wwwboard/fivewars.html
   e. Trick question: Web sites are in the public domain and do not need to be cited.

_____ 3. Plagiarism is a violation of which of the following laws:
   a. Copyright.
   b. Intellectual property.
   c. Both (a) and (b) above.
   d. None of the above; it is not a legal issue and is not punishable by law because it pertains only to students.

_____ 4. If you use a quote found in a book of quotes or from an online compilation of quotes, such as Bartlett's, how do you cite the quote?
   a. You don't—quotes found in a collection of quotations (whether online or in a book) are considered well-known and in the public domain. Just include the name of the person to whom the quote is attributed. You can also add the date if it seems relevant.

b. You should cite the original source of the quote followed by the bibliographic information from the quotation compilation, such as: Shakespeare, William. *A Midsummer Night's Dream.* Quoted in *Familiar Quotations: Being an Attempt to Trace to Their Sources Passages and Phrases in Common Use,* by John Bartlett (Boston: Little, Brown, 1886), 44.
c. You should find the original source and cite that.
d. All the above: (a) is correct, and (b) and (c) are possible options if you want to be extra careful or if the quote is extremely important to your paper. Use your common sense in this situation.

Answer Key to Plagiarism Quiz

The Plagiarism Quiz works best when the answers are discussed in class or one-on-one with a student and professor.

Section 1: Plagiarism and Academic Dishonesty

All eight incidents are forms of plagiarism or academic dishonesty. Many students are confused about the last four incidents, so please discuss them with your instructor if you need clarification.

Section 2: Common Knowledge

1. No; the basic facts about the checks-and-balances system are common knowledge and do not need to be cited.
2. No; even if you cannot remember the exact date of the assassination attempt on Reagan, it is common knowledge because the date is undisputed and can be found in a variety of sources.
3. No; writing on the Web is protected by copyright and must be cited, even if no author is listed.
4. Yes; it's common knowledge if it appears *undocumented* in five or more sources.
5. Yes; such a small program would not be widely known, so you should cite your sister as a source if you mention it. If you describe the program in more detail, it would make sense to research documents or newspaper descriptions and cite these rather than Big Sis.
6. No; the date and location of Shakespeare's birth is not in dispute and can be found in many sources, so it is common knowledge even if you did not know it.
7. Hmmm. This is a tricky situation. Because *some* but not all literary historians believe Shakespeare himself played the ghost, this is probably common knowledge among Shakespeare experts. However, You're not a Shakespeare expert, so it would be wise to cite the footnote just to be safe. So, the answer is, Yes—cite it!

8. No; undisputed dates are common knowledge.
9. Yes; conspiracy theories are controversial, and the details of such controversies need to be cited.

Section 3: Quoting, Paraphrasing, and Summarizing Texts

Illegal Trade Passage:

1. OK; an example of summary. The sentence gives the author and the title. (Remember, the bibliography would provide more publication information.)
2. X; two things are wrong: Some of the language is too similar to the original, and the citation method is incorrect. Do not list the URL in your paper. The phrase "adopt new strategies to deal with this unprecedented struggle that now shapes the world" is too close to the source—in some places, identical to it.
3. X; this paraphrase is too close to the original. The writer used a thesaurus to change key words, but the sentence structure is identical to the original. Plus, the author's last name (not first name) should appear in the parenthetical citation. (Also, using "etc." in the text is annoying!)
4. OK; This is common knowledge. The sentence is so general, it really has nothing to do with the passage from Moisés Naím, so there is no reason to cite him.

Romance Novel Passage:

1. OK; this summary is correct; the author's name appears in the sentence, so it does not need to appear in the parenthetical citation.
2. X; although the source is documented properly, some of the language is too close to the source, especially the phrases "keep women in their place" and "real female problems." These phrases need to be put into quotation marks or rewritten.
3. X; most of this sentence is copied directly from the source; it needs to be rewritten or partially enclosed in quotes.
4. X; the quote is properly attributed to Greer, but the page number refers to Modleski's book. Also, there's no need to copy the footnote from the original.
5. OK; this example shows how to properly cite one writer quoted within the work of another. Also, note how the ellipses and brackets indicate how the "-ing" part of "cherish" was deleted to make the quote flow better. The ellipses indicate that something was deleted; the brackets indicate that the ellipses were not in the original source.

Section 4: Miscellaneous

1. (c)
2. (d); (a) is an example of APA method of documenting Web sites; (b) is MLA; (c) is an APA footnote.
3. (c)
4. (d)

✓ A Checklist: Thirteen Questions to Ask Yourself When Editing

☐ Is the title of my essay at least moderately informative?

☐ Do I identify the subject of my essay (author and title) early?

☐ What is my thesis? Do I state it soon enough (perhaps even in the title) and keep it in view?

☐ Is the organization reasonable? Does each point lead into the next without irrelevancies and without anticlimaxes?

☐ Is each paragraph unified by a topic sentence or a topic idea? Are there adequate transitions from one paragraph to the next?

☐ Are generalizations supported by appropriate concrete details, especially by brief quotations from the text?

☐ Is the opening paragraph interesting and, by its end, focused on the topic? Is the final paragraph conclusive without being repetitive?

☐ Is the tone appropriate? No sarcasm, no apologies, no condescension?

☐ If there is a summary, is it as brief as possible given its purpose?

☐ Are the quotations accurate? Do they serve a purpose other than to add words to the essay?

☐ Is documentation provided where necessary?

☐ Are the spelling and punctuation correct? Are other mechanical matters (such as margins, spacing, and citations) in correct form? Have I proofread carefully?

☐ Is the paper properly identified—author's name, instructor's name, course number, and date?

A Student's Documented Essay

Jason Green

Jason Green wrote this essay not for an art history course but for an introductory course in composition. Notice that Green draws not only on his experience as an amateur photographer but also on material that he found in the college library.

Did Dorothea Lange Pose Her Subject for *Migrant Mother*?

In doing research for this essay, I was surprised to find that Dorothea Lange's *Migrant Mother* (figure 1) is one of six pictures of this woman and her children. *Migrant Mother* is so much an image of the period, an icon of the Depression, that it is hard to believe it exists in any other form than the one we all know.[1]

---

1 Curiously, Lange in her short essay on the picture, "The Assignment I'll Never Forget: Migrant Mother," in *Popular Photography* 46 (February 1960): 43, says that she made five exposures. A slightly abridged version of the essay is reprinted in Milton Meltzer, *Dorothea Lange: A Photographer's Life* (New York: Farrar Straus Giroux 1978): 132–33. Because Meltzer's book is more available than the magazine, when I quote from the article I quote from his book.

Figure 1   *Migrant Mother, Nipomo, California*
Dorothea Lange, 1936

Figure 2

Figure 3

In addition to the famous picture, four other pictures of this subject (figures 2–5) are illustrated in a recent book, Vincent Virga's *Eyes of the Nation*, and still another picture (figure 6) is illustrated in Karen Tsujimoto's *Dorothea Lange*. When you think about it, it is not surprising that Lange would take several pictures of this woman and her children. Anyone who takes snapshots knows that if photographers have the opportunity they will take several pictures of a subject. What is surprising is that the picture we all know, the one that has become an icon for the period, is so much more moving than the others.

Two of the pictures include an older child, apparently a teenager, sitting in a chair, so in a sense they are "truer" to the fact, because they give us more information about the family. The trunk, for instance, tells us that these people are on the move, and the setting—a messy field, with a shabby tent or lean-to—tells us that they are homeless. But sometimes less is more; the pictures showing the tent, trunk, and all of the children seem to sprawl. Perhaps we find ourselves wondering why people who seem to have only a trunk and some canvas would carry with them so bulky an object as a rocker. In saying that the two more inclusive pictures are less effective—less impressive, less moving—than the others, then, I don't think that I am simply expressing a personal preference. I think that most or maybe even all viewers would agree.

Putting aside the two pictures that show the setting, and also putting aside for the moment the most famous picture, we probably can agree that the three remaining pictures of the woman are approximately equally effective, one viewer might prefer one picture, another viewer another, but compared with the two that show the larger setting, all three of these pictures have the advantage of emphasizing the mother-and-child motif. But the remaining picture, the famous one, surely is far more memorable than even the other three close-up pictures. Why? Partly, perhaps, because it is a *closer* view, eliminating the tent pole and most of the hanging cloth. Partly it is more effective because the children have turned their faces from the camera, thereby conveying their isolation from everything in the world except their mother. And partly it is more effective because the woman, touching the side of her face, has a faraway look of anxiety.

Thinking about this picture in the context of the other five, if one has a cynical mind one might wonder if Lange staged it. And this is exactly what Charles J. Shindo says she did, in his recent book:

> In the course of this encounter Lange took six exposures, starting with a long shot of the lean-to with the mother and four children inside. . . . For the final shot Lange called back another of the children and had the children lean

Figure 4

Figure 5

Figure 6

upon their mother with their backs to the camera. The woman raised her hand to her chin and struck the now famous pose of the *Migrant Mother.* . . . (50)

What evidence does Shindo give for his claim that "Lange called back another of the children" and that she "had the children lean upon their mother"? Absolutely none. He does not cite Lange, or an eyewitness, or anyone who suggests that Lange customarily posed her subjects. He ignores the basic evidence, Lange's own words about how she took the picture:

> I saw and approached the hungry and desperate mother, as if drawn by a magnet. I do not remember how I explained my presence or my camera to her, but I do remember she asked me no questions. I made five exposures, working closer and closer from the same direction. I did not ask her name or her history. She told me her age, that she was thirty-two. She said that they had been living on frozen vegetables from the surrounding fields, and birds that the children killed. She had just sold the tires from her car to buy food. There she sat in that lean-to tent with her children huddled around her, and seemed to know that my pictures might help her, and so she helped me. There was a sort of equality about it.
>
> The pea crop at Nipomo had frozen and there was no work for anybody. But I did not approach the tents and shelters of other stranded pea-pickers. It was not necessary; I knew I had recorded the essence of my assignment. . . . (qtd. in Meltzer 133)

This is the *only* eyewitness account of how Lange photographed the woman and her children. Of course she may not have been telling the truth, but none of her contemporaries ever challenged the truth of her statement. Furthermore, everything that we know about Lange suggests that she did not pose her subjects. For instance, Rondal Partridge, a longtime friend and sometimes a co-worker, gave this description of Lange's method: "She did not ask people to hold a pose or repeat an action, instead she might ask a question: 'How much does that bag of cotton weigh?' And the man, wanting to give her a precise answer, would lift it onto the scales and Lange would make her photograph" (qtd. in Ohrn 61).

Rondal Partridge's comment harmonizes with comments that Lange herself made about her method. Asked about her approach to photography, she said, "First—hands off! Whatever I photograph, I do not molest or tamper with or arrange" (qtd. in Dixon 68). Elsewhere she explained that since she worked with a large camera, "You have to wait until certain decisions are made by the subject—what he's going to give to the camera, which is a very important decision; and the photographer—what he's going to choose to take" (qtd. in Ohrn 233). If I may add a personal comment, I want to say that as an amateur portrait photographer I know from my experience and from talking to other photographers, that posed photographs just don't come out successfully. You can't say to children, "Turn your faces toward your mother," and then say to the mother, "Please put your hand on your cheek," and get a good picture. Every photographer quickly learns that when the photographer specifies the poses, the pictures will be lifeless. The way to get a picture that is convincing is, as Lange's friend said, for the photographer to engage in some talk with the subject, which allows the subject to respond in some significant way. I imagine that while Lange talked, the children may have become uneasy at the sight of the woman with the big camera, and they may have turned and sought the security of their mother. (This is only a guess, but it is very different from Shindo's assertion, made without evidence, that "Lange called back another of the children and had the children lean upon their mother with their backs to the camera"). And perhaps Lange asked the woman something like, "What do you think you will do now?" or "Do you think you can get a friend to give your family a hitch to another work-site?" or some such thing, and the woman responded naturally. Again my view is different from Shindo's, who says that the woman "struck the pose of the *Migrant Mother*," where "struck the pose," in the context of his preceding sentences about Lange coldly setting up the image, suggests that the whole thing is a performance, with Lange as stage-manager and the woman as the chief actor.

Anyone who has read a book about Dorothea Lange, and has studied Lange's numerous comments about her ways of working in *Dorothea Lange*, ed. Howard M. Levin and Katherine Northrup, knows that posing figures was utterly foreign to her. In 1923 she posted on her darkroom door these words from Francis Bacon, and they guided her for the remaining thirty-odd years of her career:

> The contemplation of things as they are
> without substitution or imposture
> without error or confusion
> is in itself a nobler thing
> than a whole harvest of invention. (qtd. in Stein 59)

In her photography Lange sought to show the viewer "things as they are." She believed it was nobler to show life as it is than it is to invent compositions.

There are, of course, questions about this picture, such as "Exactly what is the mother thinking about?" Is she thinking that the situation is hopeless? Or that somehow she and the children will get through? Does her face show despair, or does it show determination? These are questions that we cannot answer definitively. But if we ask the question, "Did Lange tell the children and the woman how to position themselves?" we must answer that all of the evidence suggests that she did not set the scene. She spoke to the woman, and she moved about, looking for the best shot, but a picture as great as this one can only have come from (to repeat Lange's own belief) what the subject is "going to give to the camera" and what the photographer is "going to choose to take."

Works Cited

Dixon, Daniel. "Dorothea Lange." *Modern Photography* 16 (Dec. 1952). 68–77, 138–41. Print.

Levin, Howard M., and Katherine Northrup. *Dorothea Lange*. 2 vols. Glencoe: Text-Fiche Press, 1980. Print.

Meltzer, Milton. *Dorothea Lange: A Photographer's Life*. New York: Farrar, 1978. Print.

Ohrn, Karin Becker. *Dorothea Lange and the Documentary Tradition*. Baton Rouge: Louisiana State UP, 1980. Print.

Shindo, Charles J. *Dust Bowl Migrants in the American Imagination*. Lawrence: UP of Kansas, 1997. Print.

Stein, Sally. "Peculiar Grace: Dorothea Lange and the Testimony of the Body." *Dorothea Lange: A Visual Life*. Ed. Elizabeth Partridge. Washington, D.C.: Smithsonian Institution, 1994. 57–89. Print.

CHAPTER 4

Writing an Argument

Although in common usage an **argument** can be a noisy wrangle—baseball players argue about the umpire's decision; spouses argue about who should put out the garbage—in this chapter, we mean a discourse that uses *reasons*—rather than, say, appeals to pity or, for that matter, threats—in order to persuade readers to hold the writer's opinion or at least to persuade readers that the writer's opinion is thoughtful and reasonable. In this sense, argument is a thoroughly respectable activity.

What distinguishes argument from **exposition** (for instance, the explanation of a process) is this: Argument and exposition both consist of statements, but

- in argument, some statements are offered as reasons for other statements. Essentially, one builds an argument on the word "because."
- Another characteristic of argument is that argument assumes there may be a substantial disagreement among informed readers. Exposition assumes that the reader is unfamiliar with the subject matter—let's say, the origins of jazz or the law concerning affirmative action—but it does not assume that the reader holds a different opinion. However, the writer of an argument seeks to overcome disagreement (for instance, about the value or the fairness of something) by offering reasons that are convincing or at least worth considering carefully.

Here is Supreme Court Justice Louis Brandeis concluding a justly famous argument that government may not use evidence illegally obtained by wiretapping:

> Decency, security, and liberty alike demand that government officials shall be subjected to the same rules of conduct that are commands to the citizen. In a government of laws, existence of the government will be imperiled if it fails to observe the law scrupulously. Our Government is the potent, the omnipresent teacher. For good or for ill, it teaches the whole people by its example. Crime is contagious. If the Government becomes a lawbreaker, it breeds contempt for law; it invites every man to become a law unto himself; it invites anarchy. To declare that in the administration of the criminal law the end justifies the means—to declare that the Government may commit crimes in order to secure the conviction of a private criminal—would bring terrible retribution. Against that pernicious doctrine the Court should resolutely set its face.

Brandeis's reasoning is highlighted by his forceful style. Note the resonant use of parallel constructions ("Decency, security, and liberty," "For good or for ill," "it breeds . . . it invites," "To declare . . . to declare"), which convey a sense of dignity and authority. Notice, too, the effective variation between short and long sentences. The sentences range from three words ("Crime is contagious"—forceful because of its brevity and its alliteration) to 37 words (the next-to-last sentence—impressive because of its length and especially because the meaning is suspended until the end, when we get the crucial verb and its object: "would bring terrible retribution"). Later in our discussion of argument, we will talk about the importance of the writer's style.

The Aims of an Argumentative Essay

The aim might seem obvious—to persuade the reader to accept the writer's opinion. In fact, there are often other aims. First, writers draft argumentative essays partly in order to find out what they believe. In drafting a paper, they come to see that some of their unformed beliefs can't really be supported or that their beliefs need to be considerably modified. This point should not come as a surprise; in earlier chapters, we have said that writers get ideas and refine their beliefs by the act of writing. Second, if you read argumentative essays in, say, *National Review* (a conservative magazine), in *The Nation* (a liberal magazine), or in just about any magazine, you will see that much of the writing is really a matter of preaching to the converted. Good arguments may be offered, but they are offered not to persuade readers but to reassure them that the views they already hold are sound. After all, few liberals read *National Review,* few conservatives read *The Nation,* and so on.

When you write an argumentative essay, although you may hope to convince all readers to adopt your view, you probably also realize that the subject is complex and that other opinions are possible. What you want to do is to set forth your viewpoint as effectively as possible, not because you believe all readers will say "Yes, of course, you have converted me" but because *you want your view to be given a hearing. You want to show that it is one that can be held by a reasonable person.* Because you are a person of goodwill with an open mind, you realize that most issues are very complicated. You have formed some ideas, and now you are taking a stand and arguing on its behalf. However, you probably are not saying that no other view can possibly have the tiniest scrap of merit. As Virginia Woolf put it (with perhaps a bit of self-irony):

> When a subject is highly controversial . . . one cannot hope to tell the truth. One can only show how one came to hold whatever opinion one does hold. One can only give one's audience the chance of drawing their own conclusions as they observe the limitations, the prejudices, the idiosyncrasies of the speaker.

Again, we want to say that in drafting a paper, your chief aim is to educate yourself; in offering it to readers, your chief aim is to let others know that your views are worth considering because they are supported by reason. If you persuade your readers to accept your views, great; but you should at least persuade them that a reasonable person can hold these views.

Negotiating Agreements: The Approach of Carl R. Rogers

Carl R. Rogers (1902–1987), best known for his book entitled *On Becoming a Person,* was a psychotherapist, not a writer, but he has exerted a great influence on teachers of writing. Rogers originally intended to become a Protestant minister, but as he tells in *On Becoming a Person,* during the course of a six-month visit to East Asia, he came to recognize "that sincere and honest people could believe in very divergent religious doctrines."

He turned to the study of psychology and in the course of time developed the idea that a therapist must engage in "reflection," by which he meant that the therapist must reflect—must give back an image—of what the client said. (Rogers's use of the word "client" rather than "patient" is itself a clue to his approach; the therapist is not dealing with someone who is supposed passively to accept treatment from the all-powerful doctor.)

What does this have to do with seeking to persuade a reader? Consider two lawyers arguing a case in court. Lawyer A may seem to be arguing with lawyer B, but neither lawyer is really trying to convince the other, and neither lawyer has the faintest interest in learning from the other. The lawyers are trying to persuade not each other but the judge or jury. Similarly, the writer of a letter to a newspaper, taking issue with an editorial, probably has no thought of changing the newspaper's policy. Rather, the letter is really directed to another audience: readers of the newspaper. And we hear this sort of thing on radio and television shows with titles such as *Crossfire, Firing Line,* and *Point Counterpoint.* For the most part, the participants are not trying to learn from each other and are not trying to solve a complex problem but instead are trying to convince the audience that one side is wholly right and the other side is wholly wrong. If they are talking about an issue that we don't know much about, the arguments on both sides may seem to be equally strong, and we are likely to side with the speaker whose *style* of talk (and maybe of dress) we prefer. This point is important, and we will return to it when we talk about the *persona* or character of the writer of an argument.

Suppose that unlike a participant on a radio or television show and unlike a lawyer arguing a case, speaker X really does want to persuade speaker Y; that is, X really wants to bring Y around to X's point of view or, if X is mistaken in his or her views, X really is willing to learn from Y in the course of the give and take. Rogers points out that when we engage in an argument, if we feel that our integrity or our identity is threatened, we stiffen our resistance. Normally, we may *want* to grow, to develop our thoughts, to act in accordance with sound reasons, but when we are threatened, we erect defenses that in fact shut us off from communication. That is, we find ourselves within a circle that not only shuts others out but that also has the unintended effect of shutting us in. We—or our opponent—may have given very good reasons, but because each party has behaved in a threatening manner and has felt threatened by the other side, we have scarcely listened to each other, and therefore, little or nothing has been communicated. (If you think about your own experience, you probably can confirm Rogers's view.)

To avoid this deplorable lack of opportunity for growth, Rogers suggests that participants in arguments need to become partners, not adversaries. Here, with Rogers's insight in mind, we can digress for a moment and call attention to the combative terms normally associated with argument. For instance, *debate* is from Latin *de-* (down) and *battere* (to beat)—the same word that gives us *battery,* as in "assault and battery." We *marshal* our arguments (arrange them into a military formation), and we *attack our opponents,* seeking to *rebut* (from a Latin word meaning "to butt back") or *refute* (again from a Latin word, this time meaning "to drive back") their assertions. When we are engaged in these activities, (1) we are scarcely in a position to learn from those we are talking with—really, talking *at*—and (2) we are not likely to teach them anything because, like us, they are busy *defending* (still another military word) their own position.

Rogers suggests that a writer who wishes to communicate (as opposed to a lawyer or a debater who merely wishes to win) needs to reduce the threat. To repeat: The participants in an argument need to become partners rather than adversaries. "Mutual communication," he says, "tends to be pointed toward solving a problem rather than attacking a person or a group."

For instance, take abortion. We hear about "pro-life" (or "anti-abortion") people and about "pro-choice" (or "pro-abortion") people. It may seem that there is no common ground—nothing they can agree on. But polls reveal considerable ambiguity within some people. For example, consider a finding of a *New York Times*/CBS News poll of representative Americans in January 1998. Participants were asked which question came nearer to their opinion: Is abortion the same thing as murdering a child? Or is abortion not murder because the fetus really isn't a child? Half the sample chose "the same thing as murdering a child," and 38 percent chose "the fetus really isn't a child." However, at the same time, 58 percent—including a third of those who chose "murdering a child"—agreed that abortion was "sometimes the best course in a bad situation."

These apparently inconsistent responses have been fairly consistent for the last 20 years; some people who consider abortion equivalent to murdering a child will grant that there are situations in which abortion is "the best course," and many pro-choice people—people who insist that a woman has a right to choose and that her choice is not the government's business—also agree that abortion should not be lightly entered into. Take a particular case: A pregnant woman who regards abortion as "the same thing as murdering a child" learns that her baby will probably have Down syndrome (such persons have an average IQ of about 50, are prone to hearing problems and vision problems, and have an increased risk of heart disease and leukemia). Despite her opposition to abortion, she may become one of the people who feel abortion is "sometimes the best course in a bad situation." Given the choice of bearing or aborting, she may very reluctantly decide to abort. Yet, on the day we were drafting these pages, we happened to come across a letter in a newspaper making a point that, however obvious, we had not thought of. The writer—Maureen K. Hogan, executive director of Adopt a Special Kid—reported in her letter that "there are thousands of families around the United States that would be happy to adopt such a child. . . . In 25 years, there hasn't been a single child for whom we have not been able to find a home." We can imagine that a woman who dreaded the idea of aborting a fetus but felt that she had no choice but abortion might—on hearing this information—modify her intention and engage in a course of behavior that she and all others concerned will find more satisfactory.

We should also mention that open-minded discussions between persons who hold differing views may reveal that some of their differences are verbal rather than substantial. For instance, one can wonder if the poll would have produced the same results if the question had asked about "killing" rather than "murdering" a child. Patient, well-intentioned discussions may reveal that the parties are not as far apart as they at first seemed to be; they share some ground, and once this common ground is acknowledged, differences can be discussed.

As another example, consider a proposal in 1997 by President Clinton to introduce voluntary national tests in reading and mathematics. While not voluntary, NCLB has pushed for national standards. State tests have already started to push out some subjects from the curriculum, and a lot of what's said in this list has come true. Some people think such testing is a bad idea. Why?

- What is tested is what will get taught; teachers will soon start preparing students for the test rather than teaching the things they think are important. Why would teachers do this? Because they want to look good—they want their school to stand high in the national ratings.
- A second objection is that testing introduces an unhealthy spirit of competition.
- A third objection concerns the issue of who will make the tests. Administrators? Professors of education? The teachers who are on the firing line?
- A fourth objection is that no matter who makes the test, the testing board would have too much power, since it would in effect determine not only what things get taught but which students get to go on to college.
- A fifth objection is that a national test would have little meaning; some states have a relatively homogenous population, whereas others have a relatively heterogenous population.
- A sixth objection is that test scores don't have much value. After all, we know (or do we?) that the SAT is not really a good predictor of success in school and that tests are especially likely to fail to recognize the offbeat creative students—just look at X, who had poor grades and dropped out of school and is now recognized as a genius.

All these objections probably have some weight, but replies (also of varying weight) can be made to them. To take only the first two: It may be a good thing if teachers are jolted out of their parochialism and are made to become aware of the values of others, and second, what is wrong with some competition? Competition is sometimes healthy. But after all the pros and the cons are laid out, a Rogerian thinker will want to see what the two sides can *agree* on. They can probably agree that American school children ought to do better in reading and in mathematics. They can also probably agree that testing has some validity. And they can also probably agree that national testing by itself will not solve the problem. For instance, other possibilities include a longer school year, better pay for teachers (to attract better teachers), national tests for teachers, and so on. If the disputants can first establish the positions they *share* and realize that both sides are people of goodwill endowed with some good ideas, they may better be able to work out their differences.

Rogers was drawing on his experience as a psychotherapist, which means he was mostly writing about the relationship between two people who were literally talking to each other, whereas a writer can at best imagine a reader. But good writers do in fact bring their readers into their writings by such devices as "It may be said that . . ."—here, one summarizes or quotes a view other than one's own. Writers genuinely interested in contributing to the solution of a problem will not merely busy themselves in asserting their position but will also inform themselves of a variety of views by listening and by reading. And when they listen and read, they must do so with an open mind, giving the speaker or author (at least at first) the benefit of the doubt. (Rogers's term for this sort of activity is "empathic listening"—i.e., comprehension so complete that it grasps not only the thoughts but also the feelings and motives of another.) That is, they will listen and read sympathetically, and they will not be too quick to evaluate. In an effort to do justice to the material, they may even listen and read with the mind of a believer. Or if this is asking too much, they will act in the spirit advocated by the 17th century essayist Francis Bacon: "Read not to contradict and confute; nor to believe and take for granted; nor to find talk and discourse; but to weigh and consider."

Writers genuinely interested in persuading others will educate themselves by listening and reading. In their own writing, where they wish to contribute their views on a disputed matter, they can simultaneously reduce the psychological threat to those who hold views different from their own by doing several things: They can show sympathetic understanding of the opposing argument; they can recognize what is valid in it; and they can recognize and demonstrate that those who take a different view are nonetheless persons of goodwill.

A writer who takes Rogers seriously will usually in the first part of an argumentative essay

- state the problem, suggesting that it is an issue of concern and that the reader has a stake in it;
- show respect for persons who hold differing views;
- set forth opposing positions, *stated in such a way that their proponents will agree that the statements of their positions are fair;* and
- find some shared values—that is, grant whatever validity the writer finds in those positions, for instance, by recognizing the circumstances in which they would indeed be acceptable.

Having accurately summarized other views and having granted some concessions, the writer has presumably won the reader's attention and goodwill; the writer can now

- show how those who hold other positions will benefit if they accept the writer's position.

This last point is essentially an appeal to self-interest. In the example we gave a moment ago—concerning a pregnant woman who has contemplated aborting a fetus that, if born, will probably be a baby with Down syndrome—the appeal to self-interest might run along the lines that if she bears the child, she will be free from the remorse she might feel if she had aborted it.

Sometimes, of course, the differing positions will be so far apart that no reconciliation can be proposed, in which case the writer will probably seek to show how the issue can be best solved by adopting the writer's own position. But even in such an essay, it is desirable to state the opposing view in such a way that proponents of that view will agree that that is indeed their position and not a caricature of it.

Again Rogers was a psychologist, not a teacher of writing and not a logician. In fact, his writing shares with some recent feminist theory a distrust of logic, which can be seen as masculine and aggressive, concerned with winning, even with "annihilating the opposition." Rogers offers advice not so much on winning (in the sense of conquering) but in the sense of winning over—that is, gaining converts or at least allies.

✓ A Checklist: Rogerian Argument

☐ Have I treated other views with **respect**?

☐ Have I stated at least one other view **in a way that would satisfy its proponents and thus demonstrated my familiarity with the issue**?

☐ Have I granted **validity to any aspects of other positions and thus demonstrated my openmindedness**?

☐ Have I pointed out the **common ground**—the ground that we share—and thus prepared the reader to listen attentively to my proposals?

☐ Have I shown how the other position will be strengthened—at least in some contexts—by accepting some aspects of my position? (In short, have I **appealed to the reader's self-interest** by showing that proponents of the other view(s) will benefit from accepting at least part of my view?)

Some Ways of Arguing: Appeals to Reason and Appeals to Emotions

Appeals to Reason: Deduction and Induction

Deduction is the process of reasoning from premises to a logical conclusion. Here is the classic example:

> All men are mortal (*major premise*).
>
> Socrates is a man (*minor premise*).
>
> Therefore, Socrates is mortal (*conclusion*).

Such an argument, which takes two truths and joins them to produce a third truth, is called a **syllogism**. Deduction (from the Latin *deducere*, for "lead down from") moves from a general statement to a specific application.

Here's a second example:

> All teachers of Spanish know that *hoy* means "today" (*major premise*).
>
> John is a teacher of Spanish (*minor premise*).
>
> John knows that *hoy* means today (*conclusion*).

If indeed all teachers of Spanish know the meaning of *hoy* and if indeed John is a teacher of Spanish, the conclusion *must* be true.

However notice that *if a premise of a syllogism is not true*, one can reason logically and still come to a *false* conclusion. Example:

> All teachers are members of a union (*major premise*).
>
> John is a teacher (*minor premise*).
>
> John is a member of a union (*conclusion*).

The *process* of reasoning is correct here—*the major premise is false*—but all teachers are not members of a union—so the conclusion is worthless. John may or may not be a member of the union.

Another point: Some arguments superficially appear logical but are not. Let's take this attempt at a syllogism:

> All teachers of Spanish know that *hoy* means "today" (*major premise*).
>
> John knows that in Spanish *hoy* means today (*minor premise*).
>
> Therefore, John is a teacher of Spanish (*conclusion*).

Both of the premises are correct, but the conclusion does not follow. What's wrong? Valid deduction requires that the subject or condition of the major premise (in this case, teachers of Spanish) also appear in the minor premise, but it doesn't here. The minor premise should be "John is a teacher of Spanish," and the valid conclusion, of course, would be "Therefore, John knows that *hoy* means today."

Let's now turn to another process of reasoning: **induction.** Whereas deduction moves from a general statement ("All men are mortal") to a particular conclusion ("Socrates is mortal"), induction moves from particular instances to a general conclusion.

> I saw an elephant, and it was grayish. Six months later, I saw another elephant, and it was grayish. In fact, every elephant I have seen is grayish, so by induction (from Latin *inducere,* "lead into," "lead up to"), I conclude that all elephants are grayish.

Now consider, a second example: I have met 10 graduates of Vassar College and all are females, so I conclude that all Vassar graduates are females. However, this conclusion happens to be incorrect: Vassar was founded as a women's college, but it now admits men, so although male graduates are notably fewer than female graduates, they do exist. Induction is valid only if the sample is representative.

Because we can rarely be certain that a sample is representative, induced conclusions are usually open to doubt. Still, we live our lives largely by induction: We have dinner with a friend, we walk the dog, we write home for money—all because these actions have produced certain results in the past and we assume that actions of the same sort will produce results consistent with our earlier findings. Nelson Algren's excellent advice must have been arrived at inductively: "Never eat at a place called Mom's, and never play cards with a man called Doc."

Appeals to Emotions

"Tears are not arguments," the Brazilian writer Machado de Assis said. We understand the point, and we remember the old joke about the youngster who killed his parents and then pleaded for mercy on the grounds that he was an orphan. Still, under certain conditions, something can be said on behalf of appeals to the emotions.

An emotional appeal is legitimate if it heightens the facts rather than obscures them. In an argument about legislation that would govern police actions, surely it is legitimate to show a photograph of the battered, bloodied face of an alleged victim of police brutality. True, such a photograph cannot tell the whole truth; it cannot tell us if the subject threatened the officer with a gun or repeatedly resisted an order to surrender. But it can tell us that the victim was severely beaten, and (like a comparable description in words) it can evoke in us emotions that may properly enter into our decision about the permissible use of force.

The emotional appeals that one is most likely to encounter are:

- Appeals to pity
- Appeals to fear
- Appeals to tradition

Consider an appeal to *pity*. An animal rights activist who is arguing that calves are cruelly confined might reasonably tell us about the size of the pen in which the calf is kept (too small for the calf to turn around or even to lie down). Now, someone might argue that calves don't like to lie down or to turn around or that calves have no right to lie down or turn around, but the verbal description and the picture of the calf in the pen, which unquestionably make an emotional appeal, can hardly be called irrelevant or illegitimate.

Appeals to *fear* are commonly found in advertisements and other publications issued by insurance companies, where the argument, such as it is, plays on our concern with our property, our health, and our responsibility to provide for our spouse and our children. Appeals to *tradition* draw on our nostalgia and our fondness for and respect for the past, such as the America of the Founding Fathers—but a world—we must remember—that accepted slavery and that allowed only males to vote. The emotional appeal to tradition is not, by itself a convincing argument.

In appealing to the emotions, then, the important things are

- not to falsify the issue (for instance, by oversimplifying it),
- not to distract attention from the facts of the case, and
- not to let the emotional appeal take the place of appeals to reason.

Focus on the facts and concentrate on offering *reasons* (essentially, statements linked explicitly or implicitly with *because*). But you may also legitimately bring the facts home to your readers by seeking to induce in them the appropriate emotions. Your words will be fallacious (illegitimate, deceptive) only if you stimulate emotions that are not rightly connected to the facts of the case.

As a reader, be attentive to emotional appeals, but recognize arguments that offer *only* emotional appeals. Be especially aware of arguments that offer emotional appeals designed to keep the reader from accurately perceiving the facts—the real evidence.

Three Kinds of Evidence: Examples, Testimony, Statistics

Writers of arguments seek to persuade by showing that they themselves are persons of goodwill by offering evidence to support their thesis. The chief forms of evidence used in argument are:

- Examples
- Testimony (the citation of authorities)
- Statistics

We'll briefly consider each of these.

Examples

Example is from the Latin *exemplum,* which means "something taken out."
An **example** is the sort of thing—taken from among many similar
things—that one selects and holds up for view, perhaps after saying "for
example."

Three sorts of examples are especially common in written arguments:

- Real examples
- Invented instances
- Analogies

Real examples are just what they sound like—instances that have
occurred. If we are arguing that gun control won't work, we point to
those states that have adopted gun control laws and that nevertheless
have had no reduction in crimes using guns. Or if one wants to support
the assertion that a woman can be a capable head of state, one may find
oneself pointing to women who have actually served as heads of state,
such as Cleopatra, Queen Elizabeth I of England, Golda Meir (prime
minister of Israel), Indira Gandhi (prime minister of India), Margaret
Thatcher (prime minister of England), and Angela Merkel (German
chancellor).

The advantage of using real examples is that they are real. Of
course, an opponent might stubbornly respond that the persons
whom you name could not—for some reason or other—function as
the head of state in *our* country. For instance, one might argue that the
case of Golda Meir proves nothing, since the role of women in Israeli
society is different from the role of women in the United States (a
country in which a majority of the citizens are Christians). And one
might argue that much of Indira Gandhi's power came from her being the daughter of Nehru, an immensely popular Indian statesman.
Even the most compelling real example will inevitably be in some
ways special or particular and in the eyes of some readers may not
seem to be a fair example.

For instance, consider a student who is arguing that peer review
should be part of the writing course and points out that he or she found it
of great help in high school. An opponent argues that things in college
are different: College students should be able to help themselves, even
highly gifted college students are not competent to offer college-level
instruction, and so on. Still, as the feebleness of these objections (and the
objections against Meir and Gandhi) indicates, real examples can be very
compelling.

Invented instances are exempt from the charge that because of some
detail or another, they are not relevant as evidence. Suppose you are
arguing against capital punishment on the grounds that if an innocent
person is executed, there is no way of even attempting to rectify

the injustice. If you point to the case of X, you may be met with the reply that X was not in fact innocent. Rather than get tangled up in the guilt or innocence of a particular person, it may be better to argue that we can suppose—we can imagine—an innocent person being convicted and executed, and we can imagine that evidence later proves the person's innocence.

Invented instances have the advantage of presenting an issue clearly—free from all the distracting particularities (and irrelevancies) that are bound up with any real instance. But invented instances have the disadvantage of being invented, and they may seem remote from the real issues being argued.

Analogies are comparisons pointing out several resemblances between two rather different things. For instance, one might assert that a government is like a ship, and in times of stress—if the ship is to weather the storm—the authority of the captain must not be questioned.

But don't confuse an analogy with proof. An analogy is an extended comparison between two things: It can be useful in exposition, for it explains the unfamiliar by means of the familiar: "A government is like a ship, and just as a ship has a captain and a crew, so a government has . . ."; "Writing an essay is like building a house; just as an architect must begin with a plan, so the writer must. . . ." Such comparisons can be useful—helping to clarify what otherwise might be obscure—but their usefulness goes only so far. Everything is what it is and not something else. A government is not a ship, and what is true of a captain's power need not be true of a president's power; and a writer is not an architect. Some of what is true about ships may be roughly true of governments, and some of what is true about architects may be (again, roughly) true of writers, but there are differences too. Consider the following analogy between a lighthouse and the death penalty:

> The death penalty is a warning, just like a lighthouse throwing its beams out to sea. We hear about shipwrecks, but we do not hear about the ships the lighthouse guides safely on their way. We do not have proof of the number of ships it saves, but we do not tear the lighthouse down.
>
> J. Edgar Hoover

How convincing is Hoover's analogy as an argument—that is, as a reason for retaining the death penalty?

Testimony

Testimony—or the citation of authorities—is rooted in our awareness that some people are recognized as experts. In our daily life, we constantly turn to experts for guidance: We look up the spelling of a word in the dictionary, we listen to the weather forecast on the radio, we take an ailing cat to the vet for a checkup. Similarly, when we wish to become informed about controversial matters, we often turn to experts—first to help educate ourselves and then to help convince our readers.

Don't forget that *you* are an authority on many things. For example, today's newspaper includes an article about the cutback in funding for teaching the arts in elementary and secondary schools. Educators are responding that arts education is not a frill and that the arts provide the analytical thinking, teamwork, motivation, and self-discipline that most people agree are needed to reinvigorate American schools. If you have studied the arts in school—for instance, if you painted pictures or learned to play a musical instrument—you are in a position to evaluate these claims. Similarly, if you have studied in a bilingual educational program, your own testimony will be invaluable.

There are at least two reasons for offering testimony in an argument. The obvious reason is that expert opinion does (and should) carry some weight with the audience; the less obvious one is that a change of voice (if the testimony is not your own) in an essay may afford the reader a bit of pleasure. No matter how engaging our own voice may be, a fresh voice— whether that of Thomas Jefferson, Albert Einstein, or Toni Morrison— may provide a refreshing change of tone.

But there are dangers. The chief dangers are that the words of authorities may be taken out of context or otherwise distorted or that the authorities may not be authorities on the topic at hand. We are concerned quite rightly with what the framers of the U.S. Constitution said, but it is not entirely clear that their words can be fairly applied—on one side or the other to such an issue as abortion. We are quite rightly concerned with what Einstein said, but it is not entirely clear that his eminence as a physicist qualifies him as an authority on, say, world peace. In a moment, when we discuss errors in reasoning, we'll have more to say about the proper and improper use of authorities.

Statistics

Statistics—another important form of evidence—are especially useful in arguments concerning social issues. If we want to argue for (or against) raising the driving age, we will probably do some research in the library, and we'll offer statistics about the number of accidents caused by people in certain age groups.

But a word of caution: The significance of statistics may be difficult to assess. For instance, opponents of gun control legislation have pointed out—in support of the argument that such laws are ineffectual—that homicides in Florida *increased* after Florida adopted gun control laws. Supporters of gun control laws cried "foul," arguing that in the years after adopting these laws that Miami became (for reasons having nothing to do with the laws) the cocaine capital of the United States and the rise in homicide was chiefly a reflection of murders involved in the drug trade. That is, a significant change in the population has made a comparison of the figures meaningless. This objection seems plausible, and the statistics should therefore probably carry little weight.

How Much Evidence Is Enough?

If you allow yourself ample time to write your essay, you probably will turn up plenty of evidence to illustrate your arguments, such as examples drawn from your own experience and imagination, from your reading, and from your talks with others. Examples will not only help to clarify and to support your assertions but will also provide a concreteness that will be welcome in a paper that might be, on the whole, fairly abstract. Your sense of your audience will have to guide you in making your selection of examples. Generally speaking, a single example may not fully illuminate a difficult point, so a second example—a clincher—may be desirable. If you offer a third or fourth example, you're probably succumbing to a temptation to include something that tickles your fancy. If it is as good as you think it is, the reader will probably accept the unnecessary example and may even be grateful. But before you pile on examples, try to imagine yourself in your reader's place and ask if an example is needed. If not, ask yourself if the reader will be glad to receive the overload.

One other point: On most questions—say on the value of bilingual education or on the need for rehabilitation programs in prisons—it's not possible to make a strictly logical case in the sense of an absolutely airtight proof. Don't assume that it is your job to make an absolute proof. What you are expected to do is to offer a reasonable argument. Remember Virginia Woolf's words: "When a subject is highly controversial . . . one cannot hope to tell the truth. One can only show how one came to hold whatever opinion one does hold."

Avoiding Fallacies

Let's further examine writing reasonable arguments by considering some obvious errors in reasoning. In logic, these errors are called **fallacies** (from a Latin verb *fallere*, meaning "to deceive"). As Tweedledee says in *Through the Looking-Glass*, "If it were so, it would be; but as it isn't, it ain't. That's logic."

To persuade readers to accept your opinions, you must persuade them that you are reliable; if your argument includes fallacies, thoughtful readers will not take you seriously. More important, if your argument includes fallacies, you are misleading yourself. When you search your draft for fallacies, you are searching for ways to improve the quality of your thinking.

Here are the most common fallacies:

1. False Authority. Don't try to borrow the prestige of authorities who are not authorities on the topic in question—for example, a heart surgeon speaking on politics. Similarly, some former authorities are no longer authorities because the problems have changed or because later knowledge has superseded their views. Adam Smith, Thomas Jefferson, Eleanor Roosevelt, and Albert Einstein remain persons of genius, but an attempt to use their opinions when you are examining modern issues—even in their fields—may be questioned. Remember the last words of John B. Sedgwick, a Union Army general at the Battle of Spotsylvania in 1864: "They couldn't hit an elephant at this dist—."

In short, before you rely on an authority, ask yourself if the person in question *is* an authority on the topic. And don't let stereotypes influence your idea of who is an authority. There is an apt Yiddish proverb: "A goat has a beard, but that doesn't make him a rabbi."

2. False Quotation. If you do quote from an authority, don't misquote. For example, you may find someone who grants that "there are strong arguments in favor of abolishing the death penalty," but if she goes on to argue that, on balance, the arguments in favor of retaining it seem stronger to her, it is dishonest to quote her words so as to imply that she favors abolishing it.

3. Suppression of Evidence. Don't neglect evidence that is contrary to your own argument. You owe it to yourself and your reader to present all the relevant evidence. Be especially careful not to assume that every question is simply a matter of *either/or*. There may be some truth on both sides. Take the following thesis: "Grades encourage unwholesome competition and should therefore be abolished." Even if the statement about the evil effect of grading is true, it may not be the whole truth, and it may not follow that grades should be abolished. One might point out that grades do other things too: They may stimulate learning, and they may assist students by telling them how far they have progressed. One might nevertheless conclude, on balance, that the fault outweighs the benefits. But the argument will be more persuasive now that the benefits of grades have been considered.

Concede to the opposition what it deserves and then outscore the opposition. Failure to confront the opposing evidence will be noticed; your readers will keep wondering why you do not consider some particular point and may consequently dismiss your argument. However, if you confront the opposition, you will almost surely strengthen your own argument. As Edmund Burke said 200 years ago: "He that wrestles with us strengthens our nerves, and sharpens our skill. Our antagonist is our helper."

4. Generalization from Insufficient Evidence. In rereading a draft of an argument that you have written, try to spot your own generalizations. Ask yourself if a reasonable reader is likely to agree that the generalization is based on an adequate sample.

A visitor to a college may sit in on three classes, each taught by a different instructor, and may find all three stimulating. That's a good sign, but can we generalize and say that the teaching at this college is excellent? Are three classes a sufficient sample? If all three are offered by the biology department, which includes only five instructors, perhaps we can tentatively say that the teaching of biology at this institution is good. If the biology department contains 20 instructors, perhaps we can still say—although more tentatively—that this sample indicates that the teaching of biology is good. But what does the sample say about the teaching of other subjects at the college? It probably does say something—the institution may be much concerned with teaching across the board—but then again, it may not say a great deal, since the biology department may be exceptionally concerned with good teaching.

5. The Genetic Fallacy. Don't assume that something can necessarily be explained in terms of its birth or origin. "He wrote the novel to make money, so it can't be any good" is not a valid inference. The value of a novel does not depend on the author's motivations in writing it. Indeed, the value or worth of a novel needs to be established by reference to other criteria. Neither the highest nor the lowest motivations guarantee the quality of the product. Another example: "Capital punishment arose in days when men sought revenge, so now it ought to be abolished." Again, an unconvincing argument: Capital punishment may have some current value; for example, it may serve as a deterrent to crime. But that's another argument, and it needs evidence if it is to be believed. Be on guard too against the thoughtless tendency to judge people by their origins: Mr. X has a foreign accent, so he is probably untrustworthy or stupid or industrious.

6. Begging the Question and Circular Reasoning. Don't assume the truth of the point that you should prove. The term "begging the question" is a trifle odd. It means, in effect, "You, like a beggar, are asking me to grant you something at the outset."

Examples: "The barbaric death penalty should be abolished" and "This senseless language requirement should be dropped." Both of these statements assume what they should prove—that the death penalty is barbaric and that the language requirement is senseless. Of course, you can make such assertions, but you must go on to prove them.

Circular reasoning is usually an extended form of begging the question. What ought to be proved is covertly assumed. Example: "X is the best-qualified candidate for the office because the most informed people say so." Who are the most informed people? Those who recognize X's superiority. Circular reasoning, then, normally includes intermediate steps absent from begging the question, but the two fallacies are so closely related that they can be considered one. Another example: "I feel sympathy for her because I identify with her." Despite the "because," no reason is really offered. What follows "because" is merely a restatement, in slightly different words, of what precedes; the shift of words, from *feel sympathy* to *identify with*, has misled the writer into thinking she is giving a reason.

Other examples: "Students are interested in courses when the subject matter and the method of presentation are interesting" and "There cannot be peace in the Middle East because the Jews and the Arabs will always fight." In each case, an assertion that ought to be proved is reasserted as a reason in support of the assertion.

7. *Post hoc ergo propter hoc.* Latin: "after this, therefore because of this." Don't assume that because X precedes Y, X must cause Y. For example: "He went to college and came back a boozer; college corrupted him." He might have taken up liquor even if he had not gone to college. Another example: "When a 55-mile-per-hour speed limit was imposed in 1974, after the Arab embargo on oil, the number of auto fatalities decreased sharply, from 55,000 deaths in 1973 to 46,000 in 1974. Therefore, it is evident that a 55-mile-per-hour speed limit—still adhered to in some states—saves lives." Not quite. Because gasoline was expensive after the embargo, the number of miles traveled decreased. The number of fatalities *per mile* remained constant. The price of gas, not the speed limit, seems responsible for the decreased number of fatalities. Moreover, the national death rate has continued to fall. Why? Several factors are at work: seatbelt and child-restraint laws, campaigns against drunk driving, improved auto design, and improved roads. Medicine may have also improved, so that today, doctors can save accident victims who in 1974 would have died. In short, it probably impossible to isolate the correlation between speed and safety.

8. *Argumentum ad hominem.* Here, the argument is directed toward the person (*hominem* is Latin for *man*) rather than toward the issue. Don't shift from your topic to your opponent. A speaker argues against legalizing abortions, and her opponent—instead of facing the merits of the argument—attacks the character or the associations of the opponent: "You're a Catholic, aren't you?"

9. *False Assumption.* Consider the Scot who argued that Shakespeare must have been a Scot. Asked for his evidence, he replied, "The ability of the man warrants the assumption." Or take such a statement as "She goes to Yale, so she must be rich." Possibly the statement is based on faulty induction (the writer knows four Yale students, and all four are rich), but more likely, he is just passing on a cliché. The Yale student in question may be on a scholarship, may be struggling to earn the money, or may be backed by parents of modest means who for 18 years have saved money for her college education. Other examples: "I haven't heard him complain about French 10, so he must be satisfied" and "She's a writer, so she must be well-read." A little thought will show how weak such assertions are; they *may* be true, but they may not.

The errors we have discussed are common. In revising your writing, try to spot them and eliminate or correct them. You have a point to make, and you should make it fairly. If you can only make it unfairly, you are doing an injustice to your reader and yourself; you should try to change your view of the topic. You don't want to be like the politician whose speech had a marginal note: "Argument weak; shout here."

Drafting an Argument

Imagining an Audience

A writer's job is made easier if the audience is known. Thus, if you are writing for the college newspaper, you can assume that your readers know certain things, and you can adopt a moderately familiar tone. Similarly, if you are writing a letter to the college trustees, you can assume that they know certain things—you will not have to tell them that the institution is a small, co-educational, undergraduate college located in northern Georgia—but you will probably adopt a somewhat more formal tone than you would use in writing for your fellow students.

Your instructor may tell you to imagine a particular audience—readers of the local newspaper, alumni, high school students, your representative in Congress, or any other group. But if your instructor does not specify an audience, you will probably do best if you imagine one of two possibilities: Either write for the general reader (the person who reads *Time* or *Newsweek*) or for your classmates. Although these two audiences are similar in many respects, there is a significant difference. All your classmates may be of the same gender or the same religion, they may be of approximately the same age, and they may come from the same area. In an essay written for your classmates, then, you may not have to explain certain things that you will indeed have to explain if you are writing for the general reader. To cite an obvious example: If the school is specialized (for instance, if it is a religious school or a military school), you can assume that your readers know certain things and share certain attitudes that you cannot assume in the general public.

Getting Started

If your essay is related to one or more of the readings in this book, of course you will read the essay(s) carefully—perhaps highlighting, underlining, annotating, summarizing, and outlining, as we suggest in our first chapter. You will question the text, and you'll probably make entries in a journal, as we suggest in the second and third chapters. These entries may be ideas that come to you out of the blue or they may emerge from conscious, critical thinking—perhaps in conversations with some of your classmates. (Critical thinking means, among other things, that you will question your own assumptions and evaluate your evidence as objectively as possible.)

Discussions—with yourself and with others—will help you to improve your ideas. At this stage, you will probably have some ideas that you did not have when you began thinking about the topic, and you will probably want to abandon some of your earlier ideas that now seem less strong than you had originally thought.

Writing a Draft

By now, you probably have a fair idea of the strengths and (as you see it) the weaknesses of other positions. You also have a fair idea of what your thesis—your claim—is and what reasons you will offer to support it. And you also probably have at hand some of the supporting evidence— examples, statements by authorities, or personal experiences—that you intend to offer as support.

Some people at this point—especially if they are writing on a word processor—like to sit down and write freely, pouring out their ideas. They then print out the material and, on rereading, highlight what seems useful—perhaps indicating in the margins how the material should be re-organized. They then (again, we are speaking of writing on a word processor) move blocks of material into some reasonable organization.

Our own preference (even though we also use a word processor when we write a first draft) is to prepare a rough outline on paper—really, a list of topics. Then, after further thought, we add to it, circling items on the list and indicating (by means of arrows) better positions for these items.

Next, when we have a rough outline (perhaps a list of five or six chief items, under each of which we have written a word or phrase indicating how the point might be developed), we start writing on the word processor. It happens that our rough outline (later, much changed) for this section ran thus:

audience

  assigned? or general? or classmates

  starting

    annotating, journal? Refer to earlier chapters?

  writing

    brainstorming? outline first, then word processor

Revising a Draft

After you have written a first draft, you will read it and, almost surely, make extensive revisions. Some points will now strike you as not really worth making; others that do survive the cut you will now see as needing to be developed. You may see that you have not adequately set forth a com-monly held view that you will in effect be largely rejecting. You now realize that you must summarize this view fairly because many people hold it, and you now see the need to indicate that you are familiar with the view, that you see its merits, and that you think your own view is better and may at least in part be attractive even to those who hold this other view.

You may also see that the organization needs improvement. For instance, if you notice that a point you made in the second paragraph is pretty much the same as one in the sixth paragraph, the two should be combined, rewritten, and perhaps put into an entirely new position.

Reorganizing and providing transitional words and phrases that make the organization clear to the reader ("moreover," "a second example," "on the other hand") usually not difficult, especially if you outline your draft. When you look at the outline of what you have written, you will probably see that portions of the draft have to be moved around or (in some cases) amplified or deleted and new transitions written. Organizing an argument is so important that we will treat it separately, at some length, in a moment.

In revising, think carefully about how you use **quotations**. Keep in mind the following principles:

- Most quotations should be brief; present a long quotation only if it's extremely interesting and cannot be summarized effectively.
- Let the reader know who wrote the quotation. Identify an author who is not widely known—for example: "Judith Craft, a lawyer who specializes in constitutional matters, argues . . ."; "The warden of a maximum security prison, John Alphonso, testified that . . ."; "Anne Smith, a lesbian who has given birth to one child and adopted a second, suggests that families headed by lesbians. . . ." This sort of lead-in gives authority to the quotation.
- Let the reader know how the quotation was originally used. Examples: "The editor of the journal *Nature* argues . . ."; "The Pope rejects this view, saying . . ."; "Dr. Joycelyn Elders interprets the statistics as indicating that. . . ."
- Use the present tense: "X says," *not* "X said," although, of course, if you are treating the passage as something from the past, use the past tense: "X wrote, 20 years ago, that . . . , but today, he argues that. . . ."

After revising your draft, you may want to show it to some classmates or friends; they will doubtlessly give you helpful advice if you make it clear that you really do want their assistance.

Organizing an Argument

The writer of a persuasive essay almost always has to handle—in some sequence or other—the following matters:

- The background (for instance, the need to consider the issue)
- The readers' preconceptions
- The thesis (claim)
- The evidence that supports the claim
- The counterevidence

- Responses to counterclaims and counterevidence (perhaps a refutation but probably a concession that there *is* merit in the counterclaims, although not as much as in the writer's thesis)
- Some sort of reaffirmation—for instance, that the topic needs attention, that the thesis advanced is the most plausible or the most workable or the most moral, and that even holders of other views may find their own values strengthened by adopting the writer's view

And here, we repeat the organization that we suggested (page 85) for Rogerian argument:

- State the problem, suggesting that it is an issue of concern and that the reader has a stake in it;
- show respect for persons who hold differing views;
- set forth opposing positions, *stated in such a way that their proponents will agree that the statements of their positions are fair;* and
- find some shared values; that is, grant whatever validity the writer finds in those positions—for instance, by recognizing the circumstances in which they would indeed be acceptable.

Having accurately summarized other views and having granted some concessions, the writer presumably has won the reader's attention and goodwill; the writer can now

- show how those who hold other positions will benefit if they accept the writer's position.

Introductory and Concluding Paragraphs

Introductory Paragraphs

In the **introduction** (the first paragraph or first few paragraphs), you will usually indicate what the issue is, why it is of significance, and what your thesis is. You will also seek to gain your reader's attention and introduce yourself—which is to say that you will convey some sort of engaging personality to the reader. Obviously, it is in your interest to come across as courteous, reasonable, and well-informed. We will talk about this matter in a moment when we discuss the writer's persona.

When writing a first draft, you merely need something to break the ice—something to get you going—but in your finished paper, the opening cannot be mere throat-clearing. The opening should be interesting. Here are some common *un*interesting openings to *avoid*:

- A dictionary definition ("Webster says . . . " or "According to Webster")
- A restatement of your title. The title is (let's assume) "Poker Playing May Be Harmful to Your Health," and the first sentence says, "This

essay will study the harmful effects of poker playing." True, the sentence announces the topic of the essay, but it gives no information about the topic beyond what the title already offers, and it provides no information about you either—that is, no sense of your response to the topic, such as might be present in, say, "The people least aware of the harmful effects of poker seem to be those who play the most."

- A broad generalization, such as "Ever since the beginning of time, human beings have been violent." Again, such a sentence may be fine if it helps you to start drafting, but it should not remain in your final version: It's dull—and it tells your readers almost nothing about the essay they're about to read. (After all, our example could begin anything from an analysis of a video game to a term paper on Darfur.) To put it another way, the ever-since-the-beginning-of-time opening lacks substance—and if your opening lacks substance, it will not matter what you say next. You've already lost your reader's attention.

What is left? What is an *effective* way for an introductory paragraph to begin?

- It will be at least moderately interesting if it provides **information**.
- It will be pleasing if the information provides **focus**—that is, if it lets the reader know what your topic is and it indicates what you will say about it.
- It will capture a reader's attention if it articulates a problem and suggests why the essay is worth reading.

When you write, *you* are the teacher; it won't do to begin with a vague statement:

George Orwell says he shot the elephant because. . . .

We need some information, identifying the text you are writing about:

George Orwell, in "Shooting an Elephant," says he shot the elephant because . . .

Even better is

In "Shooting an Elephant," George Orwell set forth his reflections on his service as a policeman in Burma. He suggests that he once shot an elephant because . . . but his final paragraph suggests that we must look for additional reasons.

Why is this opening better? Because it suggests that the writer has something interesting to say. It points to a contradiction in the Orwell piece—a problem worth examining: Orwell says one thing, but that thing may not be entirely true.

Of course, you can provide interest and focus by other means, among them the following:

- A quotation
- An anecdote or other short narrative
- An interesting fact (for example, a statistic showing the reader that you know something about your topic)
- A definition of an important term—but not merely one derived from a dictionary
- A question—but an interesting one, such as "Why do we call some words obscene?"
- A glance at the opposition
- An assertion that a problem exists

Concluding Paragraphs

Concluding paragraphs, like opening paragraphs, are especially difficult if only because they are so conspicuous. Fortunately, you are not always obliged to write one. For example, descriptive essays may end merely with a final paragraph, not with a paragraph that draws a conclusion. In an expository essay explaining a process or mechanism, you may simply stop when you've finished.

But if you need to write a concluding paragraph (and an argumentative essay usually calls for one), say something interesting. It's of little interest to say "Thus, we see . . . " and then echo your title and first paragraph. A good concluding paragraph rounds out the previous discussion. Such a paragraph may offer a few sentences that summarize, but it should not begin with the dull phrase "in summary"; it might also draw an inference that has not previously been expressed. To draw such an inference is not to introduce an entirely new idea—the end of an essay is hardly the place for that. Rather, it is to see the previous material in a fresh perspective—to take the discussion perhaps one step further.

Because all writers must find out what they think about any given topic and must find the appropriate strategies for presenting their thoughts to a particular audience, we hesitate to offer a do-it-yourself kit for final paragraphs, but the following devices often work:

- End with a quotation, especially one that amplifies or varies a quotation used in the opening paragraph, but be careful not to use a quotation that is too long or too complex and that your reader would expect you to analyze.
- End with some idea or detail from the beginning of the essay and thus bring it full circle.
- End with a new (but related) point—one that takes your discussion a step further.

- End with an allusion—say, to a historical or mythological figure or event—putting your topic in a larger framework.
- End with a glance at the readers—not with a demand that they mount the barricades but with a suggestion that the next move is theirs.

If you adopt any of these devices, do so quietly; the aim is not to write a grand finale but to complete or round out a discussion.

All essayists must find their own ways of ending each essay; the five strategies we have suggested are common—you will often encounter them in the essays that you read in *The Little, Brown Reader*—but these strategies are not for you if you don't find them congenial or useful. And so, rather than ending this section with rules about how to end essays, we suggest how not to end them: *Don't* merely summarize, *don't* say "in conclusion," *don't* introduce a totally new point, and *don't* apologize.

✓ A Checklist: Revising Paragraphs

☐ Does the paragraph say anything? Does it have substance?

☐ Does the paragraph have a topic sentence? If so, is it in the best place? If the paragraph doesn't have a topic sentence, would the paragraph be improved by adding one? Or does the paragraph have a clear topic idea?

☐ If the paragraph is an opening paragraph, is it interesting enough to attract and to hold a reader's attention? If it is a later paragraph, does it easily evolve out of the previous paragraph and lead into the next paragraph?

☐ Does the paragraph contain some principle of development— for instance, from cause to effect or from general to particular? What is the purpose of the paragraph? Does the paragraph fulfill the purpose?

☐ Does each sentence clearly follow from the preceding sentence? Have you provided transitional words or cues to guide your reader? Would it be useful to repeat certain key words for clarity?

☐ Is the closing paragraph effective or is it an unnecessary restatement of the obvious?

Persona and Style

In Chapter 1, we talked about the writer's **persona**—the personality that the writer conveys through his or her words. More exactly, the persona is the image of the writer that *the readers* imagine. The writer tries to convey a certain image (courteous, fair-minded, authoritative, or all the above—and more), but if readers find the writer discourteous, well, the writer *is* discourteous (or mean-spirited or uninformed). It won't do for the writer—hearing of the readers' response—to insist that he or she did not mean to be discourteous (is not mean-spirited or is well-informed).

The persona is created by the impression that the words make—both the individual words and the kinds of sentences (long or short, complex or simple) in which they appear. A writer who says something like "It behooves us to exert all of our mental capacities on what I deem the primary issue of our era" may have a heart of gold and be well-informed, but he or she will still strike readers as a pompous ass—and the writer's argument will not get a very attentive hearing. A writer who uses many short sentences, much direct address to the reader, and lots of colloquial diction ("Let's get down to nuts and bolts. You've got to stop kidding yourselves. We all know what the problem is.") will probably strike readers as aggressive—someone they are not keen on associating with. In short, the wrong persona can alienate readers. Even though the arguments are thoughtful, readers will be put off. We would live in a better world if we could listen objectively and separate the argument (very good) from the speaker (very unpleasant), but we usually can't do so. A hundred years ago, Samuel Butler put it this way (he is overstating the case, but there is much to what he says): "We are not won by arguments that we can analyze but by tone and temper, by the manner."

Now, in fact, one often *does* find aggressive writing in magazines, but this writing is, as we said earlier, a sermon addressed to the converted. The liberal readers of *The Nation* derive pleasure from seeing conservatives roughed up a bit, just as the conservative readers of *National Review* derive pleasure from seeing liberals similarly handled. But again, these writers—utterly ignoring the principles of Carl Rogers, which we set forth on pages 81–86—are not trying to gain a hearing for their ideas; rather, they are reassuring their readers that the readers' ideas are just fine.

What kind of persona should you, as the writer of an argument, try to project? You will want to be (you will *have to be*) yourself. But just as you have different kinds of clothes suitable for different purposes, you have several or even many selves—for instance, the self you are with a close friend, the self you are with your teachers, the self you are with customers (if you have a job), and so forth. The self that you will present in your essays—the self that you hope the readers will see from the words you put down on the page—will probably include certain specific qualities. You probably want your readers to see that you are informed and fair and are presenting a thoughtful case. You want them to be interested in hearing what you have to say. If you browse through the essays in this book, you will, of course, hear different voices. Although some may have an academic tone and some may sound folksy, almost all of them have one thing in common: They are the voices of people whom we would like to get to know.

An Overview: An Examination of an Argument

Now that we have covered the ground from a more or less theoretical point of view, let's look at a specific argument. The writer is Richard Rhodes, a journalist who has written for many newspapers and magazines, including *The New York Times, Newsweek, Harper's, Playboy,* and *Rolling Stone.* Rhodes is also known as a novelist and as a writer of books about science and technology. We reprint an essay that first appeared in *The New York Times* on September 17, 2000.

Richard Rhodes

Hollow Claims about Fantasy Violence

The moral entrepreneurs are at it again, pounding the entertainment industry for advertising its Grand Guignolesque confections[1] to children. If exposure to this mock violence contributes to the development of violent behavior, then our political leadership is justified in its indignation at what the Federal Trade Commission has reported about the marketing of violent fare to children. Senators John McCain and Joseph Lieberman have been especially quick to fasten on the FTC report as they make an issue of violent offerings to children.

But is there really a link between entertainment and violent behavior? 2

The American Medical Association, the American Psychological Association, the American Academy of Pediatrics, and the National Institute of Mental Health all say yes. They base their claims on social science research that has been sharply criticized and disputed within the social science profession, especially outside the United States. In fact, no direct, causal link between exposure to mock violence in the media and subsequent violent behavior has ever been demonstrated, and the few claims of modest correlation have been contradicted by other findings, sometimes in the same studies.

History alone should call such a link into question. Private violence 4 has been declining in the West since the media-barren late Middle Ages, when homicide rates are estimated to have been 10 times what they are in Western nations today. Historians attribute the decline to improving

---

[1]*Grand Guignolesque confections* The Grand Guignol was a Parisian theater specializing in plays dealing with brutality.

---

social controls over violence—police forces and common access to courts of law—and to a shift away from brutal physical punishment in child-rearing (a practice that still appears as a common factor in the back-ground of violent criminals today).

The American Medical Association has based its endorsement of the   5
media violence theory in major part on the studies of Brandon Centerwall, a psychiatrist in Seattle. Dr. Centerwall compared the murder rates for whites in three countries from 1945 to 1974 with numbers for television set ownership. Until 1975, television broadcasting was banned in South Africa, and "white homicide rates remained stable" there, Dr. Centerwall found, while corresponding rates in Canada and the United States doubled after television was introduced.

A spectacular finding, but it is meaningless. As Franklin E. Zimring   6
and Gordon Hawkins of the University of California at Berkeley subsequently pointed out, homicide rates in France, Germany, Italy, and Japan either failed to change with increasing television ownership in the same period or actually declined, and American homicide rates have more recently been sharply declining despite a proliferation of popular media outlets—not only movies and television but also video games and the Internet.

Other social science that supposedly undergirds the theory, too, is   7
marginal and problematic. Laboratory studies that expose children to selected incidents of televised mock violence and then assess changes in the children's behavior have sometimes found more "aggressive" behavior after the exposure—usually verbal, occasionally physical.

But sometimes the control group, shown incidents judged not to be   8
violent, behaves more aggressively afterward than the test group; sometimes comedy produces the more aggressive behavior; and sometimes there's no change. The only obvious conclusion is that sitting and watching television stimulates subsequent physical activity. Any kid could tell you that.

As for those who claim that entertainment promotes violent behavior   9
by desensitizing people to violence, the British scholar Martin Barker offers this critique: "Their claim is that the materials they judge to be harmful can only influence us by trying to make us be the same as them. So horrible things will make us horrible—not horrified. Terrifying things will make us terrifying—not terrified. To see something aggressive makes us feel aggressive—not aggressed against. This idea is so odd, it is hard to know where to begin in challenging it."

Even more influential on national policy has been a 22-year study by   10
two University of Michigan psychologists, Leonard I. Eron and L. Rowell Huesmann, of boys exposed to so-called violent media. The Telecommunications Act of 1996, which mandated the television V-chip, allowing parents to screen out unwanted programming, invoked these findings, asserting, "Studies have shown that children exposed to violent video programming at a young age have a higher tendency for violent and aggressive behavior later in life than children not so exposed."

Well, not exactly. Following 875 children in upstate New York from third grade through high school, the psychologists found a correlation between a preference for violent television at age 8 and aggressiveness at age 18. The correlation—0.31—would mean television accounted for about 10 percent of the influences that led to this behavior. But the correlation only turned up in one of three measures of aggression: the assessment of students by their peers. It didn't show up in students' reports about themselves or in psychological testing. And for girls, there was no correlation at all.

Despite the lack of evidence, politicians can't resist blaming the media for violence. They can stake out the moral high ground confident that the First Amendment will protect them from having to actually write legislation that would be likely to alienate the entertainment industry. Some use the issue as a smokescreen to avoid having to confront gun control.

But violence isn't learned from mock violence. There is good evidence—causal evidence, not correlational—that it's learned in personal violent encounters, beginning with the brutalization of children by their parents or their peers.

The money spent on all the social science research I've described was diverted from the National Institute of Mental Health budget by reducing support for the construction of community mental health centers. To this day there is no standardized reporting system for emergency-room findings of physical child abuse. Violence is on the decline in America, but if we want to reduce it even further, protecting children from real violence in their real lives—not the pale shadow of mock violence—is the place to begin.

The Analysis Analyzed

Let's go through Rhodes's argument step by step, looking not only at the points he makes but also at the ways he makes them.

The title does not clearly announce the topic and the thesis, but it does give the reader a hint: Rhodes will be concerned with "hollow claims" (i.e., with assertions he thinks are insubstantial) about something he calls "fantasy violence." At this stage, the reader doesn't know what "fantasy violence" is—could it be fantasies of violence that some or all of us have, or could it be fantastic violence in films, or what? But "fantasy" and "violence" are words that interest most people, and the writer has therefore probably hooked the reader. (Give him a B+ for the title.)

The first paragraph begins with a world-weary voice: "The moral entrepreneurs are at it again. . . ." The readers do not know exactly who "the moral entrepreneurs" are or what they are doing again, but Rhodes's first words are catchy, and by the end of the sentence, the readers know the main point: People who seem to be in the business of making moral judgments—"moral entrepreneurs"—are yet again criticizing the entertainment industry because it advertises its "Grand Guignolesque confections" to children. Notice how Rhodes *diminishes* or trivializes the violent productions by calling them "Grand Guignolesque confections." For him, they are theatrical (showy but insubstantial) candies or pastries. He is already preparing us for his thesis.

The second sentence in this paragraph introduces the term "mock violence," and it makes clear Rhodes's topic: He will be concerned not with the real violence of life—assaults, robberies, rapes, murders—but with the fictional, unreal, or "mock" violence of the media. If indeed "mock violence contributes to the development of violent behavior," then the moral entrepreneurs (he will name some names in a moment) are "justified" in their indignation. But readers by now can guess that Rhodes will argue that "mock violence" (the "fantasy violence" of his title) does *not* contribute to violent behavior. By the end of the paragraph, we know what his topic is, and we have a pretty good idea of what his thesis will be. (Give him an A for his opening paragraph.)

The second paragraph consists of only one sentence: "But is there really a link between entertainment and violent behavior?" Your instructor has probably already told you, rightly, to beware of writing one-sentence paragraphs. A paragraph of one sentence is usually underdeveloped. But Rhodes knows what he is doing here. Because in an essay each paragraph is of roughly equal weight, a one-sentence paragraph must indeed contain a weighty sentence—a big point—and this one does. By letting a single sentence stand as a paragraph, Rhodes is telling us that it is very important. And clearly the answer to his question—"But is there really a link between entertainment and violent behavior?"—will be "No." (Give him an A for knowing how to make effective use of a short paragraph.)

The third paragraph shows us the opposing view. Rhodes cites the heavyweights: the medical associations that "all say yes"—that all say there is a link between entertainment and violent behavior in real life. What is Rhodes doing citing these groups that hold a view different from his own? He is letting us know that he's familiar with the opposing view; his position is not (he thus assures us) based on ignorance of the other view. And then, he firmly rejects this view: "In fact, no direct causal link between exposure to mock violence in the media and subsequent violent behavior has ever been demonstrated." Gosh, readers think, we didn't know that; we thought that there are all sorts of studies that prove. . . . But Rhodes's statement is so strong that it causes us to doubt what we thought we knew, and we realize that in fact we have not read the studies—we do *not* know of any study that really proves the connection. Gee, maybe he is right after all. (Give him an A for writing a vigorous paragraph that begins to win us to his side.)

The fourth paragraph tells us to think about history, and it offers a statistic, admittedly an uncertain one ("homicide rates are estimated to have been 10 times what they are"). By now, we can stop grading his paragraphs; he has probably won a writer's most important battle—not the battle to convince a reader but the battle to keep a reader's attention. Almost surely, the reader who has come this far will continue to read the essay to the end, and that's really as much as a writer can hope for. If the reader is also convinced, that's great, but it's an extra. When writers offer an argument, they want to tell people what their ideas are, and they want to explain why they hold these ideas. They offer reasons based on evidence, but they can offer them only to those readers who stay with them, so writers must write in ways that hold the attention of readers. The job of a writer is to make readers mentally say, "Very interesting. Tell me more."

The **fifth paragraph** sets forth opposing evidence—statistics accepted by no less an authority than the American Medical Association. Why does he do this? Because, again, if writers are to be at all convincing, they must show awareness of opposing viewpoints. However, we can be pretty sure that Rhodes will go on to dispute this opposing view.

The **sixth paragraph** does exactly what the reader expects it to do: It rejects the AMA position. The statistical findings are "spectacular"—but they are "meaningless." Of course, Rhodes cannot merely assert this; he must provide evidence. And he does. Whether this evidence is totally convincing is not our concern here; we're merely pointing out the techniques Rhodes uses in setting forth his argument.

The **seventh paragraph** returns to the strategy of setting forth the view Rhodes rejects, and we know what he will do in the eighth paragraph.

The **eighth paragraph** predictably offers evidence rejecting the view set forth in the preceding paragraph. It tells the reader that the experiments don't really prove what they are supposed to prove and that they prove only that "sitting and watching television stimulates subsequent physical activity." And then, because Rhodes's aim is to discredit the experiments, he firmly dismisses the results with "Any kid could tell you that."

The **ninth paragraph** glances at a variation of the opposing view and dismisses it by quoting an authority. Rhodes doubtlessly could have dismissed the view himself, but he wisely thought it was appropriate to let the reader know that someone else shares his view.

The **tenth paragraph** gives yet another glance at the opposing view—and we know what is coming next.

The **eleventh paragraph** dismisses the gist of the tenth with "Well, not exactly." And Rhodes now offers statistics to support his position.

The **twelfth paragraph** begins by mentioning "politicians." We're probably meant to recall Senators McCain and Lieberman, who were specifically named in the opening paragraph.

The **thirteenth paragraph** assumes that the reader has been following the argument, taking in the evidence, and perhaps is now convinced. It offers no evidence—doubtlessly, Rhodes feels that he has made his case; the paragraph is content to state the thesis bluntly: "But violence isn't learned from mock violence."

The **fourteenth (final) paragraph** mentions the National Institute of Mental Health—an organization we met in paragraph 3—but the point now is that the money used for wrong-headed social science research could have been used more wisely by the NIMH "for the construction of community mental health centers." The paragraph ends by returning to the "mock violence" of the first paragraph—a variation on the "fantasy violence" of the title.

In short,

- Rhodes's opening paragraph gets attention, although perhaps he took a risk by referring to the Grand Guignol, an allusion that not everyone will get;
- he shows he is familiar with arguments other than his own;
- his language, except for the reference to "Grand Guignolesque confections," is easily intelligible to the ordinary reader;
- his paragraphs are coherent and unified; readers are never confused about the point of a paragraph;
- his organization is clear; readers are never uncertain of how a paragraph is related to the previous paragraph;
- his concluding paragraph, with its reference to "mock violence," neatly ties things up by glancing back to the beginning of the essay.

You may strongly disagree with Rhodes's position, but if so, you ought to be able to offer some evidence. The evidence need not be the statements of authorities or statistics that you have encountered; it may be your own experience. But whether or not you disagree with Rhodes's position, we hope you will agree with our view that he sets forth his position effectively.

Joining the Conversation: Critical Thinking and Writing

1. Rhodes sets forth views other than his own, but he makes no effort to suggest that they have any merit or that they can be held by reasonable people. His essay shows no awareness of the principles that Carl Rogers set forth (see pages 84–90). Do you think Rhodes comes across as overly aggressive, arrogant, stubborn, rude? Or on this issue can there be no middle ground? In an essay of 250 words, discuss Rhodes's tone as you perceive it and its effectiveness here.

2. One reader of Rhodes's essay wrote a letter to *The New York Times,* asserting that even if violent movies and violent music cannot be directly tied to real violence, "they do set a tone and a mood. And they do send the message that in America, violence is an answer to almost any problem." If Rhodes were to write to this person, what do you think he would say? (Put your response in a letter of about 500 words.)

3. Another letter-writer said that, unfortunately, athletes are role models for young boys: "We continue to train boys to be violent men by offering them [as role models] highly paid athletes who fight, trash-talk, and assault officials." Write a 500-word essay supporting or taking issue with this position.

4. A third letter-writer said that "society at large endorses violence and killing" and went on to cite the death penalty as "society's ultimate violence." This "socially approved real violence," the letter-writer asserted, encourages violent behavior. In a 500-word essay, set forth your response to this position.

An Argument About Phoning While Driving

The following editorial appeared in *The New York Times* on December 13, 2009.

Turn Car On; Turn Phone Off

Like drivers chattering on their mobile phones, the cellphone industry was for years too distracted—by rising profits—to see the dangers ahead. As Matt Richtel wrote in the *Times* last week, the mobile phone industry promoted the glamour and convenience of "car phones" for years while failing to heed warnings that driving and phoning can be a deadly mix.

One ad from 1984 shows a bigwig driver on the phone and tellingly asks, "Can your secretary take dictation at 55 m.p.h.?"

A great measure of responsibility for safety lies with drivers. But now, as study after study shows the hazards of talking on the phone, or especially texting, while driving, it is time to ask why the wireless phone industry fought controls for so long on a product that could be used so dangerously.

It brings to mind that row of tobacco company executives who swore to a Congressional subcommittee 15 years ago that their products were not addictive. Or the car companies that went on making hefty S.U.V.'s that had a record of rolling over.

The reasons the cellphone industry representatives have given to block bans on phone use while driving sound straight out of the "Thank You for Smoking" playbook. One refrain was that the evidence was not settled, an assertion that continued as the industry itself was beginning to warn drivers about driving while phoning.

In California, the mobile industry fought off bans on talking while driving for years, at one point arguing that they were looking out for consumers. Consumers want to use their cellphones, that is true, but most who drive would also prefer to make it to their destinations. And distracted drivers put everyone else on the road at risk.

Even though the police are too seldom required to determine whether cellphone use was involved in an accident, the data about texting or phoning while driving is alarming. Harvard researchers estimated that drivers on cellphones cause about 2,600 fatal crashes a year and 570,000 accidents. Hands-free devices do not eliminate that risk. Other studies show that someone legally drunk could outperform a person texting behind the wheel.

Congress has slowly begun to focus on this issue and proposals for bans are now circulating in both houses, some with support of the cellphone industry. None of them are terribly high on Washington's agenda, however. It is time for Congress and the wireless phone industry to take highway safety a step beyond seat belts and air bags.

Joining the Conversation: Critical Thinking and Writing

1. In paragraph 5, we are told that the cell phone industry told us "that the evidence was not settled." Do you believe the evidence is now settled one way or the other? If there is still some uncertainty, should phones be banned until there is decisive evidence that they do *not* cause accidents? Or are there measures short of banning car phones that might eliminate or reduce the hazards of car phone use?

2. Paragraph 7 refers to "Harvard researchers" and to "other studies." Do these references satisfy you? Explain.

3. Some cars are equipped with voice-activated calling. One need do no more that press a button on the steering wheel to activate the system and then say "Dial home." True, one then converses but so does a driver if there is a passenger in the car. Do you believe that the government should require all phones used in cars to be voice-activated? Explain.

4. Should federal legislation prohibit all drivers from writing, sending, or reading text messages while operating a vehicle? Or is this a matter for the states, not the federal government?

5. If someone calls you and mentions that he or she is driving, do you think it is your responsibility to tell the caller to call back when the car is parked? Explain.

A Debate for Analysis: Do Credit Companies Market Too Aggressively to Youths?

After reading the following essays, consider these points:

- What assumptions does the writer make? Do you accept these assumptions?
- What evidence does the writer offer? Is the evidence convincing?
- What (if any) counterevidence can you offer?
- Does the writer seem fair to you? What has the writer done to make you hold the view that you hold? (For instance, has the writer faced objections to his or her view and answered them satisfactorily?)

Travis B. Plunkett

Travis B. Plunkett, the legislative director of Consumer Federation of America, wrote this essay for CQ Researcher in 2006.

Yes, Credit Companies Market Too Aggressively to Youths

Many credit card issuers have targeted the least sophisticated and riskiest consumers in recent years, including young people, and encouraged them to run up high, often unsustainable levels of debt. This practice has proven to be very profitable for many credit card issuers, but it can have devastating consequences for consumers.

Starting in the early 1990s, card issuers targeted massive marketing efforts at college campuses across the country, resulting in a sharp growth in credit card debt among college-age and younger Americans. As a result, Americans under age 35 continue to show more signs of trouble managing credit card debt than other age group.

Between the mid-1990s and 2004, the amount of credit card debt held by students graduating from college more than doubled, to $3,262. Americans under 35 are less likely to pay off their card balances every month than average Americans. They are paying more for debt obligations than in the past and are increasingly likely to pay more than 40 percent of their incomes on credit card debt.

Not surprisingly, more young Americans are declaring bankruptcy than in the past. Moreover, there is increasing evidence that credit card companies are now targeting high-school students, students with card offers. They are also marketing branded debit cards to adolescents, in part to encourage these young consumers to use similarly branded credit cards when they are older.

Young people are also financially vulnerable to the questionable pricing and business practices adopted by issuers to increase the profitability of lending to riskier customers. These abusive practices include "universal default," in which a consumer must suddenly pay a sharply higher interest rate on their outstanding balance with one credit card company because of a minor problem with another creditor.

Many creditors have also significantly increased their penalty fees, even for small transgressions like a payment that is made only a few hours late. Until recently, issuers also decreased the size of minimum payments that consumers had to pay, encouraging them to carry more debt for longer periods.

Several pieces of legislation have been introduced in Congress in recent years that would prevent credit card companies from targeting young people with unsustainable offers of credit and prohibit abusive fee and interest-rate practices. Unless credit card issuers adopt considerably more restraint in marketing and extending credit to less-sophisticated borrowers, the Consumer Federation of America will continue to urge Congress to adopt such restrictions.

Travis B. Plunkett: "Do Credit Companies Market Too Aggressively to Youths? Yes" from *CQ Researcher* May 26, 2006. Vol. 16 #20. Reprinted by permission of the publisher.

**Joining the Conversation:
Critical Thinking and Writing**

1. In his first paragraph, Plunkett says that issuers of credit cards encourage "young people" to run up high levels of debt. Does your experience support this assertion? Explain your answer.

2. Do you believe (with Plunkett) that legislation should be introduced to "prevent credit card companies from targeting young people with unsuitable offers of credit"? Explain your answer.

3. Whether you agree or disagree with Plunkett, give some suggestions about how he might strengthen his argument even within the space limits that governed his comments. Be specific.

Louis J. Freeh

Louis L. Freeh is vice chairman and general counsel for MBNA Corporation, and he testified before the U.S. Senate Banking Committee in 2005. CQ Researcher printed the following excerpt in 2006.

No, Credit Companies Do Not Market Too Aggressively to Youths

In discussing student marketing, it is important to note that we make every effort to ensure that credit card offers are not sent to people under the age of 18.

MBNA does promote its products to college-aged customers by partnering with more than 700 colleges and universities, primarily through the college alumni associations. By working closely with school administrators, we have earned the confidence and trust of most of America's premier educational institutions. . . .

Before granting credit to a college student, analysts familiar with the needs and abilities of college students review each application and decline more than half. . . . Most college student applicants report a separate income, and many already have an established credit history.

When evaluating an application, we consider the college student's projected performance as an alumnus, and when we grant credit, we

Louis J. Freeh: "Do Credit Companies Market Too Aggressively to Youths? No" from *CQ Researcher* May 26, 2006. Vol. 16 #20. Reprinted by permission of the publisher.

typically assign a line of between $500 and $1,000. If a college student attempts to use his or her card beyond the credit line, we typically refuse the charge. And we do not re-price these accounts based on behavior.

Once a college student becomes a cardholder, MBNA delivers its "Good Credit, Great Future" brochure in a Welcome Package. The brochure highlights sound money-management habits, including guidance on how to handle a credit card responsibly. We also maintain a Web site aimed at college-aged consumers, highlighting many of the same tips. MBNA also conducts on-campus credit-education seminars, and we provide articles concerning responsible credit use for student and parent publications.

The performance of our college-student portfolio mirrors closely that of the national experience, as reported in [Government Accountability Office] reports and several independent studies. However, our accounts have much smaller credit limits and much smaller balances than the norm, our college student customers utilize their cards less often than the norm and these accounts are less likely to incur fees. Our experience has also been that college students are no more likely to mishandle their accounts than any other group of customers.

When we grant a card to college student, we think of it as the beginning of what we hope will be a long relationship. . . . Given this, we have absolutely no interest in encouraging poor credit habits. In fact, everyone's interest is best served when college students make responsible use of credit. That is our goal in every situation, and certainly when dealing with college-aged customers.

Joining the Conversation: Critical Thinking and Writing

1. Freeh says that his organization denies credit to more than half the applicants. (He doesn't give details, but in paragraph 4, he explains that the company considers the student's projected performance as an alumnus.) Have you been denied credit? If so, do you think this action was fair and reasonable? Explain your answer. If you have been granted credit, do you think, on balance, that perhaps you should have been denied? Explain.

2. What differences do you find between Plunkett's and Freeh's accounts of college students' use of credit cards? Can you explain the differences? If not, which account are you more likely to believe and why?

3. Whether you agree or disagree with Freeh, give some suggestions about how he might strengthen his argument even within the space limits that governed his comments. Be specific.

4. Putting aside your own stand, which essay seems to you to be more convincing? Why?

✓ A Checklist: Revising Drafts of Arguments

☐ Does the introduction let the audience know what the topic is, why the topic is of some importance, and what your thesis is?

☐ Are the terms clearly defined?

☐ Are the assumptions likely to be shared by your readers? If not, are they reasonably argued rather than merely asserted?

☐ Does the essay summarize other views fairly and grant that they have some merit—at least in some contexts?

☐ Are the facts verifiable? Is the evidence reliable?

☐ Is the reasoning sound?

☐ Are the authorities really authorities on this matter?

☐ Are quotations no longer than they need to be, are they introduced with useful lead-ins, and do they make good reading?

☐ Are all the substantial counterarguments recognized and effectively responded to?

☐ Is the organization effective? Does the essay begin interestingly, keep the thesis in view, and end interestingly?

☐ Is the tone appropriate? (Do you avoid sarcasm, present yourself as fair-minded, and assume that people who hold views opposed to yours are also fair-minded?)

CHAPTER 5

Reading and Writing
Arguments about Images

I am after the one unique picture whose composition possesses such vigor and richness, and whose content so radiates outwards from it, that this single picture is a whole story in itself.

Henri Cartier-Bresson

The Language of Images

It may sound odd to talk about "reading" images and about the "language" of images, but images, like words, convey messages. Advertisers know this, and that's why their advertisements for soft drinks include images of attractive young couples frolicking at the beach. The not-so-hidden message is that consumers of these products are healthy, prosperous, relaxed, and sexually attractive.

Like compositions made of words—stories, poems, even vigorous sentences—many pictures (to use the more common word) are carefully constructed things built up in a certain way in order to make a statement. To cite an obvious example, in medieval religious pictures, Jesus or Mary may be shown larger than the surrounding figures to indicate their greater spiritual status. But even in realistic paintings, the more important figures are likely to be given a greater share of the light or a more central position than the lesser figures. Such devices of composition are fairly evident in paintings, but we occasionally forget that photographs are also almost always constructed things. The photographer—even the amateur just taking a candid snapshot—adjusts a pillow under the baby's head or suggests that the subject may want to step out of the shadow and then the photographer backs up a little and bends his or her knees before clicking the shutter. Even when photographing something inanimate, the photographer searches for the best view, waits for a cloud to pass, and perhaps pushes out of the range of the camera some trash that would spoil the effect of a lovely fern growing beside a rock. Minor White was speaking for almost all photographers when he said, "I don't take pictures; I make them."

And we often make our photographs for a particular purpose—perhaps to have a souvenir of a trip, or to show what we look like in uniform, or to show grandparents what the new baby looks like. Even professional photographers have a variety of purposes—for instance, to provide wedding portraits, to report the news, to sell automobiles, or to record some visual phenomena that they think must be recorded. Sometimes, these purposes can be mingled. For example, during the depression of the early 1930s, the Resettlement Administration employed photographers such as Dorothea Lange to help convince the nation that migrant workers and dispossessed farmers needed help. These photographers were, so to speak, selling something, but they were also reporting the news and serving a noble social purpose. (In Chapter 3, we reproduced Lange's most famous picture, *Migrant Mother*, along with some comments on it that students wrote in journals.)

Writing about an Advertisement

Most advertisements in magazines and newspapers rely heavily on pictures: We see a happy family standing by an automobile and a few lines of text tell us that we should buy such-and-such a car, or we see a sexy body and a few lines tell us to use such-and-such perfume or to put on such-and-such underwear, or we see a starving child and a few lines tell us to contribute to such-and-such charitable foundation.

Putting aside for the moment advertisements for charities, most of the ads that we see are images not so much of the product (a car, perfume) as they are images of a desirable condition, such as affluence or happiness or sexual attractiveness or health. The ads are first of all selling an *idea*, such as "You deserve to be happy" (or healthy, or sexy), and this idea is chiefly what is depicted. Once the ad has conveyed this point, it then hooks the product to it: If you buy this particular car, you and your family will have lots of fun; if you use this particular perfume or this particular underwear, you will attract a sexual partner. Again, the implication is that something is missing from your life, but you can remedy this defect if you buy X. Is cleaning the stove too much of a chore? Use X oven cleaner. Are you worried that you won't have enough money to pay for your child's college tuition? Just open a savings plan with Bank X, and you will have peace of mind. Frequently, the appeal is to our vanity: "Be the first to own" or "Use the cosmetic used by stars."

Some ads make **logical claims** ("proven," "doctors recommend," "more economical," "better value," "longer lasting"), but claims of this sort are usually impossible to validate. In any case, the picture rather than the text is usually the hook—the thing that catches the viewer's attention.

Ads for charities and other nonprofit organizations often work differently: The pictures are still the hooks (a starving child, a battered woman, a maltreated animal), but the pictures and the texts usually appeal to our sense of decency rather than to our vanity or to logic. They often **appeal to our emotions**—for instance, to our sense of pity or of fairness—and although we commonly hear that emotional appeals are an illegitimate form of argument, one can question this view. Human beings are not merely logical creatures but also compassionate, and most people would agree that compassion is a virtue.

Looking Closely: Analyzing an Ad for a Scent—*True Star*

Let's look briefly at an ad for perfume. (For a much fuller discussion of advertising techniques, please read on pages 382–83 James Twitchell's excellent analyses of images used in the campaign to sell Marlboro cigarettes.)

The ad for Tommy Hilfiger's scent (page 125) called True Star—like most ads for women's perfume—features a sexy model. The ad is unusual, however, in that it does *not* show a luxurious setting—for example, the lobby of an expensive hotel, the deck of a yacht, or simply a gold background.

Rather, the singer/actress/model Beyoncé who occupies about three-fourths of the space is shown in an indistinct, uncertain setting: She lies on what seems to be a bed, wearing what might be a nightgown. She faces us, her right arm stretched forward, her left arm across her chest, with her hand supporting her chin. From the viewer's position, Beyoncé's long hair frames her face on the left. Behind her shoulder, occupying the top quarter of the space, is what appears to be a window shade pulled down so that only a bit of night (the dark strip at the right) serves as a background for the words "A PRIVATE PERFORMANCE." What heightens the uncertainty is that the five-pointed star—obviously not a photo of a real star but an advertising artist's creation—is not in the sky but on what seems to be the window shade.

The star is important because (1) Beyoncé is a star, (2) Beyoncé is associated with a song called "Wishing on a Star," and (3) the cosmetic line is called True Star. On Google, we found that Hilfiger issued a press release characterizing its True Star line:

> Comfort and sensuality are at the essence of the True Star collection. The Eau de Parfum, body lotion, shower gel fragrance satin shimmer, contain a blend of ingredients inspired by the appeal of Beyoncé's celebrity, while also portraying the essence of her more personal and private side.

Exactly how this advertisement conveys a "personal and private side" of the famous model is unclear to us, but the words on the ad ("A PRIVATE PERFORMANCE") suggest exclusiveness, and in the context of this picture—a beautiful woman with lots of exposed flesh, on a bed, at night—the words can also suggest sex.

And what sort of woman does the viewer see? Beyoncé's beauty and sensuality hardly need to be commented on. What perhaps requires comment is the fact that she confronts the viewer head-on. She confronts us, faces reality, and more or less stares us down. In short, she is not just beautiful but also self-possessed and strong-willed. The ad—clearly aimed at women—implies that if the viewer uses True Star, she too will become strong and attractive and will be sought out for "a private performance."

Somewhat unusually, the True Star ad is in black and white. The only colors other than black, white, and shades of gray are in the tiny Hilfiger flag-like logo at the bottom of the page (between the words "Tommy" and "Hilfiger"), which uses a band of blue at its top and at its bottom and a small rectangle of red in its center-right. A viewer may at first be surprised that the advertiser gave up the use of color, given the fact that the colors of skin, lips, and hair can be highly engaging, but black and white can, as here, be sensuous and indeed even sensual. As you may recall, "sensuality" was a word that Hilfiger used when characterizing the True Star line. The soft focus, which adds to the uncertainty of the setting, and the subtle gradations of tone in the shadows and highlights give the image a moonlit night romantic effect.

Tommy Hilfiger Magazine

If your instructor asks you to analyze an advertisement, be sure to include the image with your essay. In your opening paragraph, you will probably offer some sort of lead-in ("Among the most annoying ads in the current issue of . . ." or "A good deal of today's advertising is highly sexual" rather than the bland "In this advertisement . . ."). In the body of the essay, describe the ad accurately enough so someone who hasn't seen it can visualize it and then analyze how the ad works. In your analysis, you will consider such issues as:

- To whom is the ad addressed?
- Is the appeal of the text logical ("tests prove," "doctors recommend") or emotional (for instance, addressing our sympathy, our patriotism, our love of family)?
- What is the relationship between the image and the text? How does the design of the ad make that relationship?

In your conclusion, you will probably evaluate the ad—perhaps on two grounds: How honest is the ad? Honest or not, how effective do you find it?

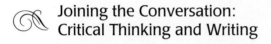

Joining the Conversation: Critical Thinking and Writing

The Little, Brown Reader includes other advertisements on pages 358 and 359. Choose one of these and then analyze its appeal and its effectiveness. The checklist below will help to stimulate responses.

✓ A Checklist: Analyzing Advertisements

☐ What is the viewer's first impression of the ad? Excitement, perhaps conveyed by a variety of colors and large type? Dignity, perhaps conveyed chiefly by grays, lots of empty space, and smaller type?

☐ What is the audience for the ad? Affluent young women? College students? Housewives? Retired persons?

☐ Does the image appeal to an emotion—for instance, to our sense of fairness, pity, patriotism, envy ("You too can get admiring looks"), fear ("Worried about aging skin? Use . . .")?

☐ Is the image intentionally shocking (for instance, a fetus being aborted, a brain being fried, lungs coated with tar)?

☐ Does the text make a logical, rational appeal ("Three out of four doctors recommend . . . " or "Tests at a leading university show . . .")?

☐ What does the text do? Is it chiefly devoted to giving information? To being entertaining?

☐ What is the relationship of image to text? Does the image do most of the work or is its job simply to get us to read the text?

☐ How successful is the ad? And how honest is it?

Writing about a Political Cartoon

Most editorial pages print political cartoons as well as editorials. These cartoons may use words in speech balloons or in captions, but generally, the drawing does most of the work. Cartoonists almost always caricature their subjects because their aim is to satirize; that is, they exaggerate the subject's distinctive features to the point where the subject becomes grotesque and ridiculous—absurd, laughable, contemptible. True, it is scarcely fair to suggest that because, say, the politician who proposes such-and-such a measure is short, fat, and bald, his proposal is ridiculous, but that is the way cartoonists work.

In addition to saying that the figures in the cartoon are ridiculous and therefore their ideas are contemptible, cartoonists often use symbolism—for instance, symbolic figures (Uncle Sam), animals (the Democratic donkey and the Republican elephant), buildings (the White House symbolically stands for the president of the United States), and things (a bag with a dollar sign on it symbolizes a bribe). For anyone brought up in our culture, these symbols (like the human figures who are represented) are obvious, and cartoonists assume that viewers will instantly recognize the symbols and figures, will get the joke, and will see the absurdity of whatever it is that they are seeking to demolish.

In writing about a cartoon, normally you will

- lead into your analysis with a sentence or two that sets the context: the date, the publication, the cartoonist's name.
- Then, even though you will include a photocopy of the cartoon with your paper, you will offer a brief but clear description of the picture. From that description your reader ought to have a pretty good idea of what the picture looks like.
- You will then offer some exposition—that is, you will explain (interpret) the drawing by identifying the persons depicted and the event or the issue the cartoonist comments on.
- You will then devote most of the essay to an analysis of the cartoon. That is, you will discuss the ways in which the cartoon makes its point. Caricature, we have said, usually says in effect, "This is ridiculous, as you can plainly see by the absurdity of the figures depicted" or "What X's proposal adds up to, despite its apparent complexity, is nothing more than. . . ." This sort of persuasion—chiefly by ridicule—is probably unfair (a thoughtful political proposal can be offered by a funny-looking person), but this is largely the way cartoons work, and we should not reject the possibility that the cartoonist has indeed put his or her finger on the absurdity of the issue.
- Your essay will probably include an evaluation of the cartoon; indeed, for example, the thesis underlying the essay may be that the cartoon is effective for such-and-such reasons, but it is also unfair for such-and-such reasons.

In analyzing the cartoon—in grasping the attitude of the cartoonist—consider such things as:

- The relative size of the figures in the image
- The quality of the lines—thin and spidery or thick and seemingly aggressive

- The amount of empty space in comparison with the amount of heavily inked space (obviously a drawing with lots of inky areas will convey a more oppressive sense than a drawing that is largely open)
- The degree to which text is important—and what the text says (Is it witty? Heavy-handed?)

Caution: If your instructor lets you choose a cartoon, be sure to choose one with sufficient complexity to make the exercise worthwhile.

✓ A Checklist: Analyzing Political Cartoons

☐ Have I provided a lead-in?

☐ Have I provided a brief but accurate description of the drawing?

☐ Have I included a brief report of the event or issue that the cartoon is dealing with and an explanation of all the symbols?

☐ Have I included an analysis of the ways in which the content and style of the drawing help to convey the message?

☐ Have I provided an adequate evaluation of the effectiveness of the drawing?

☐ Have I provided an adequate evaluation of the effectiveness of the text (caption or speech balloons) and of the fairness of the cartoon?

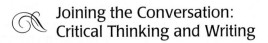 Joining the Conversation:
Critical Thinking and Writing

Write a 250-word analysis of the cartoon on the next page from *The Philadelphia Inquirer.*

Tony Auth Philadelphia Inquirer, *Universal Uclick*

Lou Jacobs Jr.

Lou Jacobs Jr., photographer and the author of several books on photography, is a frequent contributor of essays on the topic to The New York Times, *where this piece originally appeared.*

What Qualities Does a Good Photograph Have?

When amateur and professional photographers get together they often discuss equipment and techniques at some length, but it is not often that photographers take time to consider what makes a good picture.

Many photographic organizations list criteria similar to those described below when judging pictures submitted in a competition. Judges may offer opinions like "The composition is off balance," or "The expressions on peoples' faces tell the story well." But photographic criticism is not an exact art. In the media, critics tend to use esoteric terms that even an "in" group doesn't always grasp.

Therefore it's important to the average photographer that he or she develop a basis for understanding and verbalizing how pictures succeed or fail in their visual way, or how they happen to be a near-miss. The latter term describes an image that has some, but not enough, of the visual virtues discussed below.

Of course "a good picture" is a relative description because it's subjective, as is the judgment of all the qualities mentioned in the list that follows. However, there is enough agreement in the tastes of a variety of people to make certain standards general and valid, though the characteristics of a good picture are subject to flexible interpretation. A little honest controversy about the visual success of a print or slide can be a healthy thing.

Impact: This descriptive word comprises a collection of the qualities   5
that help make a photograph appealing, interesting, impressive, or memorable. For instance, Ansel Adams's "Moonrise, Hernandez, NM" is a famous image that has been selling for astronomical prices at auctions because it has enormous pictorial or visual impact—among other reasons. The picture's impact evolves from many qualities such as the drama of the light, the mood invoked, and the magic sense of realism.

It is possible to translate such qualities into your own photographs when you consider how the subjects were treated, whether landscapes or people. Too seldom do we meet dramatic opportunities in nature as grand as those in "Moonrise," but with a well developed artistic sensitivity, ideal conditions can be captured on film.

Human Interest: Here is another rather general term to encompass emotional qualities, action, and things that people do which appeal to a lot of viewers. A shot of your children laughing or a picture of vendors in

Moonrise, Hernandez, New Mexico, 1941
Ansel Adams

a marketplace might both show outstanding human interest. The success of such a photograph depends on how you compose it, on lighting, on timing to catch vivid expressions, and perhaps on camera angle or choice of lens. All of these ingredients of a good picture are coming up on the list.

There is another aspect of human interest in your own or others' photographs. Sometimes the unusualness of a subject and the way it's presented overshadows adequate technique. For instance, a good sports picture showing peak action in a scrimmage or a definitive play in baseball has intrinsic appeal.

A photograph of a pretty girl, a baby, and a sunset are in the same category, because in each case the subject matter grabs the viewer's attention. As a result, a mediocre composition, inferior lighting, a messy background, or other technical or esthetic weaknesses are ignored or excused because the subject is striking.

It's a good feeling when you can distinguish between the subject in a   10
photograph and the way it was treated.

Galleries and museums often hang photographs that are "different," but they're not necessarily worthy of distinction. Many offbeat photographs we see are likely not to have lasting visual value, while fine photographs like those of Ansel Adams or Cartier-Bresson will still be admired in future decades.

Effective Composition: Like other qualities that underlie a good picture, composition can be controversial. There are somewhat conventional principles of design that we follow because they seem "natural," like placing the horizon line or a figure off-center to avoid a static effect.

But really effective composition is usually derived from the subject, and generally the urge to keep composition as simple as possible pays off. That's why plain backgrounds are often best for portraits, and if you relate someone to his/her environment, simplicity is also a virtue. Composition may be dynamic, placid, or somewhere between.

Study the compositional tendencies of fine photographers and painters for guidance. Be daring and experimental at times too, because a "safe" composition may also be dull.

Spontaneity: This characteristic of a good picture is related to human   15
interest, realism and involvement. When you are involved with the subject, as you might be in photographing an aged father or mother, you prize most the images that include spontaneous expressions and emotional reactions. Get people involved with each other, too, so they forget the camera and your pictures are likely to be more believable—and credibility is often a pictorial asset.

If your camera lens is not fast enough to shoot at let's say 1/60th of a second at f/2.8, then you need flash. But you get more spontaneity when people aren't posed, waiting for the flash to go off. Natural light also adds to the realistic impression you capture of people and places, since flash-on-camera has an unavoidably artificial look in most cases.

Lighting: Certainly we have to shoot sometimes when the light is not pictorial, so we do the best we can. A tripod is often the answer to long exposures and exciting photographs. In some situations the light improves if we have the time and patience to wait. Outdoors plan to shoot when the sun is low in the early morning, and at sunset time. Mountains, buildings and people are more dramatic in low-angle light. Details lost in shadows don't seem to matter when the light quality itself is beautiful.

Lighting also helps to create mood, another element of a good picture. Mood is understandably an ethereal quality which includes mystery, gaiety, somberness, and other emotional aspects. Effective photographs may capitalize on the mood of a place especially when it's dramatic.

Color: In a painting a pronounced feeling of light and shadow is called chiaroscuro, and in photographs such effects are augmented by color which may be in strong contrasts, or part of important forms. Outstanding pictures may also be softly colored in pastels that can be as appealing as bright hues.

We tend to take color in photographs for granted, but we don't have to   20
settle for literal color when a colored filter or a switch in film may improve a situation. Next time it rains, shoot some pictures through a car window or windshield, or keep your camera dry and shoot on foot—using indoor color film. The cold blue effects, particularly in slides, are terrific. You may later use an 85B filter to correct the color for normal outdoor or flash use.

Keep in mind that "pretty" or striking color may influence us to take pictures where there really is no worthwhile image. And when you view prints and slides, realize that theatrical color can influence your judgment about the total quality of a picture. A beautiful girl in brightly colored clothes, or an exotic South Seas beach scene may be photographed with creative skill, or insensitively, no matter how appealing the color is.

Contrast: Outstanding pictures may be based on the fact that they contain various contrasting elements, such as large and small, near and far, old and new, bright and subtle color, etc. In taking pictures and evaluating them, keep the contrast range in mind, although these values are often integral with other aspects of the picture.

Camera Angle and Choice of Lens: If someone standing next to you shoots a mid-town Manhattan street with a 50mm lens on a 35mm camera, and you do the same scene with a 35mm or 105mm lens from a crouch rather than standing, you might get a better picture. You can dramatize a subject through your choice of camera angle and lens focal length to alter perspective as well as the relationship of things in the scene. Distortion created this way can be pictorially exciting—or awkward and distracting. You may get good pictures by taking risks in visual ways, and later deciding if what you tried seems to work.

Imagination and Creativity: These two attributes of people who take pictures might have been first on the list if they were not abused words. Look each one up in the dictionary. Ponder how you would apply the definitions to your own pictures and to photographs you see in books or exhibitions.

It takes imagination to see the commonplace in an artistic way, but a   25
certain amount of imagination and creativity should be involved every
time we press the shutter button. These human capabilities are basic to
understanding the other qualities that make good pictures.

ℰ Joining the Conversation: Critical Thinking and Writing

1. Evaluate the title and the first paragraph.

2. In paragraph 4, Jacobs says, "Of course 'a good picture' is a relative description because it's subjective. . . ." Do you agree? For example, look at Dorothea Lange's photographs of a migrant laborer and her children on pages 74–75 and 77–78. Would you be willing to argue that the famous picture (the one showing the children turned away from the camera) is clearly—objectively—a better picture than one of the other pictures? Explain.

3. In paragraph 5, Jacobs praises Ansel Adams's *Moonrise, Hernandez, NM,* but this picture—showing a cemetery with crosses illumined by a silvery moon—has been disparaged by some critics on the grounds that it is sentimental. How would you define sentimentality? And is it a bad thing in a photo-graph? Explain.

4. In paragraph 7, Jacobs speaks of "human interest," and he cites a picture of "children laughing or a picture of vendors in a marketplace." Given these examples, what does "human interest" seem to mean? What might be some examples of photographs of people that do *not* have "human interest"?

5. In paragraph 23, Jacobs says that "you can dramatize a subject through your choice of camera angle. . . ." Find an example of such a photo in a newspaper or newsmagazine—or perhaps in this book—and explain how the camera angle "dramatizes" the subject.

6. Take a photo—perhaps one in this book—and in 500 words, analyze and evaluate it in Jacobs's terms. Then, consider whether Jacobs's essay has helped you to see and enjoy the photograph.

7. Write your own short essay (250–500 words) on Jacobs's topic, "What Qualities Does a Good Photograph Have?" Illustrate it with photocopies of two or three photographs from this book or from any other source that you wish to draw from. (You may want to choose two examples of good photo-graphs or one of a good photograph and one of a poor photograph.)

A Sample Analysis of a Photograph

An Essay by a Student

If you take a course in art history, you will probably be asked to write a formal analysis. In such a context, the word *formal* is not the opposite of *informal*—as in a formal dance or a formal dinner—but simply means "related to the form or structure." Here, we print a short formal analysis of a photograph. Formal analysis is, however by no means limited to courses in art history; we follow the student's essay with a professional writer's examination—largely a formal analysis—of an advertisement.

Zoe Morales

Zoe Morales wrote the following essay in a first-year composition course at Tufts University. She is planning to go to law school, probably in her native Texas.

The instructor distributed copies of three pictures and asked students to write an analysis of any one of the three. Morales has kindly let us reproduce her final set of notes—that is, the organized notes that she jotted down after she reread material that she generated, almost at random, by asking herself questions such as "What interests me about this picture?" "What puzzles me here?" "What is the relation of one figure to another?" and "What does this all add up to?"

Dancing at Durango

(Preliminary Jottings)

Title: tourists, Navajo, in Colorado
    The tourists (white) on the train are gawking at the Navajo, and the boy seems to be interested (at least he is smiling), BUT the man with the boy looks pretty grim, looks straight ahead, *not* at dancers. Superior? Uptight?
    The Navajo are doing their stuff, at least the dancers are, BUT the girl (she's a Navajo too) is not part of the act (not dressed "Indian-style"). At side; not center-stage. Not being looked at—but she looks coolly at the photographer.
    The whole thing seems pretty grim—these Navajo (one at right even in a war bonnet) perform for a couple of minutes when the train pulls in, then probably wait an hour or maybe many hours, until the next train. They probably depend on coins or if they are lucky dollar bills that whites toss to them out of the train.
    The Navajo in the war bonnet seems to be drummer. Anyway, he is sort of offstage, with the girl.
    Pretty strong separation of whites from Navajo. A white man and a boy are on the ground with Navajo, but whites' clothes clearly separate them from Navajo. These whites belong to the group on the train, that is, to the world on wheels that will soon pull out of this town.
    Lettering on train is like lettering on a "Wanted Poster"—to make the tourists think they are in the Wild West of the nineteenth century, even though reality is 1963!

These jottings served—with considerable amplification and reorganization—as the basis of an essay on the picture. Here is the finished essay.

Navajo Dancers Entertaining a Tourist Train, June 1963, Durango, Colorado
George Hight

Dancing at Durango: White Tourists and Navajo Performers

Today when people who are not Native Americans think about
Native Americans, they probably think first of their terrible mistreatment
by whites. The lands of the Native Americans were stolen, and many of the
tribes were nearly annihilated by diseases introduced by whites. But this
view seems to be fairly recent. A common older view, forcefully presented
in the Indian Wars of the nineteenth century, can be summarized in the
blunt words, "The only good Indian is a dead Indian." These words are
reported to have been spoken by General Philip Henry Sheridan, who
achieved fame and acclaim as one of Lincoln's generals, and even more
fame and even more acclaim as an Indian fighter after the Civil War.

By the beginning of the twentieth century the Native Americans, their populations and their territories greatly reduced by war and disease, were no longer a military threat to the whites. In the popular white mind in the first half of the twentieth century, Native Americans chiefly were of two sorts, bad guys in cowboy films and quaint feather-wearing people in tourist attractions. In films they were sometimes brave but more often were cunning, and they were always defeated by whites; in tourist sites they wore their feathers and beads and moccasins, and they danced their dances, representing a colorful past that the civilized world had outgrown.

George Hight's photograph, *Navajo Dancers Entertaining a Tourist Train, June 1963, Durango, Colorado*, shows two contrasting worlds, the white world with its railroad train, and the Native American world with its costumes worn for the sake of the tourists. But this railroad train is itself a bit of a fake, a twentieth-century machine that, for the pleasure of white people, uses a style of lettering that looks like a Wanted Poster to call to mind the Wild West of a bygone day.

The train has stopped, some people have stepped off it, but the strong diagonal line conveys a sense that this self-contained world, this world which is decidedly separate from the Navajo, will soon speed away, leaving the Navajo behind. Although a white man and a boy are off the train and on the ground with the Navajo—they are in Navajo territory for a minute, so to speak—clearly there is no *real* intermingling. Their clothing separates them, and so do their expressions: The man is grim-faced, the boy is smiling and to that degree he is sympathetically entering into the Navajo world, but there is no real contact between the two dancers and the people safe in their train or the two whites who have stepped off the train. This grim white man at the left faces the same way that the Navajo in the bonnet at the right faces, but this similarity only emphasizes the difference between them. The chief connection between the two worlds, interestingly, is made by the Navajo girl at the right, who is dressed like a white and looks at the photographer and at us, that is, at the tourist world in front of the picture. She lives in what we can call the *real* Navajo world, the modern world, which whites dominate. And this is the world to which the Navajo performers probably will return. After the last performance the costumed men will put on jeans and cotton shirts, and they will replace their beaded and feathered moccasins with sneakers. But the girl, standing at the side, dressed like a white, not performing, is a Native American who scarcely exists so far as the tourists are concerned.

I find the photograph disturbing, and not simply because of the separation suggested between the worlds of the whites and the Navajo. The white man and the boy stride toward a dancer who leans, knees flexed, in their direction: Will the whites and this dancer collide? Certainly the white man does not look as though he is going to change his direction. Furthermore, the other dancer, in profile, bends forward and, as the scene is caught by the camera, blocks the movement of the white man. All of this troubling placement of the figures on the left-hand side is set in contrast to the firm vertical stances of the Indian wearing the headdress and the little girl on the right. A little to the right of the center of the picture, a man walks away (he seems to be wearing a cap, so he probably is a trainman of some sort), and further to the right two white women, also with their backs toward us, flank the bonneted Navajo and the girl. The man in the center and the two white women at the right take us in one direction, the white man and the boy at the left take us in the opposite direction. And as if all this contradictory motion were not enough, the train cars, which are stationary so that the tourists can take pictures, seem propelled forward to the left and also veering backward into the sharply receding right.

Most Native American dances had a social function: The Bear Dance was danced to appease the soul of the animal which they would kill; the Scalp Dance was a dance of victory; the Sun Dance was danced in an effort to achieve divine guidance. Judging from the hoops that hang on a post in the foreground, these Navajo perform some sort of Hoop Dance.

(According to Gladys A. Reichard, *Navaho Religions: A Study of Symbolism* [1950], hoops are used in many kinds of Navaho sacred dances.) But this dance is performed not for any ritual that is an important part of the life of the dancers; rather, it is performed for the entertainment of outsiders. It has utterly lost its religious or healing function. But not quite. It is still life-giving, since it gains some money, helping the Native Americans to survive in the narrow world that the whites have pushed them into—the space between the train and the presumably white tourist who took the picture.

To my eye and mind, it is tragic that these Navajo are performing their dances not as religious rites but just to entertain outsiders and to make a few dollars. Imagine if some Christians, Jews, Muslims, or Buddhists were so poor that today they had to make money by performing their sacred ceremonies to entertain people who do not have the faintest knowledge of or interest in their religion, but who look at the ceremonies as the strange doings of people who are not part of the modern world. On the other hand, we don't know how these Indians felt when they were dancing for tourists. Maybe they believed—and maybe they were right—that they were communicating at least some of their culture to strangers, were showing that although much of their traditional way of life had been forcibly taken from them, they nevertheless retained important parts of it, and were willing to share these with the whites. The whites in a moment will be speeding down the railroad tracks to the next tourist attraction, but maybe some of them will be mysteriously touched by what they saw. We can't know, but we can guess that the photographer was touched enough to record the image.

Joining the Conversation: Critical Thinking and Writing

1. What do the first two paragraphs contribute to the essay? What would be the effect if these were omitted?

2. Does this essay present a thesis? Does an analysis of a picture require one?

3. Do you find the ending too indefinite or just right?

CHAPTER 6

All in the Family

The Acrobat's Family with a Monkey
Pablo Picasso, 1905

Sonia
Joanne Leonard, 1966

Short Views

Higamus hogamus,
Woman's monogamous;
Hogamus higamus,
Man is polygamous.
> *Anonymous (often attributed to William James)*

After a certain age, the more one becomes oneself, the more obvious one's family traits become.
> **Marcel Proust**

All happy families resemble one another; every unhappy family is unhappy in its own fashion.
> **Leo Tolstoy**

Marriage is the best of human statuses and the worst, and it will continue to be. And that is why, though its future in some form or other is as assured as anything can be, this future is as equivocal as its past. The demands that men and women make on marriage will never be fully met; they cannot be.
> **Jessie Bernard**

Nobody who has not been in the interior of a family can say what the difficulties of any individual of that family may be.
> **Jane Austen**

Lewis Coser

Lewis Coser, born in Berlin in 1913, was educated at the Sorbonne in Paris and at Columbia University, where he received a Ph.D. in sociology in 1954. For many years, he taught at the State University of New York, Stony Brook, where he held the title Distinguished Professor. The passage below is from a textbook for college students.

The Family

Following the French anthropologist Claude Lévi-Strauss, we can define the family as a group manifesting these characteristics: it finds its origin in marriage; it consists of husband, wife and children born in their wedlock—though other relatives may find their place close to that nuclear group; and the members of the group are united by moral, legal, economic, religious, and social rights and obligations. These include a network of sexual rights and prohibitions and a variety of socially patterned feelings such as love, attraction, piety, awe, and so on.

The family is among the few universal institutions of mankind. No known society lacks small kinship groups of parents and children related through the process of reproduction. But recognition of the universality of this institution must immediately be followed by the acknowledgment that its forms are exceedingly varied. The fact that many family organizations are not monogamic, as in the West, led many nineteenth-century observers to the erroneous conclusion that in "early" stages of evolution there existed no families, and that "group marriage," institutionalized promiscuity, prevailed. This is emphatically not the case; even though patterned wife-lending shocked the sensibilities of Victorian anthropologists, such an institution is evidently predicated on the fact that men have wives in the first place. No matter what their specific forms, families in all known societies have performed major social functions—reproduction, maintenance, socialization, and social placement of the young.

Families may be monogamous or polygamous—there are systems where one man is entitled to several wives and others where several husbands share one wife. A society may recognize primarily the small nuclear, conjugal unit of husband and wife with their immediate descendants or it may institutionalize the large extended family linking several generations and emphasizing consanguinity more than the conjugal bond. Residence after marriage may be matrilocal, patrilocal or neolocal; exchanges of goods and services between families at the time of marriage

Lewis Coser: "The Family" from *Sociology Through Literature*, Prentice-Hall, 1962. pp. 250–251. Reprinted by permission.

may be based on bride price, groom price or an equal exchange; endoga-mous or exogamous regulations may indicate who is and who is not eligible for marriage; the choice of a mate may be controlled by parents or it may be left in large measure to the young persons concerned. These are but a few of the many differences which characterize family struc-tures in variant societies.

Joining the Conversation: Critical Thinking and Writing

1. At the end of paragraph 2, Coser writes: "No matter what their specific forms, families in all known societies have performed major social functions—reproduction, maintenance, socialization, and social placement of the young." What does "socialization" mean? How does it differ from "social placement of the young"? What specific forms does each take in our society?

2. What examples can you give of "moral, legal, economic, religious, and social rights and obligations" (paragraph 1) that unite members of a family?

3. As you read other selections in this chapter, what variations in form of the family do you encounter? Are there any variations in form that Coser did not mention or anticipate?

Arlie Hochschild

Arlie Hochschild, born in Boston in 1940, holds a bachelor's degree from Swarthmore College and a Ph.D. from the University of California, Berkeley, where he is now a professor in the Department of Sociology. He is the author of several important books, including The Second Shift: Working Parents and the Revolution at Home *(1989, written with Anne Machung). The material below comes from this book.*

The Second Shift: Employed Women Are Putting in Another Day of Work at Home

Every American household bears the footprints of economic and cul-tural trends that originate far outside its walls. A rise in inflation eroding the earning power of the male wage, an expanding service sector opening up jobs for women, and the inroads made by women into many professions—all these changes do not simply go on around the American family. They occur *within* a marriage or living-together arrangement and transform it. Problems between couples, problems that seem "unique" or "marital," are often the individual ripples of powerful economic and cultural shock waves. Quarrels between husbands and wives in households across the nation result mainly from a friction between faster-changing women and slower-changing men.

The exodus of women from the home to the workplace has not been accompanied by a new view of marriage and work that would make this transition smooth. Most workplaces have remained inflexible in the face of the changing needs of workers with families, and most men have yet to really adapt to the changes in women. I call the strain caused by the disparity between the change in women and the absence of change elsewhere the "stalled revolution."

If women begin to do less at home because they have less time, if men do little more, and if the work of raising children and tending a home requires roughly the same effort, then the questions of who does what at home and of what "needs doing" become a source of deep tension in a marriage.

Over the past 30 years in the United States, more and more women have begun to work outside the home, and more have divorced. While some commentators conclude that women's work *causes* divorce, my research into changes in the American family suggests something else. Since all the wives in the families I studied (over an eight-year period) worked outside the home, the fact that they worked did not account for why some marriages were happy and others were not. What *did* contribute to happiness was the husband's willingness to do the work at home. Whether they were traditional or more egalitarian in their relationship, couples were happier when the men did a sizable share of housework and child care.

In one study of 600 couples filing for divorce, researcher George Levinger found that the second most common reason women cited for wanting to divorce—after "mental cruelty"—was their husbands' "neglect of home or children." Women mentioned this reason more often than financial problems, physical abuse, drinking, or infidelity.

A happy marriage is supported by a couple's being economically secure, by their enjoying a supportive community, and by their having compatible needs and values. But these days it may also depend on a shared appreciation of the work it takes to nurture others. As the role of the homemaker is being abandoned by many women, the homemaker's work has been continually devalued and passed on to low-paid housekeepers, baby-sitters, or day-care workers. Long devalued by men, the contribution of cooking, cleaning, and care-giving is now being devalued as mere drudgery by many women, too.

In the era of the stalled revolution, one way to make housework and child care more valued is for men to share in that work. Many working mothers are already doing all they can at home. Now it's time for men to make the move.

If more mothers of young children are working at full-time jobs outside the home, and if most couples can't afford household help, who's doing the work at home? Adding together the time it takes to do a paid job and to do housework and child care and using estimates from major studies on time use done in the 1960s and 1970s, I found that women worked roughly 15 more hours each week than men. Over a year, they worked an extra month of 24-hour days. Over a dozen years, it was an extra year of 24-hour days. Most women without children spend much more time than men on housework. Women with children devote more time to both housework and child care. Just as there is a wage gap between men and women in the workplace, there is a "leisure gap" between them at home. Most women work one shift at the office or factory and a "second shift" at home.

In my research, I interviewed and observed 52 couples over an eight-year period as they cooked dinner, shopped, bathed their children, and in general struggled to find enough time to make their complex lives work. The women I interviewed seemed to be far more deeply torn between the demands of work and family than were their husbands. They talked more about the abiding conflict between work and family. They felt the second shift was *their* issue, and most of their husbands agreed. When I telephoned one husband to arrange an interview with him, explaining that I wanted to ask him how he managed work and family life, he replied genially, "Oh, this will *really* interest my *wife*."

Men who shared the load at home seemed just as pressed for time as   10
their wives, and as torn between the demands of career and small children. But of the men I surveyed, the majority did not share the load at home. Some refused outright. Others refused more passively, often offering a loving shoulder to lean on, or an understanding ear, as their working wife faced the conflict they both saw as hers. At first it seemed to me that the problem of the second shift *was* hers. But I came to realize that those husbands who helped very little at home were often just as deeply affected as their wives—through the resentment their wives felt toward them and through their own need to steel themselves against that resentment.

A clear example of this phenomenon is Evan Holt, a warehouse furniture salesman who did very little housework and played with his four-year-old son, Joey, only at his convenience. His wife, Nancy, did the second shift, but she resented it keenly and half-consciously expressed her frustration and rage by losing interest in sex and becoming overly absorbed in Joey.

Even when husbands happily shared the work, their wives *felt* more responsible for home and children. More women than men kept track of doctor's appointments and arranged for kids' playmates to come over. More mothers than fathers worried about a child's Halloween costume or a birthday present for a school friend. They were more likely to think about their children while at work and to check in by phone with the baby-sitter.

Partly because of this, more women felt torn between two kinds of urgency, between the need to soothe a child's fear of being left at day-care and the need to show the boss she's "serious" at work. Twenty percent of the men in my study shared housework equally. Seventy percent did a substantial amount (less than half of it, but more than a third), and 10 percent did less than a third. But even when couples more equitably share the work at home, women do two thirds of the daily jobs at home, such as cooking and cleaning up—jobs that fix them into a rigid routine. Most women cook dinner, for instance, while men change the oil in the family car. But, as one mother pointed out, dinner needs to be prepared every evening around six o'clock, whereas the car oil needs to be changed every six months, with no particular deadline. Women do more child care than men, and men repair more household appliances. A child needs to be tended to daily, whereas the repair of household appliances can often wait, said the men, "until I have time." Men thus have more control over when they make their contributions than women do. They may be very busy with family chores, but, like the executive who tells his secretary to "hold my calls," the man has more control over his time.

Another reason why women may feel under more strain than men is that women more often do two things at once—for example, write checks and return phone calls, vacuum and keep an eye on a three-year-old, fold laundry and think out the shopping list. Men more often will either cook dinner *or* watch the kids. Women more often do both at the same time.

Beyond doing more at home, women also devote proportionately more of their time at home to housework than men and proportionately less of it to child care. Of all the time men spend working at home, a growing amount of it goes to child care. Since most parents prefer to tend to their children than to clean house, men do more of what they'd rather do. More men than women take their children on "fun" outings to the park, the zoo, the movies. Women spend more time on maintenance, such as feeding and bathing children—enjoyable activities, to be sure, but often less leisurely or "special" than going to the zoo. Men also do fewer of the most undesirable household chores, such as scrubbing the toilet. 15

As a result, women tend to talk more intensely about being over-tired, sick, and emotionally drained. Many women interviewed were fixated on the topic of sleep. They talked about how much they could "get by on": six and a half, seven, seven and a half, less, more. They talked about who they knew who needed more or less. Some apologized for how much sleep they needed—"I'm afraid I need eight hours of sleep"—as if eight was "too much." They talked about how to avoid fully waking up when a child called them at night, and how to get back to sleep. These women talked about sleep the way a hungry person talks about food.

If, all in all, the two-job family is suffering from a speedup of work and family life, working mothers are its primary victims. It is ironic, then, that often it falls to women to be the time-and-motion experts of family life. As I observed families inside their homes, I noticed it was often the mother who rushed children, saying, "Hurry up! It's time to go." "Finish your cereal now," "You can do that later," or "Let's go!" When a bath needed to be crammed into a slot between 7:45 and 8:00, it was often the mother who called out, "Let's see who can take their bath the quickest!" Often a younger child would rush out, scurrying to be first in bed, while the older and wiser one stalled, resistant, sometimes resentful: "Mother is always rushing us." Sadly, women are more often the lightning rods for family tensions aroused by this speedup of work and family life. They are the villains in a process in which they are also the primary victims. More than the longer hours and the lack of sleep, this is the saddest cost to women of their extra month of work each year.

Raising children in a nuclear family is still the overwhelming preference of most people. Yet in the face of new problems for this family model we have not created an adequate support system so that the nuclear family can do its job well in the era of the two-career couple. Corporations have done little to accommodate the needs of working parents, and the government has done little to prod them.

We really need, as sociologist Frank Furstenberg has suggested, a Marshall Plan for the family. After World War II we saw that it was in our best interests to aid the war-torn nations of Europe. Now—it seems obvious in an era of growing concern over drugs, crime, and family instability—it is in our best interests to aid the overworked two-job families right here at home. We should look to other nations for a model of what could be done. In Sweden, for example, upon the birth of a child every working couple is entitled to 12 months of paid parental leave—nine months at 90 percent of the worker's salary, plus an additional three months at about three hundred dollars a month. The mother and father are free to divide this year off between them as they wish. Working parents of a child under eight have the opportunity to work no more than six hours a day, at six hours' pay. Parental insurance offers parents money for work time lost while visiting a child's school or caring for a sick child. That's a true pro-family policy.

A pro-family policy in the United States could give tax breaks to companies that encourage job sharing, part-time work, flex time, and family leave for new parents. By implementing comparable worth policies we could increase pay scales for "women's" jobs. Another key element of a pro-family policy would be instituting fewer-hour, more flexible options—called "family phases"—for all regular jobs filled by parents of young children. 20

Day-care centers could be made more warm and creative through generous public and private funding. If the best form of day-care comes from the attention of elderly neighbors, students, or grandparents, these people could be paid to care for children through social programs.

In these ways, the American government would create a safer environment for the two-job family. If the government encouraged corporations to consider the long-range interests of workers and their families, they would save on long-range costs caused by absenteeism, turnover, juvenile delinquency, mental illness, and welfare support for single mothers.

These are real pro-family reforms. If they seem utopian today, we should remember that in the past the eight-hour day, the abolition of child labor, and the vote for women seemed utopian, too. Among top-rated employers listed in *The 100 Best Companies to Work for in America* are many offering country-club memberships, first-class air travel, and million-dollar fitness centers. But only a handful offer job sharing, flex time, or part-time work. Not one provides on-site day-care, and only three offer child-care deductions: Control Data, Polaroid, and Honeywell. In his book *Megatrends*, John Naisbitt reports that 83 percent of corporate executives believed that more men feel the need to share the responsibilities of parenting; yet only 9 percent of corporations offer paternity leave.

Public strategies are linked to private ones. Economic and cultural trends bear on family relations in ways it would be useful for all of us to understand. The happiest two-job marriages I saw during my research were ones in which men and women shared the housework and parenting. What couples called good communication often meant that they were good at saying thanks to one another for small aspects of taking care of the family. Making it to the school play, helping a child read, cooking dinner in good spirit, remembering the grocery list, taking responsibility for cleaning up the bedrooms—these were the silver and gold of the marital exchange. Until now, couples committed to an equal sharing of housework and child care have been rare. But, if we as a culture come to see the urgent need of meeting the new problems posed by the second shift, and if society and government begin to shape new policies that allow working parents more flexibility, then we will be making some progress toward happier times at home and work. And as the young learn by example, many more women and men will be able to enjoy the pleasure that arises when family life is family life, and not a second shift.

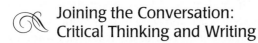 ## Joining the Conversation:
Critical Thinking and Writing

1. Here is Hochschild's opening sentence: "Every American household bears the footprints of economic and cultural trends that originate far outside its walls." Explain what Hochschild means and then—using the household you know best—test the truth of Hochschild's sentence.

2. What does Hochschild mean (paragraph 2) by the phrase "stalled revolution"?

3. Hochschild writes that "most workplaces have remained inflexible in the face of the changing needs of workers with families" (second paragraph). Assuming that he is correct, why do you think this is so?

4. The rest of the sentence we just quoted is "and most men have yet to really adapt to the changes in women." To what changes does he refer? And do you think he is right? If so, how do you account for the failure of men to adapt?

5. According to Hochschild, women "are the villains in a process in which they are also the primary victims." What does he mean? In your own experience, have you been aware that women have been cast as the villains?

6. Hochschild lists conditions in Sweden for working families and refers to them as a "pro-family policy." What are some of the conditions? In your opinion, why does a similar pro-family policy not exist in the United States?

7. In your own family, what was the division of labor for raising children and doing household chores? Who did what (and how often)? Write a brief essay (500–750 words) in which you reveal both the division of labor and your attitude toward it.

Judy Brady

Born in San Francisco in 1937, Judy Brady married in 1960 and two years later earned a bachelor's degree in painting from the University of Iowa. Active in the women's movement and in other political causes, she has worked as an author, an editor, and a secretary. The essay reprinted here—written before she and her husband separated—originally appeared in the first issue of Ms. *in 1972, when the author used her married name, Judy Syfers.*

I Want a Wife

I belong to that classification of people known as wives. I am A Wife. And, not altogether incidentally, I am a mother.

Not too long ago a male friend of mine appeared on the scene fresh from a recent divorce. He had one child, who is, of course, with his ex-wife. He is looking for another wife. As I thought about him while I was ironing one evening, it suddenly occurred to me that I, too, would like to have a wife. Why do I want a wife?

I would like to go back to school so that I can become economically independent, support myself, and, if need be, support those dependent upon me. I want a wife who will work and send me to school. And while I am going to school I want a wife to take care of my children. I want a wife to keep track of the children's doctor and dentist appointments. And to keep track of mine, too. I want a wife to make sure my children eat properly and are kept clean. I want a wife who will wash the children's clothes and keep them mended. I want a wife who is a good nurturant attendant to my children, who arranges for their schooling, makes sure that they have an adequate social life with their peers, takes them to the park, the zoo, etc. I want a wife who takes care of the children when they are sick, a wife who arranges to be around when the children need special care, because, of course, I cannot miss classes at school. My wife must arrange to lose time at work and not lose the job. It may mean a small cut in my wife's income from time to time, but I guess I can tolerate that. Needless to say, my wife will arrange and pay for the care of the children while my wife is working.

I want a wife who will take care of *my* physical needs. I want a wife who will keep my house clean. A wife who will pick up after my children, a wife who will pick up after me. I want a wife who will keep my clothes clean, ironed, mended, replaced when need be, and who will see to it that my personal things are kept in their proper place so that I can find what I need the minute I need it. I want a wife who cooks the meals, a wife who is a *good* cook. I want a wife who will plan the menus, do the necessary grocery shopping, prepare the meals, serve them pleasantly, and then do the cleaning up while I do my studying. I want a wife who will care for me when I am sick and sympathize with my pain and loss of time from school. I want a wife to go along when our family takes a vacation so that someone can continue to care for me and my children when I need a rest and change of scene.

I want a wife who will not bother me with rambling complaints about a wife's duties. But I want a wife who will listen to me when I feel the need to explain a rather difficult point I have come across in my course of studies. And I want a wife who will type my papers for me when I have written them.

I want a wife who will take care of the details of my social life. When my wife and I are invited out by my friends, I want a wife who will take care of the babysitting arrangements. When I meet people at school that I like and want to entertain, I want a wife who will have the house clean, will prepare a special meal, serve it to me and my friends, and not interrupt when I talk about things that interest me and my friends. I want a wife who will have arranged that the children are fed and ready for bed before my guests arrive so that the children do not bother us. I want a wife who takes care of the needs of my guests so that they feel comfortable, who makes sure that they have an ashtray, that they are passed the hors d'oeuvres, that they are offered a second helping of the food, that their wine glasses are replenished when necessary, that their coffee is served to them as they like it. And I want a wife who knows that sometimes I need a night out by myself.

I want a wife who is sensitive to my sexual needs, a wife who makes love passionately and eagerly when I feel like it, a wife who makes sure that I am satisfied. And, of course, I want a wife who will not demand sexual attention when I am not in the mood for it. I want a wife who assumes the complete responsibility for birth control, because I do not want more children. I want a wife who will remain sexually faithful to me so that I do not have to clutter up my intellectual life with jealousies. And I want a wife who understands that *my* sexual needs may entail more than strict adherence to monogamy. I must, after all, be able to relate to people as fully as possible.

If, by chance, I find another person more suitable as a wife than the wife I already have, I want the liberty to replace my present wife with another one. Naturally, I will expect a fresh, new life; my wife will take the children and be solely responsible for them so that I am left free.

When I am through with school and have a job, I want my wife to quit working and remain at home so that my wife can more fully and completely take care of a wife's duties.

My God, who *wouldn't* want a wife?

℘ Joining the Conversation: Critical Thinking and Writing

1. Brady uses the word "wife" in sentences where one would ordinarily use "she" or "her." Why? And why does she begin paragraphs 4, 5, 6, and 7 with the same words, "I want a wife"?

2. Drawing on your experience as observer of the world around you (and perhaps as husband, wife, or ex-spouse), do you think Brady's picture of a wife's role is grossly exaggerated? Or is it (allowing for some serious playfulness) fairly accurate, even though it was written in 1971? If grossly exaggerated, is the essay therefore meaningless? If fairly accurate, what attitudes and practices does it encourage you to support? Explain.

3. Whether or not you agree with Brady's vision of marriage in our society, write an essay (500 words) titled "I Want a Husband," imitating her style and approach. Write the best possible essay and then decide which of the two essays makes a fairer comment on current society. Or if you believe Brady is utterly misleading, write an essay titled "I Want a Wife," seeing the matter in a different light.

4. If you feel that you have been pressed into an unappreciated, unreasonable role—built-in babysitter, listening post, or girl (or boy or man or woman) Friday—write an essay of 500 words that will help the reader to see both your plight and the injustice of the system. (*Hint:* A little humor will help to keep your essay from seeming to be a prolonged whine.)

Gabrielle Glaser

Gabrielle Glaser is the author of the book Strangers to the Tribe: Portraits of Interfaith Marriage *(1997). We reprint an essay that was originally published in* The New York Times Magazine *in 1997.*

Scenes from an Intermarriage

As Alfred and Eileen Ono sit down late one evening to discuss their family's religious life, even the seating arrangement seems to reveal their spiritual divide. On one side of their sumptuous living room in Portland, Ore., Eileen settles into a comfortable wing chair. Al is across from her, on the couch, next to their 22-year-old daughter, Sarah. From time to time during the conversation, father and daughter link hands.

Gabrielle Glaser: "Faith is a Gamble: Scenes from an Intermarriage," *The New York Times Magazine*, December 7, 1997. Reprinted by permission of the author.

Sarah and her 18-year-old brother, Alistair, a college freshman, have been raised in the Buddhist faith of their Japanese-American father. Eileen, a Middle Westerner with Dutch, Lithuanian and German roots, has remained a Catholic. The Onos decided how to raise the children long ago, even before they were married, and Eileen insists that her solitary spirituality is of little import. But the religious differences in this family, in which both children shave their heads in the style of Buddhist monks and nuns, exert a gravitational pull on each relationship—between the parents and the children, between the siblings and between husband and wife.

Perhaps surprisingly, it is Eileen who is most relaxed about the family's complicated spiritual life. Over the years, her husband has become more doctrinaire. When Sarah was in her early teens and interested in Catholicism, for example, Al insisted that she continue to attend temple every Sunday. Then, in college, when she dated a devout Irish Catholic and began going to Mass with him, Al expressed his disappointment outright.

The Onos say that they try to live up to the ideal of tolerance in all matters. But it isn't any easier for them than it is for the other 33 million Americans who live in interfaith households. The United States, founded by religious dissidents and shaped by a Christian revival in the 19th century, has evolved into a rich religious pluralism. As racial and ethnic barriers have become hazier, intermarriage has become more common: according to recent surveys, 52 percent of Jews, 32 percent of Catholics and 57 percent of Buddhists marry outside the faith.

Many couples split their religious differences in the interest of family harmony, but the Onos' choice not to is evident the moment you enter their splendid turn-of-the-century home. A gold Japanese panel rests on the living room mantel, and in the library sits a black lacquer *obutsudan*, or Buddhist shrine, where Alistair, Sarah and Al recite chants over prayer beads. The three practice Jodoshinshu, a form of Japanese Buddhism, although in recent years Sarah has also included elements of Tibetan Buddhism. (Alistair refers teasingly to Sarah's interest in Tibetan Buddhism as an "upper-middle-class white thing.") 5

Al, a gentle man with thick gray hair and a kind but intense face, speaks in the drawn-out vowels of his native Minnesota. His parents, George and Masaye, were born in California; their marriage was arranged by a match-maker. They later settled in St. Louis Park, and helped to found the state's first Buddhist temple. Growing up, Al flourished there and relished the simple truths of his faith: There is suffering. There is a cause for suffering. Suffering can be overcome by thinking and living in the right way. His Buddhism, which he describes as "logical and linear," built on wisdom, knowledge, truth and compassion, filters into all aspects of his life: as a doctor—he has a thriving OB-GYN practice in Portland—a father and a husband. "When patients come to me and say, 'Oh, my God, it's cancer, I should have come to you sooner,'" Al says, "I say: 'This is not because you've done anything wrong or because you missed your last appointment. Don't blame yourself. Bodies are always changing. Now it's time to put it back on track.'"

Eileen, on the other hand, has always had questions about her faith. A plain-spoken woman with pale, luminous skin and large, hazel eyes, she was raised in a Minnesota farming town where about half the population was Catholic. As a child, she liked the music and pageantry the church offered, but some things didn't make sense to her. "I'd go to confession and have to make up sins," she says. "I just hadn't done anything horrible." By the time she married, Eileen had also begun to find much of church doctrine—on birth control and the role of women, for example— outdated. Still, she considers herself Catholic. "It's how I was brought up, and it's in my soul," she says.

From time to time, she has second thoughts about the choice she made 27 years ago to raise children in a religion not her own. "I sometimes wish we could be all the same thing," she says softly. "Sure, I do." Sometimes an "Our Father" or "Hail, Mary" will cross her lips before she falls asleep, or when she learns that someone has died. But she rarely goes to church, and like the crossword puzzles she does on Sunday mornings when the rest of her family is at temple, or the meticulous squares of fabric she sews together in her award-winning quilts, Eileen's faith lies apart, boxed and separate, from the rest of her family. "I'm happy with how my spiritual life is," she says. She pauses, then adds, "It's others who have a problem with it."

Those others included her relatives, at least at first. When Al and Eileen began dating in the late 1960's as students at the University of Minnesota, their parents couldn't believe the relationship was serious. When Al told his parents of the couple's plans to marry, his parents accepted the announcement with grim resignation. Eileen's parents reacted with similar reticence.

The wedding was to take place in Minneapolis, and the closest 10 English-speaking Buddhist clergyman lived hundreds of miles away, in Chicago, so the couple settled on a Catholic priest. They were married in a campus chapel, amid burlap banners reading "Peace" and "Love." Led by the priest, they recited Buddhist wedding vows, emphasizing not love or miracles but truth, honor and respect.

Yet the occasion did not flow as smoothly as they had hoped. Eileen's father, an Army veteran, had been stationed in the Philippines during World War II, and after the surrender had hunted the country for Japanese deserters. After several glasses of champagne at the reception, he approached George Ono's best friend with a powerful slap on the back. "Whoever would have guessed that my daughter would be marrying a Jap 25 years after I was over there shooting at them?" he declared. Eileen and Al stared at each other in disbelief. "We'd been so worried about the religious aspects of the wedding that we had overlooked the racial ones," Eileen says. "Our families had always been very cordial to each other." There were other not-so-subtle messages. As a gift, an aunt gave them a plaster statue of Christ, engraved with their names and wedding date.

The couple moved to Portland, and a few years after Sarah's birth the family started going to the Oregon Buddhist Temple there. But at first it was Eileen who took the children to and from services—while Al, caught up in building his medical practice, rarely went. Over time, she began to feel a resistance to being so involved and told Al that he would have to take the lead. "I don't care if you're in the middle of a delivery, you're going to have to be the point man on this," she finally said to him. When Al started going, she stopped.

Sometimes during the ride to temple an image would flash through his head. Of all things, he envisioned a Norman Rockwell painting he once saw, of a family driving off to church, all together. He would dismiss the picture by reminding himself: "But she's not Japanese! She doesn't even relate to this stuff. This was the agreement."

These days, Eileen attends temple occasionally and has incorporated Buddhist thought into her life as a *hakujin,* or white person, as she jokingly calls herself. Indeed, the flies she once swatted are now gently shooed outdoors, in keeping with the Buddhist belief that all forms of life deserve dignity and respect. "They get several chances," she says with a smile. But she has retained a few of her rituals, and Christmas is one of them. The family chooses a tree together, and on Dec. 24 Al and Sarah attend midnight Mass—because they like the music. Eileen doesn't go. "I'm not practicing Catholicism, so I don't feel good just going to church for the highlights," she says, "but I do encourage them to go." The next morning, the whole family opens presents together.

Al says that Christ embodied the wisdom and compassion to   15
which Buddhists aspire, so honoring his birthday has never been an issue. Even so, the holiday Eileen loved as a child, and dreamed of sharing someday with her children, is a bit of a compromise. But religious differences can't take all of the blame: Dec. 25 is also Alistair's birthday, and at noon the day turns from celebrating Christ's arrival to celebrating Alistair's.

Other holidays follow Japanese tradition. For New Year's, Al spends days preparing a feast of special rice cakes and sashimi, and the family toasts one another with sake. "It's never been, 'Well, if you get sushi, tomorrow we have to have schnitzel,'" Eileen says. "I never denied my heritage. It just wasn't a big deal."

Her children's upbringing was a world away from memorizing catechism lessons. Sarah and Alistair spent Sundays at dharma school, learning to chant and meditate. At home, they drank green tea and, as toddlers, learned to use chopsticks. (So accustomed was the family to eating rice at every meal that Alistair thought mashed potatoes were a delicacy. "I thought there was a religious meaning to having them at Thanksgiving," he says with a grin. "That's the only time we ever had them.")

Yet growing up Buddhist in Portland wasn't easy. Children taunted Sarah and Alistair on the playground. In his advanced-placement English class, Alistair once suggested that perhaps not everyone was able to recognize Biblical allusions in literature. The teacher replied, "If you don't know the story of Moses, you don't belong here."

Sarah, a recent graduate of Connecticut College, is back at home doing part-time work while she looks for a job. As a child, she could see only what her religion didn't offer her. "Buddhism didn't have any perks," she says. "Until high school, it was weird. There's no Buddhist rite of passage. My Jewish friends got bas mitzvahs, my Catholic friends got big parties at their first Communion. When you're 9 or 10, you don't want to be anything but what your friends are." So she "tried out" Catholicism and at night would drop to her knees, hands clasped together, and pray at her bedside. She thought it might be easier to "talk to God" than to sit in silent meditation and clear her head of all thoughts. She even attended Catholic summer camp. Her friends taught her prayers, walked her through the steps of Mass, including Communion. She wanted, she says, "to pass," and told people that her mother was Catholic. When a counselor found out that Sarah had taken Communion without being Catholic, she scolded her. Sarah was mortified.

In time, Sarah, a small woman with delicate Asian features, made 20
peace with Buddhism. She studied in Asia for several months and welcomed living in a Buddhist society. Her faith, she says, has taught her one true thing: "to focus on the present."

In some ways, Eileen and Al's decision to raise their children as Buddhists was reinforced by society at large. Because of their Japanese surname and their tea-with-cream-colored skin, both Alistair and Sarah say that they found themselves identifying more readily with their Asian roots than their European ones. Alistair in particular has immersed himself in Japanese culture and credits the dynamic young minister at the Portland temple with inspiring his deeper involvement in Buddhism. At a special ceremony last spring, he received his Buddhist name, a great honor. Days later, he had the name, Gu-Sen—"widespread proclamation"—tattooed in Japanese on his lower back.

Yet guilt also lurks behind Alistair's enthusiasm for his father's faith and heritage. He half-facetiously calls himself a "mama's boy," and frequently E-mails Eileen from college; he worries that he has neglected her in some way. When a high-school history teacher gave out an assignment to research family trees, Alistair filled out the Ono branches practically by heart. When he asked his mother for help with her side, she pulled out photo albums and scrapbooks and recounted details of little-known relatives. "I had never asked about them before," he says. "I felt kind of bad."

Al, too, wonders quietly if he has inadvertently dampened his wife's religious life or her ties to her culture. They don't talk about it much; Al shies from confrontation. But he does remember that on a trip to Ireland some years ago they stumbled one afternoon into a stone church in the middle of Mass. Al turned to Eileen and asked, "Do you want to take Communion?" She brushed him off, he says, by saying she couldn't, since she hadn't been to confession in years. "Was it that she didn't want to be bothered?" he wonders. "Or was it just too complicated with me there, and she didn't want to mess with it?"

What may become of the religious divide between Al and Eileen now, with both children grown, is hard to say. Their marriage is a solid one. They take trips together, go to movies, make elaborate meals, enjoy their children. As middle age gives way to senior discounts, however, the Onos are likely to have disquieting moments. For them, death poses yet another separation. "I don't necessarily believe that God will forgive all at the last minute," Eileen says. "But I do think our spirits go somewhere." Al shakes his head gently. "I'm not so sure there's any connection between this life and another one. The Buddhist perspective doesn't believe we'll all be together again somewhere. I kid Eileen sometimes, telling her: 'Gee, Eileen, if you get last rites, you'll go to heaven. We'll all go to hell, so we'll still be in different places.'"

Joining the Conversation:
Critical Thinking and Writing

1. Glaser writes of the Ono family's "complicated spiritual life" (paragraph 3). What are the complications, and what produces them?

2. Glaser casts her first paragraph in the present tense. What advantage does this focus give her?

3. Think of an intermarriage with which you are acquainted—in your family or among your friends. Then, jot down a list of "scenes" that represent it—for example, religious services, holidays, weddings, funerals. Would you label the intermarriage "complicated"?

4. In an essay of 750 to 1,000 words, write your own "Scenes from an Intermarriage" through which you reveal its ease, or strains, or both.

Andrew Sullivan

Andrew Sullivan, born in England in 1963, has lived in the United States since 1984. A gay Roman Catholic—in 2007, he married a man in Massachusetts—Sullivan is the author of several books, chiefly about American politics. Although he supports gay marriage and he opposes capital punishment (positions usually taken by liberals), Sullivan describes himself as a political conservative, especially on fiscal matters.

Why the M Word Matters to Me

As a child, I had no idea what homosexuality was. I grew up in a traditional home—Catholic, conservative, middle class. Life was relatively simple: education, work, family. I was raised to aim high in life, even though my parents hadn't gone to college. But one thing was instilled in me. What mattered was not how far you went in life, how much money you earned, how big a name you made for yourself. What really mattered was family and the love you had for one another. The most important day of your life was not graduation from college or your first day at work or a raise or even your first house. The most important day of your life was when you got married. It was on that day that all your friends and all your family got together to celebrate the most important thing in life: your happiness—your ability to make a new home, to form a new but connected family, to find love that put everything else into perspective.

But as I grew older, I found that this was somehow not available to me. I didn't feel the things for girls that my peers did. All the emotions and social rituals and bonding of teenage heterosexual life eluded me. I didn't know why. No one explained it. My emotional bonds to other boys were one-sided; each time I felt myself falling in love, they sensed it, pushed it away. I didn't and couldn't blame them. I got along fine with my buds in a nonemotional context, but something was awry, something not right. I came to know almost instinctively that I would never be a part of my family the way my siblings might one day be. The love I had inside me was unmentionable, anathema. I remember writing in my teenage journal one day, "I'm a professional human being. But what do I do in my private life?"

I never discussed my real life. I couldn't date girls and so immersed myself in schoolwork, the debate team, school plays, anything to give me an excuse not to confront reality. When I looked toward the years ahead, I couldn't see a future. There was just a void. Was I going to be alone my whole life? Would I ever have a most important day in my life? It seemed impossible, a negation, an undoing. To be a full part of my family, I had to somehow not be me. So, like many other gay teens, I withdrew, became neurotic, depressed, at times close to suicidal. I shut myself in my room with my books night after night while my peers developed the skills needed to form real relationships and loves. In wounded pride, I even voiced a rejection of family and marriage. It was the only way I could explain my isolation.

It took years for me to realize that I was gay, years more to tell others and more time yet to form any kind of stable emotional bond with another man. Because my sexuality had emerged in solitude—and without any link to the idea of an actual relationship—it was hard later to reconnect sex to love and self-esteem. It still is. But I persevered, each relationship slowly growing longer than the last, learning in my 20s and 30s what my straight friends had found out in their teens. But even then my parents and friends never asked the question they would have asked automatically if I were straight: So, when are you going to get married? When will we be able to celebrate it and affirm it and support it? In fact, no one—no one—has yet asked me that question.

When people talk about gay marriage, they miss the point. This isn't about gay marriage. It's about marriage. It's about family. It's about love. It isn't about religion. It's about civil marriage licenses. Churches can and should have the right to say no to marriage for gays in their congregations, just as Catholics say no to divorce, but divorce is still a civil option. These family values are not options for a happy and stable life. They are necessities. Putting gay relationships in some other category—civil unions, domestic partnerships, whatever—may alleviate real human needs, but by their very euphemism, by their very separateness, they actually build a wall between gay people and their families. They put back the barrier many of us have spent a lifetime trying to erase.

It's too late for me to undo my past. But I want above everything else to remember a young kid out there who may even be reading this now. I want to let him know that he doesn't have to choose between himself and his family anymore. I want him to know that his love has dignity, that he does indeed have a future as a full and equal part of the human race. Only marriage will do that. Only marriage can bring him home.

 Joining the Conversation:
Critical Thinking and Writing

1. Sullivan devotes his first paragraph to a description of the values that his family held when he was a child. To what extent does this picture describe the values you and your family held during your childhood years?

2. In his fifth paragraph, Sullivan says: "This isn't about gay marriage. It's about marriage. It's about family. It's about love." In a discussion in class, one student said that in fact Sullivan seems really to be talking not about marriage but about *weddings*, a celebration of (to quote from Sullivan's first paragraph) "that day that all your friends and all your family got together to celebrate the most important thing in your life: your happiness. . . ." How valid is the student's criticism?

Laurie Essig and Lynn Owens

Laurie Essig teaches sociology at Middlebury College. Essig, a graduate of Franklin and Marshall College, holds a Ph.D. from Columbia. She is the author of Queer in Russia: A Story of Sex, Self, and the Other *(1999) and of* American Plastic: Boob Jobs, Credit Cards, and the Spirit of Our Time *(2010).*

Lynn Owens, also a teacher of sociology at Middlebury College, is the author of a popular book, Lost in the Supermarket: An Indie Rock Cookbook *(2008), and of a scholarly book,* Cracking Under Pressure: Narrating Decline in the Amsterdam Squatters' Movement *(2009). Two of his several current projects are a cultural history of Halloween and the tactics of activists.*

...at If Marriage Is Bad for Us?

Sometimes a belief becomes so strong that suggesting it might be wrong is nearly impossible. One such belief is that marriage is good for us. Last April, when Vermont finally recognized same-sex marriage, many of our fellow Vermonters rushed to celebrate. Neither one of us did. They were puzzled by our lack of enthusiasm. "You have to support gay marriage," a straight colleague angrily shouted at one of us. But why do we have to celebrate any marriage? Unlike conservatives who attack gay marriage, it's not the gay part we object to; it's the marriage part. What does it even mean? Over the past 15 years, Americans have been fighting about that, and therefore about what it means to be a citizen and an adult.

In 1996, as Congress turned "welfare" into "workfare," it proclaimed that "marriage is the foundation of a successful society." A few years ago, President George W. Bush created the Healthy Marriage Initiative to promote marriage as a solution to poverty and for the well-being of children. Currently the government spends about $150-million annually to promote marriage among our country's poorest citizens. In *The Audacity of Hope*, President Obama claims that supporting marriage among low-income couples should be "something everyone can agree upon." As one of his earliest acts as president, with two wars and an economic meltdown on his hands, Obama took time to approve taking $5-million out of antipoverty funds to promote marriage for young people.

The belief that marriage is good for us also explains why gay and lesbian activists have been fighting so hard for same-sex marriage. According to Freedom to Marry, the national organization behind much of the gay-marriage movement, marriage is "the most powerful expression we have for the affirmation of love and commitment, a source of social recognition . . . that hold(s) two people together through life's ups and downs." Marriage is also the source of more than a thousand federal rights and responsibilities, not to mention cheaper gym memberships, social approval, and all those gifts that arrive on your wedding day.

Where there are policy disputes, you can expect social scientists to weigh in with their supposedly objective data. One noteworthy example is Mark Regnerus's recent op-ed essay in *The Washington Post* urging young people to get married. Regnerus argues that "today, as ever, marriage wisely entered into remains good for the economy and the community, good for one's personal well-being, good for wealth creation, and, yes, good for the environment, too."

Marriage promises to save the poor, empower gays and lesbians, and socialize the young. In support of those promises, the romantics wax about love and happiness, the pragmatics tout rights and security, and the experts crunch the numbers. But as critical sociologists, we find ourselves

5

Laurie Essig and Lynn Owens: "What If Marriage Is Bad For Us?" © 2009 from *The Chronicle of Higher Education*, October 9, 2009. Reprinted by permission of the publisher.

agreeing most strongly with Marx—Groucho—who quipped, "Marriage is a wonderful institution, but who wants to live in an institution?"

Institutions serve two purposes, practical and ideological. We will do well to keep both in mind in evaluating the benefits that marriage supposedly offers.

Marriage makes you rich. Advocates claim that marriage increases wealth. That makes sense; if the key to a successful marriage is hard work, you should at least get paid for it. It's true that married people are wealthier than unmarried people, but it's not marriage that makes you rich. Marriage is not randomly distributed across the population. People who get married (and stay married) tend to be wealthier and whiter than people who do not. For instance, 95 percent of white women will marry at some point in their lifetime, while only 43 percent of black women will.

To say marriage creates wealth is to confuse correlation with causation. If there is more wealth in Manhattan than in Brooklyn, that does not mean that moving to Manhattan will make you wealthier. In fact, moving—and marrying—may make you poorer, given the high start-up costs. A move requires first and last months' rent, a moving van, and lots of bubble wrap. A marriage often demands a wedding, and with the average cost of weddings at $30,000, getting married is going to cost you.

Nor will moving into marriage necessarily increase your earnings or earning potential. If you're poor and have little education, saying "I do" won't get you off welfare or make minimum wage any less a dead end. If you already have means, marriage might help. Be careful, though, because even when marriage does produce wealth, divorce often destroys it. If you are getting married for the economic benefits, better make sure it's forever.

Marriage is traditional. As Frank Sinatra once crooned: "Love and marriage/go together like a horse and carriage/. . . It's an institute you can't disparage/ Ask the local gentry and they will say it's elementary." But there is nothing elementary about the form of marriage as we practice it today. Despite the claims of sociologists, politicians, and marriage advocates on all sides, marriage has changed over time and exists differently in different cultures. 10

Marriage as we imagine it today developed during the late 1800s, when it became "for love" and "companionate." Until that point, one married for material and social reasons, not romance. Women required marriage for survival; men did not. That left men free to behave as they wished: Prostitutes and buggery were part of many a married man's sexual repertoire. But then the Victorians (with their sexual prudishness) and first-wave feminists (with their sense that what's good for the goose is good for the gander) insisted that antiprostitution and antisodomy laws be enacted, and that married men confine their sexual impulses to the conjugal bed. The result was enforced lifelong sexual monogamy for both parties, at least in theory.

That might have seemed reasonable in 1900, when the average marriage lasted about 11 years, a consequence of high death rates. But these days, when a marriage can drag on for half a century, it can be a lot of work. Laura Kipnis calls marriage a "domestic gulag," a forced-labor camp where the inmates have to spend all their time outside of work working on their marriage.

And if the dyadic couple locked in lifelong monogamy was a radical new form, so was the family structure it spawned. The nuclear family is primarily a mutant product of the nuclear age. Before World War II, most Americans lived among extended family. The definition of family was not the couple and their offspring, but brothers, sisters, aunts, uncles, and grandparents as well. With the creation of suburbs for the middle classes, large numbers of white Americans began participating in the radical family formation of two married parents plus children in a detached house separated from extended family.

Although the nuclear family is idealized as "natural" and "normal" by our culture (*Leave It to Beaver*) and our government ("family values"), it has always been both a shockingly new way of living and a minority lifestyle. Even at its height, in the early 1970s, only about 40 percent of American families lived that way. Today that number is about 23 percent, including stepfamilies. The nuclear family is not only revolutionary; it is a revolution that has failed for most of us.

Marriage makes you healthy. According to the Centers for Disease   15
Control and Prevention, married people have better health than those who are not married. A closer look at the data, however, reveals that married and never-married Americans are similar; it's the divorced who seem to suffer. The lesson might be to never divorce, but an even more obvious lesson to be drawn from the research might be to never marry.

Naomi Gerstel and Natalia Sarkisian's research shows that married couples are more isolated than their single counterparts. That is not a function just of their having children. Even empty-nesters and couples without children tent to have weak friendship networks. Marriage results in fewer rather than more social ties because it promises complete fulfillment through the claims of romance. We are instructed by movies, pop songs, state policy, and sociology to get married because "love is all you need." But actually we humans need more. We need both a sense of connection to larger networks—to community, to place—and a sense of purpose that is beyond our primary sexual relationships.

For those reasons, marriage has been self-destructing as a social form. The marriage rate in the United States is at an all-time low. In 1960 about two-thirds of adult Americans were married. Today only slightly more than half of Americans live in wedded bliss. Actually, even the bliss is declining, with fewer married Americans describing their unions as "very happy."

Maybe it's the decline in happiness that has caused an increasing number of Americans to say "I don't," despite Hollywood's presenting us with happy ending after happy ending and a government bent on distributing civil rights on the basis of marital status. Apparently no amount of propaganda or coercion can force humans to participate in a family form so out of sync with what we actually need.

With all that marriage supporters promise—wealth, health, stability, happiness, sustainability—our country finds itself confronted with a paradox: Those who would appear to gain the most from marriage are the same ones who prove most resistant to its charms. Study after study has found that it is the poor in the United States who are least likely to wed. The people who get married are the same ones who already benefit most from all our social institutions: the "haves." They benefit even more when they convince everyone that the benefits are evenly distributed.

Too often we are presented with the false choice between a lifelong, loving marriage and a lonely, unmarried life. But those are far from the only options. We should consider the way people actually live: serial monogamy, polyamory, even polygamy.

Instead of "blaming the victims" for failing to adopt the formative lifestyles of the white and middle class, we should consider that those avoiding marriage might know exactly what they are doing. Marriage is not necessarily good for all of us, and it might even be bad for most of us. When there is broad, seemingly unanimous support for an institution, and when the institution is propped up by such disparate ideas as love, civil rights, and wealth creation, we should wonder why so many different players seem to agree so strongly. Perhaps it's because they are supporting not just marriage but also the status quo.

We can dress up marriage in as many beautiful white wedding gowns as we like, but the fundamental fact remains: Marriage is a structure of rights and privileges for those who least need them and a culture of prestige for those who already have the highest levels of racial, economic, and educational capital.

So when you hear activists and advocates—gay, Christian, and otherwise—pushing to increase not only marriage rights but also marriage rates, remember these grouchy words of Marx: "Politics is the art of looking for trouble, finding it everywhere, diagnosing it incorrectly, and applying the wrong remedies." Marriage is trouble. Americans haven't failed at marriage. Marriage has failed us.

Joining the Conversation: Critical Thinking and Writing

1. If you think that you will probably marry, do you also think you want a large wedding? (If you are or were married, did you have a large wedding?) Were you surprised to learn, in paragraph 8, that the average cost of a wedding is $30,000? Do you think that spending this sort of money is well worth it? Why or why not?

2. As the authors point out in paragraph 11, the idea that "married men confine their sexual impulses to the conjugal bed" is largely a 19th-century idea. (Yes, the Hebrew Bible says, "Thou shalt not commit adultery," but the Hebrews—including Abraham, Jacob, David, and, of course, Solomon with his thousand wives—practiced polygamy. A man thus might be married but not confined to a single mate.) In your view, is sexual fidelity essential to a successful marriage? Please explain.

3. In paragraph 16, the authors report that "married couples are more isolated than their single counterparts." Do your own observations confirm this claim? If so, does the fact (if it is a fact) cause you to think that maybe marriage isn't so great an institution? Please explain.

4. In paragraph 20, the authors remind us of some alternatives to traditional marriage: "serial monogamy, polyamory, even polygamy." Two questions: What is "polyamory," and what objections can be raised against these three kinds of behavior? Another question: What, if anything, can be said on their behalf?

5. Of the various arguments that the authors advance, which one do you consider the strongest? Why?

6. It is customary for the bride's family to pay for the wedding, and it is also customary for the bride's father to hand the bride over to the groom, as though she is an object being unloaded. Should we be distressed by these conventions?

Sam Schulman

Sam Schulman writes on politics and culture for Commentary, *the* Wall Street Journal, *and other publications. We reprint an essay that appeared in the* Wall Street Journal *in 2006.*

Letting Go

In the midst of my 1950s childhood, the playwright Robert Paul Smith published a quirky little book that became a best seller called *Where Did You Go? Out. What Did You Do? Nothing*. It was a laconic evocation of the independent lives that Depression children contrived for themselves in the era before postwar affluence. And its subtitle—"How it was when you were a kid, and how things have deteriorated since"—condemned, by contrast, the coddled, structured, supervised and superabundant childhoods of my own generation.

Though *Where Did You Go?* was written for our parents, every child I knew made sure to get hold of a copy. A year after its publication, we children were the target of a sequel: *How to Do Nothing with Nobody All Alone by Yourself*. It featured seductively grim drawings of spare little toys and games you could make out of wooden matchsticks, empty spools of thread, tin cans and rubber bands. I, for one, went right to work. Trying to carve a boat out of a wine cork, I cut my thumb to the bone with my Cub Scout pocketknife. My quest for the simple life of an earlier time ended, sitting with my disgusted father, in a Chicago hospital emergency room.

But any envy that we children of the '50s felt toward the sparse childhood of our grandparents faded quickly. Now we have children of our own, and we're determined that they should never be alone, should never go out and must never do nothing. Despite all the opportunities for independence that our way of life should give them—with both parents working and huge increases in disposable income—the fact is that our children are part of the most closely watched generation in history.

The watching begins in primary school. The days are no more when knots of children wandered erratically to their schoolhouse or back home. They step out of sliding minivan doors in the morning and are quickly whisked away the moment the bell rings, driven in quick succession to gymnastics, soccer, karate or violin lessons.

And the lazy days of summer are over, too. Not only will few kids   5
be playing out on the street when the weather warms up, but the ones who go away to summer camp will be in constant contact with their parents, sending daily emails with pictures and reporting on each of their activities.

As kids grow older and begin to take an interest in something more than kickball, it turns out that even romance isn't off-limits. Today's parents don't want to be the strict, distant types of yesteryear, handing down judgments that may cause moments of unpleasantness. They want to be "friends" who hear about—and show sympathy for—the travails of dating and "relationships." As social commentator Leonard Steinhorn boasts in a recent book on the baby boomers: "Candor and openness—not rigidity and distance—have become the norms in American families today."

The parental connection does not wither away after high-school graduation. Cell phones keep college students tethered to their parents—parents who might have been sent off to college, like my freshman roommate in 1967, with 12 stamped, preaddressed envelopes in which to insert a weekly letter home. Email and text-messages now allow for minute-by-minute updates. One recent study by a college revealed that its freshmen were in touch with their parents by cell phone as many as 15 times a day.

Parental hovering has not simply produced a large number of inane conversations—"I'm on my way to class, I'm walking into the building"—it has destroyed the private lives of children. Kids no longer have the privilege of making their own worlds and participating in a separate culture. This kind of childhood was celebrated not only by Robert Paul Smith but by Peter and Iona Opie in *Lore and Language of Schoolchildren* (1959). The Opies discovered that teasing games, hide-and seek and tag, have been around at least since the time of Chaucer.

Another version of childhood as a separate realm is visible in Booth Tarkington's Penrod books, which were published in 1914 and 1916 and remained best sellers until midcentury. The American childhood that Tarkington's children experienced was beset by grown-ups, but they wanted to impose adult responsibilities on the young ones, not supervise their childhood adventures. Penrod's traumas came from haircuts, dancing lessons, school arithmetic and mixed-sex parties where he was expected to act like "a little gentleman." His parents—a stern father and a sentimental mother—knew that there were certain things he needed to be taught but generally let Penrod look after his own childhood.

So why can't parents today leave their children alone for five minutes? 10
There are probably a number of reasons. Some no doubt worry that the
coarse surrounding culture is a constant threat—and indeed it is. But it is
much more likely to intrude on the computer or on television—two aspects
of life often unmonitored by parents—than at a playground or summer
camp. Another reason may be an exaggerated sense of our own importance
in producing the persons our children are destined to become.

A recent *Wall Street Journal* story about the growing reluctance of
affluent families to send their children to boarding schools illustrates the
point. One couple, who chose not to send their daughter to a famous New
England prep school, rationalized their decision like this: "We just want
to spend a couple of more years imparting our values to our daughter."

Yes, parents impart values. But values come from other useful
sources, too. Hovering parents undermine the influence not only of other
institutions like schools and churches but of peers. Being picked for a
sports team, facing the first day at school or at a job, learning to handle
the ups and downs of courtship, enduring the apprenticeship of almost
any career—these are not only signs that our children are becoming independent adults, but acts of initiation that take them out of the family
embrace and into the wider world.

The seemingly obvious notion that kids need to be left alone sometimes if they are to grow up has been so lost that more than one American
university has been forced to station security guards outside freshmen orientation sessions to keep anxious parents out. There are no reports, encour-
agingly, of freshmen on the other side trying to pull their parents in.

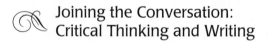

Joining the Conversation: Critical Thinking and Writing

1. Comment on the first three paragraphs of Schulman's essay. Do you think
   that it opens effectively? Why or why not?

2. Schulman claims that "parental hovering" has "destroyed the private lives of
   children." Does he provide convincing evidence to support this claim?

3. Do you think Schulman is describing such a small section of the population—
   folks who read the *Wall Street Journal* and whose kids take violin and karate
   lessons—that his essay has nothing to say to most of America? Explain your
   answer.

4. If you agree with Schulman, write an essay of one to two pages in which
   you develop and provide further support for his argument. If you disagree,
   write an essay in which you state and give evidence for your argument
   against him.

5. One student who read Schulman's essay criticized it, saying that "he doesn't
   tell us what should be done to make things better." Another student replied,
   "But that's the point of the essay." What is your view?

Anonymous

The anonymous author of this essay has revealed only that he was forty years old when he wrote it, is married, and is the father of three children. The essay originally appeared in the New Republic, *a magazine that was, at the time (1974), regarded as liberal.*

Confessions of an Erstwhile Child

Some years ago I attempted to introduce a class of Upward Bound students to political theory via More's *Utopia*. It was a mistake: I taught precious little theory and earned More a class full of undying enemies on account of two of his ideas. The first, that all members of a Utopian family were subject to the lifelong authority of its eldest male. The second, the Utopian provision that should a child wish to follow a profession different from that of his family, he could be transferred by adoption to a family that practiced the desired trade. My students were not impressed with my claim that the one provision softened the other and made for a fair compromise—for what causes most of our quarrels with our parents but our choice of life-patterns, of occupation? In objecting to the first provision my students were picturing themselves as children, subject to an unyielding authority. But on the second provision they surprised me by taking the parents' role and arguing that this form of ad lib adoption denied them a fundamental right of ownership over their children. It occurred to me that these reactions were two parts of the same pathology: having suffered the discipline of unreasonable parents, one has earned the right to be unreasonable in turn to one's children. The phenomenon has well-known parallels, such as frantic martinets who have risen from the ranks. Having served time as property, my Upward Bound students wanted theirs back as proprietors. I shuddered. It hardly takes an advanced course in Freudian psychology to realize that the perpetuation, generation after generation, of psychic lesions must go right to this source, the philosophically dubious notion that children are the property of their biological parents, compounded with the unphilosophic certitude so many parents harbor, that their children must serve an apprenticeship as like their own as they can manage.

The idea of the child as property has always bothered me, for personal reasons I shall outline. I lack the feeling that I own my children and I have always scoffed at the idea that what they are and do is a continuation or a rejection of my being. I like them, I sympathize with them, I acknowledge the obligation to support them for a term of years—but I am not so fond or

---

Anonymous: "Confessions of an Erstwhile Child" from *The New Republic*, June 15, 1974. Reprinted by permission.

foolish as to regard a biological tie as a lien on their loyalty or respect, nor to imagine that I am equipped with preternatural powers of guidance as to their success and happiness. Beyond inculcating some of the obvious social protocols required in civilized life, who am I to pronounce on what makes for a happy or successful life? How many of us can say that we have successfully managed our own lives? Can we do better with our children? I am unimpressed, to say no more, with parents who have no great track record, presuming to oracular powers in regard to their children's lives.

The current debate over the Equal Rights Amendment frequently turns to custody questions. Opponents of ERA have made the horrifying discovery that ERA will spell the end of the mother's presumed rights of custody in divorce or separation cases, and that fathers may begin custody rights. Indeed a few odd cases have been so settled recently in anticipation of the ratification of ERA. If ratified, ERA would be an extremely blunt instrument for calling the whole idea of custody into question, but I for one will applaud anything that serves to begin debate. As important as equal rights between adults may be, I think that the rights of children are a far more serious and unattended need. To me, custody by natural parents, far from being a presumed right only re-examined in case of collapsing marriages, should be viewed as a privilege.

At this point I have to explain why I can so calmly contemplate the denial of so-called parental rights.

I am the only child of two harsh and combative personalities who married, seemingly, in order to have a sparring partner always at hand. My parents have had no other consistent or lasting aim in life but to win out over each other in a contest of wills. They still live, vigorous and angry septuagenarians, their ferocity little blunted by age or human respect. My earliest memories—almost my sole memories—are of unending combat, in which I was sometimes an appalled spectator, more often a hopeless negotiator in a war of no quarter, and most often a bystander accused of covert belligerency on behalf of one side or the other, and frequently of both! I grew up with two supposed adults who were absorbed in their hatreds and recriminations to the exclusion of almost all other reality. Not only did I pass by almost unnoticed in their struggle, the Depression and World War II passed them by equally unnoticed. I figured mainly as a practice target for sarcasm and invective, and occasionally as the ultimate culprit responsible for their unhappiness. ("If it weren't for you," my mother would sometimes say, "I could leave that SOB," a remark belied by her refusal to leave the SOB during these 20 long years since I left their "shelter.")

The reader may ask, "How did you survive if your parents' house was all that bad?" I have three answers. First, I survived by the moral equivalent of running away to sea or the circus, i.e., by burying myself in books and study, especially in the history of faraway and (I thought) more idealistic times than our own, and by consciously shaping my life and tastes to be as different as possible from those of my parents (this was a reproach to them, they knew, and it formed the basis of a whole secondary area of conflict and misunderstanding). Second, I survived because statistically most people "survive" horrible families, but survival can be a qualified term, as it is in my case by a permanently impaired digestive system and an unnatural sensitivity to raised voices. And third, though I found solace in schooling and the rationality, cooperation and basic fairness in teachers that I missed in my parents, I must now question whether it is healthy for a child to count so heavily on schooling for the love and approval that he deserves from his home and family. Even if schooling can do this well, in later life it means that one is loyal and affectionate toward schooling, not toward parents, who may in some sense need affection even if they don't "deserve" it. I am not unaware that however fair and rational I may be in reaction to my parents' counterexamples, I am a very cold-hearted man. I might have done better transferred to a new family, not just by receiving love, but through learning to give it—a lack I mourn as much or more than my failure to receive.

It is little wonder then that I have an acquired immunity to the notion that parental custody is by and large a preferable thing. In my case, almost anything else would have been preferable, including even a rather callously run orphanage—anything for a little peace and quiet. Some people are simply unfit, under any conditions, to be parents, even if, indeed especially if, they maintain the charade of a viable marriage. My parents had no moral right to custody of children, and I cannot believe that my experience is unique or particularly isolated. There are all too many such marriages, in which some form of horror, congenial enough to adults too sick or crazed to recognize it, works its daily ruination on children. Surely thousands of children conclude at age 10 or 11, as I did, that marriage is simply an institution in which people are free to be as beastly as they have a mind to, which may lead either to a rejection of marriage or to a decision to reduplicate a sick marriage a second time, with another generation of victims. It is time to consider the rights of the victims.

How to implement a nascent theory of justice for children is difficult to say. One cannot imagine taking the word of a five-year-old against his parents, but what about a ten- or twelve-year-old? At *some* point, children should have the right to escape the dominance of impossible parents. The matter used to be easier than it has been since World War I. The time-honored solution—for boys—of running away from home has been made infeasible by economic conditions, fingerprints, social security and minimum wage laws. No apprenticeship system exists any more, much less its upper-class medieval version—with required exchange of boys at puberty among noble families to serve as pages and so forth. The adoption system contemplated in More's *Utopia* is a half-remembered echo of a medieval life, in which society, wiser than its theory, decreed a general exchange of children at or just before puberty, whether through apprenticeship or page-service, or more informal arrangements, like going to a university at 14 or running away with troubadors or gypsies.

Exchanging children is a wisely conceived safety valve against a too traumatic involvement between the biological parent and the child. Children need an alternative to living all their formative life in the same biological unit. They should have the right to petition for release from some sorts of families, to join other families, or to engage in other sorts of relationships that may provide equivalent service but may not be organized as a family. The nuclear family, after all, is not such an old or proven vehicle. Phillippe Aries' book, *Centuries of Childhood*, made the important point that the idea of helpless childhood is itself a notion of recent origin, that grew up simultaneously in the 16th and 17th centuries with the small and tight-knit nuclear family, sealed off from the world by another recent invention, "privacy." The older *extended* family (which is the kind More knew about) was probably more authoritarian on paper but much less productive of dependency in actual operation. There ought to be more than one way a youngster can enter adult society with more than half of his sanity left. At least no one should be forced to remain in a no-win game against a couple of crazy parents for 15–18 years. At 10 or 12, children in really messy situations should have the legal right to petition for removal from impossible families, and those rights should be reasonably easy to exercise. (This goes on de facto among the poor, of course, but it is not legal, and usually carries both stigma and danger.) The minimum wage laws should be modified to exempt such persons, especially if they wish to continue their education, working perhaps for public agencies, if they have no other means of support. If their parents can support them, then the equivalent of child support should be charged them to maintain their children, not in luxury, but adequately. Adoption of older children should be facilitated by easing of legal procedures (designed mainly to govern the adoption of *infants*) plus tax advantages for those willing to adopt older children on grounds of goodwill. Indeed children wishing to escape impossible family situations should be allowed a fair degree of initiative in finding and negotiating with possible future families.

Obviously the risk of rackets would be very high unless the exact terms of such provisions were framed very carefully, but the possibility of rackets is less frightening to anyone who thinks about it for long than the dangers of the present situation, which are evident and unrelieved by any signs of improvement. In barely a century this country has changed from a relatively loose society in which Huckleberry Finns were not uncommon, to a society of tense, airless nuclear families in which unhealthy and neurotic tendencies, once spawned in a family, tend to repeat themselves at a magnifying and accelerating rate. We may soon gain the distinction of being the only nation on earth to need not just medicare but "psychicare." We have invested far too heavily in the unproved "equity" called the nuclear family; that stock is about to crash and we ought to begin finding escape options. In colonial days many New England colonies passed laws imposing fines or extra taxes on parents who kept their children under their own roofs after age 15 or 16, on the sensible notion that a person of that age ought to be out and doing on his own, whether going to Yale or apprenticing in a foundry. Even without the benefit of Freud, the colonial fathers had a good sense of what was wrong with a closely bound and centripetal family structure—it concentrates craziness like compound interest, and so they hit it with monetary penalties, a proper Protestant response, intolerant at once of both mystery and excuses. But this was the last gasp of a medieval and fundamentally Catholic idea that children, God help them, while they may be the children of *these* particular parents biologically, spiritually are the children of God, and more appositely are the children of the entire community, for which the entire community takes responsibility. The unguessed secret of the middle ages was not that monasteries relieved parents of unwanted children; more frequently, they relieved children of unwanted parents!

 ## Joining the Conversation: Critical Thinking and Writing

1. What is the author's thesis? (Quote the thesis sentence.) Apart from his own experience, what evidence or other means does he offer to persuade you to accept his thesis?

2. What part does the *tone* of his article play in persuading you to agree with him or in alienating you? Does his tone perhaps strike you as vigorous or belligerent, as ironic or bitter, as reasonable or hysterical?

3. The author admits (paragraph 6) that he is "a very cold-hearted man." Do you remember your initial reaction to that sentence? What was it? Overall, does the author strengthen or jeopardize his argument by this admission? Explain.

4. If you did not find the article persuasive, did you find it interesting? Can you explain why?

Mary Eberstadt

Mary Eberstadt is a research fellow at the Hoover Institution and consulting editor to Policy Review, *the journal from which we reprint the following article. She is the author of numerous essays and two books on American cultural issues, and she is the editor of a book entitled* Why I Turned Right: Leading Baby Boom Conservatives Chronicle Their Political Journeys *(2007).*

Eminem Is Right

If there is one subject on which the parents of America passionately agree, it is that contemporary adolescent popular music, especially the subgenres of heavy metal and hip-hop/rap, is uniquely degraded—and degrading—by the standards of previous generations. At first blush this

Mary Eberstadt: "Eminem is Right" from *Policy Review*, December 2004 & January 2005. Reprinted by permission of Policy Review.

seems slightly ironic. After all, most of today's baby-boom parents were themselves molded by rock and roll, bumping and grinding their way through adolescence and adulthood with legendary abandon. Even so, the parents are correct: Much of today's music *is* darker and coarser than yesterday's rock. Misogyny, violence, suicide, sexual exploitation, child abuse—these and other themes, formerly rare and illicit, are now as common as the surfboards, drive-ins, and sock hops of yesteryear.

In a nutshell, the ongoing adult preoccupation with current music goes something like this: *What is the overall influence of this deafening, foul, and often vicious-sounding stuff on children and teenagers?* This is a genuinely important question, and serious studies and articles, some concerned particularly with current music's possible link to violence, have lately been devoted to it. In 2000, the American Academy of Pediatrics, the American Medical Association, the American Psychological Association, and the American Academy of Child & Adolescent Psychiatry all weighed in against contemporary lyrics and other forms of violent entertainment before Congress with a first-ever "Joint Statement on the Impact of Entertainment Violence on Children."

Nonetheless, this is not my focus here. Instead, I would like to turn that logic about influence upside down and ask this question: *What is it about today's music, violent and disgusting though it may be, that resonates with so many American kids?*

As the reader can see, this is a very different way of inquiring about the relationship between today's teenagers and their music. The first question asks what the music *does* to adolescents; the second asks what it *tells* us about them. To answer that second question is necessarily to enter the roiling emotional waters in which that music is created and consumed—in other words, actually to listen to some of it and read the lyrics.

As it turns out, such an exercise yields a fascinating and little understood fact about today's adolescent scene. If yesterday's rock was the music of abandon, today's is that of abandon*ment*. The odd truth about contemporary teenage music—the characteristic that most separates it from what has gone before—is its compulsive insistence on the damage wrought by broken homes, family dysfunction, checked-out parents, and (especially) absent fathers. Papa Roach, Everclear, Blink-182, Good Charlotte, Eddie Vedder and Pearl Jam, Kurt Cobain and Nirvana, Tupac Shakur, Snoop Doggy Dogg, Eminem—these and other singers and bands, all of them award-winning top-40 performers who either are or were among the most popular icons in America, have their own generational answer to what ails the modern teenager. Surprising though it may be to some, that answer is: dysfunctional childhood. Moreover, and just as interesting, many bands and singers explicitly link the most deplored themes in music today—suicide, misogyny, and drugs—with that lack of a quasi-normal, intact-home personal past.

To put this perhaps unexpected point more broadly, during the same years in which progressive-minded and politically correct adults have been excoriating Ozzie and Harriet as an artifact of 1950s-style oppression, many millions of American teenagers have enshrined a new generation of music idols whose shared generational signature in song after song is to rage about what *not* having had a nuclear family has done to them. This is quite a fascinating puzzle of the times. The self-perceived emotional damage scrawled large across contemporary music may not be statistically quantifiable, but it is nonetheless among the most striking of all the unanticipated consequences of our home-alone world.

Demigods of Dysfunction

To begin with music particularly popular among white teenage boys, one best-selling example of broken-home angst is that of the "nu-metal" band known as Papa Roach and led by singer/songwriter "Coby Dick" Shaddix (dubbed by one reviewer the "prince of dysfunction"). Three members of that group, Coby Dick included, are self-identified children of divorce. In 2000, as critics noted at the time, their album *Infest* explored the themes of broken homes and child and teenage rage. The result was stunning commercial success: *Infest* sold more than 3 million copies. MTV.com explained why: "The pained, confessional songs struck a nerve with disenfranchised listeners who were tired of the waves of directionless aggression spewing from the mouths of other rap-rockers. They found kinship in Papa Roach songs like 'Broken Home' and 'Last Resort.'"

In fact, even their songs about other subjects hark back to that same primal disruption. One particularly violent offering called "Revenge," about a girl hurting herself and being abused by her boyfriend, reflects on "destruction of the family design." Of all the songs on the album, however, it is the singularly direct "Broken Home" that hit its fans the hardest, which summarizes the sad domestic story it elaborates in a pair of lines: *"I know my mother loves me/ But does my father even care."*

Another band that climbed to the top of the charts recently is Everclear, led by singer Art Alexakis (also a child of divorce, as he has explained to interviewers). Like Papa Roach, Everclear/Alexakis explores the fallout of parental breakup not from the perspective of newly liberated adults, but from that of the child left behind who feels abandoned and betrayed. Several of Everclear's songs map this emotional ground in detail—from not wanting to meet mother's "new friends," to wondering how the father who walked out can sleep at night, to dreaming of that father coming back. In the song "Father of Mine," the narrator implores, *"take me back to the day / when I was still your golden boy."* Another song, "Sick and Tired," explicitly links the anger-depression-suicide teen matrix to broken homes (as indeed do numerous other contemporary groups): *"I blame my family / their damage is living in me."*

Everclear's single best-known song, a top-40 hit in 2000 that ruled the airwaves for months, is a family breakup ballad ironically titled "Wonderful"—to some fans, the best rock song about divorce ever written. Though the catchy melody cannot be captured here, the childlike simplicity of the words brings the message home loudly enough. Among them: *"I want the things that I had before / Like a Star Wars poster on my bedroom door."*

Another group successfully working this tough emotional turf is chart-topping and multiple award-winning Blink-182, which grew out of the skateboard and snowboard scene to become one of the most popular bands in the country. As with Papa Roach and Everclear, the group's intersest in the family breakdown theme is partly autobiographical: At least two members of the band say that their personal experiences as children of divorce have informed their lyrics. Blink-182's top-40 hit in 2001, "Stay Together for the Kids," is perhaps their best-known song (though not the only one) about broken homes. *"What stupid poem could fix this home,"* the narrator wonders, adding, *"I'd read it every day."*

Reflecting on the particular passion with which that song was embraced by fans, Blink-182's Tom DeLonge told an interviewer, "We get e-mails about 'Stay Together,' kid after kid after kid saying, 'I know exactly what you're talking about! That song is about my life!' And you know what? That sucks. You look at statistics that 50 percent of parents get divorced, and you're going to get a pretty large group of kids who are pissed off and who don't agree with what their parents have done."[1] Similarly, singer/bassist Mark Hoppus remarked to another interviewer curious about the band's emotional resonance, "Divorce is such a normal thing today and hardly anybody ever thinks how the kids feel about it or how they are taking it, but in the U.S. about half of all the kids go through it. They witness how their parents drift apart and all that."[2]

Then there is the phenomenon known as Pink, whose album *Missundaztood* was one of the top-10 albums of 2002, selling more than 3 million copies. Pink (dubbed by one writer the "anti-Britney") is extremely popular among young girls. Any teenager with a secular CD collection will likely own some of her songs. Pink mines the same troubled emotional territory as Blink-182 and numerous other bands, but even more exclusively: *Missundaztood* revolves entirely around the emotional wreckage and behavioral consequences of Pink's parents breaking up. A review of the album on ABCnews.com noted, "*Missundaztood* is full of painful tales of childhood—divorce, rebellion, disaffection and drugs. It's the stuff that may make parents shake their heads, but causes millions of alienated kids to nod in approval."[3] In Pink's especially mournful (and

10

[1]William Shaw, "Why Are America's Rock Bands So Goddamned Angry?" *Blender* (August 2002).
[2]Gabriella, "Interview with Mark Hoppus of Blink 182," *NY Rock* (August 2001).
[3]"Miss Pink: This Pop Star Speaks the Universal Language of Teenage Rebellion," ABCnews .com (November 6, 2003).

perhaps best-known) song, "Family Portrait," the narrator repeatedly begs her father not to leave, offering even the pitiful childish enticement, *"I won't spill the milk at dinner."*

Yet another popular group generating anthem after anthem about broken homes and their consequences is Washington, D.C.-area-based Good Charlotte, profiled on the cover of *Rolling Stone* in May 2003 as the "Polite Punks." Their first album went gold in 2002. Led by twins Benji and Joel Madden, whose father walked out one Christmas Eve and never returned, Good Charlotte is one band that would not even exist except for the broken homes in which three of its four members (guitarist Billy Martin being the third) grew up. The twins have repeatedly told interviewers it was that trauma that caused them to take up music in the first place, and family breakup figures repeatedly in Good Charlotte's songs and regularly shapes its stage appearances and publicity. (In a particular act of symbolic protest, the twins recently made the legal changeover to their mother's maiden name.)

For Good Charlotte, as for many other newly successful singers and groups, the commercial results of putting personal trauma to music have proved dramatic. Their first and eponymous album sailed up the charts partly on account of a teenage angst ballad ironically entitled "Little Things." The song opens with a dedication to every teenager wrestling with the issues of adolescence—all those "little things," including Mom's stint in a mental institution and Dad's abandonment of the kids (*"We checked his room his things were gone we didn't see him no more"*). Another song on the album is "Thank You Mom." Rather anomalously by the standards of yesterday's rock and punk, but not at all anomalously in the worlds of their descendants today, this song is devoted wholly, and without irony, to the mother who raises children after their father walks out (*"You were my mom, You were my dad / The only thing I ever had was you, It's true"*).

Rolling Stone groused about this band: "What the hell happened to punk?" Now that's a fair point. But whatever happened, the result has literally turned to gold; Good Charlotte's second album, called *The Young and the Hopeless*, sold more than a million copies. Two of its thirteen songs are apotheosized lyrics for an absent father. One is "My Old Man"(*"Last I heard he was at the bar / Doing himself in"*). Another song, "Emotionless", reads much like the related narrations of Everclear, Papa Roach, and many more. The narrator here reminds his missing father of his sons and little girl, wondering, *"How do you sleep at night?"*

Like numerous other groups, Good Charlotte weaves another prevailing theme—teenage suicide—in and out of the larger theme of parental abandonment. Perhaps the best known is the antisuicide clarion "Hold On," in which the singer implores a desperate teenager to remember that although your *"mother's gone and your father hits you . . . we all bleed the same way you do."*

Papa Roach, Everclear, Blink-182, Pink, Good Charlotte: These bands are only some of the top-40 groups now supplying the teenage demand for songs about dysfunctional and adult abandoned homes. In a remarkable 2002 article published in the pop music magazine *Blender* (remarkable because it lays out in detail what is really happening in today's metal/grunge/punk/rock music), an award-winning music journalist named William Shaw listed several other bands, observing, "If there's a theme running through rock at the beginning of the twenty-first century, it's a pervasive sense of hurt. For the past few years, bands like Korn, Linkin Park, Slip-knot, Papa Roach, and Disturbed have been thrusting forward their dark accounts of dysfunctional upbringings. . . . As the clichéd elder might mutter, what's wrong with kids today?" Shaw answers his own question this way: "[T]hese songs reflect the zeitgeist of an age group coping with the highest marital-breakdown rate ever recorded in America. If this era's music says anything, it's that this generation sees itself as uniquely fractured."

As he further observes, so powerful are the emotions roused in fans by these songs that stars and groups themselves are often surprised by it. Shaw relates the following about "Coby Dick" Shaddix of Papa Roach, who wrote the aforementioned song "Broken Home": "He's become used to [fans] coming up and telling him, over and over: 'You know that song "Broken Home?" That's my f—life, right there.' 'It's a bit sad that that's true, you know?' [Shaddix] says." Similarly, singer Chad Kroeger of Nickelback reports of a hit song he wrote on his own abandonment by his father at age two: "You should see some people who I meet after shows. . . . They break down weeping, and they're like, 'I went through the exact same thing!' Sometimes it's terrifying how much they relate to it." That Nickel-back hit song, title "Too Bad," laments that calling *"from time to time / To make sure we're alive"* just isn't enough.

Shaw's ultimate conclusion is an interesting one: that this emphasis in current music on abandoned children represents an unusually loaded form of teenage rebellion. "This is the sound of one generation reproaching another—only this time, it's the scorned, world-weary children telling off their narcissistic, irresponsible parents," he writes. "[Divorce] could be rock's ideal subject matter. These are songs about the chasm in understanding between parents—who routinely don't comprehend the grief their children are feeling—and children who don't know why their parents have torn up their world."

That is a sharp observation. Also worth noting is this historical point: The same themes of adult absence and child abandonment have been infiltrating hard rock even longer than these current bands have been around—probably for as long as family breakup rates began accelerating.

Both musically and emotionally, many of today's groups owe much to the example of the late grunge-rock idol Kurt Cobain, who prefigured today's prominent themes both autobiographically and otherwise. A star whose personal life has legendary status for his fans, Cobain was a self-described happy child until his parents' divorce when he was seven.

The years following were a miserable blur of being shuffled around to grandparents and other caretakers, including a spate of homelessness. The rage and frustration of that experience appear in some of Cobain's famously nihilistic lyrics, including the early song "Sliver," about a boy kicking and screaming upon being dropped off elsewhere by Mom and Dad yet again. The later, markedly cynical "Serve the Servants" reflects on how his traumatic childhood became exploited for personal gain. As with Cobain, so, too, with his friend Pearl Jam singer Eddie Vedder. For more than a decade Pearl Jam has reigned as one of the best-known bands in current rock, and Vedder as one of the most adulated singers; indeed, the band's distinctive sound commands instant recognition among almost every American under the age of 30 with working ears. And Pearl Jam, like the aforementioned groups, has achieved that success, according to Vedder, partly because of the group's frankness about the costs of fractured families and about related themes of alienation and suicide.

In a 1994 interview that focused on the death of Kurt Cobain, Vedder noted with particular insight:

"We [that is, Vedder and Cobain] had similar backgrounds, yeah, things that happened with our families and shit. . . . I think that's something that comes out in what we wrote in our songs, definitely. . . . But what makes it more similar is the way people responded to what we wrote and sang about, the intense identification. . . .

"And I think it was maybe a shock to both of us that so many people were going through the same things. I mean, they understood so completely what we were talking about. . . . Then all of a sudden, there's all these other people who connect with them and you're suddenly the spokesman for a f—generation. Can you imagine that! . . . when our first record came out, I was shocked how many people related to some of that stuff. . . . The kind of letters that got through to me about those songs, some of them were just frightening.

"Think about it, man," he says. "Any generation that would pick Kurt or me as its spokesman—that must be a pretty f—up generation, don't you think?"[4]

Well put. And as it turned out, Cobain and Vedder were only the beginning.

Where's Daddy?

Even less recognized than the white music emphasis on broken homes and the rest of the dysfunctional themes is that the popular black-dominated genres, particularly hip-hop/rap, also reflect themes

---

[4]Allan Jones, interview with Eddie Vedder, *Melody Maker* (May 21, 1994).

of abandonment, anger, and longing for parents. Interestingly enough, this is true of particular figures whose work is among the most adult deplored.

Once again, when it comes to the deploring part, critics have a point. It is hard to imagine a more unwanted role model (from the parental point of view) than the late Tupac Shakur. A best-selling gangsta rapper who died in a shoot-out in 1996 at age 25 (and the object of a 2003 documentary called *Tupac: Resurrection*), Shakur was a kind of polymath of criminality. In the words of a *Denver Post* review of the movie, "In a perfect circle of life imitating art originally meant to imitate life, Shakur in 1991 began a string of crimes that he alternately denied and reveled in. He claimed Oakland police beat him up in a jaywalking arrest, later shot two off-duty cops, assaulted a limo driver and video directors, and was shot five times in a robbery." Further, "At the time of his drive-by murder in Las Vegas, he was out on bail pending appeal of his conviction for sexual abuse of a woman who charged him with sodomy in New York."

Perhaps not surprising, Shakur's songs are riddled with just about every unwholesome trend that a nervous parent can name; above all they contain incitements to crime and violence (particularly against the police) and a misogyny so pronounced that his own mother, executive producer of the movie, let stand in the film a statement of protesting C. DeLores Tucker that "African-American women are tired of being called ho's, bitches and sluts by our children."   25

Yet Shakur—who never knew his father and whose mother, a long time drug addict, was arrested for possession of crack when he was a child—is provocative in another, quite overlooked way: He is the author of some of the saddest lyrics in the hip-hop/gangsta-rap pantheon, which is saying quite a lot. To sophisticated readers familiar with the observations about the breakup of black families recorded several decades ago in the Moynihan Report and elsewhere, the fact that so many young black men grow up without fathers may seem so well established as to defy further comment. But evidently some young black men—Shakur being one—see things differently. In fact, it is hard to find a rapper who does not sooner or later invoke a dead or otherwise long-absent father, typically followed by the hope that he will not become such a man himself. Or there is the flip side of that unintended bow to the nuclear family, which is the hagiography in some rappers' lyrics of their mothers.

In a song called "Papa'z Song Lyrics," Shakur opens with the narrator imagining his father showing up after a long absence, resulting in an expletive-laden tirade. The song then moves to a lacerating description of growing up fatherless that might help to explain why Shakur is an icon not only to many worse-off teenagers from the ghetto, but also to many better-off suburban ones. Here is a boy who *"had to play catch by myself,"* who prays: *"Please send me a pops before puberty."*

The themes woven together in this song—anger, bitterness, longing for family, misogyny as the consequence of a world without fathers—make regular appearances in some other rappers' lyrics, too. One is Snoop Doggy Dogg, perhaps the preeminent rapper of the 1990s. Like Shakur and numerous other rappers, his personal details cause many a parent to shudder; since his childhood he has been arrested for a variety of crimes, including cocaine possession (which resulted in three years of jail service), accomplice to murder (for which he was acquitted), and, most recently, marijuana possession. ("It's not my job to stop kids doing the wrong thing, it's their parents' job," he once explained to a reporter.) In a song called "Mama Raised Me," sung with Soulja Slim, Snoop Doggy Dogg offers this explanation of how troubled pasts come to be: *"It's probably pop's fault how I ended up/Gangbangin'; crack slangin'; not givin' a f—."*

Another black rapper who returned repeatedly to the theme of father abandonment is Jay-Z, also known as Shawn Carter, whose third and breakthrough album, *Hard Knock Life*, sold more than 500,000 copies. He also has a criminal history (he says he had been a cocaine dealer) and a troubled family history, which is reflected in his music. In an interview with MTV.com about his latest album, the reporter explained: "Jay and his father had been estranged until earlier this year. [His father] left the household and his family's life (Jay has an older brother and two sisters) when Shawn was just 12 years old. The separation had served as a major 'block' for Jay over the years. . . . His most vocal tongue lashing toward his dad was on the *Dynasty: Roc la Familia* cut 'Where Have You Been,' where he rapped 'F—you very much/You showed me the worst kind of pain.'"[5]

The fact that child abandonment is also a theme in hip-hop might help explain what otherwise appears as a commercial puzzle—namely, how this particular music moved from the fringes of black entertainment to the very center of the Everyteenager mainstream. There can be no doubt about the current social preeminence of these black- and ghetto-dominated genres in the lives of many better-off adolescents, black *and* white. As Donna Britt wrote in a *Washington Post* column noting hip-hop's ascendancy, "In modern America, where urban based hip-hop culture dominates music, fashion, dance and, increasingly, movies and TV, these kids are trendsetters. What they feel, think and do could soon play out in a middle school—or a Pottery Barn-decorated bedroom—near you."[6]

30

---

[5]Shaheem Reid, with reporting by Sway Galloway, "Jay-Z: What More Can I Say," MTV.com (November 12, 2003).

[6]Donna Britt, "Stats on Teens Don't Tell the Whole Story," *Washington Post* (January 23, 2004).

Eminem: Reasons for Rage

A final example of the rage in contemporary music against irresponsible adults—perhaps the most interesting—is that of genre-crossing bad-boy rap superstar Marshall Mathers or Eminem (sometime stage persona "Slim Shady"). Of all the names guaranteed to send a shudder down the parental spine, his is probably the most effective. In fact, Eminem has single-handedly, if inadvertently, achieved the otherwise ideologically impossible: He is the object of a vehemently disapproving public consensus shared by the National Organization for Women, the Gay & Lesbian Alliance Against Defamation, William J. Bennett, Lynne Cheney, Bill O'Reilly, and a large number of other social conservatives as well as feminists and gay activists. In sum, this rapper—"as harmful to America as any al Qaeda fanatic," in O'Reilly's opinion—unites adult polar opposites as perhaps no other single popular entertainer has done.

There is small need to wonder why. Like other rappers, Eminem mines the shock value and gutter language of rage, casual sex, and violence. Unlike the rest, however, he appears to be a particularly attractive target of opprobrium for two distinct reasons. One, he is white and therefore politically easier to attack. (It is interesting to note that black rappers have not been targeted by name anything like Eminem has.) Perhaps even more important, Eminem is one of the largest commercially visible targets for parental wrath. Wildly popular among teenagers these last several years, he is also enormously successful in commercial terms. Winner of numerous Grammys and other music awards and a perpetual nominee for many more, he has also been critically (albeit reluctantly) acclaimed for his acting performance in the autobiographical 2003 movie *8 Mile*. For all these reasons, he is probably the preeminent rock/rap star of the last several years, one whose singles, albums, and videos routinely top every chart. His 2002 album, *The Eminem Show*, for example, was easily the most successful of the year, selling more than 7.6 million copies.

This remarkable market success, combined with the intense public criticism that his songs have generated, makes the phenomenon of Eminem particularly intriguing. Perhaps more than any other current musical icon, he returns repeatedly to the same themes that fuel other success stories in contemporary music: parental loss, abandonment, abuse, and subsequent child and adolescent anger, dysfunction, and violence (including self-violence). Both in his raunchy lyrics as well as in *8 Mile*, Mathers's own personal story has been parlayed many times over: the absent father, the troubled mother living in a trailer park, the series of unwanted maternal boyfriends, the protective if impotent feelings toward a younger sibling (in the movie, a baby sister; in real life, a younger brother), and the fine line that a poor, ambitious, and unguided young man might walk between catastrophe and success. Mathers plumbs these and related themes with a verbal savagery that leaves most adults aghast.

Yet Eminem also repeatedly centers his songs on the crypto-traditional notion that children need parents and that *not* having them has made all hell break loose. In the song "8 Mile" from the movie soundtrack, for example, the narrator studies his little sister as she colors one picture after another of an imagined nuclear family, failing to understand that *"mommas got a new man."* *"Wish I could be the daddy that neither one of us had,"* he comments. Such wistful lyrics juxtapose oddly and regularly with Eminem's violent other lines. Even in one of his most infamous songs, "Cleaning Out My Closet (Mama, I'm Sorry)," what drives the vulgar narrative is the insistence on seeing abandonment from a child's point of view. *"My faggot father must have had his panties up in a bunch / 'Cause he split. I wonder if he even kissed me good-bye."*

As with other rappers, the vicious narrative treatment of women in some of Eminem's songs is part of this self-conception as a child victim. Contrary to what critics have intimated, the misogyny in current music does not spring from nowhere; it is often linked to the larger theme of having been abandoned several times—left behind by father, not nurtured by mother, and betrayed again by faithless womankind. One of the most violent and sexually aggressive songs in the last few years is "Kill You" by the popular metal band known as Korn. Its violence is not directed toward just any woman or even toward the narrator's girlfriend; it is instead a song about an abusive stepmother whom the singer imagines going back to rape and murder. **35**

Similarly, Eminem's most shocking lyrics about women are not randomly dispersed; they are largely reserved for his mother and ex-wife, and the narrative pose is one of despising them for not being better women—in particular, better mothers. The worst rap directed at his own mother is indeed gut-wrenching: *"But how dare you try to take what you didn't help me to get? / You selfish bitch, I hope you f—burn in hell for this shit!"* It is no defense of the gutter to observe the obvious: This is not the expression of random misogyny but, rather, of primal rage over alleged maternal abdication and abuse.

Another refrain in these songs runs like this: Today's teenagers are a mess, and the parents who made them that way refuse to get it. In one of Eminem's early hits, for example, a song called "Who Knew," the rapper pointedly takes on his many middle- and upper-middle-class critics to observe the contradiction between their reviling him and the parental inattention that feeds his commercial success. *"What about the make-up you allow your 12 year-old daughter to wear?"* he taunts.

This same theme of AWOL parenting is rapped at greater length in another award-nominated 2003 song called "Sing for the Moment," whose lyrics and video would be recognized in an instant by most teenagers in America. That song spells out Eminem's own idea of what connects him to his millions of fans—a connection that parents, in his view, just don't (or is that won't?) understand. It details the case of one more "problem child" created by *"His f—dad walkin' out."* "Sing for the

Moment," like many other songs of Eminem's, is also a popular video. The "visuals" show clearly what the lyrics depict—hordes of disaffected kids, with flashbacks to bad home lives, screaming for the singer who feels their pain. It concludes by rhetorically turning away from the music itself and toward the emotionally desperate teenagers who turn out for this music by the millions. If the demand of all those empty kids wasn't out there, the narrator says pointedly, then rappers wouldn't be supplying it the way they do.

If some parents still don't get it—even as their teenagers elbow up for every new Eminem CD and memorize his lyrics with psalmist devotion—at least some critics observing the music scene have thought to comment on the ironies of all this. In discussing The *Marshall Mathers* LP in 2001 for Music Box, a daily online newsletter about music, reviewer John Metzger argued, "Instead of spewing the hate that he is so often criticized of doing, Eminem offers a cautionary tale that speaks to our civilization's growing depravity. Ironically, it's his teenage fans who understand this, and their all-knowing parents that miss the point." Metzger further specified "the utter lack of parenting due to the spendthrift necessity of the two-income family."[7]

That insight raises the overlooked fact that in one important sense   40
Eminem and most of the other entertainers quoted here would agree with many of today's adults about one thing: The kids *aren't* all right out there after all. Recall, for just one example, Eddie Vedder's rueful observation about what kind of generation would make him or Kurt Cobain its leader. Where parents and entertainers disagree is over who exactly bears responsibility for this moral chaos. Many adults want to blame the people who create and market today's music and videos. Entertainers, Eminem most prominently, blame the absent, absentee, and generally inattentive adults whose deprived and furious children (as they see it) have catapulted today's singers to fame. (As he puts the point in one more in-your-face response to parents: *"Don't blame me when lil' Eric jumps off of the terrace / You shoulda been watchin him—apparently you ain't parents."*)

The spectacle of a foul-mouthed bad-example rock icon instructing the hardworking parents of America in the art of child-rearing is indeed a peculiar one, not to say ridiculous. The single mother who is working frantically because she must and worrying all the while about what her 14-year-old is listening to in the headphones is entitled to a certain fury over lyrics like those. In fact, to read through most rap lyrics is to wonder which adults or political constituencies *wouldn't* take offense. Even so, the music idols who point the finger away from themselves and toward the emptied-out homes of America are telling a

---

[7]John Metzger, review of "Eminem: the Marshall Mathers lp," *Music Box* 8:6 (June 2001).

truth that some adults would rather not hear. In this limited sense at least, Eminem is right.

Sex, Drugs, Rock and Roll, Broken Homes

To say that today's popular music is uniquely concerned with broken homes, abandoned children, and distracted or incapable parents is not to say that this is what all of it is about. Other themes remain a constant, too, although somewhat more brutally than in the alleged golden era recalled by some baby boomers.

Much of today's metal and hip-hop, like certain music of yesterday, romanticizes illicit drug use and alcohol abuse, and much of current hip-hop sounds certain radical political themes, such as racial separationism and violence against the police. And, of course, the most elementally appealing feature of all, the sexually suggestive beat itself, continues to lure teenagers and young adults in its own right—including those from happy homes. Today as yesterday, plenty of teenagers who don't know or care what the stars are raving about find enough satisfaction in swaying to the sexy music. As professor and intellectual Allan Bloom observed about rock in his bestseller, *The Closing of the American Mind* (Simon & Schuster, 1987), the music "gives children, on a silver platter, with all the public authority of the entertaining industry, everything their parents always used to tell them they had to wait for until they grew up and would understand later."

Even so, and putting aside such obvious continuities with previous generations, there is no escaping the fact that today's songs are musically and lyrically unlike any before. What distinguishes them most clearly is the fixation on having been abandoned personally by the adults supposedly in charge, with consequences ranging from bitterness to rage to bad, sick, and violent behavior.

And therein lies a painful truth about an advantage that many   45
teenagers of yesterday enjoyed but their own children often do not. Baby boomers and their music rebelled against parents *because* they were parents—nurturing, attentive, and overly present (as those teenagers often saw it) authority figures. Today's teenagers and their music rebel against parents because they are *not* parents—not nurturing, not attentive, and often not even there. This difference in generational experience may not lend itself to statistical measure, but it is as real as the platinum and gold records that continue to capture it. What those records show compared to yesteryear's rock is emotional downward mobility. Surely if some of the current generation of teenagers and young adults had been better taken care of, then the likes of Kurt Cobain, Eminem, Tupac Shakur, and certain other parental nightmares would have been mere footnotes to recent music history rather than rulers of it.

To step back from the emotional immediacy of those lyrics and to juxtapose the ascendance of such music alongside the long-standing sophisticated assaults on what is sardonically called "family values" is to meditate on a larger irony. As today's music stars and their raving fans likely do not know, many commentators and analysts have been rationalizing every aspect of the adult exodus from home—sometimes celebrating it full throttle, as in the example of working motherhood—longer than most of today's singers and bands have been alive.

Nor do they show much sign of second thoughts. Representative sociologist Stephanie Coontz greeted the year 2004 with one more op-ed piece aimed at burying poor metaphorical Ozzie and Harriet for good. She reminded America again that "changes in marriage and family life" are here to stay and aren't "necessarily a problem"; that what is euphemistically called "family diversity" is or ought to be cause for celebration. Many other scholars and observers—to say nothing of much of polite adult society—agree with Coontz. Throughout the contemporary nonfiction literature written of, by, and for educated adults, a thousand similar rationalizations about family "changes" bloom on.

Meanwhile, a small number of emotionally damaged former children, embraced and adored by millions of teenagers like them, rage on in every commercial medium available about the multiple damages of the disappearance of loving, protective, attentive adults—and they reap a fortune for it. If this spectacle alone doesn't tell us something about the ongoing emotional costs of parent-child separation on today's outsize scale, it's hard to see what could.

Joining the Conversation: Critical Thinking and Writing

1. According to Eberstadt, what is Eminem right about? To put it another way, what is Eberstadt's thesis?

2. What evidence does Eberstadt offer to support her thesis? To what extent do you agree with her?

3. Who were Ozzie and Harriet? (See paragraph 6.) What did they represent or symbolize?

4. How does Eberstadt distinguish between white and black rappers? In what ways does Eminem differ from other rappers, and in what ways is he similar?

5. According to Eberstadt, why are adolescents from happy homes also lured by rap music? Do you agree with her analysis?

6. Styles in music change rapidly. What would you add to (or subtract Eberstadt's analysis of today''s popular music? Who are the current stars, and what is their appeal and their influence?

Celia E. Rothenberg

Celia E. Rothenberg graduated from Wellesley College in 1991. A history major with a special interest in the lives of Middle Eastern women, she was awarded a Marshall fellowship and studied modern Middle Eastern history at the University of Oxford. She has served as an intern in an Israeli-Palestinian women's peace group in Jerusalem, and she plans to continue working for understanding between these two groups.

Rothenberg wrote the following essay while she was an undergraduate.

Child of Divorce

Over this past winter vacation my parents, brother, and I spent a few days together—a rare event now that the four of us live in four different states. As I watched my parents and brother engage in our usual laughter and reminiscing, accompanied by an occasional tear at a past both bitter and sweet, I listened more closely than ever before to what is a frequent topic of discussion, our relationship as a family.

Perhaps because my parents divorced when I was a small child, it seems to surprise my friends that my family's recollections of those years are filled with many pleasant memories. After all, those who don't know my family have reason to assume that the memories of growing up with divorced parents in some tough economic times might be rather dreary. In fact, however, my memories center on the results of the thoughtfulness and conscious effort exerted by both my parents to create a sense of love and protection for my brother and me. I have always felt that my family was a team, a team that sometimes fumbled, and sometimes seemed to have two, three, or even four captains, and a team that underwent a change in plan mid-game, but a team nevertheless. It is only recently, however, that I have realized how much patience and understanding went into achieving that sense of belonging and love, and how achieving it was part of the long and often painful process for us of divorce and healing.

My parents divorced, after fifteen years of marriage, when I was six. I have nearly no memories of living in a two-parent household. From the time of my earliest memories, my mother has always studied or worked full time. Immediately after the divorce, she, like many women who find

---

themselves single after many years as a "housewife," went back to school. My brother at the time was twelve. Although I remember my Cinderella-shaped cake for my seventh birthday, a few of my favorite pets, and a well-loved school teacher, I remember very little of my mom's return to school, or my own or brother's adjustment to our new surroundings. Perhaps the gaps in my memory serve as some kind of mental defense mechanism to protect me from the reality of the harder times; no matter the reason for my memory voids, however, my brother's recollections are so vivid, and my mom and dad so open about those years, that my scattered memories have been augmented by their story-telling—to the point that I often confuse my memories with theirs.

It is only recently, in fact, that I have realized how difficult the initial years following the divorce were for my mother, brother and father. Over this past winter vacation, my mom told me for the first time how taxing even the simplest tasks seemed to be. For example, locking the doors to our new, small house conjured up all the difficulties and sadnesses of this new beginning. Because my dad had customarily locked up, she had rarely been the one to lock each lock and turn off each light. Doing these tasks in a new house in a new city was a constant reminder of her changed circumstances. Late in the evening she would carefully plot the order in which to turn off the lights, so as not to be alone in the dark. She would lock a door, and then a window, pausing in between the locks to distract her mind from the task at hand—and the frightening and lonely feelings these new responsibilities brought with them.

My family now openly recalls that those years were a difficult time of   5
adjustment to new schools, a new city, and a new life. We had moved from a small suburb of St. Louis to Champaign-Urbana, a community largely centered on the life of the University of Illinois. Our first house in Champaign and my mom's tuition for the Master's degree in Library and Information Science were largely financed by the sale of the lovely Steinway baby grand piano that had graced my parents' living room since before I was born. Before the divorce, my father was an attorney until he found himself in legal difficulties, which ultimately led him to give up the practice of law. His reduced income and my mom's tuition bills placed us under a great financial strain.

My brother, who was twelve at the time of the divorce, particularly recalls how difficult communication was between the three of us and my father, and at times even among the three of us. To help ease the tension of my dad's monthly visits and maintain a relationship which included some fun, my brother and dad played checkers through the mail. They carefully conceived of a plan of multiple paper copies of the checker board and colored pencils for their game. One of my few early memories of those years focusses on the checker board we set up on the dining room table to represent the game my brother and dad played on paper. One evening, the cat we brought with us from (as my mother often said) our "other life," jumped on the board, knocking the pieces all over the table. Steve was inconsolable, and only a prolonged long-distance phone call to figure out where each piece belonged resolved the situation.

That first year my brother escaped into a world of books, often reading fiction and plays when he should have been doing homework, a coping behavior he practiced until he was nearly through high school.

But even the deepest hurts can heal over time. With encouragement and support from both my parents, Steve channeled his considerable energy and anger into planning for an early graduation from high school and a year in Israel between high school and college. The only conditions set were that he had to earn enough money to buy his own plane ticket and he had to have a college acceptance letter in hand before he left. These goals gave him something to work for at a time when he felt that he had lost friends and status in coming to a new, very different, and less comfortable environment than had been part of his early days.

As for me, perhaps because I was six years younger, I appeared to go blithely along, oblivious to most of the tensions and strains that Steve seemed to feel. With my mother studying for her classes and Steve spending almost all his time reading, I became an avid reader myself, almost in self defense. I found new friends and reveled in my new elementary school, a magnet school where we studied French every day. I wrote long, detailed stories of a young girl who lived on a farm with both parents and a dozen brothers and sisters and a beautiful horse. Perhaps I, too, was seeking some consolation in an imaginary life far removed from our little house.

It can take years for wounds to heal, and I am happy to say that my family healed more quickly than most. Perhaps we got past that initial phase early on because my parents did not make too many mistakes. They avoided some common pitfalls of divorcing families. The divorce was quick—the process was completed a few months after my parents sold their house and moved to their new homes—there were no court battles, no screaming fights, no wrenching decisions that we children were required to make. Steve and I were never asked—or allowed—to choose sides or express a preference for one parent over the other. Although my own memories are blurry, the few recollections I have of those first five years focus on my dad's regular monthly visits (he lived a few hours away by car). By the time I was ten, he was spending nearly every weekend with us at the house, a pattern which continued for the next decade, until I was out of high school and off to Wellesley.

Nothing worthwhile, my mother has always told me, is ever easy. It could not have always been easy for either of my parents to spend so much of their free time together when they had chosen to create separate lives, but at the time Steve and I rarely saw anything but civility and fondness. As parents they were determined not to let their children suffer for mistakes they may have made in their marriage. It is one of their greatest gifts to Steve and me, for it was the ultimate lesson in learning about the commitment and cost of love and the lifelong responsibilities of family.

10

The stories we have accumulated over the years have become more hilarious as I have grown older. My dad, determined not to be a "Disneyland daddy," showing up on the weekends for shopping and dinners out, was not uncomfortable in our new home. In fact, he helped us figure out how to do various home improvement projects. Under his direction, we rewired our house (and nearly electrocuted Steve in the process), insulated our attic (the family story lingers that we nearly blew off the roof), and painted the house (and, of course, ourselves). Our projects probably didn't save us very much money, since we seemed to spend as much money on fixing the mistakes we made as on the project itself, yet we were not merely building the house, or growing gardens, or mowing the lawn. We were rebuilding our lives, making memories, and creating a sense of togetherness.

My own clear and more complete memories begin at the age of eleven, when my mother, brother, and I began a new life-style, which reflected a newly achieved flexibility and confidence in our ability to manage our lives. When my brother entered the University of Illinois, we moved into a big old house and I began high school. The house was what a real estate broker fondly calls a "fixer-upper," and was perfect for my mom's income (she worked for the University after she finished her Master's degree) and our need for space for friends of mine and Steve's. Steve, in particular, brought home countless Jewish college students whom he knew from his involvement in the campus Jewish student organization. They often needed a good meal, a shoulder to lean on, an opinion on a paper, or a good night's sleep.

I remember our dining room on Shabbos, furnished with a dining room set probably beautiful in my grandmother's day but battered after three generations of use, packed with college students eating dinner. I remember vividly the talk and the laughter, the jesting and the endless debates. My mom was not only an intellectual support for those students but also an inspiration, someone who had experienced a marriage gone bad, the trials and tribulations of parenting alone (at least during the week), and the tough economics of a single-parent household. Conversations stretched from the abstract to the concrete, from the politics of the Eastern bloc to the intricacies of love and sex.

Over the years it has become clear that the divorce, although trau-   15
matic, opened our minds, enriched our relationships with each other, and loosened restraints we did not know we were subject to. I vividly remember my high school years as a busy time full of my friends and my brothers' who simply enjoyed being around the house. The slightly chaotic, easy-going atmosphere of the house was fostered in large part by our mom; she had disliked the isolated feeling of life in suburbia when she was married. She wanted to create a different atmosphere for Steve and me, a place where young people were comfortable to come and go.

My friends in high school were fascinated by my home, and I enjoyed it as much as they did. My dad was able to watch us grow and change from weekend to weekend, his place secure and comfortable at the head of the

Shabbos table surrounded by students. He helped us with science projects, participated in countless car-pools, and, most of all, was there when we needed him. Although from the point of view of the Census Bureau we were a "single parent household," in actuality we were a *family* that happened to have divorced parents. Perhaps our experience was not typical of some families in which there has been a divorce, but the labels obscure our understanding of the needs and hopes of all families, which I think are probably the same, divorced or not. My parent's expectations for Steve and me were not altered by their marital status, nor do I think that Steve and I let them get away with very much on the excuse that they were divorced!

I have always loved my family, but I find that I admire each of them increasingly as time goes on. Now, when we gather from different corners of the country and world during vacations a few times a year, we admit that the best and the worst, but always the most precious times, were when we were together on the weekends in that big old house, sometimes with the students and sometimes with only each other. On special occasions, we have a (very patient) long-distance operator connect the four of us on the same phone line, and we talk as if there is no tomorrow. We are fiercely proud of one another; I often have to restrain myself from blurting out the merits of my exceptional family to my unsuspecting friends.

At times I wonder how different we would be if we had not gone through the divorce, but for that question I can conjure up no really meaningful speculation. I know that we immensely value our time together, freely share our money (or, I should say, our student loans, as my brother is now in law school, my mom is a full-time doctoral student and my father shoulders the Wellesley burden), and exorbitantly rejoice in each other's company. What more could any of us want from family? So often, it seems to me, I see families that do not realize they possess a great wealth—time. They are together all the time. They don't miss the moments of their mother/father/brother/sister's lives that are irreplaceable.

There is no question that it is often difficult to be a family. My own family's life took a path with an unexpected curve. We weathered times of tough adjustments, economic difficulties, and typical adolescent rebellion. Through it all, though, there was a guiding (if unspoken until many years later) principle of life: family is family forever, and there is no escaping either the trials or the rewards. My parents expect my brother and me to extend ourselves and do work that in some way will bring more light into the world. I have parents who, on modest incomes and budgets, have endowed me with dreams and a sense that the impossible is possible. I have parents for whom I am extremely grateful.

When I told my family that Wellesley asked me to write an article on growing up in a single parent household, they responded in their typical chaotic fashion. My brother forced each of us to sit and write a page about the "Single-Parent Thing" before he let us eat dinner. My mother began plotting a book made up of chapters written from the different perspectives of   20 mother, father, son, and daughter in the single-parent household. My dad insisted we discuss it over dinner (and promised to write his page immediately after dessert). In the end, I took their contributions with me back to Wellesley and wrote down my own feelings, late at night in Munger Hall.

Joining the Conversation: Critical Thinking and Writing

1. What are your earliest memories of your family? How would you account for the fact that Rothenberg has "nearly no memories of living in a two-parent household"?

2. Rothenberg calls her family "exceptional." What do you find to be her strongest evidence for this claim?

3. In paragraph 2, Rothenberg refers to assumptions that her friends make about a child who grew up with divorced parents. What are or were your assumptions? On what are (or were) they based?

4. A highly personal essay runs the risk of being of little interest to persons other than the author. If you found this essay interesting, try to account for its appeal.

Black Elk

As a small boy, Black Elk, a wichasha wakon *(holy man) of the Oglala Sioux, witnessed the battle of the Little Bighorn (1876). He lived to see his people all but annihilated and his hopes for them extinguished. In 1931, toward the end of his life, he told his life story to the poet and scholar John G. Neihardt to preserve a sacred vision given him.*

"High Horse's Courting" is a comic interlude in Black Elk *Speaks, a predominantly tragic memoir.*

High Horse's Courting

You know, in the old days, it was not very easy to get a girl when you wanted to be married. Sometimes it was hard work for a young man and he had to stand a great deal. Say I am a young man and I have seen a young girl who looks so beautiful to me that I feel all sick when I think about her. I cannot just go and tell her about it and then get married if she is willing. I have to be a very sneaky fellow to talk to her at all, and after I have managed to talk to her, that is only the beginning.

Probably for a long time I have been feeling sick about a certain girl because I love her so much, but she will not even look at me, and her parents keep a good watch over her. But I keep feeling worse and worse all the time; so maybe I sneak up to her tepee in the dark and wait until she comes out. Maybe I just wait there all night and don't get any sleep at all and she does not come out. Then I feel sicker than ever about her.

Maybe I hide in the brush by a spring where she sometimes goes to get water, and when she comes by, if nobody is looking, then I jump out and hold her and just make her listen to me. If she likes me too, I can tell that from the way she acts, for she is very bashful and maybe will not say a word or even look at me the first time. So I let her go, and then maybe I sneak around until I can see her father alone, and I tell him how many horses I can give him for his beautiful girl, and by now I am feeling so sick that maybe I would give him all the horses in the world if I had them.

Well, this young man I am telling about was called High Horse, and there was a girl in the village who looked so beautiful to him that he was just sick all over from thinking about her so much and he was getting sicker all the time. The girl was very shy, and her parents thought a great deal of her because they were not young any more and this was the only child they had. So they watched her all day long, and they fixed it so that she would be safe at night too when they were asleep. They thought so much of her that they had made a rawhide bed for her to sleep in, and after they knew that High Horse was sneaking around after her, they took rawhide thongs and tied the girl in bed at night so that nobody could steal her when they were asleep, for they were not sure but that their girl might really want to be stolen.

Well, after High Horse had been sneaking around a good while and hiding and waiting for the girl and getting sicker all the time, he finally caught her alone and made her talk to him. Then he found out that she liked him maybe a little. Of course this did not make him feel well. It made him sicker than ever, but now he felt as brave as a bison bull, and so he went right to her father and said he loved the girl so much that he would give two good horses for her—one of them young and the other one not so very old.

But the old man just waved his hand, meaning for High Horse to go away and quit talking foolishness like that.

High Horse was feeling sicker than ever about it; but there was another young fellow who said he would loan High Horse two ponies and when he got some more horses, why, he could just give them back for the ones he had borrowed.

Then High Horse went back to the old man and said he would give four horses for the girl—two of them young and the other two not hardly old at all. But the old man just waved his hand and would not say anything.

So High Horse sneaked around until he could talk to the girl again, and he asked her to run away with him. He told her he thought he would

5

just fall over and die if she did not. But she said she would not do that; she wanted to be bought like a fine woman. You see she thought a great deal of herself too.

That made High Horse feel so very sick that he could not eat a bite, and he went around with his head hanging down as though he might just fall down and die any time.

Red Deer was another young fellow, and he and High Horse were great comrades, always doing things together. Red Deer saw how High Horse was acting, and he said: "Cousin, what is the matter? Are you sick in the belly? You look as though you were going to die."

Then High Horse told Red Deer how it was, and said he thought he could not stay alive much longer if he could not marry the girl pretty quick.

Red Deer thought awhile about it, and then he said: "Cousin, I have a plan, and if you are man enough to do as I tell you, then everything will be all right. She will not run away with you; her old man will not take four horses; and four horses are all you can get. You must steal her and run away with her. Then afterwhile you can come back and the old man cannot do anything because she will be your woman. Probably she wants you to steal her anyway."

So they planned what High Horse had to do, and he said he loved the girl so much that he was man enough to do anything Red Deer or anybody else could think up. So this is what they did.

That night late they sneaked up to the girl's tepee and waited until it sounded inside as though the old man and the old woman and the girl were sound asleep. Then High Horse crawled under the tepee with a knife. He had to cut the rawhide thongs first, and then Red Deer, who was pulling up the stakes around that side of the tepee, was going to help drag the girl outside and gag her. After that, High Horse could put her across his pony in front of him and hurry out of there and be happy all the rest of his life.

When High Horse had crawled inside, he felt so nervous that he could hear his heart drumming, and it seemed so loud he felt sure it would 'waken the old folks. But it did not, and afterwhile he began cutting the thongs. Every time he cut one it made a pop and nearly scared him to death. But he was getting along all right and all the thongs were cut down as far as the girl's thighs, when he became so nervous that his knife slipped and stuck the girl. She gave a big, loud yell. Then the old folks jumped up and yelled too. By this time High Horse was outside, and he and Red Deer were running away like antelope. The old man and some other people chased the young men but they got away in the dark and nobody knew who it was.

Well, if you ever wanted a beautiful girl you will know how sick High Horse was now. It was very bad the way he felt, and it looked as though he would starve even if he did not drop over dead sometime.

Red Deer kept thinking about this, and after a few days he went to High Horse and said: "Cousin, take courage! I have another plan, and I am sure, if you are man enough, we can steal her this time." And High Horse said: "I am man enough to do anything anybody can think up, if I can only get that girl."

So this is what they did.

They went away from the village alone, and Red Deer made High   20
Horse strip naked. Then he painted High Horse solid white all over, and after that he painted black stripes all over the white and put black rings around High Horse's eyes. High Horse looked terrible. He looked so terrible that when Red Deer was through painting and took a good look at what he had done, he said it scared even him a little.

"Now," Red Deer said, "if you get caught again, everybody will be so scared they will think you are a bad spirit and will be afraid to chase you."

So when the night was getting old and everybody was sound asleep, they sneaked back to the girl's tepee. High Horse crawled in with his knife, as before, and Red Deer waited outside, ready to drag the girl out and gag her when High Horse had all the thongs cut.

High Horse crept up by the girl's bed and began cutting at the thongs. But he kept thinking, "If they see me they will shoot me because I look so terrible." The girl was restless and kept squirming around in bed, and when a thong was cut, it popped. So High Horse worked very slowly and carefully.

But he must have made some noise, for suddenly the old woman awoke and said to her old man: "Old Man, wake up! There is somebody in this tepee!" But the old man was sleepy and didn't want to be bothered. He said: "Of course there is somebody in this tepee. Go to sleep and don't bother me." Then he snored some more.

But High Horse was so scared by now that he lay very still and as flat   25
to the ground as he could. Now, you see, he had not been sleeping very well for a long time because he was so sick about the girl. And while he was lying there waiting for the old woman to snore, he just forgot everything, even how beautiful the girl was. Red Deer who was lying outside ready to do his part, wondered and wondered what had happened in there, but he did not dare call out to High Horse.

Afterwhile the day began to break and Red Deer had to leave with the two ponies he had staked there for his comrade and girl, or somebody would see him.

So he left.

Now when it was getting light in the tepee, the girl awoke and the first thing she saw was a terrible animal, all white with black stripes on it, lying asleep beside her bed. So she screamed, and then the old woman screamed and the old man yelled. High Horse jumped up, scared almost to death, and he nearly knocked the tepee down getting out of there.

People were coming running from all over the village with guns and bows and axes, and everybody was yelling.

By now High Horse was running so fast that he hardly touched the   30
ground at all, and he looked so terrible that the people fled from him and
let him run. Some braves wanted to shoot at him, but the others said he
might be some sacred being and it would bring bad trouble to kill him.

High Horse made for the river that was near, and in among the brush
he found a hollow tree and dived into it. Afterwhile some braves came
there and he could hear them saying that it was some bad spirit that had
come out of the water and gone back in again.

That morning the people were ordered to break camp and move away
from there. So they did, while High Horse was hiding in his hollow tree.

Now Red Deer had been watching all this from his own tepee and
trying to look as though he were as much surprised and scared as all the
others. So when the camp moved, he sneaked back to where he had seen
his comrade disappear. When he was down there in the brush, he called,
and High Horse answered, because he knew his friend's voice. They
washed off the paint from High Horse and sat down on the river bank to
talk about their troubles.

High Horse said he never would go back to the village as long as he
lived and he did not care what happened to him now. He said he was going to go on the war-path all by himself. Red Deer said: "No, cousin, you
are not going on the war-path alone, because I am going with you."

So Red Deer got everything ready, and at night they started out on   35
the war-path all alone. After several days they came to a Crow camp just
about sundown, and when it was dark they sneaked up to where the
Crow horses were grazing, killed the horse guard, who was not thinking
about enemies because he thought all the Lakotas were far away, and
drove off about a hundred horses.

They got a big start because all the Crow horses stampeded and
it was probably morning before the Crow warriors could catch any
horses to ride. Red Deer and High Horse fled with their herd three days
and nights before they reached the village of their people. Then they drove
the whole herd right into the village and up in front of the girl's tepee. The
old man was there, and High Horse called out to him and asked if
he thought maybe that would be enough horses for his girl. The old man
did not wave him away that time. It was not the horses that he wanted.
What he wanted was a son who was a real man and good for something.

So High Horse got his girl after all, and I think he deserved her.

 ## Joining the Conversation:
Critical Thinking and Writing

Although High Horse's behavior is amusing and at times ridiculous, how does
Black Elk make it clear that he is not ridiculing the young man but is instead in
sympathy with him? Consider the following questions:

1. What is the effect of the first three paragraphs? Think about the first two sentences and then the passage beginning "Say I am a young man . . ." and ending ". . . I would give him all the horses in the world if I had them."

2. Describe the behavior of the young girl and of her father and mother. How do they contribute to the comedy? How does their behavior affect your understanding of Black Elk's attitude toward High Horse?

3. What is the function of Red Deer?

4. The narrative consists of several episodes. List them in the order in which they occur and then describe the narrative's structure. How does this structure affect the tone?

Jamaica Kincaid

Jamaica Kincaid was born in 1949 in St. Johns, Antigua, in the West Indies. She was educated at the Princess Margaret School in Antigua and, briefly, at Westchester Community College and Franconia College. Since 1974, she has been a contributor to the New Yorker, *where "Girl" was first published. "Girl" was later included in the first of Kincaid's six books,* At the Bottom of the River.*

Kincaid informs us that "benna," mentioned early in "Girl," refers to "songs of the sort your parents didn't want you to sing, at first calypso and later rock and roll."

Girl

Wash the white clothes on Monday and put them on the stone heap; wash the color clothes on Tuesday and put them on the clothesline to dry; don't walk barehead in the hot sun; cook pumpkin fritters in very hot sweet oil; soak your little clothes right after you take them off; when buying cotton to make yourself a nice blouse, be sure that it doesn't have gum on it, because that way it won't hold up well after a wash; soak salt fish overnight before you cook it; is it true that you sing benna in Sunday school?; always eat your food in such a way that it won't turn someone else's stomach; on Sundays try to walk like a lady and not like the slut you are so bent on becoming; don't sing benna in Sunday school; you mustn't speak to wharf-rat boys, not even to give directions; don't eat fruits on the street—flies will follow you; *but I don't sing benna on Sundays at all and never in Sunday school;* this is how to sew on a button; this is how to make a buttonhole for the button you have just sewed on; this is how to hem a dress when you see the hem coming down and so to prevent yourself from looking like the slut I know you are so bent on becoming; this is how you iron your father's khaki shirt so that it doesn't have a crease; this is how you iron your father's khaki pants so that they don't have a crease; this is how you grow okra—far from the house, because okra tree harbors red ants; when you are growing dasheen, make sure it gets plenty of water or else it makes your throat itch when you are eating it; this is how you sweep a corner; this is how you sweep a whole house; this is how you sweep a yard; this is how you smile to someone you don't like too much; this is how you smile to someone you don't like at all; this is how you smile to someone you like completely; this is how you set a table for tea; this is how you set a table for dinner; this is how you set a table for dinner with an important guest; this is how you set a table for lunch; this is how you set a table for breakfast; this is how to behave in the presence of men who don't know you very well, and this way they won't recognize immediately the slut I have warned you against becoming; be sure to wash every day, even if it is with your own spit; don't squat down to play marbles—you are not a boy, you know; don't pick people's flowers—you might catch something; don't throw stones at blackbirds, because it might not be a blackbird at all; this is how to make a bread pudding; this is how to make doukona; this is how to make pepper pot; this is how to make a good medicine for a cold; this is how to make a good medicine to throw away a child before it even becomes a child; this is how to catch a fish; this is how to throw back a fish you don't like, and that way something bad won't fall on you; this is how to bully a man; this is how a man bullies you; this is how to love a man, and if this doesn't work there are other ways, and if they don't work don't feel too bad about giving up; this is how to spit up in the air if you feel like it, and this is how to move quick so that it doesn't fall on you; this is how to make ends meet; always squeeze bread to make sure it's fresh; *but what if the baker won't let me feel the bread?*; you mean to say that after all you are really going to be the kind of woman who the baker won't let near the bread?

Joining the Conversation: Critical Thinking and Writing

1. In a paragraph, identify the two characters whose voices we hear in this story. Explain what we know about them (their circumstances and their relationship). Cite specific evidence from the text. For example, what is the effect of the frequent repetition of "this is how"? Are there other words or phrases frequently repeated?

2. Try reading a section of "Girl" out loud in a rhythmical pattern, giving the principal and the second voices. Then, reread the story, trying to incorporate this rhythm mentally into your reading. How does this rhythm contribute to the overall effect of the story? How does it compare to or contrast with speech rhythms that are familiar to you?

Theodore Roethke

Theodore Roethke (1908–1963) was born in Saginaw, Michigan, and educated at the University of Michigan and Harvard. From 1947 until his death, he taught at the University of Washington in Seattle, where he exerted considerable influence on the next generation of poets. Many of Roethke's best poems are lyrical memories of his childhood.

My Papa's Waltz

The whiskey on your breath
Could make a small boy dizzy;
but I hung on like death:
Such waltzing was not easy.   4

We romped until the pans
Slid from the kitchen shelf;
My mother's countenance
Could not unfrown itself.   8

The hand that held my wrist
Was battered on one knuckle;
At every step you missed
My right ear scraped a buckle.   12

You beat time on my head
With a palm caked hard by dirt,
Then waltzed me off to bed
Still clinging to your shirt.   16

[*1948*]

 ## Joining the Conversation:
Critical Thinking and Writing

1. From this recollection of a child's experience, what do we learn about the father? In what lines or images?

2. What do we learn about the mother? What contrast is there between the two?

3. Overall, from this account of the waltz, what do we learn about the child's feeling for his father? On what specific evidence?

4. Try to recall an experience you had with an adult when you were a child—a parent, a teacher, an older sibling—and write a paragraph describing that experience, from which your readers can infer how you felt about that person. You will probably not find this easy, but we think you will learn from it, not only more precisely how you then felt but also how professional writers recreate their experiences in poetry and in prose.

CHAPTER 7

Identities

Grandfather and Grandchildren Awaiting Evacuation Bus,
Hayward, California, May 9, 1942
Dorothea Lange

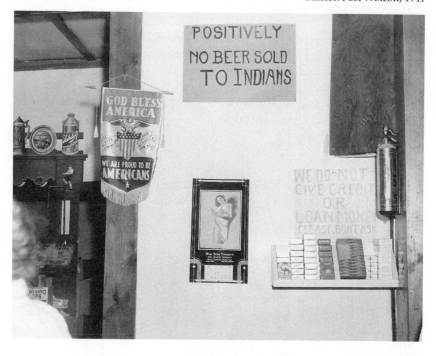

Short Views

In every known society, the male's need for achievement can be recognized. Men may cook, or weave, or dress dolls or hunt hummingbirds, but if such activities are appropriate occupations of men, then the whole society, men and women alike, votes them as important. When the same occupations are performed by women, they are regarded as less important.

Margaret Mead

This has always been a man's world, and none of the reasons hitherto brought forward in explanation of this fact has seemed adequate.

Simone de Beauvoir

America is God's crucible, the great melting pot where all the races of Europe are melting and re-forming.

Israel Zangwill

Through our own efforts and concerted good faith in learning to know, thus to respect, the wonderfully rich and diverse subcommunities of America, we can establish a new vision of America: a place where "community" may mean many things, yet retains its deeper spiritual significance. We may even learn to coincide with the 500th anniversary of the "discovery" of America by Columbus, that America, in its magnificent variety, has yet to be discovered.

Joyce Carol Oates

I have a dream that my four little children will one day live in a nation where they will not be judged by the color of their skin but by the content of their character.

Martin Luther King Jr.

Racism is so universal in this country, so wide-spread and deep-seated, that it is invisible because it is so normal.

Shirley Chisholm

Rogelio R. Gomez

Rogelio R. Gomez at the age of six was brought by his family from Mexico to the United States. His lack of competence in English caused him to fail first grade and to be labeled learning-disabled. He nevertheless earned a bachelor's degree from the University of Texas at Austin, where he majored in history, and in 1990, he earned a master's degree in English.

Foul Shots

Now and then I can still see their faces, snickering and laughing, their eyes mocking me. And it bothers me that I should remember. Time and maturity should have diminished the pain, because the incident happened more than 20 years ago. Occasionally, however, a smug smile triggers the memory, and I think, "I should have done something," Some act of defiance could have killed and buried the memory of the incident. Now it's too late.

In 1969, I was a senior on the Luther Burbank High School basketball team. The school is on the south side of San Antonio, in one of the city's many barrios. After practice one day our coach announced that we were going to spend the following Saturday scrimmaging with the ball club from Winston Churchill High, located in the city's rich, white north side. After the basketball game, we were to select someone from the opposing team and "buddy up"—talk with him, have lunch with him and generally spend the day attempting friendship. By telling us that this experience would do both teams some good, I suspect our well-intentioned coach was thinking about the possible benefits of integration and of learning to appreciate the differences of other people. By integrating us with this more prosperous group, I think he was also trying to inspire us.

But my teammates and I smiled sardonically at one another, and our sneakers squeaked as we nervously rubbed them against the waxed hardwood floor of our gym. The prospect of a full day of unfavorable comparisons drew from us a collective groan. As "barrio boys," we were already acutely aware of the differences between us and them. Churchill meant "white" to us: It meant shiny new cars, two-story homes with fireplaces, pedigreed dogs and manicured hedges. In other words, everything that we did not have. Worse, travelling north meant putting up a front, to ourselves as well as to the Churchill team. We felt we had to pretend that we were cavalier about it all, tough guys who didn't care about "nothin."

It's clear now that we entered the contest with negative images of ourselves. From childhood, we must have suspected something was inherently wrong with us. The evidence wrapped itself around our collective psyche like a noose. In elementary school, we were not allowed to speak Spanish. The bladed edge of a wooden ruler once came crashing down on my knuckles for violating this dictum. By high school, however, policies had changed, and we could speak Spanish without fear of physical reprisal. Still, speaking our language before whites brought on spasms of shame—for the supposed inferiority of our language and culture—and guilt at feeling shame. That mixture of emotions fueled our burning sense of inferiority

After all, our mothers in no way resembled the glamorized models of American TV mothers—Donna Reed baking cookies in high heels. My mother's hands were rough and chafed, her wardrobe drab and worn. And my father was preoccupied with making ends meet. His silence starkly contrasted with the glib counsel Jim Anderson offered in "Father Knows Best." And where the Beaver worried about trying to understand some difficult homework assignment, for me it was an altogether different horror, when I was told by my elementary school principal that I did not have the ability to learn.

After I failed to pass the first grade, my report card read that I had a "learning disability." What shame and disillusion it brought my parents! To have carried their dream of a better life from Mexico to America, only to have their hopes quashed by having their only son branded inadequate. And so somewhere during my schooling I assumed that saying I had a "learning disability" was just another way of saying that I was "retarded." School administrators didn't care that I could not speak English.

As teen-agers, of course, my Mexican-American friends and I did not consciously understand why we felt inferior. But we might have understood if we had fathomed our desperate need to trounce Churchill. We viewed the prospect of beating a white, north-side squad as a particularly fine coup. The match was clearly racial, our need to succeed born of a defiance against prejudice. I see now that we used the basketball court to prove our "blood." And who better to confirm us, if not those whom we considered better? In retrospect, I realize the only thing confirmed that day was that we saw ourselves as negatively as they did.

After we won the morning scrimmage, both teams were led from the gym into an empty room where everyone sat on a shiny linoleum floor. We were supposed to mingle—rub the colors together. But the teams sat separately, our backs against concrete walls. We faced one another like enemies, the empty floor between us a no man's land. As the coaches walked away, one reminded us to share lunch. God! The mere thought of offering them a taco from our brown bags when they had refrigerated deli lunches horrified us.

Then one of their players tossed a bag of Fritos at us. It slid across the slippery floor and stopped in the center of the room. With hearts beating anxiously, we Chicanos stared at the bag as the boy said with a sneer, "Y'all probably like 'em"—the "Frito Bandito" commercial being popular then. And we could see them, smiling at each other, giggling, jabbing their elbows into one another's ribs at the joke. The bag seemed to grow before our eyes like a monstrous symbol of inferiority.

We won the afternoon basketball game as well. But winning had accomplished nothing. Though we had wanted to, we couldn't change their perception of us. It seems, in fact, that defeating them made them meaner. Looking back, I feel these young men needed to put us "in our place," to reaffirm the power they felt we had threatened. I think, moreover, that they felt justified, not only because of their inherent sense of superiority, but because our failure to respond to their insult underscored our worthlessness in their eyes.

10

Two decades later, the memory of their gloating lives on in me. When a white person is discourteous, I find myself wondering what I should do, and afterward, if I've done the right thing. Sometimes I argue when a deft comment would suffice. Then I reprimand myself, for I am no longer a boy. But my impulse to argue bears witness to my ghosts. For, invariably, whenever I feel insulted I'm reminded of that day at Churchill High. And whenever the past encroaches upon the present, I see myself rising boldly, stepping proudly across the years and crushing, underfoot, a silly bag of Fritos.

Joining the Conversation:
Critical Thinking and Writing

1. Gomez is describing an experience that occurred 20 years earlier. What did he feel then, and what does he feel now?

2. How does the author make his past experiences come alive for the reader? More generally, what does it mean to say that in a piece of writing that an author has succeeded in making an experience "come alive"?

3. Have you ever suffered from a sense of inferiority similar to the one that Gomez describes? What was the situation? How did you feel at the time, and how do you feel about it now?

4. When something bad or upsetting happens to us, we are often told, "You'll have to get over it—put it behind you." Do you think that someone should offer this advice to Gomez? How do you respond when someone gives such advice to you? In your view, how would Gomez respond to someone who gave this advice to him?

Nancy Mairs

Nancy Mairs did her undergraduate work at Wheaton College in Massachusetts and her graduate work (MFA. in creative writing, Ph.D. in English Literature) at the University of Arizona. A poet and essayist, she was awarded a fellowship by the National Endowment for the Arts in 1991. Mairs often writes about her mental and physical difficulties (she spent six months in a mental hospital, and she has multiple sclerosis) and also about her spiritual journeys (raised a Congregationalist, she converted to Roman Catholicism). Among her publications are collections of essays: Waist-High in the World: A Life Among the Nondisabled *(1996) and* A Dynamic God: Living an Unconventional Catholic Faith *(2007).*

In the second paragraph of the essay that we reprint, Mairs says that she wants her readers to see her "as a tough customer, one to whom the fates/gods/viruses have not been kind, but who can face the brutal truth of her existence squarely. As a cripple, I swagger."

On Being a Cripple

To escape is nothing. Not to escape is nothing.—LOUISE BOGAN

The other day I was thinking of writing an essay on being a cripple. I was thinking hard in one of the stalls of the women's room in my office building, as I was shoving my shirt into my jeans and tugging up my zipper. Preoccupied, I flushed, picked up my book bag, took my cane down from the hook, and unlatched the door. So many movements unbalanced me, and as I pulled the door open I fell over backward, landing fully clothed on the toilet seat with my legs splayed in front of me: the old beetle-on-its-back routine. Saturday afternoon, the building deserted, I was free to laugh aloud as I wriggled back to my feet, my voice bouncing off the yellowish tiles from all directions. Had anyone been there with me, I'd have been still and faint and hot with chagrin. I decided that it was high time to write the essay.

First, the matter of semantics. I am a cripple. I choose this word to name me. I choose from among several possibilities, the most common of which are "handicapped" and "disabled." I made the choice a number of years ago, without thinking, unaware of my motives for doing so. Even now, I'm not sure what those motives are, but I recognize that they are complex and not entirely flattering. People—crippled or not—wince at the word "cripple," as they do not at "handicapped" or "disabled." Perhaps I want them to wince. I want them to see me as a tough customer, one to whom the fates/gods/viruses have not been kind, but who can face the brutal truth of her existence squarely. As a cripple, I swagger.

But, to be fair to myself, a certain amount of honesty underlies my choice. "Cripple" seems to me a clean word, straightforward and precise. It has an honorable history, having made its first appearance in the Lindisfarne Gospel in the tenth century. As a lover of words, I like the accuracy with which it describes my condition: I have lost the full use of my limbs. "Disabled," by contrast, suggests any incapacity, physical or mental. And I certainly don't like "handicapped," which implies that I have deliberately been put at a disadvantage, by whom I can't imagine (my God is not a Handicapper General), in order to equalize chances in the great race of life. These words seem to me to be moving away from my condition, to be widening the gap between word and reality. Most remote is the recently coined euphemism "differently abled," which partakes of the same semantic hopefulness that transformed countries from "undeveloped" to "underdeveloped," then to "less developed," and finally to "developing" nations. People have continued to starve in those countries during the shift. Some realities do not obey the dictates of language.

Mine is one of them. Whatever you call me, I remain crippled. But I don't care what you call me, so long as it isn't "differently abled," which strikes me as pure verbal garbage designed, by its ability to describe anyone, to describe no one. I subscribe to George Orwell's thesis that "the slovenliness of our language makes it easier for us to have foolish thoughts." And I refuse to participate in the degeneration of the language to the extent that I deny that I have lost anything in the course of this calamitous disease; I refuse to pretend that the only differences between you and me are the various ordinary ones that distinguish any one person from another. But call me "disabled" or "handicapped" if you like. I have long since grown accustomed to them; and if they are vague, at least they hint at the truth. Moreover, I use them myself. Society is no readier to accept crippledness than to accept death, war, sex, sweat, or wrinkles. I would never refer to another person as a cripple. It is the word I use to name only myself.

I haven't always been crippled, a fact for which I am soundly grateful. To be whole of limb is, I know from experience, infinitely more pleasant and useful than to be crippled; and if that knowledge leaves one open to bitterness at my loss, the physical soundness I once enjoyed (though I did not enjoy it half enough) is well worth the occasional stab of regret. Though never any good at sports, I was a normally active child and young adult. I climbed trees, played hopscotch, jumped rope, skated, swam, rode my bicycle, sailed. I despised team sports, spending some of the wretchedest afternoons of my life, sweaty and humiliated, behind a field-hockey stick and under a basketball hoop. I tramped alone for miles along the bridle paths that webbed the woods behind the house I grew up in. I swayed through countless dim hours in the arms of one man or another under the scattered shot of light from mirrored balls, and gyrated through countless more as Tab Hunter and Johnny Mathis gave way to the Rolling Stones, Creedence Clearwater Revival, Cream. I walked down the aisle. I pushed baby carriages, changed tires in the rain, marched for peace.

When I was twenty-eight I started to trip and drop things. What at first seemed my natural clumsiness soon became too pronounced to shrug off. I consulted a neurologist, who told me that I had a brain tumor. A battery of tests, increasingly disagreeable, revealed no tumor. About a year and a half later I developed a blurred spot in one eye. I had, at last, the episodes "disseminated in space and time" requisite for a diagnosis: multiple sclerosis. I have never been sorry for the doctor's initial misdiagnosis, however. For almost a week, until the negative results of the tests were in, I thought that I was going to die right away. Every day for the past nearly ten years, then, has been a kind of gift. I accept all gifts.

Multiple sclerosis is a chronic degenerative disease of the central nervous system, in which the myelin that sheathes the nerves is somehow eaten away and scar tissue forms in its place, interrupting the nerves' signals. During its course, which is unpredictable and uncontrollable, one may lose vision, hearing, speech, the ability to walk, control of bladder and/or bowels, strength in any or all extremities, sensitivity to touch, vibration, and/or pain, potency, coordination of movements—the list of possibilities is lengthy and, yes, horrifying. One may also lose one's sense of humor. That's the easiest to lose and the hardest to survive without.

In the past ten years, I have sustained some of these losses. Characteristic of MS are sudden attacks, called exacerbations, followed by remissions, and these I have not had. Instead, my disease has been slowly progressive. My left leg is now so weak that I walk with the aid of a brace and a cane; and for distances I use an Amigo, a variation on the electric wheelchair that looks rather like an electrified kiddie car. I no longer have much use of my left hand. Now my right side is weakening as well. I still have the blurred spot in my right eye. Overall, though, I've been lucky so far. My world has, of necessity, been circumscribed by my losses, but the terrain left me has been ample enough for me to continue many of the activities that absorb me: writing, teaching, raising children and cats and plants and snakes, reading, speaking publicly about MS and depression, even playing bridge with people patient and honorable enough to let me scatter cards every which way without sneaking a peek.

Lest I begin to sound like Pollyanna, however, let me say that I don't like having MS. I hate it. My life holds realities—harsh ones, some of them—that no right-minded human being ought to accept without grumbling. One of them is fatigue. I know of no one with MS who does not complain of bone-weariness; in a disease that presents an astonishing variety of symptoms, fatigue seems to be a common factor. I wake up in the morning feeling the way most people do at the end of a bad day, and I take it from there. As a result, I spend a lot of time *in extremis* and, impatient with limitation, I tend to ignore my fatigue until my body breaks down in some way and forces rest. Then I miss picnics, dinner parties, poetry readings, the brief visits of old friends from out of town. The offspring of a puritanical tradition of exceptional venerability, I cannot view these lapses without shame. My life often seems a series of small failures to do as I ought.

I lead, on the whole, an ordinary life, probably rather like the one I   10
would have led had I not had MS. I am lucky that my predilections were
already solitary, sedentary, and bookish—unlike the world-famous
French cellist I have read about, or the young woman I talked with one
long afternoon who wanted only to be a jockey. I had just begun graduate
school when I found out something was wrong with me, and I have remained, interminably, a graduate student. Perhaps I would not have if I'd
thought I had the stamina to return to a full-time job as a technical editor;
but I've enjoyed my studies.

In addition to studying, I teach writing courses. I also teach medical
students how to give neurological examinations. I pick up freelance editing jobs here and there. I have raised a foster son and sent him into the
world, where he has made me two grandbabies, and I am still escorting
my daughter and son through adolescence. I go to Mass every Saturday. I
am a superb, if messy, cook. I am also an enthusiastic laundress, capable
of sorting a hamper full of clothes into five subtly differentiated piles, but
a terrible housekeeper. I can do italic writing and, in an emergency, bathe
an oil-soaked cat. I play a fiendish game of Scrabble. When I have the
time and the money, I like to sit on my front steps with my husband
drinking Amaretto and smoking a cigar, as we imagine our counterparts
in Leningrad and make sure that the sun gets down once more behind the
sharp childish scrawl of the Tucson Mountains.

This lively plenty has its bleak complement, of course, in all the
things I can no longer do. I will never run again, except in dreams, and
one day I may have to write that I will never walk again. I like to go
camping, but I can't follow George and the children along the trails that
wander out of a campsite through the desert or into the mountains. In
fact, even on the level I've learned never to check the weather or try to
hold a coherent conversation: I need all my attention for my wayward
feet. Of late, I have begun to catch myself wondering how people can pro-
pel themselves without canes. With only one usable hand, I have to select
my clothing with care not so much for style as for ease of ingress and
egress, and even so, dressing can be laborious. I can no longer do fine
stitchery, pick up babies, play the piano, braid my hair. I am immobilized
by acute attacks of depression, which may or may not be physiologically
related to MS but are certainly its logical concomitant.

These two elements, the plenty and the privation, are never pure, nor
are the delight and wretchedness that accompany them. Almost every
pickle that I get into as a result of my weakness and clumsiness—and
I get into plenty—is funny as well as maddening and sometimes painful.
I recall one May afternoon when a friend and I were going out for a drink
after finishing up at school. As we were climbing into opposite sides of
my car, chatting, I tripped and fell, flat and hard, onto the asphalt parking
lot, my abrupt departure interrupting him in mid-sentence. "Where'd
you go?" he called as he came around the back of the car to find me
hauling myself up by the door frame. "Are you all right?" Yes, I told him,

I was fine, just a bit rattly, and we drove off to find a shady patio and some beer. When I got home an hour or so later, my daughter greeted me with "What have you done to yourself?" I looked down. One elbow of my white turtleneck with the green froggies, one knee of my white trousers, one white kneesock were bloodsoaked. We peeled off the clothes and inspected the damage, which was nasty enough but not alarming. That part wasn't funny: The abrasions took a long time to heal, and one got a little infected. Even so, when I think of my friend talking earnestly, suddenly, to the hot thin air while I dropped from his view as though through a trap door, I find the image as silly as something from a Marx Brothers movie.

I may find it easier than other cripples to amuse myself because I live propped by the acceptance and the assistance and, sometimes, the amusement of those around me. Grocery clerks tear my checks out of my checkbook for me, and sales clerks find chairs to put into dressing rooms when I want to try on clothes. The people I work with make sure I teach at times when I am least likely to be fatigued, in places I can get to, with the materials I need. My students, with one anonymous exception (in an end-of-the-semester evaluation), have been unperturbed by my disability. Some even like it. One was immensely cheered by the information that I paint my own fingernails; she decided, she told me, that if I could go to such trouble over fine details, she could keep on writing essays. I suppose I became some sort of bright-fingered muse. She wrote good essays, too.

The most important struts in the framework of my existence, of course, are my husband and children. Dismayingly few marriages survive the MS test, and why should they? Most twenty-two-and nineteen-year-olds, like George and me, can vow in clear conscience, after a childhood of chicken pox and summer colds, to keep one another in sickness and in health so long as they both shall live. Not many are equipped for catastrophe: the dismay, the depression, the extra work, the boredom that a degenerative disease can insinuate into a relationship. And our society, with its emphasis on fun and its association of fun with physical performance, offers little encouragement for a whole spouse to stay with a crippled partner. Children experience similar stresses when faced with a crippled parent, and they are more helpless, since parents and children can't usually get divorced. They hate, of course, to be different from their peers, and the child whose mother is tacking down the aisle of a school auditorium packed with proud parents like a Cape Cod dinghy in a stiff breeze jolly well stand out in a crowd. Deprived of legal divorce, the child can at least deny the mother's disability, even her existence, forgetting to tell her about recitals and PTA meetings, refusing to accompany her to stores or church or the movies, never inviting friends to the house. Many do.

But I've been limping along for ten years now, and so far George and the children are still at my left elbow, holding tight. Anne and Matthew vacuum floors and dust furniture and haul trash and rake up dog droppings and button my cuffs and bake lasagna and Toll House cookies with just enough grumbling so I know that they don't have brain fever. And far from hiding me, they're forever dragging me by racks of fancy clothes or through teeming school corridors, or welcoming gaggles of friends while I'm wandering through the house in Anne's filmy pink babydoll pajamas. George generally calls before he brings someone home, but he does just as many dumb thankless chores as the children. And they all yell at me, laugh at some of my jokes, write me funny letters when we're apart—in short, treat me as an ordinary human being for whom they have some use. I think they like me. Unless they're faking. . . .

Faking. There's the rub. Tugging at the fringes of my consciousness always is the terror that people are kind to me only because I'm a cripple. My mother almost shattered me once, with that instinct mothers have—blind, I think, in this case, but unerring nonetheless—for striking blows along the fault-lines of their children's hearts, by telling me, in an attack on my selfishness, "We all have to make allowances for you, of course, because of the way you are." From the distance of a couple of years, I have to admit that I haven't any idea just what she meant, and I'm not sure that she knew either. She was awfully angry. But at the time, as the words thudded home, I felt my worst fear, suddenly realized. I could bear being called selfish: I am. But I couldn't bear the corroboration that those around me were doing in fact what I'd always suspected them of doing, professing fondness while silently putting up with me because of the way I am. A cripple. I've been a little cracked ever since.

Along with this fear that people are secretly accepting shoddy goods comes a relentless pressure to please—to prove myself worth the burdens I impose, I guess, or to build a substantial account of goodwill against which I may write drafts in times of need. Part of the pressure arises from social expectations. In our society, anyone who deviates from the norm had better find some way to compensate. Like fat people, who are expected to be jolly, cripples must bear their lot meekly and cheerfully. A grumpy cripple isn't playing by the rules. And much of the pressure is self-generated. Early on I vowed that, if I had to have MS, by God I was going to do it well. This is a class act, ladies and gentlemen. No tears, no recriminations, no faint-heartedness.

One way and another, then, I wind up feeling like Tiny Tim,[1] peering over the edge of the table at the Christmas goose, waving my crutch, piping down God's blessing on us all. Only sometimes I don't want to play Tiny Tim. I'd rather be Caliban,[2] a most scurvy monster. Fortunately, at home no one much cares whether I'm a good cripple or a bad cripple as long as I make vichyssoise with fair regularity. One evening several years ago, Anne was reading at the dining-room table while I cooked dinner. As I opened a can of tomatoes, the can slipped in my left hand and juice spattered me and the counter with bloody spots. Fatigued and infuriated,

---

[1] **Tiny Tim** A character in Charles Dicbeus's story *A Christmas Carol.*
[2] **Caliban** A deformed brutish character in Shakespeare's *The Tempest.*

I bellowed, "I'm so sick of being crippled!" Anne glanced at me over the top of her book. "There now," she said, "do you feel better?" "Yes," I said, "yes, I do." She went back to her reading. I felt better. That's about all the attention my scurviness ever gets.

Because I hate being crippled, I sometimes hate myself for being a cripple. Over the years I have come to expect—even accept—attacks of violent self-loathing. Luckily, in general our society no longer connects deformity and disease directly with evil (though a charismatic once told me that I have MS because a devil is in me) and so I'm allowed to move largely at will, even among small children. But I'm not sure that this revision of attitude has been particularly helpful. Physical imperfection, even freed of moral disapprobation, still defies and violates the ideal, especially for women, whose confinement in their bodies as objects of desire is far from over. Each age, of course, has its ideal, and I doubt that ours is any better or worse than any other. Today's ideal woman, who lives on the glossy pages of dozens of magazines, seems to be between the ages of eighteen and twenty-five; her hair has body, her teeth flash white, her breath smells minty, her underarms are dry; she has a career but is still a fabulous cook, especially of meals that take less than twenty minutes to prepare; she does not ordinarily appear to have a husband or children; she is trim and deeply tanned; she jogs, swims, plays tennis, rides a bicycle, sails, but does not bowl; she travels widely, even to out-of-the-way places like Finland and Samoa, always in the company of the ideal man, who possesses a nearly identical set of characteristics. There are a few exceptions. Though usually white and often blonde, she may be black, Hispanic, Asian, or Native American, so long as she is unusually sleek. She may be old, provided she is selling a laxative or is Lauren Bacall. If she is selling a detergent, she may be married and have a flock of strikingly messy children. But she is never a cripple.

Like many women I know, I have always had an uneasy relationship with my body. I was not a popular child, largely, I think now, because I was peculiar: intelligent, intense, moody, shy, given to unexpected actions and inexplicable notions and emotions. But as I entered adolescence, I believed myself unpopular because I was homely: my breasts too flat, my mouth too wide, my hips too narrow, my clothing never quite right in fit or style. I was not, in fact, particularly ugly, old photographs inform me, though I was well off the ideal; but I carried this sense of self-alienation with me into adulthood, where it regenerated in response to the depredations of MS. Even with my brace I walk with a limp so pronounced that, seeing myself on the videotape of a television program on the disabled, I couldn't believe that anything but an inchworm could make progress humping along like that. My shoulders droop and my pelvis thrusts forward as I try to balance myself upright, throwing my frame into a bony S. As a result of contractures, one shoulder is higher than the other and I carry one arm bent in front of me, the fingers curled into a claw. My left arm and leg have wasted into pipestems, and I try always to keep them covered. When I think about how my body must look to others, especially to men, to whom I have been trained to display myself, I feel ludicrous, even loathsome.

At my age, however, I don't spend much time thinking about my appearance. The burning egocentricity of adolescence, which assures one that all the world is looking all the time, has passed, thank God, and I'm generally too caught up in what I'm doing to step back, as I used to, and watch myself as though upon a stage. I'm also too old to believe in the accuracy of self-image. I know that I'm not a hideous crone, that in fact, when I'm rested, well dressed, and well made up, I look fine. The self-loathing I feel is neither physically nor intellectually substantial. What I hate is not me but a disease.

I am not a disease.

And a disease is not—at least not singlehandedly—going to determine who I am, though at first it seemed to be going to. Adjusting to a chronic incurable illness, I have moved through a process similar to that outlined by Elisabeth Kübler-Ross in *On Death and Dying*. The major difference—and it is far more significant than most people recognize—is that I can't be sure of the outcome, as the terminally ill cancer patient can. Research studies indicate that, with proper medical care, I may achieve a "normal" life span. And in our society, with its vision of death as the ultimate evil, worse even than decrepitude, the response to such news is, "Oh well, at least you're not going to *die*." Are there worse things than dying? I think that there may be.

I think of two women I know, both with MS, both enough older than I   25
to have served me as models. One took to her bed several years ago and has been there ever since. Although she can sit in a high-backed wheelchair, because she is incontinent she refuses to go out at all, even though incontinence pants, which are readily available at any pharmacy, could protect her from embarrassment. Instead, she stays at home and insists that her husband, a small quiet man, a retired civil servant, stay there with her except for a quick weekly foray to the supermarket. The other woman, whose illness was diagnosed when she was eighteen, a nursing student engaged to a young doctor, finished her training, married her doctor, accompanied him to Germany when he was in the service, bore three sons and a daughter, now grown and gone. When she can, she travels with her husband; she plays bridge, embroiders, swims regularly; she works, like me, as a symptomaticpatient instructor of medical students in neurology. Guess which woman I hope to be.

At the beginning, I thought about having MS almost incessantly and because of the unpredictable course of the disease, my thoughts were always terrified. Each night I'd get into bed wondering whether I'd get out again the next morning, whether I'd be able to see, to speak, to hold a pen between my fingers. Knowing that the day might come when I'd be physically incapable of killing myself, I thought perhaps I ought to do so right away, while I still had the strength. Gradually I came to understand that the Nancy who might one day lie inert under a bedsheet, arms and legs paralyzed, unable to feed or bathe herself, unable to reach out for a gun, a bottle of pills, was not the Nancy I was at present, and that I could not presume to make decisions for that future Nancy, who might well not want in the least to die. Now the only provision I've made for the future Nancy is that when the time comes—and it is likely to come in the form of pneumonia, friend to the weak and the old—I am not to be treated with machines and medications. If she is unable to communicate by then, I hope she will be satisfied with these terms.

Thinking all the time about having MS grew tiresome and intrusive, especially in the large and tragic mode in which I was accustomed to considering my plight. Months and even years went by without catastrophe (at least without one related to MS), and really I was awfully busy, what with George and children and snakes and students and poems, and I hadn't the time, let alone the inclination, to devote myself to being a disease. Too, the richer my life became, the funnier it seemed, as though there were some connection between largesse and laughter, and so my tragic stance began to waver until, even with the aid of a brace and a cane, I couldn't hold it for very long at a time.

After several years I was satisfied with my adjustment. I had suffered my grief and fury and terror, I thought, but now I was at ease with my lot. Then one summer day I set out with George and the children across the desert for a vacation in California. Part way to Yuma I became aware that my right leg felt funny. "I think I've had an exacerbation," I told George. "What shall we do?" he asked. "I think we'd better get the hell to California," I said, "because I don't know whether I'll ever make it again." So we went on to San Diego and then to Orange, up the Pacific Coast Highway to Santa Cruz, across to Yosemite, down to Sequoia and Joshua Tree, and so back over the desert to home. It was a fine two-week trip, filled with friends and fair weather, and I wouldn't have missed it for the world, though I did in fact make it back to California two years later. Nor would there have been any point in missing it, since in MS, once the symptoms have appeared, the neurological damage has been done, and there's no way to predict or prevent that damage.

The incident spoiled my self-satisfaction, however. It renewed my grief and fury and terror, and I learned that one never finishes adjusting to MS. I don't know now why I thought one would. One does not, after all, finish adjusting to life, and MS is simply a fact of my life—not my favorite fact, of course—but as ordinary as my nose and my tropical fish and my yellow Mazda station wagon. It may at any time get worse, but no amount of worry, or anticipation can prepare me for a new loss. My life is a lesson in losses. I learn one at a time.

And I had best be patient in the learning, since I'll have to do it like it or not. As any rock fan knows, you can't always get what you want. Particularly when you have MS. You can't, for example, get cured. In recent years researchers and the organizations that fund research have started to pay MS some attention even though it isn't fatal; perhaps they have begun to see that life is something other than a quantitative phenomenon, that one may be very much alive for a very long time in a life that isn't worth living. The researchers have made some progress toward understanding the mechanism of the disease; It may well be an autoimmune reaction triggered by a slow-acting virus. But they are nowhere near its prevention, control, or cure. And most of us want to be cured. Some, unable to accept incurability, grasp at one treatment after another, no matter how bizarre: megavitamin therapy, gluten-free diet, injections of cobra venom, hypothermal suits, lymphocytopharesis, hyperbaric chambers. Many treatments are probably harmless enough, but none are curative.

The absence of a cure often makes MS patients bitter toward their doctors. Doctors are, after all, the priests of modern society, the new shamans, whose business is to heal, and many an MS patient roves from one to another, searching for the "good" doctor who will make him well. Doctors too think of themselves as healers, and for this reason many have trouble dealing with MS patients, whose disease in its intransigence defeats their aims and mocks their skills. Too few doctors, it is true, treat their patients as whole human beings, but the reverse is also true. I have always tried to be gentle with my doctors, who often have more at stake in terms of ego than I do. I may be frustrated, maddened, depressed by the incurability of my disease, but I am not diminished by it, and they are. When I push myself up from my seat in the waiting room and stumble toward them, I incarnate the limitation of their powers. The least I can do is refuse to press on their tenderest spots.

This gentleness is part of the reason that I'm not sorry to be a cripple. I didn't have it before. Perhaps I'd have developed it anyway—how could I know such a thing?—and I wish I had more of it, but I'm glad of what I have. It has opened and enriched my life enormously, this sense that my frailty and need must be mirrored in others, that in searching for and shaping a stable core in a life wrenched by change and loss, change and loss, I must recognize the same process, under individual conditions, in the lives around me. I do not deprecate such knowledge, however I've come by it.

All the same, if a cure were found, would I take it? In a minute. I may be a cripple, but I'm only occasionally a loony and never a saint. Anyway, in my brand of theology God doesn't give bonus points for a limp. I'd take a cure; I just don't need one. A friend who also has MS startled me once by asking, "Do you ever say to yourself, 'Why me, Lord?'" "No, Michael, I don't," I told him, "because whenever I try, the only response I can think of is 'Why not?'" If I could make a cosmic deal, who would I put in my place? What in my life would I give up in exchange for sound limbs and a thrilling rush of energy? No one. Nothing. I might as well do the job myself. Now that I'm getting the hang of it.

Joining the Conversation:
Critical Thinking and Writing

1. What, if anything, would be lost if the first paragraph were omitted?

2. Mairs speaks of herself not as "handicapped" or "disadvantaged" or "differently abled" but as a "cripple." Can you think of any other persons who call themselves by a term that most other people avoid using for such people?

3. In the fourth paragraph, Mairs emphatically rejects the term "differently abled." Has she convinced you not to use the term? Explain.

4. Find two or three paragraphs that you especially enjoyed reading—yes, *enjoyed* reading—and explain why they pleased you.

Zora Neale Hurston

Zora Neale Hurston (1891–1960) was brought up in Eatonville, Florida, a town said to be the first all-black self-governing town in the United States. Her early years were spent working at odd jobs (domestic servant, manicurist, waitress), but she managed to attend Howard University and then—with the aid of a scholarship—entered Barnard College, where she was the first black student. At Barnard, influenced by anthropologists Franz Boas and Ruth Benedict, she set out to study the folklore of Eatonville. Later, she published several volumes of folklore as well as stories, novels, and an autobiography entitled Dust Tracks on a Road *(1942).*

In the 1950s, Hurston's writing seemed reactionary, almost embarrassing in an age of black protest, and she herself—working as a domestic, a librarian, and a substitute teacher—was almost forgotten. She died in a county welfare home in Florida and was buried in an unmarked grave. In the 1980s, Hurston was, so to speak, rediscovered, partly because of the attention given to her by Alice Walker.

How It Feels to Be Colored Me

I am colored but I offer nothing in the way of extenuating circumstances except the fact that I am the only Negro in the United States whose grandfather on the mother's side was *not* an Indian chief.

I remember the very day that I became colored. Up to my thirteenth year I lived in the little Negro town of Eatonville, Florida. It is exclusively a colored town. The only white people I knew passed through the town going to or coming from Orlando. The native whites rode dusty horses, the Northern tourists chugged down the sandy village road in automobiles. The town knew the Southerners and never stopped cane chewing when they passed. But the Northerners were something else again. They were peered at cautiously from behind curtains by the timid. The more venturesome would come out on the porch to watch them go past and got just as much pleasure out of the tourists as the tourists got out of the village.

The front porch might seem a daring place for the rest of the town, but it was a gallery seat to me. My favorite place was atop the gate-post. Proscenium box for a born first-nighter. Not only did I enjoy the show, but I didn't mind the actors knowing that I liked it. I usually spoke to them in passing. I'd wave at them and when they returned my salute, I would say something like this: "Howdy-do-well-I-thank-you-where-you-goin'?" Usually the automobile or the horse paused at this, and after a queer exchange of compliments, I would probably "go a piece of the way" with them, as we say in farthest Florida. If one of my family happened to come to the front in time to see me, of course negotiations would be rudely broken off. But even so, it is clear that I was the first "welcome-to-our-state" Floridian, and I hope the Miami Chamber of Commerce will please take notice.

During this period, white people differed from colored to me only in that they rode through town and never lived there. They liked to hear me "speak pieces" and sing and wanted to see me dance the parse-me-la, and gave me generously of their small silver for doing these things, which seemed strange to me for I wanted to do them so much that I needed bribing to stop. Only they didn't know it. The colored people gave no dimes. They deplored any joyful tendencies in me, but I was their Zora nevertheless. I belonged to them, to the nearby hotels, to the county—everybody's Zora.

But changes came in the family when I was thirteen, and I was sent to   5
school in Jacksonville. I left Eatonville, the town of the oleanders, as Zora. When I disembarked from the river-boat at Jacksonville, she was no more. It seemed that I had suffered a sea change. I was not Zora of Orange County any more, I was now a little colored girl. I found it out in certain ways. In my heart as well as in the mirror, I became a fast brown—warranted not to rub nor run.

But I am not tragically colored. There is no great sorrow dammed up in my soul, nor lurking behind my eyes. I do not mind at all. I do not belong to the sobbing school of Negrohood who hold that nature somehow has given them a lowdown dirty deal and whose feelings are all hurt about it. Even in the helter-skelter skirmish that is my life, I have seen that the world is to the strong regardless of a little pigmentation more or less. No, I do not weep at the world—I am too busy sharpening my oyster knife.

Someone is always at my elbow reminding me that I am the grand-daughter of slaves. It fails to register depression with me. Slavery is sixty years in the past. The operation was successful and the patient is doing well, thank you. The terrible struggle that made me an American out of a potential slave said "On the line!" The Reconstruction said "Get set!"; and the generation before said "Go!" I am off to a flying start and I must not halt in the stretch to look behind and weep. Slavery is the price I paid for civilization, and the choice was not with me. It is a bully adventure and worth all that I have paid through my ancestors for it. No one on earth ever had a greater chance for glory. The world to be won and nothing to be lost. It is thrilling to think—to know that for any act of mine, I shall get twice as much praise or twice as much blame. It is quite exciting to hold the center of the national stage, with the spectators not knowing whether to laugh or to weep.

The position of my white neighbor is much more difficult. No brown specter pulls up a chair beside me when I sit down to eat. No dark ghost thrusts its leg against mine in bed. The game of keeping what one has is never so exciting as the game of getting.

I do not always feel colored. Even now I often achieve the unconscious Zora of Eatonville before the Hegira. I feel most colored when I am thrown against a sharp white background.

For instance at Barnard. "Beside the waters of the Hudson" I feel my race. Among the thousand white persons, I am a dark rock surged upon, overswept by a creamy sea. I am surged upon and overswept, but through it all, I remain myself. When covered by the waters, I am; and the ebb but reveals me again.

Sometimes it is the other way around. A white person is set down in our midst, but the contrast is just as sharp for me. For instance, when I sit in the drafty basement that is The New World Cabaret with a white person, my color comes. We enter chatting about any little nothing that we have in common and are seated by the jazz waiters. In the abrupt way that jazz orchestras have, this one plunges into a number. It loses no time in circumlocutions, but gets right down to business. It constricts the thorax and splits the heart with its tempo and narcotic harmonies. This orchestra grows rambunctious, rears on its hind legs and attacks the tonal veil with primitive fury, rending it, clawing it until it breaks through to the jungle beyond. I follow those heathen—follow them exultingly. I dance wildly inside myself; I yell within, I whoop; I shake my assegai[1] above my head, I hurl it true to the mark *yeeeeooww!* I am in the jungle and living in the jungle way. My face is painted red and yellow and my body is painted blue. My pulse is throbbing like a war drum. I want to slaughter something—give pain, give death to what, I do not know. But the piece ends. The men of the orchestra wipe their lips and rest their fingers. I creep back slowly to the veneer we call civilization with the last tone and find the white friend sitting motionless in his seat, smoking calmly.

"Good music they have here," he remarks, drumming the table with his fingertips.

---

[1]**assegai** An African spear

Music! The great blobs of purple and red emotion have not touched him. He has only heard what I felt. He is far away and I see him but dimly across the ocean and the continent that have fallen between us. He is so pale with his whiteness then and I am *so* colored.

At certain times I have no race, I am *me*. When I set my hat at a certain angle and saunter down Seventh Avenue, Harlem City, feeling as snooty as the lions in front of the Forty-Second Street Library, for instance. So far as my feelings are concerned, Peggy Hopkins Joyce on the Boule Mich[2] with her gorgeous raiment, stately carriage, knees knocking together in a most aristocratic manner, has nothing on me. The cosmic Zora emerges. I belong to no race nor time. I am the eternal feminine with its string of beads.

I have no separate feeling about being an American citizen and colored. I am merely a fragment of the Great Soul that surges within the boundaries. My country, right or wrong.

15

Sometimes, I feel discriminated against, but it does not make me angry. It merely astonishes me. How *can* any deny themselves the pleasure of my company! It's beyond me.

But in the main, I feel like a brown bag of miscellany propped against a wall. Against a wall in company with other bags, white, red and yellow. Pour out the contents, and there is discovered a jumble of small things priceless and worthless. A first-water diamond, an empty spool, bits of broken glass, lengths of string, a key to a door long since crumbled away, a rusty knife-blade, old shoes saved for a road that never was and never will be, a nail bent under the weight of things too heavy for any nail, a dried flower or two, still a little fragrant. In your hand is the brown bag. On the ground before you is the jumble it held—so much like the jumble in the bags, could they be emptied, that all might be dumped in a single heap and the bags refilled without altering the content of any greatly. A bit of colored glass more or less would not matter. Perhaps that is how the Great Stuffer of Bags filled them in the first place—who knows?

Joining the Conversation: Critical Thinking and Writing

1. Do you think that Hurston has chosen an effective title? In a sentence or two, can you summarize what she says about "how it feels to be colored me"? (Note that when Hurston wrote this essay in 1928, "colored" was the term commonly used for persons whom today we call African American or black.)

---

[2]**Peggy Hopkins Joyce on the Boule Mich** Joyce (1893–1957), an actress in racy musicals, was famous for her marriages to (and her divorces from) rich men; "Boule Mich" (pronounced "Bull Mish") refers to Michigan Avenue in Chicago, grandly compared to Boulevard St. Michel, a fashionable street in Paris.

2. Explain the following sentence: "But I am not tragically colored."

3. At one point, Hurston writes: "At certain times I have no race, I am me." What does she mean? Does her distinction here make sense to you or do you find it confusing?

4. How would you describe Hurston's style? Do you think it works well in this essay or would a different style be more effective? Explain.

5. One reader of this essay has said, "By telling us who she isn't, Hurston tells us who she is." Do you agree? If so, in a sentence or two, explain who she is.

6. Hurston was the first student of color to attend Barnard College, and this is the background for this essay, which she wrote in 1928. Do you think that the essay as it stands is still relevant?

7. Do you feel that your race, religion, ethnicity, or something else identifies you as "different"? Is this something you talk about? With whom? Or do you keep this feeling to yourself?

Gloria Naylor

Gloria Naylor—university teacher, essayist, and novelist—holds an MA in African-American Studies from Yale University. Her first novel, The Women of Brewster Place *(1983), won an American Book Award. "A Question of Language" originally appeared in* The New York Times Magazine.

A Question of Language

Language is the subject. It is the written form with which I've managed to keep the wolf away from the door and, in diaries, to keep my sanity. In spite of this, I consider the written word inferior to the spoken, and much of the frustration experienced by novelists is the awareness that whatever we manage to capture in even the most transcendent passages falls far short of the richness of life. Dialogue achieves its power in the dynamics of a fleeting moment of sight, sound, smell, and touch.

I'm not going to enter the debate here about whether it is language that shapes reality or vice versa. That battle is doomed to be waged whenever we seek intermittent reprieve from the chicken and egg dispute. I will simply take the position that the spoken word, like the written word, amounts to a nonsensical arrangement of sounds or letters without a consensus that assigns "meaning." And building from the meanings of what we hear, we order reality. Words themselves are innocuous; it is the consensus that gives them true power.

I remember the first time I heard the word *nigger*. In my third-grade class, our math tests were being passed down the rows, and as I handed the papers to a little boy in back of me, I remarked that once again he had received a much lower mark than I did. He snatched his test from me and spit out that word. Had he called me a nymphomaniac or a necrophiliac, I couldn't have been more puzzled. I didn't know what a nigger was, but I knew that whatever it meant, it was something he shouldn't have called me. This was verified when I raised my hand, and in a loud voice repeated what he had said and watched the teacher scold him for using a "bad" word. I was later to go home and ask the inevitable question that every black parent must face—"Mommy, what does 'nigger' mean?"

And what exactly did it mean? Thinking back, I realize that this could not have been the first time the word was used in my presence. I was part of a large extended family that had migrated from the rural South after World War II and formed a close-knit network that gravitated around my maternal grandparents. Their ground-floor apartment in one of the buildings they owned in Harlem was a weekend mecca for my immediate family, along with countless aunts, uncles, and cousins who brought along assorted friends. It was a bustling and open house with assorted neighbors and tenants popping in and out to exchange bits of gossip, pick up an old quarrel or referee the ongoing checkers game in which my grandmother cheated shamelessly. They were all there to let down their hair and put up their feet after a week of labor in the factories, laundries, and shipyards of New York.

Amid the clamor, which could reach deafening proportions—two or three conversations going on simultaneously, punctuated by the sound of a baby's crying somewhere in the back rooms or out on the street—there was still a rigid set of rules about what was said and how. Older children were sent out of the living room when it was time to get into the juicy details about "you-know-who" up on the third floor who had gone and gotten herself "p.r.e.g.n.a.n.t!" But my parents, knowing that I could spell well beyond my years, always demanded that I follow the others out to play. Beyond sexual misconduct and death, everything else was considered harmless for our young ears. And so among the anecdotes of the triumphs and disappointments in the various workings of their lives, the word *nigger* was used in my presence, but it was set within contexts and inflections that caused it to register in my mind as something else.

In the singular, the word was always applied to a man who had distinguished himself in some situation that brought their approval for his strength, intelligence, or drive:

"Did Johnny really do that?"

5

"I'm telling you, that nigger pulled in $6,000 of overtime last year. Said he got enough for a down payment on a house."

When used with a possessive adjective by a woman—"my nigger"— it became a term of endearment for husband or boyfriend. But it could be more than just a term applied to a man. In their mouths it became the pure essence of manhood—a disembodied force that channeled their past history of struggle and present survival against the odds into a victorious statement of being: "Yeah, that old foreman found out quick enough— you don't mess with a nigger."

In the plural, it became a description of some group within the com-   10
munity that had overstepped the bounds of decency as my family defined it: Parents who neglected their children, a drunken couple who fought in public, people who simply refused to look for work, those with excessively dirty mouths or unkempt households were all "trifling niggers." This particular circle could forgive hard times, unemployment, the occasional bout of depression—they had gone through all of that themselves— but the unforgivable sin was lack of self-respect.

A woman could never be a *nigger* in the singular, with its connotation of confirming worth. The noun *girl* was its closest equivalent in that sense, but only when used in direct address and regardless of the gender doing the addressing. *Girl* was a token of respect for a woman. The one-syllable word was drawn out to sound like three in recognition of the extra ounce of wit, nerve or daring that the woman had shown in the situation under discussion.

"G.i.r.l, stop. You mean you said that to his face?"

But if the word was used in a third-person reference or shortened so that it almost snapped out of the mouth, it always involved some element of communal disapproval. And age became an important factor in these exchanges. It was only between individuals of the same generation, or from an older person to a younger (but never the other way around), that "girl" would be considered a compliment.

I don't agree with the argument that use of the word *nigger* at this social stratum of the black community was an internalization of racism. The dynamics were the exact opposite: the people in my grandmother's living room took a word that whites used to signify worthlessness or degradation and rendered it impotent. Gathering there together, they transformed *nigger* to signify the varied and complex human beings they knew themselves to be. If the word was to disappear totally from the mouths of even the most liberal of white society, no one in that room was naive enough to believe it would disappear from white minds. Meeting the word head-on, they proved it had absolutely nothing to do with the way they were determined to live their lives.

So there must have been dozens of times that the word *nigger* was   15
spoken in front of me before I reached the third grade. But I didn't "hear" it until it was said by a small pair of lips that had already learned it could be a way to humiliate me. That was the word I went home and asked my

mother about. And since she knew that I had to grow up in America, she took me in her lap and explained.

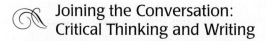

Joining the Conversation: Critical Thinking and Writing

1. According to Naylor (in paragraph 1), why is written language inferior to spoken language? Can you think of any way or any circumstance in which written language is superior? How does Naylor's essay support her position here? Or does it?

2. In paragraph 2, Naylor says, "Words themselves are innocuous; it is the consensus that gives them true power." What does this mean? In the rest of the essay, Naylor discusses meanings of the word *nigger*. To what extent does her discussion demonstrate that consensus "assigns meaning" and gives words power?

3. If as a child you were the victim of an ethnic slur, explain how you reacted to it and how others (perhaps a parent or teacher) reacted to it. Or if you ever delivered an ethnic slur, explain how you felt then and how you feel now about the incident or incidents.

Stephen Jay Gould

Stephen Jay Gould (1941–2002) taught paleontology, biology, and the history of science at Harvard University. The essays he wrote for the magazine Natural History *have been collected in several highly readable books.*

Women's Brains

In the Prelude to *Middlemarch*, George Eliot lamented the unfulfilled lives of talented women:

> Some have felt that these blundering lives are due to the inconvenient indefiniteness with which the Supreme Power has fashioned the natures of women: if there were one level of feminine incompetence as strict as the ability to count three and no more, the social lot of women might be treated with scientific certitude.

Eliot goes on to discount the idea of innate limitation, but while she wrote in 1872, the leaders of European anthropometry were trying to measure "with scientific certitude" the inferiority of women. Anthropometry, or measurement of the human body, is not so fashionable a field these days, but it dominated the human sciences for much of the nineteenth century and remained popular until intelligence testing replaced skull measurement as a favored device for making invidious comparisons among races, classes, and sexes. Craniometry, or measurement of the skull, commanded the most attention and respect. Its unquestioned leader, Paul Broca (1824–80), professor of clinical surgery at the Faculty of Medicine in Paris, gathered a school of disciples and imitators around himself. Their work, so meticulous and apparently irrefutable, exerted great influence and won high esteem as a jewel of nineteenth-century science.

Broca's work seemed particularly invulnerable to refutation. Had he not measured with the most scrupulous care and accuracy? (Indeed, he had. I have the greatest respect for Broca's meticulous procedure. His numbers are sound. But science is an inferential exercise, not a catalog of facts. Numbers, by themselves, specify nothing. All depends upon what you do with them.) Broca depicted himself as an apostle of objectivity, a man who bowed before facts and cast aside superstition and sentimentality. He declared that "there is no faith, however respectable, no interest, however legitimate, which must not accommodate itself to the progress of human knowledge and bend before truth." Women, like it or not, had smaller brains than men and, therefore, could not equal them in intelligence. This fact, Broca argued, may reinforce a common prejudice in male society, but it is also a scientific truth. L. Manouvrier, a black sheep in Broca's fold, rejected the inferiority of women and wrote with feeling about the burden imposed upon them by Broca's numbers:

> Women displayed their talents and their diplomas. They also invoked philosophical authorities. But they were opposed by *numbers* unknown to Condorcet or to John Stuart Mill. These numbers fell upon poor women like a sledge hammer, and they were accompanied by commentaries and sarcasms more ferocious than the most misogynist imprecations of certain church fathers. The theologians had asked if women had a soul. Several centuries later, some scientists were ready to refuse them a human intelligence.

Broca's argument rested upon two sets of data: the larger brains of men in modern societies, and a supposed increase in male superiority through time. His most extensive data came from autopsies performed personally in four Parisian hospitals. For 292 male brains, he calculated an average weight of 1,325 grams; 140 female brains averaged 1,144 grams for a difference of 181 grams, or 14 percent of the male weight. Broca understood, of course, that part of this difference could be attributed to the greater height of males. Yet he made no attempt to measure the effect of size alone and actually stated that it cannot account for the entire difference because we know, a priori, that women are not as intelligent as men (a premise that the data were supposed to test, not rest upon):

We might ask if the small size of the female brain depends exclusively upon the small size of her body. Tiedemann has proposed this explanation. But we must not forget that women are, on the average, a little less intelligent than men, a difference which we should not exaggerate but which is, nonetheless, real. We are therefore permitted to suppose that the relatively small size of the female brain depends in part upon her physical inferiority and in part upon her intellectual inferiority.

In 1873, the year after Eliot published *Middlemarch*, Broca measured the cranial capacities of prehistoric skulls from L'Homme Mort cave. Here he found a difference of only 99.5 cubic centimeters between males and females, while modern populations range from 129.5 to 220.7. Topinard, Broca's chief disciple, explained the increasing discrepancy through time as a result of differing evolutionary pressures upon dominant men and passive women:

> The man who fights for two or more in the struggle for existence, who has all the responsibility and the cares of tomorrow, who is constantly active in combating the environment and human rivals, needs more brain than the woman whom he must protect and nourish, the sedentary woman, lacking any interior occupations, whose role is to raise children, love, and be passive.

In 1879, Gustave Le Bon, chief misogynist of Broca's school, used these data to publish what must be the most vicious attack upon women in modern scientific literature (no one can top Aristotle). I do not claim his views were representative of Broca's school, but they were published in France's most respected anthropological journal. Le Bon concluded:

> In the most intelligent races, as among the Parisians, there are a large number of women whose brains are closer in size to those of gorillas than to the most developed male brains. This inferiority is so obvious that no one can contest it for a moment; only its degree is worth discussion. All psychologists who have studied the intelligence of women, as well as poets and novelists, recognize today that they represent the most inferior forms of human evolution and that they are closer to children and savages than to an adult, civilized man. They excel in fickleness, inconstancy, absence of thought and logic, and incapacity to reason. Without doubt there exist some distinguished women, very superior to the average man, but they are as exceptional as the birth of any monstrosity, as, for example, of a gorilla with two heads; consequently, we may neglect them entirely.

Nor did Le Bon shrink from the social implications of his views. He was horrified by the proposal of some American reformers to grant women higher education on the same basis as men:

> A desire to give them the same education, and, as a consequence, to propose the same goals for them, is a dangerous chimera. . . . The day when, misunderstanding the inferior occupations which nature has given her, women leave the home and take part in our battles; on this day a social revolution

will begin, and everything that maintains the sacred ties of the family will disappear.

Sound familiar?[1]

I have reexamined Broca's data, the basis for all this derivative pronouncement, and I find his numbers sound but his interpretation ill-founded, to say the least. The data supporting his claim for increased difference through time can be easily dismissed. Broca based his contention on the samples from L'Homme Mort alone—only seven male and six female skulls in all. Never have so little data yielded such far ranging conclusions.

In 1888, Topinard published Broca's more extensive data on the Parisian hospitals. Since Broca recorded height and age as well as brain size, we may use modern statistics to remove their effect. Brain weight decreases with age, and Broca's women were, on average, considerably older than his men. Brain weight increases with height, and his average man was almost half a foot taller than his average woman. I used multiple regression, a technique that allowed me to assess simultaneously the influence of height and age upon brain size. In an analysis of the data for women, I found that, at average male height and age, a woman's brain would weigh 1,212 grams. Correction for height and age reduces Broca's measured difference of 181 grams by more than a third, to 113 grams.

I don't know what to make of this remaining difference because I cannot assess other factors known to influence brain size in a major way. Cause of death has an important effect: degenerative disease often entails a substantial diminution of brain size. (This effect is separate from the decrease attributed to age alone.) Eugene Schreider, also working with Broca's data, found that men killed in accidents had brains weighing, on average, 60 grams more than men dying of infectious diseases. The best modern data I can find (from American hospitals) records a full 100-gram difference between death by degenerative arteriosclerosis and by violence or accident. Since so many of Broca's subjects were very elderly women, we may assume that lengthy degenerative disease was more common among them than among the men.

More importantly, modern students of brain size still have not agreed on a proper measure for eliminating the powerful effect of body size. Height is partly adequate, but men and women of the same height do not share the same body build. Weight is even worse than height, because most of its variation reflects nutrition rather than intrinsic size—fat versus skinny exerts little influence upon the brain. Manouvrier took up this subject in the 1880s and argued that muscular mass and force should be used. He tried to measure this elusive property in various ways and

---

[1]When I wrote this essay, I assumed that Le Bon was a marginal, if colorful, figure. I have since learned that he was a leading scientist, one of the founders of social psychology, and best known for a seminal study on crowd behavior, still cited today (*La psychologie des foules*, 1895), and for his work on unconscious motivation.

found a marked difference in favor of men, even in men and women of the same height. When he corrected for what he called "sexual mass," women actually came out slightly ahead in brain size.

Thus, the corrected 113-gram difference is surely too large; the true figure is probably close to zero and may as well favor women as men. And 113 grams, by the way, is exactly the average difference between a 5 foot 4 inch and a 6 foot 4 inch male in Broca's data. We would not (especially us short folks) want to ascribe greater intelligence to tall men. In short, who knows what to do with Broca's data? They certainly don't permit any confident claim that men have bigger brains than women.

To appreciate the social role of Broca and his school, we must recognize that his statements about the brains of women do not reflect an isolated prejudice toward a single disadvantaged group. They must be weighed in the context of a general theory that supported contemporary social distinctions as biologically ordained. Women, blacks, and poor people suffered the same disparagement, but women bore the brunt of Broca's argument because he had easier access to data on women's brains. Women were singularly denigrated but they also stood as surrogates for other disenfranchised groups. As one of Broca's disciples wrote in 1881: "Men of the black races have a brain scarcely heavier than that of white women." This juxtaposition extended into many other realms of anthropological argument, particularly to claims that, anatomically and emotionally, both women and blacks were like white children—and that white children, by the theory of recapitulation, represented an ancestral (primitive) adult stage of human evolution. I do not regard as empty rhetoric the claim that women's battles are for all of us.

Maria Montessori did not confine her activities to educational reform for young children. She lectured on anthropology for several years at the University of Rome, and wrote an influential book entitled *Pedagogical Anthropology* (English edition, 1913). Montessori was no egalitarian. She supported most of Broca's work and the theory of innate criminality proposed by her compatriot Cesare Lombroso. She measured the circumference of children's heads in her schools and inferred that the best prospects had bigger brains. But she had no use for Broca's conclusions about women. She discussed Manouvrier's work at length and made much of his tentative claim that women, after proper correction of the data, had slightly larger brains than men. Women, she concluded, were intellectually superior, but men had prevailed heretofore by dint of physical force. Since technology has abolished force as an instrument of power, the era of women may soon be upon us: "In such an epoch there will really be superior human beings, there will really be men strong in morality and in sentiment. Perhaps in this way the reign of women is approaching, when the enigma of her anthropological superiority will be deciphered. Woman was always the custodian of human sentiment, morality and honor."

This represents one possible antidote to "scientific" claims for the constitutional inferiority of certain groups. One may affirm the validity of biological distinctions but argue that the data have been misinterpreted by prejudiced men with a stake in the outcome, and that disadvantaged groups are truly superior. In recent years, Elaine Morgan has followed this strategy in her *Descent of Woman*, a speculative reconstruction of human prehistory from the woman's point of view—and as farcical as more famous tall tales by and for men.

I prefer another strategy. Montessori and Morgan followed Broca's philosophy to reach a more congenial conclusion. I would rather label the whole enterprise of setting a biological value upon groups for what it is: irrelevant and highly injurious. George Eliot well appreciated the special tragedy that biological labeling imposed upon members of disadvantaged groups. She expressed it for people like herself—women of extraordinary talent. I would apply it more widely—not only to those whose dreams are flouted but also to those who never realize that they may dream—but I cannot match her prose. In conclusion, then, the rest of Eliot's prelude to *Middlemarch*:

> The limits of variation are really much wider than anyone would imagine from the sameness of women's coiffure and the favorite love stories in prose and verse. Here and there a cygnet is reared uneasily among the ducklings in the brown pond, and never finds the living stream in fellowship with its own oary-footed kind. Here and there is born a Saint Theresa, foundress of nothing, whose loving heartbeats and sobs after an unattained goodness tremble off and are dispersed among hindrances instead of centering in some long-recognizable deed.

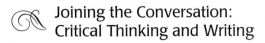 Joining the Conversation:
Critical Thinking and Writing

1. What is your understanding of anthropometry from paragraph 2? According to Gould, what does intelligence testing have in common with anthropometry? Characterize his attitude toward both. How does he reveal his attitude in this paragraph?

2. In paragraph 3, what does Gould mean when he says, "But science is an inferential exercise, not a catalog of facts"?

3. In paragraph 14, Gould says, "I do not regard as empty rhetoric the claim that women's battles are for all of us." What does he mean? What foundation for this opinion have this paragraph and paragraph 2 provided?

4. Who was Maria Montessori, and what does her work have to do with Gould's argument? If her relevance is not entirely clear to you or was not on first reading, what might Gould have done to make it clearer?

5. According to Gould, what are the social consequences of what he calls in paragraph 17 *biological labeling*? If on the whole you agree with him, what is the basis of your agreement?

6. In paragraph 14, Gould refers to the "social role of Broca and his school." What does he mean by that? On the basis of this essay (and others of Gould's that you may have read), formulate in a sentence or two the social role of Gould.

Paul Theroux

Paul Theroux was born in 1941 in Medford, Massachusetts, and was educated at the University of Maine, the University of Massachusetts, and Syracuse University. He served as a Peace Corps volunteer in Africa and has spent much of his adult life abroad, in Africa, Asia, Europe, and Central America. Although best known as a novelist and writer of travel books, he is also a poet and essayist. This essay originally appeared in The New York Times *Magazine.*

The Male Myth

There is a pathetic sentence in the chapter "Fetishism" in Dr. Norman Cameron's book *Personality Development and Psychopathology*. It goes: "Fetishists are nearly always men; and their commonest fetish is a woman's shoe." I cannot read that sentence without thinking that it is just one more awful thing about being a man—and perhaps it is the most important thing to know about us.

I have always disliked being a man. The whole idea of manhood in America is pitiful, a little like having to wear an ill-fitting coat for one's entire life. (By contrast, I imagine femininity to be an oppressive sense of nakedness.) Even the expression "Be a man!" strikes me as insulting and abusive. It means: Be stupid, be unfeeling, obedient and soldierly, and stop thinking. Man means "manly"—how can one think "about men" without considering the terrible ambition of manliness? And yet it is part of every man's life. It is a hideous and crippling lie; it not only insists on difference and connives at superiority, it is also by its very nature destructive—emotionally damaging and socially harmful.

The youth who is subverted, as most are, into believing in the masculine ideal is effectively separated from women—it is the most savage tribal logic—and he spends the rest of his life finding women a riddle and a nuisance. Of course, there is a female version of this male affliction. It begins with mothers encouraging little girls to say (to other adults), "Do you like my new dress?" In a sense, girls are traditionally urged to please adults with a kind of coquettishness, while boys are enjoined to behave like monkeys toward each other. The 9-year-old coquette proceeds to become womanish in a subtle power game in which she learns to be sexually indispensable, socially decorative and always alert to a man's sense of inadequacy.

Femininity—being ladylike—implies needing a man as witness and seducer; but masculinity celebrates the exclusive company of men. That is why it is so grotesque; and that is also why there is no manliness without inadequacy—because it denies men the natural friendship of women.

It is very hard to imagine any concept of manliness that does not be- 5
little women, and it begins very early. At an age when I wanted to meet girls—let's say the treacherous years of 13 to 16—I was told to take up a sport, get more fresh air, join the Boy Scouts, and I was urged not to read so much. It was the 1950's and, if you asked too many questions about sex, you were sent to camp—boy's camp, of course; the nightmare. Nothing is more unnatural or prisonlike than a boys' camp, but if it were not for them, we would have no Elks' Lodges, no pool-rooms, no boxing matches, no marines.

And perhaps no sports as we know them. Everyone is aware of how few in number are the athletes who behave like gentlemen. Just as high-school basketball teaches you how to be a poor loser, the manly attitude toward sports seems to be little more than a recipe for creating bad marriages, social misfits, moral degenerates, sadists, latent rapists and just plain louts. I regard high-school sports as a drug far worse than marijuana, and it is the reason that the average tennis champion, say, is a pathetic oaf.

Any objective study would find the quest for manliness essentially right wing, puritanical, cowardly, neurotic and fueled largely by a fear of women. It is also certainly philistine. There is no book hater like a Little League coach. But, indeed, all the creative arts are obnoxious to the manly ideal, because at their best the arts are pursued by uncompetitive and essentially solitary people. It makes it very hard for a creative youngster, for any boy who expresses the desire to be alone seems to be saying that there is something wrong with him.

It ought to be clear by now that I have an objection to the way we turn boys into men. It does not surprise me that when the President of the United States has his customary weekend off, he dresses like a cowboy—it is both a measure of his insecurity and his willingness to please. In many ways, American culture does little more for a man than prepare him for modeling clothes in the L. L. Bean catalogue. I take this as a personal insult because for many years I found it impossible to admit to myself that I wanted to be a writer. It was my guilty secret, because being a writer was incompatible with being a man.

There are people who might deny this, but that is because the American writer, typically, has been so at pains to prove his manliness. But first there was a fear that writing was not a manly profession—indeed, not a profession at all. (The paradox in American letters is that it has always been easier for a woman to write and for a man to be published.) Growing up, I had thought of sports as wasteful and humiliating, and the idea of manliness as a bore. My wanting to become a writer was not a flight from that oppressive role playing, but I quickly saw that it was at odds with it. Everything in stereotyped manliness goes against the life of the mind. The Hemingway personality is too tedious to go into here, but certainly it was not until this aberrant behavior was examined by feminists in the 1960's that any male writer dared question the pugnacity in Hemingway's fiction. All that bullfighting and arm-wrestling and elephant shooting diminished Hemingway as a writer: One cannot be a male writer without first proving that one is a man.

It is normal in America for a man to be dismissive or even somewhat apologetic about being a writer. Various factors make it easier. There is a heartiness about journalism that makes it acceptable—journalism is the manliest form of American writing and, therefore, the profession the most independent-minded women seek (yes, it is an illusion, but that is my point). Fiction writing is equated with a kind of dispirited failure and is only manly when it produces wealth. Money is masculinity. So is drinking. Being a drunkard is another assertion, if misplaced, of manliness. The American male writer is traditionally proud of his heavy drinking. But we are also very literal-minded people. A man proves his manhood in America in old-fashioned ways. He kills lions, like Hemingway; or he hunts ducks, like Nathanael West; or he makes pronouncements, like "A man should carry enough knife to defend himself with," as James Jones is said to have once told an interviewer. And we are familiar with the lengths to which Norman Mailer is prepared, in his endearing way, to prove that he is just as much a monster as the next man.

When the novelist John Irving was revealed as a wrestler, people took him to be a very serious writer. But what interests me is that it is inconceivable that any woman writer would be shown in such a posture. How surprised we would be if Joyce Carol Oates were revealed as a sumo wrestler or Joan Didion enjoyed pumping iron. "Lives in New York City with her three children" is the typical woman-writer's biographical note, for just as the male writer must prove he has achieved a sort of muscular manhood, the woman writer—or rather her publicists—must prove her motherhood.

There would be no point in saying any of this if it were not generally accepted that to be a man is somehow—even now in feminist-influenced America—a privilege. It is on the contrary an unmerciful and punishing burden. Being a man is bad enough; being manly is appalling. It is the sinister silliness of men's fashions that inspires the so-called dress code of the Ritz-Carlton Hotel in Boston. It is the institutionalized cheating in college sports. It is a pathetic and primitive insecurity.

And this is also why men often object to feminism, but are afraid to explain why: Of course women have a justified grievance, but most men believe—and with reason—that their lives are much worse.

Joining the Conversation: Critical Thinking and Writing

1. In paragraph 6, Theroux says that "high-school basketball teaches you how to be a poor loser." Think about this and then write a paragraph that in effect offers a definition of a "poor loser" but that also shows how a high school sport teaches one to be a poor loser.

2. Theroux speaks of "the Hemingway personality" and of "the pugnacity in Hemingway's fiction." If you have read a work by Hemingway, write a paragraph in which you explain (to someone unfamiliar with Hemingway) what Theroux is talking about.

3. Let's assume that a reader says he or she doesn't quite understand Theroux's final paragraph. Write a paragraph explaining it.

4. Theroux makes some deliberately provocative statements. For example:

> Nothing is more unnatural or prisonlike than a boys' camp (paragraph 5).

> Everyone is aware of how few in number are the athletes who behave like gentlemen (paragraph 6).

> The quest for manliness . . . [is] fueled largely by a fear of women (paragraph 7).

Choose one such statement from the essay and then consider what you would need to do to argue effectively against it. You needn't produce the argument, but you should consider how such an argument might be constructed.

Katha Pollitt

Katha Pollitt (b. 1949) writes chiefly on literary, political, and social topics. In addition to writing essays, she writes poetry; her first collection of poems, Antarctic Traveller *(1982), won the National Book Critics Circle Award. She publishes widely, especially in the* Nation, *the* New Yorker, *and* The New York Times. *We reprint an article that originally appeared in* The New York Times Magazine.

Why Boys Don't Play with Dolls

It's twenty-eight years since the founding of NOW,[1] and boys still like trucks and girls still like dolls. Increasingly, we are told that the source of these robust preferences must lie outside society—in prenatal

---

[1]**NOW** National Organization for Women (Editors' note)

---

hormonal influences, brain chemistry, genes—and that feminism has reached its natural limits. What else could possibly explain the love of preschool girls for party dresses or the desire of toddler boys to own more guns than Mark from Michigan?

True, recent studies claim to show small cognitive differences between the sexes: He gets around by orienting himself in space; she does it by remembering landmarks. Time will tell if any deserve the hoopla with which each is invariably greeted, over the protests of the researchers themselves. But even if the results hold up (and the history of such research is not encouraging), we don't need studies of sex-differentiated brain activity in reading, say, to understand why boys and girls still seem so unalike.

The feminist movement has done much for some women, and something for every woman, but it has hardly turned America into a playground free of sex roles. It hasn't even got women to stop dieting or men to stop interrupting them.

Instead of looking at kids to "prove" that differences in behavior by sex are innate, we can look at the ways we raise kids as an index to how unfinished the feminist revolution really is, and how tentatively it is embraced even by adults who fully expect their daughters to enter previously male-dominated professions and their sons to change diapers.

I'm at a children's birthday party. "I'm sorry," one mom silently mouths to the mother of the birthday girl, who has just torn open her present—Tropical Splash Barbie. Now, you can love Barbie or you can hate Barbie, and there are feminists in both camps. But *apologize* for Barbie? Inflict Barbie, against your own convictions, on the child of a friend you know will be none too pleased?   5

Every mother in that room had spent years becoming a person who had to be taken seriously, not least by herself. Even the most attractive, I'm willing to bet, had suffered over her body's failure to fit the impossible American ideal. Given all that, it seems crazy to transmit Barbie to the next generation. Yet to reject her is to say that what Barbie represents— being sexy, thin, stylish—is unimportant, which is obviously not true, and children know it's not true.

Women's looks matter terribly in this society, and so Barbie, however ambivalently, must be passed along. After all, there are worse toys. The Cut and Style Barbie styling head, for example, a grotesque object intended to encourage "hair play." The grown-ups who give that probably apologize, too.

How happy would most parents be to have a child who flouted sex conventions? I know a lot of women, feminists, who complain in a comical, eye-ball-rolling way about their sons' passion for sports: the ruined weekends, obnoxious coaches, macho values. But they would not think of discouraging their sons from participating in this activity they find so foolish. Or do they? Their husbands are sports fans, too, and they like their husbands a lot.

Could it be that even sports-resistant moms see athletics as part of manliness? That if their sons wanted to spend the weekend writing up their diaries, or reading, or baking, they'd find it disturbing? Too antisocial? Too lonely? Too gay?

Theories of innate differences in behavior are appealing. They let parents off the hook—no small recommendation in a culture that holds moms, and sometimes even dads, responsible for their children's every misstep on the road to bliss and success.

They allow grown-ups to take the path of least resistance to the dominant culture, which always requires less psychic effort, even if it means more actual work: Just ask the working mother who comes home exhausted and nonetheless finds it easier to pick up her son's socks than make him do it himself. They let families buy for their children, without *too* much guilt, the unbelievably sexist junk that the kids, who have been watching commercials since birth, understandably crave.

But the thing the theories do most of all is tell adults that the *adult* world—in which moms and dads still play by many of the old rules even as they question and fidget and chafe against them—is the way it's supposed to be. A girl with a doll and a boy with a truck "explain" why men are from Mars and women are from Venus, why wives do housework and husbands just don't understand.

The paradox is that the world of rigid and hierarchical sex roles evoked by determinist theories is already passing away. Three-year-olds may indeed insist that doctors are male and nurses female, even if their own mother is a physician. Six-year-olds know better. These days, something like half of all medical students are female, and male applications to nursing school are inching upward. When tomorrow's three-year-olds play doctor, who's to say how they'll assign the roles?

With sex roles, as in every area of life, people aspire to what is possible, and conform to what is necessary. But these are not fixed, especially today. Biological determinism may reassure some adults about their present, but it is feminism, the ideology of flexible and converging sex roles, that fits our children's future. And the kids, somehow, know this.

That's why, if you look carefully, you'll find that for every kid who fits a stereotype, there's another who's breaking one down. Sometimes it's the same kid—the boy who skateboards *and* takes cooking in his after school program; the girl who collects stuffed animals *and* A-pluses in science.

Feminists are often accused of imposing their "agenda" on children. Isn't that what adults always do, consciously and unconsciously? Kids aren't born religious, or polite, or kind, or able to remember where they put their sneakers. Inculcating these behaviors, and the values behind them, is a tremendous amount of work, involving many adults. We don't have a choice, really, about *whether* we should give our children messages about what it means to be male and female—they're bombarded with them from morning till night.

Joining the Conversation: Critical Thinking and Writing

1. In a paragraph, set forth Pollitt's answer to the question she poses in her title.

2. In paragraph 7, Pollitt says, "Women's looks matter terribly in this society." Do you agree with this generalization? If they do matter "terribly," do they matter more than men's? What evidence can you give, one way or the other? Write your answer in an essay of 250 words.

3. Look at the last sentence in paragraph 12: "A girl with a doll and a boy with a truck 'explain' why men are from Mars and women are from Venus, why wives do housework and husbands just don't understand." Why does Pollitt put "explain" within quotation marks? What is she getting at by speaking of Mars and Venus? "Do housework" and "don't understand" are not the parallel construction that a reader probably expects. Do you think Pollitt's writing is deficient here or is the variation purposeful? Explain.

4. In paragraph 14, Pollitt says that "the ideology of flexible and converging sex roles" is the one that "fits our children's future." What would be examples of "flexible and converging sex roles"? And do you agree that this ideology is the one that suits the immediate future? Why?

5. Do you believe that you have been influenced by Barbie or by any other toy? Explain.

6. In her final paragraph, Pollitt says that adults always impose an "agenda" on their children, consciously or unconsciously. What agenda did your parents (or other adults charged with your upbringing) impose or try to impose? What was your response? As you think back on it, were the agenda and the responses appropriate? Explain your answers in an essay of 500 to 750 words.

7. If you have heard that "brain chemistry" or "genes" (paragraph 1) account for "innate differences in behavior" (paragraph 10) in boys and girls, write a paragraph to explain the view and then evaluate it in another paragraph—drawing perhaps on your reading of Pollitt's essay.

Langston Hughes

Langston Hughes (1902–67), born in Joplin, Missouri, was the first African-American writer to establish an international reputation. Enormously versatile, he wrote poems, plays, stories, novels, children's books, filmscripts, essays, and autobiographies. (The selection printed below is from an autobiographical volume called The Big Sea *[1940]). Hughes also exerted a great influence on American literature by organizing poetry readings for black writers and by founding three theater groups.*

Salvation

I was saved from sin when I was going on thirteen. But not really saved. It happened like this. There was a big revival at my Auntie Reed's church. Every night for weeks there had been much preaching, singing, praying, and shouting, and some very hardened sinners had been brought to Christ, and the membership of the church had grown by leaps and bounds. Then just before the revival ended, they held a special meeting for children, "to bring the young lambs to the fold." My aunt spoke of it for days ahead. That night I was escorted to the front row and placed on the mourners' bench with all the other young sinners, who had not yet been brought to Jesus.

My aunt told me that when you were saved you saw a light, and something happened to you inside! And Jesus came into your life! And God was with you from then on! She said you could see and hear and feel Jesus in your soul. I believed her. I had heard a great many old people say the same thing and it seemed to me they ought to know. So I sat there calmly in the hot, crowded church, waiting for Jesus to come to me.

The preacher preached a wonderful rhythmical sermon, all moans and shouts and lonely cries and dire pictures of hell, and then he sang a song about the ninety and nine safe in the fold, but one little lamb was left out in the cold. Then he said: "Won't you come? Won't you come to Jesus? Young lambs, won't you come?" And he held out his arms to all us young sinners there on the mourners' bench. And the little girls cried. And some of them jumped up and went to Jesus right away. But most of us just sat there.

A great many old people came and knelt around us and prayed, old women with jet-black faces and braided hair, old men with work-gnarled hands. And the church sang a song about the lower lights are burning, some poor sinners to be saved. And the whole building rocked with prayer and song.

Still I kept waiting to *see* Jesus.

Finally all the young people had gone to the altar and were saved, but one boy and me. He was a rounder's son named Westley. Westley and I were surrounded by sisters and deacons praying. It was very hot in the church, and getting late now. Finally Westley said to me in a whisper: "God damn! I'm tired o' sitting here. Let's get up and be saved." So he got up and was saved.

Then I was left all alone on the mourners' bench. My aunt came and knelt at my knees and cried, while prayers and songs swirled all around me in the little church. The whole congregation prayed for me alone, in a mighty wail of moans and voices. And I kept waiting serenely for Jesus, waiting, waiting—but he didn't come. I wanted to see him, but nothing happened to me. Nothing! I wanted something to happen to me, but nothing happened.

I heard the songs and the minister saying: "Why don't you come? My dear child, why don't you come to Jesus? Jesus is waiting for you. He wants you. Why don't you come? Sister Reed, what is this child's name?"

"Langston," my aunt sobbed.

"Langston, why don't you come? Why don't you come and be saved? Oh, Lamb of God! Why don't you come?"   10

Now it was really getting late. I began to be ashamed of myself, holding everything up so long. I began to wonder what God thought about Westley, who certainly hadn't seen Jesus either, but who was now sitting proudly on the platform, swinging his knickerbockered legs and grinning down at me, surrounded by deacons and old women on their knees praying. God had not struck Westley dead for taking his name in vain or for lying in the temple. So I decided that maybe to save further trouble, I'd better lie, too, and say that Jesus had come, and get up and be saved.

So I got up.

Suddenly the whole room broke into a sea of shouting, as they saw me rise. Waves of rejoicing swept the place. Women leaped in the air. My aunt threw her arms around me. The minister took me by the hand and led me to the platform.

When things quieted down, in a hushed silence, punctuated by a few ecstatic "Amens," all the new young lambs were blessed in the name of God. Then joyous singing filled the room.

That night, for the last time in my life but one—for I was a big boy   15
twelve years old—I cried. I cried, in bed alone, and couldn't stop. I buried my head under the quilts, but my aunt heard me. She woke up and told my uncle I was crying because the Holy Ghost had come into my life, and because I had seen Jesus. But I was really crying because I couldn't bear to tell her that I had lied, that I had deceived everybody in the church, and I hadn't seen Jesus, and that now I didn't believe there was a Jesus any more, since he didn't come to help me.

Joining the Conversation: Critical Thinking and Writing

1. Is the piece amusing, or serious, or both? Explain.

2. How would you characterize the style or voice of the first three sentences? Childlike, or sophisticated, or what? How would you characterize the final sentence? How can you explain the change in style or tone?

3. In the paragraph beginning "Now it was really getting late," why does Hughes bother to tell us that Westley was "swinging his knickerbockered

legs and grinning"? Do you think that Westley may have also cried that night? Give your reasons.

4. Is the episode told from the point of view of someone "going on thirteen" or from the point of view of a mature man?

5. One of the Golden Rules of narrative writing is "Show, don't tell." In about 500 words, report an experience—for instance, a death in the family, or a severe (perhaps unjust) punishment, or the first day in a new school—that produced strong feelings. Like Hughes, you may want to draw on an experience in which you were subjected to group pressure. Do not explicitly state what the feelings were; rather, let the reader understand the feelings chiefly through concretely detailed actions. But, like Hughes, you might state your thesis or basic position in your first paragraph and then indicate when and where the experience took place.

Amy Tan

Amy Tan was born in Oakland, California, in 1952, of Chinese immigrant parents. When she was eight years old, she won first prize among elementary students with an essay entitled, "What the Library Means to Me." In due time, she attended Linfield College in Oregon and then transferred to San Jose State University where—while working two part-time jobs—she became an honors student and a President's Scholar. In 1973, she earned an MA in linguistics, also at San Jose, and she later enrolled as a doctoral student at the University of California, Berkeley, though she left this program after the murder of a close friend. In 1989, her novel The Joy Luck Club *was published. Other books include* The Kitchen God's Wife *(1991),* The Hundred Secret Senses *(1995),* The Bonesetter's Daughter *(2001), and* Saving Fish from Drowning *(2005). She has also written two books for children:* The Moon Lady *(1992) and* SAGWA the Chinese Siamese Cat *(1994). The essay that we reprint appeared in* Life *magazine in April 1991.*

Snapshot: Lost Lives of Women

When I first saw this photo as a child, I thought it was exotic and remote, of a faraway time and place, with people who had no connection to my American life. Look at their bound feet! Look at that funny lady with the plucked forehead!

The solemn little girl is, in fact, my mother. And leaning against the rock is my grandmother, Jingmei. "She called me Baobei," my mother told me. "It means Treasure."

The picture was taken in Hangzhou, and my mother believes the year was 1922, possibly spring or fall, judging by the clothes. At first glance, it appears the women are on a pleasure outing.

Courtesy Amy Tan

But see the white bands on their skirts? The white shoes? They are in mourning. My mother's grandmother, known to the others as Divong, "The Replacement Wife," has recently died. The women have come to this place, a Buddhist retreat, to perform yet another ceremony for Divong. Monks hired for the occasion have chanted the proper words. And the women and little girl have walked in circles clutching smoky sticks of incense. They knelt and prayed, then burned a huge pile of spirit money so that Divong might ascend to a higher position in her new world.

This is also a picture of secrets and tragedies, the reasons that warn-   ings have been passed along in our family like heirlooms. Each of these women suffered a terrible fate, my mother said. And they were not peasant women but big city people, very modern. They went to dance halls and wore stylish clothes. They were supposed to be the lucky ones.

Look at the pretty woman with her finger on her cheek. She is my mother's second cousin, Nunu Aiji, "Precious Auntie." You cannot see this, but Nunu Aiyi's entire face was scarred from smallpox. Lucky for her, a year or so after this picture was taken, she received marriage proposals from two families. She turned down a lawyer and married another man. Later she divorced her husband, a daring thing for a woman to do. But then, finding no means to support herself or her young daughter, Nunu eventually accepted the lawyer's second proposal—to become his number two concubine. "Where else could she go?" my mother asked. "Some people said she was lucky the lawyer still wanted her."

Now look at the small woman with a sour face (*third from left*). There's a reason that Jyou Ma, "Uncle's Wife," looks this way. Her husband, my great-uncle often complained that his family had chosen an ugly woman for his wife. To show his displeasure, he often insulted Jyou Ma's cooking. One time Great-Uncle tipped over a pot of boiling soup, which fell all over his niece's four-year-old neck and nearly killed her. My mother was the little niece, and she still has that soup scar on her neck. Great-Uncle's family eventually chose a pretty woman for his second wife. But the complaints about Jyou Ma's cooking did not stop.

Doomma, "Big Mother," is the regal-looking woman seated on a rock. (The woman with the plucked forehead, far left, is a servant, remembered only as someone who cleaned but did not cook.) Doomma was the daughter of my great-grandfather and Nu-pei, "The Original Wife." She was shunned by Divong, "The Replacement Wife," for being "too strong," and loved by Divong's daughter, my grandmother. Doomma's first daughter was born with a hunchback—a sign, some said, of Doomma's own crooked nature. Why else did she remarry, disobeying her family's orders to remain a widow forever? And why did Doomma later kill herself, using some mysterious means that caused her to die slowly over three days? "Doomma died the same way she lived," my mother said, "strong, suffering lots."

Jingmei, my own grandmother, lived only a few more years after this picture was taken. She was the widow of a poor scholar, a man who had the misfortune of dying from influenza when he was about to be appointed a vice-magistrate. In 1924 or so, a rich man, who liked to collect pretty women, raped my grandmother and thereby forced her into becoming one of his concubines. My grandmother, now an outcast, took her young daughter to live with her on an island outside of Shanghai. She left her son behind, to save his face. After she gave birth to another son she killed herself by swallowing raw opium buried in the New Year's rice cakes. The young daughter who wept at her deathbed was my mother.

At my grandmother's funeral, monks tied chains to my mother's ankles so she would not fly away with her mother's ghost. "I tried to take them off," my mother said. "I was her treasure. I was her life."

My mother could never talk about any of this, even with her closest friends. "Don't tell anyone," she once said to me. "People don't understand. A concubine was like some kind of prostitute. My mother was a good woman, high-class. She had no choice."

I told her I understood.

"How can you understand?" she said, suddenly angry. "You did not live in China then. You do not know what it's like to have no position in life. I was her daughter. We had no face! We belonged to nobody! This is a shame I can never push off my back." By the end of the outburst, she was crying.

On a recent trip with my mother to Beijing, I learned that my uncle found a way to push the shame off his back. He was the son my grandmother left behind. In 1936 he joined the Communist party—in large part, he told me, to overthrow the society that forced his mother into concubinage. He published a story about his mother. I told him I had written about my grandmother in a book of fiction. We agreed that my grandmother is the source of strength running through our family. My mother cried to hear this.

My mother believes my grandmother is also my muse, that she helps me write. "Does she still visit you often?" she asked while I was writing my second book. And then she added shyly, "Does she say anything about me?" 15

"Yes," I told her. "She has lots to say. I am writing it down."

This is the picture I see when I write. These are the secrets I was supposed to keep. These are the women who never let me forget why stories need to be told.

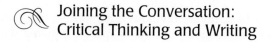

Joining the Conversation: Critical Thinking and Writing

1. Consider the title of this essay. Why are the women's lives described as "lost lives"? Can you imagine a companion piece titled "Lost Lives of Men"? If not, why not?

2. In paragraph 5, what does Tan communicate by "and they were not peasant women but big city people, very modern"? What does she imply about the lives of those who *were* peasants?

3. In the fifth paragraph and in the last, Tan refers to "secrets" that she "was supposed to keep." What were the secrets? Why does she reveal them?

4. In the first paragraph, Tan reports, "When I first saw this photo as a child, I thought it was exotic and remote, of a faraway time and place, with people who had no connection to my American life." What does she imply in this paragraph about their "connection to [her] American life" now? Where in the essay is that connection revealed or explained?

5. If you are lucky enough to have photographs of your ancestors, explore the images of the people in them and what you have been told about their lives. Do you feel "connected" or not? Explain.

A Casebook on Race

Columbia Encyclopedia

Because The Columbia Encyclopedia *is amazingly comprehensive and, for its size, relatively inexpensive, many people rightly believe that (like a good dictionary) it should be part of one's home reference library. We reprint the unsigned essay on "Race."*

Race

Race, one of the group of populations constituting humanity. The differences among races are essentially biological and are marked by the hereditary transmission of physical characteristics. Genetically a race may be defined as a group with gene frequencies differing from those of the other groups in the human species (see heredity; genetics; gene). However, the genes responsible for the hereditary differences between humans are extremely few when compared with the vast number of genes common to all human beings regardless of the race to which they belong. Many physical anthropologists believe that, because there is as much genetic variation among the members of any given race as there is between different racial groups, the concept of race is ultimately unscientific and racial categories are arbitrary designations. The term *race* is inappropriate when applied to national, religious, geographic, linguistic, or ethnic groups, nor can the biological criteria of race be equated with any mental characteristics such as intelligence, personality, or character.

All human groups belong to the same species (*Homo sapiens*) and are mutually fertile. Races arose as a result of mutation, selection, and adaptational changes in human populations. The nature of genetic variation in human beings indicates that there has been a common evolution for all races and that differentiation occurred relatively late in the history of *Homo sapiens*. Theories postulating the very early emergence of racial differentiation have been advanced (e.g., C. S. Coon, *The Origin of Races*, 1962), but they are now scientifically discredited.

To classify humans on the basis of physiological traits is difficult, for the coexistence of races through conquests, invasions, migrations, and mass deportations has produced a heterogeneous world population. Nevertheless, by limiting the criteria to such traits as skin pigmentation, color and form of hair, shape of head, stature, and form of nose, most anthropologists agree on the existence of three relatively distinct groups: the Caucasoid, the Mongoloid, and the Negroid.

The Caucasoid, found in Europe, North Africa, and the Middle East to North India, is characterized as pale reddish white to olive brown in skin color, of medium to tall stature, with a long or broad head form. The hair is light blond to dark brown in color, of a fine texture, and straight or wavy. The color of the eyes is light blue to dark brown, and the nose bridge is usually high.

The Mongoloid race, including most peoples of East Asia and the indigenous peoples of the Americas, has been described as saffron to yellow or reddish brown in skin color, of medium stature, with a broad head form. The hair is dark, straight, and coarse; body hair is sparse. The eyes are black to dark brown. The epicanthic fold, imparting an almond shape to the eye, is common, and the nose bridge is usually low or medium.

The Negroid race is characterized by brown to brown-black skin, usually a long head form, varying stature, and thick, everted lips. The hair is dark and coarse, usually kinky. The eyes are dark, the nose bridge low, and the nostrils broad. To the Negroid race belong the peoples of Africa south of the Sahara, the Pygmy groups of Indonesia, and the inhabitants of New Guinea and Melanesia.

Each of these broad groups can be divided into subgroups. General agreement is lacking as to the classification of such people as the aborigines of Australia, the Dravidian people of South India, the Polynesians, and the Ainu of North Japan.

Attempts have been made to classify humans since the 17th century, when scholars first began to separate types of flora and fauna. Johann Friedrich Blumenbach was the first to divide humanity according to skin color. In the 19th and early 20th centuries, men such as Joseph Arthur Gobineau and Houston Stewart Chamberlain, mainly interested in pressing forward the supposed superiority of their own kind of culture or nationality, began to attribute cultural and psychological values to race. This approach, called racism, culminated in the vicious racial doctrines of Nazi Germany, and especially in anti-Semitism. This same approach complicated the integration movement in the United States and underlay the former segregation policies of the Republic of South Africa (see apartheid).

See R. Benedict, *Race: Science and Politics* (rev. ed. 1943, repr. 1968); C. Lévi-Strauss, *Race and History* (1962); M. Mead et al., ed., *Science and the Concept of Race* (1968); S. M. Garn, ed., *Readings on Race* (2d ed. 1968) and *Human Races* (3d ed. 1971); J. C. King, *The Biology of Race* (1971); L. L. Cavalli-Sforza, *The Origin and Differentiation of Human Races* (1972); S. J. Gould, *The Mismeasure of Man* (1981); I. F. Haney Lopez, *White by Law: The Legal Construction of Race* (1996); A. Montagu, *Man's Most Dangerous Myth: The Fallacy of Race* (6th ed. 1998); G. M. Frederickson, *Racism: A Short History* (2002).

 ## Joining the Conversation: Critical Thinking and Writing

1. The author refers to inappropriate applications of the word "race." What applications are listed as inappropriate?

2. The author reports that physical anthropologists believe that "the concept of race is ultimately unscientific and racial categories are arbitrary designations." On what evidence does the author base this belief?

3. The author also states that "biological criteria of race" cannot "be equated with any mental characteristics such as intelligence, personality, or character." If, in a conversation, you were to hear an inappropriate use of the word "race" or an equation of race with mental characteristics, what would you do?

Armand Marie Leroi

Armand Marie Leroi, a Dutch citizen, was born in New Zealand in 1964 and educated in New Zealand, South Africa, Canada, and the United Sates. An evolutionary developmental biologist, he now teaches at Imperial College in London. He is the author of Mutants: On Genetic Variety and the Human Body *(2007).*

A Family Tree in Every Gene

Shortly after last year's tsunami devastated the lands on the Indian Ocean, *The Times* of India ran an article with this headline: "Tsunami May Have Rendered Threatened Tribes Extinct." The tribes in question were the Onge, Jarawa, Great Andamanese and Sentinelese—all living on the Andaman Islands—and they numbered some 400 people in all. The article, noting that several of the archipelago's islands were low-lying, in the direct path of the wave, and that casualties were expected to be high, said, "Some beads may have just gone missing from the Emerald Necklace of India."

The metaphor is as colorful as it is well intentioned. But what exactly does it mean? After all, in a catastrophe that cost more than 150,000 lives, why should the survival of a few hundred tribal people have any special claim on our attention? There are several possible answers to this question. The people of the Andamans have a unique way of life. True, their material culture does not extend beyond a few simple tools, and their visual art is confined to a few geometrical motifs, but they are hunter-gatherers and so a rarity in the modern world. Linguists, too, find them interesting since they collectively speak three languages seemingly unrelated to any others. But *The Times* of India took a slightly different tack. These tribes are special, it said, because they are of "Negrito racial stocks" that are "remnants of the oldest human populations in Asia and Australia."

It's an old-fashioned, even Victorian, sentiment. Who speaks of "racial stocks" anymore? After all, to do so would be to speak of something that many scientists and scholars say does not exist. If modern anthropologists mention the concept of race, it is invariably only to warn against and dismiss it. Likewise many geneticists. "Race is social concept, not a scientific one," according to Dr. Craig Venter—and he should know, since he was first to sequence the human genome. The idea that human races are only social constructs has been the consensus for at least 30 years.

But now, perhaps, that is about to change. Last fall, the prestigious journal *Nature Genetics* devoted a large supplement to the question of whether human races exist and, if so, what they mean. The journal did this in part because various American health agencies are making race an important part of their policies to best protect the public—often over the protests of scientists. In the supplement, some two dozen geneticists offered their views. Beneath the jargon, cautious phrases and academic courtesies, one thing was clear: the consensus about social constructs was unraveling. Some even argued that, looked at the right way, genetic data show that races clearly do exist.

The dominance of the social construct theory can be traced to a 1972 article by Dr. Richard Lewontin, a Harvard geneticist, who wrote that most human genetic variation can be found within any given "race." If one looked at genes rather than faces, he claimed, the difference between an African and a European would be scarcely greater than the difference between any two Europeans. A few years later he wrote that the continued popularity of race as an idea was an "indication of the power of socioeconomically based ideology over the supposed objectivity of knowledge." Most scientists are thoughtful, liberal-minded and socially aware people. It was just what they wanted to hear.

Three decades later, it seems that Dr. Lewontin's facts were correct, and have been abundantly confirmed by ever better techniques of detecting genetic variety. His reasoning, however, was wrong. His error was an elementary one, but such was the appeal of his argument that it was only a couple of years ago that a Cambridge University statistician, A. W. F. Edwards, put his finger on it.

The error is easily illustrated. If one were asked to judge the ancestry of 100 New Yorkers, one could look at the color of their skin. That would do much to single out the Europeans, but little to distinguish the Senegalese from the Solomon Islanders. The same is true for any other feature of our bodies. The shapes of our eyes, noses and skulls; the color of our eyes and our hair; the heaviness, height and hairiness of our bodies are all, individually, poor guides to ancestry.

But this is not true when the features are taken together. Certain skin colors tend to go with certain kinds of eyes, noses, skulls and bodies. When we glance at a stranger's face we use those associations to infer what continent, or even what country, he or his ancestors came from—and we usually get it right. To put it more abstractly, human physical variation is correlated; and correlations contain information.

Genetic variants that aren't written on our faces, but that can be detected only in the genome, show similar correlations. It is these correlations that Dr. Lewontin seems to have ignored. In essence, he looked at one gene at a time and failed to see races. But if many—a few hundred—variable genes are considered simultaneously, then it is very easy to do so. Indeed, a 2002 study by scientists at the University of Southern California and Stanford showed that if a sample of people from around the world are sorted by computer into five groups on the basis of genetic similarity, the groups that emerge are native to Europe, East Asia, Africa, America and Australasia—more or less the major races of traditional anthropology.

One of the minor pleasures of this discovery is a new kind of genealogy. Today it is easy to find out where your ancestors came from—or even when they came, as with so many of us, from several different places. If you want to know what fraction of your genes are African, European or East Asian, all it takes is a mouth swab, a postage stamp and $400—though prices will certainly fall.

Yet there is nothing very fundamental about the concept of the major continental races; they're just the easiest way to divide things up. Study enough genes in enough people and one could sort the world's population into 10, 100, perhaps 1,000 groups, each located somewhere on the map. This has not yet been done with any precision, but it will be. Soon it may be possible to identify your ancestors not merely as African or European, but Ibo or Yoruba, perhaps even Celt or Castilian, or all of the above.

The identification of racial origins is not a search for purity. The human species is irredeemably promiscuous. We have always seduced or coerced our neighbors even when they have a foreign look about them and we don't understand a word. If Hispanics, for example, are composed of a recent and evolving blend of European, American Indian and African genes, then the Uighurs of Central Asia can be seen as a 3,000-year-old mix of West European and East Asian genes. Even homogenous groups like native Swedes bear the genetic imprint of successive nameless migrations.

Some critics believe that these ambiguities render the very notion of race worthless. I disagree. The physical topography of our world cannot be accurately described in words. To navigate it, you need a map with elevations, contour lines and reference grids. But it is hard to talk in numbers, and so we give the world's more prominent features—the mountain ranges and plateaus and plains—names. We do so despite the inherent ambiguity of words. The Pennines of northern England are about one-tenth as high and long as the Himalayas, yet both are intelligibly described as mountain ranges.

So, too, it is with the genetic topography of our species. The billion or so of the world's people of largely European descent have a set of genetic variants in common that are collectively rare in everyone else; they are a race. At a smaller scale, three million Basques do as well; so they are a race as well. Race is merely a shorthand that enables us to speak sensibly, though with no great precision, about genetic rather than cultural or political differences.

But it is a shorthand that seems to be needed. One of the more painful spectacles of modern science is that of human geneticists piously disavowing the existence of races even as they investigate the genetic relationships between "ethnic groups." Given the problematic, even vicious, history of the word "race," the use of euphemisms is understandable. But it hardly aids understanding, for the term "ethnic group" conflates all the possible ways in which people differ from each other.

Indeed, the recognition that races are real should have several benefits. To begin with, it would remove the disjunction in which the government and public alike defiantly embrace categories that many, perhaps most, scholars and scientists say do not exist.

Second, the recognition of race may improve medical care. Different races are prone to different diseases. The risk that an African-American man will be afflicted with hypertensive heart disease or prostate cancer is nearly three times greater than that for a European-American man. On the other hand, the former's risk of multiple sclerosis is only half as great. Such differences could be due to socioeconomic factors. Even so, geneticists have started searching for racial differences in the frequencies of genetic variants that cause diseases. They seem to be finding them.

Race can also affect treatment. African-Americans respond poorly to some of the main drugs used to treat heart conditions—notably beta blockers and angiotensin-converting enzyme inhibitors. Pharmaceutical corporations are paying attention. Many new drugs now come labeled with warnings that they may not work in some ethnic or racial groups. Here, as so often, the mere prospect of litigation has concentrated minds.

Such differences are, of course, just differences in average. Everyone agrees that race is a crude way of predicting who gets some disease or responds to some treatment. Ideally, we would all have our genomes sequenced before swallowing so much as an aspirin. Yet until that is technically feasible, we can expect racial classifications to play an increasing part in health care.

The argument for the importance of race, however, does not rest purely on utilitarian grounds. There is also an aesthetic factor. We are a physically variable species. Yet for all the triumphs of modern genetics, we know next to nothing about what makes us so. We do not know why some people have prominent rather than flat noses, round rather than pointed skulls, wide rather than narrow faces, straight rather than curly hair. We do not know what makes blue eyes blue. 20

One way to find out would be to study people of mixed race ancestry. In part, this is because racial differences in looks are the most striking that we see. But there is also a more subtle technical reason. When geneticists map genes, they rely on the fact that they can follow our ancestors' chromosomes as they get passed from one generation to the next, dividing and mixing in unpredictable combinations. That, it turns out, is much easier to do in people whose ancestors came from very different places.

The technique is called admixture mapping. Developed to find the genes responsible for racial differences in inherited disease, it is only just moving from theory to application. But through it, we may be able to write the genetic recipe for the fair hair of a Norwegian, the black-verging-on-purple skin of a Solomon Islander, the flat face of an Inuit, and the curved eyelid of a Han Chinese. We shall no longer gawp ignorantly at the gallery; we shall be able to name the painters.

There is a final reason race matters. It gives us reason—if there were not reason enough already—to value and protect some of the world's most obscure and marginalized people. When *The Times* of India article is referred to the Andaman Islanders as being of ancient Negrito racial stock, the terminology was correct. Negrito is the name given by anthropologists to a people who once lived throughout Southeast Asia. They are very small, very dark, and have peppercorn hair. They look like African pygmies who have wandered away from Congo's jungles to take up life on a tropical isle. But they are not.

The latest genetic data suggest that the Negritos are descended from the first modern humans to have invaded Asia, some 100,000 years ago. In time they were overrun or absorbed by waves of Neolithic agriculturalists, and later nearly wiped out by British, Spanish and Indian colonialists. Now they are confined to the Malay Peninsula, a few islands in the Philippines and the Andamans.

Happily, most of the Andamans' Negritos seem to have survived December's tsunami. The fate of one tribe, the Sentinelese, remains uncertain, but an Indian coast guard helicopter sent to check up on them came under bow and arrow attack, which is heartening. Even so, Negrito populations, wherever they are, are so small, isolated and impoverished that it seems certain that they will eventually disappear.

Yet even after they have gone, the genetic variants that defined the Negritos will remain, albeit scattered, in the people who inhabit the littoral of the Bay of Bengal and the South China Sea. They will remain visible in the unusually dark skin of some Indonesians, the unusually curly hair of some Sri Lankans, the unusually slight frames of some Filipinos. But the unique combination of genes that makes the Negritos so distinctive, and that took tens of thousands of years to evolve, will have disappeared. A human race will have gone extinct, and the human species will be the poorer for it.

David Fitch, Herbert J. Gans, Mary T. Bassett,
Lynn M. Morgan, Martin E. Fuller,
John Waldman

Letters Responding to Armand Marie Leroi

To the Editor:

Re "A Family Tree in Every Gene," by Armand Marie Leroi (Op-Ed, March 14):

Biological diversity is real and should be celebrated, not pushed under the carpet and ignored.

This is not just about race, either. A Harvard president is being criticized for proposing that biological differences might explain why certain propensities are more common among men or women. If true, it would be important to understand what these differences are.

Understanding differences does not mean we must then use such differences to practice discrimination. The great thing about us humans is our ability to transcend biological differences, particularly if we understand them.

David Fitch
New York, March 16, 2005
The writer is an associate professor of biology
at New York University.

To the Editor:

Race remains a social construct. And no matter how Armand Marie Leroi defines it ("A Family Tree in Every Gene," Op-Ed, March 14), it is still widely used, not only to describe, but also to judge and stigmatize people. Why not choose a nonjudgmental construct like DNA type?

Herbert J. Gans
New York, March 14, 2005
The writer is a professor of sociology at
Columbia University.

To the Editor:

Now we hear that the Victorian notion of "racial stocks" could lead to improved health. Such thinking will not advance public health, which is well acquainted with the enduring impact of race. Indeed, ever since the first crude tabulation of vital statistics in Colonial America, blacks have been sicker and died younger than whites.

There has been progress: in 1981, black infants in New York City had an infant mortality rate of 22.3 per 1,000 live births. By 2003, a black infant's risk of death had fallen by almost half.

What happened? Our society changed, not our genes.

Today health disparities persist. But we can end the unfair odds by changing how people live, not by insisting on genetic explanations for these differences.

Mary T. Bassett, M.D.
Deputy Commissioner
Dept. of Health and Mental Hygiene
New York, March 15, 2005

Letters to the editor by David Fitch, Herbert J. Gans, Mary T. Bassett, M.D., Lynn M. Morgan, Martin E. Fuller, and John Waldman, published in *The New York Times*, March 20, 2005. Reprinted by permission of the authors.

To the Editor:

Race is not a fact rooted in nature, but an ideology that justifies treating people differently based on the meanings we attribute to physical differences.

When people are subjected to poor treatment, diagnostic delay and unhealthy environments because of the color of their skin, "race" impairs their health. The ideology of race can have real biological consequences.

Lynn M. Morgan
South Hadley, Mass.
March 15, 2005
The writer is an anthropology professor at
Mount Holyoke College.

To the Editor:

Armand Marie Leroi (Op-Ed, March 14) brings us a celebration of human genetic variability. That variability has enabled the human race to survive, and even thrive, in so many different and not always friendly habitats.

It would be a sad world were the races homogenized into one amorphous mass. Let us rejoice in and be grateful for our differences. They are beautiful.

Martin E. Fuller
Albuquerque, March 16, 2005

To the Editor:

Is there such a thing as "race"?

Mix 10 native Central Africans and 10 native Scandinavians together, and I'll sort them out every time. Race is real. The problem is that this easily answered question is often confounded with the far trickier and far touchier question of "how much does race matter?"

John Waldman
Flushing, Queens, March 15, 2005
The writer is a professor of biology
at Queens College, CUNY.

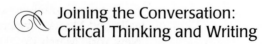 Joining the Conversation:
Critical Thinking and Writing

1. In paragraph 3, Leroi writes of the "idea that human races are only social constructs." What does this mean? With what idea about races does this idea contrast?

2. In paragraph 4, Leroi claims that the idea that races are only social constructs is about to change. What evidence does he offer to support this claim?

3. What benefits does Leroi claim for "the recognition that races are real" (paragraph 15)?

4. Leroi both begins and ends his article referring to the Negritos. Who are they? What recent event threatened their existence? According to Leroi, why should they claim our attention?

5. How does Leroi's focus on the Negritos both at the beginning and end of his essay help to define and strengthen his argument?

6. We reprint six responses to Leroi's article received by *The New York Times*. Which letter do you find most (or least) interesting and persuasive? Explain why.

Shelby Steele

Shelby Steele, a research fellow at the Hoover Institution, was educated at Coe College, Southern Illinois University, and the University of Utah. In 1990, one of his books, The Content of Our Character: A New Vision of Race in America, *was awarded the National Book Critics Circle Award for nonfiction. His most recent book is* A Dream Deferred: The Second Betrayal of Black Freedom in America. *Steele publishes widely in major journals, including* The New York Times *and (the source of the following article)* Time *magazine.*

Hailing While Black

In Manhattan recently I attempted something that is thought to be all but impossible for a black man: I tried to hail a cab going uptown toward Harlem after dark. And I'll admit to feeling a new nervousness. This simple action—black man hailing cab—is now a tableau in America's on-going culture war. If no cab swerves in to pick me up, America is still a racist country, and the entire superstructure of contemporary liberalism is bolstered. If I catch a ride, conservatives can breath easier. So, as I raise my hand and step from the curb, much is at stake.

It's all the talk these days of racial profiling that has set off my nerves in this way. Having grown up in the era of segregation, I know I can survive the racial profiling of a cabby. What makes me most nervous is the anxiety that I have wrongly estimated the degree of racism in American life. I am a conservative. But conservatism is a misunderstood identity in blacks that would be much easier to carry in a world where New York City cab drivers stopped for black fares, even after dark.

It is easy to believe that racial profiling is a serious problem in America. It fits the American profile, and now politicians have stepped forward to give it credence as a problem. But is it a real problem? Is dark skin a short-hand for criminality in the mind of America's law-enforcement officers? Studies show that we blacks are stopped in numbers higher than our per-centage in the population but lower than our documented involvement in crime. If you're trying to measure racism, isn't it better to compare police stops to actual black involvement in crime than to the mere representation of blacks in the population? The elephant in the living room—and the tragedy in black America—is that we commit crimes vastly out of propor-tion to our numbers in society.

But I can already hear "so what?" from those who believe profiling is a serious problem. And I know that the more energetic among them will move numbers and points of reference around like shells in a shill game to show racism. In other words, racial profiling is now an "identity" issue like affirmative action, black reparations or even O.J.'s innocence. It is less a real issue than a coded argument over how much racism exists in soci-ety today. We argue these issues fiercely—make a culture war around them—because the moral authority of both the left and right political identities hangs in the balance.

Racial profiling is a boon to the left because this political identity justifies its demand for power by estimating racism to be high. The more racism, the more power the left demands for social interventions that go beyond simple fairness under the law. Profiling hurts the right because it makes its fairness-under-the-law position on race seem inadequate, less than moral considering the prevalence of racism. The real debate over racial profiling is not about stops and searches on the New Jersey Turnpike. It is about the degree of racism in America and the distribution of power it justifies.

Even as individuals, we Americans cannot define our political and moral identities without making them accountable to an estimate of racism's potency in American life. Our liberalism or conservatism, our faith in government intervention or restraint and our concept of social responsibility on issues from diversity to school reform—all these will be, in part, a response to how bad we think racism is. The politically liberal identity I was born into began to fade as my estimate of American racism declined. I could identify with a wider range of American ideas and possibilities when I thought they were no longer tainted by racism. Many whites I know today, who are trying to separate themselves from the shame of America's racist past, will overestimate racism to justify a liberal identity that they hope proves that separateness. First the estima-tion, then the identity.

Recently, after a talk on a college campus, a black girl stood up and told me that she was "frequently" stopped by police while driving in this bucolic and liberal college town. A professor on the same campus told me that blacks there faced an "unwelcome atmosphere"—unwelcomeness being a newly fashionable estimation of racism's potency on college campuses today. Neither of these people offered supporting facts. But I don't think they were lying so much as "spinning" an estimation of racism that shored up their political identities.

We are terrible at discussing our racial problems in America today because we just end up defending our identities and the political power we hope those identities will align us with. On that day in Manhattan, I caught the first cab that came along. And I should have been happy just for the convenience of good service. That I also saw this minor event as evidence of something, that I was practicing a kind of political sociology as well as catching a cab—that is the problem.

 ## Joining the Conversation: Critical Thinking and Writing

1. In his essay, Steele refers to "racial profiling." What is "racial profiling," and according to Steele, how does it affect what he calls "the left" and "the right"?

2. Explain Steele's last sentence to someone who has read the article but didn't get it.

3. Have you ever been the victim, the perpetrator, or a witness to racial or ethnic profiling or prejudice? If so, in an essay of 750–1,000 words, recount the circumstances of the event—and your reaction to it—then and now. Use Steele's essay as a model if that is helpful.

Countee Cullen

Countee Cullen (1903–1946) was born Countee Porter in New York City, raised by his grand-mother, and then adopted by the Reverend Frederick A. Cullen, a Methodist minister in Harlem. Cullen received a bachelor's degree from New York University (Phi Beta Kappa) and a master's degree from Harvard University. He earned his living as a high school teacher of French, but his literary gifts were recognized in his own day.

Incident
(For Eric Walrond)

Once riding in old Baltimore,
    Heart-filled, head-filled with glee.
I saw a Baltimorean
    Keep looking straight at me.

Now I was eight and very small.   5
   And he was no whit bigger.
And so I smiled, but he poked out
   His tongue, and called me, "Nigger."

I saw the whole of Baltimore
   From May until December;   10
Of all the things that happened there
   That's all that I remember.

 ## Joining the Conversation:
Critical Thinking and Writing

1. How would you define an "incident"? A serious occurrence? A minor occurrence or what? Think about the word and then think about Cullen's use of it as a title for the event recorded in this poem. Test out one or two other possible titles as a way of helping yourself to see the strengths or weaknesses of Cullen's title.

2. The dedicatee, Eric Walrond (1898–1966), was an African-American essayist and writer of fiction who in an essay, "On Being Black," had described his experiences of racial prejudice. How does the presence of the dedication bear on our response to Cullen's account of the "incident"?

3. What is the tone of the poem? Indifferent? Angry? Or what? What do you think is the speaker's attitude toward the "incident"? What is your attitude?

4. Ezra Pound, poet and critic, once defined literature as "news that *stays* news." What do you think he meant by this? Do you think that the definition fits Cullen's poem?

CHAPTER 8

Teaching and Learning

Blackboard
Winslow Homer, 1877

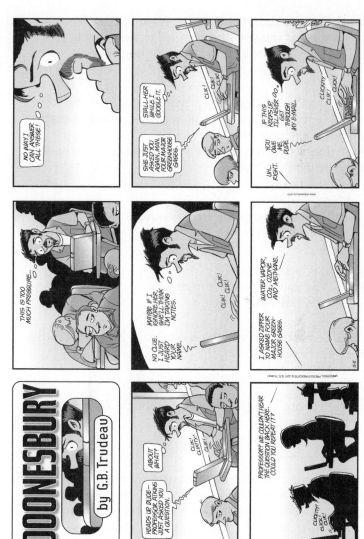

Short Views

Knowledge is power.
Francis Bacon

How people keep correcting us when we are young! There's always some bad habit or other they tell us we ought to get over. Yet most bad habits are tools to help us through life.
Johann Wolfgang von Goethe

If Johnny can't learn because he is hungry, that's the fault of poverty. But if Johnny can't pay attention because he is sleepy, that's the fault of parents.

What does it matter if we have a new book or an old book, if we open neither?
Jesse Jackson

Universities are, of course, hostile to geniuses.
Ralph Waldo Emerson

Education! Which of the various me's do you propose to educate, and which do you propose to suppress?
D. H. Lawrence

The entire object of true education is to make people not merely do the right things, but enjoy the right things.
John Ruskin

Learning without thought is labor lost; thought without learning is dangerous.
Confucius

I think [Raymond Weaver] first attracted my attention as someone worth watching when, while we were both new instructors, I heard from a bewildered freshman about the quiz he had just given. The first question written on the blackboard was, "Which of the required readings in this course did you find least interesting?" Then, after members of the class had had ten minutes in which to expatiate on what was certainly to many a congenial topic, he wrote the second question: "To what defect in yourself do you attribute this lack of interest?"
Joseph Wood Krutch

Plato

Plato (427–347 B.C.), born in Athens into an aristocratic family, wrote 30 dialogues in which Socrates is the chief speaker. Socrates, about 25 years older than Plato, was a philosopher who called himself a gadfly to Athenians. For his efforts at stinging them into thought, the Athenians executed him in 399 B.C. "The Myth of the Cave" is the beginning of Book 7 of The Republic, *a dialogue in which Socrates is talking with Glaucon.*

For Plato, true knowledge is philosophic insight or awareness of the Good, not mere opinion or the knack of getting along in this world by remembering how things have usually worked in the past. To illustrate his idea that awareness of the Good is different from the ability to recognize the things of this shabby world, Plato (through his spokesman Socrates) resorts to an allegory: Men imprisoned in a cave see on a wall in front of them the shadows or images of objects that are really behind them, and they hear echoes, not real voices. (The shadows are caused by the light from a fire behind the objects, and the echoes by the cave's acoustical properties.) Unable to perceive the real objects and the real voices, the prisoners mistakenly think that the shadows and the echoes are real, and some of them grow highly adept at dealing with this illusory world. Were Plato writing today, he might have made the cave a movie theater: We see on the screen in front of us images caused by an object (film passing in front of light) that is behind us. Moreover, the film itself is an illusory image, for it bears only the traces of a yet more real world—the world that was photographed—outside of the movie theater. And when we leave the theater to go into the real world, our eyes have become so accustomed to the illusory world that we at first blink with discomfort—just as Plato's freed prisoners do when they move out of the cave—at the real world of bright day, and we long for the familiar darkness. So too, Plato suggests, dwellers in ignorance may prefer the familiar shadows of their unenlightened world ("the world of becoming") to the bright world of the eternal Good ("the world of being") that education reveals.

We have just used the word "education." You will notice that the first sentence in the translation below (by Benjamin Jowett) says that the myth will show "how far our nature is enlightened or unenlightened." In the original Greek, the words here translated enlightened *and* unenlightened *are* paideia *and* apaideusia. *No translation can fully catch the exact meanings of these elusive words. Depending on the context,* paideia *may be translated as* enlightenment, education, civilization, culture, knowledge of the good.

The Myth of the Cave

And now, I said, let me show in a figure how far our nature is enlightened or unenlightened—Behold! human beings living in an underground den, which has a mouth open toward the light and reaching all along the den; here they have been from their childhood, and have their legs and necks chained so that they cannot move, and can only see before them, being prevented by the chains from turning round their heads. Above and behind them a fire is blazing at a distance, and between the fire and the prisoners there is a raised way; and you will see, if you look, a low wall built along the way, like the screen which marionette players have in front of them, over which they show the puppets.

I see.

And do you see, I said, men passing along the wall carrying all sorts of vessels, and statues and figures of animals made of wood and stone and various materials, which appear over the wall? Some of them are talking, others silent.

You have shown me a strange image, and they are strange prisoners.

Like ourselves, I replied; and they see only their own shadows, or the 5
shadows of one another, which the fire throws on the opposite wall of the
cave?

True, he said; how could they see anything but the shadows if they
were never allowed to move their heads?

And of the objects which are being carried in like manner they would
only see the shadows?

Yes, he said.

And if they were able to converse with one another, would they not
suppose that they were naming what was actually before them?

Very true. 10

And suppose further that the prison had an echo which came from
the other side, would they not be sure when one of the passersby spoke
that the voice which they heard came from the passing shadow?

No question, he replied.

To them, I said, the truth would be literally nothing but the shadows
of the images.

That is certain.

And now look again, and see what will naturally follow if the prison- 15
ers are released and disabused of their error. At first, when any of them is
liberated and compelled suddenly to stand up and turn his neck round
and walk and look toward the light, he will suffer sharp pains; the glare
will distress him, and he will be unable to see the realities of which in his
former state he had seen the shadows; and then conceive some one saying
to him, that what he saw before was an illusion, but that now, when he
is approaching nearer to being and his eye is turned toward more real
existence, he has a clearer vision—what will be his reply? And you may
further imagine that his instructor is pointing to the objects as they pass
and requiring him to name them—will he not be perplexed? Will he not
fancy that the shadows which he formerly saw are truer than the objects
which are now shown to him?

Far truer.

And if he is compelled to look straight at the light, will he not have
a pain in his eyes which will make him turn away to take refuge in the
objects of vision which he can see, and which he will conceive to be in
reality clearer than the things which are now being shown to him?

True, he said.

And suppose once more, that he is reluctantly dragged up a steep
and rugged ascent, and held fast until he is forced into the presence of the
sun himself, is he not likely to be pained and irritated? When he approaches the light his eyes will be dazzled, and he will not be able to see
anything at all of what are now called realities.

Not all in a moment, he said. 20

He will require to grow accustomed to the sight of the upper world.
And first he will see the shadows best, next the reflections of men and

other objects in the water, and then the objects themselves; then he will gaze upon the light of the moon and the stars and the spangled heaven; and he will see the sky and the stars by night better than the sun or the light of the sun by day?

Certainly.

Last of all he will be able to see the sun, and not mere reflections of him in the water, but he will see him in his own proper place, and not in another; and he will contemplate him as he is.

Certainly.

He will then proceed to argue that this is he who gives the season and the years, and is the guardian of all that is in the visible world, and in a certain way the cause of all things which he and his fellows have been accustomed to behold?

Clearly, he said, he would first see the sun and then reason about him.

And when he remembered his old habitation, and the wisdom of the den and his fellow-prisoners, do you not suppose that he would felicitate himself on the change, and pity them?

Certainly, he would.

And if they were in the habit of conferring honors among themselves on those who were quickest to observe the passing shadows and to remark which of them went before, and which followed after, and which were together; and who were therefore best able to draw conclusions as to the future, do you think that he would care for such honors and glories, or envy the possessors of them? Would he not say with Homer,

> Better to be the poor servant of a poor master,

and to endure anything, rather than think as they do and live after their manner?

Yes, he said, I think that he would rather suffer anything than entertain these false notions and live in this miserable manner.

Imagine once more, I said, such an one coming suddenly out of the sun to be replaced in his old situation; would he not be certain to have his eyes full of darkness?

To be sure, he said.

And if there were a contest, and he had to compete in measuring the shadows with the prisoners who had never moved out of the den, while his sight was still weak, and before his eyes had become steady (and the time which would be needed to acquire this new habit of sight might be very considerable), would he not be ridiculous? Men would say of him that up he went and down he came without his eyes; and that it was better not even to think of ascending; and if any one tried to loose another and lead him up to the light, let them only catch the offender, and they would put him to death.

No question, he said.

This entire allegory, I said, you may now append, dear Glaucon, to
the previous argument; the prison-house is the world of sight, the light of
the fire is the sun, and you will not misapprehend me if you interpret the
journey upwards to be the ascent of the soul into the intellectual world
according to my poor belief, which, at your desire, I have expressed—
whether rightly or wrongly God knows. But, whether true or false, my
opinion is that in the world of knowledge the idea of good appears last of
all, and is seen only with an effort; and, when seen, is also inferred to be
the universal author of all things beautiful and right, parent of light and
of the lord of light in this visible world, and the immediate source of reason and truth in the intellectual; and that this is the power upon which
he who would act rationally either in public or private life must have his
eye fixed.

I agree, he said, as far as I am able to understand you.

Moreover, I said, you must not wonder that those who attain to this
beatific vision are unwilling to descend to human affairs; for their souls
are ever hastening into the upper world where they desire to dwell;
which desire of theirs is very natural, if our allegory may be trusted.

Yes, very natural.

And is there anything surprising in one who passes from divine con-
templations to the evil state of man, misbehaving himself in a ridiculous
manner; if, while his eyes are blinking and before he has become accustomed to the surrounding darkness, he is compelled to fight in courts of
law, or in other places, about the images or the shadows of images of justice, and is endeavoring to meet the conceptions of those who have never
yet seen absolute justice?

Anything but surprising, he replied.

Any one who has common sense will remember that the bewilder-
ments of the eyes are of two kinds, and arise from two causes, either from
coming out of the light or from going into the light, which is true of the
mind's eye, quite as much as of the bodily eye; and he who remembers this
when he sees any one whose vision is perplexed and weak, will not be too
ready to laugh; he will first ask whether that soul of man has come out of
the brighter life, and is unable to see because unaccustomed to the dark, or
having turned from darkness to the day is dazzled by excess of light. And
he will count the one happy in his condition and state of being, and he will
pity the other; or, if he have a mind to laugh at the soul which comes from
below into the light, there will be more reason in this than in the laugh
which greets him who returns from above out of the light into the den.

That, he said, is a very just distinction.

But then, if I am right, certain professors of education must be wrong
when they say that they can put a knowledge into the soul which was not
there before, like sight into blind eyes.

They undoubtedly say this, he replied.

Whereas, our argument shows that the power and capacity of learning exists in the soul already; and that just as the eye was unable to turn

35

40

4

from darkness to light without the whole body, so too the instrument of knowledge can only by the movement of the whole soul be turned from the world of becoming into that of being, and learn by degrees to endure the sight of being, and of the brightest and best of being, or in other words, of the good.

Very true.

And must there not be some art which will effect conversion in the easiest and quickest manner; not implanting the faculty of sight, for that exists already, but has been turned in the wrong direction, and is looking away from the truth?

Yes, he said, such an art may be presumed.

And whereas the other so-called virtues of the soul seem to be akin to bodily qualities, for even when they are not originally innate they can be implanted later by habit and exercise, the virtue of wisdom more than anything else contains a divine element which always remains, and by this conversion is rendered useful and profitable; or, on the other hand, hurtful and useless. Did you never observe the narrow intelligence flashing from the keen eye of a clever rogue—how eager he is, how clearly his paltry soul sees the way to his end; he is the reverse of blind, but his keen eyesight is forced into the service of evil, and he is mischievous in proportion to his cleverness?

Very true, he said.

But what if there had been a circumcision of such natures in the days of their youth; and they had been severed from those sensual pleasures, such as eating and drinking, which, like leaden weights, were attached to them at their birth, and which drag them down and turn the vision of their souls upon the things that are below—if, I say, they had been released from these impediments and turned in the opposite direction, the very same faculty in them would have seen the truth as keenly as they see what their eyes are turned to now.

Very likely.

Yes, I said; and there is another thing which is likely, or rather a necessary inference from what has preceded, that neither the uneducated and uninformed of the truth, nor yet those who never make an end of their education, will be able ministers of State; not the former, because they have no single aim of duty which is the rule of all their actions, private as well as public; nor the latter, because they will not act at all except upon compulsion, fancying that they are already dwelling apart in the islands of the blest.

Very true, he replied.

Then, I said, the business of us who are the founders of the State will be to compel the best minds to attain that knowledge which we have already shown to be the greatest of all—they must continue to ascend until they arrive at the good; but when they have ascended and seen enough we must not allow them to do as they do now.

What do you mean?

I mean that they remain in the upper world: but this must not be allowed; they must be made to descend again among the prisoners in the den, and partake of their labors and honors, whether they are worth having or not.

But is not this unjust? he said; ought we to give them a worse life, when they might have a better?

You have again forgotten, my friend, I said, the intention of the legislator, who did not aim at making any one class in the State happy above the rest; the happiness was to be in the whole State, and he held the citizens together by persuasion and necessity, making them benefactors of the State, and therefore benefactors of one another; to this end he created them, not to please themselves, but to be his instruments in binding up the State.

True, he said, I had forgotten.

Observe, Glaucon, that there will be no justice in compelling our philosophers to have a care and providence of others; we shall explain to them that in other States, men of their class are not obliged to share in the toils of politics: and this is reasonable, for they grow up at their own sweet will, and the government would rather not have them. Being self-taught, they cannot be expected to show any gratitude for a culture which they have never received. But we have brought you into the world to be rulers of the hive, kings of yourselves and of the other citizens, and have educated you far better and more perfectly than they have been educated, and you are better able to share in the double duty. Wherefore each of you, when his turn comes, must go down to the general underground abode, and get the habit of seeing in the dark. When you have acquired the habit, you will see ten thousand times better than the inhabitants of the den, and you will know what the several images are, and what they represent, because you have seen the beautiful and just and good in their truth. And thus our State which is also yours will be a reality, and not a dream only, and will be administered in a spirit unlike that of other States, in which men fight with one another about shadows only and are distracted in the struggle for power, which in their eyes is a great good. Whereas the truth is that the State in which the rulers are most reluctant to govern is always the best and most quietly governed, and the State in which they are most eager, the worst.

Quite true, he replied.

And will our pupils, when they hear this, refuse to take their turn at the toils of State, when they are allowed to spend the greater part of their time with one another in the heavenly light?

Impossible, he answered; for they are just men, and the commands which we impose upon them are just; there can be no doubt that every one of them will take office as a stern necessity, and not after the fashion of our present rulers of State.

Yes, my friend, I said; and there lies the point. You must contrive for your future rulers another and a better life than that of a ruler, and then you may have a well-ordered State; for only in the State which offers this, will they rule who are truly rich, not in silver and gold, but in virtue and wisdom, which are the true blessing of life. Whereas if they go to the administration of public affairs, poor and hungering after their own private advantage, thinking that hence they are to snatch the chief good, order there can never be; for they will be fighting about office, and the civil and domestic broils which thus arise will be the ruin of the rulers themselves and of the whole State.

Most true, he replied.

And the only life which looks down upon the life of political ambition is that of true philosophy. Do you know of any other?

Indeed, I do not, he said.

And those who govern ought not to be lovers of the task? For, if they are, there will be rival lovers, and they will fight.

No question.

70

Who then are those whom we shall compel to be guardians? Surely they will be the men who are wisest about affairs of State, and by whom the State is best administered, and who at the same time have other honors and another and a better life than that of politics?

They are the men, and I will choose them, he replied.

And now shall we consider in what way such guardians will be produced, and how they are to be brought from darkness to light—as some are said to have ascended from the world below to the gods?

By all means, he replied.

The process, I said, is not the turning over of an oyster-shell,[1] but the turning round of a soul passing from a day which is little better than night to the true day of being, that is, the ascent from below which we affirm to be true philosophy?

75

Quite so.

Joining the Conversation: Critical Thinking and Writing

1. Plato is not merely reporting one of Socrates conversations; he is teaching. What advantages does a dialogue have over a narrative or an essay as a way of teaching philosophy? How is the form of a dialogue especially suited to solving a problem?

2. If you don't know the etymology of the word *conversion*, look it up in a dictionary. How is the etymology appropriate to Plato's idea about education?

3. In paragraph 19, describing the prisoner as "reluctantly dragged" upward and "forced" to look at the sun, Socrates asks: "Is he not likely to be pained

---

[1]An allusion to a game in which two parties fled or pursued according as an oyster shell that was thrown into the air fell with the dark or light side uppermost. (Translator's note)

and irritated?" Can you recall experiencing pain and irritation while learning something you were later glad to have learned? Can you recall learning something new *without* experiencing pain and irritation?

4. "The State in which rulers are most reluctant to govern is always the best and most quietly governed, and the State in which they are most eager, the worst" (paragraph 61). What does Socrates mean? Using examples from contemporary politics, defend this proposition or argue against it.

5. Can you account for the power of this myth or fable? In our introductory comment (page 259), we tried to clarify the message by saying that a movie theater might serve as well as a cave. But, in fact, if the story were recast using a movie theater, would the emotional power be the same? Why or why not?

6. The metaphors of education as conversion and ascent are linked by the metaphor of light. Consider such expressions as "I see" (meaning "I understand") and "Let me give an illustration" (from the Latin *in* = in, and *lustrare* = to make bright). What other expressions about light are used metaphorically to describe intellectual comprehension?

Two Debates (Four Arguments) for Analysis

Do Video Games Significantly Enhance Literacy?

James Paul Gee

James Paul Gee, a professor of reading in the School of Education at the University of Wisconsin at Madison, is the author of numerous books, including What Video Games Have to Teach Us about Learning and Literacy *(2003).*

Pro

Popular culture today often involves quite complex language, and that matters because the biggest predictor of children's school success is the size of their early vocabularies and their abilities to deal with complex language.

Consider, for example, a typical description of a "Pokémon" ("pocket monsters" found in video games, cards, books, movies and television shows): "Bulbasaur are a combination of Grass-type and Poison-type Pokémon. Because they are Grass-type Pokémon, Bulbasaur have plant-like characteristics." Or consider this from a Web site for "Yu-Gi-Oh" (another card, game, book, movie phenomenon): "The effect of '8-Claws Scorpion' is a Trigger Effect that is applied if the condition is correct on activation." Lots of low-frequency words here; complex syntax, as well.

Children as young as 6 and 7 play "Pokémon" and "Yu-Gi-Oh." To play they have to read—and read complex language.

The biggest barrier to school success is the child's ability to deal with complex "academic" language, the sort of language in textbooks. Such language starts to kick in about fourth grade and ever increases thereafter in school. Children who learn to decode, but can't read to learn in the content areas later on, are victims of the well-known "fourth-grade slump." Worse yet, research shows that even children who can pass tests in the content areas often can't apply their knowledge to real problem-solving.

Without lots of practice, humans are poor at learning from words out of their contexts of application. Good video games put young people in worlds composed of problems to be solved. They almost always give verbal information "just in time"—when players need and can use it—and "on demand," when the player asks for it. They show how language applies to the world it is about.

Research suggests that people really know what words mean only   5
when they can hook them to the sorts of actions, images or dialogues to which they apply. That is why a game manual or strategy guide makes much more sense after someone has played a game for a while than before. So, too, science textbooks, cut off from the images and actions science is about, are like a technical game manual without any game.

But, a warning: Good video games—good commercial ones like "Civilization 4" and good "serious games" made around academic content— will not work by themselves. Mentors are needed to encourage strategic thinking about the game and the complex language connected to them.

Joining the Conversation: Critical Thinking and Writing

1. Does your own experience confirm Gee's assertion (paragraph 2) that in order to play video games, youngsters "have to read"? A few games? Many games? Most games? Explain.

2. In the final paragraph, Gee speaks about the importance of mentors. If you were mentored or have served as a mentor in an enterprise involving games, briefly narrate the background and then argue that the experience did or did not serve a larger educational purpose.

Howard Gardner

Howard Gardner, a Professor of Cognition in the Harvard Graduate School of Education, has written numerous books. Among his recent publications are The Development and Education of the Mind: The Selected Works of Howard Gardner *(2006) and* Multiple Intelligences: New Horizons *(2006).*

Con

It's difficult to argue with many of Gee's points, and the jury is still out on others. Yet I'd point to several biases in the cited examples. (1) They are oriented toward competition (despite the fact that some also entail cooperation); (2) The literacy highlighted is that used in technical manuals; (3) These games, and the epistemology underlying them, are more likely to appeal to boys rather than to girls, and to "techies" rather than dreamers, humanists and conversationalists; (4) The foreground simulation, a very powerful technique, but it's not the same as real life.

I am happy to have medical students or future airplane pilots train on simulations—but they also require real, high-stake experience. Patients have feelings; simulacra and robots don't. And note that these are two areas where simulation makes sense. In many other professions, from poets to priests, they don't.

Which leads to the most important point. Literacy is far more than expertise in technical manuals or even in understanding science and technology, important as they are. It entails the capacity to immerse oneself and, ultimately, to love long, imaginative pieces of fiction, such as *Madame Bovary* or *One Hundred Years of Solitude;* poring over difficult philosophical texts and returning time and again to key passages (Kant, Wittgenstein); and spending time and exercising emotional imagination with challenging poets (Gerard Manley Hopkins, Jorie Graham).

Literacy involves linear thinking over many pages—an entirely different mental faculty than is exploited when one surfs the Web from one link to another, often randomly encountered one. I want all young persons to learn how to think like a historian, a philosopher, an economist, a literary critic (four very different "frames of mind"). I want to stimulate their imaginations to create their own worlds, not just that conjured up by the makers of "World of Warcraft."

In sum, the treasures and skills entailed in the video games of today are impressive, but they still represent only a very partial sampling of the kinds of minds that young people have and the kinds that can and should be cultivated. Some can be cultivated in front of a screen. But too much time there is not healthy on any criterion and any slice of life—no matter how engrossing—is only partial at best. So two cheers for Jim Gee—but two cheers as well for Mark Hopkins[1] on one end of a log, and an eager questioner and listener on the other.

[1]Mark Hopkins (1802–1887) was president of Williams College.

Howard Gardner: "Do Video Games Significantly Enhance Literacy?" Con, from *CQ Researcher*, November 10, 2006. Copyright © 2006. Reprinted by permission of the publisher.

Joining the Conversation:
Critical Thinking and Writing

1. Gardner's opening sentence is courteous, but he goes on to say that Gee's examples are biased. Do you agree that the examples Gee cites are severely limited and that his argument is therefore not as strong as it seems to be? Explain.

2. Gardner's "most important point" (paragraph 3) is that "Literacy is far more than expertise in technical manuals or even in understanding science." He amplifies this point in his next paragraph. Does your experience support his position? Explain.

3. Evaluate paragraph 5 as a final paragraph in an argumentative essay. Do you think it is effective? Why or why not?

Should Laptops Be Banned from the Classroom?

Andrew Goldstein

Andrew Goldstein, a student at Tufts University, submitted this essay in a first-year composition course.

Keep Online Poker Out of the Classroom: Why Professors Should Ban Laptops

Can it really be that all those students who are earnestly taking notes in my Econ class, never looking up for a moment but always tapping away, are trying to get down every word the lecturer is saying? Certainly that's the way it must seem to Prof. X, who, seeing plenty of the uplifted tops of laptops, keeps talking, and maybe even occasionally slows down so that the typists can get every detail.

From my view, behind the students and facing the professor, I see something else. I see screens that show that students are playing poker, or are shopping online, or are reading or writing e-mails. And I confess that I myself have done all these things in this course, and also in Poly Sci, another large lecture. It's not that these courses are especially boring; they aren't, they are pretty good courses. But I can get notes from my roommate, and, when you really think about it, there is no reason why both of us have to spend the hour taking notes that will be pretty much the same, so I sometimes do a little extra-curricular activity.

Actually, there *is* a reason why I should not be playing poker or surfing the web or instant messaging, and it is very simple: I should be paying attention to the lecturer, and *thinking* about what she is saying. True, there is very little discussion in the class—once in a while, maybe twice during the hour—the prof will ask if we have any questions, and maybe twice she will even toss out a question and ask for a response—but for the most part the course is a straight lecture course. Still, I know from my own experience that when I pay attention I do find myself thinking about what she is saying, sometimes wondering why I had never thought of this or that, sometimes wondering if the point also could be applied to X or Y, and so forth.

I have therefore come to the conclusion—based on my experience in the only two large lecture courses that I am taking—that professors should ban laptops from the lecture hall. There are several good reasons to support this position.

First, I'd say that when other students use laptops, they distract *me*. I cannot help but see games on the screen to my left and on the screen of the girl in front of me, and it's very distracting. The tapping noise is also distracting, and I think, that as a member of the class, I have a right to be protected from such distractions.

But what about the students who are *not* using laptops for such purposes, but who are genuinely taking notes? Well, the tapping is still an annoyance, but I suppose someone might complain that when I turn the page of the spiral notepad in which I am scribbling notes, the sound of the paper is distracting. I can only say that I don't think the two are really comparable. My noise is for a fraction of a second, not a constant sound throughout the lecture.

Second, as for the students who are using laptops in class only to take notes, not to play games or to shop or write letters, you might ask, "Why shouldn't students take advantage of technology to help them learn?" With laptops they can get down in their notes much more than they could by writing by hand. Furthermore, the notes will be easily legible when they review for the exam, and with some software the notes can easily be reorganized efficiently for certain specific purposes. All of this is true, but I think one can argue that the very fact that one can take extensive notes, almost word for word, is not good but is bad. I know from my own experience that when I take detailed notes I am *not* thinking. Instead, I am doing stenography, and it seems to me that most professors want us to *think* about what they are saying. And then, when I am reviewing for an examination and I look at my very full notes, I find lots of material that is in the textbook, and I wonder why I bothered to write all of those things down. I should have been thinking, and taking only a few notes about especially challenging ideas.

Third, in my smaller course in American Lit, where there is discussion, the five or six students (out of maybe twelve or fifteen) who are busy typing away on their laptops never contribute to the discussion. In fact, when one was called on in a recent class, he said he didn't hear the question because he was busy typing what the instructor had been saying a few minutes earlier.

In short, I don't think there are any good reasons for students to use laptops in class, and I think there are several good reasons why they should not use laptops. If professors want to ban laptops, that's fine with me. The only thing I would add is this: If a course is required, a professor should not ban laptops. Although I personally find laptops distracting, and I think that students probably learn less when they take extensive notes—and certainly when they IM or they surf the web, in the final analysis, that's their business. True, I object to the distracting noise and the distracting screens, and I suppose the prof must object to the lack of eye-contact with these students, but I think that if a course is required, a professor should allow students to take notes however they wish. But in an elective course, I think the professor can and should set the rules for the best learning conditions—and that includes banning laptops. If students want to use laptops, let them choose another course.

 ## Joining the Conversation:
Critical Thinking and Writing

1. List each argument that Golden offers in defense of his position and then evaluate each of these arguments in two or three sentences.

2. Can you think of arguments that he does not raise that would strengthen his thesis? If so, what are they?

3. What grade would you give this essay? Please explain your evaluation.

Elena Choy

Elena Choy has taught economics at several community colleges. She wrote this essay at the request of the editors of The Little, Brown Reader.

Laptops in the Classroom?
No Problem

Someone—I forget who—said, "A teacher is someone who never says anything once." I myself have quoted this comment many times—in the classroom, during conferences, at faculty meetings, and now in print. We teachers are a varied bunch, some of us are much more interesting than others, but probably all of us repeat ourselves more than we should or are sometimes boring in other ways, at least to certain students. If, then, during one of our lectures a student wants to surf the web or to play poker online, well, who am I to say that she or he hasn't the right to do so? We all claim that we value individual thinking, that we want students to think for themselves. Why, then, do we object when they decide they want to tune us out?

Let me try to give a reasoned statement of my position, a statement that will take account of the contrary position. In fact, I'll begin with what I take to be the arguments in *favor* of banning laptops. I believe the chief arguments are these: (1) the upraised lids of laptops distract the instructor, and they often prevent the instructor from making eye-contact with the students; (2) laptops distract other students, who cannot help but see what is on the screens—for instance video games; (3) students who use laptops to take notes take overly extensive notes, so they are doing stenography rather than thinking—rather, one might almost say, than paying real attention to the significant content of the course; (4) because they are so busy taking notes, laptop users tend not to participate in whatever discussion there may be in the course because they are too busy taking notes.

Let's look at each of these arguments, beginning with the first. I grant that I am not keen about seeing lots of upraised tops, but (a) the large majority of my students, even in a big lecture course, are not using laptops, and I therefore can make plenty of eye-contact; (b) I am delighted to see that students are taking notes, or at least I think they are taking notes; (c) if they are playing poker or shopping online, well, that's their business. They have paid their tuition, and it's up to them to decide how to spend their money and their time. I am not Big Brother; I don't think it is appropriate for me to assume that those with laptops are not taking notes. In any case, if they are not, it surely is not for me to tell them how to use their time in class, provided they are not disturbing others.

Which gets to the second argument offered in favor of banning laptops, that they distract other students. Do the users of laptops in class significantly damage other students? If so, of course laptops should be banned, just as we ban smoking in the classroom. I have heard students say that the poker games they see on the screens of other students prevent them from paying attention to the lecturer, but I find it hard to take this objection seriously. Such students should stop peeking, should discipline themselves, should look at the lecturer, and should occupy themselves by taking their own notes.

The third objection, that students who use laptops are engaged in stenography rather than in thoughtful thinking, seems to me to be equally without force. Different students have different methods of learning: Some students find it useful to take abundant notes, others take very few notes, perhaps preferring to think about what is being said while it is being said. Indeed, some students have different methods for different courses: I can easily imagine hearing a lecture that I would like to preserve fairly extensively, a lecture perhaps filled with facts and figures, but I can also easily imagine hearing an equally stimulating lecture that is not of the sort that I would find myself taking extensive notes—an occasional memorable phrase might be all that I might jot down. A wise student might well adopt different methods for different lecturers. It doesn't follow, then that every student who uses a laptop will take too many notes.

The fourth reason offered on behalf of banning laptops is that the note-takers tend not to participate in whatever discussion there may be in class. My response is twofold: First, in lecture classes the discussion inevitably is an extremely minor part of the class, perhaps a few minutes of discussion at the end, or possibly one or two questions that are handled during the course of the lecture. At most only three or four students can participate, so we cannot in good faith argue that the laptop user, by remaining relatively silent, is hurting himself of herself, or is depriving other students of the benefit of his or her contribution. And, for that matter, even in smaller classes, let's say of ten or fifteen, we should respect the wishes of a student who prefers not to speak much in class. In twenty years of teaching I have had three students who approached me after the first meeting of a smallish class, and explained that for one reason or another they preferred not to be called on. Ordinarily in such classes I say that part of the grade will depend upon class participation, but in their cases, because they raised the matter at the outset, I respected their wishes—I do not think it is my job to demand that shy people overcome their shyness—and I based the grade entirely on their three papers, their midterm and their final examinations—just as I base the grades in my large lecture courses. Obviously some courses—let's say Spoken Spanish—require oral participation, but in most classes I think we can comply with a student who requests that he or she not be called on to speak.

Finally, and with some hesitation, at this late stage in my essay I want to introduce a new point. It has been my experience that the call to ban laptops chiefly comes not from students but from their professors, my colleagues. Sometimes my colleagues say that they are disturbed by the lack of eye-contact, and I sympathize with them; I know what it is to see a raised lid rather than a student's face. Sometimes they say that the students are engaged in stenography, not in thinking, and I can understand this objection too, though, as I have indicated, I think different methods of note-taking work well for different students. When I was a student, in pre-laptop days, I confess, I took abundant notes in certain courses. My colleagues may say that they are concerned with helping students to *learn,* or *think,* not to be stenographers, but this sort of stenography served me well I think in some of the courses I took. It is not up to professors to prohibit students from taking the kinds of notes that the students think will be useful. We can give advice about taking notes, about preparing for the examination, and so forth, but we go too far when we prohibit students from taking notes in the way they find most useful.

In any case, and here I come to a dangerous point, I think that the chief reason instructors suggest that laptops be banned is one that they do not state, and maybe they are not even aware of. I think they fear that most students who use laptops are not taking notes, but are engaged in activities unrelated to the course—instant messaging, e-mailing, shopping, playing poker, and so on. But if students are in fact doing these things, what is the cure? Banning laptops? I don't think so. If the instructor is so boring that the students use laptops to shop and to write letters, well, when the laptops are banned the students will probably bring in crossword puzzles or exercises from other courses (for instance, Spanish vocabulary lists to be memorized) or whatever, and continue to ignore the lecturer.

I am saying, with much embarrassment, that a professor should ask himself a hard question: If students in my courses are using laptops for purposes unrelated to the course, what am I doing wrong? Perhaps we should videotape a lecture or two so that we can see and hear what we look like and sound like, or perhaps ask a colleague to visit our class and evaluate it. It may be that if we saw ourselves, we would understand why the student has chosen to act independently. It might be that we too would prefer online poker.

 ## Joining the Conversation: Critical Thinking and Writing

1. Can you think of any significant arguments *against* her case that Choy omits? If so, what are they—and how might she (or you) respond to them?

2. If you were the editor of your college newspaper, would you print this essay? Why or why not?

3. Basing your view on this essay, do you think you would want to take a course with Professor Choy? Explain your reasoning.

Frederick Douglass

Frederick Douglass (1817 or 1818–1895) was born a slave in Maryland. In 1838, he escaped to New York, and he soon became active in the abolitionist movement—both as a speaker and as the editor of a newspaper, North Star. *We give an excerpt from Chapter VII of his autobiography,* Narrative of the Life of Frederick Douglass *(1845). Douglass did not give a title to the chapter, but this passage is traditionally known by the title given here, derived from a phrase in the second sentence of the chapter.*

Learning to Read and Write

I lived in Master Hugh's family about seven years. During this time, I succeeded in learning to read and write. In accomplishing this, I was compelled to resort to various stratagems. I had no regular teacher. My mistress, who had kindly commenced to instruct me, had, in compliance with the advice and direction of her husband, not only ceased to instruct, but had set her face against my being instructed by any one else. It is due, however, to my mistress to say of her, that she did not adopt this course of treatment immediately. She at first lacked the depravity indispensable to shutting me up in mental darkness. It was at least necessary for her to have some training in the exercise of irresponsible power, to make her equal to the task of treating me as though I were a brute.

My mistress was, as I have said, a kind and tender-hearted woman; and in the simplicity of her soul she commenced, when I first went to live with her, to treat me as she supposed one human being ought to treat another. In entering upon the duties of a slaveholder, she did not seem to perceive that I sustained to her the relation of a mere chattel, and that for her to treat me as a human being was not only wrong, but dangerously so. Slavery proved as injurious to her as it did to me. When I went there, she was a pious, warm, and tender-hearted woman. There was no sorrow or suffering for which she had not a tear. She had bread for the hungry, clothes for the naked, and comfort for every mourner that came within her reach. Slavery soon proved its ability to divest her of these heavenly qualities. Under its influence, the tender heart became stone, and the lamb-like disposition gave way to one of tiger-like fierceness. The first step in her downward course was in her ceasing to instruct me. She now commenced to practice her husband's precepts. She finally became even more violent in her opposition than her husband himself. She was not satisfied with simply doing as well as he had commanded; she seemed anxious to do better. Nothing seemed to make here more angry than to see me with a newspaper. She seemed to think that here lay the danger. I have had her rush at me with a face made all up of fury, and snatch from me a newspaper, in a manner that fully revealed her apprehension. She was an apt woman; and a little experience soon demonstrated, to her satisfaction, that education and slavery were incompatible with each other.

From this time I was most narrowly watched. If I was in a separate room any considerable length of time, I was sure to be suspected of having a book, and was at once called to give an account of myself. All this, however, was too late. The first step had been taken. Mistress, in teaching me the alphabet, had given me the *inch*, and no precaution could prevent me from taking the *ell*.[1]

The plan which I adopted, and the one by which I was most successful, was that of making friends of all the little white boys whom I met in the street. As many of these as I could, I converted into teachers. With their kindly aid, obtained at different times and in different places, I finally succeeded in learning to read. When I was sent of errands, I always took my book with me, and by going one part of my errand quickly,

---

[1]**Ell** Unit of measurement equivalent to 45 inches.

I found time to get a lesson before my return. I used also to carry bread with me, enough of which was always in the house, and to which I was always welcome; for I was much better off in this regard than many of the poor white children in our neighborhood. This bread I used to bestow upon the hungry little urchins, who, in return, would give me that more valuable bread of knowledge. I am strongly tempted to give the names of two or three of those little boys, as a testimonial of the gratitude and affection I bear them; but prudence forbids:—not that it would injure me, but it might embarrass them; for it is almost an unpardonable offence to teach slaves to read in this Christian country. It is enough to say of the dear little fellows, that they live on Philpot Street, very near Durgin and Bailey's ship-yard. I used to talk this matter of slavery over with them. I would sometimes say to them, I wished I could be as free as they would be when they got to be men. "You will be free as soon as you are twenty-one, *but I am a slave for life!* Have not I as good a right to be free as you have?" These words used to trouble them; they would express for me the liveliest sympathy, and console me with the hope that something would occur by which I might be free.

I was now about twelve years old, and the thought of being *a slave for life* began to bear heavily upon my heart. Just about this time, I got hold of a book entitled "The Columbian Orator." Every opportunity I go, I used to read this book. Among much of other interesting matter, I found in it a dialogue between a master and his slave. The slave was represented as having run away from his master three times. The dialogue represented the conversation which took place between them, when the slave was re-taken the third time. In this dialogue, the whole argument in behalf of slavery was brought forward by the master, all of which was disposed of by the slave. The slave was made to say some very smart as well as impressive things in reply to his master—things which had the desired though unexpected effect; for the conversation resulted in the voluntary emancipation of the slave on the part of the master.

In the same book, I met with one of Sheridan's mighty speeches[2] on and in behalf of Catholic emancipation. These were choice documents to me. I read them over and over again with unabated interest. They gave tongue to interesting thoughts of my own soul, which had frequently lashed through my mind, and died away for want of utterance. The moral which I gained from the dialogue was the power of truth over the conscience of even a slaveholder. What I got from Sheridan was a bold denunciation of slavery, and a powerful vindication of human rights. The reading of these documents enabled me to utter my thoughts, and to meet the arguments brought forward to sustain slavery; but while they relieved

---

[2]**Sheridan's mighty speeches** Richard Brinsley Sheridan (1751–1816), Irish-born playwright and member of the English Parliament, favored the abolition of restrictions imposed by the English on catholics.

me of the difficulty, they brought on another even more painful than the one of which I was relieved. The more I read, the more I was led to abhor and detest my enslavers. I could regard them in no other light than a band of successful robbers, who had left their homes, and gone to Africa, and stolen us from our homes, and in a strange land reduced us to slavery. I loathed them as being the meanest as well as the most wicked of men. As I read and contemplated the subject, behold! that very discontentment which Master Hugh had predicted would follow my learning to read had already come, to torment and sting my soul to unutterable anguish. As I writhed under it, I would at times feel that learning to read had been a curse rather than a blessing. It had given me a view of my wretched condition, without the remedy. It opened my eyes to the horrible pit, but to no ladder upon which to get out. In moments of agony, I envied my fellow-slaves for their stupidity. I have often wished myself a beast. I preferred the condition of the meanest reptile to my own. Any thing, no matter what, to get rid of thinking! It was this everlasting thinking of my condition that tormented me. There was no getting rid of it. It was pressed upon me by every object within sight or hearing, animate or inanimate. The silver trump of freedom had roused my soul to eternal wakefulness. Freedom now appeared, to disappear no more forever. It was heard in every sound, and seen in every thing. It was ever present to torment me with a sense of my wretched condition. I saw nothing without seeing it, I heard nothing without hearing it, and felt nothing without feeling it. It looked from every star, it smiled in every calm, breathed in every wind, and moved in every storm.

I often found myself regretting my own existence, and wishing myself dead; and but for the hope of being free, I have no doubt but that I should have killed myself, or done something for which I should have been killed. While in this state of mind, I was eager to hear any one speak of slavery. I was a ready listener. Every little while, I could hear something about the abolitionists. It was some time before I found what the word meant. It was always used in such connections as to make it an interesting word to me. If a slave ran away and succeeded in getting clear, or if a slave killed his master, set fire to a barn, or did any thing very wrong in the mind of a slaveholder, it was spoken of as the fruit of *abolition*. Hearing the word in this connection very often, I set about learning what it meant. The dictionary afforded me little or no help. I found it was "the act of abolishing"; but then I did not know what was to be abolished. Here I was perplexed. I did not dare to ask any one about its meaning, for I was satisfied that it was something they wanted me to know very little about. After a patient waiting, I got one of our city papers, containing an account of the number of petitions from the north, praying for the *abolition* of slavery in the District of Columbia, and of the slave trade between the States. From this time I understood the words *abolition* and *abolitionist*, and always drew near when that word was spoken, expecting to hear something of importance to myself and fellow-slaves. The light broke in upon me by degrees. I went one day down on the wharf of Mr. Waters; and seeing two Irishmen unloading a scow of stone, I went, unasked, and helped them. When we had finished, one of them came to me and asked me if I were a slave. I told him I was. He asked, "Are ye a slave for life?" I told him that I was. The good Irishman seemed to be deeply affected by the statement. He said to the other that it was a pity so fine a little fellow as myself should be a slave for life. He said it was a shame to hold me. They both advised me to run away to the north; I should find friends there, and that I should be free. I pretended not to be interested in what they said, and treated them as if I did not understand them; for I feared they might be treacherous. White men have been known to encourage slaves to escape, and then, to get the reward, catch them and return them to their masters. I was afraid that these seemingly good men might use me so; but I nevertheless remembered their advice, and from that time I resolved to run away. I looked forward to a time at which it would be safe for me to escape. I was too young to think of doing so immediately; besides, I wished to learn how to write, as I might have occasion to write my own pass. I consoled myself with the hope that I should one day find a good chance. Meanwhile, I would learn to write.

The idea as to how I might learn to write was suggested to me by being in Durgin and Bailey's ship-yard, and frequently seeing the ship carpenters, after hewing, and getting a piece of timber ready for use, write on the timber the name of that part of the ship for which it was intended. When a piece of timber was intended for the larboard side, it would be marked thus—L." When a piece was for the starboard side, it would be marked thus—S." A piece for the larboard side forward, would be marked thus—L. F." When a piece was for starboard side forward, it would be marked thus—S. F." For larboard aft, it would be marked thus—L. A." For starboard aft, it would be marked thus—S. A." I soon learned the names of these letters, and for what they were intended when placed upon a piece of timber in the ship-yard. I immediately commenced copying them, and in a short time was able to make the four letters named. After that, when I met with any boy who I knew could write, I would tell him I could write as well as he. The next word would be, "I don't believe you. Let me see you try it." I would then make the letters which I had been so fortunate as to learn, and ask him to beat that. In this way I got a good many lessons in writing, which it is quite possible I should never have gotten in any other way. During this time, my copy-book was the board fence, brick wall, and pavement; my pen and ink was a lump of chalk. With these, I learned mainly how to write. I then commenced and continued copying the Italics in Webster's Spelling Book, until I could make them all without looking on the book. By this time, my little Master Thomas had gone to school, and learned how to write, and had written over a number of copy-books. These had been brought home, and shown to some of our near neighbors, and then laid aside. My mistress used to go to class meeting at the Wilk Street meetinghouse every Monday afternoon, and leave me to take care of the house. When left thus, I used to spend the time in writing in the spaces left in Master Thomas's copy-book, copying what he had written. I continued to do this until I could write a hand very similar to that of Master Thomas. Thus, after a long, tedious effort for years, I finally succeeded in learning how to write.

 ## Joining the Conversation: Critical Thinking and Writing

1. Douglass's autobiography reveals his intellectual gifts. In the passage that we excerpt here, what does it reveal of his character as he pursues literacy and, ultimately, freedom?

2. Take any paragraph (the first or second can serve as well as any) and analyze the style of the prose—the vocabulary and the construction of the sentences. Of course, the subject matter itself tells you that the passage was written in the days of slavery, but what characteristics of the prose make it pretty clear that this material was not written yesterday? Rewrite your selected paragraph in today's language.

3. This essay tells us about Douglass's great accomplishments, but does it have any relevance for readers today? Please explain.

Richard Rodriguez

Richard Rodriguez, the son of immigrants from Mexico, was born in San Francisco in 1944. He was educated at Stanford University, Columbia University, and the University of California, Berkeley, where he specialized in English literature of the Renaissance. In his book Hunger of Memory: The Education of Richard Rodriguez *(1982), he reports how his progress in the Anglo world was accompanied by estrangement from the Spanish-speaking world. We print an excerpt from the book; the title of the excerpt is our own.*

Rodriguez is often seen and heard as a commentator on PBS NewsHour with Jim Lehrer.

Public and Private Language

Supporters of bilingual education today imply that students like me miss a great deal by not being taught in their family's language. What they seem not to recognize is that, as a socially disadvantaged child, I considered Spanish to be a private language. What I needed to learn in school was that I had the right—and the obligation—to speak the public language of *los gringos*. The odd truth is that my first-grade classmates could have become bilingual, in the conventional sense of that word, more easily than I. Had they been taught (as upper-middle-class children are often taught early) a second language like Spanish or French, they could have regarded it simply as that: another public language. In my case such bilingualism could not have been so quickly achieved. What I did not believe was that I could speak a single public language.

Without question, it would have pleased me to hear my teachers address me in Spanish when I entered the classroom. I would have felt much less afraid. I would have trusted them and responded with ease. But I would have delayed—for how long postponed?—having to learn the language of public society. I would have evaded—and for how long could I have afforded to delay?—learning the great lesson of school, that I had a public identity.

Fortunately, my teachers were unsentimental about their responsibility. What they understood was that I needed to speak a public language. So their voices would search me out, asking me questions. Each time I'd hear them, I'd look up in surprise to see a nun's face frowning at me. I'd mumble, not really meaning to answer. The nun would persist, "Richard, stand up. Don't look at the floor. Speak up. Speak to the entire class, not just to me!" But I couldn't believe that the English language was mine to use. (In part, I did not want to believe it.) I continued to mumble. I resisted the teacher's demands. (Did I somehow suspect that once I learned public language my pleasing family life would be changed?) Silent, waiting for the bell to sound, I remained dazed, diffident, afraid.

Because I wrongly imagined that English was intrinsically a public language and Spanish an intrinsically private one, I easily noted the difference between classroom language and the language of home. At school, words were directed to a general audience of listeners. ("Boys and girls.") Words were meaningfully ordered. And the point was not self-expression alone but to make oneself understood by many others. The teacher quizzed: "Boys and girls, why do we use that word in this sentence? Could we think of a better word to use there? Would the sentence change its meaning if the words were differently arranged? And wasn't there a better way of saying much the same thing?" (I couldn't say. I wouldn't try to say.)

Three months. Five. Half a year passed. Unsmiling, ever watchful, 5 my teachers noted my silence. They began to connect my behavior with the difficult progress my older sister and brother were making. Until one Saturday morning three nuns arrived at the house to talk to our parents. Stiffly, they sat on the blue living room sofa. From the doorway of another room, spying the visitors, I noted the incongruity—the clash of two worlds, the faces and voices of school intruding upon the familiar setting of home. I overheard one voice gently wondering, "Do your children speak only Spanish at home, Mrs. Rodriguez?" While another voice added, "That Richard especially seems so timid and shy."

That Rich-heard!

With great tact the visitors continued, "Is it possible for you and your husband to encourage your children to practice their English when they are home?" Of course, my parents complied. What would they not do for their children's well-being? And how could they have questioned the Church's authority which those women represented? In an instant, they agreed to give up the language (the sounds) that had revealed and accentuated our family's closeness. The moment after the visitors left, the change was observed. "*Ahora,* speak to us *en inglés,*" my father and mother united to tell us.

At first, it seemed a kind of game. After dinner each night, the family gathered to practice "our" English. (It was still then *inglés,* a language foreign to us, so we felt drawn as strangers to it.) Laughing, we would try to define words we could not pronounce. We played with strange English sounds, often over-anglicizing our pronunciations. And we filled the smiling gaps of our sentences with familiar Spanish sounds. But that was cheating, somebody shouted. Everyone laughed. In school, meanwhile, like my brother and sister, I was required to attend a daily tutoring session. I needed a full year of special attention. I also needed my teachers to keep my attention from straying in class by calling out, *Rich-heard*—their English voices slowly prying loose my ties to my other name, its three notes. *Ri-car-do.* Most of all I needed to hear my mother and father speak to me in a moment of seriousness in broken—suddenly heartbreaking—English. The scene was inevitable: One Saturday morning I entered the kitchen where my parents were talking in Spanish. I did not realize that they were talking in Spanish however until, at the moment they saw me, I heard their voices change to speak English. Those *gringo* sounds they uttered startled me. Pushed me away. In that moment of trivial misunderstanding and profound insight, I felt my throat twisted by unsounded grief. I turned quickly and left the room. But I had no place to escape to with Spanish. (The spell was broken.) My brother and sisters were speaking English in another part of the house.

Again and again in the days following, increasingly angry, I was obliged to hear my mother and father: "Speak to us *en inglés.*" (*Speak*). Only then did I determine to learn classroom English. Weeks after, it happened: One day in school I raised my hand to volunteer an answer. I spoke out in a loud voice. And I did not think it remarkable when the entire class understood. That day, I moved very far from the disadvantaged child I had been only days earlier. The belief, the calming assurance that I belonged in public, had at last taken hold.

Shortly after, I stopped hearing the high and loud sounds of *los gringos.*   10
A more and more confident speaker of English, I didn't trouble to listen to *how* strangers sounded, speaking to me. And there simply were too many English-speaking people in my day for me to hear American accents anymore. Conversations quickened. Listening to persons who sounded eccentrically pitched voices, I usually noted their sounds for an initial few seconds before I concentrated on *what* they were saying. Conversations

became content-full. Transparent. Hearing someone's *tone* of voice—angry or questioning or sarcastic or happy or sad—I didn't distinguish it from the words it expressed. Sound and word were thus tightly wedded. At the end of a day, I was often bemused, always relieved, to realize how "silent," though crowded with words, my day in public had been. (This public silence measured and quickened the change in my life.)

At last, seven years old, I came to believe what had been technically true since my birth: I was an American citizen.

But the special feeling of closeness at home was diminished by then. Gone was the desperate, urgent, intense feeling of being at home: rare was the experience of feeling myself individualized by family intimates. We remained a loving family, but one greatly changed. No longer so close; no longer bound tight by the pleasing and troubling knowledge of our public separateness. Neither my older brother nor sister rushed home after school anymore. Nor did I. When I arrived home there would often be neighborhood kids in the house. Or the house would be empty of sounds.

Following the dramatic Americanization of their children, even my parents grew more publicly confident. Especially my mother. She learned the names of all the people on our block. And she decided we needed to have a telephone installed in the house. My father continued to use the word *gringo*. But it was no longer charged with the old bitterness or distrust. (Stripped of any emotional content, the word simply became a name for those Americans not of Hispanic descent.) Hearing him, sometimes, I wasn't sure if he was pronouncing the Spanish word *gringo* or saying gringo in English.

Matching the silence I started hearing in public was a new quiet at home. The family's quiet was partly due to the fact that, as we children learned more and more English, we shared fewer and fewer words with our parents. Sentences needed to be spoken slowly when a child addressed his mother or father. (Often the parent wouldn't understand.) The child would need to repeat himself. (Still the parent misunderstood.) The young voice, frustrated, would end up saying, "Never mind"—the subject was closed. Dinners would be noisy with the clinking of knives and forks against dishes. My mother would smile softly between her remarks; my father at the other end of the table would chew and chew at his food, while he stared over the heads of his children.

My *mother!* My *father!* After English became my primary language, I no longer knew what words to use in addressing my parents. The old Spanish words (those tender accents of sound) I had used earlier—*mamá* and *papá*—I couldn't use anymore. They would have been too painful reminders of how much had changed in my life. On the other hand, the words I heard neighborhood kids call *their* parents seemed equally unsatisfactory. *Mother* and *Father; Ma, Papa, Pa, Dad, Pop* (how I hated the all-American sound of that last word especially)—all these terms I felt were unsuitable, not really terms of address for *my* parents. As a result, I never used them at home. Whenever I'd speak to my parents, I would try to get their attention with eye contact alone. In public conversations, I'd refer to "my parents" or "my mother and father."

My mother and father, for their part, responded differently, as their children spoke to them less. She grew restless, seemed troubled and anxious at the scarcity of words exchanged in the house. It was she who would question me about my day when I came home from school. She smiled at small talk. She pried at the edges of my sentences to get me to say something more. (What?) She'd stopped her children's talking. By contrast, my father seemed reconciled to the new quiet. Though his English improved somewhat, he retired into silence. At dinner he spoke very little. One night his children and even his wife helplessly giggled at his garbled English pronunciation of the Catholic Grace before Meals. Thereafter he made his wife recite the prayer at the start of each meal, even on formal occasions, when there were guests in the house. Hers became the public voice of the family. On official business, it was she, not my father, one would usually hear on the phone or in stores, talking to strangers. His children grew so accustomed to his silence that, years later, they would speak routinely of his shyness. (My mother would often try to explain: Both his parents died when he was eight. He was raised by an uncle who treated him like little more than a menial servant. He was never encouraged to speak. He grew up alone. A man of few words.) But my father was not shy, I realized, when I'd watch him speaking Spanish with relatives. Using Spanish, he was quickly effusive. Especially when talking with other men, his voice would spark, flicker, flare alive with sounds. In Spanish, he expressed ideas and feelings he rarely revealed in English. With firm Spanish sounds, he conveyed confidence and authority English would never allow him.

The silence at home, however, was finally more than a literal silence. Fewer words passed between parent and child, but more profound was the silence that resulted from my inattention to sounds. At about the time I no longer bothered to listen with care to the sounds of English in public, I grew careless about listening to the sounds family members made when they spoke. Most of the time I heard someone speaking at home and didn't distinguish his sounds from the words people uttered in public. I didn't even pay much attention to my parents' accented and ungrammatical speech. At least not at home. Only when I was with them in public would I grow alert to their accents. Though, even then, their sounds caused me less and less concern. For I was increasingly confident of my own public identity.

I would have been happier about my public success had I not sometimes recalled what it had been like earlier, when my family had conveyed its intimacy through a set of conveniently private sounds. Sometimes in public, hearing a stranger, I'd hark back to my past. A Mexican farmworker approached me downtown to ask directions to somewhere. "Hijito ...?" he said. And his voice summoned deep longing. Another time, standing beside my mother in the visiting room of a Carmelite convent, before the dense screen which rendered the nuns shadowy figures, I heard several Spanish-speaking nuns—their busy, singsong overlapping voices—assure us that yes, yes, we were remembered, all our family was remembered in their prayers. (Their voices echoed faraway family sounds.) Another day, a dark-faced old woman—her hand light on my shoulder—steadied herself against me as she boarded a bus. She murmured something I couldn't quite comprehend. Her Spanish voice came near, like the face of a never-before-seen relative in the instant before I was kissed. Her voice, like so many of the Spanish voices I'd hear in public, recalled the golden age of my youth. Hearing Spanish then, I continued to be a careful, if sad, listener to sounds. Hearing a Spanish-speaking family walking behind me, I turned to look. I smiled for an instant, before my glance found the Hispanic-looking faces of strangers in the crowd going by.

Joining the Conversation: Critical Thinking and Writing

1. We have called this selection from Rodriguez's *The Hunger of Memory* "Public and Private Language," and, indeed, the words occur often in the text. But from reading these pages, how would you identify what is "public language" and what is "private"? What words and images would you associate with each?

2. In his first paragraph, Rodriguez identifies himself as a "socially disadvantaged child." What does he mean?

3. At the end of his second paragraph, Rodriguez identifies "the great lesson of school"—that he "had a public identity." What does Rodriguez mean by his "public identity," and would you say that your elementary school also aided you in achieving one? Explain.

4. In his 11th and 12th paragraphs, Rodriguez comes "to believe what had been technically true since [his] birth"—he was now an "American citizen." He seems to associate this truth with a change in his family relationships. Was there a period in your life when you felt such a change in your family—with or without a change in language? If so, how would you characterize it?

Maya Angelou

Maya Angelou, born in St. Louis, Missouri, in 1938, grew up in Arkansas and California. She studied music, dance, and drama (she had a role in the televised version of Alex Haley's Roots*), and she is now a professor of American studies at Wake Forest University. She has also worked as a cook, streetcar conductor, and waitress. In addition to writing books of poetry, she has written six autobiographical volumes.*

"Graduation" (editors' title) comes from her first autobiography, I Know Why the Caged Bird Sings *(1969).*

Graduation

The children in Stamps trembled visibly with anticipation. Some adults were excited too, but to be certain the whole young population had come down with graduation epidemic. Large classes were graduating from both the grammar school and the high school. Even those who were years removed from their own day of glorious release were anxious to help with preparations as a kind of dry run. The junior students who were moving into the vacating classes' chairs were tradition-bound to show their talents for leadership and management. They strutted through the school and around the campus exerting pressure on the lower grades. Their authority was so new that occasionally if they pressed a little too hard it had to be overlooked. After all, next term was coming, and it never hurt a sixth grader to have a play sister in the eighth grade, or a tenth-year student to be able to call a twelfth grader Bubba. So all was endured in a spirit of shared understanding. But the graduating classes themselves were the nobility. Like travelers with exotic destinations on their minds, the graduates were remarkably forgetful. They came to school without their books, or tablets or even pencils. Volunteers fell over themselves to secure replacements for the missing equipment. When accepted, the willing workers might or might not be thanked, and it was of no importance to the pregraduation rites. Even teachers were respectful of the now quiet and aging seniors, and tended to speak to them, if not as equals, as beings only slightly lower than themselves. After tests were returned and grades given, the student body, which acted like an extended family, knew who did well, who excelled, and what piteous ones had failed.

Unlike the white high school, Lafayette County Training School distinguished itself by having neither lawn, nor hedges, nor tennis court, nor climbing ivy. Its two buildings (main classrooms, the grade school and home economics) were set on a dirt hill with no fence to limit either its boundaries or those of bordering farms. There was a large expanse to the left of the school which was used alternately as a baseball diamond or a basketball court. Rusty hoops on the swaying poles represented the permanent recreational equipment, although bats and balls could be borrowed from the P.E. teacher if the borrower was qualified and if the diamond wasn't occupied.

Over this rocky area relieved by a few shady tall persimmon trees the graduating class walked. The girls often held hands and no longer bothered to speak to the lower students. There was a sadness about them, as if this old world was not their home and they were bound for higher ground. The boys, on the other hand, had become more friendly, more outgoing. A decided change from the closed attitude they projected while studying for finals. Now they seemed not ready to give up the old school, the familiar paths and classrooms. Only a small percentage would be continuing on to college—one of the South's A & M (agricultural and mechanical) schools, which trained Negro youths to be carpenters, farmers, handymen, masons, maids, cooks and baby nurses. Their future rode heavily on their shoulders, and blinded them to the collective joy that had pervaded the lives of the boys and girls in the grammar school graduating class.

Parents who could afford it had ordered new shoes and ready-made clothes for themselves from Sears and Roebuck or Montgomery Ward. They also engaged the best seamstresses to make the floating graduating dresses and to cut down secondhand pants which would be pressed to a military slickness for the important event.

Oh, it was important, all right. Whitefolks would attend the ceremony, and two or three would speak of God and home, and the Southern way of life, and Mrs. Parsons, the principal's wife, would play the graduation march while the lower-grade graduates paraded down the aisles and took their seats below the platform. The high school seniors would wait in empty classrooms to make their dramatic entrance.

In the Store I was the person of the moment. The birthday girl. The center. Bailey had graduated the year before, although to do so he had had to forfeit all pleasures to make up for his time lost in Baton Rouge.

My class was wearing butter-yellow piqué dresses, and Momma launched out on mine. She smocked the yoke into tiny crisscrossing puckers, then shirred the rest of the bodice. Her dark fingers ducked in and out of the lemony cloth as she embroidered raised daisies around the hem. Before she considered herself finished she had added a crocheted cuff on the puff sleeves, and a pointy crocheted collar.

I was going to be lovely. A walking model of all the various styles of fine hand sewing and it didn't worry me that I was only twelve years old and merely graduating from the eighth grade. Besides, many teachers in Arkansas Negro schools had only that diploma and were licensed to impart wisdom.

The days had become longer and more noticeable. The faded beige of former times had been replaced with strong and sure colors. I began to see my classmates' clothes, their skin tones, and the dust that waved off pussy willows. Clouds that lazed across the sky were objects of great concern to me. Their shiftier shapes might have held a message that in my new happiness and with a little bit of time I'd soon decipher. During that period I looked at the arch of heaven so religiously my neck kept a steady ache. I had taken to smiling more often, and my jaws hurt from the unaccustomed activity. Between the two physical sore spots, I suppose I could have been uncomfortable, but that was not the case. As a member of the winning team (the graduating class of 1940) I had outdistanced unpleasant sensations by miles. I was headed for the freedom of open fields.

Youth and social approval allied themselves with me and we trammeled memories of slights and insults. The wind of our swift passage remodeled my features. Lost tears were pounded to mud and then to dust.

Years of withdrawal were brushed aside and left behind, as hanging ropes of parasitic moss.

My work alone had awarded me a top place and I was going to be one of the first called in the graduating ceremonies. On the classroom blackboard, as well as on the bulletin board in the auditorium, there were blue stars and white stars and red stars. No absences, no tardinesses, and my academic work was among the best of the year. I could say the preamble to the Constitution even faster than Bailey. We timed ourselves often: "We the people of the United States in order to form a more perfect union ... " I had memorized the Presidents of the United States from Washington to Roosevelt in chronological as well as alphabetical order.

My hair pleased me too. Gradually the black mass had lengthened and thickened, so that it kept at last to its braided pattern, and I didn't have to yank my scalp off when I tried to comb it.

Louise and I had rehearsed the exercises until we tired out ourselves. Henry Reed was class valedictorian. He was a small, very black boy with hooded eyes, a long, broad nose and an oddly shaped head. I had admired him for years because each term he and I vied for the best grades in our class. Most often he bested me, but instead of being disappointed I was pleased that we shared top places between us. Like many Southern Black children, he lived with his grandmother, who was as strict as Momma and as kind as she knew how to be. He was courteous, respectful and soft-spoken to elders, but on the playground he chose to play the roughest games. I admired him. Anyone, I reckoned, sufficiently afraid or sufficiently dull could be polite. But to be able to operate at a top level with both adults and children was admirable.

His valedictory speech was entitled "To Be or Not To Be." The rigid tenth-grade teacher helped him to write it. He'd been working on the dramatic stresses for months.

The weeks until graduation were filled with heady activities. A group of small children were to be presented in a play about buttercups and daisies and bunny rabbits. They could be heard throughout the building practicing their hops and their little songs that sounded like silver bells. The older girls (non-graduates, of course) were assigned the task of making refreshments for the night's festivities. A tangy scent of ginger, cinnamon, nutmeg and chocolate wafted around the home economics building as the budding cooks made samples for themselves and their teachers.

In every corner of the workshop, axes and saws split fresh timber as the woodshop boys made sets and stage scenery. Only the graduates were left out of the general bustle. We were free to sit in the library at the back of the building or look in quite detachedly, naturally, on the measures being taken for our event.

Even the minister preached on graduation the Sunday before. His subject was, "Let your light so shine that men will see your good works and praise your Father, Who is in Heaven." Although the sermon was

15

purported to be addressed to us, he used the occasion to speak to back-sliders, gamblers, and general ne'er-do-wells. But since he had called our names at the beginning of the service we were mollified.

Among Negroes the tradition was to give presents to children going only from one grade to another. How much more important this was when the person was graduating at the top of the class. Uncle Willie and Momma had sent away for a Mickey Mouse watch like Bailey's. Louise gave me four embroidered handkerchiefs. (I gave her three crocheted doilies.) Mrs. Sneed, the minister's wife, made me an underskirt to wear for graduation, and nearly every customer gave me a nickel or maybe even a dime with the instruction "Keep on moving to higher ground," or some such encouragement.

Amazingly the great day finally dawned and I was out of bed before I knew it. I threw open the back door to see it more clearly, but Momma said, "Sister, come away from that door and put your robe on."

I hoped the memory of that morning would never leave me. Sunlight was itself still young, and the day had none of the insistence maturity would bring it in a few hours. In my robe and barefoot in the backyard, under cover of going to see about my new beans, I gave myself up to the gentle warmth and thanked God that no matter what evil I had done in my life He had allowed me to live to see this day. Somewhere in my fatalism I had expected to die, accidentally, and never have the chance to walk up the stairs in the auditorium and gracefully receive my hard-earned diploma. Out of God's merciful bosom I had won reprieve.

Bailey came out in his robe and gave me a box wrapped in Christmas paper. He said he had saved his money for months to pay for it. It felt like a box of chocolates, but I knew Bailey wouldn't save money to buy candy when we had all we could want under our noses.

He was as proud of the gift as I. It was a soft-leather-bound copy of a collection of poems by Edgar Allan Poe, or, as Bailey and I called him, "Eap." I turned to "Annabel Lee" and we walked up and down the garden rows, the cool dirt between our toes, reciting the beautifully sad lines.

Momma made a Sunday breakfast although it was only Friday. After we finished the blessing, I opened my eyes to find the watch on my plate. It was a dream of a day. Everything went smoothly and to my credit I didn't have to be reminded or scolded for anything. Near evening I was too jittery to attend to chores, so Bailey volunteered to do all before his bath.

Days before, we had made a sign for the Store and as we turned out the lights Momma hung the cardboard over the doorknob. It read clearly: CLOSED. GRADUATION.

My dress fitted perfectly and everyone said that I looked like a sunbeam in it. On the hill, going toward the school, Bailey walked behind with Uncle Willie, who muttered, "Go on, Ju." He wanted him to walk ahead with us because it embarrassed him to have to walk so slowly.

Bailey said he'd let the ladies walk together, and the men would bring up the rear. We all laughed, nicely.

Little children dashed by out of the dark like fireflies. Their crepe-paper dresses and butterfly wings were not made for running and we heard more than one rip, dryly, and the regretful "uh uh" that followed.

The school blazed without gaiety. The windows seemed cold and un-friendly from the lower hill. A sense of ill-fated timing crept over me, and if Momma hadn't reached for my hand I would have drifted back to Bailey and Uncle Willie, and possibly beyond. She made a few slow jokes about my feet getting cold, and tugged me along to the now-strange building.

Around the front steps, assurance came back. There were my fellow "greats," the graduating class. Hair brushed back, legs oiled, new dresses and pressed pleats, fresh pocket handkerchiefs and little hand-bags, all homesewn. Oh, we were up to snuff, all right. I joined my comrades and didn't even see my family go in to find seats in the crowded auditorium.

The school band struck up a march and all classes filed in as had been rehearsed. We stood in front of our seats, as assigned, and on a signal from the choir director, we sat. No sooner had this been accomplished than the band started to play the national anthem. We rose again and sang the song, after which we recited the pledge of allegiance. We remained standing for a brief minute before the choir director and the principal signaled to us, rather desperately I thought, to take our seats. The command was so un-usual that our carefully rehearsed and smooth-running machine was thrown off. For a full minute we fumbled for our chairs and bumped into each other awkwardly. Habits change or solidify under pressure, so in our state of nervous tension we had been ready to follow our usual assembly pattern: the American National Anthem, then the pledge of allegiance, then the song every Black person I knew called the Negro National Anthem. All done in the same key, with the same passion and most often standing on the same foot.

Finding my seat at last, I was overcome with a presentiment of worse things to come. Something unrehearsed, unplanned, was going to hap-pen, and we were going to be made to look bad. I distinctly remember be-ing explicit in the choice of pronoun. It was "we," the graduating class, the unit, that concerned me then.

30

The principal welcomed "parents and friends" and asked the Baptist minister to lead us in prayer. His invocation was brief and punchy, and for a second I thought we were getting back on the high road to right ac-tion. When the principal came back to the dais, however, his voice had changed. Sounds always affected me profoundly and the principal's voice was one of my favorites. During assembly it melted and lowed weakly into the audience. It had not been in my plan to listen to him, but my curiosity was piqued and I straightened up to give him my attention.

He was talking about Booker T. Washington, our "late great leader," who said we can be as close as the fingers on the hand, etc. . . . Then he said a few vague things about friendship and the friendship of kindly people to those less fortunate than themselves. With that his voice nearly faded, thin, away. Like a river diminishing to a stream and then to a trickle. But he cleared his throat and said, "Our speaker tonight, who is also our friend, came from Texarkana to deliver the commencement address, but due to the irregularity of the train schedule, he's going to, as they say, 'speak and run.'" He said that we understood and wanted the man to know that we were most grateful for the time he was able to give us and then something about how we were willing always to adjust to another's program, and without more ado—"I give you Mr. Edward Donleavy."

Not one but two white men came through the door offstage. The shorter one walked to the speaker's platform, and the tall one moved over to the center seat and sat down. But that was our principal's seat, and already occupied. The dislodged gentleman bounced around for a long breath or two before the Baptist minister gave him his chair, then with more dignity than the situation deserved, the minister walked off the stage.

Donleavy looked at the audience once (on reflection, I'm sure that he wanted only to reassure himself that we were really there), adjusted his glasses and began to read from a sheaf of papers.

He was glad "to be here and to see the work going on just as it was in the other schools."

At the first "Amen" from the audience I willed the offender to immediate death by choking on the word. But Amen's and Yes, sir's began to fall around the room like rain through a ragged umbrella.

He told us of the wonderful changes we children in Stamps had in store. The Central School (naturally, the white school was Central) had already been granted improvements that would be in use in the fall. A well-known artist was coming from Little Rock to teach art to them. They were going to have the newest microscopes and chemistry equipment for their laboratory. Mr. Donleavy didn't leave us long in the dark over who made these improvements available to Central High. Nor were we to be ignored in the general betterment scheme he had in mind.

He said that he had pointed out to people at a very high level that one of the first-line football tacklers at Arkansas Agricultural and Mechanical College had graduated from good old Lafayette County Training School. Here fewer Amen's were heard. Those few that did break through lay dully in the air with the heaviness of habit.

He went on to praise us. He went on to say how he had bragged that "one of the best basketball players at Fisk sank his first ball right here at Lafayette County Training School."

The white kids were going to have a chance to become Galileos and Madame Curies and Edisons and Gauguins, and our boys (the girls weren't even in on it) would try to be Jesse Owenses and Joe Louises.

Owens and the Brown Bomber were great heroes in our world, but what school official in the white-goddom of Little Rock had the right to decide that those two men must be our only heroes? Who decided that for Henry Reed to become a scientist he had to work like George Washington Carver, as a bootblack, to buy a lousy microscope? Bailey was obviously always going to be too small to be an athlete, so which concrete angel glued to what county seat had decided that if my brother wanted to become a lawyer he had to first pay penance for his skin by picking cotton and hoeing corn and studying correspondence books at night for twenty years?

The man's dead words fell like bricks around the auditorium and too many settled in my belly. Constrained by hard-learned manners I couldn't look behind me, but to my left and right the proud graduating class of 1940 had dropped their heads. Every girl in my row had found something new to do with her handkerchief. Some folded the tiny squares into love knots, some into triangles, but most were wadding them, then pressing them flat on their yellow laps.

On the dais, the ancient tragedy was being replayed. Professor Parsons sat, a sculptor's reject, rigid. His large, heavy body seemed devoid of will or willingness, and his eyes said he was no longer with us. The other teachers examined the flag (which was draped stage right) or their notes, or the windows which opened on our now-famous playing diamond.

Graduation, the hush-hush magic time of frills and gifts and congratulations and diplomas, was finished for me before my name was called. The accomplishment was nothing. The meticulous maps, drawn in three colors of ink, learning and spelling decasyllabic words, memorizing the whole of *The Rape of Lucrece*—it was nothing. Donleavy had exposed us.

We were maids and farmers, handymen and washerwomen, and anything higher that we aspired to was farcical and presumptuous. Then I wished that Gabriel Prosser and Nat Turner had killed all white-folks in their beds and that Abraham Lincoln had been assassinated before the signing of the Emancipation Proclamation, and that Harriet Tubman had been killed by that blow on her head and Christopher Columbus had drowned in the *Santa Maria*.   45

It was awful to be Negro and have no control over my life. It was brutal to be young and already trained to sit quietly and listen to charges brought against my color and no chance of defense. We should all be dead. I thought I should like to see us all dead, one on top of the other. A pyramid of flesh with the whitefolks on the bottom, as the broad base, then the Indians with their silly tomahawks and teepees and wigwams and treaties, the Negroes with their mops and recipes and cotton sacks and spirituals sticking out of their mouths. The Dutch children should all stumble in their wooden shoes and break their necks. The French should choke to death on the Louisiana Purchase (1803) while silkworms ate all the Chinese with their stupid pigtails. As a species, we were an abomination. All of us.

Donleavy was running for election, and assured our parents that if he won we could count on having the only colored paved playing field in that part of Arkansas. Also—he never looked up to acknowledge the grunts of acceptance—also, we were bound to get some new equipment for the home economics building and the workshop.

He finished, and since there was no need to give any more than the most perfunctory thank-you's, he nodded to the men on the stage, and the tall white man who was never introduced joined him at the door. They left with the attitude that now they were off to something really important. (The graduation ceremonies at Lafayette County Training School had been a mere preliminary.)

The ugliness they left was palpable. An uninvited guest who wouldn't leave. The choir was summoned and sang a modern arrangement of "Onward, Christian Soldiers," with new words pertaining to graduates seeking their place in the world. But it didn't work. Elouise, the daughter of the Baptist minister, recited "Invictus," and I could have cried at the impertinence of "I am the master of my fate, I am the captain of my soul."

My name had lost its ring of familiarity and I had to be nudged to go and receive my diploma. All my preparations had fled. I neither marched up to the stage like a conquering Amazon, nor did I look in the audience for Bailey's nod of approval. Marguerite Johnson, I heard the name again, my honors were read, there were noises in the audience of appreciation, and I took my place on the stage as rehearsed.

I thought about colors I hated: ecru, puce, lavender, beige and black.

There was shuffling and rustling around me, then Henry Reed was giving his valedictory address, "To Be or Not to Be." Hadn't he heard the whitefolks? We couldn't *be*, so the question was a waste of time. Henry's voice came out clear and strong. I feared to look at him. Hadn't he got the message? There was no "nobler in the mind" for Negroes because the world didn't think we had minds, and they let us know it. "Outrageous fortune"? Now, that was a joke. When the ceremony was over I had to tell Henry Reed some things. That is, if I still cared. Not "rub," Henry, "erase." "Ah, there's the erase." Us.

Henry had been a good student in elocution. His voice rose on tides of promise and fell on waves of warnings. The English teacher had helped him to create a sermon winging through Hamlet's soliloquy. To be a man, a doer, a builder, a leader, or to be a tool, an unfunny joke, a crusher of funky toadstools. I marveled that Henry could go through with the speech as if we had a choice.

I had been listening and silently rebutting each sentence with my eyes closed; then there was a hush, which in an audience warns that something unplanned is happening. I looked up and saw Henry Reed, the conservative, the proper, the A student, turn his back to the audience and turn to us (the proud graduating class of 1940) and sing, nearly speaking,

> *Lift ev'ry voice and sing*
> *Till earth and heaven ring*
> *Ring with the harmonies of Liberty . . .*

It was the poem written by James Weldon Johnson. It was the music   55
composed by J. Rosamond Johnson. It was the Negro National Anthem.
Out of habit we were singing it.

Our mothers and fathers stood in the dark hall and joined the hymn
of encouragement. A kindergarten teacher led the small children onto the
stage and the buttercups and daisies and bunny rabbits marked time and
tried to follow:

> *Stony the road we trod*
> *Bitter the chastening rod*
> *Felt in the days when hope, unborn, had died.*
> *Yet with a steady beat*
> *Have not our weary feet*
> *Come to the place for which our fathers sighed?*

Every child I knew had learned that song with his ABC's and along
with "Jesus Loves Me This I Know." But I personally had never heard it
before. Never heard the words, despite the thousands of times I had sung
them. Never thought they had anything to do with me.

On the other hand, the words of Patrick Henry had made such an impression on me that I had been able to stretch myself tall and trembling
and say, "I know not what course others may take, but as for me, give me
liberty or give me death."

And now I heard, really for the first time:

> *We have come over a way that with tears has been watered,*
> *We have come, treading our path through the blood of the slaughtered.*

While echoes of the song shivered in the air, Henry Reed bowed his   60
head, said "Thank you," and returned to his place in the line. The tears
that slipped down many faces were not wiped away in shame.

We were on top again. As always, again. We survived. The depths
had been icy and dark, but now a bright sun spoke to our souls. I was no
longer simply a member of the proud graduating class of 1940; I was a
proud member of the wonderful, beautiful Negro race.

Oh, Black known and unknown poets, how often have your auc-
tioned pains sustained us? Who will compute the lonely nights made
less lonely by your songs, or the empty pots made less tragic by your
tales?

If we were a people much given to revealing secrets, we might raise
monuments and sacrifice to the memories of our poets, but slavery cured
us of that weakness. It may be enough, however, to have it said that we
survive in exact relationship to the dedication of our poets (include
preachers, musicians and blues singers).

Joining the Conversation: Critical Thinking and Writing

1. In paragraph 1, notice such overstatements as "glorious release," "the grad-
    uating classes themselves were the nobility," and "exotic destinations." Find
    further examples in subsequent paragraphs. What do you think is the func-
    tion of this diction?

2. Characterize the writer as you perceive her through paragraph 28. Support
    your characterization with references to specific passages. Next, characterize
    her in paragraph 46, which begins "It was awful to be Negro." Next, charac-
    terize her on the basis of the entire essay. Finally, in a sentence, try to de-
    scribe the change, telling the main attitudes or moods that she goes through.

3. How would you define *poets* as Angelou uses the word in the last sentence?

Walter Kirn

---

*Walter Kirn, born in 1961, is a graduate of Princeton University. Although Kirn is perhaps best
known as an essayist—we reprint an essay that he wrote for* The New York Times Magazine—
he is also the author of several highly praised novels, including Up in the Air, *later made into a
highly successful movie.*

Class Dismissed

According to the unwritten constitution that governs ordinary
American life and makes possible a shared pop culture that even new immigrants can jump right into after a few movies and a trip to the mall, the senior year of public high school is less a climatic academic experience than an
occasion for oafish goofing off, chronic truancy, random bullying, sloppy
dancing in rented formalwear and interludes of moody, wan philosophizing
(often at sunrise while still half-drunk and staring off at a misty river or the
high-school parking lot) about the looming bummer of adulthood. In films
like "Ferris Bueller's Day Off," "Dazed and Confused" and "High School
Musical 3," senior year is a do-little sabbatical from what is presented as the
long dull labor of acquiring knowledge, honing skills and internalizing social norms. It's a spree, senior year, that discharges built-up tensions. It's an
adolescent Mardi Gras. And it's not an indulgence but an entitlement.
Remember that line in your yearbook? Seniors rule! And they rule not because they've accomplished much, necessarily (aside from surviving to age
18 or so and not dropping out or running away from home), but because it's
tradition, and seniors crave tradition. They crave it because they know, deep
down, they're lost, and tradition helps them hide this fear. From juniors.

This year of licensed irresponsibility, this two-semester recurring national holiday, was threatened recently in Utah by a Republican legislator's proposal to do away with 12th grade entirely. The idea was advanced as a budget-cutting measure—a way to shave millions from the cash-strapped state's expense sheet—and it called forth the sort of instant, intense hostility that often signals that an inspired notion, truly innovative, truly new, has, by some miracle, entered politics. The proposal drew scorn form teachers and students alike (another tribute to its possible genius) and swiftly spread across the new wires, eliciting such hostility and controversy that its sponsor flinched. Aware, perhaps, that his offbeat plan was drawing unwelcome attention to a state that has spent the modern era in a permanent defensive crouch thanks to a Mormon religious culture that many view as joyless and eccentric, the lawmaker suggested that 12th grade—that ritual time out from the march of time itself—be made optional rather than nonexistent.

But did he compromise too readily? For many American high-school seniors, especially the soberest and most studious, senior year is a holding pattern, a redundancy, a way of running out the clock on a game that has already been won. When winter vacation rolls around, many of them, thanks to college early-admissions programs, know all they need to about their futures and have no more reason to hang around the schoolhouse than prehistoric fish had need for water once they grew limbs and could crawl out of the oceans. As for students who aren't headed to four-year colleges but two-year community colleges or vocational schools, why not just get started early and read "Moby Dick" for pleasure, if they wish, rather than to earn a grade that they don't need? Kids who plan to move right into the labor force are in the same position. They may as well spend the whole year in detention—which some of them, bored and restless, end up doing. Twelfth grade, for the sorts of students I've just described, amounts to a fidgety waiting period that practically begs for descents into debauchery and concludes in a big dumb party under a mirror ball that spins in place like the minds of those beneath it.

It's not just one Utah lawmaker who has noticed this. The Bill and Melinda Gates Foundation has, too, it seems. In the interest of speeding students on their way to productive, satisfying careers, the foundation intends to give a $1.5 million grant to a project organized by the nonprofit National Center on Education and the Economy. The goal is to help certain students leapfrog the keg party and go directly from 10th grade to community colleges after passing a battery of tests. The goal is not to save money but precious time, and the program is modeled on systems now in place in Denmark, Finland, France and Singapore—countries whose young folk, in many cases, speak English more grammatically than a lot of American high-school seniors do. One of the fledgling program's backers, Terry Holliday, Kentucky's commissioner of education, calls the program's approach "move on when ready." Compared with the prevailing current system, which might be termed "move on when all your friends do" or "move on when stir-crazy" or just "move on," it seems both more pragmatic and humane, not to mention more likely to raise the G.D.P.

If senior year were to vanish from our high schools, either completely or in part, would its infamous excesses, feats of sloth, dances and stretches of absenteeism shift to junior year? To some degree. But what also might happen is that the education process, if it was shortened and compressed some, might help kids think more clearly about their paths in life and set out on them on the right foot instead of waiting to shape up later on. And what would they miss, really, under such a system? As someone who left high school a year early thanks to an offer from a progressive college that I didn't seek but hungrily accepted (anything to escape those hours of "study hall" that we passed by folding sheets of paper until they couldn't be folded any tighter, at which point we flicked them at one another's heads), I guess I wouldn't know. But I did learn from my visits home that my former classmates' senior years did them few favors maturationwise, other than to make one an unwed mother and a couple of them into victims of major car collisions. That's why, to my mind, Utah should feel to ax senior year, bank the savings and see what happens. My hunch is that nothing will happen. Nothing much. Just the loss of a year when nothing much happens anyhow.

Joining the Conversation: Critical Thinking and Writing

1. In a sentence or two, summarize Kirn's argument in his first paragraph. As you reread it and summarize its content, consider how readers might be affected by Kirn's style. Drawing on a few examples, characterize Kirn's style and evaluate it: In what ways does it contribute to or diminish his argument?

2. Kirn cites proposals from two other sources to abolish senior year. Who proposed them, and what reasons did each offer? How do these examples enhance Kirn's argument?

3. If senior year were abolished, how, according to Kirn, might that affect students in their junior year? Do you agree?

4. In his last paragraph, Kirn reveals that he was able to skip senior year to attend a progressive college and explains what he learned from visits home. Both the first paragraph of an essay and the last have a bit more emphasis than other paragraphs from their positions. If you were Kirn, would you have put this autobiographical information in the first paragraph? Or do you think it was clever of him to delay it until his conclusion?

5. How did you spend your senior year in high school? Or were you able to skip it? In a brief essay (500–750 words), evaluate Kirn's argument in light of your own experience.

Fan Shen

Fan Shen came to the United States from the People's Republic of China. A translator and writer, he also teaches at Rochester Community and Technical College, in Rochester, Minnesota.

The Classroom and the Wider Culture

Identity as a Key to Learning English Composition

One day in June 1975, when I walked into the aircraft factory where I was working as an electrician, I saw many large-letter posters on the walls and many people parading around the workshops shouting slogans like "Down with the word 'I'!" and "Trust in masses and the Party!" I then remembered that a new political campaign called "Against Individualism" was scheduled to begin that day. Ten years later, I got back my first English composition paper at the University of Nebraska–Lincoln. The professor's first comments were: "Why did you always use 'we' instead of 'I'?" and "Your paper would be stronger if you eliminated some sentences in the passive voice." The clashes between my Chinese background and the requirements of English composition had begun. At the center of this mental struggle, which has lasted several years and is still not completely over, is the prolonged, uphill battle to recapture "myself."

In this paper I will try to describe and explore this experience of reconciling my Chinese identity with an English identity dictated by the rules of English composition. I want to show how my cultural background shaped—and shapes—my approaches to my writing in English and how writing in English redefined—and redefines—my *ideological* and *logical* identities. By "ideological identity" I mean the system of values that I acquired (consciously and unconsciously) from my social and cultural background. And by "logical identity" I mean the natural (or Oriental) way I organize and express my thoughts in writing. Both had to be modified or redefined in learning English composition. Becoming aware of the process of redefinition of these different identities is a mode of learning that has helped me in my efforts to write in English, and, I hope, will be of help to teachers of English composition in this country. In presenting my case for this view, I will use examples from both my composition courses and literature courses, for I believe that writing papers for both kinds of courses contributed to the development of my "English identity." Although what I will describe is based on personal experience, many Chinese students whom I talked to said that they had had the same or similar experiences in their initial stages of learning to write in English.

Identity of the Self: Ideological and Cultural

Starting with the first English paper I wrote, I found that learning to compose in English is not an isolated classroom activity, but a social and cultural experience. The rules of English composition encapsulate values that are absent in, or sometimes contradictory to, the values of other societies (in my case, China). Therefore, learning the rules of English composition is, to a certain extent, learning the values of Anglo-American society. In writing classes in the United States I found that I had to reprogram my mind, to redefine some of the basic concepts and values that I had about myself, about society, and about the universe, values that had been imprinted and reinforced in my mind by my cultural background, and that had been part of me all my life.

Rule number one in English composition is: Be yourself. (More than one composition instructor has told me, "Just write what *you* think.") The values behind this rule, it seems to me, are based on the principle of protecting and promoting individuality (and private property) in this country. The instruction was probably crystal clear to students raised on these values, but, as a guideline of composition, it was not very clear or useful to me when I first heard it. First of all, the image or meaning that I attached to the word "I" or "myself" was, as I found out, different from that of my English teacher. In China, "I" is always subordinated to "We"—be it the working class, the Party, the country, or some other collective body. Both political pressure and literary tradition require that "I" be somewhat hidden or buried in writings and speeches; presenting the "self" too obviously would give people the impression of being disrespectful of the Communist Party in political writings and boastful in scholarly writings. The word "I" has often been identified with another "bad" word, "individualism," which has become a synonym for selfishness in China. For a long time the words "self" and "individualism" have had negative connotations in my mind, and the negative force of the words naturally extended to the field of literary studies. As a result, even if I had brilliant ideas, the "I" in my papers always had to show some modesty by not competing with or trying to stand above the names of ancient and modern authoritative figures. Appealing to Mao or other Marxist authorities became the required way (as well as the most "forceful" or "persuasive" way) to prove one's point in written discourse. I remember that in China I had even committed what I can call "reversed plagiarism"—here, I suppose it would be called "forgery"—when I was in middle school: willfully attributing some of my thoughts to "experts" when I needed some arguments but could not find a suitable quotation from a literary or political "giant."

Now, in America, I had to learn to accept the words "I" and "self" as something glorious (as Whitman did), or at least something not to be ashamed of or embarrassed about. It was the first and probably biggest step I took into English composition and critical writing. Acting upon my professor's suggestion, I intentionally tried to show my "individuality" and to "glorify" "I" in my papers by using as many "I's" as possible— "I think," "I believe," "I see"—and deliberately cut out quotations from authorities. It was rather painful to hand in such "pompous" (I mean immodest) papers to my instructors. But to an extent it worked. After a while I became more comfortable with only "the shadow of myself." I felt more at ease to put down *my* thoughts without looking over my shoulder to worry about the attitudes of my teachers or the reactions of the Party secretaries, and to speak out as "bluntly" and "immodestly" as my American instructors demanded.

But writing many "I's" was only the beginning of the process of redefining myself. Speaking of redefining myself is, in an important sense, speaking of redefining the word "I." By such a redefinition I mean not only the change in how I envisioned myself, but also the change in how *I* perceived the world. The old "I" used to embody only one set of values, but now it had to embody multiple sets of values. To be truly "myself," which I knew was a key to my success in learning English composition, meant *not to be my Chinese self* at all. That is to say, when I write in English I have to wrestle with and abandon (at least temporarily) the whole system of ideology which previously defined me in myself. I had to forget Marxist doctrines (even though I do not see myself as a Marxist by choice) and the Party lines imprinted in my mind and familiarize myself with a system of capitalist/bourgeois values. I had to put aside an ideology of collectivism and adopt the values of individualism. In composition as well as in literature classes, I had to make a fundamental adjustment: If I used to examine society and literary materials through the microscopes of Marxist dialectical materialism and historical materialism, I now had to learn to look through the microscopes the other way around, i.e., to learn to look at and understand the world from the point of view of "idealism." (I must add here that there are American professors who use a Marxist approach in their teaching.)

The word "idealism," which affects my view of both myself and the universe, is loaded with social connotations, and can serve as a good example of how redefining a key word can be a pivotal part of redefining my ideological identity as a whole.

To me, idealism is the philosophical foundation of the dictum of English composition: "Be yourself." In order to write good English, I knew that I had to be myself, which actually meant not to be my Chinese self. It meant that I had to create an English self and be *that* self. And to be that English self, I felt, I had to understand and accept idealism the way a Westerner does. That is to say, I had to accept the way a Westerner sees himself in relation to the universe and society. On the one hand, I knew a lot about idealism. But on the other hand, I knew nothing about it. I mean I knew a lot about idealism through the propaganda and objections of its opponent, Marxism, but I knew little about it from its own point of view. When I thought of the word "materialism"—which is a major part of Marxism and in China has repeatedly been "shown" to be the absolute truth—there were always positive connotations, and words like "right," "true," etc., flashed in my mind. On the other hand, the word "idealism" always came to me with the dark connotations that surround words like "absurd," "illogical," "wrong," etc. In China "idealism" is depicted as a ferocious and ridiculous enemy of Marxist philosophy. Idealism, as the simplified definition imprinted in my mind had it, is the view that the material world does not exist; that all that exists is the mind and its ideas. It is just the opposite of Marxist dialectical materialism which sees the mind as a product of the material world. It is not too difficult to see that idealism, with its idea that mind is of primary importance, provides a philosophical foundation for the Western emphasis on the value of individual human minds, and hence individual human beings. Therefore, my final acceptance of myself as of primary importance—an importance that overshadowed that of authority figures in English composition—was, I decided, dependent on an acceptance of idealism.

My struggle with idealism came mainly from my efforts to understand and to write about works such as Coleridge's *Biographia Literaria* and Emerson's "Over-Soul." For a long time I was frustrated and puzzled by the idealism expressed by Coleridge and Emerson—given their ideas, such as "I think, therefore I am" (Coleridge obviously borrowed from Descartes) and "the transparent eyeball" (Emerson's view of himself)—because in my mind, drenched as it was in dialectical materialism, there was always a little voice whispering in my ear "You are, therefore you think." I could not see how human consciousness, which is not material, could create apples and trees. My intellectual conscience refused to let me believe that the human mind is the primary world and the material world secondary. Finally, I had to imagine that I was looking at a world with my head upside down. When I imagined that I was in a new body (born with the head upside down) it was easier to forget biases imprinted in my subconsciousness about idealism, the mind, and my former self. Starting from scratch, the new inverted self—which I called my "English Self" and into which I have transformed myself—could understand and *accept*, with ease, idealism as "the truth" and "himself" (i.e., my English Self) as the "creator" of the world.

Here is how I created my new "English Self." I played a "game" similar to ones played by mental therapists. First I made a list of (simplified) features about writing associated with my old identity (the Chinese Self), both ideological and logical, and then beside the first list I added a column of features about writing associated with my new identity (the English Self). After that I pictured myself getting out of my old identity, the timid, humble, modest Chinese "I," and creeping into my new identity (often in the form of a new skin or a mask), the confident, assertive, and aggressive English "I." The new "Self" helped me to remember and accept the different rules of Chinese and English composition and the values that underpin these rules. In a sense, creating an English Self is a way of reconciling my old cultural values with the new values required by English writing, without losing the former.

An interesting structural but not material parallel to my experiences in this regard has been well described by Min-zhan Lu in her important article, "From Silence to Words: Writing as Struggle" (*College English* 49 [April 1987]: 437–48). Min-zhan Lu talks about struggles between two selves, an open self and a secret self, and between two discourses, a mainstream Marxist discourse and a bourgeois discourse her parents wanted her to learn. But her struggle was different from mine. Her Chinese self was severely constrained and suppressed by mainstream cultural discourse, but never interfused with it. Her experiences, then, were not representative of those of the majority of the younger generation who, like me, were brought up on only one discourse. I came to English composition as a Chinese person, in the fullest sense of the term, with a Chinese identity already fully formed.

Identity of the Mind: Illogical and Alogical

In learning to write in English, besides wrestling with a different ideological system, I found that I had to wrestle with a logical system very different from the blueprint of logic at the back of my mind. By "logical system" I mean two things: the Chinese way of thinking I used to approach my theme or topic in written discourse, and the Chinese critical/logical way to develop a theme or topic. By English rules, the first is illogical, for it is the opposite of the English way of approaching a topic; the second is alogical (nonlogical), for it mainly uses mental pictures instead of words as a critical vehicle.

The Illogical Pattern. In English composition, an essential rule for the logical organization of a piece of writing is the use of a "topic sentence." In Chinese composition, "from surface to core" is an essential rule, a rule which means that one ought to reach a topic gradually and "systematically" instead of "abruptly."

The concept of a topic sentence, it seems to me, is symbolic of the values of a busy people in an industrialized society, rushing to get things done, hoping to attract and satisfy the busy reader very quickly. Thinking back, I realized that I did not fully understand the virtue of the concept until my life began to rush at the speed of everyone else's in this country. Chinese composition, on the other hand, seems to embody the values of a leisurely paced rural society whose inhabitants have the time to chew and taste a topic slowly. In Chinese composition, an introduction explaining how and why one chooses this topic is not only acceptable, but often regarded as necessary. It arouses the reader's interest in the topic little by little (and this is seen as a virtue of composition) and gives him/her a sense of refinement. The famous Robert B. Kaplan "noodles" contrasting a spiral Oriental thought process with a straight-line Western approach ("Cultural Thought Patterns in Inter-Cultural Education," *Readings on English as a Second Language,* ed. Kenneth Croft, 2nd ed., Winthrop, 1980, 403–10) may be too simplistic to capture the preferred pattern of writing in English, but I think they still express some truth about Oriental writing. A Chinese writer often clears the surrounding bushes before attacking the real target. This bush-clearing pattern in Chinese writing goes back two thousand years to Kong Fuzi (Confucius). Before doing anything, Kong says in his *Luen Yu (Analects),* one first needs to call things by their proper names (expressed by his phrase "Zheng Ming"). In other words, before touching one's main thesis, one should first state the "conditions" of composition: how, why, and when the piece is being composed. All of this will serve as a proper foundation on which to build the "house" of the piece. In the two thousand years after Kong, this principle of composition was gradually formalized (especially through the formal essays required by imperial examinations) and became known as "Ba Gu," or the eightlegged essay. The logic of Chinese composition, exemplified by the eightlegged essay, is like the peeling of an onion: Layer after layer is removed until the reader finally arrives at the central point, the core.

Ba Gu still influences modern Chinese writing. Carolyn Matalene has an excellent discussion of this logical (or illogical) structure and its influence on her Chinese students' efforts to write in English ("Contrastive Rhetoric: An American Writing Teacher in China," *College English* 47 [November 1985]: 789–808). A recent Chinese textbook for composition lists six essential steps (factors) for writing a narrative essay, steps to be taken in this order: time, place, character, event, cause, and consequence (*Yuwen Jichu Zhishi Liushi Jiang [Sixty Lessons on the Basics of the Chinese Language],* ed. Beijing Research Institute of Education, Beijing Publishing House, 1981, 525–609). Most Chinese students (including me) are taught to follow this sequence in composition.

The straightforward approach to composition in English seemed to me, at first, illogical. One could not jump to the topic. One had to walk step by step to reach the topic. In several of my early papers I found that the Chinese approach—the bush-clearing approach—persisted, and I had considerable difficulty writing (and in fact understanding) topic sentences. In what I deemed to be topic sentences, I grudgingly gave out themes. Today, those papers look to me like Chinese papers with forced or false English openings. For example, in a narrative paper on a trip to New York, I wrote the forced/false topic sentence, "A trip to New York in winter is boring." In the next few paragraphs, I talked about the weather, the people who went with me, and so on, before I talked about what I learned from the trip. My real thesis was that one could always learn something even on a boring trip.

The Alogical Pattern. In learning English composition, I found that there was yet another cultural blueprint affecting my logical thinking.

I found from my early papers that very often I was unconsciously under the influence of a Chinese critical approach called the creation of "yijing," which is totally non-Western. The direct translation of the word "yijing" is: yi, "mind or consciousness," and jing, "environment." An ancient approach which has existed in China for many centuries and is still the subject of much discussion, yijing is a complicated concept that defies a universal definition. But most critics in China nowadays seem to agree on one point, that yijing is the critical approach that separates Chinese litera- ture and criticism from Western literature and criticism. Roughly speak- ing, yijing is the process of creating a pictorial environment while reading a piece of literature. Many critics in China believe that yijing is a creative process of inducing oneself, while reading a piece of literature or looking at a piece of art, to create mental pictures, in order to reach a unity of na- ture, the author, and the reader. Therefore, it is by its very nature both creative and critical. According to the theory, this nonverbal, pictorial process leads directly to a higher ground of beauty and morality. Almost all critics in China agree that yijing is not a process of logical thinking—it is not a process of moving from the premises of an argument to its conclu- sion, which is the foundation of Western criticism. According to yijing, the process of criticizing a piece of art or literary work has to involve the process of creation on the reader's part. In yijing, verbal thoughts and pic- torial thoughts are one. Thinking is conducted largely in pictures and then "transcribed" into words. (Ezra Pound once tried to capture the cre- ative aspect of yijing in poems such as "In a Station of the Metro." He also tried to capture the critical aspect of it in his theory of imagism and vorti- cism, even though he did not know the term "yijing.") One characteristic of the yijing approach to criticism, therefore, is that it often includes a de- scription of the created mental pictures on the part of the reader/critic and his/her mental attempt to bridge (unite) the literary work, the pic- tures, with ultimate beauty and peace.

In looking back at my critical papers for various classes, I discovered that I unconsciously used the approach of yijing, especially in some of my earlier papers when I seemed not yet to have been in the grip of Western logical critical approaches. I wrote, for instance, an essay entitled "Wordsworth's Sound and Imagination: The Snowdon Episode." In the major part of the essay I described the pictures that flashed in my mind while I was reading passages in Wordsworth's long poem, *The Prelude.*

> I saw three climbers (myself among them) winding up the mountain in si- lence "at the dead of night," absorbed in their "private thoughts." The sky was full of blocks of clouds of different colors, freely changing their shapes, like oily pigments disturbed in a bucket of water. All of a sudden, the moon- light broke the darkness "like a flash," lighting up the mountain tops. Under the "naked moon," the band saw a vast sea of mist and vapor, a silent ocean. Then the silence was abruptly broken, and we heard the "roaring of waters, torrents, streams/Innumerable, roaring with one voice" from a "blue chasm," a fracture in the vapor of the sea. It was a joyful revelation of divine

truth to the human mind: the bright, "naked" moon sheds the light of "higher reasons" and "spiritual love" upon us; the vast ocean of mist looked like a thin curtain through which we vaguely saw the infinity of nature beyond; and the sounds of roaring waters coming out of the chasm of vapor cast us into the boundless spring of imagination from the depth of the human heart. Evoked by the divine light from above, the human spring of imagination is joined by the natural spring and becomes a sustaining source of energy, feeding "upon infinity" while transcending infinity at the same time.

Here I was describing my own experience more than Wordsworth's. The picture described by the poet is taken over and developed by the reader. The imagination of the author and the imagination of the reader are thus joined together. There was no "because" or "therefore" in the paper. There was little *logic*. And I thought it was (and it is) criticism. This seems to me a typical (but simplified) example of the yijing approach. (Incidentally, the instructor, a kind professor, found the paper interesting, though a bit "strange.")

In another paper of mine, "The Note of Life: Williams's 'The Orchestra'," I found myself describing my experiences of pictures of nature while reading William Carlos Williams's poem. "The Orchestra." I "painted" these fleeting pictures and described the feelings that seemed to lead me to an understanding of a harmony, a "common tone," between man and nature. A paragraph from that paper reads:

> The poem first struck me as a musical fairy tale. With rich musical sounds in my ear, I seemed to be walking in a solitary, dense forest on a spring morning. No sound from human society could be heard. I was now sitting under a giant pine tree, ready to hear the grand concert of Nature. With the sun slowly rising from the east, the cello (the creeping creek) and the clarinet (the rustling pine trees) started with a slow overture. Enthusiastically the violinists (the twittering birds) and the French horn (the mumbling cow) "interpose[d] their voices," and the bass (bears) got in at the wrong time. The orchestra did not stop, they continued to play. The musicians of Nature do not always play in harmony. "Together, unattuned," they have to seek "a common tone" as they play along. The symphony of Nature is like the symphony of human life: both consist of random notes seeking a "common tone." For the symphony of life
>
> > Love is that common tone
> > shall raise his fiery head
> > and sound his note.

Again, the logical pattern of this paper, the "pictorial criticism," is illogical to Western minds but "logical" to those acquainted with yijing. (Perhaps I should not even use the words "logical" and "think" because they are so conceptually tied up with "words" and with culturally-based conceptions, and therefore very misleading if not useless in a discussion of yijing. Maybe I should simply say that yijing is neither illogical nor logical, but alogical.)

I am not saying that such a pattern of "alogical" thinking is wrong—in fact some English instructors find it interesting and acceptable—but it is very non-Western. Since I was in this country to learn the English language and English literature, I had to abandon Chinese "pictorial logic," and to learn Western "verbal logic."

If I Had to Start Again

The change is profound: Through my understanding of new meanings of words like "individualism," "idealism," and "I," I began to accept the underlying concepts and values of American writing, and by learning to use "topic sentences" I began to accept a new logic. Thus, when I write papers in English, I am able to obey all the general rules of English composition. In doing this I feel that I am writing through, with, and because of a new identity. I welcome the change, for it has added a new dimension to me and to my view of the world. I am not saying that I have entirely lost my Chinese identity. In fact I feel that I will never lose it. Any time I write in Chinese, I resume my old identity, and obey the rules of Chinese composition such as "Make the 'I' modest," and "Beat around the bush before attacking the central topic." It is necessary for me to have such a Chinese identity in order to write authentic Chinese. (I have seen people who, after learning to write in English, use English logic and sentence patterning to write Chinese. They produce very awkward Chinese texts.) But when I write in English, I imagine myself slipping into a new "skin," and I let the "I" behave much more aggressively and knock the topic right on the head. Being conscious of these different identities has helped me to reconcile different systems of values and logic, and has played a pivotal role in my learning to compose in English.

Looking back, I realize that the process of learning to write in English is in fact a process of creating and defining a new identity and balancing it with the old identity. The process of learning English composition would have been easier if I had realized this earlier and consciously sought to compare the two different identities required by the two writing systems from two different cultures. It is fine and perhaps even necessary for American composition teachers to teach about topic sentences, paragraphs, the use of punctuation, documentation, and so on, but can anyone design exercises sensitive to the ideological and logical differences that students like me experience—and design them so they can be introduced at an early stage of an English composition class? As I pointed out earlier, the traditional advice "Just be yourself" is not clear and helpful to students from Korea, China, Vietnam, or India. From "Be yourself" we are likely to hear either "Forget your cultural habit of writing" or "Write as you would write in your own language." But neither of the two is what the instructor meant or what we want to do. It would be helpful if he or she pointed out the different cultural/ideological connotations of the word "I," the connotations that exist in a group-centered culture and an individual-centered culture. To sharpen the contrast, it might be useful to design papers on topics like "The Individual vs. The Group: China vs. America" or "Different 'I's' in Different Cultures."

Carolyn Matalene mentioned in her article (789) an incident concerning American businessmen who presented their Chinese hosts with gifts of cheddar cheese, not knowing that the Chinese generally do not like cheese. Liking cheddar cheese may not be essential to writing English prose, but being truly accustomed to the social norms that stand behind ideas such as the English "I" and the logical pattern of English composition—call it "compositional cheddar cheese"—is essential to writing in English. Matalene does not provide an "elixir" to help her Chinese students like English "compositional cheese," but rather recommends, as do I, that composition teachers not be afraid to give foreign students English "cheese," but to make sure to hand it out slowly, sympathetically, and fully realizing that it tastes very peculiar in the mouths of those used to a very different cuisine.

Joining the Conversation: Critical Thinking and Writing

1. In his second paragraph, Fan Shen says, "I will try to describe and explore this experience of reconciling my Chinese identity with an English identity." What does the article tell us is part of a "Chinese identity," and what is part of an "English identity"? How does your experience in answering this question account for the value of beginning his article with two narratives?

2. His article is primarily based on "personal experience." Is this part of his "English identity" or "Chinese identity"? Explain.

3. In paragraph 4, Fan Shen says, "Rule number one in English composition is: Be yourself." Whether you are from the United States or from another country, try to explain why "being yourself" is (or is not) difficult when you enter college writing. Why did Fan Shen find it difficult?

4. Does Fan Shen's explanation (paragraphs 13–15) of the value of the topic sentence in English help to explain it to you or do you have some other account of it? Explain.

5. In his next-to-last paragraph, Fan Shen suggests topics for instructors to assign to international students. One of the two—"Different 'I's'" in Different Cultures—strikes us as a good project to assign to native students as well as those from other cultures. We suggest here that you write a journal entry taking notes on the "different 'I's'" you have experienced before attending college and now. If it suits you to do this, divide your journal entry in two down the middle, taking notes on the "I" before and the "I" after.

David Brooks

David Brooks, senior editor at the Weekly Standard *(a conservative journal), publishes frequently in* Atlantic Monthly, Newsweek, *and* The New York Times, *where he writes an op-ed column. He is the author of* Bobos in Paradise: The New Upper Class and How They Got There *(2000)—a "bobo" is a bourgeois bohemian—and* On Paradise Drive: How We Live Now (and Always Have) in the Future Tense *(2004). Brooks appears regularly on* PBS NewsHour with Jim Lehrer.

The Other Education

Like Many of you, I went to elementary school, high school and college. I took such and such classes, earned such and such grades, and amassed such and such degrees.

But on the night of Feb. 2, 1975, I turned on WMMR in Philadelphia and became mesmerized by a concert the radio station was broadcasting. The concert was by a group I'd never heard of—Bruce Springsteen and the E Street Band. Thus began a part of my second education.

We don't usually think of this second education. For reasons having to do with the peculiarities of our civilization, we pay a great deal of attention to our scholastic educations, which are formal and supervised, and we devote much less public thought to our emotional educations, which are unsupervised and haphazard. This is odd, since our emotional educations are much more important to our long-term happiness and the quality of our lives.

In any case, over the next few decades Springsteen would become one of the professors in my second education. In album after album he assigned a new course in my emotional curriculum.

This second education doesn't work the way the scholastic education works. In a normal schoolroom, information walks through the front door and announces itself by light of day. It's direct. The teacher describes the material to be covered, and then everybody works through it.

The knowledge transmitted in an emotional education, on the other hand, comes indirectly, seeping through the cracks of the windowpanes, from under the floorboards and through the vents. It's generally a byproduct of the search for pleasure, and the learning is indirect and unconscious.

From that first night in the winter of 1975, I wanted the thrill that Springsteen was offering. His manager, Jon Landau, says that each style of music elicits its own set of responses. Rock, when done right, is jolting and exhilarating.

Once I got a taste of that emotional uplift, I was hooked. The uplifting experiences alone were bound to open the mind for learning.

I followed Springsteen into his world. Once again, it wasn't the explicit characters that mattered most. Springsteen sings about teenage couples out on a desperate lark, workers struggling as the mills close down, and drifters on the wrong side of the law. These stories don't directly touch my life, and as far as I know he's never written a song about a middle-aged pundit who interviews politicians by day and makes mind-numbingly repetitive school lunches at night.

What mattered most, as with any artist, were the assumptions behind the stories. His tales take place in a distinct universe, a distinct map of reality. In Springsteen's universe, life's "losers" always retain their dignity. Their choices have immense moral consequences, and are seen on an epic and anthemic scale.

There are certain prominent neighborhoods on his map—one called defeat, another called exaltation, another called nostalgia. Certain emotional chords—stoicism, for one—are common, while others are absent. "There is no sarcasm in his writing," Landau says, "and not a lot of irony."

I find I can't really describe what this landscape feels like, especially in newspaper prose. But I do believe his narrative tone, the mental map, has worked its way into my head, influencing the way I organize the buzzing confusion of reality, shaping the unconscious categories through which I perceive events. Just as being from New York or rural Georgia gives you a perspective from which to see the world, so spending time in Springsteen's universe inculcates its own preconscious viewpoint.

Then there is the man himself. Like other parts of the emotional education, it is hard to bring the knowledge to consciousness, but I do think important lessons are communicated by that embarrassed half-giggle he falls into when talking about himself. I do think a message is conveyed in the way he continually situates himself within a tradition—deemphasizing his own individual contributions, stressing instead the R&B groups, the gospel and folk singers whose work comes out through him.

I'm not claiming my second education has been exemplary or advanced. I'm describing it because I have only become aware of it retrospectively, and society pays too much attention to the first education and not enough to the second.

In fact, we all gather our own emotional faculty—artists, friends, family and teams. Each refines and develops the inner instrument with a million strings.

Last week, my kids attended their first Springsteen concert in Baltimore. At one point, I looked over at my 15-year-old daughter. She had her hands clapped to her cheeks and a look of slack-jawed, joyous astonishment on her face. She couldn't believe what she was seeing—10,000 people in a state of utter abandon, with Springsteen surrendering himself to them in the center of the arena.

It begins again.

Joining the Conversation: Critical Thinking and Writing

1. Brooks introduces his experience of becoming "hooked" on Bruce Springsteen by distinguishing between "scholastic education" and "emotional education." Explain to someone who hasn't read the essay what he means.

2. In addition to music, what other sources of emotional education might there be?

3. For Brooks, what is appealing and uplifting about Springsteen's music? And about the man himself?

4. In his fifth paragraph, Brooks describes through metaphors "scholastic education" and in his sixth paragraph "emotional education." We won't urge you to splash your analytic essays with metaphors, but we do suggest that you try jotting some down if they occur to you—perhaps in a writer's journal. Experiencing Brooks's metaphors and thinking in or writing your own metaphors could be part of your own "emotional education."

David Gelernter

David Gelernter, a professor of computer science at Yale University, originally published this essay in the New Republic *in 1994.*

Unplugged

Over the last decade an estimated $2 billion has been spent on more than 2 million computers for America's classrooms. That's not surprising. We constantly hear from Washington that the schools are in trouble and that computers are a godsend. Within the education establishment, in poor as well as rich schools, the machines are awaited with nearly religious awe. An inner-city principal bragged to a teacher friend of mine recently that his school "has a computer in every classroom . . . despite being in a bad neighborhood!"

Computers should be in the schools. They have the potential to accomplish great things. With the right software, they could help make science tangible or teach neglected topics like art and music. They could help students form a concrete idea of society by displaying on screen a version of the city in which they live—a picture that tracks real life moment by moment.

In practice, however, computers make our worst educational nightmares come true. While we bemoan the decline of literacy, computers discount words in favor of pictures and pictures in favor of video. While we fret about the decreasing cogency of public debate, computers dismiss linear argument and promote fast, shallow romps across the information landscape. While we worry about basic skills, we allow into the classroom software that will do a student's arithmetic or correct his spelling.

David Gelernter: "Unplugged" from *The New Republic*, September 19, 1994. Reprinted by permission.

Take multimedia. The idea of multimedia is to combine text, sound and pictures in a single package that you browse on screen. You don't just *read* Shakespeare; you watch actors performing, listen to songs, view Elizabethan buildings. What's wrong with that? By offering children candy-coated books, multimedia is guaranteed to sour them on unsweetened reading. It makes the printed page look even more boring than it used to look. Sure, books will be available in the classroom, too—but they'll have all the appeal of a dusty piano to a teen who has a Walkman handy.

So what if the little nippers don't read? If they're watching Olivier instead, what do they lose? The text, the written word along with all of its attendant pleasures. Besides, a book is more portable than a computer, has a higher-resolution display, can be written on and dog-eared and is comparatively dirt cheap.

Hypermedia, multimedia's comrade in the struggle for a brave new classroom, is just as troubling. It's a way of presenting documents on screen without imposing a linear start-to-finish order. Disembodied paragraphs are linked by theme; after reading one about the First World War, for example, you might be able to choose another about the technology of battleships, or the life of Woodrow Wilson, or hemlines in the '20s. This is another cute idea that is good in minor ways and terrible in major ones. Teaching children to understand the orderly unfolding of a plot or a logical argument is a crucial part of education. Authors don't merely agglomerate paragraphs; they work hard to make the narrative read a certain way, prove a particular point. To turn a book or a document into hypertext is to invite readers to ignore exactly what counts—the story.

The real problem, again, is the accentuation of already bad habits. Dynamiting documents into disjointed paragraphs is one more expression of the sorry fact that sustained argument is not our style. If you're a newspaper or magazine editor and your readership is dwindling, what's the solution? Shorter pieces. If you're a politician and you want to get elected, what do you need? Tasty sound bites. Logical presentation be damned.

Another software species, "allow me" programs, is not much better. These programs correct spelling and, by applying canned grammatical and stylistic rules, fix prose. In terms of promoting basic skills, though, they have all the virtues of a pocket calculator.

In Kentucky, as *The Wall Street Journal* recently reported, students in grades K–3 are mixed together regardless of age in a relaxed environment. It works great, the *Journal* says. Yes, scores on computation tests have dropped 10 percent at one school, but not to worry: "Drilling addition and subtraction in an age of calculators is a waste of time," the principal reassures us. Meanwhile, a Japanese educator informs University of Wisconsin mathematician Richard Akey that in his country, "calculators are not used in elementary or junior high school because the primary emphasis is on helping students develop their mental abilities." No wonder Japanese kids blow the pants off American kids in math. Do we really think "drilling addition and subtraction in an age of calculators is a waste of time"? If we do, then "drilling reading in an age of multimedia is a waste of time" can't be far behind.

Prose-correcting programs are also a little ghoulish, like asking a   10
computer for tips on improving your personality. On the other hand, I ran this article through a spell-checker, so how can I ban the use of such programs in schools? Because to misspell is human; to have no idea of correct spelling is to be semiliterate.

There's no denying that computers have the potential to perform inspiring feats in the classroom. If we are ever to see that potential realized, however, we ought to agree on three conditions. First, there should be a completely new crop of children's software. Most of today's offerings show no imagination. There are hundreds of similar reading and geography and arithmetic programs, but almost nothing on electricity or physics or architecture. Also, they abuse the technical capacities of new media to glitz up old forms instead of creating new ones. Why not build a time-travel program that gives kids a feel for how history is structured by zooming you backward? A spectrum program that lets users twirl a frequency knob to see what happens?

Second, computers should be used only during recess or relaxation periods. Treat them as fillips, not as surrogate teachers. When I was in school in the '60s, we all loved educational films. When we saw a movie in class, everybody won: teachers didn't have to teach, and pupils didn't have to learn. I suspect that classroom computers are popular today for the same reasons.

Most important, educators should learn what parents and most teachers already know: you cannot teach a child anything unless you look him in the face. We should not forget what computers are. Like books—better in some ways, worse in others—they are devices that help children mobilize their own resources and learn for themselves. The computer's potential to do good is modestly greater than a book's in some areas. Its potential to do harm is vastly greater, across the board.

 ## Joining the Conversation: Critical Thinking and Writing

1. If you used computers in your elementary or secondary school, evaluate their contribution to your education. (This need not be an all-or-nothing issue; it may be that computers were useless in some courses, moderately useful in others, and highly useful in still others.)

2. One of Gelernter's complaints (paragraph 3) is that "computers discount words in favor of pictures and pictures in favor of video." Is this true—and if it is true, is it necessarily a bad thing? Explain.

3. Paragraph 9 touches on whether "drilling addition and subtraction in an age of calculators is a waste of time." Your views?

A Casebook on Testing and Grading

Paul Goodman

Paul Goodman (1911–1972) received his bachelor's degree from City College in New York and his Ph.D. from the University of Chicago. He taught in several colleges and universities, and he was a prolific writer on literature, politics, and education. Goodman's view that students were victims of a corrupt society made him especially popular on campuses—even in the 1960s, when students tended to distrust anyone over 30. "A Proposal to Abolish Grading" (editors' title) is an extract from Compulsory Mis-Education and the Community of Scholars *(1966).*

A Proposal to Abolish Grading

Let half a dozen of the prestigious Universities—Chicago, Stanford, the Ivy League—abolish grading, and use testing only and entirely for pedagogic purposes as teachers see fit.

Anyone who knows the frantic temper of the present schools will understand the transvaluation of values that would be effected by this modest innovation. For most of the students, the competitive grade has come to be the essence. The naïve teacher points to the beauty of the subject and the ingenuity of the research; the shrewd student asks if he is responsible for that on the final exam.

Let me at once dispose of an objection whose unanimity is quite fascinating. I think that the great majority of professors agree that grading hinders teaching and creates a bad spirit, going as far as cheating and plagiarizing. I have before me the collection of essays, *Examining in Harvard College*, and this is the consensus. It is uniformly asserted, however, that the grading is inevitable; for how else will the graduate schools, the foundations, the corporations *know* whom to accept, reward, hire? How will the talent scouts know whom to tap?

By testing the applicants, of course, according to the specific task-requirements of the inducting institution, just as applicants for the Civil Service or for licenses in medicine, law, and architecture are tested. Why should Harvard professors do the testing *for* corporations and graduate-schools?

The objection is ludicrous. Dean Whitla, of the Harvard Office of Tests, points out that the scholastic-aptitude and achievement tests used for *admission* to Harvard are a super-excellent index for all-around Harvard performance, better than high-school grades or particular

Paul Goodman: "A Proposal to Abolish Grading," from *Compulsory Mis-Education*, Horizon Press, 1964. Reprinted by permission.

Harvard course-grades. Presumably, these college-entrance tests are tailored for what Harvard and similar institutions want. By the same logic, would not an employer do far better to apply his own job-aptitude test rather than to rely on the vagaries of Harvard sectionmen. Indeed, I doubt that many employers bother to look at such grades; they are more likely to be interested merely in the fact of a Harvard diploma, whatever that connotes to them. The grades have most of their weight with the graduate schools—here, as elsewhere, the system runs mainly for its own sake.

It is really necessary to remind our academics of the ancient history of Examination. In the medieval university, the whole point of the gruelling trial of the candidate was whether or not to accept him as a peer. His disputation and lecture for the Master's was just that, a masterpiece to enter the guild. It was not to make comparative evaluations. It was not to weed out and select for an extra-mural licensor or employer. It was certainly not to pit one young fellow against another in an ugly competition. My philosophic impression is that the medievals thought they knew what a good job of work was and that we are competitive because we do not know. But the more status is achieved by largely irrelevant competitive evaluation, the less will we ever know.

(Of course, our American examinations never did have this purely guild orientation, just as our faculties have rarely had absolute autonomy; the examining was to satisfy Overseers, Elders, distant Regents— and they as paternal superiors have always doted on giving grades, rather than accepting peers. But I submit that this set-up itself makes it impossible for the student to *become* a master, to *have* grown up, and to commence on his own. He will always be making A or B for some overseer. And in the present atmosphere, he will always be climbing on his friend's neck.)

Perhaps the chief objectors to abolishing grading would be the students and their parents. The parents should be simply disregarded; their anxiety has done enough damage already. For the students, it seems to me that a primary duty of the university is to deprive them of their props, their dependence on extrinsic valuation and motivation, and to force them to confront the difficult enterprise itself and finally lose themselves in it.

A miserable effect of grading is to nullify the various uses of testing. Testing, for both student and teacher, is a means of structuring, and also of finding out what is blank or wrong and what has been assimilated and can be taken for granted. Review—including high-pressure review—is a means of bringing together the fragments, so that there are flashes of synoptic insight.

There are several good reasons for testing, and kinds of test. But if the aim is to discover weakness, what is the point of down-grading and punishing it, and thereby inviting the student to conceal his weakness, by faking and bulling, if not cheating? The natural conclusion of synthesis is the

10

insight itself, not a grade for having had it. For the important purpose of placement, if one can establish in the student the belief that one is testing *not* to grade and make invidious comparisons but for his own advantage, the student should normally seek his own level, where he is challenged and yet capable, rather than trying to get by. If the student dares to accept himself as he is, a teacher's grade is a crude instrument compared with a student's self-awareness. But it is rare in our universities that students are encouraged to notice objectively their vast confusion. Unlike Socrates, our teachers rely on power-drives rather than shame and ingenuous idealism.

Many students are lazy, so teachers try to goad or threaten them by grading. In the long run this must do more harm than good. Laziness is a character-defense. It may be a way of avoiding learning, in order to protect the conceit that one is already perfect (deeper, the despair that one *never* can). It may be a way of avoiding just the risk of failing and being down-graded. Sometimes it is a way of politely saying, "I won't." But since it is the authoritarian grown-up demands that have created such attitudes in the first place, why repeat the trauma? There comes a time when we must treat people as adult, laziness and all. It is one thing courageously to fire a do-nothing out of your class; it is quite another thing to evaluate him with a lordly F.

Most important of all, it is often obvious that balking in doing the work, especially among bright young people who get to great universities, means exactly what it says: The work does not suit me, not this subject, or not at this time, or not in this school, or not in school altogether. The student might not be bookish; he might be school-tired; perhaps his development ought now to take another direction. Yet unfortunately, if such a student is intelligent and is not sure of himself, he *can* be bullied into passing, and this obscures everything. My hunch is that I am describing a common situation. What a grim waste of young life and teacherly effort! Such a student will retain nothing of what he has "passed" in. Sometimes he must get mononucleosis to tell his story and be believed.

And ironically, the converse is also probably commonly true. A student flunks and is mechanically weeded out, who is really ready and eager to learn in a scholastic setting, but he has not quite caught on. A good teacher can recognize the situation, but the computer wreaks its will.

Joining the Conversation: Critical Thinking and Writing

1. In his opening paragraph, Goodman limits his suggestion about grading and testing to "half a dozen of the prestigious Universities." Does he offer any reason for this limitation? Can you?

2. In paragraph 3, Goodman says that "the great majority of professors agree that grading hinders teaching." What evidence does he offer to support this claim? What arguments might be made that grading assists teaching? Should Goodman have made them?

3. As a student, have grades helped you to learn or have grades hindered you? Explain.

4. If you have been a student in an ungraded course, describe the course and evaluate the experience.

Diane Ravitch

Diane Ravitch, born in Houston Texas, in 1938, holds a bachelor's degree from Wellesley College and a Ph.D. from Columbia University. She has taught history and education, served in the government with appointments first by President George H. Bush and then by his successor Bill Clinton, is the author of several books, and is now a research professor at New York University.

Note: In the eassay that we reprint, first published in 2000, Ravitch held an optimistic view of the effects that testing might have on elementary and secondary education, but in her newest book, The Death and Life of the Great American School System: How Testing and Choice Undermine Education *(2010), she takes a very different view of these tests. Ravitch now believes—based on what she saw in the first decade of the 21st century—that testing has had a disastrous effect on teaching and learning: In an effort to meet the requirements of* No Child Left Behind, *schools merely lowered the standards so students would score sufficiently high to qualify. Furthermore, in a few instances, teachers falsified scores—again so students would apparently meet the standards.*

In Defense of Testing

No one wants to be tested. We would all like to get a driver's license without answering questions about right of way or showing that we can parallel park a car. Many future lawyers and doctors probably wish they could join their profession without taking an exam.

But tests and standards are a necessary fact of life. They protect us—most of the time—from inept drivers, hazardous products, and shoddy professionals. In schools too, exams play a constructive role. They tell public officials whether new school programs are making a difference and where new investments are likely to pay off. They tell teachers what their students have learned—and have not. They tell parents how their children are doing compared with others their age. They encourage students to exert more effort.

It is important to recall that for most of this century, educators used intelligence tests to decide which children should get a high-quality education. The point of IQ testing was to find out how much children were capable of learning rather than to test what they had actually learned. Based on IQ scores, millions of children were assigned to dumbed-down programs instead of solid courses in science, math, history, literature, and foreign languages.

This history reminds us that tests should be used to improve education, not ration it. Every child should have access to a high-quality education. Students should have full opportunity to learn what will be tested; otherwise their test scores will merely reflect whether they come from an educated family.

In the past few years, we have seen the enormous benefits that flow to disadvantaged students because of the information provided by state tests. Those who fall behind are now getting extra instruction in after-school classes and summer programs. In their efforts to improve student performance, states are increasing teachers' salaries, testing new teachers, and insisting on better teacher education.

Good tests should include a mix of essay, problem-solving, short-answer, and even some multiple-choice questions. On math quizzes, students should be able to show how they arrived at their answer. The tests widely used today often rely too much on multiple-choice questions, which encourage guessing rather than thinking. Also, they frequently ignore the importance of knowledge. Today's history tests, for example, seldom expect the student to know any history—sometimes derided as "mere facts"—but only to be able to read charts, graphs, and cartoons.

Performance in education means the mastery of both knowledge and skills. This is why it is reasonable to test teachers to make sure they know their subject matter, as well as how to teach it to young children. And this is why it is reasonable to assess whether students are ready to advance to the next grade or graduate from high school. To promote students who cannot read or do math is no favor to them. It is like pushing them into a deep pool before they have learned to swim. If students need extra time and help, they should get it, but they won't unless we first carefully assess what they have learned.

Joining the Conversation: Critical Thinking and Writing

1. In paragraph 2, Ravitch says of tests that "they tell teachers what their students have learned—and have not." Thinking back on tests you took in school, to what extent do you agree with Ravitch's assertion? Do you agree with her claim that tests "encourage students to exert more effort"? Is that true of you?

2. In paragraph 4, Ravitch seems to link testing to her assertion that "every child should have access to a high-quality education." Do you believe that testing and improving education are linked? Explain.

3. In paragraph 6, Ravitch says that history tests "seldom expect the student to know any history." What history courses did you take in high school? To what extent did the tests you took support Ravitch's claim?

4. In paragraph 7, Ravitch asserts that "it is reasonable to test teachers to make sure they know their subject matter, as well as how to teach it to young children." In your schools, were teachers ever tested? If not, do you think that testing your teachers would have led to improvement in your education? What measures other than testing are there to assess the competence of teachers?

Joy Alonso

Until her retirement in 2004, Joy Alonso taught Spanish language and literature in high schools, community colleges, and four-year colleges. Her experience is therefore unusually varied. We reprint a talk that she gave at Tufts University in 2004.

Two Cheers for Examinations

First, I must say that my title is borrowed from E. M. Forster's collection of essays. I am speaking about an academic topic, to an audience of students and teachers, and I don't want to be accused of plagiarism.

Second, I want to tell a joke, a joke that I believe is highly relevant to our topic, "The Role of Examinations in College Courses." A father visited the college where he had been a student, and where his daughter was now a student. They happened to encounter an instructor who some twenty years earlier had taught the father and who last year had taught the daughter. The father said, sincerely, that he had greatly enjoyed the course and that his daughter had raved to him about the course, but he confessed that he was greatly disappointed in one respect. "The questions on the examination you gave to my daughter's class were exactly the same as the ones you gave to my class twenty years ago." "Ah, yes," the professor explained, "the questions are the same, but we have changed the answers."

A joke, but with a good deal of truth in it. No one can doubt the truth with reference to courses in the sciences. I have heard that a distinguished professor at a medical school begins his lectures by telling his students, "Half of what we are teaching you will, in twenty years, be disproved. The trouble is, we don't know which half." But even in the humanities and in the social sciences it is evident, at least to those who have been teaching the subjects for a couple of decades, that things change, that new

Joy Alonso: "Two Cheers for Examinations." Reprinted by permission of the author.

knowledge makes us look differently at the works and issues that we studied when we were students.

What are the purposes of examinations? I think most people will agree that examinations have a dual purpose: to test or measure achievement, and to stimulate learning. The first purpose serves the interests of those who want to evaluate the student, perhaps for honors within the college, for admission to a graduate or professional school, or for employment. This purpose, this business of measuring students, may even serve the students themselves or their parents, who are interested in knowing how things seem to be going, where the students stand. I take this last point seriously; many students need reassurance that they are doing just fine. I suppose I should also mention, while speaking about tests as an instrument of measuring, that tests measure the *teachers* too; they measure how well we have taught. But this is not relevant to our topic today, which is the pros and cons of tests in two- and four-year colleges.

The second purpose of a test is to stimulate learning. On the most obvious level, a vocabulary quiz or a quiz on a reading assignment forces the student to do the necessary work before the quiz. The usual metaphor is that such a test is a police measure, a device that forces the student to obey the law, in this case to master (at least to some degree) the assigned work. I don't think this is a bad thing. Yes, it would be better if all students at all times eagerly turned to their studies without any sort of compulsion, but none of us is cut from this sort of cloth. We all have lots of pressures on us, and inevitably we neglect some things—even things that we want to do—unless deadlines are imposed. A quiz tomorrow morning is a sort of deadline, a deadline that makes busy students turn for an hour or two to the assigned reading.

But when I say that tests stimulate learning, I am also thinking of something larger than this. Quizzes tend to test only details—the meanings of certain words, the uses of the subjunctive, the dates of certain events, and so forth. Midterm examinations and especially final examinations help a student to see how details may connect. In studying for examinations, a student begins to see not just the trees but the forest. The student has perhaps taken a quiz that established whether he or she had read the assigned novel—Who did what to whom?—but not until the student prepares for the final examination does the student achieve an overview, partly by reviewing notes and readings, partly by trying to anticipate examination questions, perhaps by discussing the course with fellow-students in a study group, and in any case by thinking about what the course adds up to. And finally, when the student actually faces the questions on the exam and responds thoughtfully to them, he or she is likely to experience a gratifying sense of accomplishment, an intellectual high.

I won't go so far as to say that students like examinations, but I will claim that many students experience a sense of exhilaration when the ordeal is over, when, so to speak, the initiation rite is completed and they justifiably feel that they have achieved something, they know things (at least for the moment) that they hadn't known they knew. They have met the challenge, risen to the occasion, learned (among other things) that they can do pretty well when it comes to the test—and the effort was worthwhile. Perhaps here I should say that in most of my courses, where there were several assigned papers and a midterm examination, I assured students that the final examination would count heavily if they did well, but if their grade on the final was notably lower than the average of their papers and midterm, it would count only as one unit in computing the average. I believe this system encouraged students to take the final seriously, but it protected the very rare student whose final examination was for some unfathomable reason far below his or her earlier work.

Why did I regularly put more emphasis on the final examination than on papers on topics that the students select? I did indeed assign several papers, of varying lengths, in my literature courses, but papers usually are on a relatively limited topic, rarely allowing for more than a comparison of two works. Students can write excellent papers on how the Elizabethans may have regarded the ghost in *Hamlet*, or how a director today might stage the scenes with the ghost, or they might write on, say, Shakespeare's use of prose in *Hamlet*: "Why does Hamlet sometimes speak verse, and sometimes prose?" And does Hamlet's prose differ from other prose in the play? These are worthy topics; students will learn a great deal about the play by working on them—but even the student who in a course in Shakespeare's Tragedies has written three such essays will not achieve an overview of the topic such as is afforded by studying for a final examination.

The title of my talk is "Two Cheers for Examinations." Why not three cheers? Because I know that there are drawbacks to examinations. Examinations can indeed deal with trivia, they can be badly conceived and thus can cause needless anxiety in the students who struggle to make sense out of poorly-written or poorly-focused questions.

Most damaging of all, perhaps, is the fact that professors are human 10 beings and therefore they will sometimes grade examinations unfairly. Probably very few instructors are knowingly unfair, but an instructor who grades a paper at 8:00 p.m. is not quite the same person when he or she is grading at midnight. My own practice—an effort to guard against the unfairness that may be inherent in reading dozens of papers, one after the other, was to grade the first question on all the papers, then, when I had graded all of the responses to the first question, I turned to the second, and so on, in an effort to make certain that no student had the bad luck of being the first to be graded, when I might be more demanding, and no student had the bad luck to be the last to be graded, when I may have run out of patience. Still, even this system could not insure that I was fair to those papers that were barely legible.

I confess that I often found grading examinations to be a tedious job, but I must also add that the examinations were often a learning-experience for me as well as for the students. How and why? In preparing the questions for the examination I had to think about the course as a whole, and I tried to construct questions that would help students to make connections, to go beyond the details of each day's assignment. And in reading the essays, I learned something about my failures, *my* failures, not the students'; some of the responses let me see where I had not been clear, or perhaps even where I had been misleading. On the whole, however, after reading all of the essays I felt pretty good, I felt something of the satisfaction that I hope students felt after they finished writing their examinations. It's been a lot of effort, thought, but it was worth it.

As for me, now that I am retired, well, I am preparing for my Final Examination.

 ### Joining the Conversation:
Critical Thinking and Writing

1. Alonso does not discuss take-home examinations. What are the advantages (if any) and disadvantages (if any) of this form of examination?

2. In your view, what are the advantages (if any) and disadvantages (if any) of timed examinations (i.e., of in-class examinations that run for a specific number of minutes)?

3. If you were in the audience when Alonso gave her talk, what two questions might you raise during the discussion period that followed the talk?

A Casebook: College Advice from People Who Have Been There Awhile

In September 2009, shortly before the college academic year began, *The New York Times* published advice to new students, offered by old hands. We have selected four contributions that we think are especially valuable to all incoming first-year students.

Stanley Fish

Stanley Fish, a Professor of Law at Florida International University and a contributing columnist to The New York Times, *has been teaching since 1962.*

The Hunt for a Good Teacher

I would give entering freshmen two pieces of advice. First, find out who the good teachers are. Ask your adviser; poll older students; search the Internet; and consult the teacher-evaluation guides available at most colleges. (As a professor, I am against those guides; too often they are the vehicles of petty grievances put forward by people who have no long-term stake in the enterprise. But if I were a student, I would take advantage of them.)

To some extent your options will be limited by distribution requirements (in colleges that still have them) and scheduling. But within these limits you should do everything you can to get a seat in the class of a professor known for both his or her knowledge of the material and the ability to make it a window on the larger universe. Years later you may not be able to recall the details of lectures and discussions, but the benefits of being in the company of a challenging mind will be yours forever.

Second, I would advise students to take a composition course even if they have tested out of it. I have taught many students whose SAT scores exempted them from the writing requirement, but a disheartening number of them couldn't write and an equal number had never been asked to. They managed to get through high-school without learning how to write a clean English sentence, and if you can't do that you can't do anything.

I give this advice with some trepidation because too many writing courses today teach everything but the craft of writing and are instead the vehicles of the instructor's social and political obsessions. In the face of what I consider a dereliction of pedagogical duty, I can say only, "Buyer beware." If your writing instructor isn't teaching writing, get out of that class and find someone who is.

Gerald Graff

Gerald Graff, the past president of the Modern Language Association and a Professor of English and Education at the University of Illinois at Chicago, has been teaching since 1963.

An Argument Worth Having

Freshmen are often overwhelmed by the intellectual challenge of college—so many subjects to be covered, so many facts, methods and philosophical isms to sort out, so many big words to assimilate. As if that weren't enough, what your different instructors tell you may be flatly contradictory.

Students understandably cope with this cognitive dissonance by giving each of their teachers in turn whatever he or she seems to want. Students learn to be free-market capitalists in one course and socialists in the next, universalists in the morning and relativists after lunch. This tactic has got many a student through college, but the trouble is that, even when each course is excellent in itself, jumping through a series of hoops doesn't add up to a real socialization into the ways of intellectual culture.

What the most successful college students do, in my experience is cut through the clutter of jargons, methods and ideological differences to locate the common practices of argument and analysis hidden behind it all. Contrary to the cliché that no "one size fits all" educational recipe is possible, successful academics of all fields and intellectual persuasions make some key moves that you can emulate:

1. Recognize that knowing a lot of stuff won't do you much good unless you can do something with what you know by turning it into an argument.
2. Pay close attention to what others are saying and writing and then summarize their arguments and assumptions in a recognizable way. Work especially on summarizing the views that go most against your own.
3. As you summarize, look not only for the thesis of an argument, but for who or what provoked it—the points of controversy.
4. Use these summaries to motivate what you say and to indicate why it needs saying. Don't be afraid to give your own opinion, especially if you can back it up with reasons and evidence, but don't disagree with anything without carefully summarizing it first.
5. It's too often a secret that only a minority of high achievers figure out, but the better you get at entering the conversation by summarizing it and putting in your own oar, the more you'll get out of your college education.

Gary Wills

Gary Wills, a Professor Emeritus of History at Northwestern University, has been teaching since 1962.

Play Politics

Play to your strengths. Do not make random choices from a bewildering range of subjects for study. So far as you can, choose courses and write papers on topics where you already have (or think you will have) some interest, some knowledge, some enthusiasm. Do not fear that this will narrow you. The deeper you go into one thing, the more it connects you with other things.

Learn to write well. Most incoming college students, even the bright ones, do not do it and it hampers them in courses and in later life. Read what you write to a friend, and ask the friend to read it back to you. Lack of clarity, coherence or shape will leap out at you.

Read, read, read. Students ask me how to become a writer, and I ask them who is their favorite author. If they have none, they have no love of words.

Seek out the most intellectually adventurous of your fellow students. Some are shy around "brains," but you have proximity to young minds as they are developing. That is a great opportunity. Take it.

Do not fear political activism. I was once at an event where a student asked Jimmy Carter how he, formerly the guardian of American law, felt years earlier when his freshman daughter was arrested at a protest against apartheid. He answered: "I cannot tell you how proud I was. If you young people cannot express your conscience now, when will you? Later you will have duties, jobs, families that make that harder. You will never be freer than now." Also, among the activists, you are more likely to meet the intellectually adventurous people mentioned in the last item.

Martha Nussbaum

Martha Nussbaum, a professor of philosophy, law, and divinity at the University of Chicago, has been teaching since 1975.

Go the Wrong Way

It's easy to think that college classes are mainly about preparing you for a job. But remember: this may be the one time in your life when you have a chance to think about the whole of your life, not just your job. Courses in the humanities, in particular, often seem impractical, but they are vital, because they stretch your imagination and challenge your mind to become more responsive, more critical, bigger. You need resources to prevent your mind from becoming narrower and more routinized in later life. This is your chance to get them.

**Joining the Conversation:
Critical Thinking and Writing**

Gerald Graff, one of the professors whose advice we offer, recommends that students enter "the conversation by summarizing it and putting in your own oar." What does he mean? Explain his argument in a sentence or two. Then, summarize each of the other brief articles, and put in your own oar.

Langston Hughes

Langston Hughes (1902–1967) was born in Joplin, Missouri. He lived part of his youth in Mexico, spent a year at Columbia University, served as a merchant seaman, and worked in a Paris nightclub. After returning to the United States, he showed some of his poems to Dr. Alain Locke, a strong advocate of African-American literature. Hughes went on to publish poetry, fiction, plays, essays, and biographies.

Theme for English B

The instructor said,

> *Go home and write
> a page tonight!
> And let that page come out of you—
> Then, it will be true.*

I wonder if it's that simple?

I am twenty-two, colored, born in Winston-Salem.
I went to school there, then Durham, then here
to his college on the hill above Harlem.
I am the only colored student in my class.
The steps from the hill lead down into Harlem,
through a park, then I cross St. Nicholas,
Eighth Avenue, Seventh, and I come to the Y,
the Harlem Branch Y, where I take the elevator
up to my room, sit down, and write this page:

It's not easy to know what is true for you or me
at twenty-two, my age. But I guess I'm what
I feel and see and hear, Harlem, I hear you:
hear you, hear me—we two—you, me, talk on this page.
(I hear New York, too.) Me—who?   20

Well, I like to eat, sleep, drink, and be in love.
I like to work, read, learn, and understand life.
I like a pipe for a Christmas present,
or records—Bessie,[1] bop, or Bach.
I guess being colored doesn't make me *not* like   25
the same things other folks like who are other races.

So will my page be colored that I write?
Being me, it will not be white.
But it will be
a part of you, instructor.   30

You are white—
yet a part of me, as I am a part of you.
That's American.
Sometimes perhaps you don't want to be a part of me.
Nor do I often want to be a part of you.   35
But we are, that's true!
As I learn from you,
I guess you learn from me—
although you're older—and white—
and somewhat more free.   40

This is my page for English B.

Joining the Conversation: Critical Thinking and Writing

1. Look up all the references to places, persons, and things in this poem. What does this knowledge contribute to your understanding of the poem?

2. The instructor's advice sounds good. Why, then, does the speaker question it? Do you agree with the speaker or do you think he is being oversensitive?

3. Does Hughes present an argument in this poem? If you believe he does *not*, explain. If you believe he does, summarize the argument in your own words. What is the difference, if any, between presenting this argument in a poem and presenting it in prose?

[1]*Bessie* : Bessie Smith (1898?–1937), African-American blues singer

4. A student said to us that when she first read "Theme for English B," it struck her as an "angry" poem. Is there evidence in the text that supports her response? Can you locate evidence that suggests her response might be mistaken or incomplete? If you had to sum up the poem in a single word, what would this word be?

5. In your high school courses, were you always accepted as an equal? What about in your college courses? Explain—perhaps with the help of a specific story or anecdote or two.

6. What does the speaker mean when he says "That's American"? Do you agree with his claim? In a paragraph, define what it means to be "American." Do you find this to be a hard task or an easy one?

CHAPTER 9

Work and Play

Short Views

Work and play are words used to describe the same thing under differing conditions.
Mark Twain

The Battle of Waterloo was won on the playing fields of Eton.
Attributed to the Duke of Wellington

Everyone who is prosperous or successful must have dreamed of something. It is not because he is a good worker that he is prosperous, but because he dreamed.
Lost Star, of the Maricopa

The possible quantity of play depends on the possible quantity of pay.
John Ruskin

Winning is not the most important thing; it's everything.
Vince Lombardi

Serious sport has nothing to do with fair play. It is bound up with hatred, jealousy, boastfulness, disregard of all rules and sadistic pleasure in witnessing violence: in other words, it is war minus the shooting.
George Orwell

The maturity of man—that means to have reacquired the seriousness that one has as a child at play.
Friedrich Nietzsche

The boys throw stones at the frogs in sport, but the frogs die not in sport but in earnest.
Bion

Bertrand Russell

Bertrand Russell (1872–1970) was educated at Trinity College, Cambridge. He published his first book, The Study of German Social Democracy, *in 1896; subsequent books on mathematics and on philosophy quickly established his international reputation. His pacifist opposition to* World War I *cost him his appointment at Trinity College and won him a prison sentence of six months. While serving this sentence, he wrote his* Introduction to Mathematical Philosophy. *In 1940, an appointment to teach at the College of the City of New York was withdrawn because of his unorthodox moral views. But he was not always treated shabbily; he won numerous awards, including (in 1950) a Nobel Prize. After World War II, he devoted most of his energy to warning the world about the dangers of nuclear war.*

In reading the first sentence of the essay that we reprint, you should know that the essay comes from the book The Conquest of Happiness, *published in 1930.*

Work

Whether work should be placed among the causes of happiness or among the causes of unhappiness may perhaps be regarded as a doubtful question. There is certainly much work which is exceedingly irksome, and an excess of work is always very painful. I think, however, that, provided work is not excessive in amount, even the dullest work is to most people less painful than idleness. There are in work all grades, from mere relief of tedium up to the profoundest delights, according to the nature of the work and the abilities of the worker. Most of the work that most people have to do is not in itself interesting, but even such work has certain great advantages. To begin with, it fills a good many hours of the day without the need of deciding what one shall do. Most people, when they are left free to fill their own time according to their own choice, are at a loss to think of anything sufficiently pleasant to be worth doing. And whatever they decide on, they are troubled by the feeling that something else would have been pleasanter. To be able to fill leisure intelligently is the last product of civilization, and at present very few people have reached this level. Moreover the exercise of choice is in itself tiresome. Except to people with unusual initiative it is positively agreeable to be told what to do at each hour of the day, provided the orders are not too unpleasant. Most of the idle rich suffer unspeakable boredom as the price of their freedom from drudgery. At times, they may find relief by hunting big game in Africa, or by flying round the world, but the number of such sensations is limited, especially after youth is past. Accordingly the more intelligent rich men work nearly as hard as if they were poor, while rich women for the most part keep themselves busy with innumerable trifles of whose earth-shaking importance they are firmly persuaded.

Work therefore is desirable, first and foremost, as a preventive of boredom, for the boredom that a man feels when he is doing necessary though uninteresting work is as nothing in comparison with the boredom that he feels when he has nothing to do with his days. With this advantage of work another is associated, namely that it makes holidays much more delicious when they come. Provided a man does not have to work so hard as to impair his vigor, he is likely to find far more zest in his free time than an idle man could possibly find.

The second advantage of most paid work and of some unpaid work is that it gives chances of success and opportunities for ambition. In most work success is measured by income, and while our capitalistic society continues, this is inevitable. It is only where the best work is concerned that this measure ceases to be the natural one to apply. The desire that men feel to increase their income is quite as much a desire for success as for the extra comforts that a higher income can procure. However dull work may be, it becomes bearable if it is a means of building up a reputation, whether in the world at large or only in one's own circle. Continuity of purpose is one of the most essential ingredients of happiness in the long run, and for most men this comes chiefly through their work. In this respect those women whose lives are occupied with housework are much less fortunate than men, or than women who work outside the home. The domesticated wife does not receive wages, has no means of bettering herself, is taken for granted by her husband (who sees practically nothing of what she does), and is valued by him not for her housework but for quite other qualities. Of course this does not apply to those women who are sufficiently well-to-do to make beautiful houses and beautiful gardens and become the envy of their neighbors; but such women are comparatively few, and for the great majority housework cannot bring as much satisfaction as work of other kinds brings to men and to professional women.

The satisfaction of killing time and of affording some outlet, however modest, for ambition, belongs to most work, and is sufficient to make even a man whose work is dull happier on the average than a man who has no work at all. But when work is interesting, it is capable of giving satisfaction of a far higher order than mere relief from tedium. The kinds of work in which there is some interest may be arranged in a hierarchy. I shall begin with those which are only mildly interesting and end with those that are worthy to absorb the whole energies of a great man.

Two chief elements make work interesting; first, the exercise of skill, and second, construction.

Every man who has acquired some unusual skill enjoys exercising it until it has become a matter of course, or until he can no longer improve himself. This motive to activity begins in early childhood: a boy who can stand on his head becomes reluctant to stand on his feet. A great deal of work gives the same pleasure that is to be derived from games of skill. The work of a lawyer or a politician must contain in a more delectable form a great deal of the same pleasure that is to be derived from playing bridge.

Here of course there is not only the exercise of skill but the outwitting of a skilled opponent. Even where this competitive element is absent, however, the performance of difficult feats is agreeable. A man who can do stunts in an aeroplane finds the pleasure so great that for the sake of it he is willing to risk his life. I imagine that an able surgeon, in spite of the painful circumstances in which his work is done, derives satisfaction from the exquisite precision of his operations. The same kind of pleasure, though in a less intense form, is to be derived from a great deal of work of a humbler kind. All skilled work can be pleasurable, provided the skill required is either variable or capable of indefinite improvement. If these conditions are absent, it will cease to be interesting when a man has acquired his maximum skill. A man who runs three-mile races will cease to find pleasure in this occupation when he passes the age at which he can beat his own previous record. Fortunately there is a very considerable amount of work in which new circumstances call for new skill and a man can go on improving, at any rate until he has reached middle age. In some kinds of skilled work, such as politics, for example, it seems that men are at their best between sixty and seventy, the reason being that in such occupations a wide experience of other men is essential. For this reason successful politicians are apt to be happier at the age of seventy than any other men of equal age. Their only competitors in this respect are the men who are the heads of big businesses.

There is, however, another element possessed by the best work, which is even more important as a source of happiness than is the exercise of skill. This is the element of constructiveness. In some work, though by no means in most, something is built up which remains as a monument when the work is completed. We may distinguish construction from destruction by the following criterion. In construction the initial state of affairs is comparatively haphazard, while the final state of affairs embodies a purpose: in destruction the reverse is the case; the initial state of affairs embodies a purpose, while the final state of affairs is haphazard, that is to say, all that is intended by the destroyer is to produce a state of affairs which does not embody a certain purpose. This criterion applies in the most literal and obvious case, namely the construction and destruction of buildings. In constructing a building a previously made plan is carried out, whereas in destroying it no one decides exactly how the materials are to lie when the demolition is complete. Destruction is of course necessary very often as a preliminary to subsequent construction; in that case it is part of a whole which is constructive. But not infrequently a man will engage in activities of which the purpose is destructive without regard to any construction that may come after. Frequently he will conceal this from himself by the belief that he is only sweeping away in order to build afresh, but it is generally possible to unmask this pretense, when it is a pretense, by asking him what the subsequent construction is to be. On this subject it will be found that he will speak vaguely and without enthusiasm, whereas on the preliminary destruction he has spoken precisely and with zest. This applies to not a few revolutionaries and militarists and other apostles of violence. They are actuated, usually without their own knowledge, by hatred: the destruction of what they hate is their real purpose, and they are comparatively indifferent to the question what is to come after it. Now I cannot deny that in the work of destruction as in the work of construction there may be joy. It is a fiercer joy, perhaps at moments more intense, but it is less profoundly satisfying, since the result is one in which little satisfaction is to be found. You kill your enemy, and when he is dead your occupation is gone, and the satisfaction that you derive from victory quickly fades. The work of construction, on the other hand, when completed is delightful to contemplate, and moreover is never so fully completed that there is nothing further to do about it. The most satisfactory purposes are those that lead on indefinitely from one success to another without ever coming to a dead end; and in this respect it will be found that construction is a greater source of happiness than destruction. Perhaps it would be more correct to say that those who find satisfaction in construction find in it greater satisfaction than the lovers of destruction can find in destruction, for if once you have become filled with hate you will not easily derive from construction the pleasure which another man would derive from it.

At the same time few things are so likely to cure the habit of hatred as the opportunity to do constructive work of an important kind.

The satisfaction to be derived from success in a great constructive enterprise is one of the most massive that life has to offer, although unfortunately in its highest forms it is open only to men of exceptional ability. Nothing can rob a man of the happiness of successful achievement in an important piece of work, unless it be the proof that after all his work was bad. There are many forms of such satisfaction. The man who by a scheme of irrigation has caused the wilderness to blossom like the rose enjoys it in one of its most tangible forms. The creation of an organization may be a work of supreme importance. So is the work of those few statesmen who have devoted their lives to producing order out of chaos, of whom Lenin is the supreme type in our day. The most obvious examples are artists and men of science. Shakespeare says of his verse: "So long as men can breathe, or eyes can see, so long lives this." And it cannot be doubted that the thought consoled him for misfortune. In his sonnets he maintains that the thought of his friend reconciled him to life, but I cannot help suspecting that the sonnets he wrote to his friend were even more effective for this purpose than the friend himself. Great artists and great men of science do work which is in itself delightful; while they are doing it, it secures them the respect of those whose respect is worth having, which gives them the most fundamental kind of power, namely power over men's thoughts and feelings. They have also the most solid reasons for thinking well of themselves. This combination of fortunate circumstances ought, one would think, to be enough to make any man happy. Nevertheless it is not so. Michelangelo, for example, was a profoundly unhappy man, and maintained (not, I am sure, with truth) that he would not have troubled to produce works of art if he had not had to pay the debts of his impecunious relations. The power to produce great art is very often, though by no means always, associated with a temperamental unhappiness, so great that but for the joy which the artist derives from his work, he would be driven to suicide. We cannot, therefore, maintain that even the greatest work must make a man happy; we can only maintain that it must make him less unhappy. Men of science, however, are far less often temperamentally unhappy than artists are, and in the main the men who do great work in science are happy men, whose happiness is derived primarily from their work.

One of the causes of unhappiness among intellectuals in the present day is that so many of them, especially those whose skill is literary, find no opportunity for the independent exercise of their talents, but have to hire themselves out to rich corporations directed by Philistines, who insist upon their producing what they themselves regard as pernicious nonsense. If you were to inquire among journalists in either England or America whether they believed in the policy of the newspaper for which they worked, you would find, I believe, that only a small minority do so; the rest, for the sake of a livelihood, prostitute their skill to purposes which they believe to be harmful. Such work cannot bring any real satisfaction, and in the course of reconciling himself to the doing of it, a man has to make himself so cynical that he can no longer derive whole-hearted satisfaction from anything whatever. I cannot condemn men who undertake work of this sort, since starvation is too serious an alternative, but I think that where it is possible to do work that is satisfactory to a man's constructive impulses without entirely starving, he will be well advised from the point of view of his own happiness if he chooses it in preference to work much more highly paid but not seeming to him worth doing on its own account. Without self-respect genuine happiness is scarcely possible. And the man who is ashamed of his work can hardly achieve self-respect.

The satisfaction of constructive work, though it may, as things are, be the privilege of a minority, can nevertheless be the privilege of a quite large minority. Any man who is his own master in his work can feel it; so can any man whose work appears to him useful and requires considerable skill. The production of satisfactory children is a difficult constructive work capable of affording profound satisfaction. Any woman who has achieved this can feel that as a result of her labor the world contains something of value which it would not otherwise contain.

Human beings differ profoundly in regard to the tendency to regard their lives as a whole. To some men it is natural to do so, and essential to happiness to be able to do so with some satisfaction. To others life is a series of detached incidents without directed movement and without unity. I think the former sort are more likely to achieve happiness than the latter, since they will gradually build up those circumstances from which they can derive contentment and self-respect, whereas the others will be blown about by the winds of circumstances now this way, now that, without ever arriving at any haven. The habit of viewing life as a whole is an essential part both of wisdom and of true morality, and is one of the things which ought to be encouraged in education. Consistent purpose is not enough to make life happy, but it is an almost indispensable condition of a happy life. And consistent purpose embodies itself mainly in work.

Joining the Conversation: Critical Thinking and Writing

1. Russell says (paragraph 3): "The desire that men feel to increase their income is quite as much a desire for success as for the extra comforts that a higher income can procure." In its context, what does *success* mean? In your experience, do Russell's words ring true? Why or why not?

2. In paragraphs 7–11, Russell develops a contrast between what he calls "destructive" and "constructive" work. Is the contrast clarified by the examples he offers? What examples from your own experience or knowledge can you add?

3. In paragraph 10, Russell speaks of workers who "prostitute their skill to purposes which they believe to be harmful." What work does he use as an example here? What other examples can you offer? Imagine yourself doing work that you do not respect or that you even find "harmful." Then, imagine being offered work that you do respect but at a much lower salary. How helpful would you find Russell's advice? What would you do? (Specific examples of work that you respect and work that you don't respect will help you to form a clear idea of the choice and a clear argument to support it.)

4. What new point does Russell introduce in his last paragraph? How well does this last paragraph work as a conclusion?

5. Russell is generally admired for his exceptionally clear prose. List some of the devices that make for clarity in this essay.

6. Through most of his essay, Russell writes as if only men were engaged in work. What references to women working do you find? From these references and from the predominant references to men, would you describe Russell as sexist? Why or why not?

Mike Rose

Mike Rose, the son of impoverished immigrants, received degrees from Loyola University and the University of Southern California and is a professor in the Graduate School of Education and Information Studies at the University of California, Los Angeles. Among his 10 books are Writer's Block: The Cognitive Dimension *(1984),* Lives on the Boundary: The Struggles and Achievements of America's Underprepared *(1990), and* The Promise of Public Education in America *(2004). We reprint an essay that was first published in the* Los Angeles Times *in 2004.*

Brains as Well as Brawn

I am watching a carpenter install a set of sliding French doors in a tight wall space. He stands back, surveying the frame, imagining the pieces as he will assemble them.

What angle is required to create a threshold that will shed water? Where might the sliding panels catch or snag? How must the casings be remade to match the woodwork in the rest of the room? And how can he put it all together fast enough and smart enough to make his labor pay?

This isn't the usual stuff of a Labor Day tribute. Our typical tributes spotlight the economic contribution that the labor force has made to the country, the value of the work ethic. But what about the intelligence of the laborer—the thought, the creativity, the craft it takes to do work, any work, well.

Over the last six years, I've been studying the thinking involved in what is often dismissed as manual labor, exploring the way knowledge is gained and used strategically on job sites, in trade schools and in businesses such as beauty salons and restaurants, auto factories and welding shops. And I've been struck by the intellectual demands of what I saw.

Consider what a good waitress or waiter has to do in a busy restaurant: 5
remember orders and monitor them, attend to an ever-changing environment, juggle the flow of work, make decisions on the fly. Or the carpenter: To build a cabinet, a staircase or a pitched roof requires complex mathematical calculations, a high level of precision. The hairstylist's practice is a mix of scissors technique, knowledge of biology, aesthetic judgment and communication skills. The mechanic, electrician and plumber are trouble-shooters and problem-solvers. Even the routinized factory floor calls for working smart. Yet we persist in dividing labor into the work of the hand and the work of the mind.

Distinctions between blue collar and white collar do exist. White-collar work, for example, often requires a large investment of money and time in formal schooling. And, on average, white-collar work leads to higher occupational status and income, more autonomy and less physical risk. But these distinctions carry with them unfair assumptions about the intelligence of the people who do physical work. Those assumptions have a long history, from portrayals of 18th century mechanics as illiterate and incapable of participating in government to the autoworkers I heard labeled by one supervisor as "a bunch of dummies."

Such beliefs are intensified in our high-tech era. Listen to the language we use: Work involving electronic media and symbolic analysis is "neck up" while old-style manufacturing or service work is "neck down."

If society labels whole categories of people, identified by their occupations, as less intelligent, then social separations are reinforced and divisions

---

Mike Rose: "Brains as Well as Brawn of the Blue Collar" © 2004. From the *Los Angeles Times*, September 6, 2004. Reprinted by permission of the author.

constrict the kind of civic life we can create or imagine. And if society ignores the intelligence behind the craft, it mistakes prejudice for fact.

Many Labor Day tributes will render the muscled arm, sleeve rolled tight. How many also will celebrate the link between hand and brain? It would be fitting, on this day especially, to have a truer, richer sense of all that is involved in the wide range of work that surrounds and sustains us. We need to honor the brains as well as the brawn of American labor.

 Joining the Conversation: Critical Thinking and Writing

1. Do you like Rose's title? Explain why or why not.

2. A student we know said she found Rose's first two paragraphs "confusing." Why might she have responded in this way? Do you agree with her?

3. What point about "manual labor" is Rose making here?

4. Look up the word "intelligence" in a good dictionary. What are the main meanings of this word? Is there anything in this dictionary definition that surprises you—something you had not known before?

5. What kinds of manual labor have you performed? Did all of them require brains as well as brawn? Some more than others? Did any require little or no brains at all?

Matthew Crawford

Matthew Crawford lives in Richmond, Virginia. As he mentions in the essay that we reprint, he holds a Ph.D. in political philosophy and he has taught, but he now makes a living by working with his hands. Crawford is the author of Shop Class as Soulcraft: An Inquiry into the Value of Work *(2009), from which this essay was adapted. The essay originally appeared in* The New York Times Magazine, *May 24, 2009.*

The Case for Working with Your Hands

The television show "Deadliest Catch" depicts commercial crab fishermen in the Bering Sea. Another, "Dirty Jobs," shows all kinds of grueling work; one episode featured a guy who inseminates turkeys for a living. The weird fascination of these shows must lie partly in the fact that such confrontations with material reality have become exotically unfamiliar. Many of us do work that feels more surreal than real. Working in an office, you often find it difficult to see any tangible result from your efforts. What exactly have you accomplished at the end of any give day? Where the chain of cause and effect is opaque and responsibility diffuse, the experience of individual agency can be elusive. "Dilbert," "The Office" and similar portrayals of cubicle life attest to the dark absurdism with which many Americans have come to view their white-collar jobs.

Is there a more "real" alternative (short of inseminating turkeys)?

High-school shop-class programs were widely dismantled in the 1990s as educators prepared students to become "knowledge workers." The imperative of the last 20 years to round up every warm body and send it to college, then to the cubicle, was tied to a vision of the future in which we somehow take leave of material reality and glide about in a pure information economy. This has not come to pass. To begin with, such work often feels more enervating than gliding. More fundamentally, now as ever, somebody has to actually do things: fix our cars, unclog our toilets, build our houses.

When we praise people who do work that is straightforwardly useful, the praise often betrays an assumption that they had no other options. We idealize them as the salt of the earth and emphasize the sacrifice for others their work may entail. Such sacrifice does indeed occur—the hazards faced by a lineman restoring power during a storm come to mind. But what if such work answers as well to a basic human need of the one who does it? It take this to be the suggestion of Marge Piercy's poem "To be of use," which concludes with the lines "the pitcher longs for water to carry/and a person for work that is real." Beneath our gratitude for the lineman may rest envy.

This seems to be a moment when the useful arts have an especially compelling economic rationale. A car mechanics' trade association reports that repair shops have seen their business jump significantly in the current recession: people aren't buying new cars; they are fixing the ones they have. The current downturn is likely to pass eventually. But there are also systemic changes in the economy, arising from information technology, that have the surprising effect of making the manual trades—plumbing, electrical work, car repair—more attractive as careers. The Princeton economist Alan Blinder argues that the crucial distinction in the emerging labor market is not between those with more or less education, but between those whose services can be delivered over a wire and those who must do their work in person or on site. The latter will find their livelihoods more secure against outsourcing to distant countries. As Blinder puts it, "You can't hammer a nail over the Internet." Nor can the Indians fix your car. Because they are in India.

If the goal is to earn a living, then, maybe it isn't really true that 18-year-olds need to be imparted with a sense of panic about getting into college (though they certainly need to learn). Some people are hustled off to college, then to the cubicle, against their own inclinations and natural bents, when they would rather be learning to build things or fix things. One shop teacher suggested to me that "in schools, we create artificial learning environments for our children that they know to be contrived and undeserving of their full attention and engagement. Without the opportunity to learn through the hands, the world remains abstract and distant, and the passions for learning will not be engaged."

A gifted young person who chooses to become a mechanic rather than to accumulate academic credentials is viewed as eccentric, if not self-destructive. There is a pervasive anxiety among parents that there is only one track to success for their children. It runs through a series of gates controlled by prestigious institutions. Further, there is wide use of drugs to medicate boys, especially, against their natural tendency toward action, the better to "keep things on track." I taught briefly in a public high school and would have loved to have set up a Ritalin fogger in my classroom. It is a rare person, male or female, who is naturally inclined to sit still for 17 years in school, and then indefinitely at work.

The trades suffer from low prestige, and I believe this is based on a simple mistake. Because the work is dirty, many people assume it is also stupid. This is not my experience. I have a small business as a motorcycle mechanic in Richmond, Va., which I started in 2002. I work on Japanese and European motorcycles, mostly older bikes with some "vintage" cachet that makes people willing to spend money on them. I have found the satisfactions of the work to be very much bound up with the intellectual challenges it presents. And yet my decision to go into this line of work is a choice that seems to perplex many people.

After finishing a Ph.D. in political philosophy at the University of Chicago in 2000, I managed to stay on with a one-year postdoctoral fellowship at the university's Committee on Social Thought. The academic job market was utterly bleak. In a state of professional panic, I retreated to a makeshift workshop I set up in the basement of a Hyde Park apartment building, where I spent the winter tearing down an old Honda motorcycle and rebuilding it. The physicality of it, and the clear specificity of what the project required of me, was a balm. Stumped by a starter motor that seemed to check out in every way but wouldn't work, I started asking around at Honda dealerships. Nobody had an answer; finally one service manager told me to call Fred Cousins of Triple O Service. "If anyone can help you, Fred can."

I called Fred, and he invited me to come to his independent motorcycle-repair shop, tucked discreetly into an unmarked warehouse on Goose Island. He told me to put the motor on a certain bench that was free of clutter. He checked the electrical resistance through the windings, as I had done, to confirm there was no short circuit or broken wire. He spun the shaft that ran through the center of the motor, as I had. No problem: it spun freely. Then he hooked it up to a battery. It moved ever so slightly but wouldn't spin. He grasped the shaft, delicately, with three fingers, and tried to wiggle it side to side. "Too much free play," he said. He suggested that the problem was with the bushing (a thick-walled sleeve of metal) that captured the end of the shaft in the end of the cylindrical motor housing. It was worn, so it wasn't locating the shaft precisely enough. The shaft was free to move too much side to side (perhaps a couple of hundredths of an inch), causing the outer circumference of the rotor to bind on the inner circumference of the motor housing when a current was applied. Fred scrounged around for a Honda motor. He found one with the same bushing, then used a "blind hold bearing puller" to extract it, as well as the one in my motor. Then he gently tapped the new, or rather newer, one into place. The motor worked! Then Fred gave me an impromptu dissertation on the peculiar metallurgy of these Honda starter-motor bushings of the mid-'70s. Here was a scholar.

Over the next six months I spent a lot of time at Fred's shop, learning, and put in only occasional appearances at the university. This was something of a regression: I worked on cars throughout high school and college, and one of my early jobs was at a Porsche repair shop. Now I was rediscovering the intensely absorbing nature of the work, and it got me thinking about possible livelihoods.

As it happened, in the spring I landed a job as executive director of a policy organization in Washington. This felt like a coup. But certain perversities became apparent as I settled into the job. It sometimes required me to reason backward, from desired conclusion to suitable premise. The organization had taken certain positions, and there were some facts it was more fond of than others. As its figurehead, I was making arguments I didn't fully buy myself. Further, my boss seemed intent on retraining me according to a certain cognitive style—that of the corporate world, from which he had recently come. This style demanded that I project an image of rationality but not indulge too much in actual reasoning. As I sat in my K Street office, Fred's life as an independent tradesman gave me an image that I kept coming back to: someone who really knows what he is doing, losing himself in work that is genuinely useful and has a certain integrity to it. He also seemed to be having a lot of fun.

Seeing a motorcycle about to leave my shop under its own power, several days after arriving in the back of a pickup truck, I don't feel tired even though I've been standing on a concrete floor all day. Peering into the portal of his helmet, I think I can make out the edges of a grin on the face of a guy who hasn't ridden his bike in a while. I give him a wave. With one of his hands on the throttle and the other on the clutch, I know he can't wave back. But I can hear his salute in the exuberant "bwaaAAAAP!" of a crisp throttle, gratuitously revved. That sound pleases me, as I know it does him. It's a ventriloquist conversation in one mechanical voice, and the gist of it is "Yeah!"

After five months at the think tank, I'd saved enough money to buy some tools I needed, and I quit and went into business fixing bikes. My shop rate is $40 per hour. Other shops have rates as high as $70 per hour, but I tend to work pretty slowly. Further, only about half the time I spend in the shop ends up being billable (I have no employees; every little chore falls to me), so it usually works out closer to $20 per hour—a modest but decent wage. The business goes up and down; when it is down I have supplemented it with writing. The work is sometimes frustrating, but it is never irrational.

And it frequently requires complex thinking. In fixing motorcycles 15 you come up with several imagined trains of cause and effect for manifest symptoms, and you judge their likelihood before tearing anything down. This imagining relies on a mental library that you develop. An internal combustion engine can work in any number of ways, and different manufacturers have tried different approaches. Each has it own proclivities for failure. You also develop a library of sounds and smells and feels. For example, the backfire of a too-lean fuel mixture is subtly different from an ignition backfire.

As in any learned profession, you just have to know a lot. If the motorcycle is 30 years old, from an obscure maker that went out of business 20 years ago, its tendencies are known mostly through lore. It would probably be impossible to do such work in isolation, without access to a collective historical memory; you have to embedded in a community of mechanic-antiquarians. These relationships are maintained by telephone, in a network of reciprocal favors that spans the country. My most reliable source, Fred, has such an encyclopedic knowledge of obscure European motorcycles that all I have been able to offer him in exchange is deliveries of obscure European beer.

There is always a risk of introducing new complications when working on old motorcycles, and this enters the diagnostic logic. Measured in likelihood of screw-ups, the cost is not identical for all avenues of inquiry when deciding which hypothesis to pursue. Imagine you're trying to figure out why a bike won't start. The fasteners holding the engine covers on 1970s-era Hondas are Phillips head, and they are almost always rounded out and corroded. Do you really want to check the condition of the starter clutch if each of eight screws will need to be drilled out and extracted, risking damage to the engine case? Such impediments have to be taken into account. The attractiveness of any hypothesis is determined in part by physical circumstances that have no logical connection to the diagnostic problem at hand. The mechanic's proper response to the situation cannot be anticipated by a set of rules or algorithms.

There probably aren't many jobs that can be reduced to rule-following and still be done well. But in many jobs there is an attempt to do just this, and the perversity of it may go unnoticed by those who design the work process. Mechanics face something like this problem in the factory service manuals that we use. These manuals tell you to be systematic in eliminating variables, presenting an idealized image of diagnostic work. But they never take into account the risks of working on old machines. So you put the manual away and consider the facts before you. You do this because ultimately you are responsible to the motorcycle and its owner, not to some procedure.

Some diagnostic situations contain a lot of variables. Any given symptom may have several possible causes, and further, these causes may interact with one another and therefore be difficult to isolate. In deciding how to proceed, there often comes a point where you have to step back and get a larger gestalt. Have a cigarette and walk around the lift. The gap between theory and practice stretches out in front of you, and this is where it gets interesting. What you need now is the kind of judgment that arises only from experience; hunches rather than rules. For me, at least, there is more real thinking going on in the bike shop than there was in the think tank.

Put differently, mechanical work has required me to cultivate different intellectual habits. Further, habits of mind have an ethical dimension that we don't think about. Good diagnosis requires attentiveness to the machine, almost a conversation with it, rather than assertiveness, as in the position papers produced on K Street. Cognitive psychologists speak of "metacognition," which is the activity of stepping back and thinking about your own thinking. It is what you do when you stop for a moment in your pursuit of a solution, and wonder whether your understanding of the problem is adequate. The slap of worn-out pistons hitting their cylinders can sound a lot like loose valve tappets, so to be a good mechanic you have to be constantly open to the possibility that you may be mistaken. This is a virtue that is at once cognitive and moral. It seems to develop because the mechanic, if he is the sort who goes on to become good at it, internalizes the healthy functioning of the motorcycle as an object of passionate concern. How else can you explain the elation he gets when he identifies the root cause of some problem?

This active concern for the motorcycle is reinforced by the social aspects of the job. As is the case with many independent mechanics, my business is based entirely on word of mouth. I sometimes barter services with machinists and metal fabricators. This has a very different feel than transactions with money; it situates me in a community. The result is that I really don't want to mess up anybody's motorcycles or charge more than a fair price. You often hear people complain about mechanics and other tradespeople whom they take to be dishonest or incompetent. I am sure this is sometimes justified. But it is also true that the mechanic deals with a large element of chance.

I once accidentally dropped a feeler gauge down into the crankcase of a Kawasaki Ninja that was practically brand new, while performing its first scheduled valve adjustment. I escaped a complete tear-down of the motor only through an operation that involved the use of a stethoscope, another pair of trusted hands and the sort of concentration we associate with a bomb squad. When finally I laid my fingers on that feeler gauge, I felt as if I had cheated death. I don't remember ever feeling so alive as in the hours that followed.

Often as not, however, such crises do not end in redemption. Moments of elation are counterbalanced with failures, and these, too, are vivid, taking place right before your eyes. With stakes that are often high and immediate, the manual trades elicit heedful absorption in work. They are punctuated by moments of pleasure that take place against a darker backdrop: a keen awareness of catastrophe as an always-present possibility. The core experience is one of individual responsibility, supported by face-to-face interactions between tradesman and customer.

Contrast the experience of being a middle manager. This is a stock figure of ridicule, but the sociologist Robert Jackall spent years inhabiting the world of corporate managers, conducting interviews, and he poignantly describes the "moral maze" they feel trapped in. Like the mechanic, the manager faces the possibility of disaster at any time. But in his case these disasters feel arbitrary; they are typically a result of corporate restructurings, not of physics. A manager has to make many decisions for which he is accountable. Unlike an entrepreneur with his own business, however, his decisions can be reversed at any time by someone higher up the food chain (and there is always someone higher up the food chain). It's important for your career that these reversals not look like defeats, and more generally you have to spend a lot of time managing what others think of you. Survival depends on a crucial insight: you can't back down from an argument that you initially made in straightforward language, with moral conviction, without seeming to lose your integrity. So managers learn the art of provisional thinking and feeling, expressed in corporate double-speak, and cultivate a lack of commitment to their own actions. Nothing is set in concrete the way it is when you are, for example, pouring concrete.

Those who work on the lower rungs of the information-age office hierarchy face their own kinds of unreality, as I learned some time ago. After earning a master's degree in the early 1990s, I had a hard time finding work but eventually landed a job in the Bay Area writing brief summaries of academic journal articles, which were then sold on CD-ROMs to subscribing libraries. When I got the phone call offering me the job, I was excited. I felt I had grabbed hold of the passing world—miraculously, through the mere filament of a classified ad—and reeled myself into its current. My new bosses immediately took up residence in my imagination, where I often surprised them with my hidden depths. As I was shown to my cubicle, I felt a real sense of being honored. It seemed more than spacious enough. It was my desk, where I would think my thoughts— my unique contribution to a common enterprise, in a real company with hundreds of employees. The regularity of the cubicles made me feel I had found a place in the order of things. I was to be a knowledge worker.

But the feel of the job changed on my first day. The company had gotten its start by providing libraries with a subject index of popular magazines like Sports Illustrated. Through a series of mergers and acquisitions, it now found itself offering not just indexes but also abstracts (that is, summaries), and of a very different kind of material: scholarly works in the physical and biological sciences, humanities, social sciences and law. Some of this stuff was simply incomprehensible to anyone but an expert in the particular field covered by the journal. I was reading articles in Classical Philology where practically every other word was in Greek. Some of the scientific journals were no less mysterious. Yet the categorical difference between, say, Sports Illustrated and Nature Genetics seemed not to have impressed itself on the company's decision makers. In some of the titles I was assigned, articles began with an abstract written by the author. But even in such cases I was to write my own. The reason offered was that unless I did so, there would be no "value added" by our product. It was hard to believe I was going to add anything other than error and confusion to such material. But then, I hadn't yet been trained.

My job was structured on the supposition that in writing an abstract of an article there is a method that merely needs to be applied, and that this can be done without understanding the text. I was actually told this by the trainer, Monica, as she stood before a whiteboard, diagramming an abstract. Monica seemed a perfectly sensible person and gave no outward signs of suffering delusions. She didn't insist too much on what she was telling us, and it became clear she was in a position similar to that of a veteran Soviet bureaucrat who must work on two levels at once: reality and official ideology. The official ideology was a bit like the factory service manuals I mentioned before, the ones that offer procedures that mechanics often have to ignore in order to do their jobs.

My starting quota, after finishing a week of training, was 15 articles per day. By my 11th month at the company, my quota was up to 28 articles per day (this was the normal, scheduled increase). I was always sleepy while at work, and I think this exhaustion was because I felt trapped in a contradiction: the fast pace demanded complete focus on the task, yet that pace also made any real concentration impossible. I had to actively suppress my own ability to think, because the more you think, the more the inadequacies in your understanding of an author's argument come into focus. This can only slow you down. To not do justice to an author who had poured himself into the subject at hand felt like violence against what was best in myself.

The quota demanded, then, not just dumbing down but also a bit of moral re-education, the opposite of the kind that occurs in the heedful absorption of mechanical work. I had to suppress my sense of responsibility to the article itself, and to others—to the author, to begin with, as well as to the hapless users of the database, who might naïvely suppose that my abstract reflected the author's work. Such detachment was made easy by the fact there was no immediate consequence for me; I could write any nonsense whatever.

Now, it is probably true that every job entails some kind of mutilation. I used to work as an electrician and had my own business doing it for a while. As an electrician you breathe a lot of unknown dust in crawl spaces, your knees get bruised, your neck gets strained from looking up at the ceiling while installing lights or ceiling fans and you get shocked regularly, sometimes while on a ladder. Your hands are sliced up from twisting wires together, handling junction boxes made out of stamped sheet metal and cutting metal conduit with a hacksaw. But none of this damage touches the best part of yourself.

You might wonder: Wasn't there any quality control? My supervisor would periodically read a few of my abstracts, and I was sometimes corrected and told not to begin an abstract with a dependent clause. But

30

I was never confronted with an abstract I had written and told that it did not adequately reflect the article. The quality standards were the generic ones of grammar, which could be applied without my supervisor having to read the article at hand. Rather, my supervisor and I both were held to a metric that was conjured by someone remote from the work process—an absentee decision maker armed with a (putatively) profit-maximizing calculus, one that took no account of the intrinsic nature of the job. I wonder whether the resulting perversity really made for maximum profits in the long term. Corporate managers are not, after all, the owners of the business they run.

At lunch I had a standing arrangement with two other abstracters. One was from my group, a laconic, disheveled man named Mike whom I liked instantly. He did about us well on his quota as I did on mine, but it didn't seem to bother him too much. The other guy was from beyond the partition, a meticulously groomed Liberian named Henry who said he had worked for the C.I.A. He had to flee Liberia very suddenly one day and soon found himself resettled near the office parks of Foster City, Calif. Henry wasn't going to sweat the quota. Come 12:30, the three of us would hike to the food court in the mall. This movement was always thrilling. It involved traversing several "campuses," with ponds frequented by oddly real seagulls, then the lunch itself, which I always savored. ([Karl] Marx writes that under conditions of estranged labor, man "no longer feels himself to be freely active in any but his animal functions.") Over his burrito, Mike would recount the outrageous things he had written in his abstracts. I could see my own future in such moments of sabotage—the compensating pleasures of a cubicle drone. Always funny and gentle, Mike confided one day that he was doing quite a bit of heroin. On the job. This actually made some sense.

How was it that I, once a proudly self-employed electrician, had ended up among these walking wounded, a "knowledge worker" at a salary of $23,000? I had a master's degree, and it needed to be used. The escalating demand for academic credentials in the job market gives the impression of an ever-more-knowledgeable society, whose members perform cognitive feats their unschooled parents could scarcely conceive of. On paper, my abstracting job, multiplied a millionfold, is precisely what puts the futurologist in a rapture: we are getting to be so smart! Yet my M.A. obscures a more real stupidification of the work I secured with that credential, and a wage to match. When I first got the degree, I felt as if I had been inducted to a certain order of society. But despite the beautiful ties I wore, it turned out to be a more proletarian existence than I had known as an electrician. In that job I had made quite a bit more money. I also felt free and active, rather than confined and stultified.

A good job requires a field of action where you can put your best capacities to work and see an effect in the world. Academic credentials do not guarantee this.

Nor can big business or big government—those idols of the right and the left—reliably secure such work for us. Everyone is rightly concerned about economic growth on the one hand or unemployment and wages on the other, but the *character* of work doesn't figure much in political debate. Labor unions address important concerns like workplace safety and family leave, and management looks for greater efficiency, but on the nature of the job itself, the dominant political and economic paradigms are mute. Yet work forms us, and deforms us, with broad public consequences.

The visceral experience of failure seems to have been edited out of the career trajectories of gifted students. It stands to reason, then, that those who end up making big decisions that affect all of us don't seem to have much sense of their own fallibility, and of how badly things can go wrong even with the best of intentions (like when I dropped that feeler gauge down into the Ninja). In the boardrooms of Wall Street and the corridors of Pennsylvania Avenue, I don't think you'll see a yellow sign that says "Think Safety!" as you do on job sites and in many repair shops, no doubt because those who sit on the swivel chairs tend to live remote from the consequences of the decisions they make. Why not encourage gifted students to learn a trade, if only in the summers, so that their fingers will be crushed once or twice before they go on to run the country?

There is good reason to suppose that responsibility has to be installed in the foundation of your mental equipment—at the level of perception and habit. There is an ethic of paying attention that develops in the trades through hard experience. It inflects your perception of the world and your habitual responses to it. This is due to the immediate feedback you get from material objects and to the fact that the work is typically situated in face-to-face interactions between tradesman and customer.

An economy that is more entrepreneurial, less managerial, would be less subject to the kind of distortions that occur when corporate managers' compensation is tied to the short-term profit of distant shareholders. For most entrepreneurs, profit is at once a more capacious and a more concrete thing than this. It is a calculation in which the intrinsic satisfactions of work count—not least, the exercise of your own powers of reason.

Ultimately it is enlightened self-interest, then, not a harangue about humility or public-spiritedness, that will compel us to take a fresh look at the trades. The good life comes in a variety of forms. This variety has become difficult to see; our field of aspiration has narrowed into certain channels. But the current perplexity in the economy seems to softening our gaze. Our peripheral vision is perhaps recovering, allowing us to consider the full range of lives worth choosing. For anyone who feels ill suited by disposition to spend his days sitting in an office, the question of what a good job looks like is now wide open.

Joining the Conversation:
Critical Thinking and Writing

1. In his first paragraph, Crawford writes: "Where the chain of cause and effect is opaque and responsibility diffuse, the experience of individual agency can be elusive." His language here is more abstract than elsewhere in his essay. What does he mean? Reread his first paragraph and then restate his point in your own words.

2. How, according to Crawford, has the economic recession (he was writing in 2009) affected the manual trades and attitudes toward them?

3. Crawford cites as authorities a poet (paragraph 4) and an economist (paragraph 5). In your opinion, do these citations reinforce each other? How do they strengthen his argument? (We include Piercy's poem "To be of use" at the end of this chapter (p. 355).

4. Crawford concludes his essay with brief accounts of his own work experiences (paragraphs 7 and 8). Had you been writing this essay, would you also have used this autobiographical information in your conclusion, or used it instead in your introduction? What experiences of the reader does Crawford refer to in his introduction? Evaluate his choices.

5. In a brief essay (750–1000 words), describe your own work history. Do your experiences support Crawford's argument in "The Case for Working with Your Hands"? If you find it suitable, include your own aspirations for the kind of work you hope to do.

Gabriel Thompson

Gabriel Thompson, a writer based in Brooklyn, New York, has written on a variety of topics, including hedge funds and police shootings, but chiefly he writes about poor people, especially those immigrants who earn low wages. To learn about these people, he has worked in sweatshops and as a lettuce-cutter. We print an essay based on his recent book, Working in the Shadows: A Year of Doing the Jobs That (Most) Americans Won't Do *(2010).*

A Gringo in the Lettuce Fields

I wake up staring into the bluest blue I've ever seen. I must have fallen into a deep sleep because I need several seconds to realize that I'm looking at the Arizona sky, that the pillow beneath my head is a large clump of dirt, and that a near-stranger named Manuel is standing over me, smiling. I pull myself to a sitting position. To my left, in the distance, a Border Patrol helicopter is hovering. To my right is Mexico, separated by only a few fields of lettuce. "*Buenos días*," Manuel says.

I stand up gingerly. It's only my third day in the fields, but already my 30-year-old body is failing me. I feel like someone has dropped a log on my back. And then piled that log onto a truck with many other logs, and driven that truck over my thighs. "Let's go," I say, trying to sound energetic as I fall in line behind Manuel, stumbling across rows of lettuce and thinking about "the five-day rule." The five-day rule, according to Manuel, is simple: Survive the first five days and you'll be fine. He's been a farmworker for almost two decades, so he should know. I'm on day three of five—the goal is within sight. Of course, another way to look at my situation is that I'm on day three of what I promised myself would be a two-month immersion in the work life of the people who do a job that most Americans won't do. But thinking about the next seven weeks doesn't benefit anyone. *Day three of five.*

"Manuel! Gabriel! Let's go! ¡*Vámonos!*" yells Pedro, our foreman. Our short break is over. Two dozen crew members standing near the lettuce machine are already putting on gloves and sharpening knives. Manuel and I hustle toward the machine, grab our own knives from a box of chlorinated water, and set up in neighboring rows, just as the machine starts moving slowly another endless field.

Since the early 1980s, Yuma, Ariz., has been the "winter lettuce capital" of America. Each winter, when the weather turns cold in Salinas, Calif.—the heart of the nation's lettuce industry—temperatures in sunny Yuma are still in the 70s and 80s. At the height of Yuma's growing season, the fields surrounding the city produce virtually all of the iceberg lettuce and 90 percent of the leafy green vegetables consumed in the United States and Canada.

America's lettuce industry actually needs people like me. Before applying for fieldwork at the local Dole headquarters, I came across several articles describing the causes of a farmworker shortage. The stories cited an aging workforce, immigration crackdowns, and long delays at the border that discourage workers with green cards who would otherwise commute to the fields from their Mexican homes. Wages have been rising somewhat in response to the demand for laborers (one prominent member of the local growers association tells me average pay is now between $10 and $12 an hour), but it's widely assumed that most U.S citizens wouldn't do the work at any price. Arizona's own Sen. John McCain created a stir in 2006 when he issued a challenge to a group of union members in Washington, D.C. "I'll offer anybody here $50 an hour if you'll go pick lettuce in Yuma this season, and pick for the whole season," he said. Amid jeers, he didn't back down, telling the audience, "You can't do it, my friends."

On my first day I discover that even putting on a lettuce cutter's uniform is challenging (no fieldworkers, I learn, "pick" lettuce). First, I'm handed a pair of black galoshes to go over my shoes. Next comes the *gancho,* an S-shaped hook that slips over my belt to hold packets of plastic bags. A white glove goes on my right hand, a gray glove, supposedly designed to offer protection from cuts, goes on my left. Over the cloth gloves I pull on a pair of latex gloves. I put on a black hairnet, my baseball cap, and a pair of protective sunglasses. Adding to my belt a long leather sheath, I'm good to go. I feel ridiculous.

The crew is already working in the field when Pedro walks me out to them and introduces me to Manuel. Manuel is holding an 18-inch knife in his hand. "Manuel has been cutting for many years, so watch him to see how it's done," Pedro says. Then he walks away. Manuel resumes cutting, following a machine that rolls along just ahead of the crew. Every several seconds Manuel bends down, grabs a head of iceberg lettuce with his left hand, and makes a quick cut with the knife in his right hand, separating the lettuce from its roots. Next, he lifts the lettuce to his stomach and makes a second cut, trimming the trunk. He shakes the lettuce, letting the outer leaves fall to the ground. With the blade still in his hand, he then brings the lettuce toward the *gancho* at his waist, and with a flick of the wrist the head is bagged and dropped onto one of the machine's extensions. Manuel does this over and over again, explaining each movement. "It's not so hard," he says. Five minutes later, Pedro reappears and tells me to grab a knife. Manuel points to a head of lettuce. "Try this one," he says.

I bend over, noticing that most of the crew has turned to watch. I take my knife and make a tentative sawing motion where I assume the trunk to be, though I'm really just guessing. Grabbing the head with my left hand, I straighten up, doing my best to imitate Manuel. Only my lettuce head doesn't move; it's still securely connected to the soil. Pedro steps in. "When you make the first cut, it is like you are stabbing the lettuce." He makes a quick jabbing action. "You want to aim for the center of the lettuce, where the trunk is," he says.

Ten minutes later, after a couple of other discouraging moments, I've cut maybe 20 heads of lettuce and am already feeling pretty accomplished. I'm not perfect: If I don't stoop far enough, my stab—instead of landing an inch above the ground—goes right through the head of lettuce, ruining it entirely. The greatest difficulty, though, is in the trimming. I had no idea that a head of lettuce was so humongous. In order to get it into a shape that can be bagged, I trim and trim and trim, but it's taking me upward of a minute to do what Manuel does in several seconds.

Pedro offers me a suggestion. "Act like the lettuce is a bomb," he says. "Imagine you've only got five seconds to get rid of it."

Surprisingly, that thought seems to work, and I'm able to greatly increase my speed. For a minute or two I feel euphoric. "Look at me!" I want to shout at Pedro; I'm in the zone. But the woman who is packing the lettuce into boxes soon swivels around to face me. "Look, this lettuce is no good." She's right: I've cut the trunk too high, breaking off dozens of good leaves, which will quickly turn brown because they're attached to nothing. With her left hand she holds the bag up, and with her right she smashes it violently, making a loud pop. She turns the bag over and the massacred lettuce falls to the ground. She does the same for the three other bags I've placed on the extension. "It's okay," Manuel tells me. "You shouldn't try to go too fast when you're beginning." Pedro seconds him. "That's right. Make sure the cuts are precise and that you don't rush."

So I am to be very careful and precise, while also treating the lettuce like a bomb that must be tossed aside after five seconds.

That first week on the job was one thing. By midway into week two, it isn't clear to me what more I can do to keep up with the rest of the crew. I know the techniques by this time and am moving as fast as my body will permit. Yet I need to somehow *double* my current output to hold my own. I'm able to cut only one row at a time while Manuel is cutting two. Our fastest cutter, Julio, meanwhile can handle three. But how someone could cut two rows for an hour—much less an entire day—is beyond me. "Oh, you will get it," Pedro tells me one day. "You will most definitely get it." Maybe he's trying to be hopeful or inspiring, but it comes across as a threat.

That feeling aside, what strikes me about our 31-member crew is how quickly they have welcomed me as one of their own. I encountered some suspicion at first, but it didn't last. Simply showing up on the second day seemed to be proof enough that I was there to work. When I faltered in the field and fell behind, hands would come across from adjacent rows to grab a head or two of my lettuce so I could catch up. People whose names I didn't yet know would ask me how I was holding up, reminding me that it would get easier as time went by. If I took a seat alone during a break, someone would call me into their group and offer a homemade taco or two.

Two months in, I make the mistake of calling in sick one Thursday. The day before, I put my left hand too low on a head of lettuce. When I punched my blade through the stem, the knife struck my middle finger. Thanks to the gloves, my skin wasn't even broken, but the finger instantly turned purple. I took two painkillers to get through the afternoon, but when I wake the next morning it is still throbbing. With one call to an answering machine that morning, and another the next day, I create my own four-day weekend.

The surprise is that when I return on Monday, feeling recuperated, I wind up having the hardest day of my brief career in lettuce. Within hours, my hands feel weaker than ever. By quitting time—some 10 hours after our day started—I feel like I'm going to vomit from exhaustion. A theory forms in my mind. Early in the season—say, after the first week—a farmworker's body gets thoroughly broken down. Back, legs and arms grow sore, hands and feet swell up. A tolerance for the pain is developed, though, and two-day weekends provide just enough time for the body to recover from the trauma. My four-day break had been too long: my body actually began to recuperate, and it wanted more time to continue. Instead, it was thrown right back into the mix and

15

rebelled. Only on my second day back did my body recover that middle ground. "I don't think the soreness goes away," I say to Manuel and two other co-workers one day. "You just forget what it's like not to be sore." Manuel, who's 37, considers this. "That's true, that's true," he says. "It always takes a few weeks at the end of the year to get back to normal, to recover."

An older co-worker, Mateo, is the one who eventually guesses that I have joined the crew because I want to write about it. "That is good," he says over coffee at his home one Sunday. "Americans should know the hard work that Mexicans do in this country."

Mateo is an unusual case. There aren't many other farmworkers who are still in the fields when they reach their 50s. It's simply not possible to do this work for decades and not suffer a permanently hunched back, to crooked fingers, or hands so swollen that they look as if someone has attached a valve to a finger and pumped vigorously. The punishing nature of the work helps explain why farmworkers don't live very long; the National Migrant Resources Program puts their life expectancy at 49 years.

"Are you cutting two rows yet?" Mateo asks me. "Yes more or less," I say. "I thought I'd be better by now." Mateo shakes his head. "It takes a long time to learn how to really cut lettuce. It's not something that you learn after only one season. Three, maybe four seasons—then you start understanding how to really work with lettuce."

 ## Joining the Conversation: Critical Thinking and Writing

1. Why did this "gringo," Gabriel Thompson, become a lettuce-cutter? What does he learn from the experience? What does he want us to learn?

2. How do the other members of his crew regard him? What evidence does he offer? In your view, why does he include their behavior and attitudes in his essay?

3. For the most part, Thompson's essay describes the physical labor of cutting lettuce. Choose a passage that you find striking or memorable and then explain why you like it.

4. Compare Thompson's essay with Crawford's (pp. 338–347). What experiences and values do they seem to share?

5. Compare Thompson's essay with Dorothea Lange's photograph of lettuce-cutters on page 328. What values do Thompson and Lange seem to share?

6. If you have ever, like Thompson, done "a job that most American won't do" (second paragraph), describe, analyze, and evaluate it in an essay of 750–1000 words. (If you haven't done such work, imagine it and then write about it persuasively.)

Zev Chafets

Born in 1947 in Pontiac, Michigan, Zev (or Ze'ev) Chafets was educated at the University of Michigan. In 1967, he moved to Israel, where he served in the army and later was active in government service and in politics. Among his activities was service as a delegate to the first Israel-Egyptian peace negotiations. A resident of Tel Aviv and also of New York, Chafets is the author of a dozen books (fiction, criticism, social and political commentary) and of numerous articles in newspapers throughout the world, including The New York Times, *which in 2009 published the piece that we reprint. For a further development of the material in this essay, consult his recent book,* Cooperstown Confidential: Heroes, Rogues, and the Inside Story of Baseball's Hall of Fame *(2009).*

Let Steroids into the Hall of Fame

When the Baseball Hall of Fame commemorates its 70th anniversary with an exhibition game in Cooperstown, N.Y., on Sunday, five of its members will play on the national field of dreams. At least two of them—Paul Molitor and Ferguson Jenkins—were busted in the 1980s for using cocaine. Molitor later said he sure he wasn't the only player on the team using drugs.

Given what we now know about baseball's drug habit, the remark sounds quaint. This week's report that Sammy Sosa tested positive for performance enhancing drugs in 2003 is only the latest in a long string of revelations. Barry Bonds, Roger Clemens, Alex Rodriguez, Manny Ramirez, Mark McGwire—what great players haven't been linked to drug use?

Since the dawn of baseball, players have used whatever substances they believed would help them perform better, heal faster or relax during a long and stressful season. As far back as 1889, the pitcher Pud Galvin ingested monkey testosterone. During Prohibition, Grover Cleveland Alexander, also a pitcher, calmed his nerves with federally banned alcohol, and no less an expert than Bill Veeck, who owned several major-league teams, said that Alexander was a better pitcher drunk than sober.

In 1961, during his home run race with Roger Maris, Mickey Mantle developed a sudden abscess that kept him on the bench. It came from an infected needle used by Max Jacobson, a quack who injected Mantle with a home-brew containing steroids and speed. In his autobiography, Hank Aaron admitted once taking an amphetamine tablet during a game. The Pirates' John Milner testified at a drug dealer's trial that his teammate, Willie Mays, kept "red juice," a liquid form of speed, in his locker. (Mays denied it.) After he retired, Sandy Koufax admitted the he was often "half high" on the mound from the drugs he took for his ailing left arm.

For decades, baseball beat writers—the Hall of Fame's designated electoral college—shielded the players from scrutiny. When the Internet (and exposés by two former ballplayers, Jim Bouton and Jose Canseco)

5

allowed fans to see what was really happening, the baseball writers were revealed as dupes or stooges. In a rage, they formed a posse to drive the drug users out of the game.

But today's superstars have lawyers and a union. They know how to use the news media. And they have plenty of money. The only way to punish them is to deny them a place in Cooperstown. The punishment has already been visited on Mark McGwire, and many more are on deck.

This makes no sense. On any given day, the stands are packed with youngsters on Adderall and Ritalin (stimulants used to treat attention deficit hyperactivity disorder) and college students who use Provigil (an anti-narcolepsy drug) as a study aid. The guy who sings the national anthem has probably taken a beta blocker to calm his stage fright. Like it or not, chemical enhancement is here to stay. And it is as much a part of the national game as $5.50 hot dogs, free agency and Tommy John elbow surgery.

Purists say that steroids alter the game. But since the hall opened its doors, baseball has never stopped changing. Batters now wear body padding and helmets. The pitcher's mound has risen and fallen. Bats have more pop. Night games affect visibility. Players stay in shape in the off-season. Expansion has altered the game's geography. And its demography has changed beyond recognition. Babe Ruth never faced a black pitcher. As Chris Rock put it, Ruth's record consisted of "714 affirmative-action home runs." This doesn't diminish Ruth's accomplishment, but it puts it into context.

Statistics change, too. In 1908, Ed Walsh pitched 464 innings; in 2008, C.C. Sabathia led the majors with 253. So what? They were both first under the prevailing conditions of the time.

Despite these changes, or because of them, Americans continue to love baseball. Fans will accept anything except the sense that they are being lied to. Chemical enhancement won't kill the game; it is the cover-up that could be fatal.

Baseball, led by the Hall of Fame, needs to accept this and replace mythology and spin with realism and honesty. If everyone has access to the same drugs and training methods, and the fans are told what these are, then the field is level and fans will be able to interpret what they are seeing on the diamond and in the box scores.

The purists' last argument is that players' use of performance-enhancing drugs sets a bad example for young athletes. But baseball players aren't children; they are adults in a very stressful and competitive profession. If they want to use anabolic steroids, or human growth hormone or bull's testosterone, it should be up to them. As for children, the government can regulate their use of these substances as they do with tobacco, alcohol and prescription medicine.

The Baseball Hall of Fame, which started as a local tourist attraction and a major-league publicity stunt, has since become a national field of dreams—and now, a battlefield. If it surrenders to the moralists who want to turn back the clock to some imagined golden era, and excommunicates the greatest stars anyone has ever seen, it will suffer the fate of all battlefields located on the wrong side of history. Obscurity.

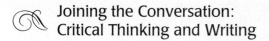

Joining the Conversation: Critical Thinking and Writing

1. As we see it, Chafets's first argument is that baseball players have always "used whatever substances they believed would help them perform better," so there is no point now in saying that those who use steroids should be denied—on that basis alone—entry into the Hall of Fame. First, evaluate this argument and then summarize each additional argument that Chafets offers.

2. You have made a list of Chafets's arguments. Which is his strongest argument? His weakest? Has he convinced you? Why or why not?

3. Evaluate Chafets's final paragraph as a piece of writing. For example, notice that he uses the phrase "a national field of dreams" and then, picking up "field," he speaks of "a battlefield," then he moves to the word "surrender," and then again to "battlefields." Notice that his final sentence also consists of only one word. Do you find these rhetorical devices effective—something you may want to incorporate into your own writing? Try to imitate Chafets's techniques in a revision of an essay you have written or one you are about to write.

Marge Piercy

Marge Piercy, born in Detroit in 1936, was the first member of her family to attend college. After earning a bachelor's degree from the University of Michigan in 1957 and a master's degree from Northwestern University in 1958, she moved to Chicago. There, she worked at odd jobs while writing novels (unpublished) and engaging in action on behalf of women and blacks and against the Vietnam War. In 1970—the year she moved to Wellfleet, Massachusetts, where she still lives— she published her first book, a novel. Since then, she has published many novels as well as short stories, poems, and essays.

To be of use

The people I love the best
jump into work head first
without dallying in the shallows
and swim off with sure strokes almost out of sight.
They seem to become natives of that element,   5
the black sleek heads of seals
bouncing like half-submerged balls.

I love people who harness themselves, an ox to a heavy cart,
who pull like water buffalo, with massive patience,
who strain in the mud and the muck to move things forward,   10
who do what has to be done, again and again.

I want to be with people who submerge
In the task, who go into the fields to harvest
and work in a row and pass the bags along,
who are not parlor generals and field deserters
but move in a common rhythm
when the food must come in or the fire be put out.

The work of the world is common as mud.
Botched, it smears the hands, crumbles to dust.
But the thing worth doing well done
has a shape that satisfies, clean and evident.
Greek amphoras for wine or oil,
Hopi vases that held corn, are put in museums
but you know they were made to be used.
The pitcher cries for water to carry
and a person for work that is real.

[197

 ## Joining the Conversation:
Critical Thinking and Writing

1. "To be of use" is a poem, but we read it also as an argument. If you agree, in a sentence or two, paraphrase (restate) the argument the poem offers.

2. The first stanza presents an image of seals; the second of oxen and water buffalo. Why does the speaker "love people" who resemble these animals? What characteristics of work does she here celebrate?

3. In the third stanza, what actions of people working remind us of the images in the first two stanzas?

4. In the last stanza, to what does the speaker compare workers? How does the title of the poem prepare us for this comparison?

CHAPTER 10

Messages

358

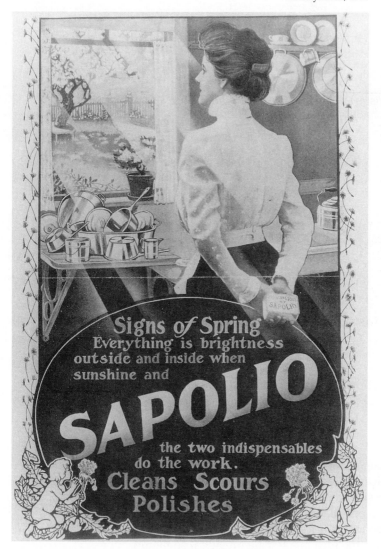

Short Views

Men . . . employ speech only to conceal their thoughts.
     Voltaire

We must be as clear as our natural reticence allows us to be.
     Marianne Moore

To change your language you must change your life.
     Derek Walcott

I personally think we developed language because of our deep inner need to complain.
     Jane Wagner

If you saw a bullet hit a bird, and he told you he wasn't shot, you might weep at his courtesy, but you would certainly doubt his word.
     Emily Dickinson

Sticks and stones may break my bones, but words will never hurt me.
     Anonymous

Language both reflects and shapes society. The textbook on American government that consistently uses male pronouns for the president, even when not referring to a specific individual (e.g., "a president may cast his veto"), reflects the fact that all our presidents have so far been men. But it also shapes a society in which the idea of a female president somehow "doesn't sound right."
     Rosalie Maggio

It is no insult to the recent, but already cherished, institution of the blogosphere to say that blogs cannot do everything well. Right now, and for the foreseeable future, the blogosphere is the friend of information but the enemy of thought.
     Alan Jacobs

Abraham Lincoln

Abraham Lincoln (1809–1865), sixteenth president of the United States, is not usually thought of as a writer, but his published speeches and writings comprise about 1,078,000 words, the equivalent of about four thousand pages of double-spaced typing. They were all composed without the assistance of a speech writer.

The Gettysburg campaign—a series of battles fought near Gettysburg in southeastern Pennsylvania—took place in June and July 1863. Each side lost something like 23,000 men. The battle is regarded as a turning point in the Civil War, but the Confederate army escaped and the war continued until April 1865.

On November 19, 1863, Lincoln delivered a short speech (printed below) at the dedication of a national cemetery on the battlefield at Gettysburg.

Address at the Dedication of the Gettysburg National Cemetery

Four score and seven years ago our fathers brought forth on this continent, a new nation, conceived in Liberty, and dedicated to the proposition that all men are created equal.

Now we are engaged in a great civil war; testing whether that nation, or any nation so conceived and so dedicated, can long endure. We are met on a great battlefield of that war. We have come to dedicate a portion of that field as a final resting-place for those who here gave their lives that that nation might live. It is altogether fitting and proper that we should do this.

But, in a larger sense, we cannot dedicate—we cannot consecrate—we cannot hallow—this ground. The brave men, living and dead, who struggled here have consecrated it, far above our poor power to add or detract. The world will little note, nor long remember, what we say here, but it can never forget what they did here. It is for us the living, rather, to be dedicated here to the unfinished work which they who fought here have thus far so nobly advanced. It is rather for us to be here dedicated to the great task remaining before us—that from these honored dead we take increased devotion to that cause for which they gave the last full measure of devotion; that we here highly resolve that these dead shall not have died in vain; that this nation, under God, shall have a new birth of freedom; and that government of the people, by the people, for the people, shall not perish from the earth.

Gilbert Highet

Gilbert Highet (1906–1978) was born in Glasgow, Scotland, and was educated at Glasgow University and at Oxford University. In 1937, he came to the United States, and in 1951, he was naturalized. Until his retirement in 1972, he taught Latin, Greek, and comparative literature at Columbia University. In addition to writing scholarly studies of classical authors, he wrote several general and more popular books.

The Gettysburg Address

Four score and seven years ago. . . .

These five words stand at the entrance to the best-known monument of American prose, one of the finest utterances in the entire language, and surely one of the greatest speeches in all history. Greatness is like granite: it is molded in fire, and it lasts for many centuries.

Fourscore and seven years ago. . . . It is strange to think that President Lincoln was looking back to the 4th of July 1776, and that he and his speech are now further removed from us than he himself was from George Washington and the Declaration of Independence. Fourscore and seven years before the Gettysburg Address, a small group of patriots signed the Declaration. Fourscore and seven years after the Gettysburg Address, it was the year 1950, and that date is already receding rapidly into our troubled, adventurous, and valiant past.

Inadequately prepared and at first scarcely realized in its full importance, the dedication of the graveyard at Gettysburg was one of the supreme moments of American history. The battle itself had been a turning point of the war. On the 4th of July 1863, General Meade repelled Lee's invasion of Pennsylvania. Although he did not follow up his victory, he had broken one of the most formidable aggressive enterprises of the Confederate armies. Losses were heavy on both sides. Thousands of dead were left on the field, and thousands of wounded died in the hot days following the battle. At first, their burial was more or less haphazard; but thoughtful men gradually came to feel that an adequate burying place and memorial were required. These were established by an interstate commission that autumn, and the finest speaker in the North was invited to dedicate them. This was the scholar and statesman Edward Everett of Harvard. He made a good speech—which is still extant: not at all academic, it is full of close strategic analysis and deep historical understanding.

Lincoln was not invited to speak, at first. Although people knew him as an effective debater, they were not sure whether he was capable of making a serious speech on such a solemn occasion. But one of the impressive   5 things about Lincoln's career is that he constantly strove to *grow*. He was anxious to appear on that occasion and to say something worthy of it. (Also, it has been suggested, he was anxious to remove the impression that he did not know how to behave properly—an impression which had been strengthened by a shocking story about his clowning on the battlefield of Antietam the previous year.) Therefore when he was invited he took considerable care with his speech. He drafted rather more than half of it in the White House before leaving, finished it in the hotel at Gettysburg the night before the ceremony (not in the train, as sometimes reported), and wrote a fair copy next morning.

There are many accounts of the day itself, 19 November 1863. There are many descriptions of Lincoln, all showing the same curious blend of grandeur and awkwardness, or lack of dignity, or—it would be best to call it humility. In the procession he rode horseback: a tall lean man in a high plug hat, straddling a short horse, with his feet too near the ground. He arrived before the chief speaker, and had to wait patiently for half an hour or more. His own speech came right at the end of a long and exhausting ceremony, lasted less than three minutes, and made little impression on the audience. In part this was because they were tired, in part because (as eyewitnesses said) he ended almost before they knew he had begun, and in part because he did not speak the Address, but read it, very slowly, in a thin high voice, with a marked Kentucky accent, pronouncing "to" as "toe" and dropping his final R's.

Some people of course were alert enough to be impressed. Everett congratulated him at once. But most of the newspapers paid little attention to the speech, and some sneered at it. The *Patriot and Union* of Harrisburg wrote, "We pass over the silly remarks of the President; for the credit of the nation we are willing . . . that they shall no more be repeated or thought of"; and the London *Times* said, "The ceremony was rendered ludicrous by some of the sallies of that poor President Lincoln," calling his remarks "dull and commonplace." The first commendation of the Address came in a single sentence of the Chicago *Tribune*, and the first discriminating and detailed praise of it appeared in the Springfield *Republican*, the Providence *Journal*, and the Philadelphia *Bulletin*. However, three weeks after the ceremony and then again the following spring, the editor of *Harper's Weekly* published a sincere and thorough eulogy of the Address, and soon it was attaining recognition as a masterpiece.

At the time, Lincoln could not care much about the reception of his words. He was exhausted and ill. In the train back to Washington, he lay down with a wet towel on his head. He had caught smallpox. At that moment he was incubating it, and he was stricken down soon after he reentered the White House. Fortunately it was a mild attack, and it evoked one of his best jokes: he told his visitors, "At last I have something I can give to everybody."

He had more than that to give to everybody. He was a unique person, far greater than most people realize until they read his life with care. The wisdom of his policy, the sources of his statesmanship—these were things too complex to be discussed in a brief essay. But we can say something about the Gettysburg Address as a work of art.[1]

A work of art. Yes: for Lincoln was a literary artist, trained both by   10
others and by himself. The textbooks he used as a boy were full of difficult exercises and skillful devices in formal rhetoric, stressing the qualities he practiced in his own speaking: antithesis, parallelism, and verbal harmony. Then he read and reread many admirable models of thought and expression: the King James Bible, the essays of Bacon, the best plays of Shakespeare. His favorites were *Hamlet, Lear, Macbeth, Richard III*, and *Henry VIII*, which he had read dozens of times. He loved reading aloud, too, and spent hours reading poetry to his friends. (He told his partner Herndon that he preferred getting the sense of any document by reading it aloud.) Therefore his serious speeches are important parts of the long and noble classical tradition of oratory which begins in Greece, runs through Rome to the modern world, and is still capable (if we do not neglect it) of producing masterpieces.

The first proof of this is that the Gettysburg Address is full of quotations—or rather of adaptations—which give it strength. It is partly religious, partly (in the highest sense) political: therefore it is interwoven with memories of the Bible and memories of American history. The first and the last words are Biblical cadences. Normally Lincoln did not say "fourscore" when he meant eighty; but on this solemn occasion he recalled the important dates in the Bible—such as the age of Abraham when his first son was born to him, and he was "fourscore and six years old." Similarly, he did not say there was a chance that democracy might die out: he recalled the somber phrasing in the Book of Job—where Bildad speaks of the destruction of one who shall vanish without a trace, and says that "his branch shall be cut off; his remembrance shall perish from the earth." Then again, the famous description of our State as "government of the people, by the people, for the people" was adumbrated by Daniel Webster in 1830 (he spoke of "the people's government, made for the people, made by the people, and answerable to the people") and then elaborated in 1854 by the abolitionist Theodore Parker (as "government of all the people, by all the people, for all the people"). There is good reason to think that Lincoln took the important phrase "under God" (which he interpolated at the last moment) from Weems, the biographer of Washington; and we know that it had been used at least once by Washington himself.

Analyzing the Address further, we find that it is based on a highly imaginative theme, or group of themes. The subject is—how can we put it

---

[1]For further reference, see W. E. Barton, *Lincoln at Gettysburg* (Indianapolis: Bobbs-Merrill, 1930); R. P. Basler, "Abraham Lincoln's Rhetoric." *American Literature* 11 (1939–1940), 167–182; and L. E. Robinson, *Abraham Lincoln as a Man of Letters* (Chicago, 1918).

so as not to disfigure it?—the subject is the kinship of life and death, that mysterious linkage which we see sometimes as the physical succession of birth and death in our world, sometimes as the contrast, which is perhaps a unity, between death and immortality. The first sentence is concerned with birth:

Our *fathers brought forth a new* nation, *conceived* in liberty.

The final phrase but one expresses the hope that

this nation, under God, shall have a *new birth* of freedom.

And that last phrase of all speaks of continuing life as the triumph over death. Again and again throughout the speech, this mystical contrast and kinship reappear: "those who *gave their lives* that that nation might *live*," "the brave men *living and dead*," and so in the central assertion that the dead have already consecrated their own burial place, while "it is for us, the *living*, rather to be dedicated . . . to the great task remaining." The Gettysburg Address is a prose poem; it belongs to the same world as the great elegies, and the adagios of Beethoven.

Its structure, however, is that of a skillfully contrived speech. The oratorical pattern is perfectly clear. Lincoln describes the occasion, dedicates the ground, and then draws a larger conclusion by calling on his hearers to dedicate themselves to the preservation of the Union. But within that, we can trace his constant use of at least two important rhetorical devices.

The first of these is *antithesis*: opposition, contrast. The speech is full   15
of it. Listen:

The world will little	*note*		
nor long	*remember*	what	*we say* here
but it can never	*forget*	what	*they did* here

And so in nearly every sentence: "brave men, *living* and *dead*"; "to *add* or *detract*." There is the antithesis of the Founding Fathers and men of Lincoln's own time:

Our *fathers brought forth* a new nation . . .

now *we* are testing whether that nation . . . can *long endure*.

And there is the more terrible antithesis of those who have already died and those who still live to do their duty. Now, antithesis is the figure of contrast and conflict. Lincoln was speaking in the midst of a great civil war.

The other important pattern is different. It is technically called *tricolon*—the division of an idea into three harmonious parts, usually of increasing power. The most famous phrase of the Address is a tricolon:

> government of the people
>   by the people
>   for the people.

The most solemn sentence is a tricolon:

> we cannot dedicate
> we cannot consecrate
> we cannot hallow   this ground.

And above all, the last sentence (which has sometimes been criticized as too complex) is essentially two parallel phrases, with a tricolon growing out of the second and then producing another tricolon: a trunk, three branches, and a cluster of flowers. Lincoln says that it is for his hearers to be dedicated to the great task remaining before them. Then he goes on.

> that from these honored dead

—apparently he means "in such a way that from these honored dead"—

> we take increased devotion to that cause.

Next, he restates this more briefly:

> that we here highly resolve . . .

And now the actual resolution follows, in three parts of growing intensity:

> that these dead shall not have died in vain

> that this nation, under God, shall have a new birth of freedom

and that (one more tricolon)

> government of the people
>   by the people
>   for the people
> shall not perish from the earth.

Now, the tricolon is the figure which, through division, emphasizes basic harmony and unity. Lincoln used antithesis because he was speaking to a people at war. He used the tricolon because he was hoping, planning, praying for peace.

No one thinks that when he was drafting the Gettysburg Address, 25 Lincoln deliberately looked up these quotations and consciously chose these particular patterns of thought. No, he chose the theme. From its development and from the emotional tone of the entire occasion, all the rest followed, or grew—by that marvelous process of choice and rejection which is essential to artistic creation. It does not spoil such a work of art to analyze it as closely as we have done; it is altogether fitting and proper that we should do this: for it helps us to penetrate more deeply into the rich meaning of the Gettysburg Address, and it allows us the very rare privilege of watching the workings of a great man's mind.

Joining the Conversation: Critical Thinking and Writing

1. At the start of his essay, after quoting the opening words of Lincoln's speech, Highet uses a metaphor and a simile: He says that the words "stand at the entrance to the best-known monument" and that "greatness is like granite: it is molded in fire, and it lasts for many centuries." Are these figures of speech effective? Why or why not? How are the two figures related to each other?

2. Analyze the structure of Highet's essay.

3. This essay was a talk given on the radio, presumably to a large general public. Find passages in the essay that suggest oral delivery to an unspecialized audience. How would you describe Highet's tone?

4. It has been suggested that "government of the people, by the people" is redundant; a government *of* the people, it is argued, must be the same as a government *by* the people. Did Lincoln repeat himself merely to get a triad: "of the people, by the people, for the people"? If so, is this a fault? Or can it be argued that "government of the people" really means "government over the people"? If so, what does the entire expression mean?

5. Highet claims that Lincoln was not only a great statesman but also a literary artist. According to Highet, what was Lincoln's training as a literary artist? Highet implies that such training is still available. To what extent has it been available to you? Traditionally, studying "admirable models of thought and expression," including poetry, was an important part of writing instruction, but it is less common now. Should such study be included in writing courses? Why or why not?

6. In paragraph 11, Highet points out that "the Gettysburg Address is full of quotations—or rather of adaptations," and he analyzes several examples of Lincoln's adaptations of sources. How is such adaptation different from plagiarism? Or is it?

Robin Lakoff

Robin Lakoff was born in 1943 and educated at Radcliffe College and Harvard University. A professor of linguistics at the University of California at Berkeley, she has been especially interested in the language that women use. The essay that we give here was first published in Ms. magazine in 1974.

You Are What You Say

Women's language is that pleasant (dainty?), euphemistic never-aggressive way of talking we learned as little girls. Cultural bias was built into the language we were allowed to speak, the subjects we were allowed to speak about, and the ways we were spoken of. Having learned our linguistic lesson well, we go out in the world, only to discover that we are communicative cripples—damned if we do, and damned if we don't.

If we refuse to talk "like a lady," we are ridiculed and criticized for being unfeminine. ("She thinks like a man" is, at best, a left-handed compliment.) If we do learn all the fuzzy-headed, unassertive language of our sex, we are ridiculed for being unable to think clearly, unable to take part in a serious discussion, and therefore unfit to hold a position of power.

It doesn't take much of this for a woman to begin feeling she deserves such treatment because of inadequacies in her own intelligence and education.

"Women's language" shows up in all levels of English. For example, women are encouraged and allowed to make far more precise discriminations in naming colors than men do. Words like *mauve, beige, ecru, aquamarine, lavender,* and so on, are unremarkable in a woman's active vocabulary, but largely absent from that of most men. I know of no evidence suggesting that women actually *see* a wider range of colors than men do. It is simply that fine discriminations of this sort are relevant to women's vocabularies, but not to men's; to men, who control most of the interesting affairs of the world, such distinctions are trivial—irrelevant.

In the area of syntax, we find similar gender-related peculiarities of speech. There is one construction, in particular, that women use conversationally far more than men: the tag question. A tag is midway between an outright statement and a yes-no question; it is less assertive than the former, but more confident than the latter.   5

A *flat statement* indicates confidence in the speaker's knowledge and is fairly certain to be believed; a *question* indicates a lack of knowledge on some point and implies that the gap in the speaker's knowledge can and

Robin Lakoff: "You Are What You Say" from *Ms.*, July 1974. Reprinted by permission of the author.

will be remedied by an answer. For example, if, at a Little League game, I have had my glasses off, I can legitimately ask someone else: "Was the player out at third?" A *tag question*, being intermediate between statement and question, is used when the speaker is stating a claim, but lacks full confidence in the truth of that claim. So if I say, "Is Joan here?" I will probably not be surprised if my respondent answers "no"; but if I say, "Joan is here, isn't she?" instead, chances are I am already biased in favor of a positive answer, wanting only confirmation. I still want a response, but I have enough knowledge (or think I have) to predict that response. A tag question, then, might be thought of as a statement that doesn't demand to be believed by anyone but the speaker, a way of giving leeway, of not forcing the addressee to go along with the views of the speaker.

Another common use of the tag question is in small talk when the speaker is trying to elicit conversation: "Sure is hot here, isn't it?"

But in discussing personal feelings or opinions, only the speaker normally has any way of knowing the correct answer. Sentences such as "I have a headache, don't I?" are clearly ridiculous. But there are other examples where it is the speaker's opinions, rather than perceptions, for which corroboration is sought, as in "The situation in Southeast Asia is terrible, isn't it?"

While there are, of course, other possible interpretations of a sentence like this, one possibility is that the speaker has a particular answer in mind—"yes" or "no"—but is reluctant to state it baldly. This sort of tag question is much more apt to be used by women than by men in conversation. Why is this the case?

The tag question allows a speaker to avoid commitment, and thereby 10 avoid conflict with the addressee. The problem is that, by so doing, speakers may also give the impression of not really being sure of themselves, or looking to the addressee for confirmation of their views. This uncertainty is reinforced in more subliminal ways, too. There is a peculiar sentence-intonation pattern, used almost exclusively by women, as far as I know, which changes a declarative answer into a question. The effect of using the rising inflection typical of a yes-no question is to imply that the speaker is seeking confirmation, even though the speaker is clearly the only one who has the requisite information, which is why the question was put to her in the first place:

(Q) When will dinner be ready?
(A) Oh . . . around six o'clock . . . ?

It is as though the second speaker was saying, "Six o'clock—if that's okay with you, if you agree." The person being addressed is put in the position of having to provide confirmation. One likely consequence of this sort of speech pattern in a woman is that, often unbeknownst to herself, the speaker builds a reputation of tentativeness, and others will refrain from taking her seriously or trusting her with any real responsibilities, since she "can't make up her mind," and "isn't sure of herself."

Such idiosyncrasies may explain why women's language sounds much more "polite" than men's. It is polite to leave a decision open, not impose your mind, or views, or claims, on anyone else. So a tag question is a kind of polite statement, in that it does not force agreement or belief on the addressee. In the same way a request is a polite command, in that it does not force obedience on the addressee, but rather suggests something be done as a favor to the speaker. A clearly stated order implies a threat of certain consequences if it is not followed, and—even more impolite—implies that the speaker is in a superior position and able to enforce the order. By couching wishes in the form of a request, on the other hand, a speaker implies that if the request is not carried out, only the speaker will suffer; non-compliance cannot harm the addressee. So the decision is really left up to the addressee. The distinction becomes clear in these examples:

Close the door.

Please close the door.

Will you close the door?

Will you please close the door?

Won't you close the door?

In the same ways as words and speech patterns used *by* women undermine their image, those used to *describe* women make matters even worse. Often a word may be used of both men and women (and perhaps of things as well); but when it is applied to women, it assumes a special meaning that, by implication rather than outright assertion, is derogatory to women as a group.

The use of euphemisms has this effect. A euphemism is a substitute for a word that has acquired a bad connotation by association with something unpleasant or embarrassing. But almost as soon as the new word comes into common usage, it takes on the same old bad connotations, since feelings about the things or people referred to are not altered by a change of name; thus new euphemisms must be constantly found.

There is one euphemism for *woman* still very much alive. The word, of course, is *lady*. *Lady* has a masculine counterpart, namely *gentleman*, occasionally shortened to *gent*. But for some reason *lady* is very much commoner than *gent(leman)*.

The decision to use *lady* rather than *woman*, or vice versa, may considerably alter the sense of a sentence, as the following examples show:

a. A woman (lady) I know is a dean at Berkeley.
b. A woman (lady) I know makes amazing things out of shoelaces and old boxes.

The use of *lady* in (a) imparts a frivolous, or nonserious, tone to the sentence: the matter under discussion is not one of great moment. Similarly, in (b), using *lady* here would suggest that the speaker considered the "amazing things" not to be serious art, but merely a hobby or an aberration. If *woman* is used, she might be a serious sculptor. To say *lady doctor* is very condescending, since no one ever says *gentleman doctor* or even *man doctor*. For example, mention in the San Francisco *Chronicle* of January 31, 1972, of Madalyn Murray O'Hair as the *lady atheist* reduces her position to that of scatterbrained eccentric. Even *woman atheist* is scarcely defensible: sex is irrelevant to her philosophical position.

Many women argue that, on the other hand, *lady* carries with it overtones recalling the age of chivalry: conferring exalted stature on the person so referred to. This makes the term seem polite at first, but we must also remember that these implications are perilous: they suggest that a "lady" is helpless, and cannot do things by herself.

Lady can also be used to infer frivolousness, as in titles of organizations. Those that have a serious purpose (not merely that of enabling "the ladies" to spend time with one another) cannot use the word *lady* in their titles, but less serious ones may. Compare the *Ladies' Auxiliary* of a men's group, or the *Thursday Evening Ladies' Browning and Garden Society* with *Ladies' Liberation* or *Ladies' Strike for Peace*.

What is curious about this split is that *lady* is in origin a euphemism—a substitute that puts a better face on something people find uncomfortable—for *woman*. What kind of euphemism is it that subtly denigrates the people to whom it refers? Perhaps *lady* functions as a euphemism for *woman* because it does not contain the sexual implications present in *woman*: it is not "embarrassing" in that way. If this is so, we may expect that, in the future, *lady* will replace woman as the primary word for the human female, since *woman* will have become too blatantly sexual. That this distinction is already made in some contexts at least is shown in the following examples, where you can try replacing *woman* with *lady*: 20

a. She's only twelve, but she's already a woman.
b. After ten years in jail, Harry wanted to find a woman.
c. She's my woman, see, so don't mess around with her.

Another common substitute for *woman* is *girl*. One seldom hears a man past the age of adolescence referred to as a boy, save in expressions like "going out with the boys," which are meant to suggest an air of adolescent frivolity and irresponsibility. But women of all ages are "girls": one can have a man—not a boy—Friday, but only a girl—never a woman or even a lady—Friday; women have girlfriends, but men do not—in a nonsexual sense—have boyfriends. It may be that this use of *girl* is euphemistic in the same way the use of *lady* is: in stressing the idea of immaturity, it removes the sexual connotations lurking in *woman*. *Girl* brings to mind irresponsibility: you don't send a girl to do a woman's errand (or even, for that matter, a boy's errand). She is a person who is both too immature and too far from real life to be entrusted with responsibilities or with decisions of any serious or important nature.

Now let's take a pair of words which, in terms of the possible relationships in an earlier society, were simple male-female equivalents, analogous to *bull: cow*. Suppose we find that, for independent reasons, society has changed in such a way that the original meanings now are irrelevant. Yet the words have not been discarded, but have acquired new meanings, metaphorically related to their original senses. But suppose these new metaphorical uses are no longer parallel to each other. By seeing where the parallelism breaks down, we discover something about the different roles played by men and women in this culture. One good example of such a divergence through time is found in the pair, *master: mistress*. Once used with reference to one's power over servants, these words have become unusable today in their original master-servant sense as the relationship has become less prevalent in our society. But the words are still common.

Unless used with reference to animals, *master* now generally refers to a man who has acquired consummate ability in some field, normally nonsexual. But its feminine counterpart cannot be used this way. It is practically restricted to its sexual sense of "paramour." We start out with two terms, both roughly paraphrasable as "one who has power over another." But the masculine form, once one person is no longer able to have absolute power over another, becomes usable metaphorically in the sense of "having power over *something*." *Master* requires as its object only the name of some activity, something inanimate and abstract. But *mistress* requires a masculine noun in the possessive to precede it. One cannot say: "Rhonda is a mistress." One must be *someone's* mistress. A man is defined by what he does, a woman by her sexuality, that is, in terms of one particular aspect of her relationship to men. It is one thing to be an *old master* like Hans Holbein,[1] and another to be an *old mistress*.

The same is true of the words *spinster* and *bachelor*—gender words for "one who is not married." The resemblance ends with the definition. While *bachelor* is a neuter term, often used as a compliment, *spinster* normally is used pejoratively, with connotations of prissiness, fussiness, and so on. To be a bachelor implies that one has a choice of marrying or not, and this is what makes the idea of a bachelor existence attractive, in the popular literature. He has been pursued and has successfully eluded his pursuers. But a spinster is one who has not been pursued, or at least not seriously. She is old, unwanted goods. The metaphorical connotations of *bachelor* generally suggest sexual freedom; of *spinster*, puritanism or celibacy.

These examples could be multiplied. It is generally considered a *faux pas*, in society, to congratulate a woman on her engagement, while it is correct to congratulate her fiancé. Why is this? The reason seems to be that it is impolite to remind people of things that may be uncomfortable to them. To congratulate a woman on her engagement is really to say, "Thank goodness! You had a close call!" For the man, on the other hand,

[1]German painter of the sixteenth century.

there was no such danger. His choosing to marry is viewed as a good thing, but not something essential.

The linguistic double standard holds throughout the life of the relationship. After marriage, bachelor and spinster become man and wife, not man and woman. The woman whose husband dies remains "John's widow"; John, however, is never "Mary's widower."

Finally, why is it that salesclerks and others are so quick to call women customers "dear," "honey," and other terms of endearment they really have no business using? A male customer would never put up with it. But women, like children, are supposed to enjoy these endearments, rather than being offended by them.

In more ways than one, it's time to speak up.

 ## Joining the Conversation: Critical Thinking and Writing

1. Lakoff's first example of "women's language" (paragraph 4) has to do with colors. She says that women are more likely than men to use such words as *mauve, beige,* and *lavender*—not because women see a wider range of colors but because men, "who control most of the interesting affairs of the world," regard distinctions of color as trivial and presumably leave them to the women. How adequate does this explanation seem to you?

2. For a day or so, try to notice if Lakoff's suggestion is correct that women are more inclined than men to use "tag questions" and to use a "rising inflection" with a declarative sentence. Jot down examples you hear, and write an essay of about 500 words, either supporting or refuting Lakoff's suggestion.

3. While you are eavesdropping, you might also notice whether in mixed company women talk more than men. Many men assume that "women talk a lot," but is it true? For example, if you spend an evening with an adult male and female couple, try to form an impression about which of the two does more of the talking. Of course, this is too small a sample to allow for a generalization; still, it is worth thinking about. If you are at a meeting—perhaps a meeting of a committee with men and women—again try to see whether the males or the females do most of the talking. Try also to see whether one sex interrupts the other more often than the other way around. And try to make some sense out of your findings.

4. In paragraph 12, Lakoff says, "Women's language sounds much more 'polite' than men's," and she implies that this politeness is a way of seeming weak. Do you associate politeness with weakness?

5. The essay originally appeared in *Ms.*, a feminist magazine, rather than in an academic journal devoted to language or to sociology. Why do you suppose Lakoff chose *Ms.*? What would you say her purpose was in writing and publishing the essay?

6. This essay was first published in 1974. Do you think it is dated? You might begin by asking yourself if women today use "women's language."

Edward T. Hall

Edward T. Hall, (1914–2009) was for many years a professor of anthropology at Northwestern University.

Hall was especially concerned with "proxemics," a word derived from the Latin proximus, "nearest." Proxemics is the study of people's responses to spatial relationships—for example, their ways of marking out their territory in public places and their responses to what they consider to be crowding. In these pages from his book The Hidden Dimension *(1966), Hall suggests that Arabs and Westerners must understand the proxemic customs of each other's culture; without such understanding, other communications between them are likely to be misunderstood.*

Proxemics in the Arab World

In spite of over two thousand years of contact, Westerners and Arabs still do not understand each other. Proxemic research reveals some insights into this difficulty. Americans in the Middle East are immediately struck by two conflicting sensations. In public they are compressed and overwhelmed by smells, crowding, and high noise levels; in Arab homes Americans are apt to rattle around, feeling exposed and often somewhat inadequate because of too much space! (The Arab houses and apartments of the middle and upper classes which Americans stationed abroad commonly occupy are much larger than the dwellings such Americans usually inhabit.) Both the high sensory stimulation which is experienced in public places and the basic insecurity which comes from being in a dwelling that is too large provide Americans with an introduction to the sensory world of the Arab.

Behavior in Public

Pushing and shoving in public places is characteristic of Middle Eastern culture. Yet it is not entirely what Americans think it is (being pushy and rude) but stems from a different set of assumptions concerning not only the relations between people but how one experiences the body as well. Paradoxically, Arabs consider northern Europeans and Americans pushy, too. This was very puzzling to me when I started investigating these two views. How could Americans who stand aside and avoid touching be considered pushy? I used to ask Arabs to explain this paradox. None of my subjects was able to tell me specifically what particulars of American behavior were responsible, yet they all agreed that the impression was widespread among Arabs. After repeated unsuccessful attempts to gain insight into the cognitive world of the Arab on this particular point, I filed it away as a question that only time would answer. When the answer came, it was because of a seemingly inconsequential annoyance.

While waiting for a friend in a Washington, D.C., hotel lobby and wanting to be both visible and alone, I had seated myself in a solitary chair outside the normal stream of traffic. In such a setting most Americans follow a rule, which is all the more binding because we seldom think about it, that can be stated as follows: as soon as a person stops or is seated in a public place, there balloons around him a small sphere of privacy which is considered inviolate. The size of the sphere varies with the degree of crowding, the age, sex, and the importance of the person, as well as the general surroundings. Anyone who enters this zone and stays there is intruding. In fact, a stranger who intrudes, even for a specific purpose, acknowledges the fact that he has intruded by beginning his request with "Pardon me, but can you tell me. . . ?"

To continue, as I waited in the deserted lobby, a stranger walked up to where I was sitting and stood close enough so that not only could I easily touch him but I could even hear him breathing. In addition, the dark mass of his body filled the peripheral field of vision on my left side. If the lobby had been crowded with people, I would have understood his behavior, but in an empty lobby his presence made me exceedingly uncomfortable. Feeling annoyed by this intrusion, I moved my body in such a way as to communicate annoyance. Strangely enough, instead of moving away, my actions seemed only to encourage him, because he moved even closer. In spite of the temptation to escape the annoyance, I put aside thoughts of abandoning my post, thinking, "To hell with it. Why should I move? I was here first and I'm not going to let this fellow drive me out even if he is a boor." Fortunately, a group of people soon arrived whom my tormentor immediately joined. Their mannerisms explained his behavior, for I knew from both speech and gestures that they were Arabs. I had not been able to make this crucial identification by looking at my subject when he was alone because he wasn't talking and he was wearing American clothes.

In describing the scene later to an Arab colleague, two contrasting   5
patterns emerged. My concept and my feelings about my own circle of privacy in a "public" place immediately struck my Arab friend as strange and puzzling. He said, "After all, it's a public place, isn't it?" Pursuing this line of inquiry, I found that an Arab thought I had no rights whatsoever by virtue of occupying a given spot; neither my place nor my body was inviolate! For the Arab, there is no such thing as an intrusion in public. Public means public. With this insight, a great range of Arab behavior that had been puzzling, annoying, and sometimes even frightening began to make sense. I learned, for example, that if *A* is standing on a street corner and *B* wants his spot, *B* is within his rights if he does what he can to make *A* uncomfortable enough to move. In Beirut only the hardy sit in the last row in a movie theater, because there are usually standees who want seats and who push and shove and make such a nuisance that most people give up and leave. Seen in this light, the Arab who "intruded" on my space in the hotel lobby had apparently selected it for the very reason

I had: it was a good place to watch two doors and the elevator. My show of annoyance, instead of driving him away, had only encouraged him. He thought he was about to get me to move.

Another silent source of friction between Americans and Arabs is in an area that Americans treat very informally—the manners and rights of the road. In general, in the United States we tend to defer to the vehicle that is bigger, more powerful, faster, and heavily laden. While a pedestrian walking along a road may feel annoyed he will not think it unusual to step aside for a fast-moving automobile. He knows that because he is moving he does not have the right to the space around him that he has when he is standing still (as I was in the hotel lobby). It appears that the reverse is true with the Arabs who apparently *take on rights to space as they move*. For someone else to move into a space an Arab is also moving into is a violation of his rights. It is infuriating to an Arab to have someone else cut in front of him on the highway. It is the American's cavalier treatment of moving space that makes the Arab call him aggressive and pushy.

Concepts of Privacy

The experience described above and many others suggested to me that Arabs might actually have a wholly contrasting set of assumptions concerning the body and the rights associated with it. Certainly the Arab tendency to shove and push each other in public and to feel and pinch women in public conveyances would not be tolerated by Westerners. It appeared to me that they must not have any concept of a private zone outside the body. This proved to be precisely the case.

In the Western world, the person is synonymous with an individual inside a skin. And in northern Europe generally, the skin and even the clothes may be inviolate. You need permission to touch either if you are a stranger. This rule applies in some parts of France, where the mere touching of another person during an argument used to be legally defined as assault. For the Arab the location of the person in relation to the body is quite different. The person exists somewhere down inside the body. The ego is not completely hidden, however, because it can be reached very easily with an insult. It is protected from touch but not from words. The dissociation of the body and the ego may explain why the public amputation of a thief's hand is tolerated as standard punishment in Saudi Arabia. It also sheds light on why an Arab employer living in a modern apartment can provide his servant with a room that is a box-like cubicle approximately 5 by 10 by 4 feet in size that is not only hung from the ceiling to conserve floor space but has an opening so that the servant can be spied on.

As one might suspect, deep orientations toward the self such as the one just described are also reflected in the language. This was brought to my attention one afternoon when an Arab colleague who is the author of an Arab-English dictionary arrived in my office and threw himself into a chair in a state of obvious exhaustion. When I asked him what had been going on, he said: "I have spent the entire afternoon trying to find the Arab equivalent of the English word 'rape.' There is no such word in Arabic. All my sources, both written and spoken, can come up with no more than an approximation, such as 'He took her against her will.' There is nothing in Arabic approaching your meaning as it is expressed in that one word."

Differing concepts of the placement of the ego in relation to the body are not easily grasped. Once an idea like this is accepted, however, it is possible to understand many other facets of Arab life that would otherwise be difficult to explain. One of these is the high population density of Arab cities like Cairo, Beirut, and Damascus. According to the animal studies described [elsewhere], the Arabs should be living in a perpetual behavioral sink. While it is probable that Arabs are suffering from population pressures, it is also just as possible that continued pressure from the desert has resulted in a cultural adaptation to high density which takes the form described above. Tucking the ego down inside the body shell not only would permit higher population densities but would explain why it is that Arab communications are stepped up as much as they are when compared to northern European communication patterns. Not only is the sheer noise level much higher, but the piercing look of the eyes, the touch of the hands, and the mutual bathing in the warm moist breath during conversation represent stepped-up sensory inputs to a level which many Europeans find unbearably intense.

The Arab dream is for lots of space in the home, which unfortunately many Arabs cannot afford. Yet when he has space, it is very different from what one finds in most American homes. Arab spaces inside their upper middle-class homes are tremendous by our standards. They avoid partitions because Arabs *do not like to be alone*. The form of the home is such as to hold the family together inside a single protective shell, because Arabs are deeply involved with each other. Their personalities are intermingled and take nourishment from each other like the roots and soil. If one is not with people and actively involved in some way, one is deprived of life. An old Arab saying reflects this value: "Paradise without people should not be entered because it is Hell." Therefore, Arabs in the United States often feel socially and sensorially deprived and long to be back where there is human warmth and contact.

Since there is no physical privacy as we know it in the Arab family, not even a word for privacy, one could expect that the Arabs might use some other means to be alone. Their way to be alone is to stop talking. Like the English, an Arab who shuts himself off in this way is not indicating that anything is wrong or that he is withdrawing, only that he wants to be alone with his own thoughts or does not want to be intruded upon. One subject said that her father would come and go for days at a time without saying a word, and no one in the family thought anything of it. Yet for this very reason, an Arab exchange student visiting a Kansas farm failed to pick up the cue that his American hosts were mad at him when they gave him the "silent treatment." He only discovered something was wrong when they took him to town and tried forcibly to put him on a bus to Washington, D.C., the headquarters of the exchange program responsible for his presence in the U.S.

Arab Personal Distances

Like everyone else in the world, Arabs are unable to formulate specific rules for their informal behavior patterns. In fact, they often deny that there are any rules, and they are made anxious by suggestions that such is the case. Therefore, in order to determine how the Arab sets distances, I investigated the use of each sense separately. Gradually, definite and distinctive behavioral patterns began to emerge.

Olfaction occupies a prominent place in the Arab life. Not only is it one of the distance-setting mechanisms, but it is a vital part of a complex system of behavior. Arabs consistently breathe on people when they talk. However, this habit is more than a matter of different manners. To the Arab good smells are pleasing and a way of being involved with each other. To smell one's friend is not only nice but desirable, for to deny him your breath is to act ashamed. Americans, on the other hand, trained as they are not to breathe in people's faces, automatically communicate shame in trying to be polite. Who would expect that when our highest diplomats are putting on their best manners they are also communicating shame? Yet this is what occurs constantly, because diplomacy is not only "eyeball to eyeball" but breath to breath.

By stressing olfaction, Arabs do not try to eliminate all the body's   15
odors, only to enhance them and use them in building human relationships. Nor are they self-conscious about telling others when they don't like the way they smell. A man leaving his house in the morning may be told by his uncle, "Habib, your stomach is sour and your breath doesn't smell too good. Better not talk too close to people today." Smell is even considered in the choice of a mate. When couples are being matched for marriage, the man's go-between will sometimes ask to smell the girl, who may be turned down if she doesn't "smell nice." Arabs recognize that smell and disposition may be linked.

In a word, the olfactory boundary performs two roles in Arab life. It enfolds those who want to relate and separates those who don't. The Arab finds it essential to stay inside the olfactory zone as a means of keeping tab on changes in emotion. What is more, he may feel crowded as soon as he smells something unpleasant. While not much is known about "olfactory crowding," this may prove to be as significant as any other variable in the crowding complex because it is tied directly to the body chemistry and hence to the state of health and emotions. It is not surprising, therefore, that the olfactory boundary constitutes for the Arabs an informal distance-setting mechanism in contrast to the visual mechanisms of the Westerner.

Facing and Not Facing

One of my earliest discoveries in the field of intercultural communication was that the position of the bodies of people in conversation varies with the culture. Even so, it used to puzzle me that a special Arab friend seemed unable to walk and talk at the same time. After years in the United States, he could not bring himself to stroll along, facing forward while talking. Our progress would be arrested while he edged ahead, cutting slightly in front of me and turning sideways so we could see each other. Once in this position, he would stop. His behavior was explained when I learned that for the Arabs to view the other person peripherally is regarded as impolite, and to sit or stand back-to-back is considered very rude. You must be involved when interacting with Arabs who are friends.

One mistaken American notion is that Arabs conduct all conversations at close distance. This is not the case at all. On social occasions, they may sit on opposite sides of the room and talk across the room to each other. They are, however, apt to take offense when Americans use what are to them ambiguous distances, such as the four- to seven-foot social-consultative distance. They frequently complain that Americans are cold or aloof or "don't care." This was what an elderly Arab diplomat in an American hospital thought when the American nurses used "professional" distance. He had the feeling that he was being ignored, that they might not take good care of him. Another Arab subject remarked, referring to American behavior, "What's the matter? Do I smell bad? Or are they afraid of me?"

Arabs who interact with Americans report experiencing a certain flatness traceable in part to a very different use of the eyes in private and in public as well as between friends and strangers. Even though it is rude for a guest to walk around the Arab home eying things, Arabs look at each other in ways which seem hostile or challenging to the American. One Arab informant said that he was in constant hot water with Americans because of the way he looked at them without the slightest intention of offending. In fact, he had on several occasions barely avoided fights with American men who apparently thought their masculinity was being challenged because of the way he was looking at them. As noted earlier, Arabs look each other in the eye when talking with an intensity that makes most Americans highly uncomfortable.

Involvement

As the reader must gather by now, Arabs are involved with each other on many different levels simultaneously. Privacy in a public place is foreign to them. Business transactions in the bazaar, for example, are not just between buyer and seller, but are participated in by everyone. Anyone who is standing around may join in. If a grownup sees a boy breaking a window, he must stop him even if he doesn't know him. Involvement and participation

20

are expressed in other ways as well. If two men are fighting, the crowd must intervene. On the political level, *to fail to intervene* when trouble is brewing is to take sides, which is what our State Department always seems to be doing. Given the fact that few people in the world today are even remotely aware of the cultural mold that forms their thoughts, it is normal for Arabs to view *our* behavior as though it stemmed from *their* own hidden set of assumptions.

Feelings about Enclosed Spaces

In the course of my interviews with Arabs the term "tomb" kept cropping up in conjunction with enclosed space. In a word, Arabs don't mind being crowded by people but hate to be hemmed in by walls. They show a much greater overt sensitivity to architectural crowding than we do. Enclosed space must meet at least three requirements that I know of if it is to satisfy the Arabs: there must be plenty of unobstructed space in which to move around (possibly as much as a thousand square feet); very high ceilings—so high in fact that they do not normally impinge on the visual field; and, in addition, there must be an unobstructed view. It was spaces such as these in which the Americans referred to earlier felt so uncomfortable. One sees the Arab's need for a view expressed in many ways, even negatively, for to cut off a neighbor's view is one of the most effective ways of spiting him. In Beirut one can see what is known locally as the "spite house." It is nothing more than a thick, fourstory wall, built at the end of a long fight between neighbors, on a narrow strip of land, for the express purpose of denying a view of the Mediterranean to any house built on the land behind. According to one of my informants, there is also a house on a small plot of land between Beirut and Damascus which is completely surrounded by a neighbor's wall built high enough to cut off the view from all windows!

Boundaries

Proxemic patterns tell us other things about Arab culture. For example, the whole concept of the boundary as an abstraction is almost impossible to pin down. In one sense, there are no boundaries. "Edges" of towns, yes, but permanent boundaries out in the country (hidden lines), no. In the course of my work with Arab subjects I had a difficult time translating our concept of a boundary into terms which could be equated with theirs. In order to clarify the distinctions between the two very different definitions, I thought it might be helpful to pinpoint acts which constituted trespass. To date, I have been unable to discover anything even remotely resembling our own legal concept of trespass.

Arab behavior in regard to their own real estate is apparently an extension of, and therefore consistent with, their approach to the body. My subjects simply failed to respond whenever trespass was mentioned. They didn't seem to understand what I meant by this term. This may be explained by the fact that they organize relationships with each other according to closed social systems rather than spatially. For thousands of years Moslems, Marinites, Druses, and Jews have lived in their own villages, each with strong kin affiliations. Their hierarchy of loyalties is: first to one's self, then to kinsman, townsman, or tribesman, coreligionist and/or countryman. Anyone not in these categories is a stranger. Strangers and enemies are very closely linked, if not synonymous, in Arab thought. Trespass in this context is a matter of who you are, rather than a piece of land or a space with a boundary that can be denied to anyone and everyone, friend and foe alike.

In summary, proxemic patterns differ. By examining them it is possible to reveal hidden cultural frames that determine the structure of a given people's perceptual world. Perceiving the world differently leads to differential definitions of what constitutes crowded living, different interpersonal relations, and a different approach to both local and international politics.

 Joining the Conversation:
Critical Thinking and Writing

1. According to Hall, why do Arabs think Americans are pushy? And, again according to Hall, why do Arabs not consider themselves pushy?

2. Explain what Hall means by "cognitive world" (paragraph 2); by "ego" (paragraph 10); by "behavioral sink" (in the same paragraph). Then, for the benefit of someone who does not understand the terms, explain how you know what Hall means by each.

3. In paragraph 9, Hall points out that there is no Arabic equivalent of the English word *rape*. Can you provide an example of a similar gap in English or in another language? Does a cultural difference account for the linguistic difference?

4. In paragraph 3, Hall says of a rule that it "is all the more binding because we seldom think about it." Is this generally true of rules? What examples or counterexamples support your view?

James B. Twitchell

James B. Twitchell teaches English and advertising at the University of Florida. He is the author of several books, including Carnival Culture: The Trashing of Taste in America *(1992) and* Twenty Ads That Shook the World: The Century's Most Groundbreaking Advertising and How It Changed Us All *(2000). The following essay comes from* Twenty Ads.

The Marlboro Man:
The Perfect Campaign

Although advertising agencies love giving themselves prizes, there has been no award for the perfect campaign. If there were, Marlboro would win. Suffice it to say that this brand went from selling less than one quarter of one percent of the American market in the early 1950s to being the most popular in the entire world in just twenty years. Every fourth cigarette smoked is a Marlboro. Leo Burnett's brilliant campaign made Marlboro the most valuable brand in the world.

First, let's dispense with the politics of the product. We all know that cigarettes are the most dangerous legal product in the world. They kill more people each year than do guns. And yes, it is dreadful that the myth of independence is used to sell addiction. But never forget as well that it is exactly this danger that animates the Marlboro Man. He came into being just as smoking became problematic and, ironically, as long as anxiety exists, so will he.

And, second, cigarettes, like domestic beer and bottled water, build deep affiliations that have absolutely nothing to do with taste. As David Ogilvy said, "Give people a taste of Old Crow and *tell* them it's Old Crow. Then give them another taste of Old Crow, *but tell them it's Jack Daniels*. Ask them which they prefer. They'll think the two drinks are quite different. *They are tasting images*" (Ogilvy 1985, 87).

In fact, it was the cigarette companies that found this out first. In the 1920s they blindfolded brand-dedicated smokers and put them into dark rooms. Then they gave them Luckies, Pall Malls, Chesterfields, and Camels, as well as European smokes, and asked the smokers to identify "their own brand"—the one they were sure they knew. By now we all know the results. Taste has basically little or nothing to do with why people choose specific brands of cigarettes.

Just as we drink the label, we smoke the advertising. So what's so   5
smokable, so tasty, about this ad?

First, everything fits around the dominant image. The heading and the logotype fall naturally in place. Product name mediates between visual and verbal. Let's start with the name, *Marlboro*. Like so many cigarette brand names, it is English and elegant and, like its counterpart Winston, deceptively vague. Like the joke about how there's gotta be a pony in there somewhere, there's gotta be prestige in here somewhere. (Oddly enough, Marlboro was first created in Victorian England, then transported to the States as a cigarette for women.) The ersatz PM crest at the apex of the "red roof" chevron on the package hints of a bloodline, and the Latin motto "Veni, Vidi, Vici"[1] (!) conveys ancient warrior strength. Clearly, the power is now both in the pack and in the buckaroo.

The buckaroo is, of course, the eponymous Marlboro Man. He is what we have for royalty, distilled manhood. (Alas, the Winston man barely exists. What little of him there is is opinionated, urbane, self-assured—and needs to tell you so.) The Marlboro Man needs to tell you nothing. He carries no scepter, no gun. He never even speaks. Doesn't need to. The difference between Marlboro and Winston is the difference between myth and reality. Winston needed to break the rules publicly to be independent ("Winston tastes good *like* a cigarette should"); the Marlboro Man has already been there, done that. Little wonder the Viceroy man ("a thinking man's filter, a smoking man's taste") couldn't even make the cut.

Generating prestige *and* independence is a crucial aspect of cigarette selling. If you are targeting those who are just entering the consumption community, and if the act of consumption is dangerous, then you do not need to stress rebellion—that's a given. What you need to announce is initiation into the pack.

When R.J. Reynolds tested Marlboro on focus groups, they found that it was not rugged machismo that was alluring to young Marlboro smokers, but separation from restraints (the tattoo) *and* a sense of belonging (Marlboro Country). This "secret" RJR report, now available on the World Wide Web, is one reason why the "I'd walk a mile for a Camel" man was subsumed into the more personable, intelligent, and independent "Cool Joe" Camel.

Let's face it, the Camel man was downright stupid. In the most repeated of his ill-fated "walk a mile" ads he is shown carrying a tire (instead of rolling it) across the desert (with no canteen), wearing no shade-providing hat. That he seemingly forgot the spare tire is as stupid as his choosing to smoke. Little wonder Cool Joe pushed him aside. A camel seems intelligent in comparison.

10

The Marlboro Man's transformation was less traumatic, but no less meaningful. In fact, it is a reversal of the most popular tabloid story of the 1950s. It was to be, as David Ogilvy would say, one of the "riskiest decisions ever made" and one "which few advertisers would take." Here's the cultural context on a thumbnail and what Philip Morris did about it:

On February 13, 1953, George Jorgenson went to Denmark and returned as Christine. The idea that one could change one's sex was profoundly unsettling to American culture. Once back at home, she uttered the perhaps apocryphal testament to his journey: "Men are wary of me and I'm wary of the ones who aren't."

---

[1]**Veni, Vidi, Vici** Latin: I came, I saw, I conquered (Julius Caesar's announcement of a victory). (Editors' note)

At almost the same time, another repositioning was occurring. Now, as any modern ten-year-old can tell you, objects have sexual characteristics, too. Philip Morris had a female cigarette, Marlboro, that wouldn't sell. So they sent her up to Chicago to be regendered by Leo Burnett. Miss Marlboro was a "sissy smoke . . . a tea room smoke," Burnett said. Although she had been in and out of production for most of the century, in her most recent incarnation she had a red filter tip (called the "beauty tip," to hide lipstick stains) and a long-running theme: "Mild as May." Men wouldn't touch her, nor would many women.

In December 1954, Burnett took Miss Marlboro out to his gentleman's farm south of Chicago and invited some of his agency cohorts over to brainstorm. Something had to be done to put some hair on her chest, to change her out of pinafores and into cowboy chaps, anything to get her out of the suffocating tea room.

"What is the most masculine figure in America?" Burnett asked. "Cab driver, sailor, marine, pilot, race car driver" came the replies. Then someone simply said, "Cowboy." Bingo! Copywriter Draper Daniels filled in the blank: this smoke "Delivers the Goods on Flavor." 15

But these admen were not thinking of a real cowboy, not some dirty, spitting, toothless, smelly wrangler. They were city boys who knew cowboys in bronzes and oils by Frederic Remington, or in oils and watercolors by Charles Russell, or in the purple prose of Owen Wister's *The Virginian* or in the pulp of Zane Grey's countless novels. Philip Morris and Leo Burnett now love to tell you that the Marlboro Man was always a "real cowboy." Just don't remind them that almost half of the real cowpunchers were black or Mexican.

No matter, Leo Burnett had just the image in mind. He remembered seeing one C. H. Long, a thirty-nine-year-old foreman at the JA Ranch in the Texas panhandle, a place described as "320,000 acres of nothing much," who had been heroically photographed by Leonard McCombe for a cover of *Life* magazine in 1949. In other words, this Marlboro cowboy was a real/reel cowboy, something like what Matt Dillon, played by James Arness, was on television. A slightly roughed-up, *High Noon* Gary Cooper, a lite-spaghetti Clint Eastwood.

To get to this image, the Leo Burnett Company tried out all manner of windblown wranglers, some professional models, some not. Then, in 1963, just as the health concerns about lung cancer really took hold, they discovered Carl "Big-un" Bradley at the 6666 Ranch in Guthrie, Texas. Carl was the first real cowboy they used, and from then on the Marlboro Men were honest-to-God cowboys, rodeo riders, and stuntmen.

One look at him and you know: no Ralph Lauren jeans, no 401(k) plans, no wine spritzers, nothing with little ducks all over it, just independence, pure and simple. He doesn't concern himself with the Surgeon General. He's his own sheriff. To make sure he stayed that way, all background was airbrushed out. Later he got a grubstake in Marlboro Country.

Even today the Philip Morris Company receives letters from all over
the world, mostly at the beginning of the summer, from travelers wishing
to know how to get to Marlboro Country.

But there's more to the ad than the free-ranging cowboy. That package with the insignia, built truck-tough as a flip-top *box*, was a badge.
With its hearty red, white, and black lettering, the smoker pinned it to his
chest on the average of twenty-three times a day. This *vade mecum*[2] of a
package was designed by Frank Gianninoto and carefully tested through
consumer surveys by Elmo Roper & Associates and the Color Research
Institute. Now the *Veni, Vidi, Vici* starts making sense. With this package
you are the decorated conqueror. You burn bridges, bust broncos, confront stuff like lung cancer.

Sure, the girlie filter was there for the women (incidentally, the famous
Marlboro red came from the lipstick red of the original "beauty filter"), but
it was battled by the box, the medallion—the manliness of it all.

Should you still not be convinced, there was always the brand, the literal brand—the tattoo. Remember, this was the 1950s, when tattoos were
not a fashion accessory, but an unambiguous sign of antisocial "otherness." But this brand was not on the biceps to signify Charles Atlas manliness; rather it was on the back of the smoking hand, or on the wrist.
A strange place for a tattoo, to be sure, but appropriate.

Although research departments may cringe to hear this, the tattoo
was not the result of motivational research showing that the image would
be super macho. Leo Burnett supposedly thought the tattoo would "say
to many men that here is a successful man who used to work with his
hands," while "to many women, we believe it will suggest a romantic
past."

But there is another story that also may be true. Alas, it doesn't emphasize virility and romance but the bugaboo of interpretation, namely,
happenstance. It seems someone at the agency had scribbled on the hand
of the *Life* magazine cowboy that there was no copyright clearance for this
particular image. The agency sent this image in a paste-up to Philip
Morris and then made another version from another cowboy photo to
avoid copyright problems. It, too, went to the client. Back came the reaction: "Where's the tattoo on the second cowboy?" Perplexed agency people dug up the original photo and saw the warning scribbled across the
wrist (McGuire 1989, 23).

No matter what the story, the tattoo stuck, not because of any massive
testing but because everyone knew the branding itself was compelling.
You are what you smoke.

When a campaign "works," every part seems compelling. In fact, in
great ads, as in great works of art, the sum of the parts is always more
than the whole. The visual and verbal rhetoric is so strong that they seem

[2]**vade mecum** Latin: "come with me" (Editors' note)

to have always been in place. They seem indestructible. In truth, however, often the greatest act of creativity is knowing when to leave well enough alone. "I have learned that any fool can write a bad ad," Burnett says in one of his pithy *100 Leo's*, "but that it takes a real genius to keep his hands off a good one" (Burnett 1995, 53).

Most of the tinkering with this campaign has been by the government. For instance, many people thought that by removing the Marlboro Man from television in the early 1970s the feds would send him into the sunset. No such luck. You can take down all the billboards and remove him from magazines. "Just a little dab" of this rhetoric "will do ya."

When Philip Morris attempted to introduce brand extension—Marlboro Light—after all the advertising bans were in place, all they did was unsaddle the cowboy and foreground the horse. Now that even mentioning the cigarette by name is becoming taboo, they are mining the original campaign by making Marlboro Country into Marlboro Unlimited and selling lots of logo'd stuff to smokers, calling it Gear Without Limits. By selling annually some 20 million T-shirts, caps, jackets, and other items bearing Marlboro logos, Philip Morris was, for a time, the nation's third-largest mail-order house.

This attempt to get around the fear of legal restrictions on advertising   30
is called "sell-through," and you see it happening with almost all the major cigarette and beer brands. So Smokin' Joe, the super-cool Camel musician, appears on a host of nontobacco products like clothing, beach towels, baseball caps, while at the same time he also appears on the hit list of the FTC as a public nuisance.

And so what is Gear Without Limits for people who want to go to the Land That Knows No Limits? Well, what about products from the Marlboro Country Store like Snake River Fishing Gear ("An outfit made to go where the cold rivers run"), the Marlboro Folding Mountain Bike, a Mountain Lantern in Marlboro red, and the Marlboro Country Cookbook (complete with their green salsa recipe for couch cowpokes). Marlboro has so captured the iconography of cowboydom that they now have ads in mass-circulation magazines consisting *only* of recipes for such grub as Huevos Rancheros, Barkeeper's Burger, and Whiskey Beef Sandwiches.

My favorite Marlboro ad, however, is an English one in which a Harleyesque motorcycle is set out in the bleak Western plains. The only color in the bleached scene is on the bike's gas tank—Marlboro red. In art lingo, this trope is called *metonymy*.

Metonymy transfers meaning because the host image, the Marlboro cowboy, is imbedded so deep not just in American culture but in world culture that we close the circuit. Ironically, slow learners are helped by the appearance of the warning box telling you that smoking is dangerous! The Marlboro Man may indeed be Dracula to his foes, but he is still the perfect icon of adolescent independence.

Ironically, the greatest danger faced by the Marlboro Man is not from lawmen armed with scientific studies, but from some wiseguy MBA in

Manhattan who will try to earn his spurs by tinkering with the campaign. This almost happened on April 22, 1993, as Michael Miles, CEO of Philip Morris, thought he could play chicken with the generics who were rustling his customers. Overnight, Miles cut the price of Marlboro by sixty cents a pack.

But the only critter he scared was the stock market, which lopped 23   35
percent off the price of PM stock in a single day. This day, still called "Marlboro Friday," will live in infamy as it seemed for a moment that other advertisers might follow. The whole point of branding is to make sure the consumer *pays* for the advertising by thinking that the interchangeable product is unique. He knows this when he pays a premium for it. When *Forbes* magazine (February 2, 1987) offered Marlboro smokers their chosen brand in a generic brown box at half the price, only 21 percent were interested. Just as the price of Marlboro is what economists call "inelastic," so is the advertising. Michael Miles lost his job and the company lost $13 billion in shareholder equity, but marketers learned a lesson: you don't fool with Mother Nature or a great campaign.

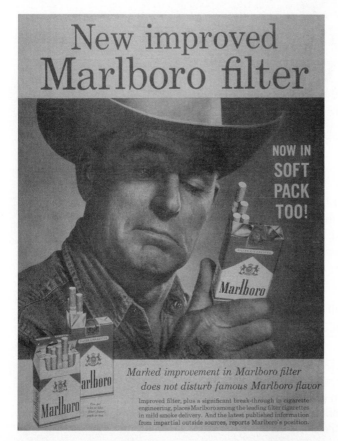

The Marlboro Man of the 1950s

The Marlboro Woman of the 1940s

Works Cited

Burnett, Leo. *100 Leo's: The Wit and Wisdom of Leo Burnett.* Lincolnwood, Ill.: NTC Business Books, 1995.

McGuide, John M. "How the Marlboro Cowboy Acquired His Tattoo." *St. Louis Post-Dispatch*, November 12, 1989.

Ogilvy, David. *On Advertising.* New York: Vintage, 1985.

 Joining the Conversation:
Critical Thinking and Writing

1. Reread the first two sentences of this essay. Does Twitchell prove the claim that he makes?

2. Did anything in this essay surprise you? Before you read it, were you familiar with the Marlboro Man? If so, in what contexts? If not, why do you think this is the case?

3. Early on, Twitchell contends that smokers and drinkers in fact cannot tell the difference between their favorite brand and other brands. Did you believe this before you read Twitchell's essay? Do you believe it now? Could you tell the difference between your favorite brand of soft drink and other brands?

4. If you are a smoker, what brand do you smoke? How much influence do you suppose has advertising had on your choice? If you are not a smoker, think of a product you use (e.g., jeans, underwear, sneakers) and, again, evaluate the effect of advertising on your choice.

5. What is Twitchell's conclusion about the importance of the Marlboro Man's tattoo? Do you have a tattoo? What made you decide to get one or perhaps more than one? If you do not have a tattoo, do you think that you might get one at some point? And what would that tattoo be?

6. Reread the essay, noting the devices Twitchell uses to persuade. Then, write a paragraph listing and analyzing these devices, providing examples for your reader.

7. The following sentences may puzzle some readers. Choose one and then explain it.

   (a) [The Marlboro Man] came into being just as smoking became problematic and, ironically, as long as anxiety exists, so will he. (paragraph 2)
   (b) The ersatz PM crest at the apex of the "red roof" chevron on the package hints of a bloodline, and the Latin motto "Vini, Vidi, Vici" (!) conveys ancient warrior strength. (paragraph 6)
   (c) The Marlboro Man may indeed be Dracula to his foes, but he is still the perfect icon of adolescent independence. (paragraph 33)

Eric Schlosser

Eric Schlosser, born in 1959, is an investigative journalist who has published in such journals as the Atlantic Monthly, Rolling Stone, *the* New Yorker, *and the* Nation. *We reprint a selection from his best-selling book,* Fast Food Nation *(2001), an exposé of the fast-food industry.*

Kid Kustomers

Twenty-five years ago, only a handful of American companies directed their marketing at children—Disney, McDonald's, candy makers, toy makers, manufacturers of breakfast cereal. Today children are being targeted by phone companies, oil companies, and automobile companies, as well as clothing stores and restaurant chains. The explosion in children's advertising occurred during the 1980s. Many working parents, feeling guilty about spending less time with their kids, started spending more money on them. One marketing expert has called the 1980s "the decade of the child consumer." After largely ignoring children for years, Madison Avenue began to scrutinize and pursue them. Major ad agencies now have children's divisions, and a variety of marketing firms focus solely on kids. These groups tend to have sweet-sounding names: Small Talk, Kid Connection, Kid2Kid, the Gepetto Group, Just Kids, Inc. At least three industry publications—*Youth Market Alert, Selling to Kids,* and *Marketing to Kids Report*—cover the latest ad campaigns and market research. The growth in children's advertising has been driven by efforts to increase not just current, but also future, consumption. Hoping that nostalgic childhood memories of a brand will lead to a lifetime of purchases, companies now plan "cradle-to-grave" advertising strategies. They have come to believe what Ray Kroc and Walt Disney realized long ago—a person's "brand loyalty" may begin as early as the age of two. Indeed, market research has found that children often recognize a brand logo before they can recognize their own name.

The discontinued Joe Camel ad campaign, which used a hip cartoon character to sell cigarettes, showed how easily children can be influenced by the right corporate mascot. A 1991 study published in the *Journal of the American Medical Association* found that nearly all of America's six-year-olds could identify Joe Camel, who was just as familiar to them as Mickey Mouse. Another study found that one-third of the cigarettes illegally sold to minors were Camels. More recently, a marketing firm conducted a survey in shopping malls across the country, asking children to describe their favorite TV ads. According to the CME KidCom Ad Traction Study II, released at the 1999 Kids' Marketing Conference in San Antonio, Texas, the Taco Bell commercials featuring a talking chihuahua were the most popular fast food ads. The kids in the survey also liked Pepsi and Nike commercials, but their favorite television ad was for Budweiser.

The bulk of the advertising directed at children today has an immediate goal. "It's not just getting kids to whine," one marketer explained in *Selling to Kids*, "it's giving them a specific reason to ask for the product." Years ago sociologist Vance Packard described children as "surrogate salesmen" who had to persuade other people, usually their parents, to buy what they wanted. Marketers now use different terms to explain the intended response to their ads—such as "leverage," "the nudge factor," "pester power." The aim of most children's advertising is straightforward: get kids to nag their parents and nag them well.

James U. McNeal, a professor of marketing at Texas A&M University, is considered America's leading authority on marketing to children. In his book *Kids As Customers* (1992), McNeal provides marketers with a thorough analysis of "children's requesting styles and appeals." He classifies juvenile nagging tactics into seven major categories. A *pleading* nag is one accompanied by repetitions of words like "please" or "mom, mom, mom." A *persistent* nag involves constant requests for the coveted product and may include the phrase "I'm gonna ask just one more time." *Forceful* nags are extremely pushy and may include subtle threats, like "Well, then, I'll go and ask Dad." *Demonstrative* nags are the most high-risk, often characterized by full-blown tantrums in public places, breath-holding, tears, a refusal to leave the store. *Sugar-coated* nags promise affection in return for a purchase and may rely on seemingly heartfelt declarations like "You're the best dad in the world." *Threatening* nags are youthful forms of blackmail, vows of eternal hatred and of running away if something isn't bought. *Pity* nags claim the child will be heartbroken, teased, or socially stunted if the parent refuses to buy a certain item. "All of these appeals and styles may be used in combination," McNeal's research has discovered, "but kids tend to stick to one or two of each that prove most effective . . . for their own parents."

McNeal never advocates turning children into screaming, breath-holding monsters. He has been studying "Kid Kustomers" for more than thirty years and believes in a more traditional marketing approach. "The key is getting children to see a firm . . . in much the same way as [they see] mom or dad, grandma or grandpa," McNeal argues. "Likewise, if a company can ally itself with universal values such as patriotism, national defense, and good health, it is likely to nurture belief in it among children."

Before trying to affect children's behavior, advertisers have to learn about their tastes. Today's market researchers not only conduct surveys of children in shopping malls, they also organize focus groups for kids as young as two or three. They analyze children's artwork, hire children to run focus groups, stage slumber parties and then question children into the night. They send cultural anthropologists into homes, stores, fast food restaurants, and other places where kids like to gather, quietly and surreptitiously observing the behavior of prospective customers. They study the academic literature on child development, seeking insights from the work of theorists such as Erik Erikson and Jean Piaget. They study the fantasy lives of young children, then apply the findings in advertisements and product designs.

Dan S. Acuff—the president of Youth Market System Consulting and the author of *What Kids Buy and Why* (1997)—stresses the importance of dream research. Studies suggest that until the age of six, roughly 80 percent of children's dreams are about animals. Rounded, soft creatures like Barney, Disney's animated characters, and the Teletubbies therefore have an obvious appeal to young children. The Character Lab, a division of Youth Market System Consulting, uses a proprietary technique called Character Appeal Quadrant Analysis to help companies develop new mascots. The technique purports to create imaginary characters who perfectly fit the targeted age group's level of cognitive and neurological development.

Children's clubs have for years been considered an effective means of targeting ads and collecting demographic information; the clubs appeal to a child's fundamental need for status and belonging. Disney's Mickey Mouse Club, formed in 1930, was one of the trailblazers. During the 1980s and 1990s, children's clubs proliferated, as corporations used them to solicit the names, addresses, zip codes, and personal comments of young customers. "Marketing messages sent through a club not only can be personalized," James McNeal advises, "they can be tailored for a certain age or geographical group." A well-designed and well-run children's club can be extremely good for business. According to one Burger King executive, the creation of a Burger King Kids Club in 1991 increased the sales of children's meals as much as 300 percent.

The Internet has become another powerful tool for assembling data about children. In 1998 a federal investigation of Web sites aimed at children found that 89 percent requested personal information from kids; only 1 percent required that children obtain parental approval before supplying the information. A character on the McDonald's Web site told children that Ronald McDonald was "the ultimate authority in everything." The site encouraged kids to send Ronald an e-mail revealing their favorite menu item at McDonald's, their favorite book, their favorite sports team—and their name. Fast food Web sites no longer ask children to provide personal information without first gaining parental approval; to do so is now a violation of federal law, thanks to the Children's Online Privacy Protection Act, which took effect in April of 2000.

Despite the growing importance of the Internet, television remains the primary medium for children's advertising. The effects of these TV ads have long been a subject of controversy. In 1978, the Federal Trade Commission (FTC) tried to ban all television ads directed at children seven years old or younger. Many studies had found that young children often could not tell the difference between television programming and television advertising. They also could not comprehend the real purpose of commercials and trusted that advertising claims were true. Michael Pertschuk, the head of the FTC, argued that children need to be shielded from advertising that preys upon their immaturity. "They cannot protect themselves," he said, "against adults who exploit their present-mindedness."

The FTC's proposed ban was supported by the American Academy of Pediatrics, the National Congress of Parents and Teachers, the Consumers Union, and the Child Welfare League, among others. But it was attacked by the National Association of Broadcasters, the Toy Manufacturers of America, and the Association of National Advertisers. The industry groups lobbied Congress to prevent any restrictions on children's ads and sued in federal court to block Pertschuk from participating in future FTC meetings on the subject. In April of 1981, three months after the inauguration of President Ronald Reagan, an FTC staff report argued that a ban on ads aimed at children would be impractical, effectively killing the proposal. "We are delighted by the FTC's reasonable recommendation," said the head of the National Association of Broadcasters.

The Saturday-morning children's ads that caused angry debates twenty years ago now seem almost quaint. Far from being banned, TV advertising aimed at kids is now broadcast twenty-four hours a day, closed-captioned and in stereo. Nickelodeon, the Disney Channel, the Cartoon Network, and the other children's cable networks are now responsible for about 80 percent of all television viewing by kids. None of these networks existed before 1979. The typical American child now spends about twenty-one hours a week watching television—roughly one and a half months of TV every year. That does not include the time children spend in front of a screen watching videos, playing video games, or using the computer. Outside of school, the typical American child spends more time watching television than doing any other activity except sleeping. During the course of a year, he or she watches more than thirty thousand TV commercials. Even the nation's youngest children are watching a great deal of television. About one-quarter of American children between the ages of two and five have a TV in their room.

Notes

[The page references have been changed to accord with pages in *The Little, Brown Reader*, 12th ed., and the bibliographic citations have been amplified where necessary.]

p. 390. *"the decade of the child consumer"*: McNeal, *Kids as Customers*, p. 6.

as early as the age of two: Cited in "Brand Aware," *Children's Business*, June 2000.

children often recognize a brand logo: See "Brand Consciousness," *IFF on Kids: Kid Focus*, no. 3.

a 1991 study . . . found: Paul Fischer et al., "Brand Logo Recognition by Children Aged 3 to 6 Years: Mickey Mouse and Old Joe the Camel," *Journal of the American Medical Association*, December 11, 1991.

Another study found: See Judann Dagnoli, "JAMA Lights New Fire Under Camel's Ads," *Advertising Age*, December 16, 1991.

the CME KidCom Ad Traction Study II: Cited in "Market Research Ages 6–17: Talking Chihuahua Strikes Chord with Kids," *Selling to Kids*, February 3, 1999.

"It's not just getting kids to whine": Quoted in "Market Research: The Old Nagging Game Can Pay off for Marketers," *Selling to Kids*, April 15, 1998.

Vance Packard described children as "surrogate salesmen": See Boas and Chain, *Big Mac*, p. 127; Vance Packard, *The Hidden Persuaders* (New York: D. McKay, 1957), pp. 158–61.

"children's requesting styles and appeals": McNeal, *Kids as Customers*, pp. 72–75.

p. 391. *"Kid Kustomers":* Ibid., p. 4.

"The key is getting children to see a firm": Ibid., p. 98.

learn about their tastes: For a sense of the techniques now being used by marketers, see Tom McGee, "Getting Inside Kids' Heads," *American Demographics,* January 1997.

roughly 80 percent of children's dreams: Cited in Acuff, *What Kids Buy and Why,* pp. 45–46.

"Marketing messages sent through a club": McNeal, *Kids As Customers,* p. 175.

increased the sales of children's meals: Cited in Karen Benezra, "Keeping Burger King on a Roll," *Brandweek,* January 15, 1996.

p. 392. *a federal investigation of Web sites aimed at children:* Cited in "Children's Online Privacy Proposed Rule Issued by FTC," press release, Federal Trade Commission, April 20, 1999.

p. 486. *"the ultimate authority in everything":* Quoted in "Is Your Kid Caught Up in the Web?" *Consumer Reports,* May 1997.

The site encouraged kids: See Matthew McAllester, "Life in Cyberspace: What's McDonald's Doing with Kids' E-mail Responses?" *Newsday,* July 20, 1997.

"They cannot protect themselves": Quoted in Linda E. Demkovich, "Pulling the Sweet Tooth of Children's TV Advertising," *National Journal,* January 7, 1978.

"We are delighted by the FTC's reasonable recommendation": Quoted in A. O. Sulzberger, Jr., "FTC Staff Urges End to Child-TV Ad Study," *New York Times,* April 3, 1981.

about 80 percent of all television viewing by kids: Cited in Steve McClellan and Richard Tedesco, "Children's TV Market May Be Played Out," *Broadcasting & Cable,* March 1, 1999.

about twenty-one hours a week: Cited in "Policy Statement: Media Education," American Academy of Pediatrics, August 1999.

more time watching television than doing: Cited in "Policy Statement: Children, Adolescents, and Television," American Academy of Pediatrics, October 1995.

p. 393. *more than thirty thousand TV commercials:* Cited in Mary C. Martin, "Children's Understanding of the Intent of Advertising: A Meta-Analysis," *Journal of Public Policy & Marketing,* Fall 1997.

one-quarter of American children: Cited in Lisa Jennings, "Baby, Hand Me the Remote," *Scripps Howard News Service,* October 13, 1999.

Joining the Conversation: Critical Thinking and Writing

1. In his opening paragraph, Schlosser asserts that advertising aimed at small children attempts "to increase not just current, but also future, consumption." Explain the reasoning of the advertising companies here. Does Schlosser provide evidence that supports their reasoning? Explain.

2. Let's assume that everything Schlosser says is true. Do you regard as unethical some or all of the practices he describes? Ethical but deplorable? Good business and thoroughly in the spirit of free enterprise? Or what?

3. Have you acquired any "brand loyalty" derived from children's advertising? If so, what are the products you are "loyal" to? When were you first exposed to the commercials, and what was memorable about them?

4. Do you think that parents should attempt to limit small children's exposure to advertising aimed at them? Or do you believe that such exposure is harmless? Explain.

5. A writing assignment: Watch a TV program for children and observe the ads. Choose one ad that you find particularly effective (whether you approve of it or not). Then, write a two or three paragraph essay in which you first describe the ad in detail and then analyze its effectiveness. (On page 124, we offer advice for writing about an advertisement. Our topic there is ads in print, but you might nevertheless find the discussion useful.)

Julia Bird

Born and educated in England, Julia Bird entered a poetry contest sponsored by a British publication, The Guardian. *The ground rules: Write a poem limited to the 160 characters of the mobile phone screen. Bird's poem won a Special Prize of £250 (about $400) for what* The Guardian *called "the most creative use of SMS 'shorthand' in a poem."*

14: a txt msg pom.

his is r bunsn brnr bl%,
his hair lyk fe filings
W/ac/dc going thru.
I sit by him in kemistry,
It splits my @oms
wen he :-)s @ me.

Translation:
14: a text message poem.
his eyes are bunsen burner blue,
his hair like iron filings
with ac/dc going through.
I sit by him in chemistry,
it splits my atoms
when he smiles at me.

Joining the Conversation:
Critical Thinking and Writing

1. Imagine that you are the person about whom Julia Bird wrote her poem. Are you pleased or not? Write a txt pom in response.

2. We print another txt pom on page 442. Suppose you were the judge in a contest and these two poems were final contenders, Which would you pick as the winner. Why?

CHAPTER 11

Social Networking

Peter Steiner
The *New Yorker* July 5, 1993 p. 61

"On the Internet, nobody knows you're a dog."

"No, Mother, I've been busy – I did
not 'unfriend' you!"

Terri Libenson
The Boston Globe November 3rd, 2009

THE FRAZZLED MOM'S DEFAULT FACEBOOK STATUS!
(FOR THOSE TOO BUSY TO THINK OF ONE)

Jill Kaplan is...

- spending quality time with the laundry.
- fishing Polly Pockets out of the DVD player.
- breaking up a baloney and mustard fight.
- attempting to--STOP IT--have an--*NOT NOW!*--uninterrupted--PUT THAT DOWN--train of--*HEY!!*
- checking out faraway fantasy resorts on Hotels.com.

11/30 © 2009 Terri Libenson; Dist By King Features Syndicate, Inc.

Libenson

Short Views

We are in great haste to construct a magnetic telegraph from Maine to Texas, but Maine and Texas it may be have nothing important to communicate. . . . We are eager to tunnel under the Atlantic and bring the Old World some weeks nearer to the New, but perhaps the first news that will leak through into the broad, flapping American ear will be that Princess Adelaide has the whooping cough.
> *Henry David Thoreau*

The value of a social network is defined not only by who's on it, but by who's excluded.
> *Paul Saffo*

The medium is the message.
> *Marshall McLuhan*

Give a person a fish and you feed them for a day; teach that person to use the Internet and they won't bother you for weeks.
> *Anonymous*

You can't take something off the Internet—it's like taking pee out of a pool.
> *Anonymous*

Christine Rosen

Christine Rosen holds a Ph.D. from Emory University. An editor at The New Atlantis *(we reprint part of an essay from this journal) and a resident fellow at the Ethics and Public Policy Center, she has published articles in the* Wall Street Journal, National Review, *and elsewhere. She is also the author of two books:* Preaching Eugenics: Religious Leaders and the American Eugenics Movement *(2004) and* My Fundamentalist Education: A Memoir of a Divine Girlhood *(2005).*

Virtual Friendship and the New Narcissism

For centuries, the rich and the powerful documented their existence and their status through painted portraits. A marker of wealth and a bid for immortality, portraits offer intriguing hints about the daily life of their subjects—professions, ambitions, attitudes, and, most importantly, social standing. Such portraits, as German art historian Hans Belting has argued, can be understood as "painted anthropology," with much to teach us, both intentionally and unintentionally, about the culture in which they were created.

Self-portraits can be especially instructive. By showing the artist both as he sees his true self and as he wishes to be seen, self-portraits can at once expose and obscure, clarify and distort. They offer opportunities for both self-expression and self-seeking. They can display egotism and modesty, self-aggrandizement and self-mockery.

Today, our self-portraits are democratic and digital; they are crafted from pixels rather than paints. On social networking websites like MySpace and Facebook, our modern self-portraits feature background music, carefully manipulated photographs, stream-of-consciousness musings, and lists of our hobbies and friends. They are interactive, inviting viewers not merely to look at, but also to respond to, the life portrayed online. We create them to find friendship, love, and that ambiguous modern thing called connection. Like painters constantly retouching their work, we alter, update, and tweak our online self-portraits; but as digital objects they are far more ephemeral than oil on canvas. Vital statistics, glimpses of bare flesh, lists of favorite bands and favorite poems all clamor for our attention—and it is the timeless human desire for attention that emerges as the dominant theme of these vast virtual galleries.

Although social networking sites are in their infancy, we are seeing their impact culturally: in language (where *to friend* is now a verb), in politics (where it is *de rigueur* for presidential aspirants to catalogue their virtues on MySpace), and on college campuses (where *not* using Facebook

Christine Rosen: "Virtual Friendship and the New Narcissism" from *The New Atlantis* 17, Summer 2007. Reprinted by permission of *The New Atlantis*.

can be a social handicap). But we are only beginning to come to grips with the consequences of our use of these sites: for friendship, and for our notions of privacy, authenticity, community, and identity. As with any new technological advance, we must consider what type of behavior online social networking encourages. Does this technology, with its constant demands to collect (friends and status), and perform (by marketing ourselves), in some ways undermine our ability to attain what it promises—a surer sense of who we are and where we belong? The Delphic oracle's guidance was *know thyself*. Today, in the world of online social networks, the oracle's advice might be *show thyself*.

The New Taxonomy of Friendship

There is a Spanish proverb that warns, "Life without a friend is death   5
without a witness." In the world of online social networking, the warning might be simpler: "Life without hundreds of online 'friends' is virtual death." On these sites, friendship is the stated *raison d'être*. "A place for friends," is the slogan of MySpace. Facebook is a "social utility that connects people with friends." Orkut describes itself as "an online community that connects people through a network of trusted friends." Friendster's name speaks for itself.

But "friendship" in these virtual spaces is thoroughly different from real-world friendship. In its traditional sense, friendship is a relationship which, broadly speaking, involves the sharing of mutual interests, reciprocity, trust, and the revelation of intimate details over time and within specific social (and cultural) contexts. Because friendship depends on mutual revelations that are concealed from the rest of the world, it can only flourish within the boundaries of privacy; the idea of public friendship is an oxymoron.

The hypertext link called "friendship" on social networking sites is very different: public, fluid, and promiscuous, yet oddly bureaucratized. Friendship on these sites focuses a great deal on collecting, managing, and ranking the people you know. Everything about MySpace, for example, is designed to encourage users to gather as many friends as possible, as though friendship were philately. If you are so unfortunate as to have but one MySpace friend, for example, your page reads: "You have 1 friends," along with a stretch of sad empty space where dozens of thumbnail photos of your acquaintances should appear.

This promotes a form of frantic friend procurement. As one young Facebook user with 800 friends told John Cassidy in *The New Yorker*, "I always find the competitive spirit in me wanting to up the number." An associate dean at Purdue University recently boasted to the *Christian Science Monitor* that since establishing a Facebook profile, he had collected more than 700 friends. The phrase universally found on MySpace is,

"Thanks for the add!"—an acknowledgment by one user that another has added you to his list of friends. There are even services like FriendFlood.com that act as social networking pimps: for a fee, they will post messages on your page from an attractive person posing as your "friend." As the founder of one such service told *The New York Times* in February 2007, he wanted to "turn cyberlosers into social-networking magnets."

The structure of social networking sites also encourages the bureaucratization of friendship. Each site has its own terminology, but among the words that users employ most often is "managing." The Pew survey mentioned earlier found that "teens say social networking sites help them manage their friendships." There is something Orwellian about the management-speak on social networking sites: "Change My Top Friends," "View All of My Friends" and, for those times when our inner Stalins sense the need for a virtual purge, "Edit Friends." With a few mouse clicks one can elevate or downgrade (or entirely eliminate) a relationship.

To be sure, we all rank our friends, albeit in unspoken and intuitive ways. One friend might be a good companion for outings to movies or concerts; another might be someone with whom you socialize in professional settings; another might be the kind of person for whom you would drop everything if he needed help. But social networking sites allow us to rank our friends publicly. And not only can we publicize our own preferences in people, but we can also peruse the favorites among our other acquaintances. We can learn all about the friends of our friends—often without having ever met them in person.

Status-Seekers

Of course, it would be foolish to suggest that people are incapable of making distinctions between social networking "friends" and friends they see in the flesh. The use of the word "friend" on social networking sites is a dilution and a debasement, and surely no one with hundreds of MySpace or Facebook "friends" is so confused as to believe those are all real friendships. The impulse to collect as many "friends" as possible on a MySpace page is not an expression of the human need for companionship, but of a different need no less profound and pressing: the need for status. Unlike the painted portraits that members of the middle class in a bygone era would commission to signal their elite status once they rose in society, social networking websites allow us to *create* status—not merely to commemorate the achievement of it. There is a reason that most of the MySpace profiles of famous people are fakes, often created by fans: Celebrities don't need legions of MySpace friends to prove their importance. It's the rest of the population, seeking a form of parochial celebrity, that does.

But status-seeking has an ever-present partner: anxiety. Unlike a portrait, which, once finished and framed, hung tamely on the wall signaling one's status, maintaining status on MySpace or Facebook requires constant vigilance. As one 24-year-old wrote in a *New York Times* essay, "I am obsessed with testimonials and solicit them incessantly. They are the ultimate social currency, public declarations of the intimacy status of a relationship. . . . Every profile is a carefully planned media campaign."

The sites themselves were designed to encourage this. Describing the work of B.J. Fogg of Stanford University, who studies "persuasion strategies" used by social networking sites to increase participation, *The New Scientist* noted, "The secret is to tie the acquisition of friends, compliments and status—spoils that humans will work hard for—to activities that enhance the site." As Fogg told the magazine, "You offer someone a context for gaining status, and they are going to work for that status." Network theorist Albert-László Barabási notes that online connection follows the rule of "preferential attachment"—that is, "when choosing between two pages, one with twice as many links as the other, about twice as many people link to the more connected page." As a result, "while our individual choices are highly unpredictable, as a group we follow strict patterns." Our lemming-like pursuit of online status via the collection of hundreds of "friends" clearly follows this rule.

What, in the end, does this pursuit of Virthal Status mean for community and friendship? Writing in the 1980s *Habits of the Heart*, sociologist Robert Bellah and his colleagues documented the movement away from close-knit, traditional communities, to "lifestyle enclaves" which were defined largely by "leisure and consumption." Perhaps today we have moved beyond lifestyle enclaves and into "personality enclaves" or "identity enclaves"–discrete virtual places in which we can be different (and sometimes contradictory) people, with different groups of like-minded, though ever-shifting, friends.

Beyond Networking

This past spring, Len Harmon, the director of the Fischer Policy and Cultural Institute at Nichols College in Dudley, Massachusetts, offered a new course about social networking. Nichols is a small school whose students come largely from Connecticut and Massachusetts; many of them are the first members of their families to attend college. "I noticed a lot of issues involved with social networking sites," Harman told me when I asked him why he created the class. How have these sites been useful to Nichols students? "It has relieved some of the stress of transitions for them," he said. "When abrupt departures occur—their family moves or they have to leave friends behind—they can cope by keeping in touch more easily."

So perhaps we should praise social networking websites for streamlining friendship the way e-mail streamlined correspondence. In the nineteenth century, Emerson observed that "friendship requires more time than poor busy men can usually command." Now, technology has given us the freedom to tap into our network of friends when it is convenient for us. "It's a way of maintaining a friendship without having to make any effort whatsoever," as a recent graduate of Harvard explained to *The New Yorker*. And that ease admittedly makes it possible to stay in contact with a wider circle of offline acquaintances than might have been possible in the era before Facebook. Friends you haven't heard from in years, old buddies from elementary school, people you might have (should have?) fallen out of touch with—it is now easier than ever to reconnect to those people.

But what kind of connections are these? In his excellent book *Friendship: An Exposé*, Joseph Epstein praises the telephone and e-mail as technologies that have greatly facilitated friendship. He writes, "Proust once said he didn't much care for the analogy of a book to a friend. He thought a book was better than a friend, because you could shut it—and be shut of it—when you wished, which one can't always do with a friend." With e-mail and caller ID, Epstein enthuses, you can. But social networking sites (which Epstein says "speak to the vast loneliness in the world") have a different effect: they discourage "being shut of" people. On the contrary, they encourage users to check in frequently, "poke" friends, and post comments on others' pages. They favor interaction of greater quantity but less quality.

This constant connectivity concerns Len Harmon. "There is a sense of, 'if I'm not online or constantly texting or posting, then I'm missing something,'" he said of his students. "This is where I find the generational impact the greatest—not the use of the technology, but the *overuse* of the technology." It is unclear how the regular use of these sites will affect behavior over the long run—especially the behavior of children and young adults who are growing up with these tools. Almost no research has explored how virtual socializing affects children's development. What does a child weaned on Club Penguin learn about social interaction? How is an adolescent who spends her evenings managing her MySpace page different from a teenager who spends her night gossiping on the telephone to friends? Given that "people want to live their lives online," as the founder of one social networking site recently told *Fast Company* magazine, and they are beginning to do so at ever-younger ages, these questions are worth exploring.

The few studies that have emerged do not inspire confidence. Researcher Rob Nyland at Brigham Young University recently surveyed 184 users of social networking sites and found that heavy users "feel less socially involved with the community around them." He also found that "as individuals use social networking more for entertainment, their level of social involvement decreases." Another recent study conducted by communications professor Qingwen Dong and colleagues at the University of the Pacific found that "those who engaged in romantic communication over MySpace tend to have low levels of both emotional intelligence and self-esteem."

The implications of the narcissistic and exhibitionistic tendencies of social networkers also cry out for further consideration. There are opportunity costs when we spend so much time carefully grooming ourselves online. Given how much time we already devote to entertaining ourselves with technology, it is at least worth asking if the time we spend on social networking sites is well spent. In investing so much energy into improving how we *present* ourselves online, are we missing chances to genuinely *improve* ourselves?   20

We should also take note of the trend toward giving up face-to-face for virtual contact—and, in some cases, a preference for the latter. Today, many of our cultural, social, and political interactions take place through eminently convenient technological surrogates—Why go to the bank if you can use the ATM? Why browse in a bookstore when you can simply peruse the personalized selections Amazon.com has made for you? In the same vein, social networking sites are often convenient surrogates for offline friendship and community. In this context it is worth considering an observation that Stanley Milgram made in 1974, regarding his experiments with obedience: "The social psychology of this century reveals a major lesson," he wrote. "Often it is not so much the kind of person a man is as the kind of situation in which he finds himself that determines how he will act." To an increasing degree, we find and form our friendships and communities in the virtual world as well as the real world. These virtual networks greatly expand our opportunities to meet others, but they might also result in our valuing less the capacity for genuine connection. As the young woman writing in the *Times* admitted, "I consistently trade actual human contact for the more reliable high of smiles on MySpace, winks on Match.com, and pokes on Facebook." That she finds these online relationships more *reliable* is telling: it shows a desire to avoid the vulnerability and uncertainty that true friendship entails. Real intimacy requires risk—the risk of disapproval, of heartache, of being thought a fool. Social networking websites my make relationships more reliable, but whether those relationships can be humanly satisfying remains to be seen.

 ## Joining the Conversation: Critical Thinking and Writing

1. In her first three paragraphs, Rosen suggests that our MySpace or Facebook pages are self-portraits. In what sense is this true? How are these digital self-portraits like or unlike the painted self-portraits of the past?

2. Rosen argues (paragraph 2) that our self-portraits "can at once expose and obscure, clarify and distort." What does she mean? Can you think of an instance in which you yourself have both exposed and obscured something

through a posting to Facebook, MySpace, or some other social networking site? If so, report the episode in about 250 words.

3. At the end of paragraph 4, Rosen implies that online social networks involve showing the self rather than knowing the self. Why does she think this is true? Based on your own experience of online social networks, is she right?

4. When Rosen argues (paragraph 9) that social networking involves the "bureaucratization of friendship," what specific evidence does she offer to back this claim up? Is her interpretation of the evidence sound? Explain.

5. Based on your own experience and the ideas you have encountered in Rosen's piece, what would you say are the key differences and similarities between online friendship and face-to-face friendship?

Jeff Howe

Jeff Howe, a contributing editor at Wired, *has written for* Time, U.S. News and World Report, Mother Jones, *and numerous other publications. In 2006, writing in* Wired, *he coined the word "crowdsourcing," a combination of "crowd" and "outsourcing." The term refers to the practice of inviting the public to do a job—for example, to solve a problem. We reprint part of Chapter 10 of his book* Crowdsourcing: Why the Power of the Crowd Is Driving the Future of Business *(2008).*

Tomorrow's Crowd: The Age of the Digital Native

There are reasons to believe that the current manifestation of crowdsourcing is just a prelude to a far more pervasive transformation. Actually, there are about 200 million reasons to believe it. That's the rough number of kids around the works that currently have Internet access. Marc Prensky, a writer and video-game developer, coined the term "digital native" to describe the cohorts that are coming of age in the Internet era. The reset of us he aptly identifies as "digital immigrants." Like most immigrants, we often struggle to understand the incomprehensible customs of the natives.

Reared on social media, always on Internet connections, cell-phone cameras, Machinima, and YouTube, digital natives live on the same planet as digital immigrants, but inhabit a very different universe. They can concentrate on multiple projects simultaneously, they collaborate seamlessly and spontaneously with people they've never met, and most important, they create media with the same avidity that previous generations consumed it. This is the crowdsourcing generation, a demographic perfectly adapted to a future in which online communities will supplant the conventional corporation.

Kids Today

In 2005, the Pew Internet & American Life Project released the findings of a large-scale survey called "Teen Content Creators and Consumers." The Pew survey revealed that well over half of all teens with Internet access weren't just surfing the Web, but were actively creating content for the Web. The portrait that emerged from the study was of a parallel information ecosystem that operated independently of professional content producers such as NBC or, say, *Wired* magazine. These kids were creating and consuming their own multimedia narratives, composed of text, photographs, and videos. The study was enormously influential and was quoted extensively in the following months.

Then in late December 2007, Pew released a sequel to the original report, "Teens and Social Media." The findings of the study, which had been conducted over the course of 2006, were even more startling. They not only reinforced Pew's original conclusions, but they demonstrated that as a trend, teen content creation is rapidly becoming even more prevalent than first indicated. "The tools needed to produce and distribute digital media are readily available and utilized in some way by most teen Internet users," the Pew authors wrote. According to Pew, about 93 percent of all American twelve-to seventeen-year-olds are regular Internet users. That means more than 23 million teenage Americans are online. Of those, some 64 percent—nearly 15 million teens—are creating content for the Internet.

Pew asked its respondents whether they engaged in several activities the researchers considered to be "hallmarks of online content creation." One, do you work on a webpage? Two, do you contribute to someone else's webpage? Three, do you share original artwork, photos, stories, or videos? And finally, do you remix content you find online? Well over half of all teens answered yes to one of those questions. But what was more significant was that 40 percent, more than 9 million teens in the United States alone, are engaged in at least three of those activities. More teens are spending more time creating more online content in a greater variety of ways then ever before, a trend that seems to be on the rise.

This has clear implications for our economy: online communities such as iStockphoto, InnoCentive, and Threadless are already making significant contributions to the overall economy, and teens make up only a small percentage of their users. When this demographic reaches adulthood, they will bring behaviors and attitudes honed through thousands of hours in front of a computer, constructing their own experience and working collaboratively in various online communities.

A profound shift is afoot, which was nowhere more evident than at the Adelphi Cybercamp. Most of the campers seemed to be working on four or five projects at once—some of which had little to do with the curriculum. One mop-headed thirteen-year-old was making an animated video in Flash, the multimedia authoring tool that powers much of the content on the Web. A few feet away a girl about the same age was using another application to make her own manga comic. (In Japanese, *manga* means "comic," but it has come to refer to any comic bearing the characteristics of that particular aesthetic.) At any given time at least five or six of the campers were using Photoshop to alter pictures from their cell phones. When one of the older campers went to lunch, a few of his cohorts altered a photograph of him to look like a "Ballchinian," a race of aliens from the movie *Men in Black II* whose genitalia appear to fall below their, well, chin. You can imagine which part of the image they imported.

In some ways these are the kids you and I grew up with. The acne, the scatological humor, the use of pop culture to create social identity—the song remains the same. But somewhere in the past fifteen years we crossed a line after which nothing will ever be the same. We—and by that I mean everyone who still gets their news from a newspaper—watch stuff, listen to stuff, and read stuff. These kids *make* stuff. A quick, informal survey of the campers indicated that Photoshop, Flash, and various blog-authoring tools have become standard technological literacy to most middle-class American kids. "Flash is really expensive," explains Josh Moran, one of the younger campers at Adelphi. "But most kids just download it off the Internet," which is to say, get it illegally using one of the file-sharing networks.

Kids are beginning to entertain themselves in a completely new way, in an emergence of what's been called "participatory culture." Henry Jenkins, the head of MIT's Comparitive Media Studies program and author of the look *Convergence Culture: Where Old and New Media Collide*, writes,

> A participatory culture [has] relatively low barriers to artistic expression and civic engagement, strong support for creating and sharing one's creations, and some type of informal mentorship whereby what is known by the most experienced is passed along to novices. [It] is also one in which members believe their contributions matter, and feel some degree of social connection with one another.

In other words, "they care what other people think about what they have created." Creative collaboration is a robust feature of the culture of many online communities, but the disparity in Pew's numbers highlights the extent to which teens exhibit this communal impulse. A full 33 percent of online teens work on other people's websites, as compared to only 13 percent of adults. Teens are more likely to help others build a blog or website than they are to create their own.

They Berkeley researcher danah boyd (her spelling) gives a telling example of this tendency to share—or, to put a fine point on it, distribute without expectation of compensation—this kind of technical knowledge. When the social networking site MySpace first began gaining popularity in 2005, early adopters noticed that unlike its predecessor, Friendster, MySpace had neglected to close a security loophole that allowed users to customize their sites by adding HTML, CSS, and JavaScript. The result is that rather than standardized profile pages, teens could create the riot of color and noise that once decorated school lockers and notebooks, but is now recognized as the MySpace aesthetic. Rather than close the loophole, the company neither encouraged nor discouraged the practice. As boyd writes, "A copy/paste culture emerged, as teens began trafficking in knowledge of how to pimp out their profiles . . . In the early days of their infatuation, teens spent innumerable hours tracking down codes, trading tips, and setting up a slick profile."

"Through this process," boyd notes, "they learn both technological *and* social codes." The italics in the sentence are mine, because it's important to emphasize that this tendency to work well not only with others, but for the sake of others, is emblematic of crowdsourcing culture. This kind of reciprocity echoes the sorts of behavior we see in other crowdsourcing communities, where money generally ranks low on the list of motivations, below community reputation and the opportunity to learn and teach in turn. Even more than the stunning technological fluency digital natives demonstrate its their adoption of social behaviors—collaboration, free sharing, promiscuous creativity—that powers crowdsourcing. The fact that so many more kids than adults exhibit this tendency indicates that the younger generation will not only be prepared to take an active role in the sorts of online communities that form the crowdsourced workplace, but will thrive there and create an even more tightly woven community fabric.

Young people are sharing more than mere tips and tricks. Some 9 million teens share artwork, stories, or videos—a significant increase from Pew's previous study. A remarkable one in seven have posted their own videos. In others words, millions of kids are making their own clips and posting them to the Internet. Teens also display a marked tendency to remix the content they find on the Internet. Just as hardcore gamers are inclined to approach their video games as malleable, something to be shaped according to their creative fancy, teens creating artistic works in other media are also inclined to create pastiches, homages, or parodies of the videos, photographs, artworks, or stories they encounter. Some 26 percent of Pew's respondents said that they had taken content off the Web and remixed it to create their own work.

All of this is a testament not only to Jenkins's observation that participatory culture features "low barriers to artistic expression" (enabled, in large part, by the proliferation of cheap, easy-to-use tools), but also to the overwhelming belief that their "contributions matter."

Undoubtedly their contributions do matter, but to whom is a subject   15
of much debate. As the Pew study makes clear, most of this creative efflorescence we're witnessing takes place on sites like MySpace and Facebook. Well over half of all American teens have a profile on a social networking site, and three-quarters of those users are actively writing stories, sharing photos and videos, and otherwise engaging in acts of creation.

Social network sites thrive by making such tasks exceedingly simple, but it's hard to know what to make of the mass visual and verbal expression that has resulted. On one hand teens are creating media on a public platform. But as researcher danah boyd points out, this requires that we redefine our concept of "public." It would be unwise to assume that their intended audience, for the most part, extends beyond an immediate circle of acquaintances. This call to mind the updated twist on Andy Warhol's maxim: In the future everyone will be famous to fifteen people.

Pew didn't ask their respondents whether they considered social networking sites to be communication tools or spaces to exhibit premeditated, creative works, but it would have been interesting to know the response. Is the prolific creativity that MySpace inspires best viewed as the stirrings of the artistic impulse or as an act of expression more analogous to passing notes in class? For anyone concerned about the future of American literacy, a tour through random MySpace sites can be a depressing experience. Most blog entries are rife with grammatical errors (intended and otherwise), spelling errors (ditto), and the sort of inane sentimentalism that make high school English teachers cringe. But then, kids aren't going on MySpace to impress their English teachers. In the words of Tiffany, a MySpace user from Houston, "Im jus on this myspace thang to have fun and meet as many cool people as I can."

For most of these young people, sites like MySpace have become an integral element in creating an identity and communicating with their peers. In other words, teens haven't changed, but their technology has. "If you look at MySpace, what kids are doing in terms of cutting and pasting and linking and forwarding is very interesting from a creative perspective," says Mimi Ito, an anthropologist whose research focuses on how children interact with new media. "But I don't think kids who participate at that level see themselves as media producers. This is simply how they hang out."

Point well taken. But while they might be "just hanging out," teens are developing radically new social behaviors and cognitive abilities. These will surely create wholesale changes to the workplace when they enter the labor force in, say, five to ten years. Most of what they make may be of little interest—or merit—to anyone outside their peer circle. But that doesn't change the fact that a legion of kids is absorbing the fundamentals of videography, among other skills. As they get older, they'll become even more adept, and the tools will continue to become cheaper and easier to use. In 2007, iStockphoto launched a separate service that applies its secret sauce to videography. Unsurprisingly, it's doing exceptionally well, earning $12 million in revenues in its first year alone. Further, to believe that as much as technology changes, people stay the same, dismisses the full social, cultural, and psychological effects of that technology, especially on those who've grown up in the networked, always-on era.

The writer and game designer Marc Prensky goes so far as to claim that digital natives have developed, as a result of near-constant exposure to digital media, a different neurological makeup than that possessed by digital immigrants. I took an informal survey during my visits to two separate Cybercamps, asking each camper when he or she had first used a computer. The kids older than fifteen generally answered that they had been four or five years old. The younger kids, however, looked at me as if I'd asked them if they remembered their first meal. None could recall their first experience using a computer, or even being on the Internet. The computer and the Internet had always been around, as much a fixture of daily life as telephones are to the rest of us.

What happens when the Adelphi teens enter the workforce? For starters, they'll help accelerate the obsolescence of such standard corporate fixtures as the management hierarchy and the nine-to-five workday. As Thomas Malone, an MIT professor and author of *The Future of Work* points out, these conventions are artifacts of an earlier age when information was scarce and all decisions, for the sake of efficiency, trickled down from on high. Information is now available to anyone with an Internet connection. The result, Malone says, "is that decision making has been decentralized." Cybercamp's Josh Block points out that the high school students he teaches during the school year "expect to be able to do their homework together, on a wiki." They'll undoubtedly carry such habits into the workplace. Even the kids who do wind up working from the proverbial cubicle will fully expect to tap their peers on the other end of the fiber-optic cable for help. Wikis don't respect corporate firewalls (or national borders), and neither will their users.

But even this considerable shift understates the transformative effects in store. Crowdsourcing has already wreaked upheaval in a few select fields like stock photography. This is because the crowd has made a once scarce resource abundant. As digital natives continue to acquire the skills it takes to build, design, and create, the scarcity of many other commodities will also decline, posing great challenges to the companies that traffic in them. "Obsolescence itself isn't a new phenomenon," Malone points out. "Kids who grew up with running water wouldn't know how to work a hand-pump, and in this new world we're entering, a lot of what's familiar will go the way of the hand pump."

 ## Joining the Conversation: Critical Thinking and Writing

1. What is the difference between a "digital native" and a "digital immigrant"? Which are you? What are the consequences of being one rather than the other?

2. The survey Howe cites discovered that most teens "weren't just surfing the Web, but were actively creating content for the web" (paragraph 3). Why does Howe think that this is an important point? What are the key differences between surfing and creating? Why do they matter?

3. What are the key features of the "participatory culture" Howe mentions? In what sense does your own experience with media consumption and production either support or refute Howe and Jenkins's sense that we now live in a participatory culture?

4. Howe argues that the "radically new social behaviors and cognitive abilities" teens are developing will reshape the workplace by pushing aside "the management hierarchy and the nine-to-five workday." Why are the skills and beliefs of the "digital native" in opposition to hierarchy and fixed working hours? Would you see the shift Howe foresees as a positive development? Explain.

Clay Shirky

Clay Shirky, born in 1964, did his undergraduate work at Yale University. A teacher in the Interactive Telecommunications Program at New York University, he also writes about the social effects of Internet technologies for a variety of publications, including The New York Times *and* Wired. *We reprint part of Chapter 3 from his book* Here Comes Everybody *(2009).*

Everyone Is a Media Outlet

Our social tools remove older obstacles to public expression, and thus remove the bottlenecks that characterized mass media. The result is the mass amateurization of efforts previously reserved for media professionals.

My uncle Howard was a small-town newspaperman, publishing the local paper for Richmond, Missouri (population 5,000). The paper, founded by my grandfather, was the family business, and ink ran in Howard's blood. I can still remember him fulminating about the rise of *USA Today*; he criticized it as "TV on paper" and held it up as further evidence of the dumbing down of American culture, but he also understood the challenge that *USA Today* presented, with its color printing and national distribution. The *Richmond Daily News* and *USA Today* were in the same business; even with the difference in scale and scope, Howard immediately got what *USA Today* was up to.

Despite my uncle's obsession, *USA Today* turned out to be nothing like the threat that old-time newspaper people feared. It took some market share from other papers, but the effect wasn't catastrophic. What was catastrophic was a less visible but more significant change, already gathering steam when *USA Today* launched. The principal threat to the *Richmond Daily News*, and indeed to all newspapers small and large, was not competition from other newspapers but radical changes in the overall ecosystem of information. The idea that someone might build four-color presses that ran around the clock was easy to grasp. The idea that the transmission of news via paper might become a bad idea, that all those huge, noisy printing presses might be like steam engines in the age of internal combustion, was almost impossible to grasp. Howard could imagine someone doing what he did, but better. He couldn't imagine someone making what he did obsolete.

Many people in the newspaper business, the same people who worried about the effects of competition like *USA Today*, missed the significance of the internet. For people with a professional outlook, it's hard to understand how something that isn't professionally produced could affect them—not only is the internet not a newspaper, it isn't a business, or even an institution. There was a kind of narcissistic bias in the profession; the only threats they tended to take seriously were from other professional media outlets, whether newspapers, TV, or radio stations. This bias had them defending against the wrong thing when the amateurs began producing material on their own. Even as web sites like eBay and Craigslist were siphoning off the ad revenues that keep newspapers viable—job listings, classified ads, real estate—and weblogs were letting people like gnarlykitty publish to the world for free, the executives of the world's newspapers were slow to understand the change, and even slower to react. How could this happen? How could the newspaper industry miss such an obvious and grave challenge to their business? The answer is the flip side of Howard's obsession with *USA Today* and has to do with the nature of professional self-definition (and occasional self-delusion).

A profession exists to solve a hard problem, one that requires some sort of specialization. Driving a race car requires special training—race car drives are professionals. Driving an ordinary car, though, doesn't require the driver to belong to a particular profession, because it's easy enough that most adults can do it with a modicum of training. Most professions exist because there is a scarce resource that requires ongoing management: librarians are responsible for organizing books on the shelves, newspaper executives are responsible for deciding what goes on the front page. In these cases, the scarcity of the resource itself creates the need for a professional class—there are few libraries but many patrons, there are few channels but many viewers. In these cases professionals become gatekeepers, simultaneously providing and controlling access to information, entertainment, communication, or other ephemeral goods.

To label something a profession means to define the ways in which it is more than just a job. In the case of newspapers, professional behavior is guided both by the commercial imperative and by an additional set of norms about what newspapers are, how they should be staffed and run, what constitutes good journalism, and so forth. These norms are enforced not by the customers but by other professionals in the same business. The key to any profession is the relations of its members to one another. In a profession, members are only partly guided by service to the public. As the UCLA sociologist James Q. Wilson put it is his magisterial *Bureaucracy*, "A professional is someone who receives important occupational rewards from a reference group whose membership is limited to people who have undergone specialized formal education and have accepted a group-defined code of proper conduct." That's a mouthful, but the two key ideas apply to newspaper publishers (as well as to journalists, lawyers, and accountants): a professional learns things in a way that differentiates her from most of the populace, and she pays as much or more attention to the judgment of her peers as to the judgment of her customers when figuring out how to do her job.

A profession becomes, for its members, a way of understanding their world. Professionals see the world through a lens created by other members of their profession; for journalists, the rewards of a Pulitzer Prize are largely about recognition from other professionals.

Much of the time the internal consistency of professional judgment is a good thing—not only do we want high standards of education and competence, we want those standards created and enforced by other members of the same profession, a structure that is almost the definition of professionalism. Sometimes, though, the professional outlook can become a disadvantage, preventing the very people who have the most at stake—the professionals themselves—from understanding major changes to the structure of their profession. In particular, when a profession has been created as a result of some scarcity, as with librarians or television programmers, the professionals are often the last ones to see it when that scarcity goes away. It is easier to understand that you face competition than obsolescence.

In any profession, particularly one that has existed long enough that no one can remember a time when it didn't exist, members have a tendency to equate provisional solutions to particular problems with deep truths about the world. This is true of newspapers today and of the media generally. The media industries have suffered first and most from the recent collapse in communications costs. It used to be hard to move words, images, and sounds from creator to consumer, and most media businesses involve expensive and complex management of that pipeline problem, whether running a printing press or a record label. In return for helping overcome these problems, media businesses got to exert considerable control over the media and extract considerable revenues from the public. The commercial viability of most media businesses involves providing those solutions, so preservation of the original problems became an economic imperative. Now, though, the problems of production, reproduction, and distribution are much less serious. As a consequence, control over the media is less completely in the hands of the professionals.

As new capabilities go, unlimited perfect copyability is a lulu, and that capability now exists in the hands of everyone who owns a computer. Digital means of distributing words and images have robbed newspapers of the coherence they formerly had, revealing the physical object of the newspaper as a merely provisional solution; now every article is its own section. The permanently important question is how society will be informed of the news of the day. The newspaper used to be a pretty good answer to that question, but like all such answers, it was dependent on what other solutions were available. Television and radio obviously changed the landscape in which the newspaper operated, but even then printed news had a monopoly on the written word—until the Web came along. The Web didn't introduce a new competitor into the old ecosystem, as *USA Today* had done. The Web created a new ecosystem.

We've long regarded the newspaper as a sensible object because it has   10
been such a stable one, but there isn't any logical connection among its many elements: stories from Iraq, box scores from the baseball game, and ads for everything from shoes to real estate all exist side by side in an idiosyncratic bundle. What holds a newspaper together is primarily the cost of paper, ink, and distribution; a newspaper is whatever group of printed items a publisher can bundle together and deliver profitably. The corollary is also true: what doesn't go into a newspaper is whatever is too expensive to print and deliver. The old bargain of the newspaper—world news lumped in with horoscopes and ads from the pizza parlor—has now ended. The future presented by the internet is the mass amateurization of publishing and a switch from "Why publish this?" to "Why not?"

The two basic organizational imperatives—acquire resources, and use them to pursue some goal or agenda—saddle every organization with the institutional dilemma, whether its goal is saving souls or selling soap. The question that mass amateurization poses to traditional media is "What happens when the costs of reproduction and distribution go away? What happens when there's nothing unique about publishing anymore, because users can do it for themselves?" We are now starting to see that question being answered.

Weblogs and Mass Amateurization

Shortly after his reelection in 2002 Trent Lott, the senior senator from Mississippi and then majority leader, gave a speech at Strom Thurmond's hundredth birthday party. Thurmond, a Republican senator form South Carolina, had recently retired after a long political career, which had included a 1948 run for president on an overtly segregationist platform. At Thurmond's hundredth birthday party Lott remembered and praised Thurmond's presidential campaign of fifty years earlier and recalled Mississippi's support for it: "I want to say this about my state: When Strom Thurmond ran for president, we voted for him. We're proud of it. And if the rest of the country had followed our lead, we wouldn't have had all these problems over all these years, either." Two weeks later, having been rebuked by President Bush and by politicians and the press on both the right and the left for this comment, Lott announced that he would not seek to remain majority leader in the new Congress.

This would have been a classic story of negative press coverage altering a political career—except that the press didn't actually cover the story, at least not at first. Indeed, the press almost completely missed the story. This isn't to say that they intentionally ignored it or even actively suppressed it; several reporters from national news media heard Lott speak, but his remark simply didn't fit the standard template of news. Because Thurmond's birthday was covered as a salutary event instead of a political one, the actual contents of the evening were judged in advance to be relatively unimportant. A related assumption is that a story that is not important one day also isn't important the next, unless something has changed. Thurmond's birthday party happened on a Thursday night, and the press gave Lott's remarks very little coverage on Friday. Not having written about it on Friday in turn became a reason not to write about it on Saturday, because if there was no story on Friday, there was even less of one on Saturday.

William O'Keefe of *The Washington Post*, one of the few reporters to think Lott's comment was important, explains the dilemma this way: "[T]here had to be a reaction" that the network could air alongside Lott's remarks, and "we had no on-camera reaction" available the evening of the party, when the news was still fresh. By the following night, he adds, "you're dealing with the news cycle: twenty-four hours later—that's old news." Like a delayed note to a friend, the initial lack of response would have meant, in any later version, having to apologize for not having written sooner.

Given this self-suppression—old stories are never revisited without a new angle—what kept the story alive was not the press but liberal and conservative bloggers, for whom fond memories of segregation were beyond the pale, birthday felicitations or no, and who had no operative sense of news cycles. The weekend after Lott's remarks, weblogs with millions of readers didn't just report his comments, they began to editorialize. The editorializers included some well-read conservatives such as Glenn Reynolds of the Instapundit blog, who wrote "But to say, as Lott did, that the country would be better off if Thurmond had won in 1948 is, well, it's proof that Lott shouldn't be majority leader for the Republicans, to begin with. And that's just to begin with. It's a sentiment as evil and loony as wishing that Gus Hall [a perennial Communist candidate for president] had been elected." Even more damaging to Lott, others began to dig deeper. After the story broke, Ed Sebesta, who maintains a database of materials related to nostalgia for the U.S. Confederacy, contacted bloggers with information on Lott, including an interview from the early 1980s in *Southern Partisan*, a neo-Confederate magazine. The simple birthday party story began looking like part of a decades-long pattern of saying one thing to the general public and another thing to his supporters.

Like the story of Ivanna's lost phone (in Chapter I), the story of Sebesta's database involves a link between individual effort and group attention. Just as Evan Guttman benefited from the expert knowledge of his readers, the bloggers posting about Lott benefited from Sebesta's deep knowledge of America's racist past, particularly of Lott's history of praise for same. Especially important, the bloggers didn't have to find Sebesta—he found them. Prior to our current generation of coordinating tools, a part-time politics junkie like Sebesta and amateur commentators like the bloggers would have had a hard time even discovering that they had mutual interests, much less being able to do anything with that information. Now, however, the cost of finding like-minded people has been lowered and, more important, deprofessionalized.

Because the weblogs kept the story alive, especially among libertarian Republicans, Lott eventually decided to react. The fateful moment came five days after the speech, when he issued a halfhearted apology for his earlier remark, characterizing it as a "poor choice of words." The statement was clearly meant to put the matter behind him, but Lott had not reckoned with the changed dynamics of press coverage. Once Lott apologized, news outlets could cover the apology as the news, while quoting the original speech as background. Only three mainstream news outlets had covered the original comment, but a dozen covered the apology the day it happened, and twenty-one covered it the day after. The traditional news cycle simple didn't apply in this situation; the story had suddenly been transformed from "not worth covering" to "breaking news."

Until recently, "the news" has meant two different things—events that are newsworthy, and events covered by the press. In that environment what identified something as news was professional judgment. The position of the news outlets (the very phrase attests to the scarcity of institutions that were able to publish information) was like that of the apocryphal umpire who says, "Some pitches are balls and some are strikes, but they ain't nothin' till I call 'em." There has always been grumbling about this system, on the grounds that some of the things the press was covering were not newsworthy (politicians at ribbon cuttings) and that newsworthy stories weren't being covered or covered enough (insert your pet issue here). Despite the grumbling, however, the basic link between newsworthiness and publication held, because there did not seem to be an alternative. What the Lott story showed us was that the link is now broken. From now on news can break into public consciousness without the traditional press weighing in. Indeed, the news media can end up covering the story *because* something has broken into public consciousness via other means.

There are several reasons for this change. The professional structuring of worldview, as exemplified by the decisions to treat Lott's remarks as a birthday party story, did not extend to the loosely coordinated amateurs publishing on their own. The decision not to cover Trent Lott's praise for a racist political campaign demonstrates a potential uniformity in the press outlook. In the world where a dozen editors, all belonging to the same professional class, can decide whether to run or kill a national story, information that might be of interest to the general public may not be published, not because of a conspiracy but because the editors have a professional bias that is aligned by the similar challenges they face and by the similar tools they use to approach those challenges. The mass amateurization of publishing undoes the limitations inherent in having a small number of traditional press outlets.

As they surveyed the growing amount of self-published content on the internet, many media companies correctly understood that the trustworthiness of each outlet was lower than that of established outlets like *The New York Times*. But what they failed to understand was that the effortlessness of publishing means that there are many more outlets. The same idea, published in dozens or hundreds of places, can have an amplifying effect that outweighs the verdict from the smaller number of professional outlets. (This is not to say that mere repetition makes an idea correct; amateur publishing relies on corrective argument even more than traditional media do.) The change isn't a shift from one kind of news institution to another, but rather in the definition of news: from news as an institutional prerogative to news as part of a communications ecosystem, occupied by a mix of formal organizations, informal collectives, and individuals.

It's tempting to regard the bloggers writing about Trent Lott or the people taking pictures of the Indian Ocean tsunami as a new crop of journalists. The label has an obvious conceptual appeal. The problem, however, is that mass professionalization is an oxymoron, since a professional class implies a specialized function, minimum tests for competence, and a minority of members. None of those conditions exist with political weblogs, photo sharing, or a host of other self-publishing tools. The individual weblogs are not merely alternate sites of publishing; they are alternatives to publishing itself, in the sense of publishers as a minority and professional class. In the same way you do not have to be a professional driver to drive, you no longer have to be a professional publisher to publish. Mass amateurization is a result of the radical spread of expressive capabilities, and the most obvious precedent is the one that gave birth to the modern world: the spread of the printing press five centuries age.

 ## Joining the Conversation: Critical Thinking and Writing

1. The concept of the "professional class" is crucial to Shirky's argument. What does he mean when he uses this term? What is the key problem that faces the newspaper industry's professional class?

2. In paragraph 4, Shirky uses librarians and newspaper executives as examples of professions that exist because of scarcity. Explain what he means by this and why he thinks the situation is changing.

3. In paragraph 18, Shirky argues that there has traditionally been a "link between newsworthiness and publication." In an essay of 500 words, explain how the story of Trent Lott's gaffe shows that this link is broken.

4. Shirky is interested in the shift from a world of "professionals" to a world in which we have what he terms "mass amateurization" (paragraph 21). Based on Shirky's arguments and on your own experiences with online news and entertainment, do you feel that this shift is a generally positive development? Explain and defend your position in an essay of 1,000 words.

A Casebook on Virtual Worlds

Brent Staples

Brent Staples, born in 1951, holds a Ph.D. in psychology from the University of Chicago. He taught briefly, then turned to journalism, and is now on the editorial board of The New York Times. *We reprint an essay that appeared in this paper in 2004.*

What Adolescents Miss When We Let Them Grow Up in Cyberspace

My 10th-grade heartthrob was the daughter of a fearsome steelworker who struck terror into the hearts of 15-year-old boys. He made it his business to answer the telephone—and so always knew who was calling—and grumbled in the background when the conversation went on too long. Unable to make time by phone, the boy either gave up or appeared at the front door. This meant submitting to the intense scrutiny that the girl's father soon became known for.

He greeted me with a crushing handshake, then leaned in close in a transparent attempt to find out whether I was one of those *bad* boys who smoked. He retired to the den during the visit, but cruised by the living room now and then to let me know he was watching. He let up after some weeks, but only after getting across what he expected of a boy who spent time with his daughter and how upset he'd be if I disappointed him.

This was my first sustained encounter with an adult outside my family who needed to be convinced of my worth as a person. This, of course, is a crucial part of growing up. Faced with same challenge today, however, I would probably pass on meeting the girl's father—and outflank him on the Internet.

Thanks to e-mail, online chat rooms and instant messages—which permit private, real-time conservations—adolescents have at last succeeded in shielding their social lives from adult scrutiny. But this comes at a cost: teenagers nowadays are both more connected to the world at large than ever, and more cut off from the social encounters that have historically prepared young people for the move into adulthood.

The Internet was billed as a revolutionary way to enrich our social   5
lives and expand our civic connections. This seems to have worked well for elderly people and others who were isolated before they got access to the World Wide Web. But a growing body of research is showing that heavy use of the Net can actually isolate younger socially connected people who unwittingly allow time online to replace face-to-face interactions with their families and friends.

Online shopping, checking e-mail and Web surfing—mainly solitary activities—have turned out to be more isolating than watching television, which friends and family often do in groups. Researchers have found that the time spent in direct contact with family members drops by as much as half for every hour we use the Net at home.

This should come as no surprise to the two-career couples who have seen their domestic lives taken over by e-mail and wireless tethers that keep people working around the clock. But a startling body of research from the Human-Computer Interaction Institute at Carnegie Mellon has shown that heavy Internet use can have stunting effect outside the home as well.

Studies show that gregarious, well-connected people actually lost friends, and experienced symptoms of loneliness and depression, after joining discussion groups and other activities. People who communicated with disembodied strangers online found the experience empty and emotionally frustrating but were nonetheless seduced by the novelty of the new medium. As Prof. Robert Kraut, a Carnegie Mellon researcher, told me recently, such people allowed low-quality relationships developed in virtual reality to replace higher-quality relationships in the real world.

No group has embraced this socially impoverishing trade-off more enthusiastically than adolescents, many of whom spend most of their free hours cruising the Net in sunless rooms. This hermetic existence has left many of these teenagers with nonexistent social skills—a point widely noted in stories about the computer geeks who rose to prominence in the early days of Silicon Valley.

Adolescents are drawn to cyberspace for different reasons than adults.   1
As the writer Michael Lewis observed in his book "Next: The Future Just Happened," children see the Net as a transformational device that lets them discard quotidian identities for more glamorous ones. Mr. Lewis illustrated the point with Marcus Arnold, who, as a 15-year-old, adopted a pseudonym a few years ago and posed as a 25-year-old legal expert for an Internet information service. Marcus did not feel the least bit guilty, and wasn't deterred,

when real-world lawyers discovered his secret and accused him of being a fraud. When asked whether he had actually read the law, Marcus responded that he found books "boring," leaving us to conclude that he had learned all he needed to know from his family's big-screen TV.

Marcus is a child of the Net, where everyone has a pseudonym, telling a story makes it true, and adolescents create older, cooler, more socially powerful selves any time they wish. The ability to slip easily into a new, false self is tailor-made for emotionally fragile adolescents, who can consider a bout of acne or a few excess pounds an unbearable tragedy.

But teenagers who spend much of their lives hunched over computer screens miss the socializing, the real-world experience that would allow them to leave adolescence behind and grow into adulthood. These vital experiences, like much else, are simply not available in a virtual form.

Joining the Conversation: Critical Thinking and Writing

1. Staples might have begun this article with the fourth paragraph. What does the argument gain through an account of his own experience in the first three paragraphs?

2. What is his argument? Try to restate it in a sentence or two and then evaluate it.

3. Do you think that parents should restrict their children's use of the Internet or supervise it? Has reading this article affected your decision? Explain.

Jeremy Rifkin

Born in Denver, Colorado, in 1945, Jeremy Rifkin is a graduate of the Wharton School of the University of Pennsylvania and of the Fletcher School of Law and Diplomacy at Tufts University. Rifkin is the author of numerous books, including The End of Work *(1995),* The Biotech Century *(1998), and* The Age of Access *(2001), and he is president of the Foundation on Economic Trends, a nonprofit organization that examines the impact of trends in science and technology on the environment and on society.*

Virtual Companionship

Over the past 20 years or so, we have preoccupied ourselves with developing ingenious new ways of communicating with each other. Our

---

Jeremy Rifkin: "Virtual Companionship." Originally published in *The Boston Globe*, October 10, 2006. Jeremy Rifkin is the author of *The Age of Access* and President of the Foundation on Economic Trends in Washington, D.C. Reprinted by permission of the author.

cellphones, personal computers, Blackberries, text messaging, e-mail, and the Internet connect 25 percent of the human race in a speed of light global village. At the same time that we are connecting the central nervous system of our species in a single, electronic embrace, the human vocabulary is plummeting all over the world, making it more difficult to express ourselves and participate in a meaningful way with our fellow human beings. It appears that we are all communicating more, but saying less.

According to a national survey conducted by the U.S. Department of Education, English literacy among college graduates has declined dramatically in the past 10 years. Only 31 percent of college graduates today are proficient in English literacy, compared with 40 percent just a decade ago. Grover J. Whitehurst, the director of the DOE Institute responsible for overseeing The National Assessment of Adult Literacy, said that he believes that literacy is declining as a result of the increase in television viewing and surfing the Internet.

Worse, it seems the more connected we are in our electronically mediated landscapes, the lonelier we find ourselves. A study conducted by the Kaiser Family Fund showed that American children now spend an average of 6.5 hours per day watching television, surfing the Internet, text messaging, and playing with video games and other electronic media.

More worrisome, the study found that most children interact with electronic media alone. For example, older children spend up to 95 percent of their time watching television alone, while children between the ages of 2 and 7 watch television alone more than 81 percent of the time. Our children are seeping further into virtual worlds and losing the emotional attachments that come with face to face real time participation with their fellow human beings. Nor are American youngsters an anomaly. Children in other high-tech countries are following close on the heels of their American peers. This new human condition can best be described as the "high-tech blues."

Are future generations to be forever lonely? No, say the technological optimists. Engineers at some of the leading technology centers are feverishly working on the next generation of technological marvels to address our lonesome high-tech existence. The field is called "affective computing" and the goal is to create technology that can express emotion, interpret and respond to the emotions of their human handlers, and even establish a sense of intimacy with their human companions. Built-in cameras allow the computers to detect even subtle changes in facial expressions, which are then processed in real time, allowing the computer to recognize the emotional state of the person. Researchers at the Massachusetts Institute of Technology have even developed an "affective wearable computer" that picks up different emotional states and subtle change of emotion by detecting changes in heart-rate, breathing, skin conductivity, temperature, pulse, and muscle activity.

5

Rosalind Picard, one of the pioneer researchers in the field of "affective computing," reports on an amazing study done at the MIT Media Lab. A computerized virtual person named "Laura" plays the role of an exercise adviser, helping real-life subjects increase their physical activity levels. Laura is capable of conversing with her subjects and is able to use hand gestures, eye gaze behavior, posture shifts, head-nods, and facial expressions. Laura, like any good exercise trainer, provides her subjects with feedback on their performance, helps them improve on their regimen, and gives empathetic verbal and facial feedback, cued to the appropriate emotional state of her human companions.

The reactions of the subjects are revealing. Compared with subjects interacting with a "nonrelational" computer interface, a number of the subjects—but not all—working with Laura reported an emotional rapport similar with what one might expect with a real-life trainer. One subject in the study remarked, "I feel Laura, in her own unique way, is genuinely concerned about my welfare." Another said, "I feel like Laura . . . likes me." A third subject confided, "Laura and I trust each other." Here is a typical response: "I like talking to Laura, especially those little conversations, about school, weather, interests, etc. She is very caring . . . I found myself looking forward to these fresh chats that pop up every now and then. They make Laura so much more like a real person." To be fair, there were skeptics as well. One subject said, "Personally, I detest Laura."

Other experiments conducted at Stanford University report similarly positive results with empathetic embodied computer agents interacting with subjects, leading researchers to conclude that "embodied computer agents are indeed social actors in the truest sense of the word 'social,' capable of forming relationships with users comparable to those found in the world of human-human interactions."

Frankly, it's hard to know whether to laugh off such technological pretensions as sadly pathological or whether to be truly frightened. There is no doubt that a growing number of young people find themselves enmeshed in virtual worlds where make believe substitutes for real-life experience. With "affective computing" looming on the horizon, the truly lonely can look forward to interacting with silicon companions, emotionally programmed to empathize and even care, to be a friend, and an intimate confidant.

Progress? Surely we can do better.   10

 ## Joining the Conversation:
Critical Thinking and Writing

1. In the first paragraph, Rifkin claims that "the human vocabulary is plummeting all over the world, making it more difficult to express ourselves and participate in a meaningful way with our fellow human beings." What does he mean?

2. In paragraph 2, Rifkin refers to a study that says that "only 31 percent of college graduates today are proficient in English literacy, compared with 40 percent just a decade ago." Rifkin does not tell us how the study defined "literacy." How do you define it? Given your definition, do you consider yourself "proficient in English literacy"? Explain.

3. In paragraph 3, Rifkin reports that American children now are "lonelier" because they "spend an average of 6.5 hours per day watching television, surfing the Internet, text messaging, and playing with video games and other electronic media." Suppose someone said to Rifkin, "For *real* loneliness, for *real* isolation, nothing beats reading a book. Reading is really a solitary pleasure. Why don't you complain about the kids who like to read?" What reply do you think Rifkin might make?

4. In paragraph 4, Rifkin says that the "new human condition can best be described as 'high-tech blues.'" What does he mean? And what is "affective computing"? Of what "technological marvels" does it now consist?

5. In paragraph 9, speaking about such developments as "Laura," Rifkin says, "Frankly, it's hard to know whether to laugh off such technological pretensions as sadly pathological or whether to be truly frightened." Your reaction to these technological developments?

Kay S. Hymowitz

Kay S. Hymowitz, born in 1948, holds degrees from Brandeis University, Tufts University, and Columbia University. Among her publications are Ready or Not: Why Treating Our Children as Small Adults Endangers Their Future and Ours *(1999) and* Liberation's Children *(2001). We reprint an essay that originally appeared in* The Wall Street Journal *in 2006.*

Big Mother Is Watching

Some years ago my older daughter, then a senior in college, listened to me fret about rumors of drinking at the parties her ninth-grade sister was begging to go to. "They're so young to deal with this sort of thing," I worried. "Mom," she began in a knowing tone, "What do you think was going on when I went to parties in the ninth grade?"

I lingered for a moment over the disconnect between this young woman standing before me, a premed student, an Organization Kid who would sooner live on bread and water than turn in a late paper, and the image of her 14-year-old self chugging a Budweiser. Then, I struggled with two contradictory responses. First, discomfiture; I had been naïve, a mental status that we been-there-done-that boomer parents find pretty embarrassing. How could I have been so out of it? And second: relief. Thank God I didn't know. If I had, I would have had to transform my parenting approach from trust-but-verify (check-in phone calls to friends' parents, "so how did the movie end again?" sort of questions, etc.) to all-out war.

This incident and my response came to mind when I read recently about the burgeoning market in parental surveillance devices. There's a gizmo that parents can plug in beneath their SUV's dashboard; when your 16-year-old daughter drives to her new boyfriend's house, it records the vehicle's speed, or any sudden stops or swerves it may have made— as well as the location of said house. There are Global Positioning Systems that you can attach to your children's cellphones; they beep your cell if your son wanders beyond his allowed haunts or notify you by email that your tween is at the mall rather than her tutoring session.

And then there are the popular Internet spy programs like eBlaster or IM Einstein that let you monitor your kid's computer activities. The more sophisticated models send an email to your work account with the content of your son or daughter's emails or Instant Messages; one of them can even show you a screen snapshot of online conversations.

Orwellian as this high-tech snooping sounds, frightening reports of abducted children, not to mention drinking parties for kids still in braces, suggest that there's a reasonable argument in its favor. A few generations ago when neighborhoods were more stable and mothers were home during the day to survey them, parents could feel pretty confident that there were familiar adult eyes watching over their kids even when they were out of parental range. Moreover, childhood had well-defined boundaries that pretty much everyone, including the corner merchant and Hollywood mediacrats, respected.

But as mothers went to work, neighborhoods emptied and the public meaning of childhood splintered, children's lives became both more anonymous and more threatened. Suddenly strangers with suspect motives were everywhere—sometimes in your own home. The Nannycam, a camera that can be secreted into the kitchen smoke alarm, for instance, to watch over babysitters, was perhaps the first of the surveillance devices to deal with the new conditions of childhood, followed quickly by the V-chip. Now with the Internet, the dangers have been globalized as online predators and porn Web sites whisper their enticements to every wired third-grader. Little wonder some parents are tempted by what one parent quoted in a Los Angeles Times article on the GPS systems, called "another set of eyes."

Still, there's a lot more behind Big Mother and Father spyware than protecting children from the dangers of an anonymous and treacherous 21st-century world. The truth is that today's parents worry about their kids' most mundane activities in a way that would baffle the legendarily meddling mothers and fathers of the 1950s. They are practitioners of what British sociologist Frank Furedi calls "paranoid parenting."

This, after all, is the generation of parents that has made bike helmets and car seats a matter of state interest and has banned such perilous pastimes as tag and dodgeball from school playgrounds. An increasing number of parents seem to be trying to control their kids' lives even after they move away from home. College administrators are now complaining about a cadre of "helicopter parents" who hassle deans with phone calls if their little one doesn't like her roommate or Chemistry grade. With a population of parents like these, Sprint's Family Locator service is bound to turn a hefty profit—even if parents have to rely on their 14-year-old, as in the case of a Kansas family described in the *Los Angeles Times*, to program the blasted thing.

Now, the obvious danger of such devices is that they raise paranoid parenting to an even more extreme level, thereby further depriving children of the chance to test their capacity for independence. Anthropologists tell us that traditional Japanese families often discouraged their babies from taking their first steps in an effort to keep them tied to their mothers. The custom makes a kind of sense in a culture that prizes group identity and interdependence above all. But Americans celebrate their children's first steps; they have always prided themselves on their self-sufficiency, which is a precondition for success in our society. The problem is that children who grow up knowing their parents keep track of them 24/7 fail to internalize the common sense and limit-setting that can only emerge from the experience of making independent judgments.

The more subtle, but equally important, objection to spyware is that it isn't good for parents either. By making snooping relatively impersonal, these technologies prompt mothers and fathers to bypass important moral questions about their relationship with their children. If it's all right to scrutinize your daughter's text messages, then it should be OK to read her diary. If it's all right to electronically monitor her driving, then it should be equally kosher to get in to your own car and follow her. Yet there are good reasons most sane adults would balk at these low-tech invasions of their children's privacy.

Equally pernicious, by making spying seem less intrusive, technology discourages parents from taking the periodic measurements of their child's maturity that are essential to guiding their development. Your 11-year-old son wants to take a public bus for the first time: Absent a GPS phone, you think about his judgment, how he handles money, how alert he is to his surroundings. With GPS, parents are trying to make an end-run around careful, and admittedly difficult, deliberation.

The fact is that raising children to become independent adults means years of worrying. Kids make stupid decisions. Terrible things can happen. How do you know when to let your toddler climb the steps on her own? Your 7-year-old walk to school? Your 12-year-old have free access to the Internet? Your 14-year-old go to a party where you suspect beer will be on the menu? No matter how much technology you buy, at some point your kids will be in a place you don't want them to be and do something you don't want them to do. Just remember, someday when they are older, they will probably tell you all about it—and you will breathe a sigh of relief.

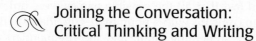

Joining the Conversation: Critical Thinking and Writing

1. Hymowitz introduces her essay with an account of a conversation she had with her daughter "some years ago." After reading the essay, evaluate the narrative as an introduction.

2. How does the title "Big Mother Is Watching" prepare readers for Hymowitz's argument? Does the title echo something else you have read?

3. What is Hymowitz's argument? How does she support it? Does she sufficiently acknowledge opinions counter to her own?

4. What is your own view of parental surveillance devices? Did reading "Big Mother Is Watching" change or strengthen your own view? Explain.

5. Imagine an issue you might have had with your parents or with your children. Would you be pleased to find an article by Hymowitz arguing on behalf of your position? Why or why not?

A Casebook on Twitter: Three Essays and Two Cartoons

David Carr

David Carr writes about culture and about business for The New York Times. *He tweets at http://twitter.com/carr2n, where—he has said—his character emerges in 140 characters.*

Why Twitter Will Endure

I can remember when I first thought seriously about Twitter. Last March, I was at the SXSW conference, a conclave in Austin, Tex., where technology, media and music are mashed up and re-imagined, and, not so coincidentally, where Twitter first rolled out in 2007. As someone who was oversubscribed on Facebook, overwhelmed by the computer-generated RSS feeds of news that came flying at me, and swamped by incoming e-mail messages, the last thing I wanted was one more Web-borne intru-sion into my life.

And then there was the name. Twitter.

In the pantheon of digital nomenclature—brands within a sector of the economy that grew so fast that all the sensible names were quickly taken—it would be hard to come up with a noun more trite than Twitter. It impugns itself, promising something slight and inconsequential, yet another way to make hours disappear and have nothing to show for it. And just in case the noun is not sufficiently indicting, the verb, "to tweet" is even more embarrassing.

Beyond the dippy lingo, the idea that something intelligent, some-thing worthy of mindshare, might occur in the space of 140 characters—Twitter's parameters were set by what would fit in a text message on a phone—seems unlikely.

But it was clear that at the conference, the primary news platform was Twitter, with real-time annotation of the panels on stage and critical updates about what was happening elsewhere at a very hectic conven-tion. At 52, I succumbed, partly out of professional necessity.

And now, nearly a year later, has Twitter turned my brain to mush? No, I'm in narrative on more things in a given moment than I ever thought possible, and instead of spending a half-hour surfing in search of illumination, I get a sense of the day's news and how people are reacting to it in the time that it takes to wait for coffee at Starbucks. Yes, I worry about my ability to think long thoughts—where was I, anyway?—but the tradeoff has been worth it.

Some time soon, the company won't say when, the 100-millionth per-son will have signed on to Twitter to follow and be followed by friends and strangers. That may sound like a MySpace waiting to happen—remember MySpace?—but I'm convinced Twitter is here to stay.

And I'm not alone.

"The history of the Internet suggests that there have been cool Web sites that go in and out of fashion and then there have been open stan-dards that become plumbing," said Steven Johnson, the author and tech-nology observer who wrote a seminal piece about Twitter for *Time* last June. "Twitter is looking more and more like plumbing, and plumbing is eternal."

Really? What could anyone possibly find useful in this cacophony of short-burst communication?

Well, that depends on whom you ask, but more importantly whom you follow. On Twitter, anyone may follow anyone, but there is very little expectation of reciprocity. By carefully curating the people you follow, Twitter becomes an always-on data stream from really bright people in their respective fields, whose tweets are often full of links to incredibly vital, timely information.

The most frequent objection to Twitter is a predictable one: "I don't need to know someone is eating a donut right now." But if that someone is a serious user of Twitter, she or he might actually be eating the curmudgeon's lunch, racing ahead with a clear, up-to-the-second picture of an increasingly connected, busy world. The service has obvious utility for a journalist, but no matter what business you are in, imagine knowing what the thought leaders in your industry were reading and considering. And beyond following specific individuals, Twitter hash tags allow you to go deep into interests and obsession: #rollerderby, #physics, #puppets and #Avatar, to name just a few of many thousands.

The act of publishing on Twitter is so friction-free—a few keystrokes and hit send—that you can forget that others are our there listening. I was on a Virgin America cross-country flight, and used its wireless connection to tweet about the fact that the guy next to me seemed to be the leader of a cult involving Axe body spray. A half-hour later, a steward approached me and said he wondered if I would be more comfortable with a seat in the bulkhead. (He turned out to be a great guy, but I was doing a story involving another part of the company, so I had to decline the offer. @VirginAmerica, its corporate Twitter account, sent me a message afterward saying perhaps it should develop a screening process for Axe. It was creepy and comforting all at once.)

Like many newbies on Twitter, I vastly overestimated the importance of broadcasting on Twitter and after a while, I realized that I was not Moses and neither Twitter nor its users were wondering what I thought. Nearly a year in, I've come to understand that the real value of the service is listening to a wired collective voice.

Not that long ago, I was at a conference at Yale and looked at the sea of open laptops in the seats in front of me. So why wasn't my laptop open? Because I follow people on Twitter who serve as my Web-crawling proxies, each of them tweeting links that I could examine and read on a Blackberry. Regardless of where I am, I surf far less than I used to. 15

At first, Twitter can be overwhelming, but think of it as a river of data rushing past that I dip a cup into every once in a while. Much of what I need to know is in that cup: if it looks like Apple is going to demo its new tablet, or Amazon sold more Kindles than actual books at Christmas, or the final vote in the Senate gets locked in on health care, I almost always learn about it first on Twitter.

The expressive limits of a kind of narrative developed from text messages, with less space to digress or explain than this sentence, has significant upsides. The best people on Twitter communicate with economy and precision, with each element—links, hash tags and comments—freighted with meaning. Professional acquaintances whom I find insufferable on every other platform suddenly become interesting within the confines of Twitter.

Twitter is incredibly customizable, with little of the social expectations that go with Facebook. Depending on whom you follow, Twitter can reveal a nation riveted by the last episode of "Jersey Shore" or a short-form conclave of brilliance. There is plenty of nonsense—Tiger had quite a run—but there are rich threads on the day's news and bravura solo performances from learned autodidacts. And the ethos of Twitter, which is based on self-defining groups, is far more well-mannered than many parts of the web—more Toastmasters than mosh pit. On Twitter, you are your avatar and your avatar is you, so best not to act like a lout and when people want to flame you for something you said, they are responding to their own followers, not yours, so trolls quickly lose interest.

"Anything that is useful to both dissidents in Iran and Martha Stewart has a lot going for it; Twitter has more raw capability for users than anything since e-mail," said Clay Shirky, who wrote "Here Comes Everybody," a book about social media. "It will be hard to wait out Twitter because it is lightweight, endlessly useful and gets better as more people use it. Brands are using it, institutions are using it, and it is becoming a place where a lot of important conversations are being held."

Twitter helps define what is important by what Mr. Shirky has called "algorithmic authority," meaning that if all kinds of people are pointing at the same thing at the same instant, it must be a pretty big deal.

Beyond the throbbing networked intelligence, there is the possibility of practical magic. Twitter can tell you what kind of netbook you should buy for your wife for Christmas—thanks Twitter!—or call you out when you complain about the long lines it took to buy it, as a tweeter on behalf of the electronics store B & H did when I shared the experience on my Blackberry while in line. I have found transcendent tacos at a car wash in San Antonio, rediscovered a brand of reporter's notepad I adore, uncovered sources for stories, all just by typing a query into Twitter.

All those riches do not come at zero cost: If you think e-mail and surfing can make time disappear, wait until you get ahold of Twitter, or more likely, it gets ahold of you. There is always something more interesting on Twitter than whatever you happen to be working on.

But in the right circumstance, Twitter can flex some big muscles. Think of last weekend, a heavy travel period marked by a terrorist incident on Friday. As news outlets were scrambling to understand the implications for travelers on Saturday morning, Twitter began lighting up with reports of new security initiatives, including one from @CharleneLi, a consultant who tweeted from the Montreal airport at about 7:30 a.m.: "New security rules for int'l flights into US. I bag, no electronics the ENTIRE flight, no getting up last hour of flight."

It was far from the whole story and getting ahead of the news by some hours would seem like no big deal, but imagine you or someone you loved was flying later that same day: Twitter might seem very useful.

Twitter's growing informational hegemony is not assured. There have been serious outages in recent weeks, leading many business and government users to wonder about the stability of the platform. And this being the Web, many smart folks are plotting ways to turn Twitter into so much pixilated mist. But I don't think so. I can go anywhere I want on the Web, but there is no guarantee that my Twitter gang will come with me. I may have quite a few followers, but that doesn't make me Moses.

Joining the Conversation: Critical Thinking and Writing

1. How would you summarize Carr's first four paragraphs? What is his strategy here? What turning points in his attitude toward Twitter does he note in his fifth and sixth paragraphs?

2. In his fourth paragraph, Carr suggests that the words "Twitter" and "Tweet" are "dippy lingo." Do you agree? Is the dippiness part of the appeal? What *is* the appeal of these words? If for some reason those words were unavailable, what words would you have suggested for the medium? Why do you choose the words you do?

3. Let's assume that you tweet, and someone tells you that you are wasting your time. What is your response? You may of course draw on Carr's essay, but if you do, be sure to give him credit. In any case, draw chiefly on your own experiences.

4. If you use Twitter, would you say that you have developed a distinctive style—something notably different from your e-mail style? Explain.

5. Begin an essay of about 500 words on Carr's style by briefly commenting on his first paragraph, in which (a) he speaks of "informational hegemony" and "pixilated mist" and (b) he says he is not Moses. Explain the terms and the allusion to Moses and then go on to write an essay in which you discuss what you consider to be the strengths and weaknesses of his style.

Steven Pinker

Steven Pinker, a specialist in the development of language in children, teaches psychology at Harvard. His most recent book for the general public is The Stuff of Thought *(2007). We reprint an essay that appeared in* The New York Times *on June 11, 2010.*

Mind Over Mass Media

New forms of media have always caused moral panics: the printing press, newspapers, paperbacks and television were all once denounced as threats to their consumers' brainpower and moral fiber.

So too with electronic technologies. PowerPoint, we're told, is reducing discourse to bullet points. Search engines lower our intelligence, encouraging us to skim on the surface of knowledge rather than dive to its depths. Twitter is shrinking our attention spans.

But such panics often fail basic reality checks. When comic books were accused of turning juveniles into delinquents in the 1950s, crime was falling to record lows, just as the denunciations of video games in the 1990s coincided with the great American crime decline. The decades of television, transistor radios and rock videos were also decades in which I.Q. scores rose continuously.

For a reality check today, take the state of science, which demands high levels of brainwork and is measured by clear benchmarks of discovery. These days scientists are never far from their e-mail, rarely touch paper and cannot lecture without PowerPoint. If electronic media were hazardous to intelligence, the quality of science would be plummeting. Yet discoveries are multiplying like fruit flies, and progress is dizzying. Other activities in the life of the mind, like philosophy, history and cultural criticism, are likewise flourishing, as anyone who has lost a morning of work to the Web site Arts & Letters Daily can attest.

Critics of new media sometimes use science itself to press their case, citing research that shows how "experience can change the brain." But cognitive neuroscientists roll their eyes at such talk. Yes, every time we learn a fact or skill the wiring of the brain changes; it's not as if the information is stored in the Pancreas. But the existence of neural plasticity does not mean the brain is a blob of clay pounded into shape by experience.   5

Experience does not revamp the basic information-processing capacities of the brain. Speed-reading programs have long claimed to do just that, but the verdict was rendered by Woody Allen after he read *War and Peace* in one sitting: "It was about Russia." Genuine multitasking, too, has been exposed as a myth, not just by laboratory studies but by the familiar sight of an S.U.V. undulating between lanes as the driver cuts deals on his cellphone.

Moreover, as the psychologists Christopher Chabris and Daniel Simons show in their new book *The Invisible Gorilla: And Other Ways Our Intuitions Deceive Us*, the effects of experience are highly specific to the experiences themselves. If you train people to do one thing (recognize shapes, solve math puzzles, find hidden words), they get better at doing that thing, but almost nothing else. Music doesn't make you better at math, conjugating Latin doesn't make you more logical, brain-training games don't make you smarter. Accomplished people don't bulk up their brains with intellectual calisthenics; they immerse themselves in their fields. Novelists read lots of novels, scientists read lots of science.

The effects of consuming electronic media are also likely to be far more limited than the panic implies. Media critics write as if the brain takes on the qualities of whatever it consumes, the informational equivalent of "you are what you eat." As with primitive peoples who believe that eating fierce animals will make them fierce, they assume that watching quick cuts in rock videos turns your mental life into quick cuts or that reading bullet points and Twitter postings turn your thoughts into bullet points and Twitter postings.

Yes, the constant arrival of information packets can be distracting or addictive, especially to people with attention deficit disorder. But distraction is not a new phenomenon. The solution is not to bemoan technology but to develop strategies of self-control, as we do with every other temptation in life. Turn off e-mail or Twitter when you work, put away your Blackberry at dinner time, ask your spouse to call you to bed at a designated hour.

And to encourage intellectual depth, don't rail at PowerPoint or Google. It's not as if habits of deep reflection, thorough research and rigorous reasoning ever came naturally to people. They must be acquired in special institutions, which we call universities, and maintained with constant upkeep, which we call analysis, criticism and debate. They are not granted by propping a heavy encyclopedia on your lap, nor are they taken away by efficient access to information on the internet.

The new media have caught on for a reason. Knowledge is increasing exponentially; human brainpower and waking hours are not. Fortunately, the Internet and information technologies are helping us manage, search and retrieve our collective intellectual output at different scales, from Twitter and previews to e-books and online encyclopedias. Far from making us stupid, these technologies are the only things that will keep us smart.

 ## Joining the Conversation: Critical Thinking and Writing

1. To whom—to what audience—does Pinker address his argument? What is your evidence? In reading "Mind Over Mass Media," did you feel that you were part of that audience? Or distinct from it? Whatever your answer, what are your reasons?

2. Pinker's first paragraph consists of a single sentence, but it easily could have been written as two sentences if he had decided to use a period rather than a colon after "panics." Which version do you prefer? Why?

3. Does the second paragraph neatly follow from the first? Do the next two sentences of the second paragraph seem to come naturally from what has preceded them? What, if anything, have they taught you about the art of writing an argument?

4. In his fifth paragraph, Pinker speaks of "cognitive neuroscientists." What is a cognitive neuroscientist?

5. In paragraph 9, Pinker says, "Turn off e-mail or Twitter when you work." If it has not been your practice to turn them off when you study or do other work, will you now do so? Why or why not?

6. In paragraph 10, Pinker speaks about "habits of deep reflection, thorough research and rigorous reasoning," with the implications that these are among the qualities that students hope to acquire during their college years. Does he speak for you? Explain.

Maureen Dowd

Maureen Dowd was born in Washington, D.C., the daughter of a police inspector and a home-maker. After graduating (as an English major) from Catholic University in D.C., she became an editorial assistant on The Washington Star, *and she has continued with a career in journalism. Dowd has worked as a reporter for* Time *and for* The New York Times, *but since 1995, she has served as a regular columnist for* The New York Times. *In the following piece, she interviews the founders of Twitter.*

To Tweet or Not To Tweet

Alfred Hitchcock would have loved the Twitter headquarters here. Birds gathering everywhere, painted on the wall in flocks, perched on the coffee table, stitched on pillows and framed on the wall with a thought bubble asking employees to please tidy up after themselves. In a droll nod to shifting technology, there's a British red telephone booth in the loftlike office that you are welcome to use but you'll have to bring in your cellphone. I was here on a simple quest: curious to know if the inventors of Twitter were as annoying as their invention. (They're not. They're charming.) I sat down with Biz Stone, 35, and Evan Williams, 37, and asked them to justify themselves.

ME: You say the brevity of Twitter enhances creativity. So I wonder if you can keep your answers to 140 characters, like Twitter users must. Twitter seems like telegrams without the news. We now know that on the president's trip to Trinidad, ABC News's Jake Tapper's shower was spewing brown water. Is there any thought that doesn't need to be published?

BIZ: The one I'm thinking right now.

ME: Did you know you were designing a toy for bored celebrities and high-school girls?

BIZ: We definitely didn't design it for that. If they want to use it for that, it's great.   5

ME: I heard about a woman who tweeted her father's funeral. Whatever happened to private pain?

EVAN: I have private pain every day.

ME: If you were out with a girl and she started twittering about it in the middle, would that be a deal-breaker or a turn-on?

BIZ (dryly): In the middle of what?

ME: Do you ever think "I don't care that my friend is having a   10
hamburger?"

BIZ: If I said I was eating a hamburger, Evan would be surprised because I'm a vegan.

ME: What do you think about the backlash to Twitter on the blogs?
Isn't that a bit like the pot calling the kettle black?

BIZ: If people are passionate about your product, whether it's because they're hating or loving it, those are both good scenarios.
People can use it to help each other during fuel shortages of revolts or
earthquakes or wildfires. That's the exciting part of it.

ME: Why did you think the answer to e-mail was a new kind of
e-mail?

BIZ: With Twitter, it's as easy to unfollow as it is to follow.   15

(They're spilling past 140 characters now, but it must feel good to climb
out of their Twitter bird cage. Evan has to leave. Biz and I continue.)

ME: Don't you get worried about being swallowed up by Google?

BIZ: They don't swallow you up. They call you up.

ME: Why did you call the company Twitter instead of Clutter?

BIZ: We had a lot of words like "Jitter" and things that reflected a   20
hyper-nervousness. Somebody threw "Twitter" in the hat. I thought
"Oh, that's the short trivial bursts of information that birds do."

ME: Oprah unleashed mayhem in the Twittersphere last week when,
in her first tweet, she greeted "Twitters" instead of "Twitterers."

BIZ: I'm still kinda old-school. We're twittering, and we're all twitterers. And we write tweets. The only thing I don't love is twits.

ME: Would Shakespeare have tweeted?

BIZ: Brevity's the soul of wit, right?

ME: Was there anything in your childhood that led you to want to de-   25
stroy civilization as we know it?

BIZ: You mean enhance civilization, make even better?

ME: What's your favorite book?

BIZ: I loved Sherlock Holmes when I was a kid.

ME: But you've helped destroy mystery.

BIZ: When you put more information out there, sometimes you can just put a little bit of it out, which just makes the mystery even broader.

ME: When newsprint blows away, I want a second career as a Twitter ghostwriter. Which celebrity on Twitter most needs my help?

BIZ: Definitely not Shaq. Britney, maybe.

ME: Gavin Newsom announced his candidacy for governor today on Twitter and elsewhere. Does that make you the new Larry King?

BIZ: Did he? I didn't know.

ME: Have you thought about using even fewer than 140 characters?

BIZ: I've seen people twitter in haiku only. Twit-u. James Buck, the student who was thrown into an Egyptian prison, just wrote "Arrested."

ME: I would rather be tied up to stakes in the Kalahari Desert, have honey poured over me and red ants eat out my eyes than open a Twitter account. Is there anything you can say to change my mind?

BIZ: Well, when you do find yourself in that position, you're gonna want Twitter. You might want to type out the message "Help."

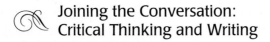

Joining the Conversation: Critical Thinking and Writing

1. In her first paragraph, Dowd uses the word "droll." What is droll about the situation she is describing?

2. In paragraph 3, what thought do you imagine Biz is thinking?

3. In paragraph 29, Dowd says that Twitter has "helped destroy mystery." What can she mean by this? (Note Biz's reply in paragraph 30.) Do you agree with Dowd or Biz? Explain as concretely as possible.

4. Conduct an interview with an avid twitterer or a dedicated opponent of tweeting. (On conducting an interview, see pages 55–58.)

Cartoonists expose what they take to be the absurdity of their subjects. (They may engage in the exposure genially—sometimes even with affection for their subject, as perhaps in these instances—or with anger, as often with political cartoonists.) Try to imagine a pro-Twitter cartoon, perhaps with Maureen Dowd (see pages 438–439) as the subject. What drawing and text can you come up with?

Two Cartoons

"hey fans! im at bat,. btm 9th, bases loaded, score tied--oops, jst got called strike1!"

Norman Silver

Norman Silver is the author of two books of poetry: Laugh Out Loud: -D *and* Age, Sex, Location. *We give a poem from the first of these. In Silver's book, the last word of the first line and the capital letters in the ninth line are printed in red.*

txt commandments

1. u shall luv ur mobil fone with all ur hart
2. u & ur fone shall neva b apart
3. u shall nt lust aftr ur neibrs fone nor thiev
4. u shall b prepard @ all times 2 tXt & 2 recv
5. u shall use LOL & othr acronyms in conversatns
6. u shall be zappy with ur ast*r*sks & exc!matns!!
7. u shall abbrevi8 & rite words like theyr sed
8. u shall nt speak 2 sum 1 face2face if u cn msg em insted
9. u shall nt shout with capitls XEPT IN DIRE EMERGNCY +
10. u shall nt consult a ninglish dictnry

 ## Joining the Conversation: Critical Thinking and Writing

1. How much depends on *seeing* this poem, as opposed to hearing it read?

2. The use of "u" for "you," "b" for "be," "2" for "to," and "8" for the syllable "ate" (in "abbreviate," in line 7) is not highly original. What *is* highly original in the poem?

CHAPTER 12

Law and Disorder

The Problem We All Live With
Norman Rockwell, 1964

Short Views

The trouble for the thief is not how to steal the chief's bugle, but where to blow it.
>   *African Proverb*

Whoever desires to found a state and give it laws, must start with assuming that all men are bad and ever ready to display their vicious nature, whenever they may find occasion for it.
>   *Niccolò Machiavelli*

If a man were permitted to make all the ballads, he need not care who should make the laws of a nation.
>   *Andrew Fletcher*

Nature has given women so much power that the law has very wisely given them very little.
>   *Samuel Johnson*

One law for the ox and the ass is oppression.
>   *William Blake*

The law, in its majestic equality, forbids the rich as well as the poor to sleep under bridges, to beg in the streets, and to steal bread.
>   *Anatole France*

The trouble about fighting for human freedom is that you have to spend much of your life defending sons of bitches; for oppressive laws are always aimed at them originally, and oppression must be stopped in the beginning if it is to be stopped at all.
>   *H. L. Mencken*

Censorship upholds the dignity of the profession, know what I mean?
>   *Mae West*

Thomas Jefferson

Thomas Jefferson (1743–1826), governor of Virginia and the third president of the United States, devoted most of his adult life, until his retirement, to the service of Virginia and of the nation. The spirit and the wording of the Declaration are almost entirely Jefferson's.

The Declaration of Independence

In CONGRESS, July 4, 1776.

The Unanimous Declaration of the Thirteen United States of America.

When in the Course of human events, it becomes necessary for one people to dissolve the political bands which have connected them with another, and to assume among the powers of the earth, the separate and equal station to which the Laws of Nature and of Nature's God entitle them, a decent respect to the opinions of mankind requires that they should declare the causes which impel them to the separation.

We hold these Truths to be self-evident, that all men are created equal, that they are endowed by their Creator with certain unalienable Rights, that among these are Life, Liberty and the pursuit of Happiness.

That to secure these rights, Governments are instituted among Men, deriving their just powers from the consent of the governed.

That whenever any Form of Government becomes destructive of these ends, it is the Right of the People to alter or to abolish it, and to institute new Government, laying its foundation on such principles and organizing its powers in such form, as to them shall seem most likely to effect their Safety and Happiness. Prudence, indeed, will dictate that Governments long established should not be changed for light and transient causes; and accordingly all experience hath shewn, that mankind are more disposed to suffer, while evils are sufferable, than to right themselves by abolishing the forms to which they are accustomed. But when a long train of abuses and usurpations, pursuing invariably the same Object evinces a design to reduce them under absolute Despotism, it is their right, it is their duty, to throw off such Government, and to provide new Guards for their future security.

Such has been the patient sufferance of these Colonies; and such is now the necessity which constrains them to alter their former Systems of Government. The history of the present King of Great Britain is a history of repeated injuries and usurpations, all having in direct object the establishment of an absolute Tyranny over these States. To prove this, let Facts be submitted to a candid world. 5

He has refused his Assent to Laws, the most wholesome and necessary for the public good.

He has forbidden his Governors to pass Laws of immediate and pressing importance, unless suspended in their operation till his Assent should be obtained; and when so suspended, he has utterly neglected to attend to them.

He has refused to pass other Laws for the accommodation of large districts of people, unless those people would relinquish the right of Representation in the Legislature, a right inestimable to them and formidable to tyrants only.

He has called together legislative bodies at places unusual, uncomfortable, and distant from the depository of their public Records, for the sole purpose of fatiguing them into compliance with his measures.

He has dissolved Representative Houses repeatedly, for opposing with manly firmness his invasions on the rights of people.

He has refused for a long time, after such dissolutions, to cause others to be elected; whereby the Legislative powers, incapable of Annihilation, have returned to the People at large for their exercise; the State remaining in the mean time exposed to all the dangers of invasion from without, and convulsions within.

He has endeavoured to prevent the population of these States; for that purpose obstructing the Laws for Naturalization of Foreigners; refusing to pass others to encourage their migrations hither, and raising the conditions of new Appropriations of Lands.

He has obstructed the Administration of Justice, by refusing his Assent to Laws for establishing Judiciary powers.

He has made Judges dependent on his Will alone, for the tenure of their offices, and the amount and payment of their salaries.

He has erected a multitude of New Offices, and sent hither swarms of Officers to harass our people, and eat out their substance.

He has kept among us, in times of peace, Standing Armies without the Consent of our legislatures.

He has affected to render the Military independent of and superior to the Civil power.

He has combined with others to subject us to a jurisdiction foreign to our constitution, and unacknowledged by our laws; giving his Assent to their Acts of pretended Legislation:

For Quartering large bodies of armed troops among us:

For Protecting them, by a mock Trial, from punishment for any Murders which they should commit on the Inhabitants of these States:

For cutting off our Trade with all parts of the world:

For imposing Taxes on us without our Consent:

For depriving us in many cases, of the benefits of Trial by Jury:

For transporting us beyond Seas to be tried for pretended offences:

For abolishing the free System of English Laws in a neighbouring Province, establishing therein an Arbitrary government, and enlarging its Boundaries so as to render it at once an example and fit instrument for introducing the same absolute rule into these Colonies:

For taking away our Charters, abolishing our most valuable Laws, and altering fundamentally the Forms of our Governments:

For suspending our own Legislatures, and declaring themselves invested with power to legislate for us in all cases whatsoever.

He has abdicated Government here, by declaring us out of his Protection and waging War against us:

He has plundered our seas, ravaged our Coasts, burnt our towns, and destroyed the lives of our people.

He is at this time transporting large Armies of foreign Mercenaries to compleat the works of death, desolation and tyranny, already begun with circumstances of Cruelty & perfidy scarcely paralleled in the most barbarous ages, and totally unworthy the Head of a civilized nation.

He has constrained our fellow Citizens taken Captive on the high Seas to bear Arms against their Country, to become the executioners of their friends and Brethren, or to fall themselves by their Hands.

He has excited domestic insurrections amongst us, and has endeavoured to bring on the inhabitants of our frontiers, the merciless Indian Savages, whose known rule of warfare, is an undistinguished destruction of all ages, sexes and conditions. In every stage of these Oppressions We have Petitioned for Redress in the most humble terms: Our repeated Petitions have been answered only by repeated injury. A Prince, whose character is thus marked by every act which may define a Tyrant, is unfit to be the ruler of a free people. Nor have We been wanting in attentions to our British brethren. We have warned them from time to time of attempts by their legislature to extend an unwarrantable jurisdiction over us. We have reminded them of the circumstances of our emigration and settlement here. We have appealed to their native justice and magnanimity, and we have conjured them by the ties of our common kindred to disavow these usurpations, which, would inevitably interrupt our connections and correspondence. They too have been deaf to the voice of justice and of consanguinity. We must, therefore, acquiesce in the necessity, which denounces our Separation, and hold them, as we hold the rest of mankind, Enemies in War, in Peace Friends.

We, THEREFORE, the Representatives of the UNITED STATES OF AMERICA, in General Congress Assembled, appealing to the Supreme Judge of the world for the rectitude of our intentions, do, in the Name and by Authority of the good People of these Colonies, solemnly publish and declare, That these United Colonies are, and of Right ought to be FREE AND INDEPENDENT STATES; that they are Absolved from all Allegiance to the British Crown, and that all political connection between them and the State of Great Britain, is and ought to be totally dissolved; and that as Free and Independent States, they have full Power to levy War, conclude Peace, contract Alliances, establish Commerce, and to do all other Acts and Things which Independent States may of right do.

And for the support of this Declaration, with a firm reliance on the protection of divine Providence, we mutually pledge to each other our Lives, our Fortunes and our sacred Honor.

⌕ Joining the Conversation: Critical Thinking and Writing

1. What audience is being addressed in the Declaration of Independence? Cite passages in the text that support your answer.

2. The Library of Congress has the original manuscript of the rough draft of the Declaration. This manuscript itself includes revisions that are indicated below, but it was later further revised. We print the first part of the second paragraph of the draft and, after it, the corresponding part of the final version. Try to account for the changes within the draft and from the revised draft to the final version.

> *self-evident,*
> We hold these truths to be ~~sacred & undeniable,~~ that all men are
> *they are endowed by their creator*
> created equal ~~& independent,~~ that ~~from that equal creation they~~
> *with*
> ~~derive equal rights some of which are in rights~~
> *rights; that   these*
> inherent & inalienable ~~among which~~ are ~~the preservation of~~ life,
> liberty, & the pursuit of happiness.

> We hold these Truths to be self-evident, that all men are created
> equal, that they are endowed by their Creator with certain
> unalienable Rights, that among these are Life, Liberty and the
> pursuit of Happiness.

   In a paragraph, evaluate the changes. Try to put yourself into Jefferson's mind and see if you can sense why Jefferson made the changes.

3. In a paragraph, define *happiness* and then, in a second paragraph, explain why, in your opinion, Jefferson spoke of "the pursuit of happiness" rather than of "happiness."

4. In "We Have No 'Right to Happiness'" (page 22), C. S. Lewis discusses the meaning of "the pursuit of happiness" in the Declaration and a current misinterpretation of the phrase. How does he explain and define the phrase? How does his interpretation differ from what he considers an erroneous interpretation?

5. What assumptions lie behind the numerous specific reasons that are given to justify the rebellion? Set forth the gist of the argument of the Declaration by using the form of reasoning known as a *syllogism*, which consists of a major premise (such as "All men are mortal"), a minor premise ("Socrates is a man"), and a conclusion ("Therefore, Socrates is mortal"). For a brief discussion of syllogisms, see page 87 (deduction).

6. In a paragraph, argue that the assertion that "all Men are created equal" is nonsense or, on the other hand, that it makes sense.

7. If every person has an unalienable right to life, how can capital punishment be reconciled with the Declaration of Independence? You need not in fact be a supporter of capital punishment; simply offer the best defense you can think of in an effort to make it harmonious with the Declaration.

Martin Luther King Jr.

Martin Luther King Jr. (1929–1968), clergyman and civil rights leader, achieved national fame in 1955–1956 when he led the boycott against segregated bus lines in Montgomery, Alabama. His policy of passive resistance succeeded in Montgomery, and King then organized the Southern Christian Leadership Conference in order to extend his efforts. In 1964, he was awarded the Nobel Peace Prize, but he continued to encounter strong opposition. On April 4, 1968, while in Memphis to support striking sanitation workers, he was shot and killed.

Nonviolent Resistance

Oppressed people deal with their oppression in three characteristic ways. One way is acquiescence: the oppressed resign themselves to their doom. They tacitly adjust themselves to oppression, and thereby become conditioned to it. In every movement toward freedom some of the oppressed prefer to remain oppressed. Almost 2800 years ago Moses set out to lead the children of Israel from the slavery of Egypt to the freedom of the promised land. He soon discovered that slaves do not always welcome their deliverers. They become accustomed to being slaves. They would rather bear those ills they have, as Shakespeare pointed out, than flee to others that they know not of. They prefer the "fleshpots of Egypt" to the ordeals of emancipation.

There is such a thing as the freedom of exhaustion. Some people are so worn down by the yoke of oppression that they give up. A few years ago in the slum areas of Atlanta, a Negro guitarist used to sing almost daily: "Been down so long that down don't bother me." This is the type of negative freedom and resignation that often engulfs the life of the oppressed.

But this is not the way out. To accept passively an unjust system is to cooperate with that system; thereby the oppressed become as evil as the oppressor. Noncooperation with evil is as much a moral obligation as is cooperation with good. The oppressed must never allow the conscience of the oppressor to slumber. Religion reminds every man that he is his brother's keeper. To accept injustice or segregation passively is to say to the oppressor that his actions are morally right. It is a way of allowing his conscience to fall asleep. At this moment the oppressed fails to be his brother's keeper. So acquiescence—while often the easier way—is not the moral way. It is the way of the coward. The Negro cannot win the respect of his oppressor by acquiescing; he merely increases the oppressor's arrogance and contempt. Acquiescence is interpreted as proof of the Negro's inferiority. The Negro cannot win the respect of the white people of the South or the peoples of the world if he is willing to sell the future of his children for his personal and immediate comfort and safety.

A second way that oppressed people sometimes deal with oppression is to resort to physical violence and corroding hatred. Violence often brings about momentary results. Nations have frequently won their independence in battle. But in spite of temporary victories, violence never brings permanent peace. It solves no social problem; it merely creates new and more complicated ones.

Violence as a way of achieving racial justice is both impractical and immoral. It is impractical because it is a descending spiral ending in destruction for all. The old law of an eye for an eye leaves everybody blind. It is immoral because it seeks to humiliate the opponent rather than win his understanding; it seeks to annihilate rather than to convert. Violence is immoral because it thrives on hatred rather than love. It destroys community and makes brotherhood impossible. It leaves society in monologue rather than dialogue. Violence ends by defeating itself. It creates bitterness in the survivors and brutality in the destroyers. A voice echoes through time saying to every potential Peter, "Put up your sword." History is cluttered with the wreckage of nations that failed to follow his command.

If the American Negro and other victims of oppression succumb to the temptation of using violence in the struggle for freedom, future generations will be the recipients of a desolate night of bitterness, and our chief legacy to them will be an endless reign of meaningless chaos. Violence is not the way.

The third way open to oppressed people in their quest for freedom is the way of nonviolent resistance. Like the synthesis in Hegelian philosophy, the principle of nonviolent resistance seeks to reconcile the truths of two opposites—acquiescence and violence—while avoiding the extremes and immoralities of both. The nonviolent resister agrees with the person who acquiesces that one should not be physically aggressive toward his opponent; but he balances the equation by agreeing with the person of violence that evil must be resisted. He avoids the nonresistance of the former and the violent resistance of the latter. With nonviolent resistance, no individual or group need submit to any wrong, nor need anyone resort to violence in order to right a wrong.

It seems to me that this is the method that must guide the actions of the Negro in the present crisis in race relations. Through nonviolent resistance the Negro will be able to rise to the noble height of opposing the unjust system while loving the perpetrators of the system. The Negro must work passionately and unrelentingly for full stature as a citizen, but he must not use inferior methods to gain it. He must never come to terms with falsehood, malice, hate, or destruction.

Nonviolent resistance makes it possible for the Negro to remain in the South and struggle for his rights. The Negro's problem will not be solved by running away. He cannot listen to the glib suggestion of those who would urge him to migrate en masse to other sections of the country. By grasping his great opportunity in the South he can make a lasting contribution to the moral strength of the nation and set a sublime example of courage for generations yet unborn.

By nonviolent resistance, the Negro can also enlist all men of good will in his struggle for equality. The problem is not a purely racial one, with Negroes set against whites. In the end, it is not a struggle between people at all, but a tension between justice and injustice. Nonviolent resistance is not aimed against oppressors but against oppression. Under its banner consciences, not racial groups, are enlisted.

10

If the Negro is to achieve the goal of integration, he must organize himself into a militant and nonviolent mass movement. All three elements are indispensable. The movement for equality and justice can only be a success if it has both a mass and militant character; the barriers to be overcome require both. Nonviolence is an imperative in order to bring about ultimate community.

A mass movement of militant quality that is not at the same time committed to nonviolence tends to generate conflict, which in turn breeds anarchy. The support of the participants and the sympathy of the uncommitted are both inhibited by the threat that bloodshed will engulf the community. This reaction in turn encourages the opposition to threaten and resort to force. When, however, the mass movement repudiates violence while moving resolutely toward its goal, its opponents are revealed as the instigators and practitioners of violence if it occurs. Then public support is magnetically attracted to the advocates of nonviolence, while those who employ violence are literally disarmed by overwhelming sentiment against their stand.

Only through a nonviolent approach can the fears of the white community be mitigated. A guilt-ridden white minority lives in fear that if the Negro should ever attain power, he would act without restraint or pity to revenge the injustices and brutality of the years. It is something like a parent who continually mistreats a son. One day that parent raises his hand to strike the son, only to discover that the son is now as tall as he is. The parent is suddenly afraid—fearful that the son will use his new physical power to repay his parent for all the blows of the past.

The Negro, once a helpless child, has now grown up politically, culturally, and economically. Many white men fear retaliation. The job of the Negro is to show them that they have nothing to fear, that the Negro understands and forgives and is ready to forget the past. He must convince the white man that all he seeks is justice, *for both himself and the white man.* A mass movement exercising nonviolence is an object lesson in power under discipline, a demonstration to the white community that if such a movement attained a degree of strength, it would use its power creatively and not vengefully.

Nonviolence can touch men where the law cannot reach them. When the law regulates behavior it plays an indirect part in molding public sentiment. The enforcement of the law is itself a form of peaceful persuasion. But the law needs help. The courts can order desegregation of the public schools. But what can be done to mitigate the fears, to disperse the hatred, violence, and irrationality gathered around school integration, to take the initiative out of the hands of racial demagogues, to release respect for the law? In the end, for laws to be obeyed, men must believe they are right.

Here nonviolence comes in as the ultimate form of persuasion. It is the method which seeks to implement the just law by appealing to the conscience of the great decent majority who through blindness, fear, pride, or irrationality have allowed their consciences to sleep.

The nonviolent resisters can summarize their message in the following simple terms: We will take direct action against injustice without waiting for other agencies to act. We will not obey unjust laws or submit to unjust practices. We will do this peacefully, openly, cheerfully because our aim is to persuade. We adopt the means of nonviolence because our end is a community at peace with itself. We will try to persuade with our words, but if our words fail, we will try to persuade with our acts. We will always be willing to talk and seek fair compromise, but we are ready to suffer when necessary and even risk our lives to become witnesses to the truth as we see it.

The way of nonviolence means a willingness to suffer and sacrifice. It may mean going to jail. If such is the case the resister must be willing to fill the jail houses of the South. It may even mean physical death. But if physical death is the price that a man must pay to free his children and his white brethren from a permanent death of the spirit, then nothing could be more redemptive.

⟨⟨⟩⟩ Joining the Conversation: Critical Thinking and Writing

1. In the first paragraph, the passage about Moses and the children of Israel is not strictly necessary; the essential idea of the paragraph is stated in the previous sentence. Why, then, does King add this material? And why the quotation from Shakespeare?

2. Pick out two or three sentences that seem to you to be especially effective and analyze the sources of their power. You can choose either isolated sentences or (because King often effectively links sentences with repetition of words or of constructions) consecutive ones.

3. In a paragraph, set forth your understanding of what nonviolent resistance is. Use whatever examples from your own experience or reading you find

useful. In a second paragraph, explain how Maya Angelou's "Graduation" (page 284) offers an example of nonviolent resistance.

Martin Luther King Jr.

Martin Luther King Jr. (1929–1968), clergyman and civil rights leader, achieved national fame in 1955–1956 when he led the boycott against segregated bus lines in Montgomery, Alabama. His policy of passive resistance succeeded in Montgomery, and King then organized the Southern Christian Leadership Conference in order to extend his efforts. In 1963, Dr. King was arrested in Birmingham, Alabama, for participating in a march for which no parade permit had been issued by the city officials. In jail, he wrote a response to a letter that eight local clergymen had published in a newspaper. In 1964, he was awarded the Nobel Peace Prize, but he continued to encounter strong opposition. On April 4, 1968, while in Memphis to support striking sanitation workers, he was shot and killed.

Note: We begin not with King's letter but with the newspaper piece by eight clergymen entitled "A Call for Unity" so you can see the context of King's response.

[Letter by Eight Local Clergymen]

A Call for Unity

April 12, 1963

We the undersigned clergymen are among those who, in January, issued "An Appeal for Law and Order and Common Sense," in dealing with racial problems in Alabama. We expressed understanding that honest convictions in racial matters could properly be pursued in the courts, but urged that decisions of those courts should in the meantime be peacefully obeyed.

Since that time there had been some evidence of increased forbearance and a willingness to face facts. Responsible citizens have undertaken to work on various problems which cause racial friction and unrest. In Birmingham, recent public events have given indication that we all have opportunity for a new constructive and realistic approach to racial problems.

However, we are now confronted by a series of demonstrations by some of our Negro citizens, directed and led in part by outsiders. We recognize the natural impatience of people who feel that their hopes are slow in being realized. But we are convinced that these demonstrations are unwise and untimely.

We agree rather with certain local Negro leadership which has called for honest and open negotiation of racial issues in our area. And we believe this kind of facing of issues can best be accomplished by citizens of our own metropolitan area, white and Negro, meeting with their knowledge and experience of the local situation. All of us need to face that responsibility and find proper channels for its accomplishment.

Just as we formerly pointed out that "hatred and violence have no sanction in our religious and political traditions," we also point out that such actions as incite to hatred and violence, however technically peaceful those actions may be, have not contributed to the resolution of our local problems. We do not believe that these days of new hope are days when extreme measures are justified in Birmingham. 5

We commend the community as a whole, and the local news media and law enforcement officials in particular, on the calm manner in which these demonstrations have been handled. We urge the public to continue to show restraint should the demonstrations continue, and the law enforcement officials to remain calm and continue to protect our city from violence.

We further strongly urge our own Negro community to withdraw support from these demonstrations, and to unite locally in working peacefully for a better Birmingham. When rights are consistently denied, a cause should be pressed in the courts and in negotiations among local leaders, and not in the streets. We appeal to both our white and Negro citizenry to observe the principles of law and order and common sense.

C.C.J. Carpenter, D.D., L.L.D., Bishop of Alabama; Joseph A. Durick, D.D., Auxiliary Bishop, Diocese of Mobile-Birmingham; Rabbi Milton L. Grafman, Temple Emanu-El, Birmingham, Alabama; Bishop Paul Hardin, Bishop of the Alabama–West Florida Conference of the Methodist Church; Bishop Nolan B. Harmon, Bishop of the North Alabama Conference of the Methodist Church; George M. Murray, D.D., L.L.D., Bishop Coadjutor, Episcopal Diocese of Alabama; Edward V. Ramage, Moderator, Synod of the Alabama Presbyterian Church in the United States; Earl Stallings, Pastor, First Baptist Church, Birmingham, Alabama.

Letter from Birmingham Jail

In Response to "A Call for Unity"

April 16, 1963

My Dear Fellow Clergymen:

While confined here in the Birmingham city jail, I came across your recent statement calling my present activities "unwise and untimely."[1] Seldom do I pause to answer criticism of my work and ideas. If I sought to answer all the criticisms that cross my desk, my secretaries would have little time for anything other than such correspondence in the course of

---

[1]This response to a published statement by eight fellow clergymen from Alabama (Bishop C.C.J. Carpenter, Bishop Joseph A. Durick, Rabbi Milton L. Grafman, Bishop Paul Hardin, Bishop Nolan B. Harmon, the Reverend George M. Murray, the Reverend Edward V. Ramage, and the Reverend Earl Stallings) was composed under somewhat constricting circumstances. Begun on the margins of the newspaper in which the statement appeared while I was in jail, the letter was continued on scraps of writing paper supplied by a friendly Negro trusty and concluded on a pad my attorneys were eventually permitted to leave me. Although the text remains in substance unaltered, I have indulged in the author's prerogative of polishing it for publication. [King's note]

---

the day, and I would have no time for constructive work. But since I feel that you are men of genuine good will and that your criticisms are sincerely set forth, I want to try to answer your statement in what I hope will be patient and reasonable terms.

I think I should indicate why I am here in Birmingham, since you have been influenced by the view which argues against "outsiders coming in." I have the honor of serving as president of the Southern Christian Leadership Conference, an organization operating in every southern state, with headquarters in Atlanta, Georgia. We have some eighty-five affiliated organizations across the South, and one of them is the Alabama Christian Movement for Human Rights. Frequently we share staff, educational, and financial resources with our affiliates. Several months ago the affiliate here in Birmingham asked us to be on call to engage in a nonviolent direct-action program if such were deemed necessary. We readily consented, and when the hour came we lived up to our promise. So I, along with several members of my staff, am here because I was invited here. I am here because I have organizational ties here.

But more basically, I am in Birmingham because injustice is here. Just as the prophets of the eighth century B.C. left their villages and carried their "thus saith the Lord" far beyond the boundaries of their home towns, and just as the Apostle Paul left his village of Tarsus and carried the gospel of Jesus Christ to the far corners of the Greco-Roman world, so am I compelled to carry the gospel of freedom beyond my own home town. Like Paul, I must constantly respond to the Macedonian call for aid.

Moreover, I am cognizant of the interrelatedness of all communities and states. I cannot sit idly by in Atlanta and not be concerned about what happens in Birmingham. Injustice anywhere is a threat to justice everywhere. We are caught in an inescapable network of mutuality; tied in a single garment of destiny. Whatever affects one directly, affects all indirectly. Never again can we afford to live with the narrow, provincial "outside agitator" idea. Anyone who lives inside the United States can never be considered an outsider anywhere within its bounds.

You deplore the demonstrations taking place in Birmingham. But your statement, I am sorry to say, fails to express a similar concern for the conditions that brought about the demonstrations. I am sure that none of you would want to rest content with the superficial kind of social analysis that deals merely with effects and does not grapple with underlying causes. It is unfortunate that demonstrations are taking place in Birmingham, but it is even more unfortunate that the city's white power structure left the Negro community with no alternative.

In any nonviolent campaign there are four basic steps: collection of the facts to determine whether injustices exist; negotiation; self-purification; and direct action. We have gone through all these steps in Birmingham. There can be no gainsaying the fact that racial injustice engulfs this community. Birmingham is probably the most thoroughly segregated city in the United States. Its ugly record of brutality is widely known. Negroes have experienced grossly unjust treatment in the courts. There have been more unsolved bombings of Negro homes and churches in Birmingham than in any other city in the nation. These are the hard, brutal facts of the case. On the basis of these conditions, Negro leaders sought to negotiate with the city fathers. But the latter consistently refused to engage in good-faith negotiation.

Then, last September, came the opportunity to talk with leaders of Birmingham's economic community. In the course of the negotiations, certain promises were made by the merchants—for example, to remove the stores' humiliating racial signs. On the basis of these promises, the Reverend Fred Shuttlesworth and the leaders of the Alabama Christian Movement for Human Rights agreed to a moratorium on all demonstrations. As the weeks and months went by, we realized that we were the victims of a broken promise. A few signs, briefly removed, returned; the others remained.

As in so many past experiences, our hopes had been blasted, and the shadow of deep disappointment settled upon us. We had no alternative except to prepare for direct action, whereby we would present our very bodies as a means of laying our case before the conscience of the local and the national community. Mindful of the difficulties involved, we decided to undertake a process of self-purification. We began a series of workshops on nonviolence, and we repeatedly asked ourselves: "Are you able to accept blows without retaliating?" "Are you able to endure the ordeal of jail?" We decided to schedule our direct-action program for the Easter season, realizing that except for Christmas, this is the main shopping period of the year. Knowing that a strong economic-withdrawal program would be the by-product of direct action, we felt that this would be the best time to bring pressure to bear on the merchants for the needed change.

Then it occurred to us that Birmingham's mayoralty election was coming up in March, and we speedily decided to postpone action until after election day. When we discovered that the Commissioner of Public Safety, Eugene "Bull" Connor, had piled up enough votes to be in the run-off, we decided again to postpone action until the day after the run-off so that the demonstrations could not be used to cloud the issues. Like many others, we waited to see Mr. Connor defeated, and to this end we endured postponement after postponement. Having aided in this community need, we felt that our direct-action program could be delayed no longer.

You may well ask: "Why direct action? Why sit-ins, marches, and so forth? Isn't negotiation a better path?" You are quite right in calling for negotiation. Indeed, this is the very purpose of direct action. Nonviolent direct action seeks to create such a crisis and foster such a tension that a community which has constantly refused to negotiate is forced to confront the issue. It seeks so to dramatize the issue that it can no longer be ignored. My citing the creation of tension as part of the work of the nonviolent resister may sound rather shocking. But I must confess that I am not afraid of the word "tension." I have earnestly opposed violent tension, but there is a type of constructive, nonviolent tension which is necessary for growth. Just as Socrates felt that it was necessary to create a tension in the mind so that individuals could rise from the bondage of myths and half-truths to the unfettered realm of creative analysis and objective appraisal, so must we see the need for nonviolent gadflies to create the kind of tension in society that will help men rise from the dark depths of prejudice and racism to the majestic heights of understanding and brotherhood.

The purpose of our direct-action program is to create a situation so crisis-packed that it will inevitably open the door to negotiation. I therefore concur with you in your call for negotiation. Too long has our beloved Southland been bogged down in a tragic effort to live in monologue rather than dialogue.

One of the basic points in your statement is that the action that I and my associates have taken in Birmingham is untimely. Some have asked: "Why didn't you give the new city administration time to act?" The only answer that I can give to this query is that the new Birmingham administration must be prodded about as much as the outgoing one, before it will act. We are sadly mistaken if we feel that the election of Albert Boutwell as mayor will bring the millennium to Birmingham. While Mr. Boutwell is a much more gentle person than Mr. Connor, they are both segregationists, dedicated to maintenance of the status quo. I have hope that Mr. Boutwell will be reasonable enough to see the futility of massive resistance to desegregation. But he will not see this without pressure from devotees of civil rights. My friends, I must say to you that we have not made a single gain in civil rights without determined legal and nonviolent pressure. Lamentably, it is an historical fact that privileged groups seldom give up their privileges voluntarily. Individuals may see the moral light and voluntarily give up their unjust posture; but as Reinhold Niebuhr[2] has reminded us, groups tend to be more immoral than individuals.

We know through painful experience that freedom is never voluntarily given by the oppressor; it must be demanded by the oppressed. Frankly, I have yet to engage in a direct-action campaign that was "well timed" in the view of those who have not suffered unduly from the disease of segregation. For years now I have heard the word "Wait!" It rings in the ear of every Negro with piercing familiarity. This "Wait" has almost always meant "Never." We must come to see, with one of our distinguished jurists, that "justice too long delayed is justice denied."[3]

We have waited for more than 340 years for our constitutional and God-given rights. The nations of Asia and Africa are moving with jetlike

---

[2]**Reinhold Niebuhr** (1892–1971) Minister, political activist, author, and professor of applied Christianity at Union Theological Seminary. (This and the following notes are the editors'.)
[3]**Justice ... denied** A quotation attributed to William E. Gladstone (1809–1898), British statesman and prime minister

speed toward gaining political independence, but we still creep at horse-and-buggy pace toward gaining a cup of coffee at a lunch counter. Perhaps it is easy for those who have never felt the stinging darts of segregation to say, "Wait." But when you have seen vicious mobs lynch your mothers and fathers at will and drown your sisters and brothers at whim; when you have seen hate-filled policemen curse, kick, and even kill your black brothers and sisters; when you see the vast majority of your twenty million Negro brothers smothering in an airtight cage of poverty in the midst of an affluent society; when you suddenly find your tongue twisted and your speech stammering as you seek to explain to your six-year-old daughter why she can't go to the public amusement park that has just been advertised on television, and see tears welling up in her eyes when she is told that Funtown is closed to colored children, and see ominous clouds of inferiority beginning to form in her little mental sky, and see her beginning to distort her personality by developing an unconscious bitterness toward white people; when you have to concoct an answer for a five-year-old son who is asking: "Daddy, why do white people treat colored people so mean?"; when you take a cross-country drive and find it necessary to sleep night after night in the uncomfortable corners of your automobile because no motel will accept you; when you are humiliated day in and day out by nagging signs reading "white" and "colored"; when your first name becomes "nigger," your middle name becomes "boy" (however old you are) and your last name becomes "John," and your wife and mother are never given the respected title "Mrs."; when you are harried by day and haunted by night by the fact that you are a Negro, living constantly at tiptoe stance, never quite knowing what to expect next, and are plagued with inner fears and outer resentments; when you are forever fighting a degenerating sense of "nobodiness"—then you will understand why we find it difficult to wait. There comes a time when the cup of endurance runs over, and men are no longer willing to be plunged into the abyss of despair. I hope, sirs, you can understand our legitimate and unavoidable impatience.

You express a great deal of anxiety over our willingness to break laws. This is certainly a legitimate concern. Since we so diligently urge people to obey the Supreme Court's decision of 1954 outlawing segregation in the public schools, at first glance it may seem rather paradoxical for us consciously to break laws. One may well ask: "How can you advocate breaking some laws and obeying others?" The answer lies in the fact that there are two types of laws: just and unjust. I would be the first to advocate obeying just laws. One has not only a legal but a moral responsibility to obey just laws. Conversely, one has a moral responsibility to disobey unjust laws. I would agree with St. Augustine that "an unjust law is no law at all."

Now, what is the difference between the two? How does one determine whether a law is just or unjust? A just law is a man-made code that squares with the moral law or the law of God. An unjust law is a code that is out of harmony with the moral law. To put it in the terms of St. Thomas Aquinas: An unjust law is a human law that is not rooted in eternal law and natural law. Any law that uplifts human personality is just. Any law that degrades human personality is unjust. All segregation statutes are unjust because segregation distorts the soul and damages the personality. It gives the segregator a false sense of superiority and the segregated a false sense of inferiority. Segregation, to use the terminology of the Jewish philosopher Martin Buber, substitutes an "I-it" relationship for an "I-thou" relationship and ends up relegating persons to the status of things. Hence segregation is not only politically, economically, and sociologically unsound, it is morally wrong and sinful. Paul Tillich[4] has said that sin is separation. Is not segregation an existential expression of man's tragic separation, his awful estrangement, his terrible sinfulness? Thus it is that I can urge men to obey the 1954 decision of the Supreme Court, for it is morally right; and I can urge them to disobey segregation ordinances, for they are morally wrong.

Let us consider a more concrete example of just and unjust laws. An unjust law is a code that a numerical or power majority group compels a minority group to obey but does not make binding on itself. This is *difference* made legal. By the same token, a just law is a code that a majority compels a minority to follow and that it is willing to follow itself. This is *sameness* made legal.

Let me give another explanation. A law is unjust if it is inflicted on a minority that, as a result of being denied the right to vote, had no part in enacting or devising the law. Who can say that the legislature of Alabama which set up that state's segregation laws was democratically elected? Throughout Alabama all sorts of devious methods are used to prevent Negroes from becoming registered voters, and there are some counties in which, even though Negroes constitute a majority of the population, not a single Negro is registered. Can any law enacted under such circumstances be considered democratically structured?

Sometimes a law is just on its face and unjust in its application. For instance, I have been arrested on a charge of parading without a permit. Now, there is nothing wrong in having an ordinance which requires a permit for a parade. But such an ordinance becomes unjust when it is used to maintain segregation and to deny citizens the First Amendment privilege of peaceful assembly and protest.

I hope you are able to see the distinction I am trying to point out. In no sense do I advocate evading or defying the law, as would the rabid segregationist. That would lead to anarchy. One who breaks an unjust law must do so openly, lovingly, and with a willingness to accept the penalty.

20

---

[4]**Paul Tillich** Tillich (1886–1965), born in Germany, taught theology at several German universities, but in 1933, he was dismissed from his post at the University of Frankfurt because of his opposition to the Nazi regime. At the invitation of Reinhold Niebuhr, he came to the United States and taught at Union Theological Seminary.

I submit that an individual who breaks a law that conscience tells him is unjust, and who willingly accepts the penalty of imprisonment in order to arouse the conscience of the community over its injustice, is in reality expressing the highest respect for law.

Of course, there is nothing new about this kind of civil disobedience. It was evidenced sublimely in the refusal of Shadrach, Meshach, and Abednego to obey the laws of Nebuchadnezzar, on the ground that a higher moral law was at stake. It was practiced superbly by the early Christians, who were willing to face hungry lions and the excruciating pain of chopping blocks rather than submit to certain unjust laws of the Roman Empire. To a degree, academic freedom is a reality today because Socrates practiced civil disobedience. In our own nation, the Boston Tea Party represented a massive act of civil disobedience.

We should never forget that everything Adolf Hitler did in Germany was "legal" and everything the Hungarian freedom fighters did in Hungary was "illegal." It was "illegal" to aid and comfort a Jew in Hitler's Germany. Even so, I am sure that, had I lived in Germany at the time, I would have aided and comforted my Jewish brothers. If today I lived in a Communist country where certain principles dear to the Christian faith are suppressed, I would openly advocate disobeying that country's anti-religious laws.

I must make two honest confessions to you, my Christian and Jewish brothers. First, I must confess that over the past few years I have been gravely disappointed with the white moderate. I have almost reached the regrettable conclusion that the Negro's great stumbling block in his stride toward freedom is not the White Citizen's Counciler or the Ku Klux Klanner, but the white moderate, who is more devoted to "order" than to justice; who prefers a negative peace which is the absence of tension to a positive peace which is the presence of justice; who constantly says: "I agree with you in the goal you seek, but I cannot agree with your methods or direct action"; who paternalistically believes he can set the timetable for another man's freedom; who lives by a mythical concept of time and who constantly advises the Negro to wait for a "more convenient season." Shallow understanding from people of good will is more frustrating than absolute misunderstanding from people of ill will. Lukewarm acceptance is much more bewildering than outright rejection.

I had hoped that the white moderate would understand that law and order exist for the purpose of establishing justice and that when they fail in this purpose they become the dangerously structured dams that block the flow of social progress. I had hoped that the white moderate would understand that the present tension in the South is a necessary phase of the transition from an obnoxious negative peace, in which the Negro passively accepted his unjust plight, to a substantive and positive peace, in which all men will respect the dignity and worth of human personality. Actually, we who engage in nonviolent direct action are not the creators of tension. We merely bring to the surface the hidden tension that is already alive. We bring it out in the open, where it can be seen and dealt with. Like a boil that can never be cured so long as it is covered up but must be opened with all its ugliness to the natural medicines of air and light, injustice must be exposed, with all the tension its exposure creates, to the light of human conscience and the air of national opinion before it can be cured.

In your statement you assert that our actions, even though peaceful, must be condemned because they precipitate violence. But is this a logical assertion? Isn't this like condemning a robbed man because his possession of money precipitated the evil act of robbery? Isn't this like condemning Socrates because his unswerving commitment to truth and his philosophical inquiries precipitated the act by the misguided populace in which they made him drink hemlock? Isn't this like condemning Jesus because his unique God-consciousness and never-ceasing devotion to God's will precipitated the evil act of crucifixion? We must come to see that, as the federal courts have consistently affirmed, it is wrong to urge an individual to cease his efforts to gain his basic constitutional rights because the quest may precipitate violence. Society must protect the robbed and punish the robber.

I had also hoped that the white moderate would reject the myth concerning time in relation to the struggle for freedom. I have just received a letter from a white brother in Texas. He writes: "All Christians know that the colored people will receive equal rights eventually, but it is possible that you are in too great a religious hurry. It has taken Christianity almost two thousand years to accomplish what it has. The teachings of Christ take time to come to earth." Such an attitude stems from a tragic misconception of time, from the strangely irrational notion that there is something in the very flow of time that will inevitably cure all ills. Actually, time itself is neutral; it can be used either destructively or constructively. More and more I feel that the people of ill will have used time much more effectively than have the people of good will. We will have to repent in this generation not merely for the hateful words and actions of the bad people but for the appalling silence of the good people. Human progress never rolls in on wheels of inevitability; it comes through the tireless efforts of men willing to be co-workers with God, and without this hard work, time itself becomes an ally of the forces of social stagnation. We must use time creatively, in the knowledge that the time is always ripe to do right. Now is the time to make real the promise of democracy and transform our pending national elegy into a creative psalm of brotherhood. Now is the time to lift our national policy from the quicksand of racial injustice to the solid rock of human dignity.

You speak of our activity in Birmingham as extreme. At first I was rather disappointed that fellow clergymen would see my nonviolent efforts as those of an extremist. I began thinking about the fact that I stand in the middle of two opposing forces in the Negro community. One is a force of complacency, made up in part of Negroes who, as a result of long years of oppression, are so drained of self-respect and a sense of "somebodiness" that they have adjusted to segregation; and in part of a few middle-class Negroes who, because of a degree of academic and economic security and because in some ways they profit by segregation, have become insensitive to the problems of the masses. The other force is one of bitterness and hatred, and it comes perilously close to advocating violence. It is expressed in the various black nationalist groups that are springing up across the nation, the largest and best-known being Elijah Muhammad's Muslim movement. Nourished by the Negro's frustration over the continued existence of racial discrimination, this movement is made up of people who have lost faith in America, who have absolutely repudiated Christianity, and who have concluded that the white man is an incorrigible "devil."

I have tried to stand between these two forces, saying that we need emulate neither the "do-nothingism" of the complacent nor the hatred and despair of the black nationalist. For there is the more excellent way of love and nonviolent protest. I am grateful to God that, through the influence of the Negro church, the way of nonviolence became an integral part of our struggle.

If this philosophy had not emerged, by now many streets of the South should, I am convinced, be flowing with blood. And I am further convinced that if our white brothers dismiss as "rabble-rousers" and "outside agitators" those of us who employ nonviolent direct action, and if they refuse to support our nonviolent efforts, millions of Negroes will, out of frustration and despair, seek solace and security in black-nationalist ideologies—a development that would inevitably lead to a frightening racial nightmare.

Oppressed people cannot remain oppressed forever. The yearning for freedom eventually manifests itself, and that is what has happened to the American Negro. Something within has reminded him of his birthright of freedom, and something without has reminded him that it can be gained. Consciously or unconsciously, he has been caught up by the *Zeitgeist*,[5] and with his black brothers of Africa and his brown and yellow brothers of Asia, South America, and the Caribbean, the United States Negro is moving with a sense of great urgency toward the promised land of racial justice. If one recognizes this vital urge that has engulfed the Negro community, one should readily understand why public demonstrations are taking place. The Negro has many pent-up resentments and latent frustrations, and he must release them. So let him march; let him make prayer pilgrimages to the city hall; let him go on freedom rides—and try to understand why he must do so. If his repressed emotions are not released in nonviolent ways, they will seek expression through violence; this is not a threat but a fact of history. So I have not said to my people: "Get rid of your discontent." Rather, I have tried to say that this normal and healthy discontent can be channeled into the creative outlet of nonviolent direct action. And now this approach is being termed extremist.

[5]*Zeitgeist* German for "spirit of the age"

But though I was initially disappointed at being categorized as an extremist, as I continued to think about the matter I gradually gained a measure of satisfaction from the label. Was not Jesus an extremist for love: "Love your enemies, bless them that curse you, do good to them that hate you, and pray for them which despitefully use you, and persecute you." Was not Amos an extremist for justice: "Let justice roll down like waters and righteousness like an ever-flowing stream." Was not Paul an extremist for the Christian gospel: "I bear in my body the marks of the Lord Jesus." Was not Martin Luther an extremist: "Here I stand; I cannot do otherwise, so help me God." And John Bunyan: "I will stay in jail to the end of my days before I make a butchery of my conscience." And Abraham Lincoln: "This nation cannot survive half slave and half free." And Thomas Jefferson: "We hold these truths to be self-evident, that all men are created equal. . . . " So the question is not whether we will be extremists, but what kind of extremists we will be. Will we be extremists for hate or for love? Will we be extremists for the preservation of injustice or for the extension of justice? In that dramatic scene on Calvary's hill three men were crucified. We must never forget that all three were crucified for the same crime—the crime of extremism. Two were extremists for immorality, and thus fell below their environment. The other, Jesus Christ, was an extremist for love, truth, and goodness, and thereby rose above his environment. Perhaps the South, the nation, and the world are in dire need of creative extremists.

I had hoped that the white moderate would see this need. Perhaps I was too optimistic; perhaps I expected too much. I suppose I should have realized that few members of the oppressor race can understand the deep groans and passionate yearnings of the oppressed race, and still fewer have the vision to see that injustice must be rooted out by strong, persistent, and determined action. I am thankful, however, that some of our white brothers in the South have grasped the meaning of this social revolution and committed themselves to it. They are still all too few in quantity, but they are big in quality. Some—such as Ralph McGill, Lillian Smith, Harry Golden, James McBride Dabbs, Ann Braden, and Sarah Patton Boyle—have written about our struggle in eloquent and prophetic terms. Others have marched with us down nameless streets of the South. They have languished in filthy, roach-infested jails, suffering the abuse and brutality of policemen who view them as "dirty nigger-lovers." Unlike so many of their moderate brothers and sisters, they have recognized the urgency of the moment and sensed the need for powerful "action" antidotes to combat the disease of segregation.

Let me take note of my other major disappointment. I have been so greatly disappointed with the white church and its leadership. Of course, there are some notable exceptions. I am not unmindful of the fact that each of you has taken some significant stands on this issue. I commend you, Reverend Stallings, for your Christian stand on this past Sunday, in welcoming Negroes to your worship service on a nonsegregated basis.

I commend the Catholic leaders of this state for integrating Spring Hill College several years ago.

But despite these notable exceptions, I must honestly reiterate that I have been disappointed with the church. I do not say this as one of those negative critics who can always find something wrong with the church. I say this as a minister of the gospel, who loves the church; who was nurtured in its bosom; who has been sustained by its spiritual blessings and who will remain true to it as long as the cord of life shall lengthen.

When I was suddenly catapulted into the leadership of the bus protest in Montgomery, Alabama, a few years ago, I felt we would be supported by the white church. I felt that the white ministers, priests, and rabbis of the South would be among our strongest allies. Instead, some have been outright opponents, refusing to understand the freedom movement and misrepresenting its leaders; all too many others have been more cautious than courageous and have remained silent behind the anesthetizing security of stained-glass windows.

In spite of my shattered dreams, I came to Birmingham with the hope that the white religious leadership of this community would see the justice of our cause and, with deep moral concern, would serve as the channel through which our just grievances could reach the power structure. I had hoped that each of you would understand. But again I have been disappointed.

I have heard numerous southern religious leaders admonish their worshipers to comply with a desegregation decision because it is the law, but I have longed to hear white ministers declare: "Follow this decree because integration is morally right and because the Negro is your brother." In the midst of blatant injustices inflicted upon the Negro, I have watched white churchmen stand on the sideline and mouth pious irrelevancies and sanctimonious trivialities. In the midst of a mighty struggle to rid our nation of racial and economic injustice, I have heard many ministers say: "Those are social issues, with which the gospel has no real concern." And I have watched many churches commit themselves to a completely other-worldly religion which makes a strange, unbiblical distinction between body and soul, between the sacred and the secular.

I have traveled the length and breadth of Alabama, Mississippi, and all the other southern states. On sweltering summer days and crisp autumn mornings I have looked at the South's beautiful churches with their lofty spires pointing heavenward. I have beheld the impressive outlines of her massive religious-education buildings. Over and over I have found myself saying: "What kind of people worship here? Who is their God? Where were their voices when the lips of Governor Barnett dripped with words of interposition and nullification? Where were they when Governor Wallace gave a clarion call for defiance and hatred? Where were their voices of support when bruised and weary Negro men and women decided to rise from the dark dungeons of complacency to the bright hills of creative protest?"

Yes, these questions are still in my mind. In deep disappointment I have wept over the laxity of the church. But be assured that my tears have been tears of love. There can be no deep disappointment where there is not deep love. Yes, I love the church. How could I do otherwise? I am in the rather unique position of being the son, the grandson, and the great-grandson of preachers. Yes, I see the church as the body of Christ. But, Oh! How we have blemished and scarred that body through social neglect and through fear of being nonconformists.

There was a time when the church was very powerful—in the time   40
when the early Christians rejoiced at being deemed worthy to suffer for what they believed. In those days the church was not merely a thermometer that recorded the ideas and principles of popular opinion; it was a thermostat that transformed the mores of society. Whenever the early Christians entered a town, the people in power became disturbed and immediately sought to convict the Christians for being "disturbers of the peace" and "outside agitators." But the Christians pressed on, in the conviction that they were "a colony of heaven," called to obey God rather than man. Small in number, they were big in commitment. They were too God-intoxicated to be "astronomically intimidated." By their effort and example they brought an end to such ancient evils as infanticide and gladiatorial contests.

Things are different now. So often the contemporary church is a weak, ineffectual voice with an uncertain sound. So often it is an archdefender of the status quo. Far from being disturbed by the presence of the church, the power structure of the average community is consoled by the church's silent—and often even vocal—sanction of things as they are.

But the judgment of God is upon the church as never before. If today's church does not recapture the sacrificial spirit of the early church, it will lose its authenticity, forfeit the loyalty of millions, and be dismissed as an irrelevant social club with no meaning for the twentieth century. Every day I meet young people whose disappointment with the church has turned into outright disgust.

Perhaps I have once again been too optimistic. Is organized religion too inextricably bound to the status quo to save our nation and the world? Perhaps I must turn my faith to the inner spiritual church, the church within the church, as the true *ekklesia* and the hope of the world. But again I am thankful to God that some noble souls from the ranks of organized religion have broken loose from the paralyzing chains of conformity and joined us as active partners in the struggle for freedom. They have left their secure congregations and walked the streets of Albany, Georgia, with us. They have gone down the highways of the South on tortuous rides for freedom. Yes, they have gone to jail with us. Some have been dismissed from their churches, have lost the support of their bishops and fellow ministers. But they have acted in the faith that right defeated is stronger than evil triumphant. Their witness has been the spiritual salt that has preserved the true meaning of the gospel in these troubled times. They have carved a tunnel of hope through the dark mountain of disappointment.

I hope the church as a whole will meet the challenge of this decisive hour. But even if the church does not come to the aid of justice, I have no despair about the future. I have no fear about the outcome of our struggle in Birmingham, even if our motives are at present misunderstood. We will reach the goal of freedom in Birmingham and all over the nation, because the goal of America is freedom. Abused and scorned though we may be, our destiny is tied up with America's destiny. Before the pilgrims landed at Plymouth, we were here. Before the pen of Jefferson etched the majestic words of the Declaration of Independence across the pages of history, we were here. For more than two centuries our forebears labored in this country without wages; they made cotton king; they built the homes of their masters while suffering gross injustice and shameful humiliation—and yet out of a bottomless vitality they continue to thrive and develop. If the inexpressible cruelties of slavery could not stop us, the opposition we now face will surely fail. We will win our freedom because the sacred heritage of our nation and the eternal will of God are embodied in our echoing demands.

Before closing I feel impelled to mention one other point in your statement that has troubled me profoundly. You warmly commended the Birmingham police force for keeping "order" and "preventing violence." I doubt that you would have so warmly commended the police force if you had seen its dogs sinking their teeth into unarmed, nonviolent Negroes. I doubt that you would so quickly commend the policemen if you were to observe their ugly and inhumane treatment of Negroes here in the city jail; if you were to watch them push and curse old Negro women and young Negro girls; if you were to see them slap and kick old Negro men and young boys; if you were to observe them, as they did on two occasions, refuse to give us food because we wanted to sing our grace together. I cannot join you in your praise of the Birmingham police department.

It is true that the police have exercised a degree of discipline in handling the demonstrators. In this sense they have conducted themselves rather "nonviolently" in public. But for what purpose? To preserve the evil system of segregation. Over the past few years I have consistently preached that nonviolence demands that the means we use must be as pure as the ends we seek. I have tried to make clear that it is wrong to use immoral means to attain moral ends. But now I must affirm that it is just as wrong, or perhaps even more so, to use moral means to preserve immoral ends. Perhaps Mr. Connor and his policemen have been rather nonviolent in public, as was Chief Pritchett in Albany, Georgia, but they have used the moral means of nonviolence to maintain the immoral end of racial injustice. As T. S. Eliot has said: "The last temptation is the greatest treason: To do the right deed for the wrong reason."

I wish you had commended the Negro sit-inners and demonstrators of Birmingham for their sublime courage, their willingness to suffer, and their amazing discipline in the midst of great provocation. One day the South will recognize its real heroes. They will be the James Merediths, with the noble sense of purpose that enables them to face jeering and hostile mobs, and with the agonizing loneliness that characterizes the life of the pioneer. They will be old, oppressed, battered Negro women, symbolized in a seventy-two-year-old woman in Montgomery, Alabama, who rose up with a sense of dignity and with her people decided not to ride segregated buses, and who responded with ungrammatical profundity to one who inquired about her weariness: "My feets is tired, but my soul is at rest." They will be the young high school and college students, the young ministers of the gospel and a host of their elders, courageously and nonviolently sitting in at lunch counters and willingly going to jail for conscience's sake. One day the South will know that when these disinherited children of God sat down at lunch counters, they were in reality standing up for what is best in the American dream and for the most sacred values in our Judaeo-Christian heritage, thereby bringing our nation back to those great wells of democracy which were dug deep by the founding fathers in their formulation of the Constitution and the Declaration of Independence.

Never before have I written so long a letter. I'm afraid it is much too long to take your precious time. I can assure you that it would have been much shorter if I had been writing from a comfortable desk, but what else can one do when he is alone in a narrow jail cell, other than write long letters, think long thoughts, and pray long prayers?

If I have said anything in this letter that overstates the truth and indicates an unreasonable impatience, I beg you to forgive me. If I have said anything that understates the truth and indicates my having a patience that allows me to settle for anything less than brotherhood, I beg God to forgive me.

I hope this letter finds you strong in the faith. I also hope that circumstances will soon make it possible for me to meet each of you, not as an integrationist or a civil-rights leader but as a fellow clergyman and a Christian brother. Let us all hope that the dark clouds of racial prejudice will soon pass away and the deep fog of misunderstanding will be lifted from our fear-drenched communities, and in some not too distant tomorrow the radiant stars of love and brotherhood will shine over our great nation with all their scintillating beauty.

50

> Yours for the cause of Peace and Brotherhood,
> Martin Luther King Jr.

 ## Joining the Conversation: Critical Thinking and Writing

1. In his first five paragraphs, how does King assure his audience that he is not a meddlesome intruder but a man of goodwill?

2. In paragraph 3, King refers to Hebrew prophets and to the Apostle Paul and, later (paragraph 10), to Socrates. What is the point of these references?

3. In paragraph 11, what does King mean when he says that "our beloved Southland" has long tried to "live in monologue rather than dialogue"?

4. King begins paragraph 23 with "I must make two honest confessions to you, my Christian and Jewish brothers." What would have been gained or lost if he had used this paragraph as his opening?

5. King's last three paragraphs do not advance his argument. What do they do?

6. Why does King advocate breaking unjust laws "openly, lovingly" (paragraph 20)? What does he mean by these words? What other motives or attitudes do these words rule out?

7. Construct two definitions of *civil disobedience*, and explain whether and to what extent it is easier (or harder) to justify civil disobedience, depending on how you have defined the expression.

8. If you feel that you wish to respond to King's letter on some point, write a letter nominally addressed to King. If you wish, you may adopt the persona of one of the eight clergymen whom King initially addressed.

9. King writes (paragraph 46) that "nonviolence demands that the means we use must be as pure as the ends we seek." How do you think King would evaluate the following acts of civil disobedience:

   (a) occupying a college administration building in order to protest the administration's unsatisfactory response to a racial incident on campus or in order to protest the failure of the administration to hire minority persons as staff and faculty;

   (b) sailing on a collision course with a whaling ship to protest against whaling;

   (c) trespassing on an abortion clinic to protest abortion?

   Write your answer in an essay of 500 words.

Michael Levin

Michael Levin, educated at Michigan State University and Columbia University, has taught philosophy at Columbia and now at City College of the City University of New York. Levin has written numerous papers for professional journals and a book entitled Metaphysics and the Mind-Body Problem *(1979). The following essay is intended for a general audience.*

The Case for Torture

It is generally assumed that torture is impermissible, a throwback to a more brutal age. Enlightened societies reject it outright, and regimes suspected of using it risk the wrath of the United States.

Michael Levin: "The Case for Torture," *Newsweek*, June 7, 1982. Reprinted by permission of the author.

I believe this attitude is unwise. There are situations in which torture is not merely permissible but morally mandatory. Moreover, these situations are moving from the realm of imagination to fact.

Death: Suppose a terrorist has hidden an atomic bomb on Manhattan Island which will detonate at noon on July 4 unless . . . (here follow the usual demands for money and release of his friends from jail). Suppose, further, that he is caught at 10 A.M. of the fateful day, but—preferring death to failure—won't disclose where the bomb is. What do we do? If we follow due process—wait for his lawyer, arraign him—millions of people will die. If the only way to save those lives is to subject the terrorist to the most excruciating possible pain, what grounds can there be for not doing so? I suggest there are none. In any case, I ask you to face the question with an open mind.

Torturing the terrorist is unconstitutional? Probably. But millions of lives surely outweigh constitutionality. Torture is barbaric? Mass murder is far more barbaric. Indeed, letting millions of innocents die in deference to one who flaunts his guilt is moral cowardice, an unwillingness to dirty one's hands. If *you* caught the terrorist, could you sleep nights knowing that millions died because you couldn't bring yourself to apply the electrodes?

Once you concede that torture is justified in extreme cases, you have   5
admitted that the decision to use torture is a matter of balancing innocent lives against the means needed to save them. You must now face more realistic cases involving more modest numbers. Someone plants a bomb on a jumbo jet. He alone can disarm it, and his demands cannot be met (or if they can, we refuse to set a precedent by yielding to his threats). Surely we can, we must, do anything to the extortionist to save the passengers. How can we tell 300, or 100, or 10 people who never asked to be put in danger, "I'm sorry, you'll have to die in agony, we just couldn't bring ourselves to . . . "

Here are the results of an informal poll about a third, hypothetical, case. Suppose a terrorist group kidnapped a newborn baby from a hospital. I asked four mothers if they would approve of torturing kidnappers if that were necessary to get their own newborns back. All said yes, the most "liberal" adding that she would like to administer it herself.

I am not advocating torture as punishment. Punishment is addressed to deeds irrevocably past. Rather, I am advocating torture as an acceptable measure for preventing future evils. So understood, it is far less objectionable than many extant punishments. Opponents of the death penalty, for example, are forever insisting that executing a murderer will not bring back his victim (as if the purpose of capital punishment were supposed to be resurrection, not deterrence or retribution). But torture, in the cases described, is intended not to bring anyone back but to keep innocents from being dispatched. The most powerful argument against using torture as a punishment or to secure confessions is that such practices disregard the rights of the individual. Well, if the individual is all that important—and he is—it is correspondingly important to protect the rights of individuals threatened by terrorists. If life is so valuable that it must never be taken, the lives of the innocents must be saved even at the price of hurting the one who endangers them.

Better precedents for torture are assassination and pre-emptive attack. No Allied leader would have flinched at assassinating Hitler, had that been possible. (The Allies did assassinate Heydrich.) Americans would be angered to learn that Roosevelt could have had Hitler killed in 1943—thereby shortening the war and saving millions of lives—but refused on moral grounds. Similarly, if nation A learns that nation B is about to launch an unprovoked attack, A has a right to save itself by destroying B's military capability first. In the same way, if the police can by torture save those who would otherwise die at the hands of kidnappers or terrorists, they must.

Idealism: There is an important difference between terrorists and their victims that should mute talk of the terrorists' "rights." The terrorist's victims are at risk unintentionally, not having asked to be endangered. But the terrorist knowingly initiated his actions. Unlike his victims, he volunteered for the risks of his deed. By threatening to kill for profit or idealism, he renounces civilized standards, and he can have no complaint if civilization tries to thwart him by whatever means necessary.

Just as torture is justified only to save lives (not extort confessions or recantations) it is justifiably administered only to those *known* to hold innocent lives in their hands. Ah, but how can the authorities ever be sure they have the right malefactor? Isn't there a danger of error and abuse? Won't We turn into Them? 10

Questions like these are disingenuous in a world in which terrorists proclaim themselves and perform for television. The name of their game is public recognition. After all, you can't very well intimidate a government into releasing your freedom fighters unless you announce that it is your group that has seized its embassy. "Clear guilt" is difficult to define, but when 40 million people see a group of masked gunmen seize an airplane on the evening news, there is not much question about who the perpetrators are. There will be hard cases where the situation is murkier. Nonetheless, a line demarcating the legitimate use of torture can be drawn. Torture only the obviously guilty, and only for the sake of saving innocents, and the line between Us and Them will remain clear.

There is little danger that the Western democracies will lose their way if they choose to inflict pain as one way of preserving order. Paralysis in the face of evil is the greater danger. Someday soon a terrorist will threaten tens of thousands of lives, and torture will be the only way to save them. We had better start thinking about this.

Joining the Conversation:
Critical Thinking and Writing

1. At the beginning of his essay, Levin presents a number of examples designed to show that torture is sometimes acceptable. Do you agree with his interpretation of these examples?

2. In paragraph 11, Levin contends, "Torture only the obviously guilty, and only for the sake of saving innocents, and the line between Us and Them will remain clear." Imagine that you are taking the other side in a debate with Levin: How would you reply to his claim?

3. How would you evaluate Levin's essay as a piece of writing? Is his argument clearly stated? Does he support it effectively? Is it convincing? If not, why not?

4. Whether or not you agree with Levin, can you imagine being the torturer yourself? Or do you think that this job should be performed by someone else? What might be the circumstances that would lead you to feel that torture would be justified?

5. Is it one thing to present an argument like Levin's in an essay and another to put Levin's ideas into practice? Do you believe that Levin's ideas could ever be put into practice in the United States? In your view, is that fortunate or unfortunate?

A Casebook on Bullying

Natalie Angier

Natalie Angier was born in New York in 1958. In college, at the University of Michigan and Barnard College, she studied English, physics, and astronomy and formed the ambition of writing for nonspecialists about literary and scientific matters. At the age of 22, she was hired by Time Inc. as a member of the staff of a new magazine, Discover, *where she wrote about biology for four years. She has also worked as a science writer for* Time *magazine and has taught at New York University's Graduate Program in Science and Environmental Reporting. In 1990, she began writing on science-related subjects for* The New York Times, *and the next year, she won a Pulitzer prize for her reporting. Angier's most recent books are* Women, an Intimate Geography *(1999),* The Best American Science and Nature Writing *(2002) and* The Canon: A Whirligig Tour of the Beautiful Business of Science *(2007).*

The Sandbox: Bully for You—
Why Push Comes to Shove

Some people are just fair game for being picked on and put down: lawyers, politicians, journalists, mothers-in-law and, now, bullies. These days, everybody is ganging up on bullies, blaming them for all that ails us.

Bullies and their taunting, arrogant ways are said to have been the driving force behind the student shootings at Columbine and Santana High Schools. Young bullies supposedly grow into sociopaths, angry drunks, wife abusers or maybe mayors of major East Coast cities.

The victims of bullying are portrayed as emotionally disfigured for life, unable to shake the feeling that they are unlovable wimps, or that everybody is out to get them.

The news bristles with reports that bullies abound. Recently, in one of the largest studies ever of child development, researchers at the National Institutes of Health reported that about a quarter of all middle-school children were either perpetrators or victims (or in some cases, both) of serious and chronic bullying, behavior that included threats, ridicule, name calling, punching, slapping, jeering and sneering.

Another highly contentious study suggested that too much time in day care may predispose a child to bullying: youngsters who spent more than 30 hours a week away from mommy had a 17 percent chance of ending up as garden-variety bullies and troublemakers, compared to only 6 percent of children who spent less than 10 hours a week in day care.

Everywhere, legislators are struggling to beat each other to the punch in demanding that schools stamp out bad behavior. In Colorado, for example, home to Columbine High School, Gov. Bill Owens has just signed legislation requiring all state school districts to develop anti-bullying programs to prevent bullying.

In a similar spirit, the familiar phys-ed game of dodgeball—also known as killerball, prison ball or bombardment—is taking a hit lately, as school authorities nationwide have moved to ban the game on the theory that it fosters hyperaggression and gives the class klutzes an inferiority complex.

Yet even as quick-fix programs with names like "Taking the Bully by the Horns" proliferate across the academic and electronic universe, experts in aggressive behavior warn that there is no easy way to stamp out bullying among children. Short of raising kids in isolation chambers, they say, bullying behaviors can never be eliminated entirely from the sustained hazing ritual otherwise known as growing up.

"Can we get rid of bullying altogether? I don't think so," said Richard J. Hazler, a professor of counselor education at Ohio University in Athens. "We can't eliminate all growing pains, either. It's tough learning to make your way in this world."

Philip C. Rodkin, an assistant professor of educational psychology at the University of Illinois at Urbana-Champaign, pointed out that, despite all the attention being paid to the subject, the root causes of bullying remain a mystery. "This is not a trivial problem," he said. "Bullies have always been with us, and we're only beginning to ask why."

Some researchers say that, despite the hype and handwringing, there is no epidemic of bullying in schools, and in fact the incidence of serious bullying has very likely declined over the years.

"It certainly was a problem when I was in boarding school, but that was ages ago," said Richard Dawkins, a professor at Oxford University who has studied the evolution of aggressive and selfish behavior. "I believe there is far less bullying now, though there probably will always be a bit."

As an example of how bad it used to be, Professor Dawkins cited a passage from the British poet John Betjeman's 1960 autobiographical poem, "Summoned by Bells."

> *Twelve to one:*
> *What chance had Angus? They surrounded him,*
> *Pulled off his coat and trousers, socks and shoes*
> *And, wretched in his shirt, they hoisted him*
> *Into the huge waste paper basket; then*
> *Poured ink and treacle on his head. With ropes*
> *They strung the basket up among the beams*
> *And as he soared I only saw his eyes*
> *Look through the slats at us who watched below.*

As Frans de Waal, a primatologist at Emory University, sees it, one of the problems in the standard approach to bully analysis is that researchers tend to ignore the subtle dynamics between a bully and the object of a bully's scorn—the scapegoat. "Some individuals may have bully characteristics, and others may have scapegoat characteristics," he said. "The two things need to be studied together, but because personality research is generally done from an individual perspective, they rarely are."

Dr. de Waal has observed that bullying behavior is quite common among most species of monkeys and apes, and that many animals at or near the top of the hierarchy will harass, charge, snap and howl at their subordinates for no other reason than because they can. But at least as striking as the presence of simian bullies, Dr. de Waal said, are the resident scapegoats, the low-ranking individuals who seem to be chosen for the role by other members of the group. Whenever a group is under strain, or when its hierarchy is in doubt, the higher-ranking primates start taking it out on the scapegoat, with the result that any time the beleaguered monkey ventures from its corner, it gets beaten up.

"This is not just a way to release frustration," said Dr. de Waal. "The scapegoat also gives the high-ranking individuals in the group a common enemy, a unifier. By uniting against the scapegoat in moments of tension, it creates a bond."

And while primate research can never be applied directly to human affairs, even when those humans are swinging from monkey bars, bully experts admit that children in groups will often encourage, or at least not discourage, a bully's nasty acts against an underling. In one study of how peers contribute to bullying, researchers from York University studied videotapes of 53 episodes of bullying among elementary school students on the school playground. The researchers found that 54 percent of the time, onlookers stood by passively as the bully picked on the victim, an inactive form of activity that the researchers said ended up reinforcing the bully's behavior. And 21 percent of the time, some of the onlookers joined in on the taunting. Only in 25 percent of the cases did a child attempt to step in and help the victim or call a teacher to help.

But as researchers lately have discovered, many bullies in fact are quite popular. "Some kids may be goaders, cheering the bully on because they want to be accepted," said Laura Hess Olson, an assistant professor of child development at Purdue University in West Lafayette, Ind. "Or they may just stand by and do nothing because they're afraid they might be targeted next." Whatever the case, she added, "We have to realize that everybody is a player in creating the atmosphere in which bullying occurs."

Another point worth noting, said Dr. Olson, is that the old stereotype of the bully as an antisocial and unpopular misfit is false. In one study of third- to fifth-graders in two East Coast schools, she and her colleagues found that, while the students described by their peers and teachers as friendly, outgoing and self-confident were the most popular, the boys known to be bullies were the second-most popular group, way beyond the perceived wimps, eggheads and teacher's pets.

"There are a fair amount of kids in a classroom who think that bullies are cool," said Dr. Rodkin, "especially when they're attractive and athletic."   20

Adding to the challenge of curbing bullies is the fact that, as researchers have learned, many students blame victims of bullying for bringing their troubles on themselves by sulking or whimpering or walking around with their head hanging low. A sizable number of students agree with the premise that bullying can help "toughen" people and teach which behaviors are laudable and which are risible to the group.

In this scenario, then, bullies are neither born nor made, but instead have bulliness thrust upon them. The group needs its whipcracking rulemeister, just as an army boot camp needs its snarling, abusive sergeant if the soft-bellied newcomers are ever to get into fighting trim.

Indeed, it's hard to see how bullying behavior in schools can be eliminated when bullying behavior among adults is not only common but often applauded—at least if it results in wild success. J. P. Morgan, for example, was thought by many of his colleagues and subordinates to be, in the words of Robert M. LaFollette, the Wisconsin progressive, "a beefy, red-faced thick-necked financial bully, drunk with wealth and power." Yet he was also lionized in his day, described by officials at Harvard University as a "prince among merchants," a man of "skill, wisdom and courage." Hey, he was the richest guy in the world, wasn't he?

It's perhaps a bit of delicious paradox that, at a time when the nation is seized with concern over school bullying, the international community views with alarm the recent moves by the United States to scuttle the Kyoto global warming treaty and to promote the construction of a space-based nuclear missile shield. To the rest of the world, it seems, America is the biggest bully of them all.

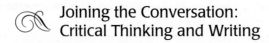

Joining the Conversation:
Critical Thinking and Writing

1. In paragraph 11, Angier cites "some researchers" who claim "that despite the hype and handwringing, there is no epidemic of bullying in schools, and in fact the incidence of serious bullying has very likely declined over the years." In addition to this reference, what evidence do you find that Angier herself believes that concern over bullying is "hype and handwringing"?

2. Compare Keen's essay (pages 478–480) with Angier's. On the basis of Keen's essay, what new data or arguments might Keen offer Angier?

3. When you were in school, were you the victim of bullying, or a bully, or both? Did you observe bullying going on around you? If so, what were your responses to bullying? (Your answer to any of these questions might provide an excellent topic for an essay of 500 words. Remember to ask yourself: Who? What? When? Where? And—most important—Why?)

4. Do you agree or disagree with the premise offered in paragraph 21 "that bullying can help 'toughen' people and teach which behaviors are laudable and which are risible to the group"? On what do you base your answer? Personal or observed experience? Reasoning? Reading? Or what? Set forth your answer in an essay of 500 words.

Andrew Keen

Andrew Keen is the author of The Cult of the Amateur *(2007), a book that is critical of user-based Web sites. We reprint an essay that originally appeared in* The Los Angeles Times, *March 1, 2008.*

Douse the Online Flames

The cartoon isn't as amusing as it once was. "On the Internet, nobody knows you're a dog," one Web-surfing canine barked to another in that 1993 classic from *The New Yorker*. Back then, of course, at the innocent dawn of the Internet Age, the idea that we might all be anonymous on the Web promised infinite intellectual freedom. Unfortunately, however, that promise hasn't been realized. Today, too many anonymous Internet users are posting hateful content about their neighbors, classmates and co-workers; today, online media is an increasingly shadowy, vertiginous environment in which it is becoming harder and harder to know other people's real identities.

Those of us who have been flamed by faceless critics in online discussion groups are intimately familiar with the problem. This isn't illegal, of course, because online speech—anonymous or otherwise—is protected by both the 1st Amendment and by the Supreme Court's much-cited 1995 McIntyre vs. Ohio Elections Commission ruling protecting anonymous speech. But is today's law adequately protecting us? What happens, for example, when anonymous Internet critics go beyond rude and irremediably blacken the reputations of innocent citizens or cause them harm? Should there be legal consequences?

The most notorious case is certainly the cyber-bullying of Megan Meier, a 13-year-old girl from a suburb of St. Louis. In 2006, Meier, a troubled, overweight adolescent, became embroiled in an intense, six-week online friendship with "Josh Evans" on MySpace. After "Josh" turned against Megan and posted a comment that "the world would be better place without you," the girl hung herself. Later, when it became clear that the fictitious Josh Evans was actually Lori Drew, a 47-year-old neighbor and mother of a girl with whom Megan Meier had argued, there were calls for a criminal prosecution. But the St. Charles County Sheriffs Department didn't charge Drew; its spokesman said that what she did "might've been rude, it might've been immature, but it wasn't illegal."

Fortunately, the Meier suicide is making officials get more serious about holding anonymous Internet users accountable. In Los Angeles, federal prosecutors were reportedly exploring whether they could charge Drew with defrauding Beverly Hills-based MySpace. In Missouri, the St. Charles County Board of Aldermen passed a law making Internet harassment a misdemeanor punishable by up to a $500 fine and 90 days in jail. And a Missouri state representative introduced legislation that could criminalize online harassment and fraud.

Online free speech fundamentalists would, no doubt, cite the 5 McIntyre vs. Ohio Elections Commission ruling in any defense. Yet that was a ruling focusing on anonymous "political speech"; Justice John Paul Stevens' opinion for the court cited the example of the Federalist Papers, originally published under pseudonyms, as proof that anonymity represents a "shield from the tyranny of the majority" and is, therefore, vital to a free society. But such a defense doesn't work for cases like the Meier suicide, in which the anonymous speech was anything but political.

The Web 2.0 revolution in self-published content is making the already tangled legal debate around anonymity even harder to unravel. Take, for example, the case of Dr. Lisa Krinsky, president of SFBC International, a Miami-based drug development firm. In 2005, Krinsky's professional and personal reputation was so vilified by anonymous critics on Yahoo message boards that she pursued a lawsuit (Krinsky vs. Doe) to subpoena the real names of 10 of her online tormentors.

Or take the case of a couple of female Yale Law School students whose reputations have been eternally sullied on an online bulletin board called AutoAdmit by "Sleazy Z," "hitlerhitlerhitler," "The Ayatollah of Rock-n-Rollah" and others. Having been publicly accused of lesbianism with the dean of admissions at Yale Law School, possessing "large false breasts" and indulging in exhibitionistic group sex, the two women filed an amended complaint (Doe vs. Ciolli) in U.S. District Court in Connecticut against the operator of AutoAdmit to reveal the identities of the anonymous critics and take down their libelous posts.

It is troubling that judges in both cases have failed to rule in favor of these victims of anonymous defamation. In the Krinsky case, a California appeals court ruled last month that her accusers had a 1st Amendment right to speak their minds. Although Doe vs. Ciolli (filed in June 2007) has yet to be ruled on, the plaintiffs had to drop Anthony Ciolli, the law student in charge of AutoAdmit, from the suit. This is because the law treats websites differently than traditional publishers in terms of their liability for libelous content. In Section 230 of the 1996 Communications Decency Act, Congress granted websites and Internet service providers immunity from liability for content posted by third parties. So a paper-and-ink newspaper can be sued for publishing a libelous letter from a reader, but, under Section 230, Web bulletin boards like AutoAdmit have no legal responsibility for the published content of their users. Thus the students are now pursuing the identities of their defamers independently of AutoAdmit—a near impossible task given the sophistication of today's software for disguising online identity.

All three of these cases indicate that the U.S. Supreme Court soon might need to rethink the civic value of anonymous speech in the digital age. Today, when cowardly anonymity is souring Internet discourse, it really is hard to understand how anonymous speech is vital to a free society. That *New Yorker* cartoon remains true: On the Internet, nobody knows you're a dog. But it is the responsibility of all of us—parents, citizens and lawmakers—to ensure that contemporary Web users don't behave like antisocial canines. And one way to achieve this is by introducing more legislation to punish anonymous sadists whose online lies are intended to wreck the reputations and mental health of innocent Americans.

 ## Joining the Conversation: Critical Thinking and Writing

1. Keen's title refers to "Online Flames"; in his 3rd paragraph, he refers to "cyber-bullying"; and in his 6th, to "the Web 2.0 revolution in self-published content." In a sentence or two, define each of these terms.

2. According to paragraph 3, Drew's malicious actions are not illegal. Does the episode demonstrate that there *should* be a law that would make such behavior illegal? Explain.

3. What do you think is an appropriate punishment (if any) for "anonymous sadists" (para. 8)?

4. Keen says that "it really is hard to understand how anonymous speech is vital to a free society" (para. 9). Spend a few minutes thinking about this issue and see whether you can come up with an example. . . . OK, time has expired: What have you come up with?

Dan Wasserman

Dan Wasserman draws cartoons for The Boston Globe. *We reproduce a cartoon devoted not to a comic but to a tragic episode.*

Editor's Note:

On January 14, 2010, a 15-year-old girl, Phoebe Prince, hanged herself with a scarf after she was bullied for three months—physically and verbally—by her classmates at South Hadley High School in Massachusetts. The bullying apparently began after it became known that she had a brief affair with a senior boy. As of the time we are writing, six teenagers have been charged with a variety of offenses: Two boys and a girl ages 16 to 18 face felony charges that include (for the males) statutory rape. Three younger girls have been charged in juvenile court with felonies including violation of civil rights and stalking.

Lawmakers in Massachusetts have been discussing legal measures, including requiring that staff and students be instructed about the dangers of bullying and also requiring that principals investigate all reports of bullying. Forty-one states already have legislation concerning bullying, but the laws vary greatly, and some are disputed on the grounds that they interfere with freedom of speech.

The subject of Wasserman's cartoon is not only the denial by South Hadley High School's officials that they had been made aware of the bullying but also that they neglected to act promptly.

School Officials Take a Test

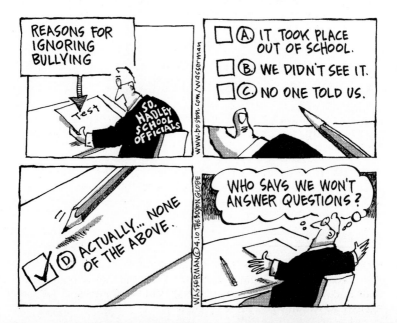

Joining the Conversation:
Critical Thinking and Writing

Describe the cartoon accurately enough so that someone who hasn't seen it can visualize it. Then, analyze the cartoon's meaning, and evaluate its effectiveness.

CHAPTER 13

Consumer Culture

American Gothic
Grant Wood, 1930

Just what is it that makes today's homes so different, so appealing?
Richard Hamilton, 1956

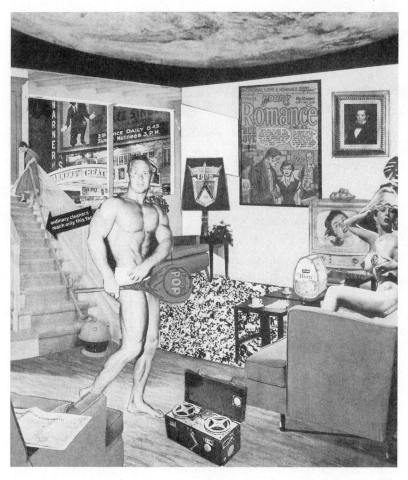

Short Views

Heaven is not as high as the desires of the human heart.
Chinese Proverb

He who desires but acts not, breeds pestilence.
William Blake

You are what you eat.
Anonymous

The great secret of vegetarianism is never to eat vegetables.
George Bernard Shaw

Coffee drunk out of wine glasses is really miserable stuff, as is meat cut at the table with a pair of scissors.
G. C. Lichtenberg

Eat, drink, and be merry, for tomorrow we die.
Ecclesiastes 8.15

Long before I am near enough to talk to you on the street, in a meeting, or at a party, you announce your sex, age and class to me through what you are wearing—and very possibly give me important information (or misinformation) as to your occupation, origin, personality, opinions, tastes, sexual desires and current mood. . . . By the time we meet and converse we have already spoken to each other in an older and more universal tongue.
Alison Lurie

Skin, if it is attractive, can be part of the design.
Rudi Gernreich

If I had to say which was telling the truth about society, a speech by a Minister of Housing or the actual buildings put up in his time, I should believe the buildings.
Kenneth Clark

A house is a machine for living.
Le Corbusier

Henry David Thoreau

Henry David Thoreau (1817–1862) was born in Concord, Massachusetts, where he spent most of his life ("I have travelled a good deal in Concord"). He taught and lectured, but he chiefly observed, thought, and wrote. From July 4, 1845, to September 6, 1847, he lived near Concord in a cabin at Walden Pond, an experience recorded in Walden *(1854).*

We reprint part of the first chapter of Walden.

Economy

The mass of men lead lives of quiet desperation. What is called resignation is confirmed desperation. From the desperate city you go into the desperate country, and have to console yourself with the bravery of minks and muskrats. A stereotyped but unconscious despair is concealed even under what are called the games and amusements of mankind. There is no play in them, for this comes after work. But it is a characteristic of wisdom not to do desperate things.

When we consider what, to use the words of the catechism, is the chief end of man, and what are the true necessaries and means of life, it appears as if men had deliberately chosen the common mode of living because they preferred it to any other. Yet they honestly think there is no choice left. But alert and healthy natures remember that the sun rose clear. It is never too late to give up our prejudices. No way of thinking or doing, however ancient, can be trusted without proof. What everybody echoes or in silence passes by as true to-day may turn out to be falsehood tomorrow, mere smoke of opinion, which some had trusted for a cloud that would sprinkle fertilizing rain on their fields. What old people say you cannot do you try and find that you can. Old deeds for old people, and new deeds for new. Old people did not know enough once, perchance, to fetch fresh fuel to keep the fire a-going; new people put a little dry wood under a pot, and are whirled round the globe with the speed of birds, in a way to kill old people, as the phrase is. Age is no better, hardly so well, qualified for an instructor as youth, for it has not profited so much as it has lost. One may almost doubt if the wisest man has learned anything of absolute value by living. Practically, the old have no very important advice to give the young, their own experience has been so partial, and their lives have been such miserable failures, for private reasons, as they must believe; and it may be that they have some faith left which belies that experience, and they are only less young than they were. I have lived some thirty years on this planet, and I have yet to hear the first syllable of valuable or even earnest advice from my seniors. They have told me nothing, and probably cannot tell me anything to the purpose. Here is life, an experiment to a great extent untried by me; but it does not avail me that they have tried it. If I have any experience which I think valuable, I am sure to reflect that this my Mentors said nothing about.

One farmer says to me, "You cannot live on vegetable food solely, for it furnishes nothing to make bones with;" and so he religiously devotes a part of his day to supplying his system with the raw material of bones; walking all the while he talks behind his oxen, which, with vegetable-made bones, jerk him and his lumbering plough along in spite of every obstacle. Some things are really necessaries of life in some circles, the most helpless and diseased, which in others are luxuries merely, and in others still are entirely unknown.

The whole ground of human life seems to some to have been gone over by their predecessors, both the heights and the valleys, and all things to have been cared for. According to Evelyn, "the wise Solomon prescribed ordinances for the very distances of trees; and the Roman prætors have decided how often you may go into your neighbor's land to gather the acorns which fall on it without trespass, and what share belongs to that neighbor." Hippocrates has even left directions how we should cut our nails; that is, even with the ends of the fingers, neither shorter nor longer. Undoubtedly the very tedium and ennui which presume to have exhausted the variety and the joys of life are as old as Adam. But man's capacities have never been measured; nor are we to judge of what he can do by any precedents, so little has been tried. Whatever have been thy failures hitherto, "be not afflicted, my child, for who shall assign to thee what thou hast left undone?"

We might try our lives by a thousand simple tests; as, for instance, that the same sun which ripens my beans illumines at once a system of earths like ours. If I had remembered this it would have prevented some mistakes. This was not the light in which I hoed them. The stars are the apexes of what wonderful triangles! What distant and different beings in the various mansions of the universe are contemplating the same one at the same moment! Nature and human life are as various as our several constitutions. Who shall say what prospect life offers to another? Could a greater miracle take place than for us to look through each other's eyes for an instant? We should live in all the ages of the world in an hour; ay, in all the worlds of the ages. History, Poetry, Mythology!—I know of no reading of another's experience so startling and informing as this would be.

The greater part of what my neighbors call good I believe in my soul to be bad, and if I repent of anything, it is very likely to be my good behavior. What demon possessed me that I behaved so well? You may say the wisest thing you can, old man—you who have lived seventy years, not without honor of a kind,—I hear an irresistible voice which invites me away from all that. One generation abandons the enterprises of another like stranded vessels.

I think that we may safely trust a good deal more than we do. We may waive just so much care of ourselves as we honestly bestow elsewhere. Nature is as well adapted to our weakness as to our strength. The incessant anxiety and strain of some is a well-nigh incurable form of disease. We are made to exaggerate the importance of what work we do; and yet how much is not done by us! or, what if we had been taken sick? How vigilant we are! determined not to live by faith if we can avoid it; all the day long on the alert, at night we unwillingly say our prayers and commit ourselves to uncertainties. So thoroughly and sincerely are we compelled to live, reverencing our life, and denying the possibility of change. This is the only way, we say; but there are as many ways as there can be drawn radii from one centre. All change is a miracle to contemplate; but it is a miracle which is taking place every instant. Confucius said, "To know that we know what we know, and that we do not know what we do not know, that is true knowledge." When one man has reduced a fact of the imagination to be a fact to his understanding, I foresee that all men will at length establish their lives on that basis.

Let us consider for a moment what most of the trouble and anxiety which I have referred to is about, and how much it is necessary that we be troubled, or at least careful. It would be some advantage to live a primitive and frontier life, though in the midst of an outward civilization, if only to learn what are the gross necessaries of life and what methods have been taken to obtain them; or even to look over the old day-books of the merchants, to see what it was that men most commonly bought at the stores, what they stored, that is, what are the grossest groceries. For the improvements of ages have had but little influence on the essential laws of man's existence; as our skeletons, probably, are not to be distinguished from those of our ancestors.

By the words, *necessary of life,* I mean whatever, of all that man obtains by his own exertions, has been from the first, or from long use has become, so important to human life that few, if any, whether from savageness, or poverty, or philosophy, ever attempt to do without it. To many creatures there is in this sense but one necessary of life. Food. To the bison of the prairie it is a few inches of palatable grass, with water to drink; unless he seeks the Shelter of the forest or the mountain's shadow. None of the brute creation requires more than Food and Shelter. The necessaries of life for man in this climate may, accurately enough, be distributed under the several heads of Food, Shelter, Clothing, and Fuel; for not till we have secured these are we prepared to entertain the true problems of life with freedom and a prospect of success. Man has invented, not only houses, but clothes and cooked food; and possibly from the accidental discovery of the warmth of fire, and the consequent use of it, at first a luxury, arose the present necessity to sit by it. We observe cats and dogs acquiring the same second nature. By proper Shelter and Clothing we legitimately retain our own internal heat; but with an excess of these, or of Fuel, that is, with an external heat greater than our own internal, may not cookery properly be said to begin? Darwin, the naturalist, says of the inhabitants of Tierra del Fuego, that while his own party, who were well clothed and sitting close to a fire, were far from too warm, these naked savages, who were farther off, were observed, to his great surprise, "to be steaming with perspiration at undergoing such a roasting." So, we are told, the New Hollander goes naked with impunity, while the European shivers in his clothes. Is it impossible to combine the hardiness of these savages with the intellectualness of the civilized man? According to Liebig, man's body is a stove, and food the fuel which keeps up the internal combustion in the lungs. In cold weather we eat more, in warm less. The animal heat is the result of a slow combustion, and disease and death take place when this is too rapid; or for want of fuel, or from some defect in the draught, the fire goes out. Of course the vital heat is not to be confounded with fire; but so much for analogy. It appears, therefore, from the above list, that the expression, *animal life*, is nearly synonymous with the expression, *animal heat*; for while Food may be regarded as the Fuel which keeps up the fire within us,—and Fuel serves only to prepare that Food or to increase the warmth of our bodies by addition from without—Shelter and Clothing also serve only to retain the *heat* thus generated and absorbed.

The grand necessity, then, for our bodies, is to keep warm, to keep the vital heat in us. What pains we accordingly take, not only with our Food, and Clothing, and Shelter, but with our beds, which are our night-clothes, robbing the nests and breasts of birds to prepare this shelter within a shelter, as the mole has its bed of grass and leaves at the end of its burrow! The poor man is wont to complain that this is a cold world; and to cold, no less physical than social, we refer directly a great part of our ails. The summer, in some climates, makes possible to man a sort of Elysian life. Fuel, except to cook his Food, is then unnecessary; the sun is his fire, and many of the fruits are sufficiently cooked by its rays; while Food generally is more various, and more easily obtained, and Clothing and Shelter are wholly or half unnecessary. At the present day, and in this country, as I find by my own experience, a few implements, a knife, an axe, a spade, a wheelbarrow, etc.; and for the studious, lamplight, stationery, and access to a few books, rank next to necessaries, and can all be obtained at a trifling cost. Yet some, not wise, go to the other side of the globe, to barbarous and unhealthy regions, and devote themselves to trade for ten or twenty years, in order that they may live—that is, keep comfortably warm,—and die in New England at last. The luxuriously rich are not simply kept comfortably warm, but unnaturally hot; as I implied before, they are cooked, of course *à la mode*.

Most of the luxuries, and many of the so-called comforts of life, are not only not indispensable, but positive hindrances to the elevation of mankind. With respect to luxuries and comforts, the wisest have ever lived a more simple and meagre life than the poor. The ancient philosophers, Chinese, Hindoo, Persian, and Greek, were a class than which none has been poorer in outward riches, none so rich in inward. We know not much about them. It is remarkable that *we* know so much of them as we do. The same is true of the more modern reformers and benefactors of their race. None can be an impartial or wise observer of human life but from the vantage ground of what *we* should call voluntary poverty. Of a life of luxury the fruit is luxury, whether in agriculture, or commerce, or literature, or art. There are nowadays professors of philosophy, but not philosophers. Yet it is admirable to profess because it was once admirable to live. To be a philosopher is not merely to have subtle thoughts, nor even to found a school, but so to love wisdom as to live accordingly to its dictates, a life of simplicity, independence, magnanimity, and trust. It is to solve some of the problems of life, not only theoretically, but practically. The success of great scholars and thinkers is commonly a courtier-like success, not kingly, not manly. They make shift to live merely by conformity, practically as their fathers did, and are in no sense the progenitors of a nobler race of men. But why do men degenerate ever? What makes families run out? What is the nature of the luxury which enervates and destroys nations? Are we sure that there is none of it in our own lives? The philosopher is in advance of his age even in the outward form of his life. He is not fed, sheltered, clothed, warmed, like his contemporaries. How can a man be a philosopher and not maintain his vital heat by better methods than other men?

When a man is warmed by the several modes which I have described, what does he want next? Surely not more warmth of the same kind, as more and richer food, larger and more splendid houses, finer and more abundant clothing, more numerous incessant and hotter fires, and the like. When he has obtained those things which are necessary to life, there is another alternative than to obtain the superfluities; and that is, to adventure on life now, his vacation from humbler toil having commenced. The soil, it appears, is suited to the seed, for it has sent its radicle downward, and it may now send its shoot upward also with confidence. Why has man rooted himself thus firmly in the earth, but that he may rise in the same proportion into the heavens above?—for the nobler plants are valued for the fruit they bear at last in the air and light, far from the ground, and are not treated like the humbler esculents, which, though they may be biennials, are cultivated only till they have perfected their root, and often cut down at top for this purpose, so that most would not know them in their flowering season.

I do not mean to prescribe rules to strong and valiant natures, who will mind their own affairs whether in heaven or hell, and perchance build more magnificently and spend more lavishly than the richest, without ever impoverishing themselves, not knowing how they live,—if, indeed, there are any such, as has been dreamed; nor to those who find their encouragement and inspiration in precisely the present condition of things, and cherish it with the fondness and enthusiasms of lovers,—and, to some extent, I reckon myself in this number; I do not speak to those who are well employed, in whatever circumstances, and they know whether they are well employed or not;—but mainly to the mass of men who are discontented, and idly complaining of the hardness of their lot or of the times, when they might improve them. There are some who complain most energetically and inconsolably of any, because they are, as they say, doing their duty. I also have in my mind that seemingly wealthy, but most terribly impoverished class of all, who have accumulated dross, but know not how to use it, or get rid of it, and thus have forged their own golden or silver fetters.

Joining the Conversation: Critical Thinking and Writing

1. In the section of *Walden* we reprint here, you will find Thoreau's observations on what is essential to our lives, and his often highly critical observations of how people live. For each of the following statements (or from others that you choose), argue whether you find it true, or partly true, or false. Take into account Thoreau's tone—for example, is he purposely exaggerating?—and supply examples from your own experience to strengthen your argument.

   a. The mass of men lead lives of quiet desperation.   (paragraph 1)
   b. A stereotyped but unconscious despair is concealed under what are called the games and amusements of mankind.   (paragraph 1)
   c. I have lived some thirty years on this planet, and I have yet to hear the first syllable of valuable or even earnest advice from my seniors. They have told me nothing and probably cannot tell me anything to the purpose.   (paragraph 2)
   d. The greater part of what my neighbors call good I believe in my soul to be bad, and if I repent of anything, it is very likely to be my good behavior. (paragraph 6)

2. If you had the opportunity to visit Thoreau in his cabin at Walden Pond, what would you like to talk with him about? What might you bring him as a house-warming gift? Would you invite him to visit you at home? Explain in a paragraph or two.

Michael Pollan

Michael Pollan holds a bachelor's degree from Bennington College and a master's degree from Columbia University. A professor of journalism at University of California, Berkeley, and the author of several books, he has been especially concerned with the ways in which societies produce the food that feeds them. We give a chapter from a recent book, In Defense of Food: An Eater's Manifesto *(2008).*

Eat Food: Food Defined

The first time I heard the advice to "just eat food" it was in a speech by Joan Gussow, and it completely baffled me. Of course you should eat food—what else is there to eat? But Gussow, who grows much of her own food on a flood-prone finger of land jutting into the Hudson River, refuses to dignify most of the products for sale in the supermarket with that title. "In the thirty-four years I've been in the field of nutrition," she said in the same speech, "I have watched real food disappear from large areas of the supermarket and from much of the rest of the eating world." Taking food's place on the shelves has been an unending stream of food-like substitutes, some seventeen thousand new ones every year—"products constructed largely around commerce and hope, supported by frighteningly little actual knowledge." Ordinary food is still out there, however, still being grown and even occasionally sold in the supermarket, and this ordinary food is what we should eat.

But given our current state of confusion and given the thousands of products calling themselves food, this is more easily said than done. So consider these related rules of thumb. Each proposes a different sort of map to the contemporary food landscape, but all should take you to more or less the same place.

DON'T EAT ANYTHING YOUR GREAT GRANDMOTHER WOULDN'T RECOGNIZE AS FOOD. Why your great grandmother? Because at this point your mother and possibly even your grandmother is as confused as the rest of us; to be safe we need to go back at least a couple generations, to a time before the advent of most modern foods. So depending on your age (and your grandmother), you may need to go back to your great- or even great-great grandmother. Some nutritionists recommend going back even further. John Yudkin, a British nutritionist whose early alarms about the dangers of refined carbohydrates were overlooked in the 1960s and 1970s, once advised, "Just don't eat anything your Neolithic ancestors wouldn't have recognized and you'll be ok."

What would shopping this way mean in the supermarket? Well, imagine your great grandmother at your side as you roll down the aisles. You're standing together in front of the dairy case. She picks up a package of Go-Gurt Portable Yogurt tubes—and has no idea what this could possibly be. Is it a food or a toothpaste? And how, exactly, do you introduce it into your body? You could tell her it's just yogurt is a squirtable form, yet if she read the ingredients label she would have every reason to doubt that that was in fact the case. Sure, there's some yogurt in there, but there are also a dozen other things that aren't remotely yogurtlike, ingredients she would probably fail to recognize as foods of any kind, including high-fructose corn syrup, modified corn starch, kosher gelatin, carrageenan, tricalcium phosphate, natural and artificial flavors, vitamins, and so forth. (And there's a whole other list of ingredients for the "berry bubblegum bash" flavoring, containing everything but berries or bubblegum.) How did Yogurt, which in your great grandmother's day consisted simply of milk inoculated with a bacterial culture, ever get to be so complicated? Is a product like Go-Gurt Portable Yogurt still a whole food? A food of any kind? Or is it just a food product?

There are in fact hundreds of foodish products in the supermarket that your ancestors simply wouldn't recognize as food breakfast cereal 5 bars transected by bright white veins representing, but in reality having nothing to do with, milk; "protein waters" and "nondairy creamer"; cheeselike food stuffs equally innocent of any bovine contribution; cakelike cylinders (with creamlike fillings) called Twinkies that never grow stale. *Don't eat anything incapable of rotting* is another personal policy you might consider adopting.

There are many reasons to avoid eating such complicated food products beyond the various chemical additives and corn and soy derivatives they contain. One of the problems with the products of food science is that, as Joan Gussow has pointed out, they lie to your body, their artificial colors and flavors and synthetic sweeteners and novel fats confound the senses we rely on to assess new foods and prepare our bodies to deal with them. Foods that lie leave us with little choice but to eat by the numbers, consulting labels rather than our senses.

It's true that foods have long been processed in order to preserve them, as when we pickle or ferment or smoke, but industrial processing aims to do much more than extend shelf life. Today foods are processed in ways specifically designed to sell us more food by pushing our evolutionary buttons—our inborn preferences for sweetness and fat and salt. These qualities are difficult to find in nature but cheap and easy for the food scientist to deploy, with the result that processing induces us to consume much more of these ecological rarities than is good for us. "Tastes great, less filling!" could be the motto for most processed foods, which are far more energy dense than most whole foods: The contain much less water, fiber, and micronutrients, and generally much more sugar and fat, making them at the same time, to coin a marketing slogan, "More fattening, less nutritious!"

The great grandma rule will help keep many of these products out of your cart. But not all of them. Because thanks to the FDA's willingness, post–1973, to let food makers freely alter the identity of "traditional foods that everyone knows" without having to call them imitations, your great grandmother could easily be fooled into thinking that that loaf of bread or wedge of cheese is in fact a loaf of bread or a wedge of cheese. This is why we need a slightly more detailed personal policy to capture these imitation foods; to wit:

AVOID FOOD PRODUCTS CONTAINING INGREDIENTS THAT ARE A) UNFAMILIAR, B) UNPRONOUNCEABLE, C) MORE THAN FIVE IN NUMBER, OR THAT INCLUDE D) HIGH-FRUCTOSE CORN SYRUP. None of these characteristics, not even the last one, is necessarily harmful in and of itself, but all of them are reliable markers for foods that have been highly processed to the point where they may no longer be what they purport to be. They have crossed over from foods to food products.

Consider a loaf of bread, one of the "traditional foods that everyone knows" specifically singled out for protection in the 1938 imitation rule. As your grandmother could tell you, bread is traditionally made using a remarkably small number of familiar ingredients: flour, yeast, water, and a pinch of salt will do it. But industrial bread—even industrial whole-grain bread—has become a far more complicated product of modern food science (not to mention commerce and hope). Here's the complete ingredients list for Sara Lee's Soft & Smooth Whole Grain White Bread. (Wait a minute—isn't "Whole Grain White Bread" a contradiction in terms? Evidently not any more.)

Enriched bleached flour [wheat flour, malted barley flour, niacin, iron, thiamin mononitrate (vitamin B_1), riboflavin (vitamin B_2), folic acid] water, whole grains [whole wheat flour, brown rice flour (rice flour, rice bran)], high fructose corn syrup [hello!], whey, wheat gluten, yeast, cellulose. Contains 2% or less of each of the following: honey, calcium sulfate, vegetable oil (soybean and/or cottonseed oils), salt, butter (cream, salt), dough conditioners (may contain one or more of the following: mono- and diglycerides, ethoxylated mono- and diglycerides, ascorbic acid, enzymes, azodicarbonamide), guar gum, calcium propionate (preservative), distilled vinegar, yeast nutrients (monocalcium phosphate, calcium sulfate, ammonium sulfate), corn starch, natural flavor, beta-carotene (color), vitamin D_3, soy lecithin, soy flour.

There are many things you could say about this intricate loaf of "bread," but note first that even if it managed to slip by your great grandmother (because it is a loaf of bread or at least is called one and strongly resembles one), the product fails every test proposed under rule number two: It's got unfamiliar ingredients (monoglycerides I've heard of before, but ethoxylated monoglycerides?); unpronounceable ingredients (try "azodicarbonamide"); it exceeds the maximum of five ingredients (by roughly thirty-six); and it contains high-fructose corn syrup. Sorry, Sara Lee, but your Soft & Smooth Whole Grain White Bread is not food and if not for the indulgence of the FDA could not even be labeled "bread."

Sara Lee's Soft & Smooth Whole Grain White Bread could serve as a monument to the age of nutritionism. It embodies the latest nutritional wisdom from science and government (which in its most recent food pyramid recommends that at least half our consumption of grain come from whole grains) but leavens that wisdom with the commercial recognition that American eaters (and American children in particular) have come to prefer their wheat highly refined—which is to say, cottony soft, snowy white, and exceptionally sweet on the tongue. In its marketing materials, Sara Lee treats this clash of interests as some sort of Gordian knot[1]—it speaks in terms of an ambitious quest to build a "no compromise" loaf—which only the most sophisticated food science could possibly cut.

---

[1]**Gordian knot** Gordius tied so intricate a knot that nobody could untie it. Alexander the Great cut it with his sword (i.e., resolved the difficulty by means of a forceful action).

And so it has, with the invention of whole-grain white bread. Because the small percentage of whole grains in the bread would render it that much less sweet than, say, all-white Wonder Bread—which scarcely waits to be chewed before transforming itself into glucose—the food scientists have added high-fructose corn syrup and honey to make up the difference; to overcome, the problematic heft and toothsomeness of a real whole grain bread, they've deployed "dough conditioners," including guar gum and the aforementioned azodicarbonamide, to simulate the texture of supermarket white bread. By incorporating certain varieties of albino wheat, they've managed to maintain that deathly but apparently appealing Wonder Bread pallor.

Who would have thought Wonder Bread would ever become an ideal of aesthetic and gustatory perfection to which bakers would actually aspire—Sara Lee's Mona Lisa?

Very often food science's efforts to make traditional foods more nutritious make them much more complicated, but not necessarily any better for you. To make dairy products low fat, it's not enough to remove the fat. You then have to go to great lengths to preserve the body or creamy texture by working in all kinds of food additives. In the case of low-fat or skim milk, that usually means adding powdered milk. But powdered milk contains oxidized cholesterol, which scientists believe is much worse for your arteries than ordinary cholesterol, so food makers sometimes compensate by adding antioxidants, further complicating what had been a simple one-ingredient whole food. Also, removing the fat makes it that much harder for your body to absorb the fat-soluble vitamins that are one of the reasons to drink milk in the first place.

All this heroic and occasionally counterproductive food science has been undertaken in the name of our health—so that Sara Lee can add to its plastic wrapper the magic words "good source of whole grain" or a food company can ballyhoo the even more magic words "low fat." Which brings us to a related food policy that may at first sound counterintuitive to a health-conscious eater:

AVOID FOOD PRODUCTS THAT MAKE HEALTH CLAIMS. For a food product to make health claims on its package it must first have a package, so right off the bat it's more likely to be a processed than a whole food. Generally speaking, it is only the big food companies that have the wherewithal to secure FDA-approved health claims for their products and then trumpet them to the world. Recently, however, some of the tonier fruits and nuts have begun boasting about their health-enhancing properties, and there will surely be more as each crop council scrounges together the money to commission its own scientific study. Because all plants contain antioxidants, all these studies are guaranteed to find something on which to base a health oriented marketing campaign.

But for the most part it is the products of food science that make the boldest health claims, and these are often founded on incomplete and often erroneous science–the dubious fruits of nutritionism. Don't forget that trans-fat-rich margarine, one of the first industrial foods to claim it was healthier than the traditional food it replaced, turned out to give people heart attacks. Since that debacle, the FDA, under tremendous pressure from industry, has made it only easier for food companies to make increasingly doubtful health claims, such as the one Frito-Lay now puts on some of its chips—that eating them is somehow good for your heart. If you bother to read the health claims closely (as food marketers make sure consumers seldom do), you will find that there is often considerably less to them than meets the eye.

Consider a recent "qualified" health claim approved by the FDA for (don't laugh) corn oil. ("Qualified" is a whole new category of health claim, introduced in 2002 at the behest of industry.) Corn oil, you may recall, is particularly high in the omega-6 fatty acids we're already consuming far too many of.

> Very limited and preliminary scientific evidence suggests that eating about one tablespoon (16 grams) of corn oil daily may reduce the risk of heart disease due to the unsaturated fat content in corn oil.

The tablespoon is a particularly rich touch, conjuring images of moms administering medicine, or perhaps cod-liver oil, to their children. But what the FDA gives with one hand, it takes away with the other. Here's the small-print "qualification" of this already notably diffident health claim:

> [The] FDA concludes that there is little scientific evidence supporting this claim.

And then to make matters still more perplexing:

> To achieve this possible benefit, corn oil is to replace a similar amount of saturated fat and not increase the total number of calories you eat in a day.

This little masterpiece of pseudoscientific bureaucratese was extracted from the FDA by the manufacturer of Mazola corn oil. It would appear that "qualified" is an official FDA euphemism for "all but meaningless." Though someone might have let the consumer in on this game. The FDA's own research indicates that consumers have no idea what to make of qualified health claims (how would they?), and its rules allow companies to promote the claims pretty much any way they want—they can use really big type for the claim, for example, and then print the disclaimers in teeny-tiny type. No doubt we can look forward to a qualified health claim for high-fructose corn syrup, a tablespoon of which probably does contribute to your health—as long as it replaces a comparable amount of, say, poison in your diet and doesn't increase the total number of calories you eat in a day.

When corn oil and chips and sugary breakfast cereals can all boast being good for your heart, health claims have become hopelessly corrupt. The American Heart Association currently bestows (for a fee) its heart-healthy seal of approval on Lucky Charms, Cocoa Puffs, and Trix cereals, Yoo-hoo lite chocolate drink, and Healthy Choice's Premium Caramel Swirl Ice Cream Sandwich—this at a time when scientists are coming to recognize that dietary sugar probably plays a more important role in heart disease than dietary fat. Meanwhile, the genuinely heart-healthy whole foods in the produce section, lacking the financial and political clout of the packaged goods a few aisles over, are mute. But don't take the silence of the yams as a sign that they have nothing valuable to say about health.

Bogus health claims and food science have made supermarkets particularly treacherous places to shop for real food, which suggests two further rules.

SHOP THE PERIPHERIES OF THE SUPERMARKET AND STAY OUT OF THE MIDDLE. Most supermarkets are laid out the same way: Processed food products dominate the center aisles of the store while the cases of ostensibly fresh food—dairy, produce, meat, and fish—line the walls. If you keep to the edges of the store you'll be that much more likely to wind up with real food in your shopping cart. The strategy is not foolproof, however, because things like high-fructose corn syrup have slipped into the dairy case under cover of Go-Gurt and such. So consider a more radical strategy.

GET OUT OF THE SUPERMARKET WHENEVER POSSIBLE. You won't find any high-fructose corn syrup at the farmers' market. You also won't find any elaborately processed food products, any packages with long lists of unpronounceable ingredients or dubious health claims, nothing microwavable, and, perhaps best of all, no old food from far away. What you will find are fresh whole foods picked at the peak of their taste and nutritional quality—precisely the kind your great grandmother, or even your Neolithic ancestors, would easily have recognized as food.

Indeed, the surest way to escape the Western diet is simply to depart the realms it rules: the supermarket; the convenience store, and the fast-food outlet. It is hard to eat badly from the farmers' market, from a CSA box (community-supported agriculture, an increasingly popular scheme in which you subscribe to a farm and receive a weekly box of produce), or from your garden. The number of farmer's markets has more than doubled in the last ten years, to more than four thousand, making it one of the fastest-growing segments of the food marketplace. It is true that most farmers' markets operate only seasonally, and you won't find everything you need there. But buying as much as you can from the farmers' market, or directly from the farm when that's an option, is a simple act with a host of profound consequences for your health as well as for the health of the food chain you've now joined.

When you eat from the farmers' market, you automatically eat food that is in season, which is usually when it is most nutritious. Eating in season also tends to diversify your diet—because you can't buy strawberries or broccoli or potatoes twelve months of the year, you'll find yourself experimenting with other foods when they come into the market. The CSA box does an even better job of forcing you out of your dietary rut because you'll find things in your weekly allotment that you would never buy on your own. Whether it's a rutabaga or an unfamiliar winter squash, the CSA box's contents invariably send you to your cookbooks to figure out what in the world to do with them. Cooking is one of the most important health consequences of buying food from local farmers; for one thing, when you cook at home you seldom find yourself reaching for the ethoxylated diglycerides or high-fructose corn syrup. But more on cooking later.

To shop at a farmers' market or sign up with a CSA is to join a short food chain and that has several implications for your health. Local produce, is typically picked ripe and is fresher than supermarket produce, and for those reasons it should be tastier and more nutritious. As for supermarket organic produce, it too is likely to have come from far away—from the industrial organic farms of California or, increasingly, China.* And while it's true that the organic label guarantees that no synthetic pesticides or fertilizers have been used to produce the food, many, if not most, of the small farms that supply farmers' markets are organic in everything but name. To survive in the farmers' market or CSA economy, a farm will need to be highly diversified, and a diversified farm usually has little need for pesticides; it's the big monocultures that can't survive without them.†

If you're concerned about chemicals in your produce, you can simply ask the farmer at the market how he or she deals with pests and fertility and begin the sort of conversation between producers and consumers that, in the end, is the best guarantee of quality in your food. So many of the problems of the industrial food chain stem from its length and complexity. A wall of ignorance intervenes between consumers and producers, and that wall fosters certain carelessness on both sides. Farmers can lose sight of the fact that they're growing food for actual eaters rather than for middlemen, and consumers can easily forget that growing good food takes care and hard work. In a long food chain, the story and identity of the food (Who grew it? Where and how was it grown?) disappear into the undifferentiated stream of commodities, so that the only information communicated between consumers and producers is a price. In a short food chain, eaters can make their needs and desires known to the

30

---

*One recent study found that the average item of organic produce in the supermarket had actually traveled farther from the farm than the average item of conventional produce.

†Wendell Berry put the problem of monoculture with admirable brevity and clarity in his essay. "The Pleasures of Eating": "But as scale increases, diversity declines; as diversity declines, so does health; as health declines, the dependence on drugs and chemicals necessarily increases."

farmer, and farmers can impress on eaters the distinctions between ordinary and exceptional food, and the many reasons why exceptional food is worth what it costs. Food reclaims its story, and some of its nobility, when the person who grew it hands it to you. So here's a subclause to the get-out-of-the-supermarket rule: *Shake the hand that feeds you*.

As soon as you do, accountability becomes once again a matter of relationships instead of regulation or labeling or legal liability. Food safety didn't become a national or global problem until the industrialization of the food chain attenuated the relationships between food producers and eaters. That was the story Upton Sinclair told about the Beef Trust in 1906, and it's the story unfolding in China today, where the rapid industrialization of the food system is leading to alarming breakdowns in food safety and integrity. Regulation is an imperfect substitute for the accountability, and trust, built into a market in which food producers meet the gaze of eaters and vice versa. Only when we participate in a short food chain are we reminded every week that we are indeed part of a food chain and dependent for our health on its peoples and soils and integrity—on its health.

"Eating is an agricultural act," Wendell Berry famously wrote, by which he meant that we are not just passive consumers of food but co-creators of the systems that feed us. Depending on how we spend them, our food dollars can either go to support a food industry devoted to quantity and convenience and "value" or they can nourish a food chain organized around *values*—values like quality and health. Yes, shopping this way takes more money and effort, but as soon you begin to treat that expenditure not just as shopping but also as a kind of vote—a vote for health in the largest sense—food no longer seems like the smartest place to economize.

✍ Joining the Conversation: Critical Thinking and Writing

1. Consider Pollan's first paragraph. Does it hold your interest? If so, what makes the material at least moderately interesting? What devices does Pollan use as a writer that you might introduce into your own argumentative essays?

2. Again, in his first paragraph, Pollan claims that "foodlike substances" have been taking the place of food in supermarkets. What "foodlike substances" are you familiar with? Do you think Pollan's essay will persuade you to avoid buying them? Explain.

3. What is the FDA (paragraph 3)?

4. In his heading for the ninth paragraph, Pollan says that we should avoid foods that contain ingredients that are unfamiliar or that have unpronounceable names. Is he in fact saying that our ignorance constitutes a

valid standard? If so, is he talking nonsense more or less equivalent to saying, "If a doctor tells you that have a disease you never heard of, pay no attention"?

5. Why does Pollan argue against buying organic produce in the supermarket? Does his evidence persuade you to avoid buying such produce? Explain.

6. In his last paragraph, Pollan acknowledges that shopping for food as he recommends is more expensive and time-consuming than shopping in supermarkets for "industrialized products." To what extent has his argument persuaded you to spend more time and money?

7. Pollan devotes his last pages (beginning with paragraph 27) to farmers' markets or, we might say, with a return to old-fashioned agriculture. In his final paragraph, he quotes Wendell Berry, "Eating is an agricultural act," which Pollan takes to mean that we are "cocreators of the systems that feed us." If you have made purchases at a farmers' market, in 500 words, explain why you shop at farmers' markets or why you made those particular purchases.

Michael Ableman

Michael Ableman, of the Center for Ecoliteracy, is a farmer, author, and photographer. His most recent book is Fields of Plenty: A Farmer's Journey in Search of Real Food and the People Who Grow It *(2005). We reprint an essay from a series called "Thinking Outside the Lunchbox," published in 2005 by the Center for Ecoliteracy.*

Feeding Our Future

Lunchtime at Goleta Valley Junior High starts at 12:07. Within 28 minutes, 700 students have to be "fed" before returning to classes. The scene is pandemonium. Students are either standing in lines, clustered in small bands, or racing around as if lost. The lunch tables are folded and stacked with their accompanying chairs; students eat outside while standing up (a food fight a couple years ago resulted in the administration's removing any opportunity for students to sit down and eat together).

The cool stainless tubular slides that once carried plastic trays of hot food dished out by hair-netted women in starched white uniforms remain. But no milk machines squirt columns of regular or chocolate milk;

no bottom-heated tables keep mashed potatoes or lasagna warm; no fishcakes wait in stacks; no coleslaw sits at the ready; no clam chowder simmers, ready to be ladled into waiting bowls.

The heating table's large pans are now filled with prepackaged barbe-cued beef sandwiches and cheeseburgers prepared at anonymous kitchens, miles away, with ingredients from U.S. government commodi-ties programs. On the wall a faded sign reads, "Fruits and vegetables are always in season. Whether they're fresh, frozen, canned, or dried, they all count." The cardboard "No pizza today" sign brings audible sighs of disappointment.

A salad bar graces one corner of the room, laden with shredded ice-berg lettuce, grated cheese, pickles, peppers, yogurt, granola, peanuts, and apple and orange pieces. Another station is stacked with Italian subs, ham sandwiches, and celery pieces with containers of peanut butter. With a pair of plastic tongs, the lady in charge of the salad bar makes a futile at-tempt to conceal the brown lettuce leaves. She asks if I'm an inspector, then apologizes for the condition of the lettuce. She tells me that it's the last day before the break and that they're trying to "get rid of" the old product.

The longest lines of students lead to two wire mesh-covered windows   5
outside the building, where attendants dispense nachos—orange gooey imitation cheese squirted from a machine onto chips. Every purchased item is placed in a thick cardboard tray. I watch as students pay for their food, then immediately toss the trays, foil wrappers, napkins, and cans into rapidly filling trash barrels.

Just a few blocks away, in the fertile fields of Fairview Gardens, a small community farm, long rows of asparagus poke their heads out of sandy soil, crimson strawberries dot a nearby field, and multicolored lettuces stand up straight and tall. Peach, plum, apricot, and nectarine trees have just shed their pink and white flower petals, revealing branches loaded with small fruit. In neighboring fields, the last of the mandarin oranges hang like orange beacons, and the first avocados cluster from huge grandfather trees in the "cathedral" orchard that dominates the land.

The farm is often referred to as "the little farm that could" for its un-precedented diversity of products and as a model of urban agriculture and public education. It has operated since 1895, holding out against the tide of development, withstanding a range of threats to its existence, and now permanently preserved under an agricultural conservation easement.

In the large field along Fairview Avenue, the main thoroughfare used by most students going to and from the school, carrots, beets, spinach, onions, broccoli, artichokes, and snap and English peas provide food for the burgeoning suburban population that now inhabits this once agricul-tural valley. In the surrounding neighborhood, fields containing some of the richest and deepest topsoil on the West Coast now yield housing developments, shopping centers, and clogged roadways.

It takes about 10 minutes to walk from Goleta Valley Junior High to Fairview Gardens farm, about four minutes by bicycle, and about one minute by car. This stunning twelve-and-a-half-acre outdoor classroom is open to the public. Thousands of people come each year to enjoy a different kind of educational experience, starting with soil and moving through a range of food crops and animals. Hundreds of students from the school have toured the farm. The farm helped the school to start a garden and has done assembly presentations about food and farming. But while those experiences are well received, the ideas and inspiration they engender stop at the cafeteria door. As founder and executive director of the Center for Urban Agriculture at Fairview Gardens, I've tried to interest the school in replacing some of the highly processed, distantly grown items that its cafeteria serves. I've offered the alternative of fresh, organic food grown by the school's neighbor down the street, but have never been able to generate interest.

Recently, the school district spent $150,000 on a computer system to manage the inflow of anonymous food from distant sources. But it doesn't require a computer to figure out that young people need whole food— food that tastes better because it's grown in living soil and harvested locally, food that makes clear the relationship between human health and the health of the Earth. It doesn't require a computer to tell us that by feeding young people the best, not just the cheapest, we are in effect feeding and nourishing our own future.

Why shouldn't students be eating the sweet French carrots, the Clementine mandarins, the year-round salad greens, the radishes and beets and avocados that grow so near the school? How difficult would it be to replace nachos with real corn on the cob? How much more time and expense would be required to serve farm-fresh eggs, or ripe strawberries, or bean or vegetable soups and stew produced with real local ingredients? How difficult would it be to spend less on hardware and more on providing professional development so that cafeteria staff can help students make connections between the food they eat and the farms where it's grown?

Imagine if students could plant, harvest, and cultivate the very foods that later appear in their lunch at the cafeteria. Shouldn't all 700 students at Goleta Valley Junior High be required, as part of their education, to develop a relationship with the farm in order to understand the connections between soil life and their own life—between taste and health?

For more than 20 years I have hosted local students on the farm, walking and grazing from the fields with them, allowing them to settle into a different rhythm for an hour or two. I always take a few moments to get to know them, to ask a few simple questions before we begin; How many of you live on farms, how many have ever visited one, what did you eat for breakfast? Over the years I have seen a dramatic shift in young people's responses and in their relationship to food and the land.

It used to be that a handful in every group lived on farms; most had at least visited one. Their breakfast might have included an egg or a piece of fruit or bread, or even some whole grain. Now it is rare to find a kid who lives on a farm, or has even visited one. Many have not had breakfast, and those who have often tell me that it consisted of a granola bar, a corn dog, or even a can of Coke. It is not just kids' answers that tell me that something has changed. When young people come to the farm, I look at each of them, study them the way I do the farm's soil and plants and trees, try to get a feel for how they are doing. These days, many are overweight; they seem to lack focus and have difficulty being still. Our task with our young visitors is different now, our goals very basic. We want to provide them with something real to eat—a fresh carrot or strawberry—and an hour or two outside of the walls of the classroom, a chance to slow down and an opportunity to touch the Earth for just one moment and to be calmed and settled by it. Change, I have to remind myself, comes slowly and incrementally.

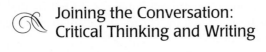

Joining the Conversation: Critical Thinking and Writing

1. Do you think Ableman is a good writer? Cite and comment on passages from the essay to support your view.

2. Describe how this essay is organized.

3. What is Ableman's main point? Is this point new to you or is it familiar?

4. A student said that she liked Ableman's essay but wished that he had omitted the references in it to himself. She thinks that the essay would have been more effective that way. Why would she say that? Do you agree or disagree? Explain.

5. Describe what you typically eat for breakfast, lunch, and dinner. Be as specific as you can. How do you think that Ableman would respond to your food choices? What would be your response to him?

David Gerard Hogan

David Gerard Hogan, a historian of food, is the author of Sell 'Em by the Sack *(1997), an account of the first (pre-McDonald) promoter of fast-food hamburger. He is also the author of* The Creation of American Food *(1999). We print part of an essay that originally appeared in* Encyclopedia of Food and Culture *(2003).*

Fast Food

Criticism of Fast Food

Despite the widespread popularity of fast food in modern American culture, critics abound. Since the 1930s, articles and books have condemned the industry, exposing allegedly poor sanitary conditions, unhealthy food products, related environmental problems, and unfair working conditions. Whether it warrants the attention or not, the fast-food industry is still regularly cited for exploiting young workers, polluting, and contributing to obesity and other serious health problems among American consumers. American beef consumption, and more specifically the fast-food hamburger industry, is often blamed for the burning of the Amazon rain forests to make way for more grazing lands for beef cattle. Early foes of fast food cited the deplorable filth of many hamburger stands, in addition to claiming that the beef ground for their sandwiches was either spoiled, diseased, or simply of low quality. In fact, many critics maintained that much of the meat used in fast-food hamburgers came from horse carcasses. The high fat content of fast food was also controversial. Despite deceptive industry claims about the high quality and the health benefits of their products, in the 1920s and 1930s concerned nutritionists warned the public about the medical dangers of regular burger consumption. This distrust and criticism of fast food continue today, extending even further to include dire warnings about the industry's use of genetically modified and antibiotic-laden beef products. Most major chains have responded to recent attacks by prominently posting calorie and nutritional charts in their restaurants, advertising fresh ingredients, and offering alternatives to their fried foods. Despite a few more health-conscious items on the menu, fast-food chains now aggressively advertise the concept that bigger is better, offering large "super-size" or "biggie" portions of french fries, soft drinks, and milkshakes. Critics point to this marketing emphasis as a reason for an excessive and greatly increasing per-capita caloric intake among fast-food consumers, resulting in fast-growing rates of obesity in the United States.

Increased litter is another problem that critics have blamed on the fast-food industry. Selling their products in paper wrappings and paper bags, early outlets created a source of litter that had not previously existed. Wrappers strewn about city streets, especially those close to fast-food restaurants, brought harsh criticism, and often inspired new local ordinances to address the problem. Some municipalities actually forced chains to clean up litter that was imprinted with their logos, but such sanctions were rare. Fast-food wrappers became part of the urban, and later suburban, landscape. Since bags and wrappers were crucial in the delivery of fast food, the industry as a whole continued to use disposable packaging, superficially assuaging public criticism by providing outside trash receptacles for the discarded paper. Years later, environmentalists again attacked the industry for excessive packaging litter, criticizing both the volume and the content of the refuse. By the early 1970s, the harshest criticisms focused more on the synthetic materials used in packaging, and less on the carelessly discarded paper. Critics derided the industry's use of styrofoam sandwich containers and soda cups, claiming that these products were not sufficiently biodegradable and were clogging landfills. Facing mounting opposition from a growing environmental movement, most of the major chains returned to packaging food in paper wrappings or small cardboard boxes.

Labor activists have criticized fast-food chains' tendency to employ inexpensive teenage workers. Usually offering the lowest possible wages, with no health or retirement benefits, these restaurants often find it difficult hiring adults for stressful, fast-paced jobs. Many critics claim that the industry preys on teenagers, who will work for less pay and are less likely to organize. Though these accusations may have merit, the industry's reliance on teenage labor also has inherent liabilities, such as a high employee turnover rate, which result in substantial re-cruiting and training costs. Companies have countered criticism about their use of teenage workers with the rationale that they offer young people entry-level work experience, teaching them: both skills and responsibility.

Despite the relentless attacks, hundreds of millions of hungry customers eat fast food daily. The media constantly remind American consumers about its supposed evils. Most are conscious of the health risks from fatty, greasy meals; most realize that they are being served by a poorly paid young worker; and if they choose to ponder it, most are aware that the excessive packaging causes millions of tons of trash each year. But they continue to purchase and eat fast food on a regular basis. Fast food remains central to the American diet because it is inexpensive, quick, con-venient, and predictable, and because it tastes good. Even more impor-tant, Americans eat fast food because it is now a cultural norm. As American culture homogenized and became distinctively "American" in the second half of the twentieth century, fast food, and especially the hamburger, emerged as the primary American ethnic food. Just as the Chinese eat rice and Mexicans eat tamales, Americans eat burgers.

And fast food has grown even beyond being just a distinctive ethnic food. Since the 1960s, the concept has extended far beyond the food itself, with the term becoming a common descriptor for other quick-service operations, even a metaphor for many of the negative aspects of main-stream American life. Theorists and pundits sometimes use the term "fast food" to denigrate American habits, institutions, and values, referring to them as elements of a "fast-food society." In fact, "fast-food" has become a frequently used adjective, implying not only ready availability but also superficiality, mass-produced standardization, lack of authenticity, or just poor quality.

In the last two decades of the twentieth century, fast food gained additional economic and cultural significance, becoming a popular American export to nations around the world. Some detractors claim that it is even deliberately used by the United States, as a tool of cultural imperialism. The appearance of a McDonald's or Kentucky Fried Chicken restaurant on the streets of a foreign city signals to many the demise of indigenous culture, replacing another country's traditional practices and values with American materialism. In fact, the rapid spread of American fast food is probably not an organized conspiracy, rather more the result of aggressive corporate marketing strategies. Consumers in other countries are willing and able to buy fast-food products, so chains are quick to accommodate demand. Thought of around the world as "American food," fast food continues its rapid international growth.

 ## Joining the Conversation: Critical Thinking and Writing

1. How would you define fast food?

2. What fast foods, if any, do you consume? What criticisms of fast food does Hogan list? To what extent do you share these criticisms?

3. In his last paragraph, Hogan writes, "Some detractors claim that it [fast food] is even deliberately used by the United States, as a tool of cultural imperialism." What does Hogan mean here? To what extent do you find this claim reasonable?

4. How would you classify Hogan's essay? Is it expository? Or is it, in part, an argument? Explain your answer. It might be helpful to compare Hogan's essay with Donna Maurer's essay below to answer this question.

Donna Maurer

Donna Maurer, author of Vegetarianism: Movement or Moment *(2002), has co-edited several books on food and nutrition. We reprint material that she contributed to* Encyclopedia of Food and Culture, *ed. Solomon H. Katz (2003).*

Vegetarianism

Varieties of Vegetarianism

A wide range of dietary practices falls under the rubric of "vegetarianism." People who practice the strictest version, veganism, do not use

---

any animal products or by-products. They do not eat meat, poultry, or seafood, nor do they wear leather or wool. They avoid foods that contain such animal by-products as whey and gelatin and do not use products that have been tested on animals.

Other vegetarians limit their avoidances to food. For example, ovo-lacto vegetarians consume eggs and dairy products but not meat, poultry, and seafood. Ovo vegetarians do not consume dairy products, and lacto vegetarians consume dairy products but not eggs. Semivegetarians occasionally consume some or all animal products and may or may not consider themselves vegetarians. Studies suggest that semivegetarians outnumber "true" vegetarians by about four to one.

These terms define the various types of vegetarians by what they do not consume. Consequently, many vegetarians are concerned that non-vegetarians view vegetarian diets as primarily prohibitive and restrictive. They emphasize that following a vegetarian diet often leads people to consume a wider variety of foods than many meat eaters do, as vegetarians often include a wider range of fruits, vegetables, grains, and legumes in their diets.

•   •   •

Characteristics of Contemporary Vegetarians

While vegetarians probably exhibit more differences than similarities, researchers have discerned several patterns regarding their social backgrounds and statuses. Vegetarians tend to come from predominantly middle-class backgrounds, and a substantially smaller percentage comes from lower social classes. This can be explained by the fact that people who have less money view meat as desirable and associate it with upward social mobility. Therefore, when they have discretionary income, they are likely to use it to purchase meat products. In North America meat is often associated with success and social status. People are only likely to reject meat once they have the opportunity to consume as much as they want.

Gender is another patterned feature of vegetarians in North America. Studies have consistently found that about 70 percent of all vegetarians are female. Several explanations are possible. First, the foods embraced by vegetarian diets are those already symbolically linked with feminine attributes, that is, foods that are light, low-fat, and not bloody (as people often equate blood with strength). For many people meat and masculinity are inextricably linked; therefore it is easier for women than for men to escape cultural expectations. In addition, women tend to be more concerned with weight loss, and many pursue a vegetarian diet as the means to that end. Finally, some researchers hold that women are more likely than men to hold a compassionate attitude toward animals, leading them to have more concern about killing animals for food. All of these factors contribute to the reality that women are more likely than men to become vegetarians.

Studies have suggested that vegetarians may share a variety of other characteristics as well. For example, while vegetarians are less likely than the general population to follow a conventional religion, they are more likely to describe themselves as spiritual and to practice some form of yoga or meditation. They are more likely to describe themselves as "liberal" and less likely to adhere to traditional values that embrace upholding the existing social order. They are also less likely than the general population to smoke cigarettes and drink alcohol. Yet it is important to point out that vegetarians are more different than similar in their social backgrounds, political beliefs, and health practices.

Reasons for Vegetarianism

People become vegetarians for a variety of reasons, including personal health, a concern for the treatment of farm animals and the environment, spiritual beliefs, and sometimes simply a physical disgust toward meat. Most commonly North Americans follow a gradual path toward vegetarianism that starts with a health motivation. They perceive that a vegetarian diet will give them more energy, will help them lose weight, or will assuage a health condition, such as heart disease or cancer. Other people become vegetarians out of a concern for the rights of animals or a belief that meat production causes devastating effects to the environment. Some grew up with or adopted a religion (for example, Hinduism, Jainism, Seventh Day Adventism) that encourages or requires a vegetarian diet. Still others are concerned with world hunger and take the view that many more people can be fed on a vegetarian diet than on a meat-based one.

People tend to first stop eating the foods they view as the most offensive or unhealthy. For most gradual vegetarians this is red meat. The typical path for a new vegetarian is to stop eating red meat first, then poultry, and then fish. Some move to further prohibitions by adopting a vegan lifestyle as they eliminate eggs, dairy products, and other animal by-products. As people progress along the vegetarian "path," they tend to adopt new reasons to support their lifestyle practices. Most commonly people begin with a health motivation and gradually become concerned with the humane treatment of animals and protecting the environment, and many develop a disgust response to meat products.

Joining the Conversation: Critical Thinking and Writing

1. How would you define vegetarianism? Do all vegetarians observe similar practices? If not, what is the range of vegetarian practices? If you do not know the answers to these questions, what sources might you use to retrieve reliable explanations?

2. According to Maurer, why do people become vegetarians?

3. A writing exercise (two paragraphs): If you are a vegetarian, what do you consume (or refuse to consume), and what were your reasons for becoming vegetarian? If you are not a vegetarian, interview one or two vegetarians and then explain their practices and their reasons.

Jonathan Foer

Jonathan Foer, born in Washington, D.C., in 1977, was educated at Princeton University. Foer, who teaches in the creative writing program at New York University, is primarily a novelist, but he is also the author of a nonfiction work: Eating Animals *(2009). The essay that we reprint is adapted from this book.*

Against Meat (or at Least 99% of It)

The Fruits of Family Trees

When I was young, I would often spend the weekend at my grandmother's house. On my way in, Friday night, she would lift me from the ground in one of her fire-smothering hugs. And on the way out, Sunday afternoon, I was again taken into the air. It wasn't until years later that I realized she was weighing me.

My grandmother survived World War II barefoot, scavenging Eastern Europe for other people's inedibles: rotting potatoes, discarded scraps of meat, skins and the bits that clung to bones and pits. So she never cared if I colored outside the lines, as long as I cut coupons along the dashes. I remember hotel buffets: while the rest of us erected Golden Calves of breakfast, she would make sandwich upon sandwich to swaddle in napkins and stash in her bag for lunch. It was my grandmother who taught me that one tea bag makes as many cups of tea as you're serving, and that every part of the apple is edible.

Her obsession with food wasn't an obsession with money. (Many of those coupons I clipped were for foods she would never buy.)

Her obsession wasn't with health. (She would beg me to drink Coke.)

My grandmother never set a place for herself at family dinners. Even   5
when there was nothing more to be done—no soup bowls to be topped off, no pots to be stirred or ovens checked—she stayed in the kitchen, like a vigilant guard (or prisoner) in a tower. As far as I could tell, the sustenance she got from the food she made didn't require her to eat it.

We thought she was the greatest chef who ever lived. My brothers and I would tell her as much several times a meal. And yet we were worldly enough kids to know that the greatest chef who ever lived would probably have more than one recipe (chicken with carrots), and that most great recipes involved more than two ingredients.

And why didn't we question her when she told us that dark food is inherently more healthful than light food, or that the bulk of the nutrients are found in the peel or crust? (The sandwiches of those weekend stays were made with the saved ends of pumpernickel loaves.) She taught us that animals that are bigger than you are very good for you, animals that are smaller than you are good for you, fish (which aren't animals) are fine for you, then tuna (which aren't fish), then vegetables, fruits, cakes, cookies and sodas. No foods are bad for you. Sugars are great. Fats are tremendous. The fatter a child is, the fitter it is—especially if it's a boy. Lunch is not one meal, but three, to be eaten at 11, 12:30 and 3. You are always starving.

In fact, her chicken with carrots probably *was* the most delicious thing I've ever eaten. But that had little to do with how it was prepared, or even how it tasted. Her food was delicious because we believed it was delicious. We believed in our grandmother's cooking more fervently than we believed in God.

More stories could be told about my grandmother than about anyone else I've ever met—her otherwordly childhood, the hairline margin of her survival, the totality of her loss, her immigration and further loss, the triumph and tragedy of her assimilation—and while I will one day try to tell them to my children, we almost never told them to one another. Nor we did we call her by any of the obvious and earned titles. We called her the Greatest Chef.

The story of her relationship to food holds all of the other stories that could be told about her. Food, for her, is not *food*. It is terror, dignity, gratitude, vengeance, joy, humiliation, religion, history and, of course, love. It was as if the fruits she always offered us were picked from the destroyed branches of our family tree.

Possible Again

When I was 2, the heroes of all my bedtime books were animals. The first thing I can remember learning in school was how to pet a guinea pig without accidentally killing it. One summer my family fostered a cousin's dog. I kicked it. My father told me we don't kick animals. When I was 7, I mourned the death of a goldfish I'd won the previous weekend. I discovered that my father had flushed it down the toilet. I told my father—using other, less familial language—we don't flush animals down the toilet. When I was 9, I had a baby sitter who didn't want to hurt anything. She put it just like that when I asked her why she wasn't having chicken with my older brother and me.

"*Hurt* anything?" I asked.

"You know that chicken is chicken, right?"

Frank shot me a look: Mom and Dad entrusted this stupid woman with their precious babies?

Her intention might or might not have been to convert us, but being a   15
kid herself, she lacked whatever restraint it is that so often prevents a full
telling of this particular story. Without drama or rhetoric, skipping over
or euphemizing, she shared what she knew.

My brother and I looked at each other, out mouths full of hurt chickens, and had simultaneous how-in-the-world-could-I-have-never-thought-
of-that-before-and-why-on-earth-didn't-someone-tell-me? moments. I put
down my fork. Frank finished the meal and is probably eating a chicken as
I type these words.

What our baby sitter said made sense to me, not only because it
seemed so self-evidently true, but also because it was the extension to
food of everything my parents had taught me. We don't hurt family
members. We don't hurt friends or strangers. We don't even hurt uphol-
stered furniture. My not having thought to include farmed animals in
that list didn't make them the exceptions to it. It just made me a child, ignorant of the world's workings. Until I wasn't. At which point I had to
change my life.

Until I didn't. My vegetarianism, so bombastic and unyielding in the
beginning, lasted a few years, sputtered and quietly died. I never thought
of a response to our baby sitter's code but found ways to smudge, diminish and ignore it. Generally speaking, I didn't cause hurt. Generally
speaking, I strove to do the right thing. Generally speaking, my conscience was clear enough. Pass the chicken, I'm starving.

Mark Twain said that quitting smoking is among the easiest things
you can do; he did it all the time. I would add vegetarianism to the list of
easy things. In high school I became vegetarian more times than I can
now remember, most often as an effort to claim a bit of identity in a world
of people whose identities seemed to come effortlessly. I wanted a slogan
to distinguish my mom's Volvo's bumper; a bake-sale cause to fill the self-
conscious half-hour of school break, an occasion to get closer to the
breasts of activist women. (And I continued to think it was wrong to hurt
animals.) Which isn't to say that I refrained from eating meat. Only that I
refrained in public. Many dinners of those years began with my father
asking, "Any dietary restrictions I need to know about tonight?"

When I went to college, I started eating meat more earnestly. Not "be-   2
lieving in it"—whatever that would mean—but willfully pushing the
questions out of my mind. It might well have been the prevalence of vegetarianism on campus that discouraged my own—I find myself less likely
to give money to a street musician whose case is overflowing with bills.

But when, at the end of my sophomore year, I became a philosophy
major and started doing my first seriously pretentious thinking, I became
a vegetarian again. The kind of active forgetting that I was sure meat eating required felt too paradoxical to the intellectual life I was trying to
shape. I didn't know the details of factory farming, but like most everyone, I knew the gist: it is miserable for animals, the environment, farmers,
public health, biodiversity, rural communities, global, poverty and so on.

I thought life could, should and must conform to the mold of reason, period. You can imagine how annoying this made me.

When I graduated, I ate meat—lots of every kind of meat—for about two years. Why? Because it tasted good. And because more important than reason in shaping habits are the stories we tell ourselves and one another. And I told a forgiving story about myself to myself: I was only human.

Then I was set up on a blind date with the women who would become my wife. And only a few weeks later we found ourselves talking about two surprising topics: marriage and vegetarianism.

Her history with meat was remarkably similar to mine: there were things she believed while lying in bed at night, and there were choices made at the breakfast table the next morning. There was a gnawing (if only occasional and short-lived) dread that she was participating in something deeply wrong, and there was the acceptance of complexity and fallibility. Like me, she had intuitions that were very strong, but apparently not strong enough.

People marry for many different reasons, but one that animated our   25
decision to take that step was the prospect of explicitly marking a new beginning. Jewish ritual and symbolism strongly encourage this notion of demarcating a sharp division with what came before—the most well-known example being the smashing of the glass at the end of the wedding ceremony. Things were as they were, but they will be different now. Things will be better. We will be better.

Sounds and feels great, but better how? I could think of endless ways to make myself better (I could learn foreign languages, be more patient, work harder), but I'd already made too many such vows to trust them anymore. I could also think of ways to make "us" better, but the meaningful things we can agree on and change in a relationship are few.

Eating animals, a concern we'd both had and had both forgotten, seemed like a place to start. So much intersects there, and so much could flow from it. In the same week, we became engaged and vegetarian.

Of course our wedding wasn't vegetarian, because we persuaded ourselves that it was only fair to offer animal protein to our guests, some of whom traveled from great distances to share our joy. (Find that logic hard to follow?) And we ate fish on our honeymoon, but we were in Japan, and when in Japan. . . . And back in our new home, we did occasionally eat burgers and chicken soup and smoked salmon and tuna steaks. But only whenever we felt like it.

And that, I thought, was that. And I thought that was just fine. I assumed we'd maintain a diet of conscientious inconsistency. Why should eating be different from any of the other ethical realms of our lives? We were honest people who occasionally told lies, careful friends who sometimes acted clumsily. We were vegetarians who from time to time ate meat.

But then we decided to have a child, and that was a different story   30
that would necessitate a different story.

About half an hour after my son was born, I went into the waiting
room to tell the gathered family the good news.

"You said 'he'! So it's a boy?"

"What's his name?"

"Who does he look like?"

"Tell us everything!"   35

I answered their questions as quickly as I could, then went to the corner and turned on my cellphone.

"Grandma," I said. "We have a baby."

Her only phone is in the kitchen. She picked up halfway into the
first ring. It was just after midnight. Had she been clipping coupons?
Preparing chicken with carrots to freeze for someone else to eat at some
future meal? I'd never once seen or heard her cry, but tears pushed
through her words as she asked, "How much does it weigh?"

A few days after we came home from the hospital, I sent a letter to a
friend, including a photo of my son and some first impressions of father-
hood. He responded, simply, "Everything is possible again." It was the
perfect thing to write, because that was exactly how it felt. The world itself had another chance.

Eating Animals

Seconds after being born, my son was breast-feeding. I watched him   40
with an awe that had no precedent in my life. Without explanation or experience, he knew what to do. Millions of years of evolution had wound
the knowledge into him, as it had encoded beating into his tiny heart and
expansion and contraction into his newly dry lungs.

Almost four years later, he is a big brother and a remarkably sophisticated little conversationalist. Increasingly the food he eats is digested together with stories we tell. Feeding my children is not like feeding myself:
it matters more. It matters because food matters (their physical health
matters, the pleasure they take in eating matters), and because the stories
that are served with food matter.

Some of my happiest childhood memories are of sushi "lunch dates"
with my mom, and eating my dad's turkey burgers with mustard and
grilled onions at backyard celebrations, and of course my grandmother's
chicken with carrots. Those occasions simply wouldn't have been the
same without those foods—and that is important. To give up the taste of
sushi, turkey or chicken is a loss that extends beyond giving up a pleasurable eating experience. Changing what we eat and letting tastes fade from
memory create a kind of cultural loss, a forgetting. But perhaps this kind
of forgetfulness is worth accepting—even worth cultivating (forgetting,
too, can be cultivated). To remember my values, I need to lose certain

tastes and find other handles for the memories that they once helped me carry.

My wife and I have chosen to bring up our children as vegetarians. In another time or place, we might have made a different decision. But the realities of our present moment compelled us to make that choice. According to an analysis of U.S.D.A. data by the advocacy group Farm Forward, factory farms now produce more than 99 percent of the animals eaten in this country. And despite labels that suggest otherwise, genuine alternatives—which do exist, and make many of the ethical questions about meat moot—are very difficult for even an educated eater to find. I don't have the ability to do so with regularity and confidence. ("Free range," "cage free," "natural" and "organic" are nearly meaningless when it comes to animal welfare.)

According to reports by the Food and Agriculture Organization of the U.N. and others, factory farming has made animal agriculture the No. 1 contributor to global warming (it is significantly more destructive than transportation alone), and one of the Top 2 or 3 causes of all of the most serious environmental problems, both global and local: air and water pollution, deforestation, loss of biodiversity. . . . Eating factory-farmed animals—which is to say virtually every piece of meat sold in supermarkets and prepared in restaurants—is almost certainly the single worst thing that humans do to the environment.

Every factory-farmed animal is, as a practice, treated in ways that would be illegal if it were a dog or a cat. Turkeys have been so genetically modified they are incapable of natural reproduction. To acknowledge that these things matter is not sentimental. It is a confrontation with the facts about animals and ourselves. We know these things matter.   45

Meat and seafood are in no way necessary for my family—unlike some in the world; we have easy access to a wide variety of other foods. And we are healthier without it. So our choices aren't constrained.

While the cultural uses of meat can be replaced—my mother and I now eat Italian, my father grills veggie burgers, my grandmother invented her own "vegetarian chopped liver"—there is still the question of pleasure. A vegetarian diet can be rich and fully enjoyable, but I couldn't honestly argue, as many vegetarians try to, that it is as rich as a doet that includes meat. (Those who eat chimpanzee look at the Western diet as sadly deficient of a great pleasure.) I love calamari, I love roasted chicken, I love a good steak. But I don't love them without limit.

This isn't animal experimentation, where you can imagine some proportionate good at the other end of the suffering. This is what we feel like eating. Yet taste, the crudest of our senses, has been exempted from the ethical rules that govern our other senses. Why? Why doesn't horny person have as strong a claim to raping an animal as a hungry one does to confining, killing and eating it? It's easy to dismiss that question but hard to respond to it. Try to imagine any end other than taste for which it would be justifiable to do what we do to farmed animals.

Children confront us with our paradoxes and dishonesty, and we are exposed. You need to find an answer for every why—Why do we do this? Why don't we do that?—and often there isn't a good one. So you say, simply, because. Or you tell a story that you know isn't true. And whether or not your face reddens, you blush. The shame of parenthood—which is a good shame—is that we want our children to be more whole than we are, to have satisfactory answers. My children not only inspired me to reconsider what kind of eating animal I would be, but also shamed me into reconsideration.

And then, one day, they will choose for themselves. I don't know what my reaction will be if they decide to eat meat. (I don't know what my reaction will be if they decide to renounce their Judaism, root for the Red Sox or register Republican.) I'm not as worried about what they will choose as much as my ability to make them conscious of the choices before them. I won't measure my success as a parent by whether my children share my values, but by whether they act according to their own.

In the meantime, my choice on their behalf means they will never eat their great-grandmother's singular dish. They will never receive that unique and most direct expression of her love, will perhaps never think of her as the greatest chef who ever lived. Her primal story, our family's primal story, will have to change.

Or will it? It wasn't until I became a parent that I understood my grandmother's cooking. The greatest chef who ever lived wasn't preparing food, but humans. I'm thinking of those Saturday afternoons at her kitchen table, just the two of us—black bread in the glowing toaster, a humming refrigerator that couldn't be seen through its veil of family photographs. Over pumpernickel ends and Coke, she would tell me about her escape from Europe, the foods she had to eat and those she wouldn't. It was the story of her life—"Listen to me," she would plead—and I knew a vital lesson was being transmitted, even if I didn't know, as a child, what that lesson was. I know, now, what it was.

Listen to Me

"We weren't rich, but we always had enough. Thursday we baked bread, and challah and rolls, and they lasted the whole week. Friday we had pancakes. Shabbat we always had a chicken and soup with noodles. You would go to the butcher and ask for a little more fat. The fattiest piece was the best piece. It wasn't like now. We didn't have refrigerators, but we had milk and cheese. We didn't have every kind of vegetable, but we had enough. The things that you have here and take for granted. . . . But we were happy. We didn't know any better. And we took what we had for granted, too.

"Then it all changed. During the war it was hell on earth, and I had nothing. I left my family, you know. I was always running, day and night, because the Germans were always right behind me. If you stopped, you died. There was never enough food. I became sicker and sicker from not eating, and I'm not just talking about being skin and bones. I had sores all over my body. It became difficult to move. I wasn't too good to eat from a garbage can. I ate the parts others wouldn't eat. If you helped yourself, you could survive. I took whatever I could find. I ate things I wouldn't tell you about.

"Even at the worst times, there were good people, too. Someone taught me to tie the ends of my pants so I could fill the legs with any potatoes I was able to steal. I walked miles and miles like that, because you never knew when you would be lucky again. Someone gave me a little rice, once, and I traveled two days to a market and traded it for some soap, and then traveled to another market and traded the soap for some beans. You had to have luck and intuition.

"The worst it got was near the end. A lot of people died right at the end, and I didn't know if I could make it another day. A farmer, a Russian, God bless him, he saw my condition, and he went into his house and came out with a piece of meat for me."

"He saved your life."

"I didn't eat it."

"You didn't eat it?"

"It was pork. I wouldn't eat pork."

"Why?"

"What do you mean why?"

"What, because it wasn't kosher?"

"Of course."

"But not even to save your life?"

"If nothing matters, there's nothing to save."

Joining the Conversation: Critical Thinking and Writing

1. There is much narrative (storytelling) in this essay, but we think that it is fundamentally an argument. What do you think Foer's chief point is?

2. In paragraph 44, Foer says that "factory farming has made animal agriculture the No. 1 contributor to global warming," but he does not explain the connection. Can you explain it? If so, write a 250-word explanation. If you cannot explain it, find out and then write a 300-word explanation, devoting your opening paragraph to explaining how you found out.

3. Toward the end of his essay, recounting the last of several anecdotes about his grandmother, Foer argues that within the episode, "a vital lesson was being transmitted." His concluding line is his grandmother's "If nothing matters, there's nothing to save." To what, specifically, did his grandmother refer? In your opinion, why does Foer conclude his argument with this quotation?

Paul Goldberger

Paul Goldberger, formerly the architecture critic for The New York Times, *has contributed articles to various magazines and is the author of many books about architecture.*

Quick! Before It Crumbles!

An Architecture Critic Looks at Cookie Architecture

Sugar Wafer (Nabisco)

There is no attempt to imitate the ancient forms of traditional, individually baked cookies here—this is a modern cookie through and through. Its simple rectangular form, clean and pure, just reeks of mass production and modern technological methods. The two wafers, held together by the sugar-cream filling, appear to float, and the Nabisco trademark, stamped repeatedly across the top, confirms that this is a machine-age object. Clearly the Sugar Wafer is the Mies van der Rohe of cookies.

Fig Newton (Nabisco)

This, too, is a sandwich but different in every way from the Sugar Wafer. Here the imagery is more traditional, more sensual even; a rounded form of cookie dough arcs over the fig concoction inside, and the whole is soft and pliable. Like all good pieces of design, it has an appropriate form for its use, since the insides of Fig Newtons can ooze and would not be held in place by a more rigid form. The thing could have had a somewhat different shape, but the rounded top is a comfortable, familiar image, and it's easy to hold. Not a revolutionary object but an intelligent one.

Milano (Pepperidge Farm)

This long, chocolate-filled cookie summons up contradictory associations. Its rounded ends suggest both the traditional image of stodgy ladyfingers and the curves of Art Deco, while the subtle yet forceful "V" embossed onto the surface creates an abstract image of force and movement. The "V" is the kind of ornament that wishes to appear modern without really being modern, which would have meant banning ornament altogether. That romantic symbolism of the modern was an Art Deco characteristic, of course; come to think of it the Milano is rather Art Deco in spirit.

Mallomar (Nabisco)

This marshmallow, chocolate and cracker combination is the ultimate sensual cookie—indeed, its resemblance to the female breast has been cited so often as to sound rather trite. But the cookie's imagery need not be read so literally—the voluptuousness of the form, which with its nipped waist rather resembles the New Orleans Superdome, is enough. Like all good pieces of design, the form of the cookie is primarily derived from functional needs, but with just enough distinction to make it instantly identifiable. The result is a cultural icon—the cookie equivalent, surely, of the Coke bottle.

Lorna Doone (Nabisco)

Like the Las Vegas casino that is overwhelmed by its sign, image is all in the Lorna Doone. It is a plain, simple cookie (of shortbread, in fact), but a cookie like all other cookies—except for its sign. The Lorna Doone logo, a four-pointed star with the cookie's name and a pair of fleur-de-lis-like decorations, covers the entire surface of the cookie in low relief. Cleverly, the designers of this cookie have placed the logo so that the points of the star align with the corners of the square, forcing one to pivot the cookie forty-five degrees, so that its shape appears instead to be a diamond. It is a superb example of the ordinary made extraordinary.

Oatmeal Peanut Sandwich (Sunshine)

If the Sugar Wafer is the Mies van der Rohe of cookies, this is the Robert Venturi—not pretentiously modern but, rather, eager to prove its ordinariness, its lack of real design, and in so zealous a way that it ends up looking far dowdier than a *really* ordinary cookie like your basic gingersnap. The Oatmeal Peanut Sandwich is frumpy, like a plump matron in a flower-print dress, or an old piece of linoleum. But it is frumpy in an intentional way and not by accident—one senses that the designers of this cookie knew the Venturi principle that the average user of architecture (read eater of cookies) is far more comfortable with plain, ordinary forms that do not require him to adjust radically any of his perceptions.

Joining the Conversation:
Critical Thinking and Writing

1. How seriously do you take these descriptions? Do they have any point or are they sheer fooling around?

2. Explain to someone who does not understand them the references to Mies van der Rohe, Art Deco, the New Orleans Superdome, and Robert Venturi. If you had to do some research, explain what sources you used and how you located the sources. What difficulties, if any, did you encounter?

3. Explain Goldberger's final sentence on "Mallomar"; "The result is a cultural icon—the cookie equivalent, surely, of the Coke bottle."

4. Write a similar description of some cookie not discussed by Goldberger. Or write a description, along these lines, of a McDonald's hamburger, a BLT, and a hero sandwich. Other possibilities: a pizza, a bagel, and a taco.

Peter Singer and Jim Mason

Peter Singer, a professor of bio-ethics at Princeton University, became internationally known in 1973 with an essay on animal liberation. In his writings about animals, Singer argues that if a creature can suffer, it deserves consideration. He has not argued—so far as we know—that human beings ought not to eat animals, but he has argued that, given the horrific treatment of animals in farms and slaughterhouses, a vegetarian diet is a reasonable solution.

Jim Mason grew up on a family farm in Missouri. With Peter Singer, he is the co-author of Animal Factories *(1980) and the author of* Why We Are Destroying the Planet and Each Other *(1997).*

We reprint below an extract from a new book by Singer and Mason, The Way We Eat: Why Our Food Choices Matter *(2006). The authors introduce three families and examine their food choices. One of these families consists of Jake Hilliard (age 36), her husband, and their two small children, who live in Mabelvale, Arkansas. Jake does most of the family shopping at a Wal-Mart Supercenter because, she explains, it is hard to beat their prices and she can get everything at one stop.*

Wal-Mart: Everyday Low Prices—At What Cost?

If Jake's chicken is an iconic American food, the place she buys it is equally characteristic of America today. Wal-Mart is the biggest everything—world's largest grocer, world's largest retailer, world's largest corporation.

Short of being a nation, nothing gets bigger than that. (If Wal-Mart were a nation, it would have a bigger economy than 80 percent of the world's countries.) Each week, 138 million people go to one of Wal-Mart's 5,000 stores in the United States and nine other countries, giving the corporation annual sales of more than $300 billion. With a global workforce of 1.6 million, it is the largest private employer in the United States, as well as in Mexico and Canada. The ethics of what we eat encompasses not only how our food is produced, but also how our food is sold. If so many people do it, can there be anything wrong with shopping at Wal-Mart?

One reason for concern about Wal-Mart is simply its size. Wal-Mart already has 11 percent of all U.S. grocery store sales, and according to Merrill Lynch analyst Daniel Berry, by 2013 that figure is likely to rise to 21 percent.[1] Being the biggest buyer of food gives Wal-Mart a lot of clout over how the food it buys is produced. Do we really want a single corporation to have so great a sway over that? The answer might depend on how the corporation behaves.

No corporation as big as Wal-Mart can avoid criticism, and Wal-Mart gets so much flak that it has set up a "war room" to fight back.[2] So let's focus our discussion on something that Wal-Mart does not deny, and indeed boasts of: the way it seeks to drive down costs in order to provide "everyday low prices." As Wal-Mart CEO Lee Scott said to CNBC's David Faber when discussing Wal-Mart's approach to its suppliers, "The idea is that we say—we sit down with you and say, 'How do we take cost out of doing business with you.'"[3] As a result, according to a UBS-Warburg study, Wal-Mart has grocery prices 17 to 20 percent lower than other supermarkets. Our question is: In constantly striving to reduce costs, has Wal-Mart breached any ethical limits?

Low prices are a good thing. If customers like Jake pay less for their food at Wal-Mart than they would at another store, they have more money to spend on meeting their other needs, or, if they are so inclined, to increase their contributions to good causes. Low food prices are particularly good for the poor, who spend a higher proportion of their income on food than the rich. People living in poor areas often have few places to buy fresh food, and the stores they do have charge higher prices than stores in more affluent neighborhoods. When a Wal-Mart moves in—and Wal-Mart's stores are disproportionately located in the poorer parts of the country—that changes, and the poor can save significant sums.[4]

[1]Jennifer Waters, "Wal-Mart Grocery Share Seen Doubling," *CBS MarketWatch*, June 24, 2004, cited from RetailWire Discussions, www.retailwire.com/Discussions/Sngl_Discussion.cfm/9953.

[2]Michael Barbaro, "A New Weapon for Wal-Mart: A War Room," *New York Times*, November 1, 2005.

[3]John Dicker, *The United States of Wal-Mart*, Tarcher/Penguin, New York, 2005, p. 122.

[4]Pankaj Ghemawat and Ken Mark, "The Price Is Right," *New York Times*, August 3, 2005.

The positive value of a store with low prices can, however, turn negative   5
if the low prices are achieved by passing costs onto others. In 2004, Wal-
Mart's spokesperson Mona Williams told *Forbes* that a full-time store assistant
takes home around $18,000 annually. Some think this estimate is generous,
but assuming that it is accurate, it still means that if the employee is the only
income earner in a family of four, the family is living below the poverty line.
According to documents released as part of a gender-discrimination suit
against Wal-Mart, researchers found that the average non-salaried Wal-Mart
associate in California gets nearly $2,000 in public welfare benefits each year,
including health care, food stamps, and subsidized housing. If all California's
retailers lowered their wages and benefits to Wal-Mart's level, that would
pass an additional burden of $400 million to the state.[5] In 2005 Wal-Mart
acknowledged that nearly half of the children of its employees either have no
health insurance or are on Medicaid. Wal-Mart itself admits that for the
national labor force as a whole, that figure is only one-third. M. Susan
Chambers, a senior Wal-Mart executive who led the investigation that
produced this finding, admits that she was "startled" by the discovery. Wal-
Mart's critics would not have been. Wal-Mart subsequently announced that
it would improve the health care benefits it offers its workers.[6]

Nevertheless, Wal-Mart says "it doesn't make sense to say that we
cost taxpayers money" and then cites the substantial amounts of federal,
state, and local taxes the corporation pays, including sales taxes.[7] But
that's no answer to the charge. If Wal-Mart were replaced by stores that
paid better wages and gave better health benefits, consumers would still
buy food. So the various taxes Wal-Mart now pays would be paid by the
corporations or family-owned businesses that sold the food Wal-Mart
now sells—and their better-paid workers, instead of needing assistance
from taxpayers, would pay taxes themselves.

Wal-Mart's impact on wages and benefits was most clearly shown in
2002 when it announced plans to open 40 Supercenters in California over
the next three years. California was then a stronghold for Safeway,
Albertsons, and Kroger, three of the largest grocery chains in the country. In
contrast to Wal-Mart, which has succeeded in keeping unions out of its U.S.
stores, these three chains have unionized workforces, and their workers
were paid about 50 percent more than workers at Wal-Mart and had much
better health insurance programs. The big three chains believed, with some
justification, that these costs would be a fatal handicap in the coming battle
to defend their market share against Wal-Mart. They therefore demanded
that their workers accept a new contract that contained no wage increases
and would require workers to contribute substantially to their health insurance. In effect, the workers were being asked to take a pay cut. The result

---

[5]John Dicker, *The United States of Wal-Mart*, Tarcher/Penguin, New York, 2005, p. 86.
[6]Michael Barbaro, "Wal-Mart to Expand Health Plan for Workers," *New York Times*, October
24, 2005; Reed Abelson, "Wal-Mart's Health Care Struggle Is Corporate America's Too,"
New York Times, October 29, 2005.
[7]"Wal-Mart Sets the Record Straight" www.walmartfacts.com/newsdesk/article.aspx?id=1091

was the biggest strike in California's history, but against their employers' fear of Wal-Mart, even 70,000 united workers could gain little. After 20 weeks on strike, they agreed to take a contract with reduced benefits. Wal-Mart, or the threat of it, was forcing wages and benefits down.

Wal-Mart applies a similar strategy of cost-reduction to its suppliers. Gib Carey is a partner with Bain & Co., a management consultant firm that has Wal-Mart suppliers among its clients. For many suppliers, Carey says, maintaining their business with Wal-Mart becomes indispensable, but it isn't easy to do so. "Year after year," Carey says, "for any product that is the same as what you sold them last year, Wal-Mart will say, 'Here's the price you gave me last year. Here's what I can get a competitor's product for. Here's what I can get a private-label version for. I want to see a better value that I can bring to my shopper this year. Or else I'm going to use that shelf space differently.' " As business writer Charles Fishman sums it up, "The Wal-Mart squeeze means vendors have to be as relentless and as microscopic as Wal-Mart is at managing their own costs. They need, in fact, to turn themselves into shadow versions of Wal-Mart itself."[8] As a result, suppliers of American-made goods often have to look for cheaper goods made in countries with lower wage costs. If they don't, Wal-Mart will go to a Chinese manufacturer and cut them out entirely. Wal-Mart acknowledges that it bought $18 billion worth of goods from China last year.

Is it wrong to buy goods from China if they can be made more cheaply there than in the U.S.? We don't think so. People in China, Bangladesh, and Indonesia need work too, and since they are, in general, poorer than Americans, they probably need it even more than Americans do. So we are not going to chastise Wal-Mart for buying goods made abroad. The issue is, rather, whether in countries with deep poverty and endemic corruption, the unremitting drive to reduce costs can stop short of sweatshop conditions that include hazards to workers' health, child labor, and debt bondage that verges on forced labor.

In this area, Wal-Mart acknowledges past mistakes. A 1993 *Dateline* exposé showed that clothes sold in Wal-Mart stores under a "Made in the USA" banner were actually made in Bangladesh, and, worse still, were made by child labor. Four years later it emerged that a Wal-Mart line of clothing brand-named Kathie Lee, after ABC morning show cohost Kathie Lee Gifford, was also made by factories that used child labor. Now, however, Wal-Mart insists that it has strict supplier standards that absolutely forbid the employment of anyone younger than 14. Yet Wal-Mart's standards still allow workers to be pushed very hard. Employees may be made to work for 72 hours in a six-day week—that's 12 hours a day, for six days solid—and to work for 14 hours in a single day.[9]

---

[8]Charles Fishman, "The Wal-Mart You Don't Know," *Fast Company*, December 2003, www.fastcompany.com/magazine/77/walmart.html; the quote from Gib Carey is also from this article.
[9]Wal-Mart Stores, Inc., "Standards for Suppliers," www.walmartstores.com/Files/Supplier Standards-June2005.pdf

In the minds of Wal-Mart's critics, however, the problem is more one of enforcement than of the standards Wal-Mart espouses. Some corporations, like Gap, allow independent organizations to inspect the foreign factories of its suppliers. Wal-Mart prefers to use only inspectors it hires. Their impartiality can be questioned.

Wal-Mart is a member of the Food Marketing Institute and as such has been taking part in the discussions that this Institute and the National Council of Chain Restaurants have been holding to set standards for animal welfare. As we saw when looking at McDonald's, the move to set standards was triggered by measures taken first by McDonald's and then matched by other chain restaurants. In many areas of animal production, the FMI/NCCR standards do little more than describe existing factory farm practices, although in a few places they tinker with some of the details, to the modest benefit of the animals. For example, they adopt wholesale most of the National Chicken Council's Animal Welfare Guidelines, which, as we have seen, give chickens a space allowance the size of a standard sheet of typing paper, permit their beaks to be seared off, and allow the breeder birds to be kept half-starved. They also allow catchers to pick up the birds by one leg and dangle five live chickens from each hand.[10] Regrettably, as we have already seen, there is a tension between strong animal welfare policies and "everyday low prices." We'll learn more about that in Part II, when we consider the animal welfare standards being set by Whole Foods Market, a food retailer at the other end of the spectrum from Wal-Mart.

In his book *The United States of Wal-Mart*, John Dicker writes that the success of Wal-Mart says something about us: "The cult of low prices has become so ingrained in the consumer culture that deep discounts are no longer novelties. They are entitlements."[11] Bargain-seeking seems to be such a basic aspect of human nature that to question it can appear quixotic. But at Wal-Mart, the bargains hide costs to taxpayers, the community, animals, and the environment. That is why, despite the undoubted benefits of Wal-Mart's low prices, a very large ethical question-mark hangs over buying our food at Wal-Mart.

Joining the Conversation: Critical Thinking and Writing

1. Do you think Singer and Mason are fair? Support your response by citing a few sentences or passages from their essay.

2. In paragraph 6, the authors say that Wal-Mart does not adequately answer the charge that it costs taxpayers money. Your view? (Reread paragraphs 5 and 6 carefully.)

[10]Food Marketing Institute, "Status FMI-NCCR Animal Welfare Guidelines, Updated May 2005," www.fmi.org/animal_welfare/guideline_status_chart_May_2005.pdf
[11]John Dicker, *The United States of Wal-Mart*, Tarcher/Penguin, New York, 2005, p. 213.

3. Judging from this essay, do you think Wal-Mart's practices are ethical? Ethical but ungenerous? Unethical? Good business? Or what?

4. In paragraph 9, the authors ask, "Is it wrong to buy goods from China if they can be made more cheaply there than in the U.S?" Their answer to the question—based on a reason that perhaps surprised you—is "We don't think so." Your answer? And your reasons? By the way, what do you think of *their* reason why it is not wrong to buy goods that are made cheaply abroad?

5. In their final paragraph, the authors use the word "quixotic." If you don't know the meaning of the word, check a dictionary. Do you think Singer and Mason are quixotic? Explain.

6. Singer is a professor. If he taught at your institution, would you be eager to take a course with him? Explain.

Sheldon Richman

Sheldon Richman, a libertarian, is the editor of The Freeman, *published by the Foundation for Economic Education, and the author of several books, including* Why We Must Abolish the Income Tax.

The *Chutzpah* of Wal-Mart's Critics

When critics attack a big, successful corporation no matter what it does, maybe it's the critics who have the problem. Wal-Mart pleases tens of millions of customers every day and provides desirable jobs to thousands of workers. The company is a blessing particularly to the "working families" whom the politicians and social activists love to champion with words. Yet these same politicians and activists have a bottomless bag of charges against Wal-Mart. In their eyes nothing the corporation does is right.

Consider this: Wal-Mart is the biggest corporate donor in the country. The Foundation Center says the Wal-Mart Foundation is second to none in contributing money to charitable causes, with annual donations totaling $120 million. If for no other reason, you'd think this would win some plaudits from Wal-Mart's critics—and you'd be wrong.

According to the National Committee for Responsive Philanthropy (NCRP), Wal-Mart's efforts hardly qualify as charity at all. "Unfortunately, their philanthropy is more about corporate advertising than it is about helping nonprofits or communities." That's how NCRP deputy director Jeffrey Krehely sees it. Anyone surprised?

Sheldon Richman: "The Chutzpah of Wal-Mart's Critics" by Sheldon Richman, posted on The Future of Freedom Foundation website, August 12, 2005. Reprinted by permission of The Future of Freedom Foundation.

It seems that Wal-Mart's giving is too locally oriented. Store managers pick the beneficiaries. Now this is a funny sort of criticism, since Wal-Mart is routinely accused of destroying communities. Yet Wal-Mart gives lots of small donations of the Little League, Girl Scouts, United Way, literacy programs, teacher recognition, police and fire departments, and the Children's Miracle Network, an alliance of children's hospitals. How cynical! says the NCRP. It's all geared to make the company look good! Why isn't it contributing to international causes?

Whatever happened to "think globally, act locally"? Smell some hypocrisy here?   5

Wal-Mart has also been criticized for giving money to 261 women's clinics, some of which don't approve of abortion, and for giving money to the Sons of Confederate Veterans, which, while condemning racism, supports use of the Confederate Battle Flag.

But this issue is not about whom Wal-Mart gives money to or how much. One can make a case that corporations shouldn't engage in philanthropy at all. A corporation is owned by its shareholders, who buy stock to increase their wealth. Corporate money given away is money that cannot be paid in dividends or used to improve the company, which in turn would raise the stock price. Thus, donated money is diverted from shareholders, employees, and customers, who are perfectly capable of giving to charity if they choose.

On the other hand, charity can create goodwill, which is good for shareholders and employees. At any rate, if shareholders think the company diverts too much money from the business, they can sell their stock and invest elsewhere. Obviously that isn't happening.

The real issue here is the chutzpah of Wal-Mart's critics. The NCRP supports the estate tax, opposes income-tax cuts, and favors government intervention in private economic affairs. Thus, ironically, if the NCRP and its ilk had their way, Wal-Mart would have far less money to contribute. As Ayn Rand wrote in *The Fountainhead*, "Men have been taught that the highest virtue is not to achieve, but to give. Yet one cannot give that which has not been created. Creation comes before distribution—or there will be nothing to distribute. The need of the creator comes before the need of any possible beneficiary. Yet we are taught to admire the second-hander who dispenses gifts he has not produced above the man who made the gifts possible. We praise an act of charity. We shrug at an act of achievement."

The criticism of Wal-Mart amounts to people telling other people who satisfy countless consumers every day what to do with their money.   10

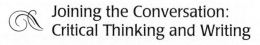

Joining the Conversation: Critical Thinking and Writing

1. Exactly what is *chutzpah*? (Check a dictionary if you are in doubt.) Why is Richman's title better than—or worse than—a title with some synonym that you might substitute for *chutzpah*?

2. Does Richman's first paragraph provide an effective opening? Why or why not?

3. What is your response to paragraph 6? Do you find the actions that Richman specifies objectionable? Why or why not?

4. What is Richman's thesis? Does he offer enough evidence to support it? Be specific.

5. In paragraph 7, Richman quotes Ayn Rand. Do you find the quotation effective? (Note that our question is *not* "Do you agree with Rand?"; rather, it concerns Richman's use of the quotation.)

6. Evaluate paragraph 10 as a concluding paragraph.

7. If you have read Singer and Mason (page 521), do you believe that they exhibit the *chutzpah* that Richman attributes to Wal-Mart's critics? Explain.

Jonathan Swift

Jonathan Swift (1667–1745) was born in Ireland of an English family. He was ordained in the Church of Ireland in 1694, and in 1714, he became dean of St. Patrick's Cathedral, Dublin. He wrote abundantly on political and religious topics, often motivated (in his own words) by "savage indignation." It is ironic that Gulliver's Travels, the masterpiece by this master of irony, is most widely thought of as a book for children.

From the middle of the sixteenth century, the English regulated the Irish economy so it would enrich England. Heavy taxes and other repressive legislation impoverished Ireland, and in 1728, the year before Swift wrote "A Modest Proposal," Ireland was further weakened by a severe famine. Deeply moved by the injustice, the stupidity, and the suffering that he found in Ireland, Swift adopts the disguise or persona of an economist and offers an ironic suggestion on how Irish families may improve their conditions.

A Modest Proposal

For Preventing the Children of Poor People in Ireland from Being a Burden to Their Parents or Country, and for Making Them Beneficial to the Public

It is a melancholy object to those who walk through this great town or travel in the country, when they see the streets, the roads, and cabin doors, crowded with beggars of the female sex, followed by three, four, or six children, all in rags and importuning every passenger for an alms. These mothers, instead of being able to work for their honest livelihood, are forced to employ all their time in strolling to beg sustenance for their helpless infants: who as they grow up either turn thieves for want of work, or leave their dear native country to fight for the pretender in Spain, or sell themselves to the Barbadoes.

I think it is agreed by all parties that this prodigious number of children in the arms, or on the backs, or at the heels of their mothers, and frequently of their fathers, is in the present deplorable state of the kingdom a very great additional grievance; and, therefore, whoever could find out a fair, cheap, and easy method of making these children sound, useful members of the commonwealth, would deserve so well of the public as to have his statue set up for a preserver of the nation.

But my intention is very far from being confined to provide only for the children of professed beggars; it is of a much greater extent, and shall take in the whole number of infants at a certain age who are born of parents in effect as little able to support them as those who demand our charity in the streets.

As to my own part, having turned my thoughts for many years upon this important subject, and maturely weighed the several schemes of our projectors, I have always found them grossly mistaken in their computation. It is true, a child just dropped from its dam may be supported by her milk for a solar year, with little other nourishment; at most not above the value of 2s.,[1] which the mother may certainly get, or the value in scraps, by her lawful occupation of begging; and it is exactly at one year old that I propose to provide for them in such a manner as instead of being a charge upon their parents or the parish, or wanting food and raiment for the rest of their lives, they shall on the contrary contribute to the feeding, and partly to the clothing, of many thousands.

There is likewise another great advantage in my scheme, that it will prevent those voluntary abortions, and that horrid practice of women murdering their bastard children, alas! too frequent among us! sacrificing the poor innocent babes I doubt more to avoid the expense than the shame, which would move tears and pity in the most savage and inhuman breast.

The number of souls in this kingdom being usually reckoned one million and a half, of these I calculate there may be about 200,000 couple whose wives are breeders; from which number I subtract 30,000 couple who are able to maintain their own children (although I apprehend there cannot be so many, under the present distress of the kingdom); but this being granted, there will remain 170,000 breeders. I again subtract 50,000 for those women who miscarry, or whose children die by accident or disease within the year. There only remain 120,000 children of poor parents annually born. The question therefore is, how this number shall be reared and provided for? which, as I have already said, under the present situation of affairs, is utterly impossible by all the methods hitherto proposed. For we can neither employ them in handicraft or agriculture; we neither build houses (I mean in the country) nor cultivate land; they can very seldom pick up a livelihood by stealing, till they arrive at six years

5

---

[1]**2s** Two shillings. Later in the essay, "£" and "1" stand for pounds and "d" for pence. (Editors' note)

old, except where they are of towardly parts; although I confess they learn the rudiments much earlier; during which time they can, however, be properly looked upon only as probationers; as I have been informed by a principal gentleman in the country of Cavan, who protested to me that he never knew above one or two instances under the age of six, even in a part of the kingdom so renowned for the quickest proficiency in that art.

I am assured by our merchants, that a boy or a girl before twelve years old is no saleable commodity; and even when they come to this age they will not yield above 3l. or 3l. 2s. 6d. at most on the exchange; which cannot turn to account either to the parents or kingdom, the charge of nutriment and rags having been at least four times that value.

I shall now therefore humbly propose my own thoughts, which I hope will not be liable to the least objection.

I have been assured by a very knowing American of my acquaintance in London, that a young healthy child well nursed is at a year old a most delicious, nourishing, and wholesome food, whether stewed, roasted, baked, or broiled; and I make no doubt that it will equally serve in a fricassee or a ragout.

I do therefore humbly offer it to public consideration that of the 120,000 children already computed, 20,000 may be reserved for breed, whereof only one-fourth part to be males; which is more than we allow to sheep, black cattle, or swine; and my reason is, that these children are seldom the fruits of marriage, a circumstance not much regarded by our savages; therefore one male will be sufficient to serve four females. That the remaining 100,000 may, at a year old, be offered in sale to the persons of quality and fortune through the kingdom; always advising the mother to let them suck plentifully in the last month, so as to render them plump and fat for a good table. A child will make two dishes at an entertainment for friends; and when the family dines alone, the fore or hind quarter will make a reasonable dish, and seasoned with a little pepper or salt will be very good boiled on the fourth day, especially in winter.

I have reckoned upon a medium that a child just born will weigh 12 pounds, and in a solar year, if tolerably nursed, will increase to 28 pounds.

I grant this food will be somewhat dear, and therefore very proper for landlords, who, as they have already devoured most of the parents, seem to have the best title to the children.

Infant's flesh will be in season throughout the year, but more plentiful in March, and a little before and after: for we are told by a grave author, an eminent French physician, that fish being a prolific diet, there are more children born in Roman Catholic countries about nine months after Lent than at any other season; therefore, reckoning a year after Lent, the markets will be more glutted than usual, because the number of popish infants is at least three to one in this kingdom: and therefore it will have one other collateral advantage, by lessening the number of papists among us.

I have already computed the charge of nursing a beggar's child (in which list I reckon all cottagers, laborers, and four-fifths of the farmers) to be about 2s. per annum, rags included; and I believe no gentleman would repine to give 10s. for the carcass of a good fat child, which, as I have said, will make four dishes of excellent nutritive meat, when he has only some particular friend or his own family to dine with him. Thus the squire will learn to be a good landlord, and grow popular among the tenants; the mother will have 8s. net profit, and be fit for work till she produces another child.

Those who are more thrifty (as I must confess the times require) may flay the carcass; the skin of which artificially dressed will make admirable gloves for ladies, and summer boots for fine gentlemen. 15

As to our city of Dublin, shambles may be appointed for this purpose in the most convenient parts of it, and butchers we may be assured will not be wanting: although I rather recommend buying the children alive, and dressing them hot from the knife as we do roasting pigs.

A very worthy person, a true lover of his country, and whose virtues I highly esteem, was lately pleased in discoursing on this matter to offer a refinement upon my scheme. He said that many gentlemen of this kingdom, having of late destroyed their deer, he conceived that the want of venison might be well supplied by the bodies of young lads and maidens, not exceeding fourteen years of age nor under twelve; so great a number of both sexes in every country being now ready to starve for want of work and service; and these to be disposed of by their parents, if alive, or otherwise by their nearest relations. But with due deference to so excellent a friend and so deserving a patriot, I cannot be altogether in his sentiments; for as to the males, my American acquaintance assured me from frequent experience that their flesh was generally tough and lean, like that of our schoolboys by continual exercise, and their taste disagreeable; and to fatten them would not answer the charge. Then as to the females, it would, I think, with humble submission be a loss to the public, because they soon would become breeders themselves: and besides, it is not improbable that some scrupulous people might be apt to censure such a practice (although indeed very unjustly), as a little bordering upon cruelty; which, I confess, has always been with me the strongest objection against any project, how well soever intended.

But in order to justify my friend, he confessed that this expedient was put into his head by the famous Psalmanazar, a native of the island Formosa, who came from thence to London about twenty years ago: and in conversation told my friend, that in his country when any young person happened to be put to death, the executioner sold the carcass to persons of quality as a prime dainty; and that in his time the body of a plump girl of fifteen, who was crucified for an attempt to poison the emperor, was sold to his imperial majesty's prime minister of state, and other great mandarins of the court, in joints from the gibbet, at 400 crowns. Neither indeed can I deny, that if the same use were made of several plump young girls in this town, who without one single groat to their fortunes cannot stir abroad without a chair, and appear at the playhouse and assemblies in foreign fineries which they never will pay for, the kingdom would not be the worse.

Some persons of a desponding spirit are in great concern about that vast number of poor people, who are aged, diseased, or maimed, and I have been desired to employ my thoughts what course may be taken to ease the nation of so grievous an encumbrance. But I am not in the least pain upon that matter, because it is very well known that they are every day dying and rotting by cold and famine, and filth and vermin, as fast as can be reasonably expected. And as to the young laborers, they are now in as hopeful a condition: they cannot get work, and consequently pine away for want of nourishment, to a degree that if at any time they are accidentally hired to common labor, they have not strength to perform it; and thus the country and themselves are happily delivered from the evils to come.

I have too long digressed, and therefore shall return to my subject. I think the advantages by the proposal which I have made are obvious and many, as well as of the highest importance.

For first, as I have already observed, it would greatly lessen the number of papists, with whom we are yearly overrun, being the principal breeders of the nation as well as our most dangerous enemies; and who stay at home on purpose to deliver the kingdom to the Pretender, hoping to take their advantage by the absence of so many good Protestants, who have chosen rather to leave their country than stay at home and pay tithes against their conscience to an Episcopal curate.

Secondly, The poor tenants will have something valuable of their own, which by law may be made liable to distress and help to pay their landlord's rent, their corn and cattle being already seized, and money a thing unknown.

Thirdly, Whereas the maintenance of 100,000 children from two years old and upward, cannot be computed at less than 10s, a-piece per annum, the nation's stock will be thereby increased £50,000 per annum, beside the profit of a new dish introduced to the tables of all gentlemen of fortune in the kingdom who have any refinement in taste. And the money will circulate among ourselves, the goods being entirely of our own growth and manufacture.

Fourthly, The constant breeders beside the gain of 8s. sterling per annum by the sale of their children, will be rid of the charge of maintaining them after the first year.

Fifthly, This food would likewise bring great custom to taverns, where the vintners will certainly be so prudent as to procure the best receipts for dressing it to perfection, and consequently have their houses frequented by all the fine gentlemen, who justly value themselves upon their knowledge in good eating; and a skilful cook who understands how to oblige his guests, will contrive to make it as expensive as they please.

Sixthly, This would be a great inducement to marriage, which all wise nations have either encouraged by rewards or enforced by laws and penalties. It would increase the care and tenderness of mothers toward their children, when they were sure of a settlement for life to the poor babes, provided in some sort by the public, to their annual profit instead of expense. We should see an honest emulation among the married women, which of them would bring the fattest child to the market. Men would become as fond of their wives during the time of their pregnancy as they are now of their mares in foal, their cows in calf, their sows when they are ready to farrow; nor offer to beat or kick them (as is too frequent a practice) for fear of a miscarriage.

Many other advantages might be enumerated. For instance, the addition of some thousand carcasses in our exportation of barreled beef, the propagation of swine's flesh, and improvement in the art of making good bacon, so much wanted among us by the great destruction of pigs, too frequent at our table; which are no way comparable in taste or magnificence to a well-grown, fat, yearling child, which roasted whole will make a considerable figure at a lord mayor's feast or any other public entertainment. But this and many others I omit, being studious of brevity.

Supposing that 1,000 families in this city would be constant customers for infants' flesh, besides others who might have it at merry-meetings, particularly at weddings and christenings, I compute that Dublin would take off annually about 20,000 carcasses; and the rest of the kingdom (where probably they will be sold somewhat cheaper) the remaining 80,000.

I can think of no one objection that will possibly be raised against this proposal, unless it should be urged that the number of people will be thereby much lessened in the kingdom. This I freely own, and it was indeed one principal design in offering it to the world. I desire the reader will observe, that I calculate my remedy for this one individual kingdom of Ireland and for no other that ever was, is, or I think ever can be upon earth. Therefore let no man talk to me of other expedients: of taxing our absentees at 5s. a pound: of using neither clothes nor household furniture except what is of our own growth and manufacture: of utterly rejecting the materials and instruments that promote foreign luxury: of curing the expensiveness of pride, vanity, idleness, and gaming in our women: of introducing a vein of parsimony, prudence, and temperance: of learning to love our country, in the want of which we differ even from Laplanders and the inhabitants of Topinamboo: of quitting our animosities and factions, nor acting any longer like the Jews, who were murdering one another at the very moment their city was taken: of being a little cautious not to sell our country and conscience for nothing: of teaching landlords to have at least one degree of mercy toward their tenants: lastly, of putting a spirit of honesty, industry, and skill into our shopkeepers; who, if a resolution could now be taken to buy only our native goods, would immediately unite to cheat and exact upon us in the price, the measure, and the goodness, nor could ever yet be brought to make one fair proposal of just dealing, though often and earnestly invited to it.

Therefore, I repeat, let no man talk to me of these and the like expedients, till he has at least some glimpse of hope that there will be ever some hearty and sincere attempt to put them in practice. 30

But as to myself, having been wearied out for many years with offering vain, idle, visionary thoughts, and at length utterly despairing of success, I fortunately fell upon this proposal; which, as it is wholly new, so it has something solid and real, of no expense and little trouble, full in our own power, and whereby we can incur no danger in disobliging England. For this kind of commodity will not bear exportation, the flesh being of too tender a consistence to admit a long continuance in salt, although perhaps I could name a country which would be glad to eat up our whole nation without it.

After all, I am not so violently bent upon my own opinion as to reject any offer proposed by wise men, which shall be found equally innocent, cheap, easy, and effectual. But before something of that kind shall be advanced in contradiction to my scheme, and offering a better, I desire the author or authors will be pleased maturely to consider two points. First, as things now stand, how they will be able to find food and raiment for 100,000 useless mouths and backs. And secondly, there being a round million of creatures in human figure throughout this kingdom, whose subsistence put into a common stock would leave them in debt 200,000,000 pounds sterling, adding those who are beggars by profession to the bulk of farmers, cottagers, and laborers, with the wives and children who are beggars in effect; I desire those politicians who dislike my overture, and may perhaps be so bold as to attempt an answer, that they will first ask the parents of these mortals, whether they would not at this day think it a great happiness to have been sold for food at a year old in the manner I prescribe, and thereby have avoided such a perpetual scene of misfortunes as they have since gone through by the oppression of landlords, the impossibility of paying rent without money or trade, the want of common sustenance, with neither house nor clothes to cover them from the inclemencies of the weather, and the most inevitable prospect of entailing the like or greater miseries upon their breed for ever.

I profess, in the sincerity of my heart, that I have not the least personal interest in endeavoring to promote this necessary work, having no other motive than the public good of my country, by advancing our trade, providing for infants, relieving the poor, and giving some pleasure to the rich. I have no children by which I can propose to get a single penny; the youngest being nine years old, and my wife past child-bearing.

Joining the Conversation:
Critical Thinking and Writing

1. Characterize the pamphleteer (not Swift but his persona) who offers his "modest proposal." What sort of man does he think he is? What sort of man do we regard him as? Support your assertions with evidence.

2. In the first paragraph, the speaker says that the sight of mothers begging Is "melancholy." In this paragraph, what assumption does the speaker make about women that in part gives rise to this melancholy? Now that you are familiar with the entire essay, explain Swift's strategy in his first paragraph.

3. Explain the function of the "other expedients" (listed in paragraph 29).

4. How might you argue that although this satire is primarily ferocious, it also contains some playful touches? What specific passages might support your argument?

James Wright

James Wright (1927–1980) was born in Martins Ferry, Ohio, which provided him with the locale for many of his poems. He is often thought of as a poet of the Midwest, but (as in the example that we give) his poems move beyond the scenery. Wright was educated at Kenyon College in Ohio and at the University of Washington. He wrote several books of poetry and published many translations of European and Latin American poetry.

Lying in a Hammock
at William Duffy's Farm
in Pine Island, Minnesota

Over my head, I see the bronze butterfly,
Asleep on the black trunk,
Blowing like a leaf in green shadow.
Down the ravine behind the empty house,
The cowbells follow one another
Into the distances of the afternoon.
To my right,

5

In a field of sunlight between two pines,
The droppings of last year's horses
Blaze up into golden stones.   10
I lean back, as the evening darkens and comes on.
A chicken hawk floats over, looking for home.
I have wasted my life.

Joining the Conversation:
Critical Thinking and Writing

1. How important is it that the poet is "lying in a hammock"? That he is at some place other than his own home?

2. Do you take the last line as a severe self-criticism, or as a joking remark, or as something in between, or what?

3. Write an imitation of Wright's poem, placing yourself somewhere specific— your eye taking in the surroundings. End with a judgment or concluding comment, as Wright does. Try to imitate the sentence structure as well as the form of Wright's poem. Here is an imitation written by a student at Wellesley College:

> Near my side, I feel his strong body,
> Asleep on the blue sheet,
> Smiling like a babe in soft blankets,
> Behind the house, past the blooming garden,
> The children chase one another
> Through the haziness of the morning.
> In the yard,
> In a pool of shadow behind high hedges,
> The hummings of late summer's honeybees
> Sound among the yellow flowers.
> I stand up, as the morning brightens and comes on.
> A wild goose cries somewhere, looking for the path.
> I have enjoyed my life.

CHAPTER 14

Our Environment: Present and Future

A Victim of the Gulf Oil disaster 2010
Charlie Riedel

Short Views

First, there is the power of the Wind, constantly exerted over the globe. . . . Here is an almost incalculable power at our disposal, yet how trifling the use we make of it! It only serves to turn a few mills, blow a few vessels across the ocean, and a few trivial ends besides. What a poor compliment do we pay to our indefatigable and energetic servant!"
   — *Henry David Thoreau*

"To waste, to destroy, our natural resources, to skin and exhaust the land instead of using it so as to increase its usefulness, will result in undermining in the days of our children the very prosperity which we ought by right to hand down to them."
   — *Theodore Roosevelt*

The world's forests need to be seen for what they are . . . giant global utilities, providing essential services to humanity on a vast scale. Rainforests store carbon, which is lost to the atmosphere when they burn, increasing global warming. The life they support cleans the atmosphere of pollutants and feeds it with moisture. They help regulate our climate and sustain the lives of some of the poorest people on this Earth.
   —*Prince Charles*

We have many advantages in the fight against global warming, but time is not one of them. Instead of idly debating the precise extent of global warming, or the precise timeline of global warming, we need to deal with the central facts of rising temperatures, rising waters, and all the endless troubles that global warming will bring. We stand warned by serious and credible scientists across the world that time is short and the dangers are great. The most relevant question now is whether our own government is equal to the challenge.
   —*John McCain*

With the collapse of Marxism, environmentalism has become the new refuge of socialist thinking. The environment is a great way to advance a political agenda that favors central planning and an intrusive government. What better way to control someone's property than to subordinate one's private property rights to environmental concern?

—*Rush Limbaugh*

There is hope if people will begin to awaken that spiritual part of themselves, that heartfelt knowledge that we are caretakers of this planet.

—*Brooke Medicine Eagle*

We do not inherit the earth from our ancestors, we borrow it from our children.

—*Native American Proverb*

Edward Abbey

Edward Abbey (1927–1989), born in Indiana, Pennsylvania, and educated there and at the University of New Mexico, where he earned a master's degree, wrote a thesis entitled "Anarchism and the Morality of Violence." A vigorous advocate on behalf of environmental issues, he wrote a novel, The Monkey Wrench Gang *(1975), in which some eco-terrorists destroy property belonging to road-builders and other companies that endanger the desert by seeking to "develop" it. The book is said to have inspired radical environmentalists, persons who engage in unlawful activities—including terrorism—in the defense of the environment. (Abbey's response: "The most common form of terrorism in the U.S.A. is that carried on by bulldozers and chain saws.")*

Even before Abbey wrote The Monkey Wrench Gang, *his reputation had been established with* Desert Solitaire *(1968), a nonfictional account of his experiences as a park ranger at Arches National Monument (now a national park) in Utah. In accordance with his dying wish ("I want my body to help fertilize the growth of a cactus or cliff rose or sagebrush or tree"), he is buried in the Cabeza Prieta Desert in Arizona.*

Eco-Defense

If a stranger batters your door down with an axe, threatens your family and yourself with deadly weapons, and proceeds to loot your home of whatever he wants, he is committing what is universally recognized—by law and in common morality—as a crime. In such a situation the householder has both the right and the obligation to defend himself, his family, and his property by whatever means are necessary. This right and this obligation is universally recognized, justified, and praised by all civilized human communities. Self-defense against attack is one of the basic laws not only of human society but of life itself, not only of human life but of all life.

The American wilderness, what little remains, is now undergoing exactly such an assault. With bulldozer, earth mover, chainsaw, and dynamite the international timber, mining, and beef industries are invading our public lands—property of all Americans—bashing their way into our forests, mountains, and rangelands and looting them for everything they can get away with. This for the sake of short-term profits in the corporate sector and multimillion-dollar annual salaries for the three-piece-suited gangsters (MBA—Harvard, Yale, University of Tokyo, et alia) who control and manage these bandit enterprises. Cheered on, naturally, by *Time, Newsweek,* and *The Wall Street Journal,* actively encouraged, inevitably, by those jellyfish government agencies that are supposed to *protect* the public lands, and as always aided and abetted in every way possible by the compliant politicians of our Western states, such as Babbitt, DeConcini, Goldwater, McCain, Hatch, Garn, Simms, Hansen, Andrus, Wallop, Domenici and Co. Inc.—who would sell the graves of their mothers if there's a quick buck in the deal, over or under the table, what do they care.

Representative government in the United States has broken down. Our legislators do not represent the public, the voters, or even those who voted for them but rather the commercial-industrial interests that finance their political campaigns and control the organs of communication—the TV, the newspapers, the billboards, the radio. Politics is a game for the rich only. Representative government in the USA represents money, not people, and therefore has forfeited our allegiance and moral support. We owe it nothing but the taxation it extorts from us under threats of seizure of property, imprisonment, or in some cases already, when resisted, a violent death by gunfire.

Such is the nature and structure of the industrial megamachine (in Lewis Mumford's term) which is now attacking the American wilderness. That wilderness is our ancestral home, the primordial homeland of all living creatures including the human, and the present final dwelling place of such noble beings as the grizzly bear, the mountain lion, the eagle and the condor, the moose and the elk and the pronghorn antelope, the redwood tree, the yellow pine, the bristlecone pine, and yes, why not say it?—the streams, waterfalls, rivers, the very bedrock itself of our hills, canyons, deserts, mountains. For many of us, perhaps for most of us, the wilderness is more our home than the little stucco boxes, wallboard apartments, plywood trailerhouses, and cinderblock condominiums in which the majority are now confined by the poverty of an overcrowded industrial culture.

And if the wilderness is our true home, and if it is threatened with invasion, pillage, and destruction—as it certainly is—then we have the right to defend that home, as we would our private quarters, by whatever means are necessary. (An Englishman's home is his castle; the American's home is his favorite forest, river, fishing stream, her favorite mountain or desert canyon, his favorite swamp or woods or lake.) We have the right to resist and we have the obligation; not to defend that which we love would be dishonorable. The majority of the American people have demonstrated on every possible occasion that they support the ideal of wilderness preservation; even our politicians are forced by popular opinion to *pretend* to support the idea; as they have learned, a vote against wilderness is a vote against their own reelection. We are justified then in defending our homes—our private home and our public home—not only by common law and common morality but also by common belief. We are the majority; they—the powerful—are in the minority.

How best defend our homes? Well, that is a matter of the strategy, tactics, and technique which eco-defense is all about.

What is eco-defense? Eco-defense means fighting back. Eco-defense means sabotage. Eco-defense is risky but sporting; unauthorized but fun; illegal but ethically imperative. Next time you enter a public forest scheduled for chainsaw massacre by some timber corporation and its flunkies in the US Forest Service, carry a hammer and a few pounds of 60-penny nails in your creel, saddlebag, game bag, backpack, or picnic basket. Spike those trees; you won't hurt them; they'll be grateful for the protection; and you may save the forest. Loggers hate nails. My Aunt Emma

5

back in West Virginia has been enjoying this pleasant exercise for years. She swears by it. It's good for the trees, it's good for the woods, and it's good for the human soul. Spread the word.

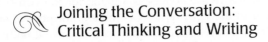 Joining the Conversation: Critical Thinking and Writing

1. Abbey's opening paragraph speaks of a stranger battering down the reader's door, threatening the family, and so on. His second paragraph begins, "The American wilderness, what little remains of it, is now undergoing exactly such an assault." Really? "Exactly such an assault"? Do you find Abbey's analogy appropriate, helpful, convincing—or do you think he weakens his case by overstating it? Explain.

2. Abbey lists 11 "compliant politicians" who, he says, would "sell the graves of their mothers" (paragraph 2) if the price were right. Choose two or three from the list, and investigate their voting records in Congress. What does your investigation tell you about the legitimacy of Abbey's scorn?

3. In a somewhat cute manner, Abbey writes "yes, why not say it?" (paragraph 4), followed by a list of seven items in the physical environment. Why the cute comment? Does it advance his argument or not? Explain.

4. How do these seven items compare with the 10 "noble beings" (also paragraph 4) that precede the list of seven? What others might belong on either of these lists?

5. Evaluate the final paragraph as a piece of writing (Is it effective?) and as a piece of advice (Is it good advice?). Support your responses with reasons.

Daniel Goleman and Gregory Norris

Daniel Goleman, a science journalist who often writes for The New York Times, *is the author of several books, including* How Knowing the Hidden Impacts of What We Buy Can Change Everything. *Gregory Norris, a lecturer at the Harvard School of Public Health, is developing Earthstar, an open-source software system that conducts life cycle assessments. This essay appeared in* The New York Times *on April 19, 2009.*

How Green Was My Bottle

Earth Day is this Wednesday, and all things "green" will be celebrated. But it's worth asking: how environmentally friendly are "green" products, really? Consider, for example, this paragon of eco-virtue: the stainless steel water bottle that lets us hydrate without discarding endless plastic bottles. Using a method called life cycle assessment, we have evaluated the environmental and health impact of a stainless steel thermos—from the extraction and processing of its ingredients, to its manufacture, distribution, use and final disposal. There were some surprises. What we think of as "green" turns out to be less so (and, yes, sometimes more so) than we assume.

Extraction Processing: Producing stainless steel requires a global supply chain involving more than 1,400 steps, each with its own impact on the environment. For example, the mining of chromium ore, an essential component of stainless steel, can expose workers to a heightened risk of cancer. Next, the ores have to be processed to extract useful metal. This usually involves energy-intensive heating, a process that not only requires enormous amounts of fossil fuel but also releases greenhouse gases, carcinogens, particulates and toxic material into the air, water, and soil.

Manufacture: Making stainless steel—which requires the processing of nickel and chromium ores—results in about 10 times more pollution than regular steel. But if the steel mills use recycled iron, instead of newly mined pig iron, the environmental and health impact can be reduced by 10 percent to 15 percent. In addition, simple innovations like a lighter single-wall design—rather than the double walls typically found in insulated bottles—can reduce the ecological impact by about 35 percent.

Distribution: The bottle's journey from factory to distribution center to you uses up oil and energy and results in particulates, greenhouse gases and other emissions. The good news: shipping the bottle from a factory in Asia in a tightly packed cargo container, plus a few hundred miles by truck, adds only 1 percent to 5 percent to the environmental burden. The bad: the heating, cooling, lighting and ventilation of the store where you buy the bottle could have nearly as much of a negative effect on the environment as producing the bottle itself.

Use: Obviously, one danger of any reusable water bottle is bacteria buildup, so you have to keep it clean. If you wash your stainless steel water bottle in a dishwasher that uses a half-liter of electrically heated water, 50 to 100 washes can result in the same amount of pollution that was caused by making the bottle in the first place. Washing it in cold water still demands electricity to pump the water and chemicals to treat it—but the impact is tiny by comparison.

Disposal: Steel lasts forever; so disposal probably comes the day you lose the top. Try to ensure that the discarded bottle finds its way to a steel recycler—not just to a landfill, where it could sit for centuries. By recycling stainless steel, you return not only steel but also nickel and chromium alloys to the production chain, reducing the need to mine and process more of these essential ingredients. These benefits are well worth the impact of transporting the steel back to the mill for recycling.

So, is stainless steel really better than plastic?

One stainless steel bottle is—obviously much worse than one plastic bottle. Producing that 300-gram stainless steel bottle requires seven times as much fossil fuel, releases 14 times more greenhouse gases, demands the extraction of hundreds of times more metal resources and causes hundreds of times more toxic risk to people and ecosystems than making a 32-gram plastic bottle. If you're planning to take only one drink in your life, buy plastic.

But chances are buying that stainless steel bottle will prevent you from using and then throwing away countless plastic bottles. And think of the harm done to the environment by making more and more plastic—the electricity needed to form polyethylene terephthalate resin into bottles, the fossils fuels burned to produce this electricity the energy used and emissions released from mining the coal and converting crude oil to fuel, and on and on. What it comes down to is this: if your stainless steel bottle takes the place of 50 plastic bottles, the climate is better off, and if it gets used 500 times, it beats plastic in all the environment-impact categories studied in a life cycle assessment.

It's important to keep in mind that the 21st century has inherited from the 20th (and sometimes the 19th) manufacturing processes and industrial chemicals that were developed when no one knew—of cared that much—about environmental damage. But even though climate change demands urgent ecological action, this crisis also offers vast entrepreneurial opportunities; we need to re-invent everything with an eye to protecting the planet.

Then again, some old solutions we shouldn't discount. Before stainless steel thermoses before bottled water, we already had an eco-friendly method of getting water: drinking fountains.

Joining the Conversation: Critical Thinking and Writing

1. In their first paragraph, the authors label a stainless steel water bottle "this paragon of eco-virtue." What do they mean? Are they being serious or ironic? Explain.

2. For the most part, the essay is expository—it explains and evaluates "the environmental and health impact of a stainless steel thermos" (first paragraph). What argument does the exposition support? Summarize it in a sentence or two.

3. The essay was published shortly before Earth Day, April 22, a day that celebrates awareness of our environment. Have you ever participated in the ceremony? Might the essay influence you to participate in the future? Why or why not?

4. If you do not have a stainless steel bottle, are you considering getting one? Why or why not?

5. When you make a purchase, are you much concerned about how "green" it is? If you dare, in an essay of 250 words, indicate why you did or did not buy a certain item.

Al Gore

Albert Arnold Gore Jr. was born in 1948 in Washington, D.C., where his father served as a congressman from Tennessee. Gore himself became a congressman, then a senator, and from 1993–2001, he served as vice president, when William Jefferson Clinton was president. The Democratic nominee for president in the 2000 election, Gore won the popular vote but lost the electoral college vote.

Among the awards that Gore has received is the Nobel Peace Prize, 2007, won jointly with the Intergovernmental Panel on Climate Change.

We Can't Wish Away Climate Change

It would be an enormous relief if the recent attacks on the science of global warming actually indicated that we do not face an unimaginable calamity requiring large-scale, preventive measures to protect human civilization as we know it.

Of course, we would still need to deal with the national security risks of our growing dependence on a global oil market dominated by dwindling reserves in the most unstable region of the world, and the economic risks of sending hundreds of billions of dollars a year overseas in return for that oil. And we would still trail China in the race to develop smart grids, fast trains, solar power, wind, geothermal and other renewable sources of energy—the most important sources of new jobs in the 21st century.

But what a burden would be lifted! We would no longer have to worry that our grandchildren would one day look back on us as a criminal generation that had selfishly and blithely ignored clear warnings that their fate was in our hands. We could instead celebrate the naysayers who had doggedly persisted in proving that every major National Academy of Sciences report on climate change had simply made a huge mistake.

I, for one, genuinely wish that the climate crisis were an illusion. But unfortunately, the reality of the danger we are courting has not been changed by the discovery of at least two mistakes in the thousands of pages of careful scientific work over the last 22 years by the Intergovernmental Panel on Climate Change. In fact, the crisis is still growing because we are continuing to dump 90 million tons of global-warming pollution every 24 hours into the atmosphere—as if it were an open sewer.

It is true that the climate panel published a flawed overestimate of the   5
melting rate of debris-covered glaciers in the Himalayas, and used information about the Netherlands provided to it by the government, which was later found to be partly inaccurate. In addition, e-mail messages stolen from the University of East Anglia in Britain showed that scientists besieged by an onslaught of hostile, make-work demands from climate skeptics may not have adequately followed the requirements of the British freedom of information law.

But the scientific enterprise will never be completely free of mistakes. What is important is that the overwhelming consensus on global warming remains unchanged. It is also worth noting that the panel's scientists—acting in good faith on the best information then available to them—probably underestimated the range of sea-level rise in this century, the speed with which the Arctic ice cap is disappearing and the speed with which some of the large glacial flows in Antarctica and Greenland are melting and racing to the sea.

Because these and other effects of global warming are distributed globally, they are difficult to identify and interpret in any particular location. For example, January was seen as unusually cold in much of the United States. Yet from a global perspective, it was the second-hottest January since surface temperatures were first measured 130 years ago.

Similarly, even though climate deniers have speciously argued for several years that there has been no warming in the last decade, scientists confirmed last month that the last 10 years were the hottest decade since modern records have been kept.

The heavy snowfalls this month have been used as fodder for ridicule by those who argue that global warming is a myth, yet scientists have long pointed out that warmer global temperatures have been increasing the rate of evaporation from the oceans, putting significantly more moisture into the atmosphere—thus causing heavier downfalls of both rain and snow in particular regions, including the Northeastern United States. Just as it's important not to miss the forest for the trees, neither should we miss the climate for the snowstorm.

Here is what scientists have found is happening to our climate: man-   10
made global-warming pollution traps heat from the sun and increases atmospheric temperatures. These pollutants—especially carbon dioxide—have been increasing rapidly with the growth in the burning of coal, oil, natural gas and forests, and temperatures have increased over the same period. Almost all of the ice-covered regions of the Earth are melting—and seas are rising. Hurricanes are predicted to grow stronger and more destructive, though their number is expected to decrease. Droughts are

getting longer and deeper in many mid-continent regions, even as the severity of flooding increases. The seasonal predictability of rainfall and temperatures is being disrupted, posing serious threats to agriculture. The rate of species extinction is accelerating to dangerous levels.

Though there have been impressive efforts by many business leaders, hundreds of millions of individuals and families throughout the world and many national, regional and local governments, our civilization is still failing miserably to slow the rate at which these emissions are increasing— much less reduce them.

And in spite of President Obama's efforts at the Copenhagen climate summit meeting in December, global leaders failed to muster anything more than a decision to "take note" of an intention to act.

Because the world still relies on leadership from the United States, the failure by the Senate to pass legislation intended to cap American emissions before the Copenhagen meeting guaranteed that the outcome would fall far short of even the minimum needed to build momentum toward a meaningful solution.

The political paralysis that is now so painfully evident in Washington has thus far prevented action by the Senate—not only on climate and energy legislation, but also on health care reform, financial regulatory reform and a host of other pressing issues.

This comes with painful costs. China, now the world's largest and fastest-growing source of global-warming pollution, had privately signaled early last year that if the United States passed meaningful legislation, it would join in serious efforts to produce an effective treaty. When the Senate failed to follow the lead of the House of Representatives, forcing the president to go to Copenhagen without a new law in hand, the Chinese balked. With the two largest polluters refusing to act, the world community was paralyzed. 15

Some analysts attribute the failure to an inherent flaw in the design of the chosen solution—arguing that a cap-and-trade approach is too unwieldy and difficult to put in place. Moreover, these critics add, the financial crisis that began in 2008 shook the world's confidence in the use of any market-based solution.

But there are two big problems with this critique: First, there is no readily apparent alternative that would be any easier politically. It is difficult to imagine a globally harmonized carbon tax or a coordinated multilateral regulatory effort. The flexibility of a global market-based policy—supplemented by regulation and revenue-neutral tax policies—is the option that has by far the best chance of success. The fact that it is extremely difficult does not mean that we should simply give up.

Second, we should have no illusions about the difficulty and the time needed to convince the rest of the world to adopt a completely new approach. The lags in the global climate system, including the buildup of heat in the oceans from which it is slowly reintroduced into the atmosphere,

means that we can create conditions that make large and destructive consequences inevitable long before their awful manifestations become apparent:
the displacement of hundreds of millions of climate refugees, civil unrest,
chaos and the collapse of governance in many developing countries, large-
scale crop failures and the spread of deadly diseases.

It's important to point out that the United States is not alone in its inaction. Global political paralysis has thus far stymied work not only on
climate, but on trade and other pressing issues that require coordinated
international action.

The reasons for this are primarily economic. The globalization of the
economy, coupled with the outsourcing of jobs from industrial countries,
has simultaneously heightened fears of further job losses in the industrial
world and encouraged rising expectations in emerging economies. The
result? Heightened opposition, in both the industrial and developing
worlds, to any constraints on the use of carbon-based fuels, which remain
our principal source of energy.

The decisive victory of democratic capitalism over communism in the
1990s led to a period of philosophical dominance for market economics
worldwide and the illusion of a unipolar world. It also led, in the United
States, to a hubristic "bubble" of market fundamentalism that encouraged
opponents of regulatory constraints to mount an aggressive effort to shift
the internal boundary between the democracy sphere and the market
sphere. Over time, markets would most efficiently solve most problems,
they argued. Laws and regulations interfering with the operations of the
market carried a faint odor of the discredited statist adversary we had
just defeated.

This period of market triumphalism coincided with confirmation by
scientists that earlier fears about global warming had been grossly under-
stated. But by then, the political context in which this debate took form
was tilted heavily toward the views of market fundamentalists, who
fought to weaken existing constraints and scoffed at the possibility that
global constraints would be needed to halt the dangerous dumping of
global-warming pollution into the atmosphere.

Over the years, as the science has become clearer and clearer, some industries and companies whose business plans are dependent on unrestrained pollution of the atmospheric commons have become ever more
entrenched. They are ferociously fighting against the mildest regulation—
just as tobacco companies blocked constraints on the marketing of cigarettes for four decades after science confirmed the link of cigarettes to
diseases of the lung and the heart.

Simultaneously, changes in America's political system—including the
replacement of newspapers and magazines by television as the dominant
medium of communication—conferred powerful advantages on wealthy
advocates of unrestrained markets and weakened advocates of legal
and regulatory reforms. Some news media organizations now present
showmen masquerading as political thinkers who package hatred and

divisiveness as entertainment. And as in times past, that has proved to be a potent drug in the veins of the body politic. Their most consistent theme is to label as "socialist" any proposal to reform exploitive behavior in the marketplace.

From the standpoint of governance, what is at stake is our ability to use the rule of law as an instrument of human redemption. After all has been said and so little done, the truth about the climate crisis—inconvenient as ever—must still be faced.   25

The pathway to success is still open, though it tracks the outer boundary of what we are capable of doing. It begins with a choice by the United States to pass a law establishing a cost for global warming pollution. The House of Representatives has already passed legislation, with some Republican support, to take the first halting steps for pricing greenhouse gas emissions.

Later this week, Senators John Kerry, Lindsey Graham and Joe Lieberman are expected to present for consideration similar cap-and-trade legislation. I hope that it will place a true cap on carbon emissions and stimulate the rapid development of low-carbon sources of energy.

We have overcome existential threats before. Winston Churchill is widely quoted as having said, "Sometimes doing your best is not good enough. Sometimes, you must do what is required." Now is that time. Public officials must rise to this challenge by doing what is required; and the public must demand that they do so—or must replace them.

Letters of Response

To the Editor:

Al Gore's attempt to sweep "two mistakes" by the Intergovernmental Panel on Climate Change under the carpet provoked a wry smile; no mention of the nine major factual errors that a British high court judge noted in a case challenging the showing of "An Inconvenient Truth" in schools.

The sad fact is that these mistakes do matter, and they are not isolated. I.P.C.C. collaborators have been voicing their concern that there is too much pressure to simplify and exaggerate their work and to ignore their doubts. Bottom line: We know that the climate changes, but we are not sure why nor what is short term and what is long term.

By pushing and alarmist stance to promote huge expenditures at a time of deep recession, Mr. Gore is undermining the case for much-needed but more mundane work. We do need to improve our use of natural resources, clean our water, restore land and forests, and move sensibly

Letters to the Editor by Simon Noble and Generoso Pope published in The New York Times March 2, 2010. Reprinted by permission of the authors.

to better energy use. Smaller, more local initiatives will get support and will have positive results.

By swinging for the fences, we are missing the singles and doubles.

The more Mr. Gore huffs and puffs and the corrections roll in, the more I hear the catch phrase from "Saturday Night Live": "Never mind."

Simon Noble
Larchmont, N.Y., Feb. 28, 2010

To the Editor:

Al Gore makes a cogent argument. What is distressing to me is the attempt to combine what are two completely separate issues.

The first is whether the earth is warming or cooling, or neither. The second is whether the human race is substantially contributing to this effect.

Mr. Gore's point is well taken taken that climate change in and of itself is here to stay (and, as theorized, has always been a fact of life on this planet). But the "mistakes" alluded to affect the much more important second aspect of the issue—whether we as a species are in charge of our climate, or merely passengers along for the ride. Going forward, we should keep this scientific segregation always in mind.

Generoso Pope
Bedford, N.Y., March 1, 2010

 ## Joining the Conversation: Critical Thinking and Writing

1. Evaluate Gore's first four paragraphs as the beginning of an argumentative essay. In your remarks, consider the sort of persona that he projects.

2. In paragraph 6, Gore speaks about "the overwhelming consensus" concerning global warming. Is there an overwhelming consensus on the degree to which human beings are contributing to climate change? On what do you base your answer?

3. In paragraph 16, Gore speaks about "a cap-and-trade approach." Exactly what is this approach?

4. In paragraph 21, Gore speaks about "market fundamentalism." What does he mean by the term?

5. In paragraph 23, Gore refers to "some industries" that fight against the mildest regulations, but he does not specify any of these industries. Which industries do you think he has in mind? Should he have specified them? Why or why not?

6. In paragraph 24, Gore speaks about "showmen masquerading as political thinkers." Can you name two of the people Gore probably has in mind? Given the fact that Gore is presenting an argument, should he have named them? Why or why not?

7. What argumentative strategies does Gore use in his final paragraph? How successful—as the final paragraph in an argument—do you think this paragraph is?

Nicolette Hahn Niman

Nicolette Hahn Niman, an environmental lawyer and livestock rancher, is the author of Righteous Porkchop: Finding a Life and Good Food Beyond Factory Farming *(2009). Although Niman is a vegetarian, she has argued that meat consumption is not necessarily more dangerous to the environment than is vegetarianism. We reprint an essay that she published in* The New York Times, *October 30, 2009.*

The Carnivore's Dilemma

Is eating a hamburger the global warming equivalent of driving a Hummer? This week an article in *The Times* of London carried a headline that blared: "Give Up Meat to Save the Planet." Former Vice President Al Gore, who has made climate change his signature issue, has even been assailed for omnivorous eating by animal rights activists.

It's true that food production is an important contributor to climate change. And the claim that meat (especially beef) is closely linked to global warming has received some credible backing, including by the United Nations and University of Chicago. Both institutions have issued reports that have been widely summarized as condemning meat-eating.

But that's an overly simplistic conclusion to draw from the research. To a rancher like me, who raises cattle, goats and turkeys the traditional way (on grass), the studies show only that the prevailing methods of producing meat—that is, crowding animals together in factory farms, storing their waste in giant lagoons and cutting down forests to grow crops to feed them—cause substantial greenhouse gases. It could be, in fact, that a conscientious meat eater may have a more environmentally friendly diet than your average vegetarian.

So what is the real story of meat's connection to global warming? Answering the question requires examining the individual greenhouse gases involved: carbon dioxide, methane and nitrous oxides.

Carbon dioxide makes up the majority of agriculture-related greenhouse emissions. In American farming, most carbon dioxide emissions come from fuel burned to operate vehicles and equipment. World

5

agricultural carbon emissions, on the other hand, result primarily from the clearing of woods for crop growing and livestock grazing. During the 1990s, tropical deforestation in Brazil, India, Indonesia, Sudan and other developing countries caused 15 percent to 35 percent of annual global fossil fuel emissions.

Much Brazilian deforestation is connected to soybean cultivation. As much as 70 percent of areas newly cleared for agriculture in Mato Grosso State in Brazil is being used to grow soybeans. Over half of Brazil's soy harvest is controlled by a handful of international agribusiness companies, which ship it all over the world for animal feed and food products, causing emissions in the process.

Meat and dairy eaters need not be part of this. Many smaller, traditional farms and ranches in the United States have scant connection to carbon dioxide emissions because they keep their animals outdoors on pasture and make little use of machinery. Moreover, those farmers generally use less soy than industrial operations do, and those who do often grow their own, so there are no emissions from long-distance transport and zero chance their farms contributed to deforestation in the developing world.

In contrast to traditional farms, industrial livestock and poultry facilities keep animals in buildings with mechanized systems for feeding, lighting, sewage flushing, ventilation, heating and cooling, all of which generate emissions. These factory farms are also soy guzzlers and acquire much of their feed overseas. You can reduce your contribution to carbon dioxide emissions by avoiding industrially produced meat and dairy products.

Unfortunately for vegetarians who rely on it for protein, avoiding soy from deforested croplands may be more difficult: as the Organic Consumers Association notes, Brazilian soy is common (and unlabeled) in tofu and soymilk sold in American supermarkets.

Methane is agriculture's second-largest greenhouse gas. Wetland rice fields alone account for as much 29 percent of the world's human-generated methane. In animal farming, much of the methane comes from lagoons of liquefied manure at industrial facilities, which are as nauseating as they sound.

This isn't a problem at traditional farms. "Before the 1970s, methane emissions from manure were minimal because the majority of livestock farms in the U.S. were small operations where animals deposited manure in pastures and corrals," the Environmental Protection Agency says. The E.P.A. found that with the rapid rise of factory farms, liquefied manure systems became the norm and methane emissions skyrocketed. You can reduce your methane emissions by seeking out meat from animals raised outdoors on traditional farms.

CRITICS of meat-eating often point out that cattle are prime culprits in methane production. Fortunately, the cause of these methane emissions is understood, and their production can be reduced.

Much of the problem arises when livestock eat poor quality forages, throwing their digestive systems out of balance. Livestock nutrition experts have demonstrated that by making minor improvements in animal diets (like providing nutrient-laden salt licks) they can cut enteric methane by half. Other practices, like adding certain proteins to ruminant diets, can reduce methane production per unit of milk or meat by a factor of six, according to research at Australia's University of New England. Enteric methane emissions can also be substantially reduced when cattle are regularly rotated onto fresh pastures, researchers at University of Louisiana have confirmed.

Finally, livestock farming plays a role in nitrous oxide emissions, which make up around 5 percent of this country's total greenhouse gases. More than three-quarters of farming's nitrous oxide emissions result from manmade fertilizers. Thus, you can reduce nitrous oxide emissions by buying meat and dairy products from animals that were not fed fertilized crops—in other words, from animals raised on grass or raised organically.

In contrast to factory farming, well-managed, non-industrialized animal farming minimizes greenhouse gases and can even benefit the environment. For example, properly timed cattle grazing can increase vegetation by as much as 45 percent, North Dakota State University researchers have found. And grazing by large herbivores (including cattle) is essential for well-functioning prairie ecosystems, research at Kansas State University has determined.

Additionally, several recent studies show that pasture and grassland areas used for livestock reduce global warming by acting as carbon sinks. Converting croplands to pasture, which reduces erosion, effectively sequesters significant amounts of carbon. One analysis published in the journal *Global Change Biology* showed a 19 percent increase in soil carbon after land changed from cropland to pasture. What's more, animal grazing reduces the need for the fertilizers and fuel used by farm machinery in crop cultivation, things that aggravate climate change.

Livestock grazing has other noteworthy environmental benefits as well. Compared to cropland, perennial pastures used for grazing can decrease soil erosion by 80 percent and markedly improve water quality, Minnesota's Land Stewardship Project research has found. Even the United Nations report acknowledges, "There is growing evidence that both cattle ranching and pastoralism can have positive impacts on biodiversity."

As the contrast between the environmental impact of traditional farming and industrial farming shows, efforts to minimize greenhouse gases need to be much more sophisticated than just making blanket condemnations of certain foods. Farming methods vary tremendously, leading to widely variable global warming contributions for every food we eat. Recent research in Sweden shows that, depending on how and where a food is produced, its carbon dioxide emissions vary by a factor of 10.

And it should also be noted that farmers bear only a portion of the blame for greenhouse gas emissions in the food system. Only about one-fifth of the food system's energy use is farm-related, according to University of Wisconsin research. And the Soil Association in Britain estimates that only half of food's total greenhouse impact has any connection to farms. The rest comes from processing, transportation, storage, retailing and food preparation. The seemingly innocent potato chip, for instance, turns out to be a dreadfully climate-hostile food. Foods that are minimally processed, in season and locally grown, like those available at farmers' markets and backyard gardens, are generally the most climate-friendly.

Rampant waste at the processing, retail and household stages compounds the problem. About half of the food produced in the United States is thrown away, according to University of Arizona research. Thus, a consumer could measurably reduce personal global warming impact simply by more judicious grocery purchasing and use.   20

None of us, whether we are vegan or omnivore, can entirely avoid foods that play a role in global warming. Singling out meat is misleading and unhelpful, especially since few people are likely to entirely abandon animal-based foods. Mr. Gore, for one, apparently has no intention of going vegan. The 90 percent of Americans who eat meat and dairy are likely to respond the same way.

Still there are numerous reasonable ways to reduce our individual contributions to climate change through our food choices. Because it takes more resources to produce meat and dairy than, say, fresh locally grown carrots, it's sensible to cut back on consumption of animal-based foods. More important, all eaters can lower their global warming contribution by following these simple rules: avoid processed foods and those from industrialized farms; reduce food waste; and buy local and in season.

Joining the Conversation: Critical Thinking and Writing

1. Niman's argument rests in part on the contrasts between family farms and industrial farms. According to Niman, how do they contrast?

2. What is her argument? Summarize it in a sentence or two.

3. What is a carnivore? What is a dilemma? Is "The Carnivore's Dilemma" an apt title for this essay? Explain.

4. In her final paragraph, Niman tells her readers how—by changing their patterns of eating and yet without becoming vegetarians—they can reduce their bad contributions to climate change. Will her essay have any effect on your choice of foods? In an essay of 250–500 words, explain why or why not.

Robert Frost

Robert Frost (1874–1963) was born in California. After his father's death in 1885, Frost's mother brought the family to New England, where she taught in high schools in Massachusetts and New Hampshire. Frost studied for part of one term at Dartmouth College in New Hampshire, then did odd jobs (including teaching), and from 1897 to 1899 was enrolled as a special student at Harvard. He then farmed in New Hampshire, published a few poems in local newspapers, left the farm and taught again, and in 1912 left for England, where he hoped to achieve more popular success as a writer. By 1915, he had won a considerable reputation, and he returned to the United States, settling on a farm in New Hampshire and cultivating the image of the country-wise farmer-poet.

Among his numerous comments about poetry is his observation that a poem "begins in de-light and ends in wisdom. . . . It runs a course of lucky events, and ends in a clarification of life—not necessarily a great clarification, such as sects and cults are founded on, but in a momentary stay against confusion."

Fire and Ice

Some say the world will end in fire,
Some say in ice,
From what I've tasted of desire
I hold with those who favor fire.
But if it had to perish twice,
I think I know enough of hate
To say that for destruction ice
Is also great
And would suffice.

Joining the Conversation:
Critical Thinking and Writing

1. This poem was first published in 1920, long before there was talk about global warming or nuclear bombs. Who, then, are those who "say the world will end in fire" or will end in "ice"?

2. Why does Frost match "fire" with "desire"? And why "hate" with "ice"?

3. Certainly, the destruction of the world (whether because of "desire" or "hate") is a serious matter, but can one also say that the poem is in some ways comic? If you find it is in some ways entertaining, point out the light qualities to a serious-minded friend who finds only glumness in "Fire and Ice."

4. In our biographical headnote, we quote Frost's comment that a poem offers a reader "a momentary stay against confusion." Does this comment make any sense to you as a person who has just read a poem by Frost?

A Writer's Glossary

analogy. An analogy (from the Greek *analogos*, proportionate, resembling) is a kind of comparison. Normally, an analogy compares substantially different kinds of things and reports several points of resemblance. A comparison of one city with another ("New York is like Chicago in several ways") does not involve an analogy because the two things are not substantially different. And a comparison giving only one resemblance is usually not considered an analogy ("Some people, like olives, are an acquired taste"). But if we claim that a state is like a human body and we find in the state equivalents for the brain, heart, and limbs, we are offering an analogy. Similarly, one might construct an analogy between feeding the body with food and supplying the mind with ideas: the diet must be balanced, taken at approximately regular intervals, in proper amounts, and digested. An analogy may be useful in explaining the unfamiliar by comparing it to the familiar ("The heart is like a pump . . . "), but, of course, the things compared are different, and the points of resemblance can go only so far. For this reason, analogies cannot prove anything, although they are sometimes offered as proof.

analysis. Examination of the parts and their relation to the whole.

argument. Discourse in which some statements are offered as reasons for other statements. Argument, then—like emotional appeal and wit—is a form of persuasion, but argument seeks to persuade by appealing to reason. (See Chapter 4.)

audience. The writer's imagined readers. An essay on inflation written for the general public—say, for readers of *Time*—will assume less specialized knowledge than will an essay written for professional economists—say, the readers of *Journal of Economic History*. In general, the imagined audience in a composition course is *not* the instructor (although in fact the instructor may be the only reader of the essay); the imagined audience usually is the class or, to put it a little differently, someone rather like the writer but without the writer's specialized knowledge of the topic.

cliché. Literally, a *cliché* was originally (in French) a stereotype or an electrotype plate for printing; in English, the word has come to mean an oft-repeated expression, such as "a sight for sore eyes," "a heartwarming experience," "the acid test," "a meaningful relationship," "last but not least." Because these expressions implicitly claim to be impressive or forceful, they can be distinguished from such unpretentious common expressions as "good morning," "thank you," and "see you tomorrow." Clichés are not impressive or forceful; they strike the hearer as tired, vague, and unimaginative.

compare/contrast. Strictly speaking, to compare is to examine in order to show similarities. (It comes from the Latin *comparare*, "to pair," "to match.") To contrast is to set into opposition in order to show differences. (It comes from the Latin *contra*, "against," and *stare*, "to stand.") But in ordinary usage, a comparison may include not only similarities but also differences. (For a particular kind of comparison—emphasizing similarities—see *analogy*.) In comparing and contrasting, a writer usually means not simply to list similarities or differences but to reveal something clearly by calling attention either to its resemblances to something we might not think it resembles or to its differences from something we might think it does resemble.

connotation. The associations that cluster around a word. *Mother* has connotations that *female parent* does not have, yet both words have the same denotation or explicit meaning.

convention. An agreed-on usage. Beginning each sentence with a capital letter is a convention.

denotation. The explicit meaning of a word, as given in a dictionary, without its associations. *Daytime serial* and *soap opera* have the same denotation, although *daytime serial* probably has a more favorable connotation (see *connotation*).

description. Discourse that aims chiefly at producing a sensory response (usually a mental image) to, for example, a person, object, scene, taste, smell, and so on. A descriptive essay or a passage in an essay uses concrete words (words that denote observable qualities such as *hair* and *stickiness*), and it uses specific language (words such as *basketball* rather than *game* and *steak, potatoes, and salad* rather than *hearty meal*).

diction. Choice of words. Examples: between *car, auto*, and *automobile*, between *lie* and *falsehood*, between *can't* and *cannot*.

euphemism. An expression, such as *passed away* for *died*, used to avoid realities that the writer finds unpleasant. Thus, oppressive governments "relocate people" (instead of putting them in concentration camps).

evaluation. Whereas an interpretation seeks to explain the meaning, an evaluation judges worth. After we interpret a difficult piece of writing, we may evaluate it as not worth the effort.

explication. An attempt to reveal the meaning by calling attention to implications, such as the connotations of words and the tone conveyed by the brevity or length of a sentence. Unlike a paraphrase, which is a rewording or rephrasing in order to set forth the gist of the meaning, an explication is a commentary that makes explicit what is implicit. If we paraphrased the beginning of the Gettysburg Address (page 361), we might turn "Four score and seven years ago our fathers brought forth" into "Eighty-seven years ago our ancestors established" or some such statement. In an explication, however, we would mention that *four score* evokes the language of the Bible and that the biblical echo helps to establish the solemnity and holiness of the occasion. In an explication, we would also mention that *fathers* initiates a chain of images of birth, continued in *conceived in liberty, any nation so conceived*, and *a new birth*. (See Highet's explication of the Gettysburg Address, page 362.)

exposition. An expository essay is chiefly concerned with giving information—how to register for classes, the causes of the French Revolution, or the tenets of Zen Buddhism. The writer of exposition must, of course, have a point of view (an attitude or a thesis), but because exposition—unlike persuasion—does not assume that the reader's opinion differs from the writer's, the point of view in exposition is often implicit rather than explicit.

general and **specific** (or **particular**). A general word refers to a class or group; a specific (particular) word refers to a member of the class or group. Example: *vehicle* is general compared with *automobile* or with *motorcycle*. But *general* and *specific* are relative. *Vehicle* is general when compared to *automobile*, but *vehicle* is specific when compared to *machine*, for *machine* refers to a class or group that includes not only vehicles but clocks, typewriters, and dynamos. Similarly, although *automobile* is specific in comparison with *vehicle*, *automobile* is general in comparison with *Volkswagen* or *sports car*.

generalization. A statement relating to every member of a class or category or, more loosely, to most members of a class or category. Example: "Students from Medford High are well-prepared." Compare: (1) "Janet Kuo is well-prepared" (a report of a specific condition); (2) "Students from Medford High are well-prepared" (a low-level generalization because it is limited to one school); (3) "Students today are well-prepared" (a high-level generalization, covering many people in many places).

imagery and **symbolism.** When we read *rose*, we may more or less call to mind a picture of a rose or perhaps we are reminded of the odor or texture of a rose. Whatever in a piece of writing appeals to any of our senses (including sensations of heat and pressure as well as of sight, smell, taste, touch, sound) is an image. In short, images are the sensory content of a work, whether literal (the roses discussed in an essay on rose-growing) or figurative (a comparison in a poem of a girl to a rose). It is usually easy to notice images in literature, particularly in poems, which often include comparisons such as "I wandered lonely as a cloud," "a fiery eye," and "seems he a dove? His feathers are but borrowed." In literature, imagery (again, literal as well as figurative) plays a large part in communicating the meaning of the work. For example, in *Romeo and Juliet* abundant imagery of light and dark re-enforces the conflict between life and death. Juliet is especially associated with light (Romeo says, "What light through yonder window breaks? It is the east and Juliet is the sun"), and at the end of the play, when the lovers have died, we are told that the morning is dark: "The sun for sorrow will not show his head."

If we turn from imaginative literature to the essay, we find, of course, that descriptive essays are rich in images. But other kinds of essays may also make use of imagery—and not only by literal references to real people or things. Such essays may use figures of speech, as Thoreau does when he says that the imagination as well as the body should "both sit down at the same table." After all, the imagination, does not literally sit down at a table—but Thoreau personifies the imagination, seeing it as no less concrete than the body.

The distinction between an image and a symbol is partly a matter of emphasis and partly a matter of a view of reality. If an image is so insisted on that we feel that the writer sees it as highly significant in itself and also as a way of representing something else, we can call it a symbol. A symbol is what it is, and yet it is also much more. We may feel that a passage about the railroad—emphasizing its steel tracks and its steel cars, its speed, and its noise—may be not only about the railroad but also about industrialism and, even further, about an entire way of life—a way of thinking and feeling—that came into being in the nineteenth century.

A symbol, then, is an image so loaded with significance that it is not simply literal, and it does not simply stand as a figure for something else; it is both itself *and* something else that it richly suggests—a kind of manifestation of something too complex or too elusive to be otherwise revealed. Still, having said all this, one must add that the distinction between *image* and *symbol* is not sharp, and usage allows us to even say such things as, "The imagery of light symbolizes love," meaning that the imagery stands for or represents or is in part about love.

interpretation. An explanation of the meaning. If we see someone clench his fist and tighten his mouth, we may interpret these signs as revealing anger. When we say that in the New Testament the passage alluding to the separation of sheep from goats is to be understood as referring to the saved and the damned, we are offering an interpretation.

irony. In *verbal irony*, the meaning of the words intentionally contradicts the literal meaning, as in "that's not a very good idea," where the intended meaning is "that's a terrible idea."

Irony, in distinction from sarcasm, employs at least some degree of wit or wryness. Sarcasm reveals contempt obviously and heavily, usually by asserting the opposite of what is meant: "You're a great guy" (if said sarcastically) means "It's awful of you to do this to me." Notice that the example of irony we began with was at least a trifle more ingenious than this sarcastic remark, for the sarcasm here simply is the opposite of what is meant, whereas our example of verbal irony is not quite the opposite. The opposite of "that's not a very good idea" is "that is a very good idea," but (in our example) the speaker's meaning is clearly something else. Put it this way: Sarcasm is irony at its crudest, and finer irony commonly uses overstatement or especially understatement rather than a simple opposite. (For a brief discussion of the use of irony in satire, see *satire*, page 565.)

If the speaker's words have an unintentional double meaning, the irony may be called *dramatic irony:* a character, about to go to bed, says, "I think I'll have a sound sleep" and dies in her sleep. Similarly, an action can turn dramatically ironic: a character seeks to help a friend and unintentionally harms her. Finally, a situation can be ironic: thirsty sailors are surrounded by water that cannot be drunk.

All these meanings of irony are held together, then, by the sense of a somewhat bitter contrast.

jargon. Technical language used inappropriately or inexactly. *Viable* means *able to survive*. To speak of a *viable building* is to use jargon. "A primary factor in my participation in the dance" is jargon if what is meant is "I dance because. . . ."

metaphor. Words have literal meanings: A lemon is a yellow, egg-shaped citrus fruit; to drown is to suffocate in water or other fluid. But words can also have metaphoric meanings: We can call an unsatisfactory automobile a *lemon,* and we can say that we are *drowning* in paperwork. Metaphoric language is literally absurd; if we heed only the denotation, it is clearly untrue, for an automobile cannot be a kind of citrus fruit, and we cannot drown in paperwork. (Even if the paper literally suffocated someone, the death could not be called a drowning.) Metaphor, then, uses not the denotation of the word but the associations—the connotations. Because we know that the speaker is not crazy, we turn from the literal meaning (which is clearly untrue) to the association.

myth. (1) A traditional story dealing with supernatural beings or with heroes, often accounting for why things are as they are. Myths tell of the creation of the world, the creation of man, the changes of the season, the achievements of heroes. For example, Zulu myth explains that rain is the tears of a god weeping for a beloved slain bird. *Mythology* is a system or group of such stories, so we speak of

Zulu mythology, Greek mythology, or Norse mythology. (2) Mark Schorer, in *William Blake*, defines myth as "a large controlling image that gives philosophic meaning to the facts of ordinary life. . . . All real convictions involve a mythology. . . . Wars may be described as the clash of mythologies." In this sense, then, a myth is not a traditional story we do not believe but any idea, true or false, to which people subscribe. Thus, one can speak of the "myth" of democracy or of communism.

narration. Discourse that recounts a real or a fictional happening. An anecdote is a narrative and so is a history of the decline and fall of the Roman Empire. Narration may, of course, include substantial exposition ("four possible motives must be considered") and description ("the horse was an old gray mare"), but the emphasis is on a sequence of happenings ("and then she says to me, . . . ").

parable. A short narrative from which a moral or a lesson can be drawn. A parable may—but need not—be an allegory wherein, say, each character stands for an abstraction that otherwise would be hard to grasp. Usually, the parable lacks the *detailed* correspondence of an allegory.

paradox. An apparent self-contradiction, such as "He was happiest when miserable."

paraphrase. A rewording of a passage, usually in order to clarify the meaning. A paraphrase is a sort of translating within the same language; it can help to make clear the gist of the passage. But one must recognize the truth of Robert Frost's charge that when one paraphrases a line of good writing, one puts it "in other and worse English." Paraphrase should not be confused with *explication*, page 561.

parody. A parody (from the Greek for *counter song*) seeks to amuse by imitating the style—the diction, the sentence structure—of another work, but the parody normally substitutes a very different subject. Thus, it might use tough-guy Hemingway talk to describe not a bullfighter but a butterfly catcher. Often, a parody of a writer's style is a good-natured criticism of it.

persona. The writer or speaker in a role adopted for a specific audience. When Abraham Lincoln wrote or spoke, he sometimes did so in the persona of commander in chief of the Union army, but at other times, he did so in the persona of the simple man from Springfield, Illinois. The persona is a mask put on for a performance (*persona* is the Latin word for *mask*). If *mask* suggests insincerity, we should remember that whenever we speak or write, we do so in a specific role—as friend, or parent, or teacher, or applicant for a job, or whatever. Although Lincoln was a husband, a father, a politician, a president, and many other things, when he wrote a letter or speech, he might write solely as one of these; in a letter to his son, the persona (or, we might say, personality) is that of father, not that of commander in chief. The distinction between the writer (who necessarily fills many roles) and the persona who writes or speaks a work is especially useful in talking about satire because the satirist often invents a mouthpiece very different from himself. The satirist—say, Jonathan Swift—may be strongly opposed to a view, but his persona (his invented essayist) may favor the view; the reader must perceive that the real writer is ridiculing the invented essayist.

persuasion. Discourse that seeks to change a reader's mind. Persuasion usually assumes that the writer and the reader do not agree or do not fully agree at the outset. Persuasion may use logical argument (appeal to reason), but it may also try to win the reader over by other means—by appeal to the emotions, by wit, by geniality.

rhetoric. Although in much contemporary usage the word's meaning has sadly decayed to "inflated talk or writing," it can still mean "the study of elements such as content, structure, and cadence in writing or in speech." In short, in the best sense, rhetoric is the study of the art of communicating with words.

satire. A work ridiculing identifiable objects in real life, meant to arouse in the reader contempt for its object. Satire is sometimes distinguished from comedy in that comedy aims simply to evoke amusement, whereas satire aims to bring about moral reform by ridicule. According to Alexander Pope, satire "heals with morals what it hurts with wit." Satire sometimes uses invective (direct abuse), but if the invective is to entertain the reader, it must be witty, as in a piling up of ingenious accusations. Invective, however, is probably less common in satire than is irony, a device in which the tone somehow contradicts the words. For example, a speaker may seem to praise ("well, that's certainly an original idea that you have"), but we perceive that she is ridiculing a crackpot idea. Or the satirist may invent a naïve speaker (a persona) who praises, but the praise is really dispraise because a simpleton offers it; the persona is sincere, but the writer is ironic and satiric. Or, adopting another strategy, the writer may use an apparently naïve persona to represent the voice of reason; the persona dispassionately describes actions that we take for granted (a political campaign), and through this simple, accurate, rational description, we see the irrationality of our behavior. (For further comments on *irony*, see page 563.)

style. A distinctive way of expression. If we see a picture of a man sitting on a chair, we may say that it looks like a drawing for a comic book or we may say that it looks like a drawing by Rembrandt, Van Gogh, or Andrew Wyeth. We have come to recognize certain manners of expression—independent of the content— as characteristic of certain minds. The content, it can be said, is the same—a man sitting in a chair—but the creator's way of expressing the content is individual.

Similarly, "Four score and seven years ago" and "Eighty-seven years ago" are the same in content, but the styles differ because "Four score and seven years ago" distinctively reflects a mind familiar with the Bible and an orator speaking solemnly. In fact, many people (we include ourselves) believe that the content is not the same if the expression is not the same. The "content" of "Four score and seven years ago" includes suggestions of the Bible and of God-fearing people not present in "eighty-seven years ago." In this view, a difference in style is a difference in content and therefore a difference in meaning. Surely, it is true that in the work of the most competent writers—those who make every word count—one cannot separate style and content.

Let C. S. Lewis have the next-to-last word: "The way for a person to develop a style is (a) to know exactly what he wants to say, and (b) to be sure he is saying exactly that. The reader, we must remember, does not start by knowing what we mean. If our words are ambiguous, our meaning will escape him. I sometimes think that writing is like driving sheep down a road. If there is any gate open to the left or the right the readers will most certainly go into it." And let the Austrian writer Karl Kraus have the last word: "There are two kinds of writers, those who are and those who aren't. With the first, content and form belong together like soul and body; with the second, they match each other like body and clothes."

thesis. The writer's position; the proposition advanced.

thesis statement. A sentence or two summarizing the writer's position or attitude. An essay may or may not have an explicit thesis statement.

tone. The prevailing spirit of an utterance. The tone may be angry, bitter, joyful, solemn, or expressive of any similar mood or emotion. Tone usually reflects the writer's attitude toward the subject, the audience, and the self. (For further comments on *tone*, see pages 11–13.)

PHOTO ACKNOWLEDGMENTS

Index

READINGS

Vernon Can Read!

Vernon E. Jordan Jr.

In the summer of 1955, at the end of my sophomore year in college, I worked as a chauffeur in my hometown of Atlanta, Georgia. It had not been my first choice of jobs. I was originally supposed to work as a salesman for the Continental Insurance Company, which had made me an offer during a campus interview at my school, DePauw University. When the interviewer said there was an opening for me in the company's Atlanta office, I jumped at the chance. It was the perfect arrangement for me. I would have a job in the place where I most wanted to be — at home in Atlanta. At the end of the term, brimming with the confidence of a young man with two years of college behind me, I packed my bags and headed south thinking everything was in place.

After a few days settling in with my family, I put on my best suit and headed downtown to the Fulton National Bank Building, where Continental had its offices. I went up to the receptionist's desk to present myself.

"My name is Vernon Jordan," I said. "I'm a student at DePauw University, and I'm here to begin my summer internship."

The receptionist seemed in need of a translator to help clarify what I had just said. She was, at that moment, like a machine whose gears had ground to a halt and was struggling to get restarted. When she finally realized she'd heard what she thought she'd heard, she called for the man in charge of summer workers. "You won't believe this," she told him, "but there's a colored boy out here who says he's a summer intern."

The supervisor, a tall fellow who looked to be in his mid-thirties, came out. I introduced myself. [5]

"I'm Vernon Jordan. I was hired to be a summer intern in your office." [6]

His reaction was not unlike the receptionist's. But he quickly composed himself and took me inside his office. An awkward moment passed before he said, "They didn't tell us." [7]

"They didn't tell you what?" I asked, even though I suspected where he was heading. [8]

"They didn't tell us you were colored," he replied. At that time in history, we had not yet become "black." [9]

He went on. "You know, you can't work here. It's just impossible. You just can't." [10]

Of course, segregation was still very much a fact of life in Georgia in   11
the summer of 1955. I was well aware of that, and of the rules that were
still propping up the system. But I had thought — hoped — during those
months after my interview that I had somehow made my way around
them. It was my policy then, and it remains the same today, never to
expect defeat before making an honest effort. Also, by then I'd come to
think of Jim Crow as a lame horse that was about to be put down. The
feeling was in the air. And I wanted to do whatever I could to help speed
the process along. But it wouldn't happen on that day at the Continental
Insurance Company.

Although I was disappointed, I knew there was nothing to be done   12
about the situation at that particular moment. As I got up to go, my
never-to-be-supervisor, not wanting to leave things as they stood, said,
"I'll tell you what I'll do. I'm going to call J. L. Wolfe Realty. We do business with them sometimes, and we can see if they can give you an office."

While Continental was willing to honor its commitment to hire me,   13
under no circumstances could I sit in its offices as an employee. J. L. Wolfe
Realty, a black-owned real estate and insurance business on Auburn
Avenue — "Sweet Auburn," the heart of Atlanta's black business district —
was the proposed solution.

The Continental representative called Wolfe Realty and explained the   14
situation. The head of the company agreed to give me an office out of
which I sold Continental's income-protection insurance policies to black
businesses employing five or more people. On occasion, my white supervisor came down to my office to make calls.

It was absurd. As a black person, I could not sell the policies of a   15
white company to black businesses while sitting in the white company's
office. Yet my white supervisor could come in to the black business office
and sell the white company's policies to black firms. This was a prime
example of the craziness, the backwardness, the inefficiency of Southern
life.

The job was also very boring. . . . When I could stand it no longer, my   16
mother, who knew I was deeply unhappy, suggested an alternative. The
summer was passing, and the opportunities for other office jobs had
dwindled. I wanted to work. So why not, she asked, work the balance of
the time using other skills I had? I was a good driver and, like many
young men in the 1950s, I was in love with cars. My mother ran a catering
business, which meant she had contacts within most, if not all, the prominent white households in Atlanta.

That is how I became a chauffeur for Robert F. Maddox.   17

Robert Maddox was one of the leading figures in Atlanta's white elite   18
for most of the early part of the twentieth century. He was mayor of the
city in 1910, and before that he had been active in the civic and social affairs of the town. A man of finance, he was the president of the First
National Bank of Atlanta and president of the American Banking

Association. Maddox's interests and influence were wide-ranging. He had a fabulous garden on his grounds and was, for a time, the president of the Garden Clubs of America.

In many ways Maddox was a symbol of the New South — open to business and economic development and devoted to progress, as long as it was within certain boundaries. When Booker T. Washington gave his famous Atlanta Exposition address (sometimes called the Atlanta Compromise), Maddox had been among the dignitaries on the platform, listening while the "wizard of Tuskegee" assured whites that blacks would make no immediate press for social equality. 19

Maddox was very proud of having built the first very large home in Buckhead, one of Atlanta's most exclusive neighborhoods. When I encountered him, he was well into his eighties, a widower living alone in that spectacular house, attended by a small group of servants: Joe, the chauffeur and butler, whose place I took for the month of August, when he was away; Lizzie, the cook, a middle-aged woman who played the piano at the Mount Zion Baptist Church; and Troy, the yardman. 20

Every morning I picked up Lizzie and brought her to work. If needed, I would then press one of Maddox's Palm Beach suits as Lizzie fixed his breakfast. When she finished doing that, she would take the meal up to Maddox and then return to prepare my breakfast, which I ate in the butler's pantry. Lizzie also made breakfast for Troy. But Troy worked in the yard and, according to age-old protocol, was not allowed to eat inside the house. His meal was handed out to him by Lizzie, and he sat on the back porch of that huge southern house and had his breakfast. 21

My routine varied little. Maddox, in his old age, was a creature of habit. He would come downstairs, get his hat, and select one of his many walking canes. We'd go out to the car, a four-door blue Cadillac. In a bid for independence, Maddox usually insisted upon opening the passenger door himself, although he could have used my help. I would drive him from the back of the house around to the front and stop near the rose garden. At that moment, Troy, cued by the idling of the car's engine, would appear from the garden with a single rose — sometimes red, sometimes white or yellow — for Maddox's lapel. Then our day's journey began. 22

At Maddox's insistence, we took the same route each day: down West Paces Ferry Road, right on Habersham, down to Peachtree Battle, left on Peachtree Street, and down to the First National Bank Building, where Maddox kept an office. He would go up and stay sometimes ten minutes, sometimes two hours — I never knew what to expect. But I knew that whenever he finished, our next destination would be the Capital City Club, where Maddox, and sometimes a companion we might pick up along the way, went to have a drink and lunch. Then it was back home for Maddox's afternoon nap. So, by 1:30 at the latest, my duties as chauffeur were over. I had nothing to do until six o'clock, when I took on the mantle of butler and served dinner. 23

Maddox had a wonderful library that soon became a place of refuge   24
for me during the dead hours of the afternoon. Shakespeare, Thoreau,
Emerson — it had everything. What I read most eagerly, however, were
the various books of speeches in his collection. There are few things I enjoy more than a good speech and good preaching. I've tried my hand at
doing both. The experience of saying aloud what needs to be said in front
of a group of willing listeners is intoxicating. The good speaker or
preacher is apart from the audience but always with them in some fundamental way — rising when they rise, falling when they fall, directing
them but being directed as well. When a speaker has a talent for doing
this, there is nothing more exciting to watch. This is all better as live theater, but the power of a truly well-written speech can come through even
when read silently.

One book in Maddox's library contained Booker T. Washington's   25
Atlanta Exposition address. Maddox was deeply impressed with
Washington, as the well-thumbed pages of that part of the book showed.
Maddox had vigorously underlined one particular passage, to the point
of damaging the page, where Washington had said of the races, "In all
things purely social we can be as separate as the fingers yet one as the
hand in all things essential to mutual progress." This was Maddox's
credo, but, obviously, not mine. I was, after all, sitting in his private
library.

I sat there day after day, drinking in the atmosphere of the place —   26
the smell of the books, the feel of them, the easy chairs. The way of life
that the library symbolized — the commitment to knowledge and the
leisure to pursue it — struck a chord in me that still resonates. I wanted
all this for myself and my family. This was what going to college was for,
to become a part of a community that appreciated and had access to a
place like this. I knew I belonged there. . . .

One afternoon, as I sat reading, Maddox walked in on me. He had   27
awakened early from his afternoon nap and had come down in his underwear, with a bottle of Southern Comfort in one hand and a glass in the
other. He was clearly startled to see me there.

"What are you doing in the library, Vernon?"   28

"I'm reading, Mr. Maddox."   29

"Reading? I've never had a nigger work for me who could read," he said.   30

"Mr. Maddox, I can read. I go to college."   31

"You do what?" he asked.   32

"I go to college."   33

"You go to college over there at those colored schools?"   34

"No, sir. I go to DePauw University in Greencastle, Indiana."   35

He pondered this for a moment.   36

"White children go to that school."   37

"Yes, sir."   38

Then the inevitable.   39

"White *girls* go to that school." 40

"Yes, sir." 41

"What are you studying to be, a preacher or a teacher?" 42

"Actually, I'm going to be a lawyer, Mr. Maddox." 43

"Niggers aren't supposed to be lawyers." 44

"I'm going to be a lawyer, Mr. Maddox." 45

"Hmmm. Well, don't you know I have some place downstairs for you all to sit and do what you want to do?" 46

"I know. But I didn't think you'd want me to take these books down there. They should stay in the library." 47

He looked around and finally said, "Just read then — just go ahead." He turned and walked out. I thought the matter was closed. I soon found out it was not. 48

His children and their spouses came for dinner that evening, which was not uncommon. Ed Smith, married to Maddox's daughter, Laura, was the chairman of the First National Bank, and Maddox's son, Baxter, was its executive vice president. Maddox was at his customary place at the head of the table. As I moved among them serving soup in my white jacket and bow tie with a napkin draped over my arm, Maddox said, "I have an announcement to make." 49

"Yes, Papa?" one of his children said. 50

Silence. 51

"Vernon can read." 52

More silence. Maddox went on. 53

"And he's going to school with white children." 54

No one made a sound. Finally, and with a great deal of emotion, Maddox said, "I knew all this was coming. But I'm glad I won't be here when it does." 55

The truth is that his guests were all quite embarrassed by this display because they knew I could read. They knew I was a college student. Maddox's children had hired me, through my mother. My ability to read was not a detail they had thought to mention to him. Why should they have? 56

For my part, the whole business seemed so absurd that there was nothing to say. I served dinner, poured the water and wine, and left them to themselves. This was not the last of it. . . . 57

When I have told this story to younger people, they often ask why I was not more angry at Maddox. How could I have continued working for him under those circumstances? While I was certainly annoyed by what was going on, I did not think then — and I do not think now — that it would have done any good to lash out at this elderly man for his aggressive backwardness. Each of us has to decide for ourselves how much nonsense we can take in life, and from whom we are willing to take it. It all depends, of course, on the situation and people involved. 58

I knew Maddox, or more precisely, I knew his type. I was aware of and had borne the brunt of the forces that helped shape him. He had lived his life as though Booker T. Washington's program for black-white relations in the South had been enacted. To me, Robert Maddox was not an evil man. He was just an anachronism. And with the brashness of youth I mentally noted (and counted on) the fact that his time was up. I do not mean just his physical time on earth — but I believed that the "time" that helped shape him was on its way out. His half-mocking, half-serious comments about my education were the death rattle of his culture. When he saw that I was in the process of crafting a life for myself that would make me a man in some of the same ways he thought of being a man, he was deeply unnerved. That I was doing it with money gained from working in his household was probably even more unnerving. These things, however, were his problem. As far as I was concerned, I was executing a plan for my life and had no time to pause and reeducate him. 59

I kept reading in Maddox's library, but he never again announced to anyone that I could read. This story does not have a happy ending, with the old man coming to see the error of his ways and taking on the role of mentor to the young man; I would find mentors in other places. The character of our relationship, however, did change slightly, but perceptibly, after he was forced to focus on who I really was. He became much more inclined to speak to me at times other than when he wanted me to do something for him. As we drove around, he sometimes tossed out a comment about a current issue with the expectation that I might know something about it. At the very least we could have a conversation. That held true over the course of the next few years when I worked for him during the summers and on vacations from school. 60

The story is told, and I am not sure it is true, that in 1961, when I escorted Charlayne Hunter through the mobs at the University of Georgia to desegregate that institution, Maddox was watching the well-publicized event on television. By that time he was no longer living in the house (in 1963 he would sell the property to the state of Georgia, where the governor's mansion now stands), and he was living in a smaller place in Atlanta attended by a nurse. 61

The nurse recognized me and said, "Mr. Maddox, do you know who that colored lawyer is?" 62

"I don't believe I do." 63

"It's your chauffeur, Vernon." 64

Maddox looked hard at the screen and said, "I always knew that nigger was up to no good." 65

Discovering the Power of My Words

Russell Baker

The notion of becoming a writer had flickered off and on in my head . . . but it wasn't until my third year in high school that the possibility took hold. Until then I'd been bored by everything associated with English courses. I found English grammar dull and baffling. I hated the assignments to turn out "compositions," and went at them like heavy labor, turning out leaden, lackluster paragraphs that were agonies for teachers to read and for me to write. The classics thrust on me to read seemed as deadening as chloroform.

When our class was assigned to Mr. Fleagle for third-year English I anticipated another grim year in that dreariest of subjects. Mr. Fleagle was notorious among City students for dullness and inability to inspire. He was said to be stuffy, dull, and hopelessly out of date. To me he looked to be sixty or seventy and prim to a fault. He wore primly severe eyeglasses, his wavy hair was primly cut and primly combed. He wore prim vested suits with neckties blocked primly against the collar buttons of his primly starched white shirts. He had a primly pointed jaw, a primly straight nose, and a prim manner of speaking that was so correct, so gentlemanly, that he seemed a comic antique.

I anticipated a listless, unfruitful year with Mr. Fleagle and for a long time was not disappointed. We read *Macbeth*. Mr. Fleagle loved *Macbeth* and wanted us to love it, too, but he lacked the gift of infecting others with his own passion. He tried to convey the murderous ferocity of Lady Macbeth one day by reading aloud the passage that concludes

> . . . I have given suck, and know
> How tender 'tis to love the babe that milks me.
> I would, while it was smiling in my face,
> Have plucked my nipple from his boneless gums . . .

The idea of prim Mr. Fleagle plucking his nipple from boneless gums was too much for the class. We burst into gasps of irrepressible snickering. Mr. Fleagle stopped.

"There is nothing funny, boys, about giving suck to a babe. It is the — the very essence of motherhood, don't you see."

He constantly sprinkled his sentences with "don't you see." It wasn't a question but an exclamation of mild surprise at our ignorance. "Your pronoun needs an antecedent, don't you see," he would say, very primly.

Reprinted from *Growing Up* (1982), by permission of Don Congdon Associates, Inc.

"The purpose of the Porter's scene, boys, is to provide comic relief from the horror, don't you see."

Late in the year we tackled the informal essay. "The essay, don't you   6
see, is the . . ." My mind went numb. Of all forms of writing, none seemed so boring as the essay. Naturally we would have to write informal essays. Mr. Fleagle distributed a homework sheet offering us a choice of topics. None was quite so simpleminded as "What I Did on My Summer Vacation," but most seemed to be almost as dull. I took the list home and dawdled until the night before the essay was due. Sprawled on the sofa, I finally faced up to the grim task, took the list out of my notebook, and scanned it. The topic on which my eye stopped was "The Art of Eating Spaghetti."

This title produced an extraordinary sequence of mental images.   7
Surging up from the depths of memory came a vivid recollection of a night in Belleville when all of us were seated around the supper table — Uncle Allen, my mother, Uncle Charlie, Doris, Uncle Hal — and Aunt Pat served spaghetti for supper. Spaghetti was an exotic treat in those days. Neither Doris nor I had ever eaten spaghetti, and none of the adults had enough experience to be good at it. All the good humor of Uncle Allen's house reawoke in my mind as I recalled the laughing arguments we had that night about the socially respectable method for moving spaghetti from plate to mouth.

Suddenly I wanted to write about that, about the warmth and good   8
feeling of it, but I wanted to put it down simply for my own joy, not for Mr. Fleagle. It was a moment I wanted to recapture and hold for myself. I wanted to relive the pleasure of an evening at New Street. To write it as I wanted, however, would violate all the rules of formal composition I'd learned in school, and Mr. Fleagle would surely give it a failing grade. Never mind. I would write something else for Mr. Fleagle after I had written this thing for myself.

When I finished it the night was half gone and there was no time left   9
to compose a proper, respectable essay for Mr. Fleagle. There was no choice next morning but to turn in my private reminiscence of Belleville. Two days passed before Mr. Fleagle returned the graded papers, and he returned everyone's but mine. I was bracing myself for a command to report to Mr. Fleagle immediately after school for discipline when I saw him lift my paper from his desk and rap for the class's attention.

"Now, boys," he said, "I want to read you an essay. This is titled 'The   10
Art of Eating Spaghetti.'"

And he started to read. My words! He was reading *my words* out loud   11
to the entire class. What's more, the entire class was listening. Listening attentively. Then somebody laughed, then the entire class was laughing, and not in contempt and ridicule, but with open-hearted enjoyment. Even Mr. Fleagle stopped two or three times to repress a small prim smile.

I did my best to avoid showing pleasure, but what I was feeling was   12
pure ecstasy at this startling demonstration that my words had the power

to make people laugh. In the eleventh grade, at the eleventh hour as it were, I had discovered a calling. It was the happiest moment of my entire school career. When Mr. Fleagle finished he put the final seal on my happiness by saying, "Now that, boys, is an essay, don't you see. It's — don't you see — it's of the very essence of the essay, don't you see. Congratulations, Mr. Baker."

For the first time, light shone on a possibility. It wasn't a very heartening possibility, to be sure. Writing couldn't lead to a job after high school, and it was hardly honest work, but Mr. Fleagle had opened a door for me. After that I ranked Mr. Fleagle among the finest teachers in the school. 13

The Maker's Eye: Revising Your Own Manuscripts

Donald M. Murray

When students complete a first draft, they consider the job of writing done — and their teachers too often agree. When professional writers complete a first draft, they usually feel that they are at the start of the writing process. When a draft is completed, the job of writing can begin.

That difference in attitude is the difference between amateur and professional, inexperience and experience, journeyman and craftsman. Peter F. Drucker, the prolific business writer, calls his first draft "the zero draft" — after that he can start counting. Most writers share the feeling that the first draft, and all of those which follow, are opportunities to discover what they have to say and how best they can say it.

To produce a progression of drafts, each of which says more and says it more clearly, the writer has to develop a special kind of reading skill. In school we are taught to decode what appears on the page as finished writing. Writers, however, face a different category of possibility and responsibility when they read their own drafts. To them the words on the page are never finished. Each can be changed and rearranged, can set off a chain reaction of confusion or clarified meaning. This is a different kind of reading which is possibly more difficult and certainly more exciting.

Writers must learn to be their own best enemy. They must accept the criticism of others and be suspicious of it; they must accept the praise of others and be even more suspicious of it. Writers cannot depend on others. They must detach themselves from their own pages so that they can apply both their caring and their craft to their own work.

Such detachment is not easy. Science-fiction writer Ray Bradbury supposedly puts each manuscript away for a year to the day and then rereads it as a stranger. Not many writers have the discipline or the time to do this. We must read when our judgment may be at its worst, when we are close to the euphoric moment of creation.

Then the writer, counsels novelist Nancy Hale, "should be critical of everything that seems to him most delightful in his style. He should excise what he most admires, because he wouldn't thus admire it if he weren't . . . in a sense protecting it from criticism." John Ciardi, the poet, adds, "The last act of the writing must be to become one's own reader. It is, I suppose, a schizophrenic process, to begin passionately and to end

Reprinted from *The Writer* (1973), by permission of The Rosenberg Group on behalf of the author's estate. Copyright © 1973 by Donald M. Murray.

critically, to begin hot and to end cold; and, more important, to be passion-hot and critic-cold at the same time."

Most people think that the principal problem is that writers are too   7
proud of what they have written. Actually, a greater problem for most
professional writers is one shared by the majority of students. They are
overly critical, think everything is dreadful, tear up page after page,
never complete a draft, see the task as hopeless.

The writer must learn to read critically but constructively, to cut what   8
is bad, to reveal what is good. Eleanor Estes, the children's book author,
explains: "The writer must survey his work critically, coolly, as though he
were a stranger to it. He must be willing to prune, expertly and hard-
heartedly. At the end of each revision, a manuscript may look . . . worked
over, torn apart, pinned together, added to, deleted from, words changed
and words changed back. Yet the book must maintain its original fresh-
ness and spontaneity."

Most readers underestimate the amount of rewriting it usually takes to   9
produce spontaneous reading. This is a great disadvantage to the student
writer, who sees only a finished product and never watches the craftsman
who takes the necessary step back, studies the work carefully, returns to the
task, steps back, returns, steps back, again and again. Anthony Burgess, one
of the most prolific writers in the English-speaking world, admits, "I might
revise a page twenty times." Roald Dahl, the popular children's writer,
states, "By the time I'm nearing the end of a story, the first part will have
been reread and altered and corrected at least 150 times. . . . Good writing is
essentially rewriting. I am positive of this."

Rewriting isn't virtuous. It isn't something that ought to be done. It is   10
simply something that most writers find they have to do to discover what
they have to say and how to say it. It is a condition of the writer's life.

There are, however, a few writers who do little formal rewriting,   11
primarily because they have the capacity and experience to create and
review a large number of invisible drafts in their minds before they
approach the page. And some writers slowly produce finished pages,
performing all the tasks of revision simultaneously, page by page,
rather than draft by draft. But it is still possible to see the sequence
followed by most writers most of the time in rereading their own work.

Most writers scan their drafts first, reading as quickly as possible to   12
catch the larger problems of subject and form, and then move in closer
and closer as they read and write, reread and rewrite.

The first thing writers look for in their drafts is *information*. They know   13
that a good piece of writing is built from specific, accurate, and interesting
information. The writer must have an abundance of information from
which to construct a readable piece of writing.

Next, writers look for *meaning* in the information. The specifics must   14
build to a pattern of significance. Each piece of specific information must
carry the reader toward meaning.

Writers reading their own drafts are aware of *audience*. They put   15
themselves in the reader's situation and make sure that they deliver
information which a reader wants to know or needs to know in a manner
which is easily digested. Writers try to be sure that they anticipate and
answer the questions a critical reader will ask when reading the piece of
writing.

Writers make sure that the *form* is appropriate to the subject and the   16
audience. Form, or genre, is the vehicle which carries meaning to the
reader, but form cannot be selected until the writer has adequate information to discover its significance and an audience which needs or wants
that meaning.

Once writers are sure the form is appropriate, they must then look at   17
the *structure*, the order of what they have written. Good writing is built on
a solid framework of logic, argument, narrative, or motivation which
runs through the entire piece of writing and holds it together. This is the
time when many writers find it most effective to outline as a way of visu-
alizing the hidden spine by which the piece of writing is supported.

The element on which writers may spend a majority of their time is   18
development. Each section of a piece of writing must be adequately developed. It must give readers enough information so that they are satisfied.
How much information is enough? That's as difficult as asking how
much garlic belongs in a salad. It must be done to taste, but most
beginning writers underdevelop, underestimating the reader's hunger
for information.

As writers solve development problems, they often have to consider   19
questions of *dimension*. There must be a pleasing and effective proportion
among all the parts of the piece of writing. There is a continual process of
subtracting and adding to keep the piece of writing in balance.

Finally, writers have to listen to their own voices. *Voice* is the force   20
which drives a piece of writing forward. It is an expression of the writer's
authority and concern. It is what is between the words on the page, what
glues the piece of writing together. A good piece of writing is always
marked by a consistent, individual voice.

As writers read and reread, write and rewrite, they move closer and   21
closer to the page until they are doing line-by-line editing. Writers read
their own pages with infinite care. Each sentence, each line, each clause,
each phrase, each word, each mark of punctuation, each section of white
space between the type has to contribute to the clarification of meaning.

Slowly the writer moves from word to word, looking through   22
language to see the subject. As a word is changed, cut, or added, as a
construction is rearranged, all the words used before that moment and all
those that follow that moment must be considered and reconsidered.

Writers often read aloud at this stage of the editing process, mutter-   23
ing or whispering to themselves, calling on the ear's experience with language. Does this sound right — or that? Writers edit, shifting back and

forth from eye to page to ear to page. I find I must do this careful editing in short runs, no more than fifteen or twenty minutes at a stretch, or I become too kind with myself. I begin to see what I hope is on the page, not what actually is on the page.

This sounds tedious if you haven't done it, but actually it is fun. 24 Making something right is immensely satisfying, for writers begin to learn what they are writing about by writing. Language leads them to meaning, and there is the joy of discovery, of understanding, of making meaning clear as the writer employs the technical skills of language.

Words have double meanings, even triple and quadruple meanings. 25 Each word has its own potential of connotation and denotation. And when writers rub one word against the other, they are often rewarded with a sudden insight, an unexpected clarification.

The maker's eye moves back and forth from word to phrase to sen- 26 tence to paragraph to sentence to phrase to word. The maker's eye sees the need for variety and balance, for a firmer structure, for a more appropriate form. It peers into the interior of the paragraph, looking for coherence, unity, and emphasis, which make meaning clear.

I learned something about this process when my first bifocals were 27 prescribed. I had ordered a larger section of the reading portion of the glass because of my work, but even so, I could not contain my eyes within this new limit of vision. And I still find myself taking off my glasses and bending my nose toward the page, for my eyes unconsciously flick back and forth across the page, back to another page, forward to still another, as I try to see each evolving line in relation to every other line.

When does this process end?. Most writers agree with the great 28 Russian writer Tolstoy, who said, "I scarcely ever reread my published writings; if by chance I come across a page, it always strikes me: all this must be rewritten; this is how I should have written it."

The maker's eye is never satisfied, for each word has the potential to 29 ignite new meaning. This article has been twice written all the way through the writing process [. . .]. Now it is to be republished in a book. The editors made a few small suggestions, and then I read it with my maker's eye. Now it has been re-edited, re-revised, re-read, and re-re-edited, for each piece of writing to the writer is full of potential and alternatives.

A piece of writing is never finished. It is delivered to a deadline, torn 30 out of the typewriter on demand, sent off with a sense of accomplishment and shame and pride and frustration. If only there were a couple more days, time for just another run at it, perhaps then . . .

The Case for Short Words

Richard Lederer

When you speak and write, there is no law that says you have to use   1
big words. Short words are as good as long ones, and short, old words —
like *sun* and *grass* and *home* — are best of all. A lot of small words, more
than you might think, can meet your needs with a strength, grace, and
charm that large words do not have.

Big words can make the way dark for those who read what you write   2
and hear what you say. Small words cast their clear light on big things —
night and day, love and hate, war and peace, and life and death. Big
words at times seem strange to the eye and the ear and the mind and the
heart. Small words are the ones we seem to have known from the time we
were born, like the hearth fire that warms the home.

Short words are bright like sparks that glow in the night, prompt like   3
the dawn that greets the day, sharp like the blade of a knife, hot like salt
tears that scald the cheek, quick like moths that flit from flame to flame,
and terse like the dart and sting of a bee.

Here is a sound rule: Use small, old words where you can. If a long   4
word says just what you want to say, do not fear to use it. But know that
our tongue is rich in crisp, brisk, swift, short words. Make them the spine
and the heart of what you speak and write. Short words are like fast
friends. They will not let you down.

The title of this chapter and the four paragraphs that you have just read   5
are wrought entirely of words of one syllable. In setting myself this task, I
did not feel especially cabined, cribbed, or confined. In fact, the structure
helped me to focus on the power of the message I was trying to put across.

One study shows that twenty words account for twenty-five percent   6
of all spoken English words, and all twenty are monosyllabic. In order of
frequency they are: *I, you, the, a, to, is, it, that, of, and, in, what, he, this, have,
do, she, not, on,* and *they.* Other studies indicate that the fifty most common
words in written English are each made of a single syllable.

For centuries our finest poets and orators have recognized and   7
employed the power of small words to make a straight point between
two minds. A great many of our proverbs punch home their points with
pithy monosyllables: "Where there's a will, there's a way," "A stitch in
time saves nine," "Spare the rod and spoil the child," "A bird in the hand
is worth two in the bush."

Reprinted from *The Miracle of Language* (1991), by permission of Pocket Books, a division of
Simon & Schuster, Inc. Copyright © 1991 by Richard Lederer.

Nobody used the short word more skillfully than William Shakespeare,   8
whose dying King Lear laments:

> And my poor fool is hang'd! No, no, no life!
> Why should a dog, a horse, a rat have life,
> And thou no breath at all? . . .
> Do you see this? Look on her; look, her lips.
> Look there, look there!

Shakespeare's contemporaries made the King James Bible a center-   9
piece of short words — "And God said, Let there be light: and there was
light. And God saw the light, that it was good." The descendants of
such mighty lines live on in the twentieth century. When asked to explain his policy to Parliament, Winston Churchill responded with these
ringing monosyllables: "I will say: It is to wage war, by sea, land, and
air, with all our might and with all the strength that God can give us." In
his "Death of the Hired Man" Robert Frost observes that "Home is the
place where, when you have to go there, / They have to take you in."
And William H. Johnson uses ten two-letter words to explain his secret
of success: "If it is to be, / It is up to me."

You don't have to be a great author, statesman, or philosopher to tap   10
the energy and eloquence of small words. Each winter I ask my ninth
graders at St. Paul's School to write a composition composed entirely of
one-syllable words. My students greet my request with obligatory moans
and groans, but, when they return to class with their essays, most feel
that, with the pressure to produce high-sounding polysyllables relieved,
they have created some of their most powerful and luminous prose. Here
are submissions from two of my ninth graders:

> What can you say to a boy who has left home? You can say that he has
> done wrong, but he does not care. He has left home so that he will not have to
> deal with what you say. He wants to go as far as he can. He will do what he
> wants to do.
>
> This boy does not want to be forced to go to church, to comb his hair, or
> to be on time. A good time for this boy does not lie in your reach, for what
> you have he does not want. He dreams of ripped jeans, shorts with no starch,
> and old socks.
>
> So now this boy is on a bus to a place he dreams of, a place with no rules.
> This boy now walks a strange street, his long hair blown back by the wind.
> He wears no coat or tie, just jeans and an old shirt. He hates your world, and
> he has left it.
>
> —Charles Shaffer

> For a long time we cruised by the coast and at last came to a wide bay
> past the curve of a hill, at the end of which lay a small town. Our long boat
> ride at an end, we all stretched and stood up to watch as the boat nosed its
> way in.

The town climbed up the hill that rose from the shore, a space in front of it left bare for the port. Each house was a clean white with sky blue or grey trim; in front of each one was a small yard, edged by a white stone wall strewn with green vines.

As the town basked in the heat of noon, not a thing stirred in the streets or by the shore. The sun beat down on the sea, the land, and the back of our necks, so that, in spite of the breeze that made the vines sway, we all wished we could hide from the glare in a cool, white house. But, as there was no one to help dock the boat, we had to stand and wait.

At last the head of the crew leaped from the side and strode to a large house on the right. He shoved the door wide, poked his head through the gloom, and roared with a fierce voice. Five or six men came out, and soon the port was loud with the clank of chains and creak of planks as the men caught ropes thrown by the crew, pulled them taut, and tied them to posts. Then they set up a rough plank so we could cross from the deck to the shore. We all made for the large house while the crew watched, glad to be rid of us.

—Celia Wren

You, too, can tap into the vitality and vigor of compact expression. Take a suggestion from the highway department. At the boundaries of your speech and prose place a sign that reads "Caution: Small Words at Work." 11

The Ways of Meeting Oppression

Martin Luther King Jr.

Oppressed people deal with their oppression in three characteristic ways. One way is acquiescence: The oppressed resign themselves to their doom. They tacitly adjust themselves to oppression, and thereby become conditioned to it. In every movement toward freedom some of the oppressed prefer to remain oppressed. Almost 2,800 years ago Moses set out to lead the children of Israel from the slavery of Egypt to the freedom of the promised land. He soon discovered that slaves do not always welcome their deliverers. They become accustomed to being slaves. They would rather bear those ills they have, as Shakespeare pointed out, than flee to others that they know not of. They prefer the "fleshpots of Egypt" to the ordeals of emancipation.

There is such a thing as the freedom of exhaustion. Some people are so worn down by the yoke of oppression that they give up. A few years ago in the slum areas of Atlanta, a Negro guitarist used to sing almost daily: "Been down so long that down don't bother me." This is the type of negative freedom and resignation that often engulfs the life of the oppressed.

But this is not the way out. To accept passively an unjust system is to cooperate with that system; thereby the oppressed become as evil as the oppressor. Noncooperation with evil is as much a moral obligation as is cooperation with good. The oppressed must never allow the conscience of the oppressor to slumber. Religion reminds every man that he is his brother's keeper. To accept injustice or segregation passively is to say to the oppressor that his actions are morally right. It is a way of allowing his conscience to fall asleep. At this moment the oppressed fails to be his brother's keeper. So acquiescence — while often the easier way — is not the moral way. It is the way of the coward. The Negro cannot win the respect of his oppressor by acquiescing; he merely increases the oppressor's arrogance and contempt. Acquiescence is interpreted as proof of the Negro's inferiority. The Negro cannot win the respect of the white people of the south or the peoples of the world if he is willing to sell the future of his children for his personal and immediate comfort and safety.

A second way that oppressed people sometimes deal with oppression is to resort to physical violence and corroding hatred. Violence often brings about momentary results. Nations have frequently won their independence in battle. But in spite of temporary victories, violence never brings permanent peace. It solves no social problem; it merely creates new and more complicated ones.

Violence as a way of achieving racial justice is both impractical and   5
immoral. It is impractical because it is a descending spiral ending in destruction for all. The old law of an eye for an eye leaves everybody blind. It is immoral because it seeks to humiliate the opponent rather than win his understanding; it seeks to annihilate rather than to convert. Violence is immoral because it thrives on hatred rather than love. It destroys community and makes brotherhood impossible. It leaves society in monologue rather than dialogue. Violence ends by defeating itself. It creates bitterness in the survivors and brutality in the destroyers. A voice echoes through time saying to every potential Peter, "Put up your sword." History is cluttered with the wreckage of nations that failed to follow this command.

If the American Negro and other victims of oppression succumb to   6
the temptation of using violence in the struggle for freedom, future generations will be the recipients of a desolate night of bitterness, and our chief legacy to them will be an endless reign of meaningless chaos. Violence is not the way.

The third way open to oppressed people in their quest for freedom is   7
the way of nonviolent resistance. Like the synthesis in Hegelian philosophy, the principle of nonviolent resistance seeks to reconcile the truths of two opposites — the acquiescence and violence — while avoiding the extremes and immoralities of both. The nonviolent resister agrees with the person who acquiesces that one should not be physically aggressive toward his opponent; but he balances the equation by agreeing with the person of violence that evil must be resisted. He avoids the nonresistance of the former and the violent resistance of the latter. With nonviolent resistance, no individual or group need submit to any wrong, nor need anyone resort to violence in order to right a wrong.

It seems to me that this is the method that must guide the actions of   8
the Negro in the present crisis in race relations. Through nonviolent resistance the Negro will be able to rise to the noble height of opposing the unjust system while loving the perpetrators of the system. The Negro must work passionately and unrelentingly for full stature as a citizen, but he must not use inferior methods to gain it. He must never come to terms with falsehood, malice, hate, or destruction.

Nonviolent resistance makes it possible for the Negro to remain in the   9
South and struggle for his rights. The Negro's problem will not be solved by running away. He cannot listen to the glib suggestion of those who would urge him to migrate en masse to other sections of the country. By

grasping his great opportunity in the South he can make a lasting contribution to the moral strength of the nation and set a sublime example of courage for generations yet unborn.

By nonviolent resistance, the Negro can also enlist all men of good will in his struggle for equality. The problem is not a purely racial one, with Negroes set against whites. In the end, it is not a struggle between people at all, but a tension between justice and injustice. Nonviolent resistance is not aimed against oppressors but against oppression. Under its banner consciences, not racial groups, are enlisted.

I Have a Dream

Martin Luther King Jr.

Five score years ago, a great American, in whose symbolic shadow 1
we stand, signed the Emancipation Proclamation. This momentous
decree came as a great beacon light of hope to millions of Negro slaves
who had been seared in the flames of withering injustice. It came as a joyous daybreak to end the long night of captivity.

But one hundred years later, we must face the tragic fact that the 2
Negro is still not free. One hundred years later, the life of the Negro is still
sadly crippled by the manacles of segregation and the chains of discrimination. One hundred years later, the Negro lives on a lonely island of
poverty in the midst of a vast ocean of material prosperity. One hundred
years later, the Negro is still languishing in the corners of American society and finds himself an exile in his own land. So we have come here
today to dramatize an appalling condition.

In a sense we have come to our nation's Capitol to cash a check. 3
When the architects of our republic wrote the magnificent words of the
Constitution and the Declaration of Independence, they were signing a
promissory note to which every American was to fall heir. This note was a
promise that all men would be guaranteed the unalienable rights of life,
liberty, and the pursuit of happiness.

It is obvious today that America has defaulted on this promissory note 4
insofar as her citizens of color are concerned. Instead of honoring this sacred obligation, America has given the Negro people a bad check; a check
which has come back marked "insufficient funds." But we refuse to
believe that the bank of justice is bankrupt. We refuse to believe that there
are insufficient funds in the great vaults of opportunity of this nation. So
we have come to cash this check — a check that will give us upon demand
the riches of freedom and the security of justice. We have also come to this
hallowed spot to remind America of the fierce urgency of *now*. This is no
time to engage in the luxury of cooling off or to take the tranquilizing drug
of gradualism. *Now* is the time to make real the promises of Democracy.
Now is the time to rise from the dark and desolate valley of segregation to
the sunlit path of racial justice. *Now* is the time to open the doors of opportunity to all of God's children. *Now* is the time to lift our nation from the
quicksands of racial injustice to the solid rock of brotherhood.

It would be fatal for the nation to overlook the urgency of the moment and to underestimate the determination of the Negro. This sweltering summer of the Negro's legitimate discontent will not pass until there is an invigorating autumn of freedom and equality. Nineteen sixty-three is not an end, but a beginning. Those who hope that the Negro needed to blow off steam and will now be content will have a rude awakening if the nation returns to business as usual. There will be neither rest nor tranquility in America until the Negro is granted his citizenship rights. The whirlwinds of revolt will continue to shake the foundations of our nation until the bright day of justice emerges.

But there is something I must say to my people who stand on the warm threshold which leads into the palace of justice. In the process of gaining our rightful place we must not be guilty of wrongful deeds. Let us not seek to satisfy our thirst for freedom by drinking from the cup of bitterness and hatred. We must forever conduct our struggle on the high plane of dignity and discipline. We must not allow our creative protest to degenerate into physical violence. Again and again we must rise to the majestic heights of meeting physical force with soul force. The marvelous new militancy which has engulfed the Negro community must not lead us to a distrust of all white people, for many of our white brothers, as evidenced by their presence here today, have come to realize that their destiny is tied up with our destiny and their freedom is inextricably bound to our freedom. We cannot walk alone.

And as we walk, we must make the pledge that we shall march ahead. We cannot turn back. There are those who are asking the devotees of civil rights, "When will you be satisfied?" We can never be satisfied as long as the Negro is the victim of the unspeakable horrors of police brutality. We can never be satisfied as long as our bodies, heavy with the fatigue of travel, cannot gain lodging in the motels of the highways and the hotels of the cities. We cannot be satisfied as long as the Negro's basic mobility is from a smaller ghetto to a larger one. We can never be satisfied as long as a Negro in Mississippi cannot vote and a Negro in New York believes he has nothing for which to vote. No, no, we are not satisfied, and we will not be satisfied until justice rolls down like waters and righteousness like a mighty stream.

I am not unmindful that some of you have come here out of great trials and tribulations. Some of you have come fresh from narrow jail cells. Some of you have come from areas where your quest for freedom left you battered by the storms of persecution and staggered by the winds of police brutality. You have been the veterans of creative suffering. Continue to work with the faith that unearned suffering is redemptive.

Go back to Mississippi, go back to Alabama, go back to South Carolina, go back to Georgia, go back to Louisiana, go back to the slums and ghettoes of our northern cities, knowing that somehow this situation can and will be changed. Let us not wallow in the valley of despair.

I say to you today, my friends, that in spite of the difficulties and   10
frustrations of the moment I still have a dream. It is a dream deeply
rooted in the American dream.

I have a dream that one day this nation will rise up and live out the   11
true meaning of its creed: "We hold these truths to be self-evident; that all
men are created equal."

I have a dream that one day on the red hills of Georgia the sons of   12
former slaves and the sons of former slaveowners will be able to sit down
together at the table of brotherhood.

I have a dream that the state of Mississippi, a desert state sweltering   13
with the heat of injustice and oppression, will be transformed into an
oasis of freedom and justice.

I have a dream that my four little children will one day live in a nation   14
where they will not be judged by the color of their skin but by the content
of their character.

I have a dream today.   15

I have a dream that the state of Alabama, whose governor's lips are   16
presently dripping with the words of interposition and nullification, will
be transformed into a situation where little black boys and black girls will
be able to join hands with little white boys and white girls and walk
together as sisters and brothers.

I have a dream today.   17

I have a dream that one day every valley shall be exalted, every hill   18
and mountain shall be made low, the rough places will be made plain,
and the crooked places will be made straight, and the glory of the Lord
shall be revealed, and all flesh shall see it together.

This is our hope. This is the faith with which I return to the South.   19
With this faith we will be able to hew out of the mountain of despair a
stone of hope. With this faith we will be able to transform the jangling
discords of our nation into a beautiful symphony of brotherhood. With
this faith we will be able to work together, to pray together, to struggle
together, to go to jail together, to stand up for freedom together, knowing
that we will be free one day.

This will be the day when all of God's children will be able to sing   20
with new meaning.

> My country, 'tis of thee
> Sweet land of liberty,
>   Of thee I sing:
> Land where my fathers died,
> Land of the pilgrims' pride,
> From every mountainside
>   Let freedom ring.

And if America is to be a great nation this must become true. So let   21
freedom ring from the prodigious hilltops of New Hampshire. Let freedom

ring from the mighty mountains of New York. Let freedom ring from the heightening Alleghenies of Pennsylvania!

Let freedom ring from the snowcapped Rockies of Colorado!   22

Let freedom ring from the curvaceous peaks of California!   23

But not only that; let freedom ring from Stone Mountain of Georgia!   24

Let freedom ring from Lookout Mountain of Tennessee!   25

Let freedom ring from every hill and molehill of Mississippi.   26

From every mountainside, let freedom ring.

When we let freedom ring, when we let it ring from every village and   27
every hamlet, from every state and every city, we will be able to speed up that day when all of God's children, black men and white men, Jews and Gentiles, Protestants and Catholics, will be able to join hands and sing in the words of the old Negro spiritual, "Free at last! free at last! thank God almighty, we are free at last!"

Shitty First Drafts

Anne Lamott

Now, practically even better news than that of short assignments is   1
the idea of shitty first drafts. All good writers write them. This is how
they end up with good second drafts and terrific third drafts. People tend
to look at successful writers, writers who are getting their books published and maybe even doing well financially, and think that they sit
down at their desks every morning feeling like a million dollars, feeling
great about who they are and how much talent they have and what a
great story they have to tell; that they take in a few deep breaths, push
back their sleeves, roll their necks a few times to get all the cricks out, and
dive in, typing fully formed passages as fast as a court reporter. But this is
just the fantasy of the uninitiated. I know some very great writers, writers
you love who write beautifully and have made a great deal of money, and
not *one* of them sits down routinely feeling wildly enthusiastic and confident. Not one of them writes elegant first drafts. All right, one of them
does, but we do not like her very much. We do not think that she has a
rich inner life or that God likes her or can even stand her. (Although when
I mentioned this to my priest friend Tom, he said you can safely assume
you've created God in your own image when it turns out that God hates
all the same people you do.)

Very few writers really know what they are doing until they've done   2
it. Nor do they go about their business feeling dewy and thrilled. They do
not type a few stiff warm-up sentences and then find themselves bound-
ing along like huskies across the snow. One writer I know tells me that he
sits down every morning and says to himself nicely, "It's not like you
don't have a choice, because you do — you can either type or kill yourself." We all often feel like we are pulling teeth, even those writers whose
prose ends up being the most natural and fluid. The right words and sentences just do not come pouring out like ticker tape most of the time. Now,
Muriel Spark is said to have felt that she was taking dictation from God
every morning — sitting there, one supposes, plugged into a Dictaphone,
typing away, humming. But this is a very hostile and aggressive position.
One might hope for bad things to rain down on a person like this.

For me and most of the other writers I know, writing is not rapturous.   3
In fact, the only way I can get anything written at all is to write really,
really shitty first drafts.

Reprinted from *Bird By Bird: Some Instructions on Writing and Life* (1994), Anchor Books, a
division of Random House, Inc.

The first draft is the child's draft, where you let it all pour out and 4
then let it romp all over the place, knowing that no one is going to see it
and that you can shape it later. You just let this childlike part of you channel whatever voices and visions come through and onto the page. If one
of the characters wants to say, "Well, so what, Mr. Poopy Pants?," you let
her. No one is going to see it. If the kid wants to get into really sentimental, weepy, emotional territory, you let him. Just get it all down on paper,
because there may be something great in those six crazy pages that you
would never have gotten to by more rational, grown-up means. There
may be something in the very last line of the very last paragraph on page
six that you just love, that is so beautiful or wild that you now know what
you're supposed to be writing about, more or less, or in what direction
you might go — but there was no way to get to this without first getting
through the first five and a half pages.

I used to write food reviews for *California* magazine before it folded. 5
(My writing food reviews had nothing to do with the magazine folding,
although every single review did cause a couple of canceled subscrip-
tions. Some readers took umbrage at my comparing mounds of vegetable
puree with various ex-presidents' brains.) These reviews always took two
days to write. First I'd go to a restaurant several times with a few opinionated, articulate friends in tow. I'd sit there writing down everything anyone said that was at all interesting or funny. Then on the following
Monday I'd sit down at my desk with my notes, and try to write the
review. Even after I'd been doing this for years, panic would set in. I'd try
to write a lead, but instead I'd write a couple of dreadful sentences, xx
them out, try again, xx everything out, and then feel despair and worry
settle on my chest like an X-ray apron. It's over, I'd think, calmly. I'm not
going to be able to get the magic to work this time. I'm ruined. I'm
through. I'm toast. Maybe, I'd think, I can get my old job back as a
clerk-typist. But probably not. I'd get up and study my teeth in the mirror
for a while. Then I'd stop, remember to breathe, make a few phone calls,
hit the kitchen and chow down. Eventually I'd go back and sit down at
my desk, and sigh for the next ten minutes. Finally I would pick up my
one-inch picture frame, stare into it as if for the answer, and every time
the answer would come: All I had to do was to write a really shitty first
draft of, say, the opening paragraph. And no one was going to see it.

So I'd start writing without reining myself in. It was almost just typ- 6
ing, just making my fingers move. And the writing would be *terrible*. I'd
write a lead paragraph that was a whole page, even though the entire
review could only be three pages long, and then I'd start writing up
descriptions of the food, one dish at a time, bird by bird, and the critics
would be sitting on my shoulders, commenting like cartoon characters.
They'd be pretending to snore, or rolling their eyes at my overwrought
descriptions, no matter how hard I tried to tone those descriptions down,

no matter how conscious I was of what a friend said to me gently in my early days of restaurant reviewing. "Annie," she said, "it is just a piece of *chicken*. It is just a bit of *cake*."

But because by then I had been writing for so long, I would eventu- 7 ally let myself trust the process — sort of, more or less. I'd write a first draft that was maybe twice as long as it should be, with a self-indulgent and boring beginning, stupefying descriptions of the meal, lots of quotes from my black-humored friends that made them sound more like the Manson girls than food lovers, and no ending to speak of. The whole thing would be so long and incoherent and hideous that for the rest of the day I'd obsess about getting creamed by a car before I could write a decent second draft. I'd worry that people would read what I'd written and believe that the accident had really been a suicide, that I had panicked because my talent was waning and my mind was shot.

The next day, though, I'd sit down, go through it all with a colored 8 pen, take out everything I possibly could, find a new lead somewhere on the second page, figure out a kicky place to end it, and then write a second draft. It always turned out fine, sometimes even funny and weird and helpful. I'd go over it one more time and mail it in.

Then, a month later, when it was time for another review, the whole 9 process would start again, complete with the fears that people would find my first draft before I could rewrite it.

Almost all good writing begins with terrible first efforts. You need to 10 start somewhere. Start by getting something — anything — down on paper. A friend of mine says that the first draft is the down draft — you just get it down. The second draft is the up draft — you fix it up. You try to say what you have to say more accurately. And the third draft is the dental draft, where you check every tooth, to see if it's loose or cramped or decayed, or even, God help us, healthy.

What I've learned to do when I sit down to work on a shitty first draft 11 is to quiet the voices in my head. First there's the vinegar-lipped Reader Lady, who says primly, "Well, *that's* not very interesting, is it?" And there's the emaciated German male who writes these Orwellian memos detailing your thought crimes. And there are your parents, agonizing over your lack of loyalty and discretion; and there's William Burroughs, dozing off or shooting up because he finds you as bold and articulate as a houseplant; and so on. And there are also the dogs: let's not forget the dogs, the dogs in their pen who will surely hurtle and snarl their way out if you ever *stop* writing, because writing is, for some of us, the latch that keeps the door of the pen closed, keeps those crazy ravenous dogs contained.

Quieting these voices is at least half the battle I fight daily. But this is 12 better than it used to be. It used to be 87 percent. Left to its own devices, my mind spends much of its time having conversations with people who aren't there. I walk along defending myself to people, or exchanging repartee with them, or rationalizing my behavior, or seducing them with gossip, or pretending I'm on their TV talk show or whatever. I speed or run an aging yellow light or don't come to a full stop, and one nanosecond later am explaining to imaginary cops exactly why I had to do what I did, or insisting that I did not in fact do it.   13

I happened to mention this to a hypnotist I saw many years ago, and he looked at me very nicely. At first I thought he was feeling around on the floor for the silent alarm button, but then he gave me the following exercise, which I still use to this day.   14

Close your eyes and get quiet for a minute, until the chatter starts up. Then isolate one of the voices and imagine the person speaking as a mouse. Pick it up by the tail and drop it into a mason jar. Then isolate another voice, pick it up by the tail, drop it in the jar. And so on. Drop in any high-maintenance parental units, drop in any contractors, lawyers, colleagues, children, anyone who is whining in your head. Then put the lid on, and watch all these mouse people clawing at the glass, jabbering away, trying to make you feel like shit because you won't do what they want — won't give them more money, won't be more successful, won't see them more often. Then imagine that there is a volume-control button on the bottle. Turn it all the way up for a minute, and listen to the stream of angry, neglected, guilt-mongering voices. Then turn it all the way down and watch the frantic mice lunge at the glass, trying to get to you. Leave it down, and get back to your shitty first draft.   15

A writer friend of mine suggests opening the jar and shooting them all in the head. But I think he's a little angry, and I'm sure nothing like this would ever occur to you.

Coming to an Awareness of Language

Malcolm X

I've never been one for inaction. Everything I've ever felt strongly about, I've done something about. I guess that's why, unable to do anything else, I soon began writing to people I had known in the hustling world, such as Sammy the Pimp, John Hughes, the gambling house owner, the thief Jumpsteady, and several dope peddlers. I wrote them all about Allah and Islam and Mr. Elijah Muhammad. I had no idea where most of them lived. I addressed their letters in care of the Harlem or Roxbury bars and clubs where I'd known them. 1

I never got a single reply. The average hustler and criminal was too uneducated to write a letter. I have known many slick, sharp-looking hustlers, who would have you think they had an interest in Wall Street; privately, they would get someone else to read a letter if they received one. 2

Besides, neither would I have replied to anyone writing me something as wild as "the white man is the devil." 3

What certainly went on the Harlem and Roxbury wires was that Detroit Red was going crazy in stir, or else he was trying some hype to shake up the warden's office.

During the years that I stayed in the Norfolk Prison Colony, never did any official directly say anything to me about those letters, although, of course, they all passed through the prison censorship. I'm sure, however, they monitored what I wrote to add to the files which every state and federal prison keeps on the conversion of Negro inmates by the teachings of Mr. Elijah Muhammad. 4

But at that time, I felt that the real reason was that the white man knew that he was the devil. 5

Later on, I even wrote to the Mayor of Boston, to the Governor of Massachusetts, and to Harry S. Truman. They never answered; they probably never even saw my letters. I handscratched to them how the white man's society was responsible for the black man's condition in this wilderness of North America. 6

It was because of my letters that I happened to stumble upon starting to acquire some kind of a homemade education. 7

I became increasingly frustrated at not being able to express what I wanted to convey in letters that I wrote, especially those to Mr. Elijah 8

Reprinted from *The Autobiography of Malcolm X* (1964), Random House, Inc.

Muhammad. In the street, I had been the most articulate hustler out there — I had commanded attention when I said something. But now, trying to write simple English, I not only wasn't articulate, I wasn't even functional. How would I sound writing in slang, the way I would *say* it, something such as, "Look, daddy, let me pull your coat about a cat. Elijah Muhammad —"

Many who today hear me somewhere in person, or on television, or those who read something I've said, will think I went to school far beyond the eighth grade. This impression is due entirely to my prison studies. 9

It had really begun back in the Charlestown Prison, when Bimbi first made me feel envy of his stock of knowledge. Bimbi had always taken charge of any conversation he was in, and I had tried to emulate him. But every book I picked up had few sentences which didn't contain anywhere from one to nearly all of the words that might as well have been in Chinese. When I just skipped those words, of course, I really ended up with little idea of what the book said. So I had come to the Norfolk Prison Colony still going through only book-reading motions. Pretty soon, I would have quit even these motions, unless I had received the motivation that I did. 10

I saw that the best thing I could do was get hold of a dictionary — to study, to learn some words. I was lucky enough to reason also that I should try to improve my penmanship. It was sad. I couldn't even write in a straight line. It was both ideas together that moved me to request a dictionary along with some tablets and pencils from the Norfolk Prison Colony school. 11

I spent two days just riffling uncertainly through the dictionary's pages. I'd never realized so many words existed! I didn't know *which* words I needed to learn. Finally, just to start some kind of action, I began copying. 12

In my slow, painstaking, ragged handwriting, I copied into my tablet everything printed on that first page, down to the punctuation marks. 13

I believe it took me a day. Then, aloud, I read back, to myself, everything I'd written on the tablet. Over and over, aloud, to myself, I read my own handwriting. 14

I woke up the next morning, thinking about those words — immensely proud to realize that not only had I written so much at one time, but I'd written words that I never knew were in the world. Moreover, with a little effort, I also could remember what many of these words meant. I reviewed the words whose meanings I didn't remember. Funny thing, from the dictionary first page right now, that "aardvark" springs to my mind. The dictionary had a picture of it, a long-tailed, long-eared, burrowing African mammal, which lives off termites caught by sticking out its tongue as an anteater does for ants. 15

I was so fascinated that I went on — I copied the dictionary's next page. And the same experience came when I studied that. With every succeeding page, I also learned of people and places and events from 16 history. Actually the dictionary is like a miniature encyclopedia. Finally the dictionary's A section had filled a whole tablet — and I went on into the B's. That was the way I started copying what eventually became the entire dictionary. It went a lot faster after so much practice helped me to pick up handwriting speed. Between what I wrote in my tablet, and writing letters, during the rest of my time in prison I would guess I wrote a million words.

I suppose it was inevitable that as my word-base broadened, I could for the first time pick up a book and read and now begin to understand what the book was saying. Anyone who has read a great deal can imagine the new world that opened. Let me tell you something: from then until I left that prison, in every free moment I had, if I was not reading in the library, I was reading on my bunk. You couldn't have gotten me out of books with a wedge. Between Mr. Muhammad's teachings, my correspondence, my visitors . . . and my reading of books, months passed without my even thinking about being imprisoned. In fact, up to then, I never had been so truly free in my life. 17

Campus Racism 101

Nikki Giovanni

There is a bumper sticker that reads: TOO BAD IGNORANCE ISN'T PAINFUL.   1
I like that. But ignorance is. We just seldom attribute the pain to it or even
recognize it when we see it. Like the postcard on my corkboard. It shows a
young man in a very hip jacket smoking a cigarette. In the background is a
high school with the American flag waving. The caption says: "Too cool for
school. Yet too stupid for the real world." Out of the mouth of the young
man is a bubble enclosing the words "Maybe I'll start a band." There could
be a postcard showing a jock in a uniform saying, "I don't need school. I'm
going to the NFL or NBA." Or one showing a young man or woman studying and a group of young people saying, "So you want to be white." Or
something equally demeaning. We need to quit it.

I am a professor of English at Virginia Tech. I've been here for four   2
years, though for only two years with academic rank. I am tenured,
which means I have a teaching position for life, a rarity on a predominantly white campus. Whether from malice or ignorance, people who
think I should be at a predominantly Black institution will ask, "Why are
you at Tech?" Because it's here. And so are Black students. But even if
Black students weren't here, it's painfully obvious that this nation and
this world cannot allow white students to go through higher education
without interacting with Blacks in authoritative positions. It is equally
clear that predominantly Black colleges cannot accommodate the numbers of Black students who want and need an education.

Is it difficult to attend a predominantly white college? Compared   3
with what? Being passed over for promotion because you lack credentials? Being turned down for jobs because you are not college-educated?
Joining the armed forces or going to jail because you cannot find an alternative to the streets? Let's have a little perspective here. Where can you
go and what can you do that frees you from interacting with the white
American mentality? You're going to interact; the only question is, will
you be in some control of yourself and your actions, or will you be controlled by others? I'm going to recommend self-control.

What's the difference between prison and college? They both pre-   4
scribe your behavior for a given period of time. They both allow you to
read books and develop your writing. They both give you time alone to
think and time with your peers to talk about issues. But four years of

Reprinted from *Essence Magazine* (September 1991).

prison doesn't give you a passport to greater opportunities. Most likely that time only gives you greater knowledge of how to get back in. Four years of college gives you an opportunity not only to lift yourself but to serve your people effectively. What's the difference when you are called nigger in college from when you are called nigger in prison? In college you can, though I admit with effort, follow procedures to have those students who called you nigger kicked out or suspended. You can bring issues to public attention without risking your life. But mostly, college is and always has been the future. We, neither less nor more than other people, need knowledge. There are discomforts attached to attending predominantly white colleges, though no more so than living in a racist world. Here are some rules to follow that may help:

Go to class. No matter how you feel. No matter how you think the professor feels about you. It's important to have a consistent presence in the classroom. If nothing else, the professor will know you care enough and are serious enough to be there.   5

Meet your professors. Extend your hand (give a firm handshake) and tell them your name. Ask them what you need to do to make an A. You may never make an A, but you have put them on notice that you are serious about getting good grades.   6

Do assignments on time. Typed or computer-generated. You have the syllabus. Follow it, and turn those papers in. If for some reason you can't complete an assignment on time, let your professor know before it is due and work out a new due date — then meet it.   7

Go back to see your professor. Tell him or her your name again. If an assignment received less than an A, ask why, and find out what you need to do to improve the next assignment.   8

Yes, your professor is busy. So are you. So are your parents who are working to pay or help with your tuition. Ask early what you need to do if you feel you are starting to get into academic trouble. Do not wait until you are failing.   9

Understand that there will be professors who do not like you; there may even be professors who are racist or sexist or both. You must discriminate among your professors to see who will give you the help you need. You may not simply say, "They are all against me." They aren't. They mostly don't care. Since you are the one who wants to be educated, find the people who want to help.   10

Don't defeat yourself. Cultivate your friends. Know your enemies. You cannot undo hundreds of years of prejudicial thinking. Think for yourself and speak up. Raise your hand in class. Say what you believe no matter how awkward you may think it sounds. You will improve in your articulation and confidence.   11

Participate in some campus activity. Join the newspaper staff. Run for office. Join a dorm council. Do something that involves you on campus.   12

You are going to be there for four years, so let your presence be known, if not felt.

You will inevitably run into some white classmates who are troubling because they often say stupid things, ask stupid questions — and expect an answer. Here are some comebacks to some of the most common inquiries and comments: 13

Q: What's it like to grow up in a ghetto? 14
A: I don't know. 15

Q: (from the teacher) Can you give us the Black perspective on Toni Morrison, Huck Finn, slavery, Martin Luther King Jr., and others? 16
A: I can give you *my* perspective. (Do not take the burden of 22 million people on your shoulders. Remind everyone that you are an individual, and don't speak for the race or any other individual within it.) 17

Q: Why do all the Black people sit together in the dining hall? 18
A: Why do all the white students sit together? 19

Q: Why should there be an African American studies course? 20
A: Because white Americans have not adequately studied the contributions of Africans and African Americans. Both Black and white students need to know our total common history. 21

Q: Why are there so many scholarships for "minority" students? 22
A: Because they wouldn't give my great-grandparents their forty acres and the mule. 23

Q: How can whites understand Black history, culture, literature, and so forth? 24
A: The same way we understand white history, culture, literature, and so forth. That is why we're in school: to learn. 25

Q: Should whites take African American studies courses? 26
A: Of course. We take white-studies courses, though the universities don't call them that. 27

Comment: When I see groups of Black people on campus, it's really intimidating. 28
Comeback: I understand what you mean. I'm frightened when I see white students congregating. 29

Comment: It's not fair. It's easier for you guys to get into college than for other people. 30
Comeback: If it's so easy, why aren't there more of us? 31

Comment: It's not our fault that America is the way it is. 32
Comeback: It's not our fault, either, but both of us have a responsibility to make changes. 33

It's really very simple. Educational progress is a national concern;   34
education is a private one. Your job is not to educate white people; it is to
obtain an education. If you take the racial world on your shoulders, you
will not get the job done. Deal with yourself as an individual worthy of
respect, and make everyone else deal with you the same way. College is a
little like playing grown-up. Practice what you want to be. You have been
telling your parents you are grown. Now is your chance to act like it.

Ain't I a Woman?

Sojourner Truth

Well, children, where there is so much racket there must be some-   1
thing out of kilter. I think that 'twixt the Negroes of the South and the
women of the North, all talking about rights, the white men will be in a
fix pretty soon. But what's all this here talking about?

That man over there says that women need to be helped into   2
carriages, and lifted over ditches, and to have the best place everywhere.
Nobody ever helps me into carriages, or over mudpuddles, or gives me
any best place! And ain't I a woman? Look at me! Look at my arm! I have
ploughed and planted, and gathered into barns, and no man could head
me! And ain't I a woman? I could work as much and eat as much as a
man — when I could get it — and bear the lash as well! And ain't I a
woman? I have borne thirteen children, and seen them most all sold off to
slavery, and when I cried out with my mother's grief, none but Jesus
heard me! And ain't I a woman?

Then they talk about this thing in the head; what's this they call it?   3
[Intellect, someone whispers.] That's it, honey. What's that got to do with
women's rights or negro's rights? If my cup won't hold but a pint, and
yours holds a quart, wouldn't you be mean not to let me have my little
half-measure full?

Then that little man in black there, he says women can't have as much   4
rights as men, 'cause Christ wasn't a woman! Where did your Christ
come from? Where did your Christ come from? From God and a woman!
Man had nothing to do with Him.

If the first woman God ever made was strong enough to turn the   5
world upside down all alone, these women together ought to be able to
turn it back, and get it right side up again! And now they is asking to do
it, the men better let them.

Obliged to you for hearing me, and now old Sojourner ain't got nothing   6
more to say.